Children's Writers' & Artists' YEARBOOK 2020

SIXTEENTH EDITION

The essential guide for children's writers and artists
on how to get published and who to contact

BLOOMSBURY

LONDON · OXFORD · NEW YORK · NEW DELHI · SYDNEY

BLOOMSBURY YEARBOOKS
Bloomsbury Publishing Plc
50 Bedford Square, London, WC1B 3DP, UK

BLOOMSBURY YEARBOOKS, WRITERS' & ARTISTS' and the Diana logo are
trademarks of Bloomsbury Publishing Plc

This edition published 2019

A catalogue record for this book is available from the British Library

ISBN: PB: 978-1-4729-4763-5; eBook: 978-1-4729-4762-8

2 4 6 8 10 9 7 5 3 1

Typeset by DLxml, a division of RefineCatch Limited, Bungay, Suffolk
Printed and bound in Great Britain by CPI Group (UK) Ltd, Croydon CR0 4YY

To find out more about our authors and books visit www.bloomsbury.com and sign up for our
newsletters.

Writers' & Artists' team
Editor Alysoun Owen
Assistant editor Eden Phillips Harrington
Articles copy-editor Virginia Klein
Listings editors Lisa Carden, Rebecca Collins, Lauren Simpson
Editorial assistance Sophia Blackwell (poetry)
Production controller Ben Chisnall

Children's
Writers'
& Artists'
# YEARBOOK
# 2020

Other Writers & Artists titles include

Writers' & Artists' Companions
Series Editors: Carole Angier and Sally Cline
Each title is full of expert advice and tips from bestselling authors.

Writing Children's Fiction by Yvonne Coppard and Linda Newbery
'. . . a book for anyone interested in children's books: the authors
manage – with a very light touch – to pass on masses of information
and ideas.' **Wendy Cooling**

Crime and Thriller Writing by Michelle Spring and Laurie R. King
Life Writing by Sally Cline and Carole Angier
Literary Non-fiction by Sally Cline and Midge Gillies
Writing Historical Fiction by Celia Brayfield and Duncan Sprott
Writing Short Stories by Courttia Newland and Tania Hershman
Novel Writing by Romesh Gunesekera and A.L. Kennedy
Playwriting by Fraser Grace and Clare Bayley
Writing for TV and Radio by Sue Teddern and Nick Warburton

NEW in October 2019
Writers' & Artists' Guide to Writing for Children and YA by Linda Strachan
Writers' & Artists' Guide to Getting Published by Alysoun Owen

You can buy copies from your local bookseller or online at
www.writersandartists.co.uk/shop

About the *Yearbook*

The Editor welcomes readers to this edition of the *Children's Writers' & Artists' Yearbook.*

I'm delighted to introduce you to this year's edition of the *Children's Writers' & Artists' Yearbook* and to the inspiring set of articles and practical details you will find inside. Every year we review, update and add to the information in the hundreds of listings we include. New to every edition are articles that complement those from previous editions and which, collectively, provide expert and considered advice on how to develop your writing and get your work published.

Caroline Horn gives her annual update on the market in *News and trends in children's publishing 2018-19* on page 12). If you are just starting out as an author or illustrator, turn to Davinia Andrew-Lynch's *A message for under-represented writers: We Want You!* (page 237) or Salvatore Rubbino's *The craft of the illustrator* (page 266). Clémentine Beauvais promotes the benefits of translation in order to improve your own writing in *Writing and translating children's fiction* (page 100) and Deirdre Sullivan, in *Reinventing old stories for new readers* (page 148), describes how she breathes new creative life into traditional tales.

Kiran Millwood Hargrave shares her experience of *Writing magic into fiction* on page 145. If you are seeking support on how to deal with more realistic elements in your writing, then let Holly Bourne (*Dealing with tough issues in YA fiction*, page 169) and Natasha Farrant (*Writing about love and loss for children*, page 173) be your guides. Jayne Kirkham advises on reaching a market or audience that lies beyond words on the page in *Writing for visual broadcast media* on page 319.

Whatever your chosen media or the age of your target market, I hope there is something here to entice and support you. Whether you are writing picture books, for middle grade or YA, fiction or non-fiction, if you are wanting to break into comics or magazines, or if you are a fledging poet or dramatist – you are all welcome.

Alysoun Owen, Editor

Contents

Praise for the *Yearbook*

'How to get published? 1. Write a good book.
2. Read a good book – this one.'
Charlie Higson

'Riffle these pages and turn your dream into an ambition.'
Frank Cottrell Boyce

'Take the great advice that's in this *Yearbook*.'
David Almond

'Contains a wealth of essays, articles and advice.'
Frances Hardinge

'Every writer has to take a first step. Make the *Children's Writers' &
Artists' Yearbook* yours.'
Meg Cabot

'Between the covers of this book is everything you need to know
to get published.'
Julia Donaldson

'... absolutely essential. If it were a person, it would
be your most knowledgeable and trusted confidant.'
Andy Stanton

'The *Children's Writers' & Artists' Yearbook* has two
great virtues: one is the wealth of information it contains
and the other is the impressive raft of advice and
notes on every aspect of the business.'
Quentin Blake

'Stuffed full of useful facts to help you get writing
(and drawing).'
Liz Pichon

More than a book

The Writers & Artists **website** (www.writersandartists.co.uk) provides up-to-the-minute writing advice, blogs, competitions and the chance to share work with other writers. You can sign up to our regular **newsletter**; browse our **Writing Calendar**; and learn about the **editorial services** we offer. We also run **courses, workshops** and other events, including **How to Hook an Agent** lunches and one-day **How to Get Published** conferences around the country, including some specifically related to writing and publishing for children.

Our **listings service** can be accessed at www.writersandartists.co.uk/listings. In addition to all the contacts in this edition of the *Yearbook*, subscribers are able to search hundreds of additional organisations and companies.

Whatever your needs, we hope that Writers & Artists resources, whether delivered in print, online or at our events, will provide you with the information, advice and inspiration you are looking for.

Short story competition

The annual *Writers' & Artists' Yearbook* Short Story Competition offers published and aspiring writers the chance to win a place on an Arvon residential writing course (worth £1,000). In addition, the winner's story will be published on the Writers & Artists website.

To enter the competition, submit a short story (for adults) of no more than 2,000 words, on any theme by 13 February 2020 to competition@bloomsbury.com. For full details, terms and conditions, and to find out more about how to submit your entry, visit www.writersandartists.co.uk/competitions.

You can find details of competitions for children's writing under *Children's book and illustration prizes and awards* on page 379.

ARVON runs three historic writing houses in the UK, where published writers lead week-long residential courses. Covering a diverse range of genres, from poetry and fiction to screenwriting and comedy, Arvon courses have provided inspiration to thousands of people at all stages of their writing lives. You can find out more and book a course online at www.arvon.org.

Foreword

William Sutcliffe

In the 23 years that I have been writing and publishing books I have been to scores of literary events, both as a speaker and an audience member. If I had to agglomerate all the questions I've heard put to authors into one overarching meta-question, it would be this: 'How do you do it?'. Sadly, my agglomerated meta-answer to that question would have to be 'I don't know.' Every published writer frequently gets asked for advice, and most of them have only one truly essential tip to offer: buy the *Writers' & Artists' Yearbook*. The key turning point in every professional writer's life is when writing shifts from being a hobby or a dream into a source of income. For making that transition, this book is the Bible.

To get published, you don't have to know someone; you don't have to know someone who knows someone; you don't have to live in Hampstead; and you don't need a degree in English literature. You do, however, need to understand that publishing is a business and that, like every other business, it operates in a way that seems obvious and transparent to insiders, but is opaque and confusing to outsiders. This is what makes the *Writers' & Artists' Yearbook* an essential reference book for everyone who hopes to make a living as a writer. Trying to get published without it is like setting off on a hike without a map.

When put to a writer, the question 'How do you do it?' can mean two things. If it means 'How do you get published?', you are holding the answer in your hands right now. Not everyone who hopes to find a publisher will achieve that, not by a long shot, but if you want to give your work in progress the best possible chance of finding an agent and ultimately a publisher, all the answers you need are right here. Of course, the other thing that question often means is 'How do you write a good book?'; and for that one, there are no clear-cut answers. Moreover, when it comes to key questions such as getting started, editing, plotting, characterisation, getting unstuck when you are stuck, for every writer there is a different solution. There is a right and a wrong way to make a submission to an agent; there isn't a right and a wrong way to write a novel. Everyone finds their own method.

The fascinating essays in this volume contain a wealth of experience from many of Britain's finest children's authors. You will find Jacqueline Wilson on 20 years of perseverance before her big breakthrough; J.K. Rowling on rejection letters; ten writers' commandments by Michael Morpurgo; Michael Rosen analysing who children's writers write for; and many more fascinating pieces. None of these essays will tell you how to write like those authors, but they will open your thoughts onto how you should write – how to get your personality onto the page; how to tell a unique story in an original way; how to navigate your own path through the craft of writing. These essays are the second-best resource there is for hearing the secrets of good children's writing. The best resource, of course, is the novels themselves.

Read them. Read them once as a reader, then again as a writer – which is to say with the eyes of a hyena. Pull the books to pieces. Think about the word choices, the structure, the characterisation, the pacing, the world-building. Read the books you love ruthlessly and critically. Read the books you don't love in the same way, and hone your sense of where your literary taste sits. There is no objective scale of good and bad. You need to make your own. This gimlet-eyed reading is essential, because only when you have done it to others will you be able to do it to your own prose. To write for children you have to tap into a playfulness in your imagination, but when it comes to editing and rewriting you have to be brutal. Any word or sentence that isn't doing a useful job has to go.

This book is filled with practical and creative advice for writers at every stage of a writing career, but I would like to leave you with the simplest and most important advice there is: enjoy it. When you write, pour yourself into the work. Think of the blank page not as a scary place but as a path to freedom. Writing can take you anywhere. If you really apply yourself to the task, whether you get published or not, that journey will be worthwhile.

William Sutcliffe writes for adults, young adults and children and is the author of 12 novels, including three titles in his *Circus of Thieves* series, published by Simon & Schuster Children's: *Circus of Thieves and the Raffle of Doom* (2014), *Circus of Thieves on the Rampage* (2015) and *Circus of Thieves and the Comeback Caper* (2016). His YA books are *The Wall* (2014) which was shortlisted for the CILIP Carnegie Medal, *Concentr8* (2016), shortlisted for the YA Book Prize, *We See Everything* (2017), and *The Gifted, The Talented and Me* (2019), all published by Bloomsbury. William's novels for adults include the international bestseller *Are You Experienced?* (Hamish Hamilton 1997), *New Boy* (Penguin 1996), *Bad Influence* (Hamish Hamilton 2004), and *Whatever Makes You Happy* (Bloomsbury 2008), which was adapted into a Netflix film with the new title, *Otherhood*, in 2019. He is also a screenwriter. His work has been translated into 28 languages.

Books
Spotting talent

Publishers and literary agents are not looking for what *they* like but for what children will like. Barry Cunningham famously accepted the manuscript of the first *Harry Potter* book which – as everyone knows – turned out to be the first of an international bestselling series. He explains here what he is looking for when he reads a new manuscript.

I'm a fan: I love reading and I love great stories. My background is in sales and marketing, and for many years I travelled with Penguin the length and breadth of the country – on tours with authors like Roald Dahl, to schools with the Puffin Book Club or to lonely writers' festivals. It was during this time that I learnt the most important part of my trade – how children react to the books they love, the authors that they adore, and how they put up with the material that they are coerced into reading. Reluctant readers indeed!

So what I'm looking for is what *they* want, not what I like or what you think is good. More of this later.

First steps

All publishers get streams of brown envelopes – especially, like divorces, after Christmas or the summer holidays – when writers finally feel something must be done with that story they've been working on.

So, how do you get your manuscript read by a publisher? Firstly, find out what the publisher wants: A sample? The complete manuscript? Perhaps, like us, they only accept submissions at certain times of the year. For most editors, first on the reading list are the submissions from agents, manuscripts recommended by other authors or by someone whose judgement they trust. So, if you know someone who knows someone, use the contact.

Next, know a little about the list you are submitting to: look at their catalogue or read some of their books. Let publishers know how much you like their publications (we all like those sorts of comments!) and how you think your novel might sit with the rest of their titles.

Then, write a short snappy synopsis – a page will do (I've had some that are as long as half the novel itself!). It should tell the publisher what the book is about, its characters and why they should read it. Also include a little bit about you, the author. Don't forget that. It can be almost as important as anything else in these days of marketing and personality promotion (no, you don't *have* to have had an exciting job, but it does give an impetus to read on …).

I worked with a very famous editor in my first job who was talking one day about her regular advice to first-time writers. Her advice began with a simple question: 'Have you thought of starting at Chapter 2?' Strangely, I find myself repeating this regularly. Often I find the first chapter is tortured and difficult, before the writer relaxes into the flow of the story in Chapter 2. And often things improve if we start straight into the action, and come back and explain later. But more importantly, first novels often fail because the editor doesn't get past a poor opening section. Beginnings are crucial, because I know children won't persevere if the story has a poor start, either.

So what am I looking for?

Back to the heart of things ... There are writers who know a lot about children – they might be teachers or parents – so does this mean they can write more relevantly for young people? There are authors who know nothing about modern children, don't even really like children – does this mean they will never understand what a child wants? There are 'crossover' books that don't appear to be for real children at all. There are books with children in them that aren't children's books. Confused?

To me it's simple. Books that really work for children are written from a child's perspective through an age-appropriate memory of how the author felt and dreamed and wondered. The best children's writers carry that childhood wonder, its worry and concern, or even its fear and disappointment, around with them. They have kept the child within alive – so writing is not a professional task of storytelling for tiny tots but a simple glorious act of recreating the excitement of childhood.

That's part one of what you need. Part two, in my view, is a concentration on your audience. I've worked with adult writers too and there is a difference here. Children's authors are creating for a distinctly different readership – they need to think in a more *humble* way than if their work was for their contemporaries. What I mean is that they have to be mindful of how their work will impact on children. Characters must have convincing voices, descriptions must be good enough for children to visualise, and authors must be aware of things like children's attention span when it comes to detailed explanations.

But perhaps even more important is an awareness of the emotional effect of a story on a child. We must always remember their hunger for hope and a bright tomorrow, the closeness and importance of relationships – how easily a world can be upset by parents, or loss of an animal or a friend – and the way in which action really does speak to children, for fantasy and adventure is part of the process of literally growing an imagination.

(If all this means nothing to you, and writing for children is just another category, then I don't think you should bother. That's not to say all this should operate consciously in the mind of the new writer – but that's what a publisher seeks, and that's what I'm looking for.)

Categories and concepts

Everyone has read about the older children's market, and its lucrative crossover into the kind of children's book that adults buy for themselves. I think this will continue to be a growing phenomenon – but the best books in the field will still be clear in their intent: not looking 'over their shoulder' at adults, but true to themselves and their subjects.

I'm sure fantasy will continue to hold a firm following – but with the best books based around character and not simply wild lands and strange people. Historical fiction is poised for a comeback for older children – showing the rich material and heritage we have in our shared everyday culture, as well as the 'big battles' of yore.

At last all kinds of young adult fiction has found a firm market and any number of clear voices: hard-edged, romantic, comic, or a wild mixture of all three! Both here and in the USA, the 13–18 age group is firmly established as a permanent adjunct to the children's market, buying for themselves thrillers, dystopian adventures and books that speak to crises and concerns.

But my favourite category is the most neglected – real stories and novels for 7–9 year-olds. This was once the classic area of children's books, with the biggest names and the greatest longevity of appeal. Sadly, it has become the haunt of derivative series and boring chapter books. But there are clear signs of revival, with bestselling stories for this age group and the slightly older 9–12 category coming thick and fast. It's a great area for new talent; our own *Beetle Boy* by M.G. Leonard (Chicken House 2016) is a prime example.

Picture books have had a great revival – seeing off the apparent challenges of apps and new technology to reassert the love of a beautifully-produced picture story, so I expect more innovations coming here. The success of cartoon novels and graphic story treatments for older readers has shown how story and illustration can work together in amusing and stimulating ways, enticing those who are looking for something a little bit different.

Language and setting

It's often said that, like exams, children's books are getting easier, that the language is getting 'younger' while the plots are getting more sophisticated. I don't think this is true. Certainly, for all markets, dialogue is more important than ever – and less time is taken in description. Children are used to characters who say what they mean, and whose motivations and subtleties emerge in speech. But largely I think this makes for more interpretation and imagination. Descriptions now concentrate on setting and atmosphere, rather than telling us authoritatively what the hero or heroine feels. All to the good in my view, and something new writers for children should absorb.

Also welcome in contemporary children's books is the freeing up of the adult! These characters are no longer confined to small walk-on parts and 'parental' or 'villainous' roles. Nowadays, adults in children's novels are as well drawn as the children, sometimes as touchingly vulnerable people themselves. But as in life, the most potent and frightening image in any children's book remains the bad or exploitative parent.

International scope

Children's literature is truly one of our most glorious 'hidden exports'. British writers continue to be very successful around the world, particularly in the USA and Europe. It is worth remembering this – while setting is not so important as inspiration, obviously UK-centred plots, regional dialogue and purely domestic issues, if not absolutely necessary, are best avoided. But there is no need either – like a creaky old British film – to introduce 'an American boy' or mid-Atlantic slang to your work to appeal to another audience. This seldom works and is often excruciating!

The marketplace

The market still remains delightfully unpredictable. It is hopeless to look at last year's trends and try to speculate. The sound and timelessly good advice is to find your own voice and, above all, to write from the heart. If you can touch what moved you as a child or still moves the child within you, then there's your 'market appeal'. Whether it's aboard the frigate of your imagination or in the quieter but equally dangerous seas of the lonely soul, skill and inspiration will win you your readership.

Oh, and finally, don't give up. As I once said to a certain young woman about a boy called Harry …

Barry Cunningham OBE was the editor who originally signed J.K. Rowling to Bloomsbury Children's Books. He now runs his own publishing company, Chicken House (see page 25), specialising in introducing new children's writers to the UK and USA. Notable recent successes include James Dashner, Cornelia Funke, M.G. Leonard, Kiran Millwood Hargrave, James Nicol, Maz Evans and Lucy Christopher. Chicken House and *The Times* jointly run an annual competition to find new writers; visit www.chickenhousebooks.com or see page 386. Barry was awarded an OBE in 2010 for services to publishing.

Books

What makes a children's classic?

David Fickling describes how he chooses a story for publication and hints at how it is crafted into the final book.

This is a variation of the age-old exam question, the general one you attempted in a hyperventilating panic as a last resort and with a plunging heart because the question you had swotted up on had been unaccountably and unfairly omitted. This was the make-weight question that looked deceptively easy but you knew was a trap. But you couldn't resist it because it looked like you could write *something*. It was really only meant for the brainiest, to sort them out from us goats. So, if you want a considered, deeply reflective and wonderfully good-humoured and, more to the point, *beautifully written* answer, then may I respectfully refer you to Italo Calvino and his essay *Why Read the Classics?*. Answers to all the 'whys' and most of the 'whats' are in there. Calvino offers 14 increasingly mysterious and connected answers in all, and each one is a gem. There is little more to be added by way of definition. By implication Calvino leads the reader onto '*How* do you write a classic?'. Of course the question asked of an editor is entirely different: 'How do you recognise a classic?', and that is the one I propose to attempt here in a deeply personal way with special reference to younger readers.

Recognising a good story

Recognition is everything. We publishers don't do much but recognise and act on the recognition. (The famous editor Maxwell Perkins just said we add enthusiasm.) 'No!' we say, 'We won't publish that'. Or 'Yes!' we say, 'I *love* this. Please please can we publish your story?' We are often wrong but at least we make a decision.

For good or ill, I am a potato print publisher. By which I mean that I do not analyse the decision (much) once it has been made. I am sent a story to consider for publication. I read the story (eventually). And if it moves me to laughter or tears or affects me in some other mysterious and powerful way and seems to be better than all the other things I am being asked to consider at that time, I say to myself 'Let's publish that'. In short, I *recognise* it. I *see* it, *make* it happen, *publish* it – 'there!' – like a potato print. I try to do all that as quickly as possible to the highest possible standard of manufacture. For the reader! Oh and I really like to meet the author, to see if we'll get on, and most of all to make sure they have tons of stories in them. There is really nothing in the world more exciting than meeting a writer with new stories to tell and a singing voice with which to tell them. And then to help bring those stories to readers. I am blessed.

A story is a whole thing in itself, like a melody, to which it is related. It must make sense in relation to itself. It is a wonderful pattern snatched out of the chaos. I try not to take it apart like a pocket watch fearing that I may not be able to reassemble it. It is not good if an author says back to you, 'Well if you know so much David, why don't you write it?'. As a young editor I once sent a five-page letter of quite brilliant, or so I thought, closely argued and typed editorial comments to an elderly experienced author who lived in Wales. My then boss received a sad note from his wife to the effect that Arthur (name changed) had been unfortunately taken to hospital after a heart attack. Nothing to do with David's letter of course, but ... I have never since written such a letter even though I always write myself copious notes on a book. If I can, I boil those notes down to four or five practical points to say to the author in a relaxed way over lunch or a cup of coffee. Things 'said' can be more easily ignored, discarded, digested or given to the writer. Nowadays I never suggest that the author puts in any different ingredients. I never say, can we have some 'Tanks at the beginning' or could we have some 'Nude Women' or have you tried 'Vampires'? When I suggested to the late Jan Mark that she write about Japan, she reserved for me some choice language (not bad language, *choice*) that previously I had only heard her use about Tony Blair. Of course it was me that was interested in Japan, not Jan. I might venture something like, 'There seems to be something missing in Chapter Four, tho' I don't know what it is.' And the author might say, 'No there isn't, it's absolutely fine you fool'. To which I shall not demur. Or the author might say, 'Wow David, you are so right, you're a genius, we need some heavy artillery in there. I didn't tell you but I left out the pomegranates but now I am going to put them right back in. Thank you! Thank you!'. At this point my demeanour must be that of Beech the butler, or Jeeves. I may allow myself a raised eyebrow: 'Pomegranates' (*no inflection*). 'Very good sir. Will that be all?' P.G. Wodehouse contains in his butlers nearly all the editorial advice a good editor will ever need. The point here is that the story – however long – is the whole thing. I am interested in the whole thing and not just the parts.

When I was nine years-old I can remember getting bored while reading the *Wind in the Willows* by Kenneth Graham, an acknowledged classic. The story seemed to be winging along quite merrily. I had been enjoying it. Mole, Rat, Badger and Toad were up and adventuring and then I came to Chapter Seven: *The Piper at the Gates of Dawn*. At that point the story gets interrupted by some long-winded poetical interlude (as it seemed to me at the time). Nowadays I am fond of poetical interludes. Not then. 'What was all that about?' my nine-year-old self asked. This is not to say my nine year-old self was right. Recently I found myself editing the accumulated essays and articles of that amazing writer, Diana Wynne-Jones. Her young self was electrified by reading *Piper at the Gates of Dawn* at an even younger age and she believed reading and recognising the poetic brilliance of that chapter almost kick-started her career as a writer. My point is not about being correct but understanding all readers change over the course of their lives. My editorial point to Kenneth Grahame would be this chapter may stop some readers and his answer could have been but it will inspire some too. I hope I would have said 'Okay, we'll leave it in.' Which brings me to the special circumstances in publishing for children. There really aren't any, apart from the fact that most of us are woefully bad at remembering what our minds were like when we were only seven years old. The single biggest error made by all of us publishers is to fail to empathise properly with the reader. Children suffer in particular.

I don't conduct research beforehand. I don't consult other people, unless they are members of the DFB editorial team. The DFB editorial team is like a gestalt mind, a hive mind. We are the editorial Borg. We always agree and no one can tell our opinions apart – in public. Behind the scenes we argue away like (polite) snarling dogs over a bone. Editors work well in teams. When I write 'I' I always mean 'We'. I certainly don't consult the accounts department, the marketing team, the sales department or the bookshop owner or anybody else in the book trade. I listen to them and respect them too, of course I do, but I don't consult them. I might pretend to consult them but I never really take any notice. (Please don't worry on my account as none of them ever bother reading this kind of article because they are usually too busy grappling with the appalling reality of sales figures.) But most of all, I *never* consult children. How much better it is to be told a wonderful story rather than be asked to choose one. Sometimes I feel I'm sailing against the world's prevailing wind. Children don't want to be asked. They want to be given. Actually all human beings want to be given stories and to learn how to give them to others. If a child likes something, you learn that very quickly. If they don't like something, you learn that quicker. They are the most honest audience on this Earth. Anybody who has read to five year-olds and seen them peel off courteously to the sand pit will know this. Don't listen to all those comedians who talk about 'dying' in the clubs in Glasgow. They know nothing if they haven't 'died' in a nursery school. The test of a story for children is the intentness with which they listen and then how quickly they get their pencils out and start to write, draw or act their own stories. It is a guiding rule: Good stories promote creation, Classic stories promote a culture.

The editing secret

The point is, I have already made the decision to publish before the editorial stage, before any possibility of consultation, exulting inside myself as a reader. The recognition has already happened. I am in love. It's just a case of when, not if.

It is in the editorial phase with the author where we check that the story is in as good a shape as it can be. This is really just another phase of the writer's work. It is the author who matters here, not the editor. This is the holy of holies, now, when classics are made. Editors may be useful in the early days, telling authors things they already know but haven't admitted to themselves or learned yet. Later on, good writers invariably know how to edit themselves. Then we editors are happy to be friends and supporters. This editorial phase is a secret, to be kept forever. The editing is important, not the editor. Any editing is like the scaffolding on a house: once the building is finished the scaffolding is taken away and forgotten. Once the story is published, that is how it is. Any new versions are new versions. The original story still stands and if we read it and loved it, we love it as we first read it. Were changes made? I am not saying. Was the first version different? None of your business! The author can talk about the building process if they want. The editor must never speak. It's not polite.

Another kind of group writing that is becoming more and more popular is where teams of writers get together to write stories. It happens a lot in films and television series, for example *The Simpsons*, etc. It has been done before: the great French storyteller Dumas had a lot of help. I admire this kind of writing but am not a practitioner. I like it because it raises the text and the reader's response above all other considerations. However, the set-up and the way of working needs to be established from the outset and all participants need to be given and to accept their due recognition as co-creators. This can be difficult, and besides, I suspect that there is always a presiding authorial mind that takes the decisions. For this reason I am happier with a clear editor/author demarcation. However it is written, the final version is the one to read.

Fairies and money

So you see it is not initially a matter of money, though the definition of Calvino's that most applies is No 6: 'A classic is a book that has never finished saying what it has to say.' And clearly, if that is the case then it need never go out of print. And it will keep making money for the author and the publisher forever – publisher heaven! A publisher's definition of a classic is a book that never stops selling. But this does *not* mean that everything that sells is a classic, nor that all classics sell immediately.

I have no desire to rehearse the reasons why money is in charge as it will be obvious to all of you: the huge agglomeration into mighty international corporations, the demise of the Net Book Agreement, the adoption of new technology, the internet, the withering of story value, as stories become 'loss leaders' for other more profitable products and thus we crazily sell the most desired books at a loss and the newest and least reader-tested books are priced highest. All this is driven by the insane, bonkers drumbeat of the vast corporations searching for double-digit growth forever … In my experience the people who work within corporations are nicer and cleverer than those outside. But they have been 'taken' and are dancing under the hill with the fairies and cannot stop. When the corporation throws them out eventually, they are bemused and cannot remember where they have been or why. I have seen the sales graphs soaring into the future, and still they climb on and on, faster and faster. Speed is killing the book. Everything has to happen faster these days. Mark my words, there will be a crash. The fairies are powerful but they are no good with money. Put the sales graphs away. Stop consulting. Put the story horse before the sales cart and pile the sales in the back. Of course the sales are important. We need to earn a living. I *love* sales. Like everyone else, I want more. But the way to more is to make things; stop fiddling and checking and get writing and making.

It is the story that matters. When I read a text that is new and original and hits the mark, I know. You know. Everyone knows. You would be deaf and blind not to feel the thrill of it. It is like seeing the northern lights or hearing the horns of elfland and the trumpets of the seventh cavalry sounding together. Or it could be just hearing Christopher's voice in *The Curious Incident of the Dog in the Night-Time*, it is not loud but is so clear and it sounds as if it has always been there and never been heard before.

Why you might ask do I get to choose? Who do I think I am? What gives me the right? You do, dear reader. You do. Thank you. Oh, and a favour, please stop asking our very best storytellers to do so many things. Personal appearances, opening shops, writing reviews, giving quotes. Hush children! They are working. There will be a new story all in good time.

What makes a children's classic? Wait and see.

David Fickling is an award-winning children's book editor and publisher. He started his career with Oxford University Press in 1977, moving on to Transworld and then to Scholastic UK. In 1999, David formed his own imprint, the Oxford-based storyhouse David Fickling Books, which he then set up as an independent company in July 2013. DFB's successful fiction titles include Philip Pullman's *The Book of Dust*, Mark Haddon's *The Curious Incident of the Dog in the Night-Time*, John Boyne's *The Boy in the Striped Pyjamas*, Jenny Downham's *Before I Die* and Lisa Williamson's *The Art of Being Normal*, as well as four novels by the late Siobhan Dowd. In January 2012 David independently launched *The Phoenix Comic*, which has now passed 300 issues. David published three, and commissioned a fourth, of the titles on the 2016 World Book Day's list of 'Top 10 Future Classics', and was shortlisted for Editor of the Year at the 2018 British Book Awards.

See also...
- *Spotting talent*, page 1
- *Who do children's authors write for?*, page 104

Breaking down the market: where does your book sit?

Author and editor Jasmine Richards provides a breakdown of the established market categories used by publishers and booksellers, to help budding authors know where their own work might fit in.

Writing for children is big business. Around 10,000 children's books are published every year in the UK. Publishers and agents are saying that children's books are having a renaissance. That's despite the fact that, ten years ago, some in the industry were pronouncing the death of the printed book for young readers. We now know that parents are worried about screen time and its effects. Parents want their children to turn pages rather than swipe left. To tell the truth, adults still seem to prefer reading printed text also. There is something comforting and nourishing about the physical book and that realisation is why sales of that format will continue to increase.

So, if the children's market is so buoyant, why is it so hard to get published? The fact is, the children's market is a very established and mature business, and competition is ferocious. It also has some very big players who have a lot of the market share. Amazingly, the three biggest-selling authors of 2018 (for the second year running) were children's authors. David Walliams' sales totalled more than £17.1, J.K. Rowling sold £14.2m worth of books and Julia Donaldson £13.2m.

Thrown into the mix, you also have celebrity fiction from musicians, TV personalities, YouTubers and sports stars. Then you have the perennial children's classics that book buyers return to again and again because they are excellent stories that stand the test of time. Established adult writers have also entered the marketplace, creating books for young adults and increasing their range of readers downwards. Finally, you have several well-established series each written by a team of writers on a rapid publishing cycle (such as the *Rainbow Magic* and *Beast Quest* series). There are an awful lot of books on the shelves and, for a new book to go on, another will have to come off. Obviously, there is infinite space online – but that doesn't help with discoverability.

In this fiercely competitive market, publishers are looking for exceptional books – novels that will stand out in this crowded arena and grab, not just the readers' attention, but also the attention of all the gatekeepers who will encounter the book before it even reaches the bookshop. A new book needs to convince sales directors selling in and also the head buyers at the main book chains, planning their offering. The book will need to be able to hold its own; it needs to be 'sticky' or, in other words, memorable and really easy to pitch. People in the industry love books, but the bottom line is that publishing is a business. Each book needs to have the potential to perform, if it is going to be published and if it is going to stay in print.

So, what can an author do to give themselves the best chance? Well – write a great story! A story with characters that readers will care about. A plot that turns the pages for the reader. A world that feels real and rich. A children's author must produce all those things, but it would be wise for them also to master an understanding of the market so they can appreciate the universe their book will operate in. There are a few ways to do this:

• Attend writing conferences or children's book events put on by people like SCBWI (see page 353) where you'll see people in the industry talking about what they are buying and why.
• Spend lots of time in bookshops and see what kind of books are on the table tops or in promotion.
• Keep an eye on what novels are winning key children's book awards or getting a lot of reviews in the print media.
• Read publications like the *Bookseller* to see what is happening in the world of publishing.
• Follow authors, book publicists, agents, booksellers and editors on social media to see what they are saying about the industry.
• It's also worth visiting libraries or talking to teachers about what books kids are reading.
• Most importantly, chat to children and ask what they are enjoying about the books they're reading. Their answers might surprise and inspire you.

Authors also need to get an understanding of the age ranges of children's books, a sense of word lengths for each of those age brackets, and some of the other features that are unique to certain parts of the market. Editors, including this one, can be a bit reticent when it comes to defining word counts. There is a good reason for this caginess. Books are works of art. They are an author's creative endeavour and thus not something that will always sit neatly in predefined categories. Still, if a book is going to sit outside some of the established norms when it comes to word count, then that needs to be for a good reason.

There are also some practical considerations to do with word counts; the bigger the book, the more it costs to print, after all, but there are set price points at the different age ranges. For instance, a middle-grade book will normally have a higher price point than a book for a 5–7 year-old and the middle-grade book can take a heftier page count because the publisher can charge more for that book.

You also need to consider the reading stamina of the children at the different age ranges. If an author writes a 70,000-word book for a 7–9 year-old, when the average is 10,0-00–15,000 words, then they are asking an awful lot of that reader. That's not to say that some readers won't be up to the task, but is that extended word count really serving the story well? Is it giving the book its best chance of being published? Is it giving the child reader the best reading experience? The guidelines provided below are just that: a guide – the average word count for the different age ranges of books – but there will always be exceptions. Ultimately, a story should be as long or as short as it *needs* to be.

Picture books

Golden rule: keep picture book text short! Remember, the pictures will do a lot of the telling in the story. The best picture books really take advantage of that fact. Picture books are often split out into two categories:

Books for age 0-2. These will not have many words at all (300 words or fewer) but they will have very strong images that tend to relate to the everyday and familiar rather than more fantastical settings or themes.

Books for 2-5 year-olds (although older children will still get a lot out of picture books and will be reading these alongside first chapter books). These books are on average be-tween 300 and 1,500 words, but some books might just be one word! Although short, these books need to have definite story beats, and twists and turns that will delight both the adult reader and child listener. They should explore the experiences and possible feelings that young children may be dealing with for the first time. The best picture books are those where a kind of magic happens in that space between the images and the text, and in which that interplay brings new meaning. The picture book should be a pleasure to read out loud, with rhythm but not necessarily rhyme – as this could have an impact on how well the book sells internationally. Rhyme can be pretty tricky to make work in translation, although not impossible!

Printing a book in full colour is not cheap; the publishing house that commissions the title needs to be sure that they will achieve co-editions with overseas publishers to keep printing costs down and make the book profitable. When writing a picture book, it is worth keeping the 32-page format front and centre – this roughly works out at 24 pages or 12 spreads in which to tell the story. The narrative needs to offer ample opportunity for illustration, but that does not mean the author should dictate what these illustrations might be. It is a collaboration. Part of the publisher's role in the process of publishing a picture book is to find the perfect pairing of author and illustrator.

Younger readers
Books for readers aged 5-7. These tend to have shorter sentences and simpler diction. Some may feature chapters, and illustration can either be in colour or in black-and-white. They average between 500 and 4,000 words.

Books for readers 7-9. These are on average between 10,000 and 15,000 words but can be longer. Readers at this age will have a bit more confidence and may be devouring a lot of series fiction and enjoying the fact that they are reading whole novels. The age of the protagonists in these books will tend to be at the top end of the actual readership or perhaps even older.

Middle-grade fiction or core readers
Novels for 9-12 year-olds will be significantly longer than the previous category and average at about 30,000-40,000 words. A novel can be much longer for this age range, especially if it is a fantasy title. Whatever the number, the words should serve the story and ensure that it is being delivered in the optimal way. If the novel is going to be 80,000 words that can work, but there should be a very good reason for it.

Generally, readers in this age range have a lot more stamina. They will identify strongly with the hero, so a close third-person perspective or first-person narrative can work very well here. The protagonist tends to be aspirational and so often they are aged around 13. Readers in this age range can deal with more complex stories and themes, but a more challenging style choice might be off-putting.

Books for teenagers and YA
Books for readers aged 12+ can be anything from 30,000 words upwards. There is series fiction for teenagers, but the idea of author as the main brand is perhaps something teenagers identify with more commonly, rather than a series title. Teenagers are interested in exploring big ideas, regardless of the genre, and an author can take a few more risks with the style choice or perspective in order to help get those big ideas across.

The protagonists in these books tend to be teenagers rather than 20+ year-olds. There is also a burgeoning category – called NA or New Adult – of books which feature protagonists in their early 20s. In the UK this age range has not become firmly fixed as yet, but may well do in the future.

Jasmine Richards is an author who has written over a dozen books for children and teenagers. Her most recent novel is *Keeper of Myths* (2017), sequel to *Secrets of Valhalla* (2016), both published by HarperCollins Children's Books. She is also a publishing consultant with over 15 years worth of experience working at Puffin, Working Partners and Oxford University Press as an editor and story developer. In 2018 Jasmine founded Storymix: The Inclusive Fiction Development Studio (www.storymix.co.uk), which focuses on developing stories with BAME protagonists and working with talented writed from diverse backgrounds. Her website is www.jasminerichards.com and you can follow her on Facebook and Twitter @JRichardsAuthor.

See also...
- *Children's books: genres and categorisation*, page 17
- *News and trends in children's publishing 2018–19*, page 12

Books

News and trends in children's publishing 2018–19

Caroline Horn reports on the latest areas of growth and success, challenge and change in children's publishing over the last year, with strong sales in middle-grade fiction, a drive towards inclusivity, and a boom in non-fiction.

Debuts, diversity – and David Walliams – were the key words of 2018, and the signs are that these will get even more attention moving ahead. Debut writers should be encouraged that, despite a concentration of sales in the hands of a few well-known authors – particularly David Walliams – the demand for strong new voices endures, while debut writers from diverse backgrounds should also take heart from a long overdue, but increasingly urgent, call for inclusivity in children's books.

Sales of children's books in the UK are bearing up in the age of austerity and represent nearly one third of the overall market, with 106 million children's and YA books sold in 2018 (Nielsen Book Research 2018).[1] That compares with an overall market of 355 million books sold. In value terms, Nielsen's figures show that the children's and YA market was worth a quarter of adult sales, or £623m, out of total book sales revenue of £2.4bn in 2018.

The strongest area of sales of children's books remains the core market for publishers – fiction for 7-12 year-olds – or 'middle grade' – which accounted for around one third (36%) of children's book sales (Nielsen Book Research 2018). Key trends in children's fiction include 'classic-in-the-making fantasy and adventure, with storytelling that feels timeless – and then properly funny books', says Rebecca McNally, publishing director at Bloomsbury Children's Books. A handful of authors dominate the middle-grade bestseller charts, including Walliams – who sold 2.6 million books in the UK in 2018, as well as Liz Pichon (author-illustrator of the *Tom Gates* series) and US author Jeff Kinney with his *Wimpy Kid* series; both the *Tom Gates* and *Wimpy Kid* series are long-term successes which continue to find readers. Beyond the bestsellers, however, the underlying story in children's fiction is the strength of today's rising stars, says McNally: 'When you look at middle-grade fiction over the long term, it's really clear that this is where our brilliant, hard-working, committed authors can build really long-term careers, where we get strongest support from schools and teachers, and where books really stick – where we build backlist.'

Bloomsbury made a strategic commitment to its middle-grade list and has been rewarded with a 40% growth in its middle-grade sales during 2018 (*Harry Potter* sales are stripped out). Bloomsbury Children's 'rising stars' of middle-grade include Katherine Rundell, whose *The Explorer* (2017) won the Costa Children's Book Award and has sold over 100,000 copies in paperback; Greg James and Chris Smith's *Kid Normal* books (2018-), which have sold in 24 languages; as well as emerging names Catherine Doyle (*The Storm Keeper's Island* 2018) and Sibeal Pounder's two series *Witch Wars* (2015-) and *Bad Mermaids* (2017-).

Publishers know they need to nurture new voices and there is a continuing and dedicated hunt for new names. Strong debuts are flourishing, and this is an exciting and vibrant

1. Nielsen Book Research provides BookScan sales data for both print and e-books alongside industry research from their Books & Consumers Survey.

part of children's books where the standard is also incredibly high. One only needs look at the books longlisted for the Branford Boase Award for debut writers to see how competitive the market now is; several of the contenders for its latest award – Sophie Andersen's *The House with Chicken Legs* (Usborne Books 2018), Adam Baron's *Boy Underwater* (HarperCollins Children's 2018), *Me Mam. Me Dad. Me.* (Head of Zeus 2018) by Malcolm Duffy, and *The Boy at the Back of the Class* (Orion Children's Books 2018) by Onjali Q. Raúf – were also longlisted for the Carnegie Medal, the most prestigious children's book award that is voted for entirely by specialist children's librarians.

There is also an urgent and committed drive to inclusivity in the industry; every publisher is looking to publish more diverse voices and seeking more authors and illustrators from BAME backgrounds. 'Better reflecting the diversity of our communities is essential for our creative and commercial future as publishers of books for children', says McNally. 'It's also a long-term project for all of us – it takes time to build careers in middle-grade.' Indeed, a study into ethnic representation in children's literature by the Centre for Literacy in Primary Education, *Reflecting Realities: Ethnic Diversity in UK Children's Books* (CLPE 2018) confirmed a worrying lack of BAME characters in children's books, with just 4% of the children's books published in the UK in 2017 featuring black, Asian or minority ethnic (BAME) characters. The report concluded with the startling – if not unexpected – fact that every ethnic minority in the UK is significantly under-represented in children's literature; while 32% of children of school age in England are from BAME backgrounds, only 1% of books written for them have a BAME central character. CLPE ceo Louise Johns-Shepherd said, 'These figures are alarming ... When I read these statistics I wonder about the cost to the imaginations of all our children, and particularly to BAME children.'

Part of the problem is perceived to be within publishing itself (the industry is dominated by white, middle-class people), while publishers have historically pointed to a lack of demand for greater diversity. However, the success of *The Boy at the Back of the Class* (Orion Children's Books 2018) by Onjali Q. Raúf, which won both the Blue Peter and Waterstones children's book awards in 2019, the creativity of *Children of Blood and Bone* by Tomi Adeyemi (Macmillan Children's Books 2018), and the commercial and critical success of Angie Thomas's *The Hate U Give* (Walker Books 2017) have put paid to that argument. In fact, publisher Knights Of launched in 2017 specifically to publish stories by BAME writers.

Children's picture books have tended to be at the forefront of moves towards inclusivity in children's books – look at publishers like Tiny Owl and Lantana Publishing, which have traditionally focused on stories from other cultures, or picture books such as Mary Hoffman's *The Great Big Book Of ...* series (Frances Lincoln) and the *Lulu* books by Anna McQuinn (Alanna Books) for diverse characters. Picture books have also been challenging the gender imbalance, says Chloe Morgan, agent at Plum Pudding Illustration: 'Strong female lead characters were also a strong trend as well as books that challenge gender stereotypes.' Examples are Frances Lincoln Children's Books' *Little People, Big Dreams* series (about famous women's early lives) and Kate Pankhurst's *Fantastically Great Women* series (Bloomsbury Children's), although Morgan points out that alongside these were also 'a variety of picture book and activity books based on unicorns, mermaids and sloths'.

As well as up-ending stereotypes, picture books are being used to explore areas that would typically be seen in older fiction, including political issues, but told in a gentle and sensitive way, says Morgan. One good example is *Dear Mr President* (Templar 2019) by Sophie Siers, illustrated by Anne Villeneuve, which addresses finding consensus rather than wall-building. Non-fiction picture books about our world are also becoming more popular, covering subjects like the environment, sea pollution, animal habitats, and the importance of recycling. Look out for *The Sea: Exploring our Blue Planet* (Bloomsbury Children's Books 2019) by Miranda Krestovnikoff and illustrator Jill Calder and the National Trust's *How to Help a Hedgehog and Protect a Polar Bear* (Nosy Crow 2018). Morgan says this trend will most likely be explored further, through 2019 and beyond, as there is a real push on the importance of the environment and ensuring that awareness about these issues are being highlighted to children at a young age.

While picture book sales saw a fall in 2018, non-fiction was one of the success stories that year; there is ongoing interest in large-format illustrated books like Templar's *Welcome to the Museum* series and Yuval Zommer's *The Big Book Of…* series, published by Thames & Hudson, as well as a focus on inspirational books such as Matthew Syed's *You Are Awesome* (Hachette Children's 2018) which have helped to drive sales. Non-fiction books focusing on mental health are becoming more and more popular, says Laura Knowles, author and editorial director at Quarto: 'This is quite a big trend because there is so much in the news about children being under pressure, and the issues they now face in relation to social media that earlier generations haven't had to deal with. Parents and librarians are trying to find ways to help with that, and as a publisher, we are keen to keep developing that area with books like *50 Ways to Feel Happy* (QED Publishing 2018).' Other books that have done well in this area include the picture book *Feelings: Inside My Heart and Inside My Head* (Caterpillar Books 2016) by Libby Walden and Richard Jones (or for a more up to date example you could use Ed Vere's picture book about empowerment, *How to Be a Lion* (Puffin 2018)), and for older children *Positively Teenage* (Franklin Watts 2018) by Nicola Morgan.

Knowles also points to a shift in non-fiction to books that feature factual information – but that might also include fiction, art or poetry, for example *It Starts with a Seed* (Aurum Press 2016), by Laura Knowles and Jennie Webber, or of course *The Lost Words* (Hamish Hamilton 2017) by Robert Macfarlane and Jackie Morris. 'The lines between fiction and non-fiction are blurring, so we no longer read non-fiction just to find out facts', explains Knowles. She points to the *Maps* book published by the Big Picture Press in 2013: 'It shifted the idea of non-fiction being just about discovering facts to becoming more of an experience, a book that parents and children can share together.'

Narrative non-fiction has become increasingly popular – an area that was opened up by the success of William Grill's illustrated narrative non-fiction account, *Shackleton's Journey* (Flying Eye Books 2014), which won the Kate Greenaway Medal for illustrated books in 2015. The acceptance and success of *Shackleton's Journey* has encouraged other publishing into this area. Author and illustrator David Roberts, for example, wrote his own narrative non-fiction book, *Suffragette: The Battle for Equality* (Pan Macmillan 2018), a subject he had wanted to write about for years, after reading *Shackleton's Journey*.

Suzanne Carnell, publishing director at Two Hoots, says that a passion for a subject is vital. 'As publishers, we acquire books and give briefs to meet particular parts of the market, but the real successes come from passions', she says. 'Try to find your own way, your own style, develop your own voice in illustration and find something you want to say.' This might involve exploring a niche area, as with *The Colours of History* (QED Publishing 2018) by Clive Gifford – a book about how pigments have developed, which won the Blue Peter Book Award for factual books – or the design-led *Professor Astro Cat* series (Penguin Random House 2013-) by Dominic Walliman and Ben Newman, that tackles complex science subjects for children.

If non-fiction has been a success story of 2018, the YA market is where the challenges have been, and YA authors in particular have felt the squeeze; many have opted to move out of writing altogether or to write for younger children as advances have shrunk. This is a market that is dependent on the 'next big thing' more than others – past successes like *The Hunger Games* and *The Fault in our Stars* have really driven the trend and demand for YA fiction, so publishers are hopeful that upcoming TV adaptations of books including Malorie Blackman's *Noughts and Crosses* (Doubleday 2000) and *All the Bright Places* (Knopf 2015) by Jennifer Niven can help transform its fortunes once again.

Emma Matthewson, publishing director at Bonnier Zaffre, says that the area of greatest challenge during 2018 was in hard-hitting fiction for older readers aged 14+, but adds that, with the right author, sales can still be 'stellar' and points to high expectations for upcoming debut *All the Things We Never Said* by author Yasmin Rahman (Hot Key Books, due July 2019). YA fantasy, though, continues to sell strongly, and authors like Holly Black and Sebastien de Castell have done well here, as have accomplished debuts including Tomi Adeyemi's *Children of Blood and Bone* (Macmillan Children's Books 2018) and *We Are Blood and Thunder* (Bloomsbury YA 2019) by Kesia Lupo. Looking ahead, Matthewson predicts 'less dystopia, more fantasy and more feelgood fiction, from diverse authors'.

While YA sales might be challenging, research by The Insights People, reported during the London Book Fair in early 2019, gave more hopeful signs for the future health of YA publishing, with findings that showed reading is now the most popular hobby among teenage girls aged 13-18, followed by swimming, listening to music and dancing. Surprisingly, watching videos on YouTube was in 21st place, using the internet at 22nd and using a smartphone at 28th. Getting more teenagers reading, though, is largely dependent on children catching the reading bug before they hit their teenage years and – with library and bookshop closures, the attractions of the internet and gaming, and the government's focus on 'literacy' turning many children off reading – publishers have their work cut out to encourage children to read, and this depends not only on the kinds of books they publish. Industry campaigns are ongoing, especially to persuade busy parents to continue sharing books with their children beyond the age at which they can read. According to Nielsen Book Research's *Understanding the Children's Book Consumer* survey into the reading habits of UK children aged 0-17, only one third of children aged 0-13 are read to daily. That figure has fallen 4% since last year and 9% since 2012. Nielsen's data also shows a strong correlation between older children being read to and those who choose to read independently for pleasure, since a huge proportion (74%) of 8-13 year-olds who are read to each day also read independently daily for pleasure, a figure that drops to just 29% for children who are read to less than once a week.

Authors themselves can help to influence children to decide whether or not they will read a book, and there is growing pressure on children's authors and illustrators, especially debut authors, to get out and about to meet their readers and to sell their books. Being a 'Waterstones Children's Author of the Month' has been very influential for debut authors including, for Chicken House, Maz Evans (*Who Let The Gods Out* 2017) and M.G. Leonard (*Beetle Boy* 2016) – but it has been the authors' drive to get out and meet their readers as their series have grown that has really made the difference in their success. And while school events, bookshop and library visits can tip the balance in getting word out about new books, just as important is to develop a strong viral presence where the 'influencers' – teachers, librarians and reviewers with high profiles – are increasingly found.

With just one influential bookselling chain, Waterstones, now in the high street, the days of relying on booksellers to hand-sell your book are long gone. These days, it's the author who is the most important advocate, and sales person, for their work.

Caroline Horn is Editor of www.readingzone.com.

See also...
- *Breaking down the market: where does your book sit?*, page 8
- *Including LGBT+ characters in children's fiction*, page 176
- *Children's bookshops*, page 71
- *Children's book and illustration prizes and awards*, page 379

Children's books: genres and categorisation

When you walk into any high street bookstore or search online the range of children's books can seem overwhelming. Caroline Horn guides us through the maze of books and explains how publishers and booksellers categorise titles.

Retailers – both physical and online – generally organise their children's book displays according to age ranges, making it easier for buyers to go straight to the section they want, be it baby board books or children's fiction. This approach also reflects how publishers 'segment' their lists.

Categorising children's books according to age groups is helpful as these categories generally reflect children's interests and reading abilities at key stages in their development. A book's format and subject matter, the presence of illustrations, and the size of text and pagination signal the intended age of its reader. So, for example, toddlers and preschool titles comprise short, illustrated picture books while young fiction books are mainly black and white text with short chapters, large text and, increasingly, a smattering of black-and-white illustrations.

Large publishing houses will tend to cover the whole gamut of age ranges for children, from nought to young adult. They want their titles to win the loyalty of new parents from day one and to keep that loyalty all the way through to that child's teen years. Smaller, specialist publishers will often focus their lists on specific areas of children's publishing that reflect their in-house skills. Nosy Crow, for example, is strong in preschool and junior fiction while Hot Key Books is known for its Young Adult (YA) fiction, books that appeal to readers aged 11 years plus.

Broadly speaking, children's books fit one of the following age groups: baby books (0–2 years), picture books (2–5 years), beginner readers (5–7 years), young fiction (6–8 years) and core fiction (8–11 years). Teen, or YA titles, are in the top age range, i.e. 11 years plus. The increasing number of books for older teenagers has led to calls for publishers to distinguish between books for teenagers (11+) and YA readers (14+), as YA books push the boundaries of what can be explored in books for older children. These titles may include swearing, drinking and drug-taking, or sex, and address sensitive issues such as sexual identity, abuse, suicide, etc.

Many readers at the top end of this age range are themselves adults; some 60% of YA books purchased are thought to be bought for adult readers. A more recent category, New Adult, has been introduced for older readers (aged 18+) who are happy to have sexual content in the books they buy. Traditionally the sexual content in YA books is limited, but the success of *Fifty Shades of Grey* by E.L. James has opened the market to more explicit fiction. Non-fiction is also categorised according to age range and, often, National Curriculum subject areas.

There are, though, always exceptions and children's varied abilities and interests will mean that young readers will often cross these age bands. This is why age guidance on books themselves – as shown on children's toys and clothing – is often absent. A nine-year-old boy with reading difficulties could, for example, find himself reading a title that he sees is recommended for a child aged six, and there's nothing more guaranteed to put off a child from picking up another book – ever! Lists have been developed by publishers like Bloomsbury (*White Wolves* series) and Barrington Stoke to fill the gap for titles that can be enjoyed by older readers who are still struggling to read fluently, and reluctant readers. In other cases, where perhaps an eight-year-old child has the reading ability of an 11- or 12-year-old, that child would probably struggle with the subject matter intended for older readers.

Age ranging

However, while there are very good reasons for not giving specific age recommendations on book covers, this has not helped parents and other book buyers who are struggling to find the right title for children. Publishers remain heavily reliant on the ability of booksellers, librarians and teachers to recommend the best book for individual children, although a limited number of fiction titles do now include an age guidance on the back cover, for example covering ages 5+, 7+, 9+, 11+ or 13+.

For those browsing online, very similar categories are used to those of physical bookshops. Amazon, for example, enables searches according to age ranges (0–2, 3–5, 6–8 and 9–11), as well as the type of book, such as picture book or pop-up book in the younger age ranges, while for older children you can search according to categories such as humour, themed or classic books. The more child-centred websites like Scholastic Book Club uses age-ranging to help narrow selections, and there is often a function to enable children to pick from an area of interest, either by subject (aliens, school, animals) or genre (humour, myths, thrillers, etc).

Age ranging is the broadest tool publishers can use in categorising their lists but they will also build their lists' depth and range according to a variety of other factors, particularly genres that are popular such as romance, fantasy, adventure, horror, etc. Publishers will frequently revisit their lists to check where their 'gaps' are and look for new titles according to how well a particular genre is doing.

Recent developments in fiction

In recent years, the British and US markets for children's fiction has flourished thanks to authors such as David Walliams (*Awful Auntie*, *Demon Dentist*) and Liz Pichon (*Tom Gates*), while a growing body of adults as well as teenage readers are enjoying bestselling authors including John Green (*The Fault in our Stars*) and Veronica Roth (*Divergent* series).

While it was once hard to envisage any demand by adults for children's books prior to the *Twilight* (Stephenie Meyer) and *Hunger Games* (Suzanne Collins) series, many YA books are now bought to be read by adults and publishers will look closely at a title's potential for crossover appeal. After all, selling to adults as well as to teenagers instantly doubles a book's market. A few short years ago, publishers would create separate editions of books for adult and younger readers. David Fickling Books and Random House, for example, created distinct children's and adult covers for *The Curious Incident of the Dog in the Night-Time* by Mark Haddon and John Boyne's *The Boy in the Striped Pyjamas*, with identical text for both versions of each book. That rarely happens now, as so many YA books are already being bought by adults, but it has made publishers careful to use covers that are not defined by the age of the potential reader. The covers of Sarah J. Maas's *A*

Court of Thorns and Roses (Bloomsbury) and Leslye Walton's *The Strange and Beautiful Sorrows of Ava Lavender* (Walker Books), for example, do not limit the readership to a particular age range.

The growing interest from adult readers and bloggers in YA fiction, as well as the number of authors wanting to write for young adults, means that YA fiction itself has really come of age, although it takes a bestseller like *The Fault in Our Stars* or *Divergent* to really push sales for this age group

Books are also sometimes categorised by author 'brand'. David Walliams, Jacqueline Wilson, Michael Morpurgo, and Julia Donaldson are all regarded as brands in their own right and, while they might write for many different age ranges, their titles will often be displayed together on an author's 'shelf' in bookshops. These key author 'brands' will regularly outsell adult bestseller titles and now take the biggest proportion of top ten places in the annual bestseller tables. Readers are also loyal to series – Liz Pichon's *Tom Gates* and Robin Stevens' *A Murder Most Unladylike* mystery series have shown how successful these can be.

At the younger end of the market, sales of the *Horrid Henry* series by Francesca Simon (Orion) encouraged publishers to develop more mass market series such as *Rainbow Magic* (Orchard Books) and the *Beast Quest* series (Orchard Books). Mass market series like these help to get 6–8 year-olds into the reading habit because they can recognise the books they have enjoyed and go back for more. Since young fiction books also tend to be relatively thin, a set of five or six books will help give them a presence on booksellers' shelves. Publishers are also turning to established picture book characters to help young fiction series stand out. Characters like Jonny Duddle's *Jolley Rogers* pirate family (from *The Pirates Next Door*) and Valerie Thomas's *Winnie the Witch* are now successful young fiction series.

The next 'big thing'

But publishers know that they would be unwise to focus exclusively on areas that are ahead in today's climate – children's books is a cyclical business and what works today could be out of favour a few months down the line. The partnership of Julia Donaldson and Axel Scheffler – beginning with *The Gruffalo* – helped to reinvigorate the picture book market over the last decade, while more recently large format, heavily illustrated books have helped drive up sales of non-fiction titles – an area that was previously struggling.

YA fiction, on the other hand, once the preserve of a dedicated but small band of readers, was blown open with the advent of ebooks, blogging and blockbuster films like *The Hunger Games*. It only takes a new taste, design or development to flip sales up or down, and trends will have a huge influence on what is published into these markets. After the dystopian trend in YA publishing, inspired by *The Hunger Games*, the trend was for more sci-fi, horror and romance and more focus on LGBT characters; today, YA publishers are waiting for the 'next big thing' – often driven by a film – to increase YA sales once again. Among younger readers, humour is what children are looking for, as well as the traditional adventure stories.

Demographics are also responsible for changing tastes and shifting emphasis in publishers' lists. The number of children aged under 12 years was falling, until a recent baby boom helped to grow the picture book market; that, however, is now falling back. The teen market has also grown, which partly accounts for the increasing interest in YA books, but it is general children's fiction that is currently seeing growth.

Books

Publishers will regularly revisit and reshape their lists as a result of market changes like these. Egmont Press, a notable fiction publisher for younger readers, has in recent years strengthened its teen fiction list with an imprint for this age range, Electric Monkey; the Bonnier Zaffre group bought the Piccadilly Press list to cement its move into younger fiction, while traditional non-fiction publisher Raintree moved into the fiction market with its imprint Curious Fox.

It goes without saying that writers need to know what areas a publisher specialises in before approaching them with manuscripts. A brilliant teenage title is likely to be rejected if the publisher's list does not include YA books. Still worse, an inexperienced publisher could take on a YA novel but let it fall into oblivion by failing to market it to the correct audience. That said, it is hard to second-guess what type of book publishers are looking for at any one time. A picture book publisher may still turn down a title, no matter how much they like it, or if they have over-commissioned in that area or if it is too similar to a title they are already publishing. Equally, even though booksellers' shelves may be groaning with middle-grade fantasy adventures, a book that stands out from the crowd will always find a home – publishers are continuously hunting for talented 'new voices'. In fact, 'debut author' has almost become a category in its own right as publishers strive to get unknown but promising authors into the hands of bloggers and booksellers.

It is also worth remembering that across the board, large publishing houses are reducing their children's output and that their lists are more structured and more focused than ever. If a company has filled the gap for a dragon fantasy for a ten-year-old reader, they won't be looking for any more. Another publisher, however, might be looking for exactly that.

Caroline Horn is Editor of www.readingzone.com.

See also...
- *Writing for a variety of ages*, page 124
- *News and trends in children's publishing 2018–19*, page 12
- *Breaking down the market: where does your book sit?*, page 8
- *Writing for reluctant readers*, page 112

Children's book publishers UK and Ireland

*Member of the Publishers Association or Publishing Scotland
†Member of Publishing Ireland, the Irish Book Publishers' Association

Abbey Home Media Group Ltd
435–7 Edgware Road, London W2 1TH
tel 020-7563 3910
email info@abbeyhomemedia.com
website www.abbeyhomemedia.com
Chairman Ian Miles, *Directors* Anne Miles, Dan Harriss, Emma Evans

Activity books, board books, novelty books, picture books, non-fiction, reference books and CDs. Advocates learning through interactive play. Age groups: preschool, 5–10 years.

Alanna Max
38 Oakfield Road, London N4 4NL
email info@alannamax.com
website www.alannamax.com
Publisher Ken Wilson Max, *Editor-at-Large* Anna McQuinn

Children's picture books. See website for submissions guidelines. Founded 2012.

Amgueddfa Cymru – National Museum Wales
Cathays Park, Cardiff CF10 3NP
tel 029-2057 3235
email post@museumwales.ac.uk
website www.museumwales.ac.uk
Twitter @AmgueddfaBooks
Head of Publishing Mari Gordon

Books based on the collections and research of Amgueddfa Cymru for adults, schools and children, in both Welsh and English. Founded 1907.

Andersen Press Ltd*
20 Vauxhall Bridge Road, London SW1V 2SA
tel 020-7840 8703 (editorial), 020-7840 8701 (general)
email anderseneditorial@penguinrandomhouse.co.uk
website www.andersenpress.co.uk
Managing Director Mark Hendle, *Publisher* Klaus Flugge, *Directors* Philip Durrance, Joëlle Flugge, Libby Hamilton (editorial picture books), Sue Buswell (editorial picture books), Charlie Sheppard (editorial fiction), Liz White (rights)

A leading children's publisher of picture books, fiction for 5–8 and 9–12 years and young adult fiction. Successes include the *Elmer* series by David McKee, the *Little Princess* series by Tony Ross, *Who's in the Loo?* by Jeanne Willis and Adrian Reynolds,

The Lonely Beast by Chris Judge, *Out of Shadows* by Jason Wallace and *Liar & Spy* by Rebecca Stead. Will consider unsolicited MSS. Include sae and allow three months for response. For novels, send three sample chapters and a synopsis only. No poetry or short stories. Do not send MSS via email. Founded 1976.

Arcturus Publishing Ltd
26–27 Bickels Yard, 151–153 Bermondsey Street, London SE1 3HA
tel 020-7407 9400
email info@arcturuspublishing.com
website www.arcturuspublishing.com
Editorial Manager Joe Harris (children's)

Children's non-fiction, including activity books, reference, education, practical art, geography, history and science. No unsolicited MSS. Founded 1993.

Atlantic Europe Publishing Co. Ltd
The Barn, Bottom Farm, Bottom Lane, Henley-on-Thames, Oxon RG8 0NR
tel (01491) 684028
email info@atlanticeurope.com
website www.atlanticeurope.com,
www.curriculumvisions.com
Director Dr B.J. Knapp

Educational: children's colour illustrated information books, co-editions and primary school class books covering science, geography, technology, mathematics, history, religious education. Recent successes include the *Curriculum Visions* series and *Science at School* series. Submit via email to contactus@atlanticeurope.com with no attachments. No MSS accepted by post. Established teacher authors only. Founded 1990.

Aurora Metro
67 Grove Avenue, Twickenham TW1 4HX
tel 020-3261 0000
email info@aurorametro.com
website www.aurorametro.com
Facebook www.facebook.com/AuroraMetroBooks
Twitter @aurorametro
Managing Director Cheryl Robson

Adult fiction, young adult fiction, biography, drama (including plays for young people), non-fiction, theatre, cookery and translation. Submissions: send synopsis and three chapters via our website:

www.aurorametro.com/contact-us/submit-your-work/. Runs a biennial competition for women novelists over 18 (odd years): Virginia Prize For Fiction. Entry fee for submission of either adult or young adult novel. See website: www.aurorametro.com/VirginiaPrize. Founded 1996.

Award Publications Ltd
The Old Riding School, The Welbeck Estate, Worksop, Notts. S80 3LR
tel (01909) 478170
email info@awardpublications.co.uk
Facebook www.facebook.com/awardpublications
Twitter @award_books

Children's books: picture story books; early learning, information and activity books from birth to 12. No unsolicited material. Founded 1972.

b small publishing limited
website www.bsmall.co.uk
Managing Director Catherine Bruzzone, *Publisher* Sam Hutchinson

Activity books and foreign language learning books for 2–12 years. Written in-house. No unsolicited MSS. Founded 1990.

Badger Learning*
Suite F32, Business & Technology Centre, Bessemer Drive, Stevenage, Herts. SG1 2DX
tel (01553) 816083
email info@badgerlearning.co.uk
website www.badgerlearning.co.uk
Publisher Danny Pearson

Educational publishing for pupils and teachers across the curriculum, from Foundation Stage to Year 13, dual language books and science books for KS3–KS5. Specialists in publishing teen fiction and books for children and young adults who are struggling or reluctant readers. Range covers high interest age/low reading age titles. Series include *Teen Reads, YA Reads, Papercuts, Between the Lines, Strange Town, Snow-Man, The League of Enchanted Heroes, Full Flight, First Flight* and *Graphic Novels*. Email for submission guidelines. Founded 2001.

Barrington Stoke*
18 Walker Street, Edinburgh EH3 7LP
tel 0131 225 4113
email info@barringtonstoke.co.uk
website www.barringtonstoke.co.uk

Fiction for reluctant, dyslexic or under-confident readers: fiction for children 8–12 years with a reading age of 8+, fiction for teenagers with a reading age of 8+, fiction for 8–12 years with a reading age of below 8, fiction for teenagers with a reading age of below 8, non-fiction for children 10–14 years with a reading age of 8+, fiction for adults with a reading age of 8+, graphic novels. Resources for readers and their teachers. Publishes approx. 70 titles a year and has over 350 books in print.

No unsolicited MSS. All work is commissioned from well-known authors and adapted for reluctant readers. Founded 1998.

A&C Black – see Bloomsbury Publishing Plc

Bloomsbury Publishing Plc*
50 Bedford Square, London WC1B 3DP
tel 020-7631 5600
website www.bloomsbury.com
Co-founder & Chief Executive Nigel Newton

A medium-sized independent book publishing house and digital content services provider with two worldwide publishing divisions: Consumer and Non-Consumer. Offices in the UK, the USA (page 51), India and Australia (page 42). Has acquired imprints dating back to 1807. MSS must normally be channelled through literary agents. Bloomsbury runs training for authors on getting published via www.writersandartists.co.uk and Bloomsbury Institute events. Founded 1986.

BLOOMSBURY CONSUMER DIVISION
Managing Director Emma Hopkin
Imprints include: Absolute Press, Bloomsbury Activity Books, Bloomsbury Children's Books, Bloomsbury Circus, Bloomsbury India, Bloomsbury Press, Bloomsbury Publishing, Bloomsbury Reader, Bloomsbury USA, Bloomsbury USA Children's Books, Raven Books.

Bloomsbury Adult Trade Publishing
Adult Editor-in-Chief Alexandra Pringle, *Publishing Directors* Alexis Kirschbaum, Michael Fishwick, *Editorial Director Raven Books* Alison Hennessey
Part of Bloomsbury Consumer Division, Bloomsbury Adult Trade publishes fiction and non-fiction.

Bloomsbury Children's Books
Publishing Director & International Editor-in-Chief Rebecca McNally, *Publishing Directors* Sharon Hutton (non-fiction), Emma Blackburn (illustrated books), *Head of Fiction* Ellen Holgate, *Editorial Directors* Zoe Griffiths (fiction), Saskia Gwinn (non-fiction)
Authors include J.K. Rowling, Louis Sachar, Neil Gaiman, Sarah J. Maas, Sarah Crossan and Brian Conaghan. No complete MSS; send a synopsis with three chapters.

Bloomsbury Education
Head of Education Rachel Lindley, *Editorial Directors* Helen Diamond (education) and Hannah Rolls (educational fiction and poetry), *Commissioning Editor* Hannah Marston (education – CPD)
Publishes around 75 print titles per year and apps and digital platforms for children, young people and those working with them. Titles for teachers and practitioners cover the areas of early years, primary and secondary education, and include both practical resources and professional development titles. Imprints include Bloomsbury Education, A&C Black, Andrew Brodie and Featherstone Education.

No submissions by email. Look at recently published titles and catalogues to gauge current publishing interests. Much of the list is educationally focused and publishes in series. Allow 8–10 weeks for a response.

BLOOMSBURY ACADEMIC AND PROFESSIONAL DIVISION
website www.bloomsburyprofessional.com
website www.bloomsburyacademic.com
Managing Director Jonathan Glasspool

Part of Bloomsbury Non-Consumer Division.

Bloomsbury Special Interest
Managing Director Sarah Broadway

Publishes a wide variety of non-fiction.

Digital Resources
Managing Director Kathryn Earle

Digital content services.

Bodley Head Children's Books – see Penguin Random House Children's UK

Bonnier Zaffre*
80–81 Wimpole Street, London W1G 9RE
tel 020-7490 3875
email info@bonnierzaffre.co.uk
website www.bonnierzaffre.co.uk
Facebook www.facebook.com/BonnierZaffre
Twitter @BonnierZaffre
Ceo tbc, *Executive Director* Kate Parkin (adult), *Executive Director* Jane Harris (children's), *Executive Director* James Horobin (sales and marketing)

Publishes award-winning fiction for all ages, including crime, thrillers, women's fiction, general fiction, children's fiction and picture books and young adult. Imprints include: Zaffre Publishing, Twenty7 Books, Hot Key Books (page 30), Piccadilly Press (page 36) and Manilla Publishing. A division of Bonnier Books UK. Founded 2015.

The Book Guild Ltd
14 Priory Business Park, Wistow Road, Kibworth, Leics. LE8 0RX
tel 0800 999 2982
email info@bookguild.co.uk
website www.bookguild.co.uk
Facebook www.facebook.com/thebookguild
Twitter @BookGuild
Directors Jeremy Thompson (managing), Jane Rowland (operations)

Offers traditional and partnership publishing arrangements, with all titles published being funded or co-funded by The Book Guild Ltd (does not offer self-publishing). MSS accepted in fiction, children's and non-fiction genres, please see the website for details. The Book Guild is part of parent company Troubador Publishing Ltd. Founded 1996.

Boxer Books Ltd
70 Cowcross Street, London EC1M 6EJ
email info@boxerbooks.com
website www.boxerbooks.com

No unsolicited MSS in any form unless via a recognised agency. Publishes innovative baby board books, picture books, young fiction and stunning story collections. Founded 2005.

Bright Red Publishing
1 Torphichen Street, Edinburgh EH3 8HX
tel 0131 220 5804
email info@brightredpublishing.co.uk
website www.brightredpublishing.co.uk
Facebook www.facebook.com/BrightRedBooks
Twitter @_BrightRed
Instagram bright_red_publishing
Directors John MacPherson, Alan Grierson

Educational publishing for Scotland's students and teachers. Founded 2008.

Brilliant Publications Ltd*
Unit 10, Sparrow Hall Farm, Edlesborough, Dunstable LU6 2ES
tel (01525) 222292
email info@brilliantpublications.co.uk
website www.brilliantpublications.co.uk
Facebook www.facebook.com/Brilliant-Publications-340005555138
Twitter @Brilliantpub
Twitter @BrillCreative
Managing Director Priscilla Hannaford

Creates easy-to-use educational resources, featuring engaging approaches to learning, across a wide range of curriculum areas, including English, foreign languages, maths, art and design, thinking skills and PSHE. No children's picture books, non-fiction books or one-off fiction books. See Guidelines for Authors on website before sending proposal. Founded 1993.

The British Museum Press
38 Russell Square, London WC1B 3QQ
tel 020-3073 4946
email publicity@britishmuseum.org
website www.britishmuseum.org/about_us/services/the_british_museum_press.aspx
Head of Business Planning Susan Walby

Award-winning illustrated books for children, young readers and families, inspired by the famous collections of the British Museum. Titles range across picture books, activity books and illustrated non-fiction. Founded 1973.

Andrew Brodie – see Bloomsbury Publishing Plc

Burning Chair Publishing
71–75 Shelton Street, Covent Garden, London WC2H 9JQ

Books

email info@burningchairpublishing.com
website www.burningchairpublishing.com
Facebook www.facebook.com/
BurningChairPublishing
Twitter @Burning_Chair
Directors Simon Finnie, Peter Oxley

Burning Chair is an independent publishing company based in the UK but covering readers and authors across the globe. Welcomes unsolicited young adult fiction submissions (from authors direct as well as through agents) in the following genres: mystery, thriller, suspense, crime, action and adventure, science fiction, fantasy, paranormal, horror, historical fiction. See the submissions page: www.burningchairpublishing.com/submissions. Founded 2018.

Buster Books

16 Lion Yard, Tremadoc Road, London SW4 7NQ
tel 020-7720 8643
email enquiries@mombooks.com
website www.mombooks.com/buster
Facebook www.facebook.com/BusterBooks
Twitter @BusterBooks
Reference, activity, board and picture books for 0+ years. Publishes approx. 70 titles a year. Buster's publications include puzzle books, with the *Clever Kids* series, and a wide selection of children's illustrated non-fiction, colouring, drawing, sticker, picture and activity books. Titles range from self-discovery titles such as *Picture Me, I am a Wonder Woman* and *All About Me*, to quirky titles such as *The Magical Unicorn Society Official Handbook, Sherlock Bones and the Times Table Adventure* and *BTS: Test Your Super-Fan Status*. Bestselling colouring books include the *I Heart Colouring* series and *Colourtronic*. Unable to guarantee a reply to every submission received, please send sae for return of submission. Allow between one and two months for response. Founded 1985.

Cambridge University Press*

University Printing House, Shaftesbury Road,
Cambridge CB2 8BS
tel (01223) 358331
email information@cambridge.org
website www.cambridge.org
Facebook www.facebook.com/
CambridgeUniversityPress
Twitter @CambridgeUP
Chief Executive Peter Phillips; *Managing Directors* Mandy Hill (academic), Paul Colbert (ELT), Rod Smith (Cambridge Education)

For children: curriculum-based education books and software for schools and colleges (primary, secondary and international). ELT for adult and younger learners. Founded 1534.

Campbell – see Pan Macmillan

Candy Jar Books

Mackintosh House, 136 Newport Road,
Cardiff CF24 1DJ
tel 029-2115 7202
email shaun@candyjarbooks.co.uk
website www.candy-jar.co.uk/books
Facebook www.facebook.com/CandyJarLimited
Twitter @Candy_Jar
Head of Publishing Shaun Russell

Non-fiction and fiction for children aged 7+. Will consider unsolicited MSS. Check website for submission details. Founded 2010.

Carlton Publishing Group

20 Mortimer Street, London W1T 3JW
tel 020-7612 0400
email enquiries@carltonbooks.co.uk
website www.carltonbooks.co.uk

No unsolicited MSS; synopses and ideas welcome, but no fiction or poetry. Acquired by Welbeck Publishing Group 2019. Founded 1992.

Caterpillar Books – see Little Tiger Group

Catnip Publishing Ltd

320 City Road, London EC1V 2NZ
tel 020-7138 3650
email editorial@catnippublishing.co.uk
website www.bouncemarketing.co.uk/publisher/
catnip-publishing
Twitter @catnipbooks
Managing Director Robert Snuggs

New and previously published titles from picture books to teen fiction. Acquires new titles from overseas publishers, reissues out-of-print titles by top authors and commissions original fiction for 7–9 years, 9–12 years and young adult readers. Publishes 15–20 books a year. Recently published books by Pippa Goodhart, Jason Beresford, Berlie Doherty, Sarah Baker, Sophie Plowden, Joan Lingard, Keris Stainton and Anne Booth. Will only consider agented submissions. Founded 2005.

CGP

Coordination Group Publications,
Broughton House, Broughton-in-Furness,
Cumbria LA20 6HH
tel (01229) 715753
email ewt@cgpbooks.co.uk
website www.cgpbooks.co.uk

Educational books centred around the National Curriculum, including revision guides and study books for KS1, KS2, KS3, GCSE and A level. Subjects include maths, English, science, history, geography, ICT, psychology, business studies, religious studies, design and techology, PE, music, French, German, Spanish, sociology, 11+ and functional skills. On the lookout for top teachers at all levels, in all subjects. Potential authors and proofreaders should email the external writing team with their name, subject area, level and experience, plus contact address, ready for when a project comes up in their subject area. Founded 1996.

Chicken House

2 Palmer Street, Frome, Somerset BA11 1DS
tel (01373) 454488
email hello@chickenhousebooks.com
website www.chickenhousebooks.com
Twitter @chickenhsebooks
Managing Director & Publisher Barry Cunningham,
Deputy Managing Director Rachel Hickman

Fiction for ages 7+ and young adult. No unsolicited MSS. Successes include James Dashner (the *Maze Runner* series), Cornelia Funke (*Inkheart* and *Dragon Rider* series) and Kiran Millwood Hargrave (*The Girl of Ink & Stars*). See website for details of *Times*/Chicken House Children's Fiction Competition for unpublished writers. Founded 2000.

Child's Play (International) Ltd

Ashworth Road, Bridgemead, Swindon,
Wilts. SN5 7YD
tel (01793) 616286
email office@childs-play.com
website www.childs-play.com
Facebook www.facebook.com/ChildsPlayBooks
Twitter @ChildsPlayBooks
Chairman Adriana Twinn, *Publisher* Neil Burden

Children's educational books: board, picture, activity and play books; fiction and non-fiction. Founded 1972.

Christian Education

5/6 Imperial Court, 12 Sovereign Road,
Birmingham B30 3FH
tel 0121 472 4242
email anstice.hughes@christianeducation.org.uk
website http://shop.christianeducation.org.uk/
website www.retoday.org.uk
Facebook www.facebook.com/RETodayServices
Twitter @IBRAbibleread

Incorporating RE Today Services and International Bible Reading Association. Publications and services for teachers and other professionals in religious education including *REtoday* magazine, curriculum booklets and classroom resources. Also publishes bible reading materials. Founded 2001.

Claret Press

51 Iveley Road, London SW4 0EN
tel 020-622 0436
email contact@claretpress.com
website www.claretpress.com
Facebook www.facebook.com/ClaretPublisher
Twitter @Claret_Press
Founder & Editor-in-Chief Katie Isbester

Selects on the basis of quality and readability in the belief that those criteria create modern classics.

Publishes quirky, tilt to young adult cross-over. Flexible about genre. Founded 2016.

Classical Comics

PO Box 177, Ludlow, Shrops. SY8 9DL
tel 0845 812 3000
email info@classicalcomics.com
website www.classicalcomics.com
Managing Director Gary Bryant

Graphic novel adaptations of classical literature. Founded 2007.

Colourpoint Creative Ltd[†]

Colourpoint House, Jubilee Business Park,
21 Jubilee Road, Newtownards, Co. Down BT23 4YH
tel 028-9182 6339 (within UK), 048-9182 6339 (Republic of Ireland)
email sales@colourpoint.co.uk
website www.colourpoint.co.uk
Twitter @colourpointedu
Commissioning Editor Wesley Johnston, *Marketing* Jacky Hawkes

Textbooks for Northern Ireland CCEA board. Educational textbooks for KS3 (11–14 years) KS3 Special Needs (10–14 years), GCSE (14–16 years) and A-Level/undergraduates (age 17+). Not primary. Subjects include, but not limited to, biology, business studies, chemistry, English, geography, history, HE, ICT, Irish, life and health sciences, LLW, MVRUS, PE, physics, politics, technology and design, science and RE. Short queries by email. Full submission in writing including details of proposal, sample chapter/section to show ability to connect with target age group, qualification/experience in the subject, full contact details and return postage. Textbooks, workbooks and electronic resources all considered. Founded 1993.

Corner to Learn

Willow Cottage, 26 Purton Stoke, Swindon SN5 4JF
tel 07976 574627
email neil@cornertolearn.co.uk
website www.cornertolearn.co.uk
Publisher Neil Griffiths

Books and learning materials aimed at teachers and parents with young children. Imprint: Red Robin Books (picture books).

Cranachan Publishing

Blacksheep Croft, 52 North Galson,
Isle of Lewis HS2 0SJ
tel (01851) 850700
email hello@cranachanpublishing.co.uk
website www.cranachanpublishing.co.uk
Twitter @cranachanbooks
Publishing Director Anne Glennie, *Publicity & Sales Manager* Kelly Macdonald

A small independent publisher based on the Isle of Lewis, publishes high-quality children's fiction and non-fiction, under the Pokey Hat imprint, with a focus on exciting historical fiction set in Scotland, for the 9–12 age range. Also publishes educational resources for teachers. Young adult fiction imprint: Gob Stopper. Founded 2015.

Cranthorpe Millner Publishers
18 Soho Square, London W1D 3QL
tel 020-3441 9212
email Kirstyellen.smillie@cranthorpemillner.com
website www.cranthorpemillner.com
Facebook www.facebook.com/CranthorpeMillner
Twitter @CMPublishers
Instagram cranthorpemillnerpublishers
Directors Kirsty-Ellen Smillie (managing), David Hahn (chairman)

Titles include fiction and non-fiction: memoir, celeb autobiographies, history, science fiction, young adult, historical fiction, crime/thriller, literary fiction. Founded 2018.

Crown House Publishing Ltd
Crown Buildings, Bancyfelin, Carmarthen SA33 5ND
tel (01267) 211345
email books@crownhouse.co.uk
website www.crownhouse.co.uk
Facebook www.facebook.com/Crown-House-Publishing
Twitter @CrownHousePub
Directors David Bowman (managing), Karen Bowman

Education publisher with a large range of classroom resources and materials for professional teacher development. The list includes the Independent Thinking Press imprint, as well as books on health and wellbeing, NLP, hypnosis, counselling, psychotherapy and coaching. Founded 1998.

Independent Thinking Press
email books@independentthinkingpress.com
website www.independentthinkingpress.com

Publishes CPD books and resources for teachers and school leaders. The list includes books on business, training and development, coaching, health and wellbeing, NLP, hypnosis, counselling and psychotherapy and a range of children's books.

Dinosaur Books Ltd
88 Turney Road, London SE21 7JH
tel 020-7737 6737
email info@dinosaurbooks.co.uk
website www.dinosaurbooks.co.uk
Twitter @dinosaurbooksco
Director Sonya McGilchrist

Submit by email only: submissions@dinosaurbooks. co.uk. Website as above. Publishing chapter books for children aged 5–14. Founded 2014.

DK
80 Strand, London WC2R 0RL
tel 020-625 5678
website www.dk.com
Ceo Ian Hudson

Publishes illustrated titles. A member of the Penguin Random House division of Bertelsmann, publishing highly visual books for adults and children: travel, children's, reference, education, gardening, food and drink (page 35). Founded 1974.

Dorling Kindersley – see DK

Doubleday Children's Books – see Penguin Random House Children's UK

Dref Wen
28 Church Road, Whitchurch, Cardiff CF14 2EA
tel 029-2061 7860
website www.drefwen.com
Directors Roger Boore, Anne Boore, Gwilym Boore, Alun Boore, Rhys Boore

Welsh language publisher. Original, adaptations and translations of foreign and English language full-colour picture story books for children. Also activity books, novelty books, Welsh language fiction for children 7–14 years, teenage fiction, reference, religion, audiobooks and poetry. Educational material for primary and secondary schoolchildren in Wales and England, including dictionaries, revision guides and Welsh as a Second Language. Publishes approx. 50 titles a year and has 450 in print. No unsolicited MSS. Phone first. Founded 1970.

The Educational Company of Ireland
Ballymount Road, Walkinstown, Dublin D12 R25C, Republic of Ireland
tel +353 (0)14 500611
email info@edco.ie
website www.edco.ie
Ceo Martina Harford

Educational (primary and post-primary) books in the Irish language. Publishes approx. 60–70 titles each year and has 600–700 in print. Ancillary materials include digital resources, concrete resources and CDs. A member of the Smurfit Kappa Group plc. Founded 1910. Submissions to: amolumby@edco.ie. Please include: a brief description of the project's scope and content; table of contents; sample chapter and biographical details. Allow three months for response.

Educational Explorers (Publishers)
Unit 5, Feidr Castell Business Park, Fishguard SA65 9BB
tel (01348) 874890
website www.cuisenaire.co.uk
Directors J. Hollyfield, D.M. Gattegno

Educational. Recent successes include: mathematics: *Numbers in Colour with Cuisenaire Rods*; languages:

The Silent Way; literacy, reading: *Words in Colour*; educational films. No longer accepting unsolicited MSS. Founded 1962.

Egmont UK Ltd*

First Floor, The Yellow Building, 1 Nicholas Road, London W11 4AN
tel 020-3220 0400
email info@egmont.co.uk
website www.egmont.co.uk
Twitter @EgmontUK

Large specialist children's publisher. Publishes a diverse portfolio of inclusive, child-friendly books and magazines. Egmont UK is part of the Egmont Group and owned by the Egmont Foundation, a charitable trust. Submission details: visit website to see current policy. Publishes classics as well as exciting new voices. Authors include: Michael Morpurgo, Laura Ellen Anderson, Andy Stanton, Enid Blyton, Anne Fine, Tahereh Mafi, Jim Smith and Katherine Woodfine. Picture Book and Gift list offers an inclusive range of picture books (ages 0–5), gift books, classics and non-fiction titles (ages 5–16) featuring bestselling authors and illustrators, such as Julia Donaldson, Jim Field, Chris Packham, Steven Lenton, Peter Bently, Adam and Charlotte Guillain. Founded 1878.

Egmont Heritage

Publishes high-quality bound editions of classics in European literature.

Electric Monkey

Contact Alison Dougal
Young adult imprint. Authors on the list include: Michael Grant (writer of the GONE series), Em Bailey and Siobhan Curham. Founded 2012.

Jelly Pie

Humour for 5-8 years olds, including the Mr Gum series of books. Awards received include: The People's Book Prize, The Roald Dahl Funny Prize, the Nestle Children's Book Prize, the Red House Children's Book Award and the Blue Peter award. Founded 2013.

Electric Monkey – see Egmont UK Ltd

Everything With Words Ltd

16 Limekiln Place, London SE19 2RE
tel 020-8771 2974
email info@everythingwithwords.com
website www.everythingwithwords.com
Managing Director & Publisher Mikka Bott

Children's fiction for ages 5 to young adult. Publishes innovative, quality fiction. Accepts unsolicited manuscripts. Founded 2016.

Faber and Faber Ltd*

Bloomsbury House, 74–77 Great Russell Street, London WC1B 3DA

tel 020-7927 3800
website www.faber.co.uk
Twitter @FaberChildrens
Chief Executive Stephen Page, *Publisher* Leah Thaxton (children's), *Communications Director & Associate Publisher* Rachel Alexander, *Operations Director* Nigel Marsh

High-quality picture books, general fiction and non-fiction, drama, film, music, poetry. For children: fiction for 5–8 and 9–12 years, teenage fiction, poetry and some non-fiction. Authors include T.S. Eliot, Ted Hughes, Philip Ardagh, Justin Fletcher, Harry Hill, Betty G. Birney, Francesca Simon, Karen McCombie, Jennifer Gray, Mackenzie Crook, Natasha Frarrant. Founded 1929.

CJ Fallon

Ground Floor, Block B, Liffey Valley Office Campus, Dublin D22 X0Y3, Republic of Ireland
tel +353 (0)16 166400
email editorial@cjfallon.ie
website www.cjfallon.ie
Executive Directors Brian Gilsenan (managing), John Bodley (financial)

Educational textbooks. Founded 1927.

Fat Fox Books

The Den, PO Box 579, Tonbridge TN9 9NG
tel (01580) 857249
email hello@fatfoxbooks.com
website http://fatfoxbooks.com
Facebook www.facebook.com/Fat-Fox/
Twitter @FatFoxBooks
Managing Director Holly Millbank

Independent publisher of children's books for children 3–14 years. Founded 2014.

Featherstone Education – see Bloomsbury Publishing Plc

David Fickling Books

31 Beaumont Street, Oxford OX1 2NP
tel (01865) 339000
website www.davidficklingbooks.com
Publisher David Fickling

Independent publisher of picture books and novels for all ages, as well as graphic novels, with a focus on brilliant storytelling and world-class illustration. Founded 1999.

Fircone Books Ltd

The Holme, Church Road, Eardisley, Herefordshire HR3 6NJ
tel (01544) 327182
email info@firconebooks.com
website www.firconebooks.com
Facebook www.facebook.com/firconebooks
Twitter @firconebooks
Directors Richard Wheeler, Su Wheeler

Books

Nostalgic illustrated books on church art and architecture. Welcomes submission of ideas: send synopsis first. Founded 2009.

Firefly Press Ltd*

25 Gabalfa Road, Llandaff North, Cardiff CF14 2JJ
email fireflypress@yahoo.co.uk
website www.fireflypress.co.uk
Facebook www.facebook.com/FireflyPress
Twitter @fireflypress
Publisher Penny Thomas, *Editor* Janet Thomas,
Marketing & Publicity Manager Megan Farr,
Commercial Director Robin Bennett

Award-winning publisher of quality fiction for ages 5 to 19. Founded 2013.

Fisherton Press

email general@fishertonpress.co.uk
website www.fishertonpress.co.uk
Facebook www.facebook.com/FishertonPress
Twitter @fishertonpress
Director Ellie Levenson

A small independent publisher producing picture books for children under 7. Not currently accepting proposals but illustrators are welcome to send links to their portfolio. Founded 2013.

Flame Tree Publishing

6 Melbray Mews, Fulham, London SW6 3NS
tel 020-7751 9650
email info@flametreepublishing.com
website www.flametreepublishing.com
Ceo & Publisher Nick Wells

Occasional children's novelty books and early learning. Founded 1992.

Floris Books*

2a Robertson Avenue, Edinburgh EH11 1PZ
tel 0131 337 2372
email floris@florisbooks.co.uk
website www.florisbooks.co.uk
Facebook www.facebook.com/FlorisBooks
Twitter @FlorisBooks
Commissioning Editors Sally Polson, Eleanor Collins

Children's activity books, novels, board and picture books. Approx. 70 titles each year. Founded 1978.

Kelpies

website www.discoverkelpies.co.uk
Contemporary Scottish fiction – picture books (for 3–6 years), young readers series (for 6–8 years) and novels (for 8–15 years). Recent successes include *The Nowhere Emporium* by Ross MacKenzie and *There Was a Wee Lassie Who Swallowed a Midgie* by Rebecca Colby. See website for submission details.

Galore Park Publishing Ltd*

338 Euston Road, London NW1 3BH
tel 020-7873 6412
website www.galorepark.co.uk

Educational textbooks and revision guides for students studying at independent schools. *So You Really Want To Learn* range of textbooks for children 11+ years and *Junior* range for children 8–10 years. Courses include Latin, French, English, Spanish, maths and science. Founded 1999.

Gardner Education Ltd

Unit 2, Aston Way, Middlewich, Cheshire CW10 0HS
tel 0845 230 0775
email education@gardnereducation.co.uk
website www.gardnereducation.co.uk
Facebook www.facebook.com/GardnerEducation
Twitter @Gardner_Edu
Managing Director Stuart Withers

A specialist supplier of primary and secondary literacy books to schools and parents. Range includes book banded publications, dyslexia friendly texts, Accelerated Reader and Catch Up Literacy approved titles, books tailored for struggling and reluctant readers, and a massive selection of titles to cater for all primary and secondary reading preferences. Founded 1999.

Ginn – see Pearson UK

GL Assessment

1st Floor Vantage London, Great West Road, Brentford TW8 9AG
tel 020-8996 3333
email information@gl-assessment.co.uk
website www.gl-assessment.co.uk
Chairman Philip Walters

Independent provider of tests, assessments and assessment services for education. Aims to help educational professionals to understand and maximise the potential of their pupils and students. Publishes assessments for the 0–19 age group, though the majority of its assessments are aimed at children 5–14 years. Testing and assessment services include literacy, numeracy, thinking skills, ability, learning support and online testing. Founded 1981.

Gomer Press

33–35 Lammas Street, Carmarthen SA31 3AL
tel (01267) 221400
email meirion@gomer.co.uk
website www.gomer.co.uk
website www.pontbooks.co.uk
Managing Director Jonathan Lewis, *Editors* Dr Ashley Owen (children's English), Nia Parry (children's Welsh)

History, travel, photography, biography, art, poetry and fiction of relevance to Welsh culture, in English and in Welsh. Picture books, novels, stories, poetry and teaching resources for children. Preliminary enquiry essential. Welcomes submissions by email. Founded 1892.

W.F. Graham
2 Pondwood Close, Moulton Park,
Northampton NN3 6RT
tel (01604) 645537
email books@wfgraham.co.uk
website www.wfgraham.co.uk

Activity books including colouring, dot-to-dot, magic painting, puzzle, word search and sticker books.

Granada Learning*
1st Floor Vantage London, Great West Road,
Brentford TW8 9AG
tel 020-8996 3333
website www.gl-education.com

Educational multimedia company publishing innovative assessment and curriculum-based resources for the UK and abroad. It has a catalogue of over 200 products for preschool children, primary and secondary, through to A level. Products are developed by teachers and educationalists. The Granada Learning Group includes Granada Learning Professional Development, GL Assessment (page 28) and schoolcentre.net. Founded 1991.

The Greystones Press
37 Lawton Avenue, Carterton, Oxon OX18 3JY
tel (01993) 841219
email editorial@greystonespress.com
website www.greystonespress.com
Directors Mary Hoffman, Stephen Barber

A small independent publishing company specializing in adult and young adult fiction and adult non-fiction in areas of interest, like literature, art, history, music, myths and legends. Currently closed to submissions. No middle grade or younger or illustrated books. Founded 2014.

Hachette Children's Group*
Carmelite House, 50 Victoria Embankment,
London EC4Y 0DZ
email editorial@hachettechildrens.co.uk
website www.hachettechildrens.co.uk
Ceo Hilary Murray Hill

Children's non-fiction, reference, information, gift, fiction, picture, novelty and audiobooks. Unsolicited material is not considered other than by referral or recommendation. Formed by combining Watts Publishing with Hodder Children's Books in 2005. Founded 1986.

Hodder Children's Group
Facebook www.facebook.com/hodderchildrensbooks
Twitter @hodderchildrens
Publishing Director Anne McNeil
Fiction, picture books, novelty, general non-fiction and audiobooks.

Little, Brown Books for Young Readers
Facebook www.facebook.com/lbkidsuk
Twitter @lbkidsuk

Publisher Megan Tingley
Fiction, novelty, general non-fiction and audiobooks.

Orchard Books
Facebook www.facebook.com/orchardchildrensbooks
Twitter @orchardbooks
Publishing Director Megan Larkin
Fiction, picture and novelty books.

Orion Children's Books
Facebook www.facebook.com/TheOrionStar
Twitter @the_orionstar
Fiction, picture books, novelty, general non-fiction and audiobooks.

Pat-a-Cake
New baby, preschool and early years imprint.

Quercus Children's Books
Imprint poducing quality teen and young adult fiction.

Franklin Watts
Twitter @franklinwatts
Editorial Director Sarah Peutrill
Non-fiction and information books.

Wayland
Twitter @waylandbooks
Editorial Director Paul Rockett
Non-fiction and information books.

Wren & Rook
Publishing Director Debbie Foy
Imprint publishing brave, diverse and imaginative books for children and young people.

Hachette UK*
Carmelite House, 50 Victoria Embankment,
London EC4Y 0DZ
tel 020-3122 6000
website www.hachette.co.uk
Chief Executive David Shelley, *Directors* Richard Kitson, Jamie Hodder Williams (Ceo, Hodder & Stoughton, Headline, John Murray Press, Quercus & Director of Trade Publishing, Hachette UK), Alison Goff (Ceo, Octopus), Hilary Murray Hill (Ceo, Hachette Children's Group), Lis Tribe (managing, Hodder Education) Chris Emerson (Coo), Pierre de Cacqueray (Group Finance Director), Melanie Tansey (Group HR Director), Clare Harington (Group Communications Director), Oliver Rhodes (Chief Executive Bookouture).

Part of Hachette Livre SA since 2004. Hachette UK group companies: Hachette Children's Group (see above), Headline Book Publishing, Hodder Education Group, Hodder & Stoughton, Hodder Faith, John Murray, Little, Brown Book Group, Orion Group, Octopus Group, Hachette Ireland, Hachette Australia (page 42), Hachette New Zealand. Founded 1986.

Haldane Mason Ltd

PO Box 34196, London NW10 3YB
tel 020-8459 2131
email info@haldanemason.com
website www.haldanemason.com
Directors Sydney Francis, Ron Samuel

Illustrated non-fiction books and box sets, mainly for children. No unsolicited material. Imprints: Haldane Mason (adult), Red Kite Books (children's). Founded 1995.

HarperCollins Publishers*

The News Building, 1 London Bridge Street, London SE1 9GF
tel 020-8741 7070
Alternative address Westerhill Road, Bishopbriggs, Glasgow G64 2QT
tel 0141 772 3200
website www.harpercollins.co.uk
Ceo Charlie Redmayne

For adults: fiction (commercial and literary) and non-fiction. Subjects include history; celebrity memoirs; biographies; popular science; mind, body & spirit; dictionaries; maps and reference. All fiction and trade non-fiction must be submitted through an agent. Owned by News Corporation. Founded 1817.

Harper Audio

Offers bestselling in CD and other audio formats.

HarperCollins Children's Books

Publisher Ann-Janine Murtagh

Annuals, activity books, novelty books, pre-school brands, picture books, pop-up books and book and CD sets. Fiction for 5–8 and 9–12 years, young adult fiction and series fiction; film/TV tie-ins. Publishes approx. 265 titles each year. Picture book authors include Oliver Jeffers, Judith Kerr and Emma Chichester Clark, and fiction by David Walliams, Michael Morpurgo, David Baddiel and Lauren Child. Books published under licence include *Dr Seuss*, *Bing*, *Twirlywoos* and *Paddington Bear*. No unsolicited MSS: only accepts submissions via agents.

HQ

Publisher Lisa Milton, *Editorial Director, Fiction* Manpreet Grewal

General, crime and thrillers, women's fiction, historical, book club and young adult.

Hawthorn Press

1 Lansdown Lane, Stroud, Glos. GL5 1BJ
tel (01453) 757040
email info@hawthornpress.com
website www.hawthornpress.com
Director Martin Large

Publishes books and ebooks for a more creative, peaceful and sustainable world. Series include *Early Years*, *Steiner/Waldorf Education*, *Crafts*, *Personal Development*, *Art and Science*, *Storytelling*. Founded 1981.

Head of Zeus - Zephyr

Clerkenwell House, 5–8 Hardwick Street, London EC1R 4RG
tel 020-7253 5557
email hello@headofzeus.com
website www.headofzeus.com
Facebook www.facebook.com/headofzeus/
Twitter @HoZ_Books
Chairman Anthony Cheetham, *Publishing Director* Laura Palmer

Children's imprint. Founded 2002.

Hodder Children Group – see Hachette Children's Group

Hogs Back Books Ltd

34 Long Street, Devizes, Wilts. SN10 1NT
tel (01483) 506030
email enquiries@hogsbackbooks.com
website www.hogsbackbooks.com
Director & Commissioning Editor Karen Stevens

Children's picture books and teenage fiction. Welcomes texts and submissions from illustrators but cannot return material without prior arrangement. Founded 2009.

Hopscotch

St Jude's Church, Dulwich Road, London SE24 0PB
tel 020-7501 6736
email orders@hopscotchbooks.com
website www.hopscotchbooks.com
Associate Publisher Angela Morano Shaw

A division of MA Education. Teaching resources for primary school teachers. Founded 1997.

Practical Pre-School Books

Early years teacher resources.

Hot Key Books

80–81 Wimpole Street, London W1G 9RE
tel 020-7490 3875
email enquiries@hotkeybooks.com
website www.hotkeybooks.com
Facebook www.facebook.com/HotKeyBooks/
Twitter @HotKeyBooks
Editor-at-Large Emma Matthewson

Publishes books targeted at teen and older readers, some of which appeal to an adult audience. The content of a Hot Key book is defined by originality of voice and challenging, thought-provoking stories that resonate on a global stage. An imprint of Bonnier Books UK. Founded 2012.

Hutchinson Children's Books – see Penguin Random House Children's UK

Igloo Books Ltd

Cottage Farm, Mears Ashby Road, Sywell,
Northants NN6 0BJ
tel (01604) 741116
email customerservices@igloobooks.com
website www.igloobooks.com
Twitter @igloo_books

Adult and children's: cookery, lifestyle, gift, trivia,
fiction, non-fiction (adult), licensed books, novelty,
board, picture, activity books, audio (children's),
education, ebooks and apps. Not currently accepting
submissions. Founded 2005.

Imagine That Publishing Ltd

Marine House, Tide Mill Way, Woodbridge,
Suffolk IP12 1AP
tel (01394) 386651
email customerservice@imaginethat.com
website www.imaginethat.com
Facebook www.facebook.com/
ImagineThatPublishing/
Twitter @imaginethatbook
Instagram imaginethatbook
Chairman Barrie Henderson, *Managing Director*
David Henderson

Children's activity books, novelty books, picture
books, reference, character, gift books, early learning
books, apps and digital animations. Imprint: Willow
Tree, Top That. Founded 1999.

IWM (Imperial War Museums) Publishing

Lambeth Road, London SE1 6HZ
tel 020-7416 5000
email publishing@iwm.org.uk
website www.iwm.org.uk
Facebook www.facebook.com/iwm.london
Twitter @I_W_M

IWM tells the stories of people who have lived,
fought and died in conflicts involving Britain and the
Commonwealth since 1914. IWM Publishing
produces a range of books drawing on the expertise
and archives of the museum. Books are produced
both in-house and in partnership with other
publishers. Founded 1917.

Jelly Pie – see Egmont UK Ltd

Jolly Learning Ltd*

Tailours House, High Road, Chigwell, Essex IG7 6DL
tel 020-8501 0405
email info@jollylearning.co.uk
website www.jollylearning.co.uk
Director Christopher Jolly

Educational: primary and English as a Bilingual
Language. The company is committed to enabling
high standards in the teaching of reading and writing.
Publishes approx. 25 titles each year and has 300 in

print. Recent successes include *Jolly Phonics Extra*,
My Jolly Phonics and *Jolly Dictionary*. Imprint: Jolly
Phonics. Unsolicited MSS are only considered for
add-ons to existing products. Founded 1987.

Miles Kelly Publishing

Harding's Barn, Bardfield End Green, Thaxted,
Essex CM6 3PX
tel (01371) 832440
email hello@mileskelly.net
website www.mileskelly.net
Director Gerard Kelly

High-quality illustrated non-fiction and fiction titles
for children and family: activity books, board books,
story books, picture books, poetry, reference, posters
and wallcharts. Age groups: preschool, 5–10, 10–15,
15+. Founded 1996.

Kelpies – see Floris Books

The King's England Press

111 Meltham Road, Lockwood, Huddersfield,
West Yorkshire HD4 7BG
tel (01484) 663790
email sales@kingsengland.com
website www.kingsengland.com

Poetry collections for both adults and children plus
history books. Successes include *The Spot on My
Bum: Horrible Poems for Horrible Children* by Gez
Walsh, *Revudeville* and *Turned Out Nice Again* by
Deborah Tyler-Bennett and *Jordan's Guide to British
Steam Locomotives* by Owen Jordan. Also publishes
reprints of Arthur Mee's *The King's England* series of
1930s guidebooks and books on folklore, and local
and ecclesiastical history, plus children's and adult
fiction. See website for guidelines. However, currently
not accepting new unsolicited proposals. Founded
1989.

Kings Road Publishing

Suite 2.08 The Plaza, 535 Kings Road,
London SW10 0SZ
tel 020-770 3888
email info@kingsroadpublishing.co.uk
website www.kingsroadpublishing.co.uk
Ceo Perminder Mann, *Managing Director* Ben Dunn,
Acquisitions Director & Publisher Natalie Jerome, *UK
Sales & Marketing Director* Andrew Sauerwine, *Head
of Children's Publishing* Lisa Edwards

Part of Bonnier Publishing UK. The children
imprints are Studio Press, Weldon Owen, which
includes it's new sub imprint 20 Watt, Templar
Publishing (page 40), which contains Big Picture
Press. They focus on illustrated non-fiction, picture
books, novelty titles, activity books, fiction and family
reference. Submissions to be sent to the address
above indicating which imprint they are addressed to.
Founded 2015.

Kube Publishing Ltd
Markfield Conference Centre, Ratby Lane,
Markfield, Leics. LE67 9SY
tel (01530) 249230
email info@kubepublishing.com
website www.kubepublishing.com
Managing Director Haris Ahmad

Formerly the Islamic Foundation. Books on Islam
and the Muslim world for adults and children.
Founded 2006.

Ladybird Books
80 Strand, London WC2R 0RL
tel 020-7010 3000
email ladybird@penguinrandomhouse.co.uk
website www.ladybird.co.uk
Publisher Jackie McCann

Ladybird publishes books across a wide range of
formats for children aged from birth to 7 years. They
include tactile books for babies, nursery rhymes,
classic fairy tales and reading schemes, alongside
licensed character publishing. Part of Penguin
Random House UK (page 35). Founded 1867.

Leckie & Leckie*
Dipford House, Queens Square Business Park,
Huddersfield Road, Honley, Holmfirth HD9 6QZ
tel 0141 772 3200
email info@leckieandleckie.co.uk
website www.leckieandleckie.co.uk

Educational resources. Dedicated to the ongoing
development of materials specifically for education in
Scotland, from Standard Grade Foundation to
Advanced Higher Level and including new resources
for the Curriculum for Excellence. Over 220 titles are
currently available in the study guide range.
Subsidiary of HarperCollins Publishers (page 30).
Founded 1989.

Lincoln Children's Books
The Old Brewery, 6 Blundell Street, London N7 9BH
tel 020-7700 6700
email rachel.williams@quarto.com
website www.quartoknows.com/Lincoln-Childrens-
Books
Facebook www.facebook.com/Quartokids
Twitter @QuartoKids
Publisher Rachel Williams

Imprint of The Quarto Group. Illustrated Children's
Books: art and the great outdoors, as well as visual
storytelling, cultural diversity. Founded 1983.

Lion Hudson Ltd
Wilkinson House, Jordan Hill Business Park,
Banbury Road, Oxford OX2 8DR
tel (01865) 302750
email info@lionhudson.com
website www.lionhudson.com
Managing Director Suzanne Wilson-Higgins

Bible story retellings, prayer books, picture
storybooks, illustrated non-fiction and information
books on the Christian faith and world religions. Also
specialises in gift books, occasion books, seasonal
books for Christmas and Easter and bible activity
books. Submissions: hardcopy with sae if return
required. Founded 1971.

Lion Fiction
Historical fiction, cosy crime, women's fiction and
some fantasy from authors with a Christian world-
view.

Lion Scholar
Bible related reference works for the serious reader or
first year undergraduate.

Little Tiger Group
1 Coda Studios, 189 Munster Road,
London SW6 6AW
tel 020-7385 6333
email contact@littletiger.co.uk
website www.littletiger.co.uk
Ceo Monty Bhatia

Children's picture books, novelty books, board books
and pop-up books for preschool age to 7 years, and
fiction for 6–12 years and young adult. See imprint
websites for submissions guidelines. Imprints:
Caterpillar Books (novelty), Little Tiger Press (picture
books), Stripes (fiction), 360 Degrees (non-fiction).
Acquired by Penguin Random House (page 60) in
2019. Founded 1987.

Caterpillar Books
email contact@littletiger.co.uk
website www.littletiger.co.uk/imprint/caterpillar-
books
Publisher Thomas Truong, *Editorial Director* Pat
Hegarty
Books for children, including novelty board and
picture books. Founded 2003.

Little Tiger Press
email contact@littletiger.co.uk
website www.littletiger.co.uk
Publisher Jude Evans, *Editorial Director* Barry Timms
Children's picture books, board books and novelty
books for preschool–7 years. See website for
submissions guidelines. Founded 1987.

Stripes
email contact@littletiger.co.uk
website www.littletiger.co.uk/imprint/stripes-
publishing
Publisher Thomas Truong, *Editorial Director* Ruth
Bennett, *Commissioning Editor* Katie Jennings
Fiction for children aged 6–12 years and young adult.
Quality standalone titles and series publishing in all
age groups. Will consider new material from authors
and illustrators; see website for guidelines. Founded
2005.

360 Degrees
email contact@littletiger.co.uk
website www.littletiger.co.uk/special/360degrees/
Publisher Thomas Truong, *Editorial Director* Pat Hegarty
Non-fiction novelty for children aged 5–12 years. Founded 2015.

LOM ART
16 Lion Yard, Tremadoc Road, London SW4 7NQ
tel 020-7720 8643
email enquiries@mombooks.com
website www.mombooks.com/lom
Facebook www.facebook.com/MichaelOMaraBooks
Twitter @OMaraBooks
Managing Director Lesley O'Mara, *Publisher* Philippa Wingate

Illustrated non-fiction for children and adults. Publishes approx. 10 titles a year. Titles include *Fantomorphia*, *Maybe the Moon*, *The Van Gogh Activity Book* and *Life Lessons From My Cat*, plus a range of artist-led drawing, colouring and picture book titles. Unable to guarantee a reply to every submission received, but the inclusion of a sae is necessary for submission to be returned. Imprint of Michael O'Mara Books Ltd. Founded 2015.

Longman – see Pearson UK

Mabecron Books ltd
3 Briston Orchard, St Mellion, Saltash, Cornwall Pl 12 6RQ
tel (01579) 350885
email ronjohns@mabecronbooks.co.uk
website www.mabecronbooks.co.uk
Twitter @mabecronbooks

Award-winning publisher. Producing beautiful children's picture books and books with a Cornish or west country subject. Linked to bookshops in Falmouth, St Ives, Dartmouth and Padstow. Founded 1998.

McGraw-Hill School Education*
Head Office, 338 Euston Road, London NW1 3BH
tel (01628) 502730
email helpme@mheducation.com
website www.mheducation.co.uk
Facebook www.facebook.com/UKSchoolsMHE
Twitter @UKSchoolsMHE

Educational publisher for primary and secondary education in English, maths, science, humanities and other subject areas, including intervention and learning support. Founded 1888.

Mantra Lingua Ltd
Global House, 303 Ballards Lane, London N12 8NP
tel 020-8445 5123
email info@mantralingua.com
website http://uk.mantralingua.com/

website www.discoverypen.co.uk
Facebook www.facebook.com/Mantralingua
Twitter @mantralingua
Managing Directors R. Dutta, M. Chatterji

Publishes picture books and educational resources. The unique talking pen technology enables any book to be sound activated. All resources can be narrated in multiple languages and educational posters for schools and museums have audio visual features. Looking for illustrators, authors, translators and audio narrators. Museums and Heritage: looking for illustrators and trail writers. Looking for specialist audio recordings of birds, frogs and other animals from around the world, tel: 0845 600 1361. Founded 2002.

Maverick Books
Studio 3A, City Business Centre, 6 Brighton Road, Horsham, West Sussex RH13 5BB
tel (01403) 256941
email submissions@maverickbooks.co.uk
website www.maverickbooks.co.uk
Facebook www.facebook.com/Maverick-Childrens-Books
Twitter @maverickbooks
Managing Director Steve Bicknell, *Editor & Designer* Kimara Nye

Publishes titles across the formats of board books, picture books, early readers, graphic reluctant readers, junior fiction and activity books and another. Has a strong ethos of championing new authors and emerging illustrators, with a big emphasis on supporting them once their book is published. For submissions, please see submissions page on website. Founded 2009.

Kevin Mayhew Ltd
Buxhall, Stowmarket, Suffolk IP14 3BW
tel (01449) 737978
email info@kevinmayhew.com
website www.kevinmayhew.com
Directors Kevin Mayhew, Barbara Mayhew

Christianity: prayer and spirituality, pastoral care, preaching, liturgy worship, children's, youth work, drama, instant art, educational. Music: hymns, organ and choral, contemporary worship, piano and instrumental, tutors. Greetings cards: images, spiritual texts, birthdays, Christian events, musicians, general occasions. Read submissions section on website before sending MSS/synopses. Founded 1976.

The Mercier Press†
Unit 3B, Oak House, Bessboro Road, Blackrock, Cork T12 D6CH, Republic of Ireland
tel +353 (0)21 4614700
email info@mercierpress.ie
website www.mercierpress.ie
General Manager Deirdre Roberts, *Commissioning Editor* Patrick O'Donoghue (non-fiction)

Books for adults and children. Subjects include Irish literature; folklore; history; politics; humour; current affairs; health; mind, body & spirit and general non-fiction. Founded 1944.

Nobrow Books

27 Westgate Street, London E8 3RL
tel 020-7033 4430
email nobrowsubs@gmail.com
website http://nobrow.net/
Twitter @NobrowPress

Publishes picture books, illustrated fiction and non-fiction and graphic novels. Nobrow Books aims to combine good design and storytelling, quality production value and environmental consciousness. Founded 2008.

Flying Eye Books

email info@nobrow.net
website www.flyingeyebooks.com
Twitter @FlyingEyeBooks

Children's imprint. Focuses on the craft of children's storytelling and non-fiction. Founded 2013.

Nosy Crow*

14 Baden Place, Crosby Row, London SE1 1YW
tel 020-7089 7575
email hello@nosycrow.com
website www.nosycrow.com
Managing Director Kate Wilson, *Editorial Director* Camilla Reid, *Head of Fiction* Kirsty Stansfield, *Head of Picture Books* Louise Bolongaro, *Head of Non-Fiction* Rachel Kellehar, *Head of Sales & Marketing* Catherine Stokes, *Commercial Director* Adrian Soar

Award-winning children's books and apps, children's publisher for The National Trust and The British Museum. IPG Children's Publisher of the Year 2012, 2013, 2016 and 2017; IPG Independent Publisher of the Year 2016; BIA Childrens Publisher of the Year 2017. Submit by email: submissions@nosycrow.com. Founded 2010.

Oberon Books

521 Caledonian Road, London N7 9RH
tel 020-7607 3637
email info@oberonbooks.com
website www.oberonbooks.com
Managing Director Charles Glanville, *Publisher* James Hogan, *Senior Editor* Chris Campbell

New and classic play texts, programme texts and general theatre, dance and performing arts books. Founded 1986.

The O'Brien Press Ltd†

12 Terenure Road East, Rathgar, Dublin D06 HD27, Republic of Ireland
tel +353 (0)14 923333
email books@obrien.ie
website www.obrien.ie

Directors Michael O'Brien, Ivan O'Brien, Kunak McGann

Children: fiction for all ages; illustrated fiction for ages 3+, 5+, 6+, 8+ years, novels (10+ and young adult): contemporary, historical, fantasy. Adult non-fiction: biography, politics, history, true crime, sport, humour, reference. Adult fiction, crime (Brandon). No poetry or academic. Unsolicited MSS (sample chapters only), synopses and ideas for books welcome – submissions will not be returned. Founded 1974.

Orchard Books – see Hachette Children's Group

Oxford University Press*

Great Clarendon Street, Oxford OX2 6DP
tel (01865) 556767
email enquiry@oup.com
website www.oup.com
Ceo Nigel Portwood, *Group Finance Director* Giles Spackman, *Global Academic Business Managing Director* David Clark, *Managing Director, Oxford Education* Fathima Dada, *ELT Division Managing Director* Peter Marshall, *Human Resources Director* Lesley Sommerville, *Academic Sales Director* Alastair Lewis

Archaeology, architecture, art, belles lettres, bibles, bibliography, children's books (fiction, non-fiction, picture), commerce, current affairs, dictionaries, drama, economics, educational (foundation, primary, secondary, technical, university), encyclopedias, ELT, electronic publishing, essays, foreign language learning, general history, hymn and service books, journals, law, medical, music, oriental, philosophy, political economy, prayer books, reference, science, sociology, theology and religion; educational software; *Grove Dictionaries of Music & Art*. Trade paperbacks published under the imprint of Oxford Paperbacks. Founded 1478.

Children's and Educational Division

Managing Director, Oxford Education Fathima Dada, *Sales, Marketing & Operations Director* Richard Hodson, *Business & Strategy Director* Rod Theodorou, *Children's Publisher* Liz Cross, *Dictionaries Publisher* Vineeta Gupta, *Director, Digital & Home/School Services* Simon Tanner-Tremaine, *Director, Secondary* Clare Varlet-Baker, *Publishing Director, International* Elspeth Boardley, *Director, Primary* Jane Harley, *Managing Director of Asia Education* Adrian Mellor

Picture books, fiction, poetry and dictionaries. Authors include Tim Bowler, Gillian Cross, Julie Hearne and Geraldine McCaughrean.

Pan Macmillan*

20 New Wharf Road, London N1 9RR
tel 020-7014 6000
email webqueries@macmillan.co.uk
website www.panmacmillan.com

Managing Director Anthony Forbes Watson, *Sales & Brand Director* Anna Bond, *Publishers* Jeremy Trevathan (adult), Robin Harvie (non-fiction), Paul Baggaley (Picador), Carole Tonkinson (Bluebird)

Novels, literary, crime, thrillers, romance, science fiction, fantasy and horror. Autobiography, biography, business, gift books, health and beauty, history, humour, natural history, travel, philosophy, politics, world affairs, theatre, film, gardening, cookery, popular reference. No unsolicited MSS except through Macmillan New Writing. Founded 1843.

Campbell

Early learning, pop-up, novelty, board books for the preschool market.

Macmillan Children's Books

Imprint for Macmillan's children's books composed of two divisions: Macmillan Under 6s and Macmillan Over 6s.

Two Hoots

Illustrated children's books.

Tor

Science fiction and fantasy published in hardback and paperback.

Patrician Press

51 Free Rodwell House, School Lane,
Mistley CO11 1HW
tel 07968 288651
email patricia@patricianpress.com
website www.patricianpress.com
Facebook www.facebook.com/patricianpress,
www.facebook.com/puddingpress
Twitter @PatricianCom
Publisher Patricia Borlenghi

Paperback and digital publisher of fiction and poetry. Publisher of children's books under the imprint Pudding Press. Founded 2012.

Pavilion Children's Books*

43 Great Ormond Street, London WC1N 3HZ
tel 020-7462 1500
website www.pavilionbooks.com
Publisher Neil Dunnicliffe

Children's books: from baby books to illustrated non-fiction and classics. Part of Pavilion Books Company Ltd. Submissions via an agent only. Successes include *The Story of the Little Mole* by Werner Holzwarth, *The King Who Banned the Dark* by Emily Haworth-Booth, *The Journey Home* by Fran Preston-Gannon and *War Game* by Michael Foreman. Founded 2005.

Pearson UK*

Edinburgh Gate, Harlow, Essex CM20 2JE
tel 0845 313 6666
email schools@longman.co.uk
website www.pearsoned.co.uk
President Rod Bristow

Founded 1998.

Harcourt

Educational resources for teachers and learners at primary, secondary and vocational level. Provides a range of published resources, teachers' support, and pupil and student material in all core subjects for all ages. Imprints: Ginn, Heinemann, Payne-Gallway, Raintree, Rigby.

Longman

Educational: primary and secondary. Primary: literacy and numeracy. Secondary: English, maths, science, history, geography, modern languages, design and technology, business and economics, psychology and sociology.

Penguin Longman

ELT.

York Notes

Literature guides for students.

Penguin Longman – see Pearson UK

Penguin Random House Children's UK*

80 Strand, London WC2R 0RL
tel 020-7139 3000
website www.penguin.co.uk
Managing Director Francesca Dow, *Publishing Director* Amanda Punter (Puffin Fiction, non-fiction, licensing and picture books), *Publisher* Ruth Knowles (Puffin Fiction, non-fiction and licensing), *Publisher* Ben Horslen (Puffin Fiction), *Publisher* Lara Hancock (Puffin, picture books, partnerships and illustrated non-fiction), *Publishing Director* Shannon Cullen (Ladybird trade, licensing and education), *Publisher* Jacquie Bloese (Ladybird education and international), *Licensing & Consumer Products Director* Susan Bolsover (Penguin Ventures), *Art Director* Anna Billson

Part of Penguin Random House UK (see below). Children's paperback and hardback books: wide range of picture books, board books, gift books and novelties; fiction; non-fiction, popular culture, digital and audio. Preschool illustrated developmental books for 0–6 years; licensed brands; children's classic publishing and merchandising properties. No unsolicited MSS or original artwork or text. Imprints: Ladybird, Puffin, Penguin. Founded 2013.

Penguin Random House UK*

20 Vauxhall Bridge Road, London SW1V 2SA
tel 020-7840 8400
website www.penguin.co.uk
Directors Markus Dohle (Ceo Penguin Random House), Tom Weldon (Ceo Penguin Random House UK)

Penguin Random House UK group companies which publish books for children: Ebury, Michael Joseph and Penguin Random House Children's UK (see above). Founded 2013.

Phaidon Press Ltd

Regent's Wharf, All Saints Street, London N1 9PA
tel 020-7843 1000
email enquiries@phaidon.com
website www.phaidon.com
Managing Director James Booth-Clibborn

Visual arts, lifestyle, culture and food. Founded 1923.

Phoenix Yard Books

18 Dean House Studios, 27 Greenwood Place, Kentish Town, London NW5 1LB
tel 020-7239 4968
email hello@phoenixyardbooks.com
website www.phoenixyardbooks.com
Facebook www.facebook.com/PhoenixYardBooks
Twitter @phoenixyardbks

Picture books, poetry and fiction for children 3–13 years. Particularly seeking young fiction (6–9 years). Please read the detailed submissions guidelines on website before submitting. Founded 2009.

Piccadilly Press

80–81 Wimpole St, Marylebone, London W1G 9RF
tel 020-7490 3875
email hello@piccadillypress.co.uk
website www.piccadillypress.co.uk

Early picture books, parental advice, trade paperbacks, trade paperback children's fiction, young adult non-fiction and fun, family-orientated stories in any genre, that possess the ability to capture readers' imagination and inspire them to develop a life-long love of reading. An imprint of Bonnier Books UK. Founded 1983.

Poolbeg Press Ltd

123 Grange Hill, Baldoyle, Dublin D13 N529, Republic of Ireland
tel +353 (0)18 063825
email info@poolbeg.com
website www.poolbeg.com
Directors Kieran Devlin, Barbara Delvin

Children's and teenage fiction. Also adult popular fiction, non-fiction, current affairs. Imprints: Poolbeg, In a Nut Shell. Founded 1976.

Priddy Books

Chancery House, 53–64 Chancery Lane, London WC2A 1QT
tel 020-7418 5515
website www.priddybooks.com
Publisher Roger Priddy

Specialises in baby/toddler and preschool books: activity books, board books, novelty books, picture books. Founded 2000.

Prim-Ed Publishing

Marshmeadows, New Ross, Co. Wexford Y34 TA46, Republic of Ireland
tel 0851 440075
email marketing@prim-ed.com
website www.prim-ed.com
Managing Director Seamus McGuinness

Educational publisher specialising in copymasters (photocopiable teaching resources) for primary school and special needs lower second level pupils. Books written by practising classroom teachers.

Puffin – see Penguin Random House Children's UK

Pure Indigo Ltd

Publishing Department, 17 The Herons, Cottenham, Cambridge CB24 8XX
tel 07981 395258
email ashley.martin@pureindigo.co.uk
website www.pureindigo.co.uk/publishing
Commissioning Editor Ashley Martin

Pure Indigo Publishing develops innovative junior series fiction. All titles are available in both print and digital formats and are distributed internationally with select partners. The company also develops software products that complement the product range. The junior series fiction titles are developed in-house and on occasion authors and illustrators are commissioned to complete project-based work. For consideration for commissions visit the website. Not currently accepting submissions. Founded 2005.

Pushkin Press*

Unit 43 Pall Mall Deposit, 124–128 Barlby Road, London W10 6BL
tel 020-3735 9078
email books@pushkinpress.com
website www.pushkinpress.com
Facebook www.facebook.com/PushkinPress
Twitter @pushkinpress
Publisher Adam Freudenheim, *Deputy Publisher* Laura Macaulay, *Commissioning Editor* Daniel Seton

Having first rediscovered European classics of the 20th century, Pushkin now publishes novels, essays, memoirs, children's books (Pushkin's Children's) and everything from timeless classics to the urgent and contemporary. Imprints: Pushkin Press, Pushkin Children's Books, Pushkin Vertigo, ONE. Founded 1997.

QED Publishing

6 Blundell Street, London N7 9BH
tel 020-7812 8600
email qedpublishing@quarto.com
website www.quartoknows.com/QED-Publishing
Facebook www.facebook.com/qedpublishingofficial
Twitter @QEDPublishing
Directors Zeta Jones, Maxime Boucknooghe

Imprint of the Quarto Group, Inc. 'Edutainment' is the key focus of QED's approach – aims to both educate and entertain. Humour, fresh design and great illustrations combine to make learning engaging and fun for children 4–11 years. QED's diverse range of titles covers innovative non-fiction to clever and original picture books. Founded 1974.

The Quarto Group, Inc.
The Old Brewery, 6 Blundell Street, London N7 9BH
tel 020-7700 9000, 020-7700 8066
email dan.rosenberg@quarto.com
website www.quarto.com
Chairman Peter Read

The Quarto Group is a leading global illustrated book publisher and distribution group. It is composed of three publishing divisions: Quarto International Co-editions Group; Quarto Publishing Group USA; and Quarto Publishing Group UK; plus Books & Gifts Direct (a direct seller of books and gifts in Australia and New Zealand) and Regent Publishing Services, a specialist print services company based in Hong Kong. Quarto has nine children's imprints across its three publishing divisions; these are: Quarto International Co-editions Group (Quarto Children's Books, QED Publishing (above), Ivy Kids, small world creations, words & pictures (page 41), Marshall Children's Books); Quarto Publishing Group UK (Wide Eyed Editions (page 41) Lincoln Children's Books (page 32)); Quarto Publishing Group US (Walter Foster Jr.). Founded 1976.

Ransom Publishing Ltd
Unit 7, Brocklands Farm, West Meon GU32 1JN
tel (01730) 829091
email ransom@ransom.co.uk
website www.ransom.co.uk
Directors Jenny Ertle (managing), Steve Rickard (creative)

Teen fiction, reading programmes and books for children and adults who are reluctant and struggling readers. Range covers high interest age/low reading age titles, quick reads, reading schemes and titles for young able readers. Series include *Reading Stars, The Outer Reaches, Shades 2.0, Boffin Boy, PIG* and *Dark Man*. Email for submission guidelines. Founded 1995.

Raven Books
Publishes fiction for children and young adults 8–18 years. Actively looking for strong new fiction, either from published authors or new authors.

Really Decent Books
191 Newbridge Road, Bath BA1 3HH
tel (01225) 334747
email info@reallydecentbooks.co.uk
website www.reallydecentbooks.co.uk
Facebook www.facebook.com/reallydecentbooks

Twitter @ReallyDecent
Publisher Phil Dauncey

Independent publisher of books for babies, toddlers and children. Founded 2012.

Red Bird Publishing
Kiln Farm, East End Green, Brightlingsea, Colchester, Essex CO7 0SX
tel (01206) 303525
email info@red-bird.co.uk
website www.red-bird.co.uk
Publisher Martin Rhodes-Schofield

Innovative children's activity packs and books produced with a mix of techniques and materials such as Glow in the Dark, Mirrors, Stereoscopic 3D, Moiré and other optical illusions. Authors are specialists in their fields. Activity books, novelty books, picture books, painting and colouring books, teaching books, posters: hobbies, nature and the environment, science. Age groups: preschool, 5–10, 10–15. No unsolicited MSS. Founded 1998.

Red Kite Books – see Haldane Mason Ltd

Rising Stars
PO Box 105, Rochester, Kent ME2 4BE
tel 0800 091 1602
email info@risingstars-uk.com
website www.risingstars-uk.com
Managing Director Andrea Carr

Educational publisher of books and software for primary school age children. Titles are linked to the National Curriculum Key Stages, QCA Schemes of Work, National Numeracy Framework or National Literacy Strategy. Approach by email with ideas for publishing. Part of Hodder Education. Founded 2001.

Rockpool Children's Books Ltd
6 Kitchener Terrace, Ferryhill, Co. Durham DL17 8AX
tel 07711 351691
email stuarttrotter3@gmail.com
website www.rockpoolchildrensbooks.co.uk
Facebook www.facebook.com/RockpoolChildrensBooks/
Twitter @rockpooltweets
Publisher & Creative Director Stuart Trotter

Print-on-demand picture books, packager, co-editions, 'All About Picture Books' school visits. Blog: www.rockpoolchildrensbooks.blogspot.com. Founded 2006.

Ruby Tuesday Books Ltd
6 Newlands Road, Tunbridge Wells, Kent TN4 9AT
tel (01892) 557767
email shan@rubytuesdaybooks.com
website www.rubytuesdaybooks.com
Twitter @RubyTuesdaybk

Books

Publisher & Author Ruth Owen, *All Sales & Rights* Shan White

Publisher of children's books. Founded 2008.

SAGE Publications Ltd*
1 Oliver's Yard, 55 City Road, London EC1Y 1SP
tel 020-7324 8500
email info@sagepub.co.uk
website www.sagepublishing.com
Facebook www.facebook.com/SAGEPublications
Twitter @SAGE_News

Independent company that disseminates journals, books and library products for the educational, scholarly and professional markets. LinkedIn: www.linkedin.com/company/sage-publications. Founded 1965.

Salariya Book Company Ltd
Book House, 25 Marlborough Place, Brighton BN1 1UB
tel (01273) 603306
email salariya@salariya.com
website www.salariya.com
Facebook www.facebook.com/theSalariya
Twitter @theSalariya
Managing Director David Salariya

Children's art, picture books, fiction and non-fiction. Imprints: Book House, Scribblers, Scribo. No unsolicited MSS. Founded 1989.

Schofield & Sims Ltd*
Unit 11, The Piano Works, 113–117 Farringdon Road, London EC1R 3BX
tel (01484) 607080
email post@schofieldandsims.co.uk
website www.schofieldandsims.co.uk

Educational: nursery, infants, primary; posters. Founded 1901.

Scholastic Ltd*
Euston House, 24 Eversholt Street, London NW1 1DB
tel 020-7756 7756
website www.scholastic.co.uk
Chairman M.R. Robinson, *Co-Group Managing Directors* Catherine Bell, Steve Thompson

Children's fiction, non-fiction and picture books, education resources for primary schools. Owned by Scholastic Inc. Founded 1964.

Chicken House
See page 25.

Scholastic Book Fairs
See page 70.

Scholastic Children's Books
tel 020-7756 7761
email submissions@scholastic.co.uk
website www.scholastic.co.uk
Twitter @scholasticuk

UK Publisher Miriam Farbey, *Editorial Director* Elizabeth Scoggins (non-fiction), *Publisher* Samantha Smith (fiction and picture books)

Activity books, novelty books, picture books, fiction for 5–12 years, teenage fiction, series fiction and film/TV tie-ins. Recent successes include *Tom Gates* series by Liz Pichon, *Horrible Histories* by Terry Deary and Martin Brown, *His Dark Materials trilogy* by Philip Pullman, *The Hunger Games* by Suzanne Collins, and picture books by Julia Donaldson and Axel Scheffler including *Stick Man, Zog, Tiddler* and *The Highway Rat*. Imprints: Scholastic, Alison Green Books. No unsolicited MSS. Unsolicited illustrations are accepted, but do not send any original artwork as it will not be returned.

Scholastic Educational Resources
Book End, Range Road, Witney, Oxon OX29 0YD
tel (01993) 893456
Publishing Director Robin Hunt

Professional books, classroom materials, home learning books and online resources for primary teachers.

Scripture Union
Trinity House, Opal Court, Fox Milne, Milton Keynes MK15 0DF
tel (01908) 856000
email info@scriptureunion.org.uk
website www.scriptureunion.org.uk
Director of Ministry Development (Publishing) Terry Clutterham

Christian books and bible reading materials for people of all ages; educational and worship resources for churches; adult fiction and non-fiction; children's fiction and non-fiction (age groups: under 5, 5–8 years, 8–10 years and youth). Publishes approx. 40 titles each year for children/young people and has 200–250 in print. Recent successes include the *Bible Storybook* series and *Essential 100* by Whitney Kuniholm. Scripture Union works as a charity in over 120 countries and publishes in approx. 20. Will not consider unsolicited MSS. Founded 1867.

SEN Press Ltd
1 Necton Road, Wheathampstead AL4 8AT
tel (01582) 833205
email info@senpress.co.uk
website www.senpress.co.uk
Publisher Janie Nicholas

Literacy and life skills resources for ages 14–19 with special needs. Founded 2003.

Simon & Schuster UK Ltd*
222 Gray's Inn Road, London WC1X 8HB
tel 020-7316 1900
email enquiries@simonandschuster.co.uk
website www.simonandschuster.co.uk
Facebook www.facebook.com/simonschusterUK
Twitter @simonschusteruk

Directors Ian Chapman (ceo), Helen Mackenzie Smith (editorial, picture books), Jane Griffiths (editorial, fiction)

Children's and young adult fiction, picture books, novelty, pop-up and licensed character. Founded 1986.

Smart Learning
Unit 2, Aston Way, Middlewich, Cheshire CW10 0HS
tel (01423) 206 200
email admin@smart-learning.co.uk
website www.smart-learning.co.uk

High-quality teaching and learning resources for both teachers and children – from Foundation Stage through to KS3. Publishes software and books to enhance the teaching and learning of ICT, phonics, literacy, PSHE and citizenship and English.

Stacey Publishing Ltd
14 Great College Street, London SW1P 3RX
tel 020-7221 7166
email info@stacey-international.co.uk
website www.stacey-international.co.uk
Founder Tom Stacey

Illustrated books for children 3–12 years. Publishers of the *Musgrove* series.

Strident Publishing Ltd
22 Strathwhillan Drive, Hairmyres, Glasgow G75 8GT
tel (01355) 220588
email info@stridentpublishing.co.uk
website www.stridentpublishing.co.uk
Executive Director Keith Charters

Fiction for children 7–18 years, including young adult/adult crossover, 7+ years: 'timeless classic' feel, 9+ years: general, teen: general, but especially contemporary social realism, young adult/adult crossover: high quality accessible (often edgy) literature. Publishes approx. 15 books a year. Renowned for taking provocative young adult titles and for the energetic marketing of all of its titles. Works closely with authors who present in schools/at festivals. Authors include: young adult/adult: Gillian Philip (*Firebrand*) and Janne Teller (*Nothing*); teen: Linda Strachan (*Spider* – winner of the Catalyst Award); 9+ years: D.A. Nelson (*DarkIsle* – winner of the Scottish Children's Book Awards), Catherine MacPhail (*Granny Nothing*), Matt Cartney (*The Sons of Rissouli*), Nick Green (*The Cat Kin*) and Hazel Allan (*Bree McCready*); 7+ years: Emma Barnes (*Jessica Haggerthwaite* – Branford Boase shortlisted) and Paul Biegel (*The King of the Copper Mountains*). Email proposed blurb together with the first three chapters and covering letter stating why book is likely to appeal to readers. Founded 2005.

Stripes – see Little Tiger Group

Studio Fun International Ltd
The Ice House, 124–126 Walcot Street, Bath BA1 5BG
tel (01225) 463401
email jennifer.fifield@studiofun.com
website www.studiofun.com
International Director Jennifer Fifield

Innovative, high-quality books designed to encourage children to use their creativity and imagination. Board, novelty, film/TV tie-ins. Licensed characters and brands. Also a wide range of children's religious titles. Imprint of Printers Row Publishing Group (PRPG). Founded 1981.

Sweet Cherry Publishing*
Unit 36, Vulcan Business Complex, Vulcan Road, Leicester LE5 3EF
tel 0116 253 6796
email submissions@sweetcherrypublishing.com
website www.sweetcherrypublishing.com
Facebook www.facebook.com/sweetcherrypublishing
Twitter @sweetcherrypub
Director A. Thadha

Children's series fiction specialist. Children's picture books, novelty books, gift books, board books, educational books and fiction series for all ages. Also welcomes young adult novels, trilogies or longer series. Likes to publish a set of books as a box set or in a slipcase. See website for submission guidelines. Founded 2011.

Tarquin Publications
Suite 74, 17 Holywell Hill, St Albans AL1 1DT
tel (01727) 833866
email info@tarquinbooks.com
website www.tarquinbooks.com

Mathematical models, puzzles, codes and logic and paper engineering books for intelligent children. Publishes 7–8 titles each year and has 103 in print. Recent successes include *Magic Moving Images* and *Mini Mathematical Murder Mysteries*. Do not send unsolicited MSS. Send a one-page proposal of idea. Founded 1970.

Taylor & Francis Group*
2 and 4 Park Square, Milton Park, Abingdon, Oxon OX14 4RN
tel 020-7017 6000
email enquiries@taylorandfrancis.com
website http://taylorandfrancis.com/
Ceo Annie Callanan, Managing Director (Taylor & Francis Books) Jeremy North

Academic and reference books, including education. Imprints include CRC Press, Europa, Garland Science, Psychology Press, Routledge, Spon and Taylor & Francis. Founded 1988.

Focal Press
Animation, audio, film, gaming, music technology, photography and theatre.

Templar Publishing

Suite 2.08 The Plaza, 535 Kings Road,
London SW10 0SZ
tel 020-3770 8888
email social@bonnierpublishing.co.uk
website www.templarco.co.uk
Facebook www.facebook.com/templarpublishing
Twitter @templarbooks

Templar has become one of the world's most
respected publishers of illustrated children's non-
fiction, picture books, fiction, gift and novelty books
for all ages. An imprint of Bonnier Books UK.
Founded 1978.

Three Hares Publishing

2 Dukes Avenue, London N10 2PT
tel 020-8245 8989
email submissions@threeharespublishing.com
website www.threeharespublishing.com
Facebook www.facebook.com/threeharespublishing
Twitter @threeharesbooks
Publisher Yasmin Standen

Submissions are open for children's and young adult
books. No picture books. The children's list is
currently expanding. Interested in discovering new
talent. Visit website for submission guidelines – email
submissions only. Founded 2014.

Tiny Owl Publishing Ltd

1 Repton House, Charlwood Street,
London SW1V 2LD
email info@tinyowl.co.uk
website www.tinyowl.co.uk
Facebook www.facebook.com/tinyowlpublishing
Twitter @TinyOwl_Books
Publisher Delaram Ghanimifard

An independent leading publisher of global children's
literature. Publishes high-quality picture books for
children 3–11 years. Aims to promote diversity and
human rights values. Founded 2015.

Tiptoe Books

United House, North Road, London N7 9DP
tel 020-7520 7600
email enquiries@amberbooks.co.uk
website www.tiptoebooks.co.uk
Chairman Stasz Gnych, *Managing Director* Sara
McKie, *Editorial Director* Charles Catton, *Head of
Production* Peter Thompson, *Design Manager* Mark
Batley, *Picture Manager* Terry Forshaw

Illustrated non-fiction, multi-volume sets, calendars
and sticker books for children of all ages. Subjects
include history, ancient civilisations, the natural
world, fantasy and general reference. Opportunities
for freelancers. Children's books imprint of Amber
Books Ltd.

Troika

Troika Books Ltd, Well House, Green Lane,
Ardleigh, Colchester, Essex CO7 7PD

tel (01206) 233333
email info@troikabooks.com
website www.troikabooks.com
Publisher Martin West, *Rights* Petula Chaplin, *Sales &
Marketing* Roy Johnson

Publishes picture books, poetry and fiction for all
ages, with an emphasis on quality and accessibility.
Though a determinedly small list, it publishes some
big name authors including prize-winners Michelle
Magorian, Bernard Ashley, Pippa Goodhart together
with new authors Savita Kalhan and Miriam
Halahmy. Our poetry list includes Zaro Weil, Brian
Moses, John Foster, Hilda Offen and Neal Zetter.
Founded 2012.

Usborne Publishing Ltd

Usborne House, 83–85 Saffron Hill,
London EC1N 8RT
tel 020-7430 2800
email mail@usborne.co.uk
website www.usborne.com
Directors Peter Usborne, Jenny Tyler (editorial),
Nicola Usborne, Andrea Parsons

An independent, family business which creates
engaging, innovative books for children of all ages.
Including baby, preschool, novelty, activity, non-
fiction and fiction. Looking for high-quality
imaginative children's fiction. No unsolicited MSS.
Founded 1973.

Wacky Bee Books*

Shakespeare House, 168 Lavender Hill,
London SW11 5TG
tel 020-7801 6300
email hello@wackybeebooks.com
website www.wackbeebooks.com
Facebook www.facebook.com/wackybeebooks
Twitter @wackybeebooks
Director Louise Jordan

Publishing books with a buzz for children 3–12 years.
Picture books for 3+, early readers for 5–7, general
fiction for 8–12 years. Submission enquiries by email
to submissions@wackybeebooks.com. Founded 2014.

Walker Books Ltd*

87 Vauxhall Walk, London SE11 5HJ
tel 020-7793 0909
website www.walker.co.uk
Facebook www.facebook.com/walkerbooks
Twitter @walkerbooksuk
Directors Roger Alexander (chairman, non-
executive), Karen Lotz (group managing), Ian Mablin
(non-executive), Mike McGrath (cfo), Jane
Winterbotham (publishing), Ed Ripley (sales and
marketing), Alan Lee (production), Annette Watson
(business affairs)

An independent company with a global reach,
publishing activity books, novelty books, picture
books, fiction for 5–8 and 9–12 years, young adult

fiction, series fiction, film/TV tie-ins, plays, poetry, digital and audio. Publishes approx. 300 titles each year and has 1,800 in print. Continuing successes include the *Alex Rider* series by Anthony Horowitz, *Chaos Walking* by Patrick Ness, *Maisy* by Lucy Cousins, *Where's Wally?* by Martin Handford, the *Mortal Instruments* series by Cassandra Clare and a wide range of award-winning novels and picture books by other authors and illustrators. Imprint: Walker Books, Walker Studio and Walker Entertainment. Write to the editor, enclosing return postage, and allow six months for response. Founded 1980.

Ward Lock Educational Co. Ltd

BIC Ling Kee House, 1 Christopher Road, East Grinstead, West Sussex RH19 3BT
tel (01342) 318980
email wle@lingkee.com
website http://wle.lingkee.com/wle/
Director Wai Kwok Allen Au

Primary and secondary pupil materials, Kent Mathematics Project: *KMP BASIC* and *KMP Main* series covering Reception to GCSE, *Reading Workshops*, *Take Part* series and *Take Part* starters, teachers' books, music books, *Target* series for the National Curriculum: *Target Science* and *Target Geography*, religious education. Founded 1952.

Franklin Watts – see Hachette Children's Group

Wayland – see Hachette Children's Group

Wide Eyed Editions

The Old Brewery, 6 Blundell Street, London N7 9BH
tel 020-7700 6700
website www.quartoknows.com/Wide-Eyed-Editions

Imprint of the Quarto Group, Inc. (page 37). Wide Eyed Editions creates original non-fiction for children and families and believes that books should encourage curiosity about the world, inspiring readers to set out on their own journey of discovery. Founded 2014.

words & pictures

The Old Brewery, 6 Blundell Street, London N7 9BH
tel 020-7800 8043
website www.quartoknows.com/words-pictures
Publisher Zeta Jones

Imprint of the Quarto Group, Inc. (page 37). The imprint has three main focuses: imagination, innovation and inspiration. Always on the lookout for authors and artists with creative ideas that

enhance and broaden the children's publishing list. See the submission guidelines on the website. Founded 2012.

Y Lolfa Cyf

Talybont, Ceredigion SY24 5HE
tel (01970) 832304
email ylolfa@ylolfa.com
website www.ylolfa.com
Director Garmon Gruffudd, *Editor* Lefi Gruffudd

Welsh language books and English books of Welsh and Celtic interest, popular biographies and sports books. Founded 1967.

ZigZag Education

Unit 3, Greenway Business Centre, Doncaster Road, Bristol BS10 5PY
tel 0117 950 3199
email submissions@publishmenow.co.uk
website www.zigzageducation.co.uk
website www.publishmenow.co.uk
Development Director John-Lloyd Hagger, *Strategy Director* Mike Stephens

Secondary school teaching resources: English, maths, ICT, geography, history, science, business, politics, P.E., media studies. Founded 1998.

ZooBooKoo International Ltd

4 Gurdon Road, Grundisburgh, Woodbridge, Suffolk IP13 6XA
tel (01473) 735346
email karen@zoobookoo.com
website www.zoobookoo.com

Designer/manufacturer of ZooBooKoo Original Cube Books, multi-level educational folding cube books. Recent successes include *World Football*, *Human Body*, *Kings and Queens*, *French Phrases* and *United Kingdom*.

ZunTold

email elainebous@gmail.com
website https://zuntold.com/
Facebook www.facebook.com/zuntoldbooks
Twitter @zuntold
Instagram zuntold_books
Director Elaine Bousfield

Publishes new fiction for children and young people and young adults. Also supports young people in their own writing. Interested in middle grade fiction (9–12), teens, young adults and crossover fiction. For submission please send a copy of synopsis and the first five chapters. Founded 2016.

Children's book publishers overseas

Listings are given for children's book publishers in Australia (below), Canada (page 43), France (page 46), Germany (page 46), Italy (page 47), the Netherlands (page 47), New Zealand (page 48), South Africa (page 49), Spain (page 50) and the USA (page 51).

AUSTRALIA

Member of the Australian Publishers Association

ACER Press*
19 Prospect Hill Road, Private Bag 55, Camberwell, VIC 3124
tel +61 (0)3 9277 5555
email proposals@acer.org
website www.acer.org/au

Publisher of the Australian Council for Educational Research. Produces a range of books and assessments including professional resources for teachers, psychologists and special needs professionals. Founded 1930.

Allen & Unwin Pty Ltd*
83 Alexander Street, Crows Nest, NSW 2065
Postal address PO Box 8500, St Leonards, NSW 1590
tel +61 (0)2 8425 0100
website www.allenandunwin.com
Chairman Patrick Gallagher, *Ceo* Robert Gorman, *Publishing Director* Sue Hines

Fiction for children 5–9 and 10–13 years, teenage fiction, series fiction and narrative non-fiction. Also adult/general trade books, including fiction, academic, especially social science and history. Imprints include: Allen & Urwin, Inspired Living, Crows Nest, House of Books, Murdoch Books. Will consider unsolicited MSS (but not picture book texts). Prefers to receive full MSS by post, with a brief synopsis and biography. Allow three months for response. Seeking junior fiction, quirky non-fiction by wise, funny, inventive authors with a distinctive voice. Founded 1990.

Bloomsbury Publishing Pty Ltd*
Level 4, 387 George Street, Sydney, NSW 2000
tel +61 (0)2 8820 4900
email au@bloomsbury.com
website www.bloomsbury.com/au
Facebook www.facebook.com/bloomsburypublishingaustralia
Twitter @BloomsburySyd
Managing Director Liz Bray

Supports the worldwide publishing activities of Bloomsbury Publishing: caters for the Australia and New Zealand territories. Bloomsbury Publishing Plc founded 1986.

Cengage Learning Australia*
Level 7, 80 Dorcas Street, South Melbourne, VIC 3205
tel +61 (0)3 9685 4111
website www.cengage.com.au

Educational books. Founded 2007.

Hachette Australia Pty Ltd*
Level 17, 207 Kent Street, Sydney, NSW 2000
tel +61 (0)2 8248 0800
email auspub@hachette.com.au
website www.hachette.com.au
Ceo Louise Sherwin-Stark, *Group Publishing Director* Fiona Hazard

General, children's: picture books, fiction for children 5–8 and 9–12 years, teenage fiction and series fiction. Accepts MSS via website. Founded 1971.

HarperCollins Publishers (Australia) Pty Ltd Group*
Postal address PO Box A565, Sydney South, NSW 1235
tel +61 (0)2 9952 5000
website www.harpercollins.com.au

Literary fiction and non-fiction, popular fiction, children's, reference, biography, autobiography, current affairs, sport, lifestyle, health/self-help, humour, true crime, travel, Australiana, history, business, gift, religion. Founded 1989.

Little Hare Books*
(imprint of Hardie Grant Egmont)
Ground Floor, Building 1, 658 Church Street, Richmond, VIC 3121
tel +61 (0)3 8520 6444
email info@hardiegrantegmont.com.au
website www.hardiegrant.com.au/egmont/our-books/little-hare

Publishes high-quality children's books in Australia, New Zealand and the UK: early childhood and picture books. Check website for details of when submissions are accepted. Founded 2010.

McGraw-Hill Australia Pty Ltd*
Level 2, 82 Waterloo Road, North Ryde, NSW 2113
Postal address Private Bag 2233, Business Centre, North Ryde, NSW 1670
tel +61 (0)2 9900 1800
email cservice_sydney@mcgraw-hill.com
website www.mcgraw-hill.com.au

Educational publisher: higher education, primary education and professional (including medical, general and reference). Division of the McGraw-Hill Companies. Founded 1964.

New Frontier Publishing*

48 Ross Street, Glebe, NSW 2037
tel +61 (0)2 9660 4614
email info@newfrontier.com.au
website www.newfrontier.com.au
Director Peter Whitfield

Aims to uplift, educate and inspire through its range of children's books. Activity books, picture books, fiction, dictionaries, textbooks. Caters for children 5–10 years. Unsolicited MSS accepted. Understanding of existing list crucial. Downloadable submissions pack available via website. Founded 2002.

Pan Macmillan Australia Pty Ltd*

Level 25, 1 Market Street, Sydney, NSW 2000
tel +61 (0)2 9285 9100
email pan.reception@macmillan.com.au
website www.panmacmillan.com.au
Directors Cate Paterson (publishing), Katie Crawford (sales), Tracey Cheetham (publicity and marketing)

Commercial and literary fiction; children's fiction, non-fiction and character products; general non-fiction; sport. Founded 1843.

Penguin Random House Australia Pty Ltd*

Sydney office Level 3, 100 Pacific Highway, North Sydney, NSW 2060
tel +61 (0)2 9954 9966
email information@penguinrandomhouse.com.au
Melbourne office 707 Collins Street, Melbourne, VIC 3008
website www.penguinrandomhouse.com.au
Ceo Julie Burland, *Group Publishing Director* Nikki Christer, *Publishing Director, Penguin Young Readers* Laura Harris, *Publicity Director* Karen Reid

General fiction and non-fiction; children's, illustrated. MS submissions for non-fiction accepted, unbound in hard copy addressed to Submissions Editor. Fiction submissions are only accepted from previously published authors, or authors represented by an agent or accompanied by a report from an accredited assessment service. Imprints: Arrow, Bantam, Ebury, Hamish Hamilton, Knopf, Michael Joseph, Penguin, Viking, Vintage and William Heinemann. Subsidiary of Bertelsmann AG. Founded 2013.

University of Queensland Press*

PO Box 6042, St Lucia, QLD 4067
tel +61 (0)7 3365 7244
email uqp@uqp.uq.edu.au
website www.uqp.uq.edu.au

Founded 1948.

R.I.C. Publications Pty Ltd

5 Bendsten Place, Balcatta, WA 6021
tel +61 (0)8 9240 9888
website www.ricpublications.com.au

Educational publisher specialising in blackline master or copymasters and student workbooks for schools and homeschoolers. Founded 1986.

Rhiza Edge

PO Box 1519, Capalaba, QLD 4157
tel +61 (0)7 3245 1938
email editor@rhizaedge.com.au
website www.rhizaedge.com.au
Facebook www.facebook.com/rhizaedge
Commissioning Editor Emily Lighezzolo

Aims to publish relatable, issue-based stories for today's young adult readers, ranging from books with a light, humorous touch through to deeper, more challenging tales. Founded 2018.

Scholastic Australia Pty Ltd*

76–80 Railway Crescent, Lisarow, Gosford, NSW 2250
tel +61 (0)2 4328 3555
website www.scholastic.com.au
Chairman David Peagram

Children's fiction and non-fiction. Founded 1968.

Wombat Books*

PO Box 1519, Capalaba, QLD 4157
tel +61 (0)7 3245 1938
email wombat@wombatbooks.com.au
website www.wombatbooks.com.au
Facebook www.facebook.com/wombatbooks
Publisher Rochelle Manners, *Editor & Publicity Coordinator* Emily Lighezzolo

An independent publisher of children's picture books and books for early readers. Always on the lookout for the next story to be shared. Young adult and adult imprint: Rhiza Edge (page 43). Founded 2009.

CANADA

*Member of the Canadian Publishers' Council
†Member of the Association of Canadian Publishers

Annick Press Ltd†

15 Patricia Avenue, Toronto, ON M2M 1H9
tel +1 416-221-4802
email annickpress@annickpress.com
website www.annickpress.com
Owner/Director Rick Wilks, *Office Manager* Asiya Awale

Preschool to young adult fiction and non-fiction. Approximately 25% of books are by first-time authors. Founded 1975.

Dundurn Press†

500–503 Church Street, Toronto, ON M5E 1M2
tel +1 416-214-5544
email submissions@dundurn.com
Publisher Kirk Howard

Young adult fiction and non-fiction. Founded 1972.

Fitzhenry & Whiteside Ltd

195 Allstate Parkway, Markham, ON L3R 4T8
tel +1 800-387-9776
email bookinfo@fitzhenry.ca
website www.fitzhenry.ca
Ceo Sharon Fitzhenry

Fiction and non-fiction (social studies, visual arts, biography, environment). Publishes ten picture books, five early readers/chapter books, six middle novels and seven young adult books each year. Approximately 10% of books are by first-time authors. Emphasis is on Canadian authors and illustrators, subject or perspective. Will review MS/ illustration packages from artists. Submit outline and copy of sample illustration. For illustrations only, send samples and promotional sheet. Responds in three months. Samples returned with sase. Founded 1966.

HarperCollins Publishers Ltd*

22 Adelaide Street West, 41st Floor, Toronto, ON M5H 4E3
tel +1 416-975-9334
email hcOrder@harpercollins.com
website www.harpercollins.ca
President & Publisher Jonathan Burnham

Literary fiction and non-fiction, history, politics, biography, spiritual and children's books. Founded 1989.

Kids Can Press Ltd†

25 Dockside Drive, Toronto, ON M5A 0B5
tel +1 416-479-7000
email customerservice@kidscan.com
website www.kidscanpress.com
Editorial Director Yvette Ghione

Middle grade/young adult fiction and non-fiction. Publishes 16–22 picture books, 8–12 young readers, 10–18 middle readers and 2–3 young adult titles each year. Recent successes include *Virginia Wolf* by Kyo Maclear and Isabelle Arsenault, Melanie Watt's award-winning *Scaredy Squirrel* series, *If the World Were a Village* by David J. Smith – part of the CitizenKid series – and the *Binky the Space Cat* books. Publishers of *Franklin the Turtle* and *Elliot Moose* characters. Approximately 10–15% of books are by first-time authors. Submit outline/synopsis and between two and three sample chapters. For picture books, submit complete MS. Responds in six months. Only accepts MSS from Canadian authors. Fiction length: picture books – 1,000–2,000 words; young readers – 750–1,500 words; middle readers –

10,000–15,000 words; young adult – over 15,000 words. Non-fiction length: picture books – 500–1,250 words; young readers – 750–2,000 words; middle readers – 5,000–15,000 words. Founded 1973.

McGraw-Hill Ryerson Ltd*

145 Kings Street West, Suite 1501, Toronot ON M5H 1J8
tel +1 800-565-5758
website www.mheducation.ca

Educational and trade books. Founded 1972.

Nelson Education*

1120 Birchmount Road, Toronto, ON M1K 5G4
tel +1 416-752-9448
website www.nelson.com
President & Ceo Steve Brown

Educational publishing: school (K–12), college and university, career education, measurement and guidance, professional and reference, ESL titles. Division of Thomson Canada Ltd. Founded 1914.

Oberon Press

145 Spruce Street, Ottawa, ON K1R 6P1
tel +1 613-238-3275
email oberon@sympatico.ca
website www.oberonpress.ca

General fiction, short stories, poetry, some biographies, art and children's. Only publishes Canadian writers. Founded 1985.

Orca Book Publishers†

1016 Balmoral Road Victoria, BC V8T 1A8
tel +1 800-210-5277
email orca@orcabook.com
website www.orcabook.com

Books for children and young adults. Will consider MSS from Canadian writers only. No submissions by fax or email. See website for submission guidelines. No poetry. Founded 1984.

Pearson Canada*

26 Prince Andrew Place, North York, ON M3C 2T8
tel +1 800-361-6128
website www.pearsoned.com/ca
Ceo Dan Lee

Academic, technical, educational, children's and adult, trade. Founded 1998.

Penguin Random House Canada Ltd*

320 Front Street, Suite 1400, Toronto, ON M5V 3B6
tel +1 416-364-4449
website www.penguinrandomhouse.ca
Ceo Kristin Cochrane

Literary fiction, commercial fiction, memoir, non-fiction (history, business, current events, sports), adult, teen and children's young readers. No unsolicited MSS; submissions via an agent only.

Imprints: Allen Lane Canada, Anchor Canada, Appetite by Random House, Bond Street Books, Doubleday Canada, Emblem, Hamish Hamilton Canada, Knopf Canada, McClelland & Stewart, Penguin Canada, Penguin Teen, Portfolio Canada, Puffin Canada, Random House Canada, Seal Books, Signal, Strange Light, Tundra Books, Viking Canada, Vintage Canada. Subsidiary of Penguin Random House. Founded 2013.

Pippin Publishing Corporation

PO Box 242, Don Mills, ON M3C 2S2
tel +1 416-510-2918
email arayner@utphighereducation.com
website www.utppublishing.com

ESL/EFL, teacher reference, adult basic education, school texts (all subjects), general trade (non-fiction) – acquired by University of Toronto Press in 2014 (page 45). Founded 1995.

Red Deer Press

195 Allstate Parkway, Markham, ON L3R 4T8
tel +1 800-387-9776
email rdp@reddeerpress.com
website www.reddeerpress.com
Publisher Richard Dionne, *Children's Editor* Peter Carver

Literary fiction, science fiction, non-fiction, children's illustrated books, young adult fiction, teen fiction. Publishes books that are written or illustrated by Canadians and that are about or of interest to Canadians. Imprints: RJS (Robert J. Sawyer) Books (science fiction). Publishes 14–18 new books a year. Children's picture books MSS from established authors with a demonstrable record of publishing success are preferred. Currently accepting new MSS. Founded 1975.

Ronsdale Press[†]

3350 West 21st Avenue, Vancouver, BC V6S 1G7
tel +1 604-738-4688
email ronsdale@shaw.ca
website www.ronsdalepress.com
Facebook www.facebook.com/ronsdalepress
Twitter @ronsdalepress
Director Ronald B. Hatch

Ronsdale is a Canadian publisher based in Vancouver with some 290 books in print. Not currently accepting picture books. Founded 1988.

Scholastic Canada Ltd*

175 Hillmount Road, Markham, ON L6C 1Z7
tel +1 800-268-3860
email custserv@scholastic.ca
website www.scholastic.ca
Facebook www.facebook.com/ScholasticCanada
Twitter @scholasticCDA
Instagram scholasticcda
Pinterest scholasticcda

Art Director Andrea Casault

Serves children, parents and teachers through a variety of businesses including Scholastic Reading Club and Book Fairs, Scholastic Education, Classroom Magazines, Trade and Éditions Scholastic. Publishes recreational reading for children and young people from preschoolers to teens and educational materials for kindergarten to Grade 8 in both official languages. Its publishing focus is on books by Canadians. Wholly owned subsidiary of Scholastic Inc. Scholastic Canada is interested in reviewing indigenous material in all genres and at all levels. No other unsolicited MSS are being accepted at this time. Canadian artists may submit electronic samples of their work along with their website/contact information to the art director. Never send originals. Please see website for submission guidelines. Founded 1920.

University of Toronto Press

800 Bay Street, Mezzanine,
Toronto Ontario M5S 3A9
tel +1 416-978-2239
email publishing@utpress.utoronto.ca
website www.utpress.utoronto.ca
President Meric Gertler

Publishers of academic books, ESL/EFL, teacher reference, adult basic education and school texts. Founded 1901.

Tundra Books

320 Front Street West, Suite 1400, Toronto, ON M5V 3B6
tel +1 888-523-9292
email submissions@tundrabooks.com
email art@tundrabooks.com
website www.penguinrandomhouse.ca/imprints/TU/tundra-books
Facebook www.facebook.com/tundrabooks
Twitter @TundraBooks
Publisher Tara Walker

Publisher of high-quality children's picture books and novels, renowned for its innovations. Publishes books for children to teens. Imprints: Penguin Teen Canada, Puffin Canada, Tundra Books. A division of Penguin Random House Canada Ltd. Founded 1967.

Whitecap Books Ltd[†]

209–314 West Cordova Street, Vancouver, BC V6B 1E8
tel +1 800-387-9776
website www.whitecap.ca
Facebook www.facebook.com/whitecapbooks
Twitter @whitecapbooks
Ceo Sharon Fitzhenry

Diverse list features books on food, wine, gardening, health and well-being, regional history and regional guidebooks. Market expanded into the United States through Midpoint Books. Submissions must be sent by mail. Full details can be found on website. Founded 1977.

FRANCE

l'école des loisirs

11 rue de Sevres, 75006 Paris
tel +33 (0)1 4222 9410
email edl@ecoledesloisirs.com
website www.ecoledesloisirs.com
Managing Director Louis Delas

Specialises in children's literature from picture books to young adult fiction. Founded 1965.

Flammarion

87 quai Panhard et Levassor, 75647 Paris
tel +33 (0)1 4051 3100
website https://editions.flammarion.com
Ceo Gilles Hae'ri

Leading French publisher. Children's imprints include: Albums du Père Castor, Castor Poche, Tribal, Etonnants Classiques, GF – Flammarion, Chan – OK. Founded 1875.

Père Castor
Children's Publisher Céline Dehaine

Children's picture books, junior fiction, activity books, board books, how-to books, comics, gift books, fairy tales, dictionaries and records and tapes. Covers 0–16 years.

Gallimard Jeunesse

5 rue Gaston Gallimard, 75328 Paris
tel +33 (0)1 4954 4200
website www.gallimard-jeunesse.fr
Children's Publisher Hedwige Pasquet

Publisher of high-quality children's fiction and non-fiction including board books, novelty books, picture books, pop-up books. Founded 1911.

Hachette Livre/Gautier-Languereau

53 rue Jean Bleuzen, 92170 Vanves
tel +33 (0)1 4392 3030
website www.hachette.com
Director Arnaud Nourry

Picture books and poetry. Publishes approximately 55 titles each year. Recent successes include *Cyrano* by Tai Marc Le Thanh and Rébecca Dautremer and *Princesses* by Philippe Lechermeier and Rébecca Dautremer. Will consider unsolicited MSS. Allow two months for response. Founded 1992.

Kaléidoscope

11 rue de Sèvres, F75006 Paris
tel +33 (0)1 4544 0708
email infos@editions-kaleidoscope.com
website www.editions-kaleidoscope.com
Children's Publisher Isabel Finkenstaedt

Specialises in up-market picture books for children 0–6 years. Founded 1988.

Editions Sarbacane

35 rue d'Hauteville, 75010 Paris
tel +33 (0)1 4246 3727
email e.beulque@sarbacane.net
website www.editions-sarbacane.com

High-quality activity books, board books, picture books and young adult fiction, fiction for children from preschool age to adult.

Le Sorbier

25 boulevard Romain Rolland, 75014 Paris
tel +33 (0)1 4148 8000
website www.editionsdelamartiniere.fr

High-quality picture books for children up to 10 years and illustrated reference books for 9–12 years. Imprint of Editions de la Martiniere.

GERMANY

Carlsen Verlag

Postfach 50 03 80, 22703 Hamburg
tel +49 (0)40 398040
email info@carlsen.de
website www.carlsen.de
Directors Renate Herre, Joachim Kaufmann

Children's picture books, board books and novelty books. Illustrated fiction and non-fiction. Teenage fiction and non-fiction. Publishes both German and international authors including Stephenie Meyer, J.K. Rowling and Philip Pullman. Publisher of the *Harry Potter* series. Imprint: Chicken House Deutschland. Age groups: preschool, 5–10, 10–15, 15+. Unsolicited MSS welcome but must include a sae for return. Do not follow up by phone or post. For illustrations, submit no more than three colour photocopies and unlimited b&w copies. Founded 1953.

dtv Verlagsgesellschaft mbH & Co. KG

Tumblingerstraße 21, 80337 Munich
tel +49 (0)89 38167282
email verlag@dtv.de
website www.dtvjunior.de
Facebook www.facebook.com/dtvVerlag
Twitter @dtv_verlag
Children's Publishing Director Susanne Stark

Fiction and non-fiction for children, teenagers and young adults. Authors include Kate DiCamillo, Kevin Brooks, Colleen Hoover, Sarah J. Maas, Libba Bray, Eva Ibbotson, Sarah Dessen. Founded 1971.

Bold

Young general fiction. Authors include: Hank Green, Atticus, K.A. Tucker a.o. Founded 2018.

Carl Hanser Verlag
Vilshofener Straße 10, 81679 Munich
tel +49 (0)89 998300
email info@hanser.de
website www.hanser-literaturverlage.de
Facebook www.facebook.com/HanserLiteraturverlage
Twitter @hanserliteratur
Instagram hanserliteratur, hanser.hey
Children's Publisher Saskia Heintz

High-quality hardback books for all ages from
preschool to young adults. Board books, picture
books, fiction and non-fiction. Age groups: 3–10,
10–15, 15+. Founded 1993.

Ravensburger Buchverlag
Robert-Bosch-Straße 1, 88214 Ravensburg
tel +49 (0)751 860
email buchverlag@ravensburger.de
website www.ravensburger.de

Activity books, novelty books, picture books, fiction
for children 5–8 and 9–12 years, teenage fiction,
series fiction and educational games and puzzles.
Publishes approx. 450 titles each year and has 1,500
in print. Will consider unsolicited MSS for fiction
only. Allow two months for response. Founded 1883.

ITALY

De Agostini Editore
Via Giovanni da Verrazano 15, 28100 Novara
tel +39 03-214241
website www.deagostini.it
Publisher Annachiara Tassan

Illustrated and children's books. Founded 1901.

Edizioni Arka srl
Via Raffaello Sanzio 7, 20149, Milan
tel +39 02-4818230
email edizioniel@edizioniel.it
website www.arkaedizioni.it
Publisher Ginevra Viscardi

Picture books and some general fiction for preschool
children and children up to 10 years.

Edizioni El/Einaudi Ragazzi/Emme Edizioni
Via J. Ressel 5, 34018 San Dorligo della Valle TS
tel +39 040-3880311
email edizioniel@edizioniel.it
website www.edizioniel.com
Children's Publisher Orietta Fatucci

Activity books, board books, picture books, pop-up
books, non-fiction, novels, poetry, fairy tales, fiction.
Age groups: preschool, 5–10, 10–15, 15+. Publishes
over 270 new titles a year.

Giunti Editore S.p.A.
Via Bolognese 165, 50139, Florence
tel +39 055-50621
email info@giunti.it
website www.giunti.it
President Sergio Giunti

Activity books, board books, novelty books, picture
books, colouring books, pop-up books and some
educational textbooks. Founded 1956.

Arnoldo Mondadori Editore S.p.A. (Mondadori)
Via private Mondadori 1, 20090 Segrate, Milan
tel +39 02-75421
email infolibri@mondadori.it
website www.mondadori.it

Activity books, board books, novelty books, picture
books, painting and colouring books, pop-up books,
how-to books, hobbies, leisure, pets, sport, comics,
poetry, fairy tales, education, fiction and non-fiction.
Age groups: preschool, 5–10, 10–15, 15+. Founded
1907.

Adriano Salani Editore S.p.A.
Via Gherardini 10, 20145 Milan
tel +39 02-34597624
email info@salani.it
website www.salani.it

Picture books, how-to books, comics, gift books,
fiction, novels, poetry, fairy tales. Age groups:
preschool, 5–10, 10–15, 15+. Founded 1862.

THE NETHERLANDS

Baeckens Books
Frederik de Merodestraat 18, 2800 Mechelen
tel +32 15-715653
email info@baeckensbooks.be
website www.baeckensbooks.com
Children's Publisher Klaas Demeulemeester

High-quality picture books, activity books, board
books, novelty books, pop-up books, poetry, fiction
and some non-fiction. Founded 2004.

Lemniscaat BV
Vijverlaan 48, 3062 HL, Rotterdam
tel +31 10-2062929
email info@lemniscaat.nl
website www.lemniscaat.nl
Publisher Jean Christophe Boele van Hensbroek

Well-known independent children's book publishers
based in the Netherlands, publishing picture books,
juvenile novels and young adult literature.
Lemniscaat has its own list of titles in the
Netherlands, China, Italy and the USA. Founded
1963.

Books

Rubinstein Publishing

Prinseneiland 43, 1013 LL, Amsterdam
tel +31 20-4200772
email info@rubinstein.nl
website www.rubinstein.nl
Children's Publisher Mascha de Vries

Independent publisher specialising in audiobooks for children. Also produces novelty books. Founded 1985.

Van Goor/Van Holkema & Warendorf

PO Box 23202, 1100 DS, Amsterdam
tel +31 20-2364200
website www.de-leukste-kinderboeken.nl
website www.bestofyabooks.nl

High-quality picture books, learn-to-read books, middle grade and (literary) fiction and non-fiction, young adult. Founded 2009.

NEW ZEALAND

*Member of the New Zealand Book Publishers' Association

Cengage Learning New Zealand*

Unit 4B, Rosedale Office Park, 331 Rosedale Road, Albany, North Shore 0632
Postal address PO Box 33376, Takapuna, North Shore 0740
tel +64 (0)9 415 6850
Publishing Editor Jenny Thomas

Educational books. Founded 2007.

Edify Ltd*

Level 1, 39 Woodside Avenue, Northcote, Auckland 0627
tel +64 (0)9 972 9428
email mark@edify.co.nz
website www.edify.co.nz
Ceo Adrian Keane

Edify is a publishing, sales and marketing business providing its partners with opportunities for their products and solutions in the New Zealand educational market. Exclusive representatives of Pearson and the New Zealand based educational publisher, Sunshine Books. Founded 2013.

Gecko Press*

PO Box 9335, Marion Square, Wellington 6141
tel +64 (0)4 801 9333
email info@geckopress.com
website www.geckopress.com
Publisher Julia Marshall

Children's books: picture books, junior fiction and non-fiction. Translates and publishes award-winning children's books from around the world. Selects books strong in story, illustration and design, with a

strong 'heart factor'. See website for submission guidelines. Founded 2005.

HarperCollins Publishers (New Zealand) Ltd*

Unit D, 63 Apollo Drive, Rosedale, Auckland 0632
tel +64 (0)9 443 9400
email publicity@harpercollins.co.nz
Postal address PO Box 1, Shortland Street, Auckland 1140
website www.harpercollins.co.nz

General literature, non-fiction, reference, children's. HarperCollins New Zealand does not accept proposals or MSS for consideration, except via the Wednesday Post portal on its website. Founded 1989.

McGraw-Hill Book Company New Zealand Ltd

Level 8, 56–60 Cawley Street, Ellerslie, Auckland 1005
Postal address Private Bag 11904, Ellerslie, Auckland 1005
tel +64 (0)9 526 6200
website www.mcgraw-hill.com.au

Educational publisher: higher education, primary and secondary education (grades K–12) and professional (including medical, general and reference). Division of the McGraw-Hill Companies. Always looking for potential authors. Has a rapidly expanding publishing programme. See website for author's guide. Founded 1974.

New Zealand Council for Educational Research

Box 3237, Education House, 178–182 Willis Street, Wellington 6140
tel +64 (0)4 384 7939
email david.ellis@nzcer.org.nz
website www.nzcer.org.nz
Publishing Manager David Ellis

Education, including educational policy and practice, early childhood education, educational achievement tests, Māori education, schooling for the future, curriculum and assessment. Founded 1934.

Penguin Random House New Zealand Ltd*

Private Bag 102902, North Shore, Auckland 0745
tel +64 (0)9 442 7400
email publishing@penguinrandomhouse.co.nz
website www.penguinrandomhouse.co.nz
Facebook www.facebook.com/ PenguinBooksNewZealand
Publishing Director Debra Millar, *Head of Publishing* Claire Murdoch

Adult and children's fiction and non-fiction. Imprints: Penguin, Vintage, Black Swan, Godwit,

Viking, Puffin Books. Part of Penguin Random House. Founded 2013.

SOUTH AFRICA

Member of the Publishers' Association of South Africa

Cambridge University Press, Africa*

Lower Ground Floor, Nautica Building,
The Water Club, Beach Road, Granger Bay,
Cape Town 8005
tel +27 (0)21 412 7800
email capetown@cambridge.org
website www.cup.co.za
Publishing Director Johan Traut

Textbooks and literature for sub-Sahara African countries, as well as primary reading materials in 28 African languages. Founded 1534.

Educat Publishers Pty Ltd

4 Clifford Street, Ottery, Cape Town
tel +27 (0)21 697 3669
email takeeducat@gmail.com
website www.educat.co.za

Educational products including science and maths, product designs for schools and retail, as well as mass markets. Age groups: preschool, 5–10, 10–15, 15+.

Human & Rousseau

12th Floor, Naspers, 40 Heerengracht,
Roggebaai 8012
tel +27 (0)21 406 3033
email nb@nb.co.za
website www.humanrousseau.com

General Afrikaans and English titles. Quality Afrikaans literature, popular literature, general children's and youth literature, cookery, self-help. Founded 1959.

Best Books
Education.

Jacklin Enterprises (Pty) Ltd

PO Box 521, Parklands 2121
tel +27 (0)11 265 4200
website www.jacklin.co.za
Managing Director Mike Jacklin

Children's fiction and non-fiction; Afrikaans large print books. Subjects include aviation, natural history, romance, general science, technology and transportation. Founded 1901.

Macmillan Education South Africa

4th Floor, Building G, Hertford Office Park,
90 Bekker Road, Vorna Valley, Midrand 1685
tel +27 (0)11 731 3300
Postal address Private Bag X19, Northlands 2116
website www.macmillan.co.za
Managing Director Preggy Naidoo

Educational titles for the RSA market. Founded 1843.

NB Publishers (Pty) Ltd*

PO Box 879, Cape Town 8000
tel +27 (0)21 406 3033
email nb@nb.co.za
website www.nb.co.za

General: Afrikaans fiction, politics, children's and youth literature in all the country's languages, non-fiction. Imprints: Tafelberg, Human & Rousseau, Queillerie, Pharos, Kwela, Best Books and Lux Verbi. Founded 1950.

New Africa Books (Pty) Ltd

Unit 13, Athlone Industrial Park,
10 Mymoena Crescent, Cape Town 7764
tel +27 (0)21 467 5860
email info@newafricabooks.co.za
Postal address PostNet, Suite 144, Private Bag X9190, Cape Town 8000

New Africa Books, incorporating David Philip Publishers, is an independent publishing house. Currently publishes fiction and non-fiction books for young people in all South African languages. Also publishes children's illustrated books and comics. Founded 1971.

Oxford University Press Southern Africa*

Vasco Boulevard, N1 City, Goodwood,
Cape Town 7460
tel +27 (0)21 596 2300
email oxford.za@oup.com
Postal address PO Box 12119, N1 City,
Cape Town 7463
website www.oxford.co.za
Managing Director Steve Cilliers

Oxford University Press is one of the leading educational publishers in South Africa, producing a wide range of quality educational material in print and digital format. The range includes books from Grade R to Grade 12, as well as higher education textbooks, school literature, dictionaries and atlases. Committed to transforming lives through education by providing superior quality learning material and support. Founded 1586.

Pearson South Africa*

4th Floor, Auto Atlantic Building,
Cnr Hertzog Boulevard and Heerengracht Boulevard,
Cape Town 8001
Postal address PO Box 396, Cape Town 8000
tel +27 (0)21 532 6008
email pearsonza.enquiries@pearson.com
website https://za.pearson.com/
Managing Director Ebrahim Matthews

Pearson South Africa provides learning materials, technologies and services for use in schools, TVET colleges, higher education institutions and in home and professional environments. Also graduates

Books

thousands of students every year through the Pearson Institute of Higher Education. Founded 2010.

Shuter and Shooter Publishers (Pty) Ltd*

110 CB Downes Road, Pietermaritzburg, KwaZulu-Natal 3201
tel +27 (0)33 846 8700
email sales@shuters.com
Postal address PO Box 61, Mkondeni, KwaZulu-Natal 3212
website www.shuters.co.za
Ceo Primi Chetty

Core curriculum-based textbooks for use at foundation, intermediate, senior and FET phases. Supplementary readers in various languages; dictionaries; reading development kits, charts. Literature titles in English, isiXhosa, Sesotho, Sepedi, Setswana, Tshivenda, Xitsonga, Ndebele, isiZulu and Siswati. Founded 1925.

Via Afrika Publishers

11th Floor, 40 Heerengracht, Cape Town 8001
Postal address PO Box 5197, Cape Town 8001
tel +27 (0)21 406 3528
email customerservices@viaafrika.com
website www.viaafrika.com
Ceo Christina Watson

Educational materials for South African schools and FET colleges, for all learning areas and subjects at all grades/levels: in all official languages of South Africa. Imprints: Acacia, Action, Afritech, Afro, Atlas, Bateleur Books, Collegium, Idem, Juta/Gariep, KZN Books, Nasou; Stimela, Van Schaik (literature), Via Afrika. Founded 1949.

SPAIN

Grupo Anaya

C/Juan Ignacio Luca de Tena 15, 28027 Madrid
tel +34 913 938 800
website www.anaya.es
Managing Director Carlos Lamadrid

Non-fiction: education textbooks for preschool–15+.

Editorial Cruilla

C/Roger de Llúria 44, 4th, 08009 Barcelona
tel +34 902 123 336
email editorial@cruilla.cat
website www.cruilla.cat
Publishing Director Josep Maria Cervera

Activity books, novelty books, fiction for children 5–8 and 9–12 years, teenage fiction and poetry. Publishes approx. 120–130 titles each year. Recent successes include *El Vaixell de Vapor* (series), *Vull Llegir!* and *Molly Moon Stops the World/Molly Moon's Incredible Book of Hypnotism*. Subsidiary of Ediciones SM. Founded 1984.

Destino Infantil & Juvenil

Edificio Planeta, Diagonal 662–664, 08034 Barcelona
tel +34 934 496 7001
email infoinfantilyjuvenil@planetao.es
website www.librosdelzorrorojo.com
Children's & Young Adult Director Marta Bueno Miró

Fiction for children 6–16 years. Picture books, pop-up books, fiction and some unusual illustrated books.

Libros del Zorro Rojo

Carrer de Llull 51, 60–4A, 08005 Barcelona
tel +34 933 076 850
email editorial@librosdelzorrorojo.com
website https://novedades.librosdelzorrorojo.com/
Editorial Director Fernando Diego García

Small independent publisher specialising in children's and young adult books. Main focus is picture books for young children and classics with high-quality illustrations for young readers. Founded 2004.

Editorial Libsa

Calle de San Rafael 4, 28108 Alcobendas/Madrid
tel +34 916 572 580
email libsa@libsa.es
website www.libsa.es
President Amado Sanchez, *Children's Books Editor* Maria Dolores Maeso

Publisher and packager of highly-illustrated mass market books: activity books, board books, picture books, colouring books, how-to books, fairy tales.

Penguin Random House Grupo Editorial

Luchana 23, 1A, 28010 Madrid
tel +34 915 358 190
website www.penguinrandomhousegrupoeditorial.com

Preschool activity, novelty and picture books through to young adult fiction. Also a packager and printer. Part of Penguin Random House. Founded 2013.

Beascoa

Character publishing, including Disney and Fisher-Price.

Nube de Tinta

Provides novels to a broad range of readers from young adult to adult who share a love of reading.

Montena

Contemporary literary fiction including fantasy.

Vicens Vives SA

Avenida Sarriá 130–132, 08017 Barcelona
tel +34 932 523 700
email rrhh@vicensvives.es
website www.vicensvives.es

Activity and novelty books, fiction, art, encyclopedias, dictionaries, education, geography, history, music, science, textbooks, posters. Age groups: preschool, 5–10, 10–15, 15+.

USA

Member of the Association of American Publishers Inc.

Abingdon Press

2222 Rosa L. Parks Boulevard, Nashville, TN 37228
tel +1 800-251-3320
website www.abingdonpress.com
Facebook www.facebook.com/AbingdonPress
Twitter @AbingdonPress
President & Publisher Neil Alexander

General interest, professional, academic and reference, non-fiction and fiction, youth and children's non-fiction and Vatican Bible School; primarily directed to the religious market. Imprint of United Methodist Publishing House with tradition of crossing denominational boundaries. United Methodist Publishing founded 1789.

Harry N. Abrams, Inc.

195 Broadway, 9th Floor, New York, NY 10007
tel +1 212-206-7715
email abrams@abramsbooks.com
website www.abramsbooks.com

Art and architecture, photography, natural sciences, performing arts, children's books. No fiction. Imprints include: Abrams, Abrams Appleseed, Abrams Books for Young Readers, Abrams Comicarts, Abrams Images, Abrams Noterie, Abrams Press, Amulet Books, Amulet Paperbacks. Founded 1949.

Abrams Books for Young Readers

tel +1 212-519-1200
website www.abramsyoungreaders.com
Fiction and non-fiction: picture books, young readers, middle readers, young adult.
For picture books submit covering letter and complete MS, for longer works and non-fiction send query and sample chapter with sase.

Aladdin Paperbacks – see Simon & Schuster Children's Publishing Division

All About Kids Publishing

PO Box 159, Gilroy, CA 95021
tel +1 408-337-1152
email lguevara@allaboutkidspub.com
website www.allaboutkidspub.com
Publisher Mike G. Guevara, *Editor* Linda L. Guevara

Fiction and non-fiction picture books and chapter books. Recent successes include *Don't Let the Dead Bugs Bite!* by Stephen Zmina (picture book) and *Cold Waves, Cold Blood* by Patrick Doherty (teen novel). Founded 2000. See website for submission guidelines. Not currently taking submissions.

Amistad – see HarperCollins Publishers

Atheneum Books for Young Readers – see Simon & Schuster Children's Publishing Division

Avon – see HarperCollins Publishers

Barefoot Books

2067 Massachusetts Avenue, Cambridge, MA 02140
tel +1 617-576-0660
email publicity@barefootbooks.com
website www.barefootbooks.com
Facebook www.facebook.com/barefootbooks
Twitter @BarefootBooks

Currently not accepting MS submissions or queries. Accepts illustrator samples via mail only. Please mail samples (no original artwork) for the attention of the editor. Recent successes include *Mindful Kids* by Whitney Stewart, illustrated by Mina Braun; and *The Barefoot Book of Children* by Kate DePalma and Tessa Strickland, illustrated by David Dean (3–7 years, picture book). Length: 500–1,000 words (picture books), 2,000–3,000 words (young readers). Founded 1993 (UK); 1998 (USA).

Bick Publishing House

75 Mungertown Road, Madison, CT 06443
tel +1 203-605-0341
email bickpubhse@aol.com
website https://bickpubhouse.com/

Adults: health and recovery, living with disabilities, wildlife rehabilitation. Non-fiction for young adults: philosophy, psychology, self-help, social issues, science. Recent successes include *What Are You Doing with Your Life? Books on Living for Teenagers* by J. Krishnamurti; *The Teen Brain Book: Who and What Are You?*, *Talk: Teen Art of Communication*, *Cosmic Calendar: The Big Bang to Your Consciousness* by Dale Carlson and *The Challenged Addict: Addiction Recovery with Concuring Developmental Disorders* by Hannah Carlsen Jurewicz. Founded 1993.

Bloomsbury Publishing USA*

1385 Broadway, New York, NY 10018
tel +1 212-419-5300
email ChildrensPublicityUSA@bloomsbury.com
website www.bloomsbury.com/us
Vice President & Publishing Director Cindy Loh (consumer publishing)

Supports the worldwide publishing activities of Bloomsbury Publishing Plc: caters for the US market. For submission guidelines see website: www.bloomsbury.com/us/authors/submissions/. Bloomsbury Publishing Plc founded 1986.

The Blue Sky Press – see Scholastic, Inc.

Boyds Mills Press

815 Church Street, Honesdale, PA 18431
website www.boydsmillspress.com
Facebook www.facebook.com/BoydsMillsPressBooks

Books

Twitter @boydsmillspress

Activity books, picture books, fiction, non-fiction and poetry for 18 years and under. Successes include *Drive* by Nathan Clement, *One Whole and Perfect Day* by Judith Clarke and *I'm Being Stalked by a Moonshadow* by Doug MacLeod. Publishes approx. 80 titles each year. Will consider both unsolicited MSS and queries. Send to above address and label package 'Manuscript Submission'. Looking for middle grade fiction with fresh ideas and subject matter, and young adult novels of real literary merit. Non-fiction should be fun and entertaining as well as informative, and non-fiction MSS should be accompanied by a detailed bibliography. Interested in imaginative picture books and welcomes submissions from both writers and illustrators. Submit samples as b&w and/or colour copies or transparencies; submissions will not be returned. Include sase with all submissions. Send art samples to above address and label package 'Art Sample Submission'. Founded 1991.

Calkins Creek Books

US history and historical fiction.

Highlights Press

Publishes activity books and innovative novelty formats, with a variety of types of puzzle books.

WordSong

Poetry.

Calkins Creek Books – see Boyds Mills Press

Candlewick Press

99 Dover Street, Somerville, MA 02144
tel +1 617-661-3330
email bigbear@candlewick.com
website www.candlewick.com
President & Publisher Karen Lotz, *Creative Director & Associate Publisher* Chris Paul, *Executive Editorial Director & Associate Publisher* Liz Bicknell, *Editorial Director & Director of Editorial Operations* Mary Lee Donovan

Books for babies through teens: board books, picture books, early readers, first chapter books, novels, non-fiction, novelty books, poetry, graphic novels. Publishes 70 picture books, 40 middle readers and 30 young adult titles each year. Founded 1991.

Candlewick Entertainment

Group Editorial Director Joan Powers

Media-related children's books, including film/TV tie-ins.

Carolrhoda Books – see Lerner Publishing Group

Cartwheel Books – see Scholastic, Inc.

Charlesbridge Publishing

85 Main Street, Watertown, MA 02472
tel +1 617-926-0329
email tradeeditorial@charlesbridge.com
website www.charlesbridge.com
President & Publisher Brent Farmer

Fiction and non-fiction board books, picture books and middle grade books for preschool–14 years. Young Adult novels for readers 14+. Dedicated to diversity titles and new voices across genres. Non-fiction list specialises in nature, concept, history and science. Publishes roughly 60% non-fiction, 40% fiction. Recent successes include *Samurai Rising* by Pamela S. Turner, *The Cazuela That the Farm Maiden Stirred* by Samantha Vamos, *Trapped!: A Whale's Rescue* by Robert Burleigh, *A Black Hole Is Not a Hole* by Carolyn DeCristofano, *Currents* by Jane Smolik and *Feathers: Not Just for Flying* by Melissa Stewart. Send full MSS; no queries. Responds to MSS of interest. For illustrations, send query with samples, tearsheets and résumé. Founded 1980.

Chicago Review Press

814 North Franklin Street, Chicago, IL 60610
tel +1 312-337-0747
email frontdesk@jpg.com
website www.chicagoreviewpress.com
Publisher Cynthia Sherry

General publisher. Non-fiction activity books for children. Imprint Zephyr publishes professional development titles for teachers. Interested in hands-on educational books. See website for submission guidelines. Founded 1973.

Chronicle Books*

680 Second Street, San Francisco, CA 94107
tel +1 415-537-4200
email hello@chroniclebooks.com
website www.chroniclebooks.com
website www.chroniclebooks.com/titles/kids-teens
Facebook www.facebook.com/ChronicleBooks
Twitter @ChronicleKids
Chairman & Ceo Nion McEvoy, *Publisher* Christine Carswell

Traditional and innovative children's books. Looking for projects that have a unique bent – in subject matter, writing style or illustrative technique – that will add a distinctive flair. Interested in fiction and non-fiction for children of all ages as well as board books, decks, activity kits and other unusual or 'novelty' formats. Publishes 60–100 books each year. Also for adults: cooking, how-to books, nature, art, biographies, fiction, gift. For picture books submit MS. For older readers, submit outline/synopsis and three sample chapters. No submitted materials will be returned. Response approx. three months. Founded 1967.

Clarion Books – see Houghton Mifflin Harcourt

Books

Clear Light Books

823 Don Diego, Santa Fe, NM 87505
tel +1 505-989-9590
website www.clearlightbooks.com

For adults: art and photography, cookbooks, ecology/environment, health, gift books, history, Native America, Tibet, Western Americana. Non-fiction for children and young adults: multicultural, American Indian, Hispanic. Looking for authentic American Indian art and folklore. Send complete MS with sase.

CMX – see DC Comics

David C Cook

4050 Lee Vance View, Colorado Springs, CO 80918
tel +1 719-536-0100
website www.davidccook.com

Christian education resources for preschool to teenagers. Founded 1875.

Cooper Square Publishing

4501 Forbes Boulevard, Suite 200, Lanham, MD 20706
tel +1 301-459-3366

Part of the Rowman & Littlefield Publishing Group (page 61). Founded 1949.

Cricket Books

1751 Pinnacle Drive, Suite 600, McLean, Virginia 22102
email customerservice@caruspub.com
website https://shop.cricketmedia.com/

Picture books, chapter books, poetry, non-fiction and novels for children and young adults. Recent successes include *Breakout* by Paul Fleischman and *Robert and the Weird & Wacky Facts* by Barbara Seuling, illustrated by Paul Brewer. Also publishes *Cricket*, the award-winning magazine of outstanding stories and art for 9–14 year-olds, and other magazines for young readers. Division of Carus Publishing. Not accepting MSS submissions at this time. Founded 1973.

Darby Creek Publishing – see Lerner Publishing Group

Dawn Publications

12402 Bitney Springs Road, Nevada City, CA 95959
tel +1 800-545-7475
email chris@deep-books.co.uk
website www.dawnpub.com
Editor & Art Director Carol Malnor

Dedicated to inspiring in children a deeper understanding and appreciation for all life on Earth. The aim is to help parents and teachers encourage children to bond with the Earth in a relationship of love, respect and intelligent cooperation, through the books published and the educational materials

offered online. Recent successes include: *Why Should I Walk? I Can FLY!*, *Scampers Thinks Like a Scientist*, *Over on a Desert: Somewhere in the World*, *He's Your Daddy: Ducklings, Joeys, Kits, and More*, *I Am the Rain*, *Paddle Perch Climb*, *Tall Tall Tree*, *Daytime Nighttime*, *Baby on Board*, *There's a Bug on My Book*, *A Moon of My Own*. See website for submission guidelines. Founded 1979.

DC Comics

4000 Warner Boulevard, Burbank, CA 91522
website www.dccomics.com

Activity books, board books, novelty books, picture books, painting and colouring books, pop-up books, fiction, fairy tales, art, hobbies, how-to books, leisure, entertainment, film/TV tie-ins, calendars, comics, gift books, periodicals, picture cards, posters, CD-Roms, CD-I, internet for preschool age to 15+ years. DC Comics has published and licensed comic books for over 60 years in all genres for all ages, including super heroes, fantasy, horror, mystery and high-quality graphic stories for mature readers. Imprints: WildStorm, Vertigo. A Warner Bros. Company. Founded 1934.

CMX

Translated manga from Japan in its original format.

MINX

Original graphic novels for teenage girls.

Dial Books – see Penguin Young Readers

Tom Doherty Associates, LLC

175 5th Avenue, New York, NY 10010
tel +1 212-388-0100
email enquiries@tor.com
website www.torforgeblog.com

Fiction and non-fiction for middle readers and young adults. Publishes 5–10 middle readers and 5–10 young adult books each year. Successes include *Hidden Talents, Flip* by David Lubar (fantasy, 10+ years), *Briar Rose* by Jane Yolen (fiction, 12+ years), *Strange Unsolved Mysteries* by Phyllis Rabin Amert (non-fiction). For adults: fiction – general, historical, western, suspense, mystery, horror, science fiction, fantasy, humour, juvenile, classics (English language); non-fiction. Imprints: Tor Books, Forge Books, Orb Books, Starscope, Tor Teen. Founded 1980.
For both fiction and non-fiction, submit outline/synopsis and complete MS. Responds to queries in one month; MSS in six months for unsolicited work. Fiction length: middle readers – 30,000 words; young adult – 60,000–100,000 words. Non-fiction length: middle readers – 25,000–35,000 words; young adult – 70,000 words. For illustrations, query with samples to Irene Gallo, Art Director. Responds only if interested.

StarScape

Science fiction and fantasy for children 10–12 years.

Tor

Science fiction and fantasy published in hardback and paperback.

Tor Teen

website www.torteen.com

Science fiction and fantasy for children 12+ years.

Doubleday – see Penguin Random House

Dover Publications, Inc.

31 East 2nd Street, Mineola, NY 11501
tel +1 516-294-7000
website http://store.doverpublications.com/

Activity books, novelty books, picture books, fiction for children 5–8 and 9–12 years, teenage fiction, series fiction, reference, plays, religion, poetry, audio and CD-Roms. Also adult non-fiction. Publishes approx. 150 children's titles and has over 2,500 in print. Successes include *Easy Noah's Ark Sticker Picture, How to Draw a Funny Monster* and *Pretty Ballerina Sticker Paper Doll*. Will consider unsolicited MSS but write for guidelines. Founded 1941.

Dragon Books – see Pacific View Press

EDCON Publishing Group

30 Montauk Boulevard, Oakdale, NY 11769–1399
tel +1 631-567-7227
email info@edconpublishing.com
website www.edconpublishing.com

Supplemental instructional materials for use by education professionals to improve reading and maths skills. Includes early reading, *Classics* series, *Easy Shakespeare*, fiction and non-fiction, reading diagnosis and vocabulary books. Founded 1970.

Eerdmans Publishing Company

2140 Oak Industrial Drive NE, Grand Rapids, MI 49505
tel +1 616-459-4591
website www.eerdmans.com
President & Publisher Bill Eerdmans

Independent publisher of a wide range of religious books, from academic works in theology, biblical studies, religious history and reference to popular titles in spirituality, social and cultural criticism and literature. Founded 1911.

Eerdmans Books for Young Readers

website www.eerdmans.com/Pages/YoungReaders/EBYR-About.aspx

Picture books, biographies, middle reader and young adult fiction and non-fiction. Publishes 12–18 books a year. Seeks MSS that are honest, wise and hopeful but also publishes stories that delight with their storyline, characters or good humour. Stories that celebrate diversity, stories of historical significance, and stories that relate to current issues are of special interest. Accepts unsolicited submissions. Send to Acquisitions Editor; responds in four months only to submissions of interest. For illustrations, send photocopies or printed media and include a list of previous illustrated publications. Send to Gayle Brown. Samples will be kept on file; they will not be returned.

Encyclopaedia Britannica Inc.

325 North La Salle Street, Suite 200, Chicago, IL 60654-2682
tel +1 312-347-7159
email contact@eb.com
website www.britannica.com

Encyclopedias, reference books, almanacs, videos and CD-Roms for adults and children 5–15+ years.

Enslow Publishers, Inc.

101 West 23rd Street, Suite #240, New York NY1011
tel +1 800-398-2504
email customerservice@enslow.com
website www.enslow.com
President Mark Enslow, *Vice President & Publisher* Brian Enslow

Provides fiction and non-fiction content across the K-12 space. Aims to inspire readers to become lifelong learners. Founded 1976.

Evan-Moor Educational Publishers

18 Lower Ragsdale Drive, Monterey, CA 93940
tel +1 800-714-0971
email marketing@evan-moor.com
website www.evan-moor.com/
Founder & Ceo William E. Evans

Educational materials for parents and teachers of children (3–12 years): activity books, textbooks, how-to books, CD-Roms. Subjects include maths, geography, history, science, reading, writing, social studies, art and craft. Publishes approx. 50 titles each year and has over 500 in print. Less than 10% of books are by first-time authors. Query or submit outline, table of contents and sample pages. Responds to queries in two months; MSS in four months. See website for submission guidelines. For illustrations, send résumé, samples and tearsheets to the Art Director. Primarily uses b&w material. Founded 1979.

Farrar Straus Giroux Books for Young Readers

175 Fifth Avenue, New York, NY 10010
website http://us.macmillan.com/publishers/farrar-straus-giroux#FYR

An imprint of Macmillan Children's Publishing Group. Books for toddlers through to young adults: picture books, fiction and non-fiction for all ages, and poetry (occasionally). Publishes 70 hardcover originals plus ten paperback reprints each year and has approx. 500 titles in print. Submission details: Approx. 10% of books are by first-time authors. No unsolicited MSS. Founded 1946.

Flux

2297 Waters Drive, Mendota Heights, MN 55120
tel +1 888-917-0145
email publicity@northstareditions.com
email submissions@northstareditions.com
website www.fluxnow.com
Facebook www.facebook.com/FluxBooks
Twitter @FluxBooks
Managing Editor Mari Kesselring

From their very first Young Adult novels in 2006, Flux set out to be different. Consistently provocative, independently alternative and striving to find unique voices that unsettle, surprise, inform and ignite. See website above for submission guidelines. Accepts electronic submissions only. Flux is an imprint of North Star Editions, Inc.

Free Spirit Publishing

6325 Sandburg Road, Suite 100, Golden Valley, MN 5542
tel +1 612-338-2068
email help4kids@freespirit.com
website www.freespirit.com
Facebook www.facebook.com/freespiritpublishing
Twitter @freespiritbooks
President Judy Galbraith

Award-winning publisher of non-fiction materials for children and teens, parents, educators and counsellors. Specialises in materials for self-help for kids and teens which empower young people and promote positive self-esteem through improved social and emotional health. Topics include self-esteem and self-awareness, stress management, school success, creativity, friends and family, peacemaking, social action and special needs (i.e. gifted and talented, children with learning differences). Publishes approx. 18–22 new products each year, adding to a backlist of over 200 books and posters. Free Spirit authors are expert educators and mental health professionals who have been honoured nationally for their contributions on behalf of children. Founded 1983.

Front Street

815 Church Street, Honesdale, PA 18431
tel +1 570-253-1164
email contact@boydsmillpress.com
website www.boydsmillspress.com/bmp/book-imprint/front-street
Editorial Director Larry Rosler

Books for children and young adults: picture books, fiction (5–8, 9–12, teenage). For fiction, submit the first three chapters and a plot summary. For picture books, submit the entire MSS. Include an sase if return required. Allow three to four months for response. Imprint of Boyds Mills Press (page 51). Founded 1994.

Fulcrum Publishing

4690 Table Mountain Drive, Suite 100, Golden, CO 80403
tel +1 303-277-1623
website www.fulcrum-books.com

Publishes a wide variety of educational non-fiction texts and children's books, also books and support materials for teachers, librarians, parents and elementary through middle school children. Subjects include: science and nature, literature and storytelling, history, multicultural studies and Native American and Hispanic cultures. Founded 1965.

Gale Cengage Learning*

27500 Drake Road, Farmington Hills, MI 48331–3535
tel +1 248-699-4253
website www.gale.com

Education publishing for libraries, schools and businesses. Serves the K–12 market with the following imprints: Blackbirch Press, Greenhaven Press, KidHaven Press, Lucent Books, Sleeping Bear Press, UXL. Founded 1954.

Greenhaven Press

353 3rd Avenue, Suite 255, New York, NY 10010
website https://greenhavenpublishing.com/

High-quality non-fiction resources for the education community. Publishes 220 young adult academic reference titles each year. Successes include the *Opposing Viewpoints* series. Approx. 35% of books are by first-time authors. No unsolicited MSS. All writing is done on a work-to-hire basis. Send query, résumé and list of published works. Founded 1970.

KidHaven Press

Non-fiction references for younger researchers.

Lucent Books

Non-fiction resources for upper-elementary to high school students. Successes include *Women in the American Revolution* and *Civil Liberties and the War on Terrorism*. No unsolicited MSS. Query with résumé.

Sleeping Bear Press

email sleepingbearpress@cengage.com
website www.sleepingbearpress.com
High-quality picture books.

Gibbs Smith

tel 801-544-9800
email info@gibbs-smith.com
website www.gibbs-smith.com

A Utah-based publisher. Its trade and special interest division publishes home reference, cookbook and children's titles. The Gibbs Smith Education division is the nation's leading publisher of state history programs. All unsolicited queries, submissions and correspondence should be via email. Due to the number of submissions received, the policy is to respond only to projects the company wishes to explore. Founded 1969.

Books

Greenhaven Press – see Gale Cengage Learning

Grosset & Dunlap – see Penguin Young Readers

Gryphon House, Inc.

PO Box 10, 6848 Leon's Way, Lewisville, NC 27023
tel +1 800-636-0928
website www.gryphonhouse.com

Early childhood (0–8 years) resource books for teachers and parents.
Looking for books that are developmentally appropriate for the intended age group, are well researched and based on current trends in the field, and include creative, participatory learning experiences with a common conceptual theme to tie them together. Send query and/or a proposal. Founded 1971.

Hachai Publishing

527 Empire Boulevard, Brooklyn, New York, NY 11225
tel +1 718-633-0100
email info@hachai.com
website www.hachai.com

Jewish books for children 0–8+ years.
Welcomes unsolicited MSS. Specialises in books for children 2–4 years and 3–6 years. Looking for stories that convey the traditional Jewish experience in modern times or long ago, traditional Jewish observance and positive character traits. Founded 1970.

Hachette Book Group*

1290 Avenue of the Americas, New York, NY 10104
tel +1 212-364-1100
website www.hachettebookgroup.com

Divisions: Grand Central Publishing; Hachette Audio; Hachette Nashville; Little, Brown and Company; Little, Brown and Company Books for Young Readers; Orbit, Perseus Books. Imprints: Grand Central: Forever, Forever Yours, Goop Press, Twelve, Vision. Hachette Nashville: Center Street, FaithWords, Worthy Books. Hachette Books: Little, Brown and Company: Back Bay Books, JIMMY Patterson, Little, Brown Spark, Mulholland Books. Little, Brown Books for Young Readers: LB Kids, Poppy Orbit: Orbit, Redhook. Perseus Books: Avalon Travel, Basic Books, Black Dog & Leventhal, Bold Type Books, DaCapo Press, Hachette Books, Running Press, PublicAffairs, Seal Press, Weinstein Books, Westview. Founded 1996.

Handprint Books

413 Sixth Avenue, Brooklyn, New York, NY 11215–3310
tel +1 718-768-3696
email info@handprintbooks.com
website www.handprintbooks.com
Publisher Christopher Franceschelli

A range of children's books: picture and story books through to young adult fiction. Imprints: Handprint Books, Ragged Bears, Blue Apple. Welcomes submissions of MSS of quality for works ranging from board books to young adult novels. For novels, first query interest on the subject and submit a 7,500-word max. sample. Accepts MSS on an e-submission basis only, sent as attachments in a word processing format readily readable on a PC. Artwork should be sent as small jpgs; artists' website addresses may also be submitted. No series fiction, licensed character (or characters whose primary avatar is meant to be as licences), 'I-Can-Read'-type books, or titles intended primarily for mass merchandise outlets. Founded 2000.

HarperCollins Publishers*

195 Broadway, New York, NY 10007
tel +1 212-207-700
website http://corporate.harpercollins.com/us
President & Ceo Brian Murray

Adult fiction (commercial and literary) and non-fiction. Subjects include biography, business, cookbooks, educational, history, juvenile, poetry, religious, science, technical and travel. Imprints: Avon, Avon Inspire, Avon Red (mass market romance); Broadside Books (conservative non-fiction); Custom House (thought-provoking non-fiction); Day Street Books; Ecco (distinguished fiction and non-fiction); Harper Books (best-selling fiction and non-fiction); Harper Business; Harper Design (popular culture and the arts); Harper Luxe; Harper Perennial; Harper Voyager (science fiction); Harper Wave (health and wellness); HarperAudio; HarperCollins 360; HarperOne (spirituality); Morrow Gift; William Morrow; Witness. No unsolicited material; all submissions must come through a literary agent. Founded 1817.

History Compass LLC

25 Leslie Road, Auburndale, MA 02466
tel +1 617-332-2202
email info@historycompass.com
website www.historycompass.com

The history of the USA presented through the study of primary source documents. Successes include *Get a Clue!* (grades 2–8) and *Adventures in History* series (grades 4–8). Other series include *Perspectives on History* (grades 5–12+) and *Researching American History* (8–15 year-olds and ESL students). Also historical fiction for younger readers. Founded 1990.

Holiday House, Inc.

425 Madison Avenue, New York, NY 10017
tel +1 212-688-0085
email info@holidayhouse.com
website www.holidayhouse.com

General fiction for children. Publishes 35 picture books, ten young reader, 15 middle reader and eight young adult titles each year. Recent successes include *Lafayette and the American Revolution* by Russell Freedman. Approx. 20% of books are by first-time authors. Send entire MS. Only responds to projects of interest. Will review MS/illustration packages from artists: send MS with dummy and colour photocopies. Founded 1935.

Henry Holt Books for Young Readers

175 Fifth Avenue, New York, NY 10010
website https://us.macmillan.com/mackids/,
www.fiercereads.com
Vice President & Publisher Laura Godwin

Imprint of Macmillan Children's Publishing Group. Publishes picture books, chapter books, middle grade titles and young adult titles. Founded 1866.

Houghton Mifflin Harcourt*

3 Park Avenue, Floor 19, New York, NY 10016
tel +1 212-598-5730
website www.hmhco.com

Reference, fiction and non-fiction for adults and young readers. Also educational content and solutions for K-12 teachers and students. Founded 1832.

Houghton Mifflin Harcourt Books for Young Readers

Boston office 222 Berkeley Street, Boston, MA 02116-3764
tel +1 617-351-5000
New York office 215 Park Avenue South, New York, NY 10003
tel +1 215-420-5800
website www.hmhbooks.com

Picture books, fiction, poetry and non-fiction for children, preschool through high school. Recent successes include *The Testing* by Joelle Charbonneau and *Sleep Like a Tiger* by Mary Logue and illustrated by Pamela Zagarenski. Imprint: Clarion Books. For fiction, submit complete MS. For non-fiction, submit outline/synopsis and sample chapters. Responds only if interested. For illustrations, query with samples (colour photocopies and tearsheets). Responds in four months.

Houghton Mifflin Harcourt/Clarion Books

215 Park Avenue South, New York, NY 10003
tel +1 212-420-5800
Vice-President & Publisher, Clarion Books Dinah Stevenson, *Creative Director* Christine Kettner

Picture books, fiction, poetry and non-fiction for children preschool through to high school. Recent successes include *Mr. Wuffles!* by David Wiesner. For fiction and picture books, send complete MS. For non-fiction, send query with up to three sample chapters. Founded 1965.

Hunter House Publishers

4507 Charlotte Ave, Suite 100, Nashville, TN 3720
tel +1 615-255-2665
email submissions@turnerpublishing.com
website www.hunterhouse.com

Imprint of Turner Publishing Company. Non-fiction books on children's physical, mental and emotional health, including books for tweens and children's life skills and activity books (games, classroom and fitness activities) for use by parents, teachers, youth leaders, camp counselors, coaches. Imprint of Turner Publishing Company. Founded 1978.

Hyperion Books for Children*

237 Park Avenue, New York, NY 10017
tel +1 212-633-4400
website www.hyperionbooks.com

Board and novelty books, picture books, young readers, middle grade, young adult, non-fiction (all subjects at all levels). Recent successes include *Don't Let the Pigeon Drive the Bus*, written and illustrated by Mo Willems, *Dumpy The Dump Truck* series by Julie Andrews Edwards and Emma Walton Hamilton (3–7 years) and *Artemis Fowl* by Eoin Colfer (young adult novel, *New York Times* bestseller). Imprints include Michael di Capua Books, Jump at the Sun, Volo. Founded 1991. Approx. 10% of books are by first-time authors. Only interested in submissions via literary agents. For illustrations, send résumé, business card, promotional literature or tearsheets to be kept on file to Anne Diebel, Art Director.

Illumination Arts Publishing

PO Box 1865, Bellevue, WA 98009
tel +1 425-968-5097
email liteinfo@illumin.com
website www.illumin.com
Editorial Director John Thompson

Picture books. Publishes books to inspire the mind, touch the heart and uplift the spirit. Successes include *The Right Touch*. Length: 300–1,500 words. Founded 1987.

Impact Publishers Inc.

5674 Shattuck Avenue, Oakland, CA 94609
tel +1 805-466-5917
email customerservice@newharbinger.com
website www.newharbinger.com/imprint/impact-publishers

Psychology and self-improvement books and audio tapes for adults, children, families, organisations and communities. Imprint of New Harbinger Publications. Only publishes non-fiction books which serve human development and are written by highly respected psychologists and other human service professionals. Rarely publishes authors outside of the USA. See website for guidelines. Founded 1970.

Incentive Publications by World Book

180 N. LaSalle, Suite 900, Chicago, IL 60601
tel +1 888-482-9764
website https://incentivepublications.com/

Produces supplemental resources for student use and instruction and classroom management improvement materials for teachers. Specializes in supplemental resources for middle grade students and teaching strategies for grades K–12. More than 300 titles are available. Send a letter of introduction, table of contents, a sample chapter and sase for return of material. Acquired by World Book in 2013. Founded 1969.

Jolly Fish Press

2297 Waters Drive, Mendota Heights, MN 55120
tel +1 888-417-0195
email publicity@jollyfishpress.com
email submit@jollyfishpress.com
website www.jollyfishpress.com
Facebook www.facebook.com/JollyFishPress
Twitter @JollyFishPress
Managing Editor Mari Kesselring

Jolly Fish Press is dedicated to promoting exceptional, unique new voices in middle grade fiction and jumpstarting writing careers. See website above for submission guidelines. Accepts electronic submissions only. Jolly Fish Press is an imprint of North Star Editions, Inc. Founded 2011.

Just Us Books, Inc.

356 Glenwood Avenue East Orange, NJ 07017
tel +1 973-672-7701
email info@justusbooks.com
website http://justusbooks.com/
Publishers Cheryl Hudson, Wade Hudson

Publishers of Black-interest books for young people, including preschool materials, picture books, biographies, chapter books and young adult fiction. Focuses on Black history, Black culture and Black experiences. Imprint: Sankofa Books. Currently accepting queries for young adult titles, targeted to 13–16 year-old readers. Work should contain realistic, contemporary characters, compelling plot lines that introduce conflict and resolution, and cultural authenticity. Also considers MSS for picture books and middle reader chapter books. Send a query letter, 1–2pp synopsis, a brief author biography that includes any previously published work, plus an sase. Founded 1988.

Kaeden Books

PO Box 16190, Rocky River, OH 44116
tel +1 800-890-7323
email info@kaeden.com
website www.kaeden.com

Educational publisher specialising in early literacy books and beginning chapter books. Accepts samples of all styles of illustration but is primarily looking for samples that match the often humorous style appropriate for juvenile literature. Send samples, no larger than 8.5 x 11ins to keep on file. Seeking beginning chapter books and unique non-fiction MSS (25–3,000 words). Vocabulary and sentence structure must be appropriate for young readers. No sentence fragments. See website for complete guidelines. Founded 1986.

Kar-Ben Publishing – see Lerner Publishing Group

KidHaven Press – see Gale Cengage Learning

Klutz – see Scholastic, Inc.

Alfred A. Knopf – see Penguin Random House

LB Kids – see Little, Brown & Company

Lee & Low Books, Inc.

95 Madison Avenue, Suite 1205, New York, NY 10016
tel +1 212-779-4400
email general@leeandlow.com
website www.leeandlow.com
Editor-at-Large Louise May, *Editorial Director* Cheryl Klein

Children's book publisher specialising in multicultural literature that is relevant to young readers. The company's goal is to meet the need for stories that children of colour can identify with and that all children can enjoy and which promote a greater understanding of one another. Focuses on fiction, non-fiction and poetry for children 5–12 years, and for middle graders and young adults ages 13–18. Of special interest are realistic fiction, historical fiction and non-fiction with a non-white protagonist, a distinct voice, or unique approach. Does not consider folktales or animal stories. Imprints: Lee & Low, Bebop Books, Tu Books, Children's Book Press, Dive Into Reading, Shen's Books and Lee & Low Games. For picture books send complete MS, no longer than 1,500 words for fiction and 3,000 words for non-fiction. For middle grade and young adult MSS, send first three chapters and synopsis of entire story. Send with a covering letter that includes a brief biography of the author, including publishing history, and stating if the MS is a simultaneous or an exclusive submission. No submissions via email. Do not include an sase. Potential authors will be contacted by email or phone within six months if interested. Makes a special effort to work with authors and artists of colour. Founded 1991.

Lerner Publishing Group

1251 Washington Ave N Minneapolis, MN 55401
tel +1 800-328-4929

email info@lernerbooks.com
website www.lernerbooks.com
Publisher Adam Lerner

Independent publisher of high-quality children's books for K–12 schools and libraries: picture books, fiction for children 5–8 and 9–12 years, teenage fiction, series fiction and non-fiction. Subjects include biography, social studies, science, sports and curriculum. Publishes approx. 300 titles each year and has about 1,500 in print. Imprints and partners include: Anderson Press USA; Big & Small; Carolrhoda Lab; Creston Books; Darby Creek; ediciones Lerner; First Avenue Editions; Full Tilt Press; Gecko Press USA; Graphic Universe; Hungry Tomato; JR Comics; Kane Press; Kar-Ben Publishing; Lantana Publishing; LernerClassroom; Lerner Digital; Lerner Publications; Live Oak Media; Lorimer Children & Teens; Maverick Arts; Millbrook Press; Quarto Library; Red Chair Press; StarBerry Books; Twenty-First Century Books; and We Do Listen Foundation; and Zest Books. Details can be found on the website: https://lernerbooks.com/Pages/Our-Imprints#imprints. No unsolicited submissions for any imprint. Founded 1959.

Arthur A. Levine Books – see Scholastic, Inc.

Little, Brown & Company

1290 Ave of the Americas, New York, NY 10104
tel +1 212-364-1100
email lbpublicity.Generic@hbgusa.com
website www.littlebrown.com

General literature, fiction, non-fiction, biography, history, trade paperbacks, children's. Founded 1837.

Jimmy Patterson
website www.littlebrown.com/imprint/little-brown-and-company/jimmy-patterson
Publishes James Patterson's *Middle School Years* series and other books by the same author and other popular writers of middle grade fiction.

Little, Brown Spark
Publishes books for young people and adults that spark ideas, feelings and change. Looking for authors who are experts and thought leaders in the fields of health, lifestyle, psychology and science.

Lucent Books – see Gale Cengage Learning

Margaret K. McElderry Books – see Simon & Schuster Children's Publishing Division

McGraw-Hill Professional*

2 Penn Plaza, 12th Floor, New York, NY 10121
tel +1 212-904-2000
website www.mhprofessional.com

Macmillan Publishers, Inc.*

175 Fifth Avenue, New York, NY 10010
tel +1 646-307-5151

email press.inquiries@macmillanusa.com
website http://us.macmillan.com

Imprints: Farrar, Straus and Giroux; Henry Holt and Company; Picador; St. Martin's Press; Tor/Forge; Macmillan Audio; and Macmillan Children's Publishing Group. Macmillan Publishers is based in New York City, with many publishers located in the historic Flatiron Building. Founded 1843.

Marshall Cavendish Benchmark

Marshall Cavendish Corporation,
99 White Plains Road, Tarrytown, NY 10591
tel +1 914-332-8888
email marketing@mceducation.com
website www.mceducation.com/mce-intl

Non-fiction books for young, middle grade and young adult readers. Subjects include: American studies, the arts, biographies, health, mathematics, science, social studies, history, world cultures. Imprint of Marshall Cavendish Corporation. Non-fiction subjects should be curriculum-related and are published in series form. Length: 1,500–25,000 words. Send synopsis with one or more sample chapters and sample table of contents. Founded 1968.

Marshall Cavendish Children's Books

Marshall Cavendish Corporation,
99 White Plains Road, Tarrytown, NY 10591
tel +1 914-332-8888
email marketing@mceducation.com
website www.mceducation.com/mce-intl

Picture books and novels for middle grade and teens. Does not accept submissions via email. Imprint of Marshall Cavendish Corporation. Founded 1968.

Millbrook Press – see Lerner Publishing Group

MINX – see DC Comics

Mitchell Lane Publishers, Inc.

2001 S.W. 31st Avenue, Hallandale, FL 33009
tel +1 800 223 3251
email customerservice@mitchelllane.com
website www.mitchelllane.com
President Phil Comer

Non-fiction titles for young readers, middle readers and young adults. Founded 1962.

Mondo Publishing*

980 Avenue of the Americas, New York, NY 10018
tel +1 888-886-6636
email info@mondopub.com
website www.mondopub.com

Classroom materials and professional development for K–5 educators. Founded 1986.

Thomas Nelson Publisher

PO Box 141000, Nashville, TN 37214
tel +1 800-251-4000

email publicity@thomasnelson.com
website www.thomasnelson.com

Bibles, religious, non-fiction and fiction general trade books for adults and children. Acquired by HarperCollins in 2012. Founded 1798.

NorthSouth Books

600 Third Avenue, 2nd Floor, New York, NY 10016
tel +1 917-210-5868
website www.northsouth.com

Successes include *The Rainbow Fish* by Marcus Pfister, *Little Polar* by Hans de Beer, *Wonderment* by Lisbeth Zwerger, *Lindbergh: The Tale of a Flying Mouse* by Torben Kuhlmann, *Mr. Squirrel and the Moon* by Sebastian Meschenmoser, *The Green Sea Turtle* by Isabel Mueller and *Surf's Up* by Kwame Alexander and Daniel Miyares. Publishes 100 titles a year. Publishes fresh, original, fiction and non-fiction with universal themes that could appeal to children 3–8 years. Accepting picture book submissions from US authors and illustrators. Guidelines on submissions: accepts picture book MSS (1,000 words or less); typically does not acquire rhyming texts (although have been exceptions for simple/original text); authors do not need to include illustrations; illustrators to send sample sketches in pdf or jpg form. Submit via email: submissionsnsb@gmail.com. Founded 1961.

NorthWord Books for Young Readers – see Cooper Square Publishing

Orchard Books – see Scholastic, Inc.

The Overlook Press

141 Wooster Street #4B, New York, NY 10012
tel +1 212-673-2210
website www.overlookpress.com
Facebook www.facebook.com/overlookpress
Twitter @overlookpress

Non-fiction, fiction, children's books (*Freddy the Pig* series). Imprints: Ardis Publishing, Duckworth. Now an imprint of Abrams. Founded 1971.

Richard C. Owen Publishers, Inc.

PO Box 585, Katonah, NY 10536
tel +1 914-232-3903
website www.rcowen.com
Publisher Richard C. Owen

Books for grades K–6.
All work must be submitted as hard copy. Books for young learners: Seeks high-interest stories with charm and appeal that children 5–7 years can read by themselves. Interested in original, realistic, contemporary stories, as well as folktales, legends and myths of all cultures. Non-fiction content must be supported with accurate facts. Length: 45–1,000 words. Also beginning chapter books up to 3,000 words.

Pearson Education*

One Lake Street, Upper Saddle River, NJ 07458
tel +1 201-236-7000
email communications@pearsoned.com
website www.phschool.com, www.pearsoned.com

Educational secondary publisher of scientifically researched and standards-based instruction materials for today's Grade 6–12 classrooms with a mission to create exceptional educational tools that ensure student and teacher success in language arts, mathematics, modern and classical languages, science, social studies, careers and technology, and advanced placements, electives and honors. Part of the Curriculum Division of Pearson Education, Inc. Founded 1966.

Pearson Scott Foresman

One Lake Street, Upper Saddle River, NJ 07458
tel +1 201-236-7000
website www.pearsonschool.com

Elementary educational publisher. Teacher and student materials: reading, science, mathematics, language arts, social studies, music, technology, religion. Its educational resources and services include textbook-based instructional programmes, curriculum websites, digital media, assessment materials and professional development. Part of the Curriculum Division of Pearson Education, Inc. Founded 1896.

Pelican Publishing Company

1000 Burmaster Street, Gretna, LA 70053
tel +1 504-368-1175
email editorial@pelicanpub.com
website www.pelicanpub.com
Publisher & President Kathleen Calhoun Nettleton

Children's books. Also art and architecture books, biographies, holiday books, local and international cookbooks, motivational works, political science, social commentary, history, business. Send a query letter, outline if chapter book, résumé and sase. No queries or submissions by email. No unsolicited MSS for chapter books. Most young children's books are 32 illustrated pages when published; their MSS will be 1,100 words maximum. Proposed books for middle readers (8+ years) should be at least 90pp. Brief books for readers under 9 years may be submitted in their entirety. Founded 1926.

Penguin Random House*

1745 Broadway, New York, NY 10019
tel +1 212-782-9000
website www.penguinrandomhouse.com
Ceo Madeline McIntosh

With 250 independent imprints and brands on five continents, more than 15,000 new titles and close to 800 million print, audio and ebooks sold annually, Penguin Random House is the world's leading trade book publisher. The company, which employs about

12,500 people globally, was formed on July 1, 2013 by Bertelsmann and Pearson, who own 53% and 47%, respectively. Like its predecessor companies, Penguin Random House is committed to publishing adult and children's fiction and non-fiction print editions, and is a pioneer in digital publishing. Its book brands include storied imprints such as Doubleday, Viking and Alfred A. Knopf (USA); Ebury, Hamish Hamilton and Jonathan Cape (UK); Plaza & Janés and Alfaguara (Spain); and Sudamericana (Argentina); as well as the international imprint DK. Founded 2013.

Penguin Young Readers*

1745 Broadway, New York, NY 10019
tel +1 212-366-2000
website www.penguin.com/children
President Jen Loja

Penguin Young Readers is one of the leading children's book publishers in the USA. The company owns a wide range of imprints and trademarks including Dial Books, Dutton, Grosset & Dunlap, Kathy Dawson Books, Kokila, Nancy Paulsen Books, Penguin Workshop, Philomel, Puffin, G.P. Putnam's Sons, Viking, Razorbill, Speak and Frederick Warne. Penguin Young Readers is also the proud publisher of perennial brand franchises such as the *Nancy Drew* and *Hardy Boys* series, *Peter Rabbit, Corduroy, The Very Hungry Caterpillar, Llama Llama, Mad Libs, Last Kids On Earth, Who Was?*, Roald Dahl, Jacqueline Woodson, S.E. Hinton, and John Green among many others. Penguin Young Readers is a division of Penguin Group LLC, a Penguin Random House company. Founded 1935.

Philomel – see Penguin Young Readers

Poppy – see Little, Brown & Company

Puffin Books – see Penguin Young Readers

Simon Pulse Books – see Simon & Schuster Children's Publishing Division

Quarto Publishing Group – Walter Foster Publishing Jr.

26391 Crown Valley Parkway, STE 220, Mission Viejo, CA 92691
tel +1 949-380-7510
email pauline.molinari@quarto.com
website www.quartoknows.com/Walter-Foster-Jr
Group Publisher Anne Landa, *Publisher* Rebecca Razo
Editorial Director Pauline Molinari

Imprint of The Quarto Group. Instructional art books for children and adults. Also art and activity kits for children. A division of Quarto Publishing Group US. Founded 1976.

Random House Children's Books*

1745 Broadway, New York, NY 10019
tel +1 212-782-9000
website www.randomhousekids.com
website www.randomhouse.com/teachers
President & Publisher Barbara Marcus

Random House Children's Books is the world's largest English-language children's trade book publisher. Creates books for preschool children through young adult readers, in all formats from board books to activity books to picture books, graphic novels, novels and non-fiction. Imprints: Alfred A. Knopf Books for Young Readers, Crown Books for Young Readers, Delacorte Press, Doubleday Books for Young Readers, Random House Books for Young Readers, Rodale Kids, Little Golden Books, Make Me A World, Schwartz & Wade Books, Wendy Lamb Books, Random House Graphic, Ember, Dragonfly, Yearling Books, Laurel-Leaf, Princeton Review and Sylvan Learning. Part of Penguin Random House (page 60). Founded 1925.

Razorbill – see Penguin Young Readers

Rising Moon – see Cooper Square Publishing

Roaring Brook Press

175 Fifth Avenue, New York, NY 10010
tel +1 646-600-7861
website https://us.macmillan.com/publishers/roaring-brook-press/
Publisher Jennifer Besser

Picture books, fiction (including graphic novels) and non-fiction for young readers, from toddler to teen. Publishes about 40 titles a year. Awards for titles include: 2014 Michael L. Printz Award, the 2011, 2004 and 2003 Caldecott Medals, seven Caldecott Honor awards and a Newbery Honor award. Imprint: First Second Books. Division of Holtzbrink Publishers. Part of Macmillan. Does not accept unsolicited MSS or submissions. Founded 2002.

Rowman & Littlefield

4501 Forbes Boulevard, Suite 200, Lanham, MD 20706
tel +1 301-459-3366
email customercare@rowman.com
website www.rowman.com
Facebook www.facebook.com/rowmanuk
Twitter @rowmanuk
President & Ceo James E. Lyons

Rowman & Littlefield is an independent publisher specialising in academic publishing in the humanities and social sciences, government and official data and educational publishing. Founded 1925.

Running Press Book Publishers

2300 Chestnut Street, Suite 200, Philadelphia, PA 19103
tel +1 215-567-5080
email perseus.promos@perseusbooks.com
website www.runningpress.com

General non-fiction, science, history, children's fiction and non-fiction, cookbooks, pop culture, lifestyle, illustrated gift books, Miniature Editions. Imprints: Running Press, Running Press Miniature Editions, Running Press Kids, Running Press Adults. Member of the Perseus Books Group. Recent successes include *You Are a Badass* by Jen Sincero, *Ripe* by Cheryl Sternman Rule, *Cats in Hats* by Sara Thomas, and *Slow Beauty* by Shel Pink. Founded 1972.

Running Press Kids
Picture books, activity books, young adult fiction. Recent successes include the *Doodles* series.

Sasquatch Books
1904 Third Ave, Suite 710 Seattle, WA 98101
tel +1 206-467-4300
email custserv@sasquatchbooks.com
website www.sasquatchbooks.com

Independent press, located in downtown Seattle. The mission is to seek out and work with gifted writers, chefs, naturalists, artists and thought leaders in the Pacific Northwest and bring their talents to a national audience. Publishes a variety of non-fiction books, as well as children's books under the Little Bigfoot imprint. Are happy to consider queries and proposals from authors and agents for new projects that fit into the company's West Coast regional publishing programme. Founded 1986.

Scholastic, Inc.*
557 Broadway, New York, NY 10012
tel +1 212-343-6100
email news@scholastic.com
website www.scholastic.com
Facebook www.facebook.com/scholastic
Twitter @scholastic

Scholastic is the world's largest publisher and distributor of children's books and a leader in education technology and children's media. Divisions: Scholastic Trade Publishing, Scholastic Book Clubs, Scholastic Book Fairs, Scholastic Education, Scholastic International, Media, Licensing and Advertising. Imprints include: Arthur A. Levine Books, Cartwheel Books, Chicken House, David Fickling Books, Graphix, Orchard Books, Point, PUSH, Scholastic en español, Scholastic Focus, Scholastic Licensed Publishing, Scholastic Nonfiction, Scholastic Paperbacks, Scholastic Press, Scholastic Reference and The Blue Sky Press. In addition, Scholastic Trade Books includes Klutz, a highly innovative publisher and creator of "books plus" for children. Founded 1920.

Scholastic Trade Books, Children's Book Publishing
Award-winning publisher of original children's books. Publishes over 600 new titles a year including bestselling brands such as *Harry Potter*, *Captain Underpants*, *The Hunger Games*, *Clifford The Big Red Dog*, *I Spy* and *The Magic School Bus*.

Scholastic Education*
557 Broadway, New York, NY 10012
tel +1 212-343-6100
website www.scholastic.com/

Educational publisher of research-based core and supplementary instructional materials. A leading provider in reading improvement and professional development products, as well as learning services that address the needs of the developing reader – from grades pre-K to high school. Publishes 32 curriculum-based classroom magazines used by teachers in grades pre-K–12 as supplementary educational materials to raise awareness about current events in an age-appropriate manner and to help children develop reading skills. Scholastic Education has also developed technology-based reading assessment and management products to help administrators and educators quickly and accurately assess student reading levels, match students to the appropriate books, predict how well they will do on district and state standardised tests, and inform instruction to improve reading skills. Founded 1923.

Scholastic Library Publishing
90 Sherman Turnpike, Danbury, CT 06816
tel +1 203-797-3500
website www.scholastic.com
Online and print publisher of reference products.

Silver Moon Press
400 East 85th Street, New York, NY 10028
tel +1 800-874-3320
email mail@silvermoonpress.com
website www.silvermoonpress.com

Children's book publisher: test preparation, science, multiculture, biographies, historical fiction. Successes include *Stories of the States*, *Mysteries in Time* and the *Adventures in America* series.

Simon & Schuster Children's Publishing Division*
1230 Avenue of the Americas, New York, NY 10020
tel +1 212-698-7200
website www.simonandschuster.com/kids
President & Publisher Jon Anderson

Preschool to young adult, fiction and non-fiction, trade, library and mass market. Imprints: Aladdin Paperbacks, Atheneum Books for Young Readers, Beach Lane Books, Little Simon, Margaret K. McElderry Books, Simon & Schuster Books for Young Readers, Simon Pulse, Salaam Reads, Simon Spotlight, Paula Wiseman Books. More details on some of the imprints are given below. Division of Simon & Schuster, Inc. Founded 1924.

Aladdin Books
Reprints successful hardbacks from other Simon & Schuster imprints.

Accepts query letters with proposals for middle grade series and single-title fiction, beginning readers, middle grade and commercial non-fiction. Send MS for the attention of the Submissions Editor.

Atheneum Books for Young Readers
Vice-President & Publisher Justin Chanda

Picture books, chapter books, mysteries, biography, science fiction, fantasy, graphic novels, middle grade and young adult fiction and non-fiction. Covers preschool–young adult. Publishes 20–30 picture books, 4–5 young readers, 20–25 middle readers and 10–15 young adult books each year. Approximately 10% of books are by first-time authors. No unsolicited MSS. Send query letter only. Responds in one month.

Margaret K. McElderry Books
Vice-President & Publisher Justin Chanda

Picture books, easy-to-read books, fiction (8–12 years, young adult), poetry, fantasy. Covers preschool to young adult. Publishes 10–12 picture books, 2–4 young reader titles, 8–10 middle reader titles and 5–7 young adult books each year. Approximately 10% of books are by first-time authors. No unsolicited MSS. Fiction length: picture books – 500 words; young readers – 2,000; middle readers – 10,000–20,000; young adult – 45,000–50,000. Non-fiction length: picture books – 500–1,000 words; young readers – 1,500–3,000 words; middle readers – 10,000–20,000 words; young adult – 30,000–45,000 words. Responds in three months. Samples returned with sase.

Simon Pulse Books
Publisher Mara Anastas

Young adult series and fiction. Focuses on high-concept commercial fiction.
Accepts query letters. Send MS for the attention of the Submission Editor.

Simon & Schuster Books for Young Readers
Publisher Justin Chandu

Publishes a wide range of contemporary, commercial, award-winning fiction and non-fiction that spans every age of children's publishing.
No unsolicited MSS. Send query letter only. Responds in two months. Seeking challenging and psychologically-complex young adult novels; also imaginative and humorous middle grade fiction.

Paula Wiseman
email paulawiseman@simonandschuster.com
Vice-President & Publisher Paula Wiseman

Publishes award-winning and bestselling books, including picture books, novelty books and novels. The imprint focuses on stories and art that are childlike, timeless, innovative and centered in emotion. Approx. 10% of books are by first-time authors. Submit complete MS. Length: picture books – 500 words; others standard length. Considers all categories of fiction. Will review MS/illustration packages from artists. Send MS with dummy.

Sleeping Bear Press – see Gale Cengage Learning

StarScape – see Tom Doherty Associates, LLC

Sterling Publishing Co., Inc.
1166 Avenue of the Americas, 17th Floor, New York, NY 10036
tel +1 212-532-7160
email editorial@sterlingpublishing.com
website www.sterlingpublishing.com
Executive Vice-President Theresa Thompson

Adult non-fiction and children's board books, picture books and non-fiction. Subsidiary of Barnes & Noble. Founded in 1949.

Flashkids
Workbooks and flash cards for preschool, elementary and middle school students.

Sterling Children's Books
Non-fiction: crafts, hobbies, games, activities, origami, optical illusions, mazes, dot-to-dots, science experiments, puzzles (maths/word/picture/logic), chess, card games and tricks, sports, magic. Non-fiction: Write explaining the idea and enclose an outline and a sample chapter. Include information and a résumé with regard to the subject area and publishing history, and sase for return of material. No email submissions. Send submissions FAO Children's Book Editor.

Teacher Created Resources
12621 Western Ave, Garden Grove, CA 92841
tel +1 800-662-4321
email custserv@teachercreated.com
website www.teachercreated.com

Educational materials. See website for guidelines. Founded 1977.

Katherine Tegen Books – see HarperCollins Publishers

Twenty-first Century Books – see Lerner Publishing Group

Two-Can Publishing – see Cooper Square Publishing

Viking – see Penguin Young Readers

Walker & Co.
175 Fifth Avenue, New York, NY 10010
tel +1 212-674-5151
website www.walkerbooks.com
website www.bloomsburykids.com

Picture books, non-fiction and fiction (middle grade and young adult). Publishes 20 picture books, five to eight middle readers and five to eight young adult books each year. Walker Books and Walker Books for Young Readers are imprints of Bloomsbury Publishing Plc (page 22). Approx. 5% of books are by first-time authors. Approx. 65% of books are acquired via literary agents. Particularly interested in picture books, illustrated non-fiction, middle-grade and young adult fiction. No series ideas. Send 50–75pp and synopsis for longer works; send the entire MS for picture books. Include sase for response only. Founded 1959.

Weigl Publishers Inc.
350 5th Avenue, 59th Floor, New York, NY 10118
tel +1 866-649-3445
email linda@weigl.com
website www.weigl.com

Educational publisher: children's non-fiction titles. Successes include *The AV2 Collection* (av2books.com). Founded 1979.

Albert Whitman & Company
250 South Northwest Highway, Suite 320, Park Ridge, Illinois, IL 60068
tel +1 847-581-0033
email mail@awhitmanco.com
website www.albertwhitman.com

Books that respond to cultural diversity and the special needs and concerns of children and their families (e.g. divorce, bullying). Also novels for middle grade readers, picture books and non-fiction for children 2–12 years. Send to submissions@awhitmanco.com. For submissions guidelines see website. Founded 1919.

Paula Wiseman – see Simon & Schuster Children's Publishing Division

WordSong – see Boyds Mills Press

Workman Publishing Company*
225 Varick Street, New York, NY 10014
tel +1 212-254-5900
email info@workman.com
website www.workman.com
Director, Children's Publishing Traci Todd

General non-fiction for adults and children. Calendars. Founded 1968.

World Book, Inc.
233 North Michigan Avenue, Suite 2000, Chicago, IL 60601
tel +1 800-975-3250
email international@worldbook.com
website www.worldbook.com
Facebook www.facebook.com/WorldBook
Twitter @worldbookinc

EA leading publisher of authoritative, age-appropriate and reliable print and digital educational and reference materials for children and adults. Committed to creating educational products that meet the highest standards aiming to inspire a lifelong love of learning. Trade companies include children's book publisher Bright Connections Media and Incentive Publications which specialises in supplemental resources for children and teachers. Founded 1917.

WorthyKids
6100 Tower Circle, Suite 210, Franklin, TN 37067
email IdealsInfo@hbgusa.com
website www.worthypublishing.com
Facebook www.Facebook.com/worthykidsideals

An imprint of Worthy Publishing Group. Picture books and board books for young children (2–8 years). See website for submission guidelines. Digital submissions not accepted. Due to the large volume of submissions, the company only responds to those that are of interest to the publishing program. Potential authors should become familiar with current books before submitting.

Yen Press*
Hachette Book Group, 1290 Avenue of the Americas, New York, NY 10104
email yenpress@hbgusa.com
website www.yenpress.com
Facebook www.facebook.com/yenpress
Twitter @yenpress

Graphic novels and manga in all formats for all ages. Currently not seeking original project pitches from writers who are not already working with an illustrator. For submission guidelines see under Contact on website. Division of Hachette Book Group (page 56). Founded 2006.

Children's audio publishers

Many of the audio publishers listed below are also publishers of print and electronic books.

Abbey Home Media Group Ltd

435–437 Edgware Road, London W2 1TH
tel 020-7563 3910
email info@abbeyhomemedia.com
website www.abbeyhomemedia.com
Chairman Ian Miles, *Directors* Anne Miles, Dan Harriss, Emma Evans

Activity books, board books, novelty books, picture books, as well as audio and other multimedia formats. Advocates learning through interactive play. Age groups: preschool, five to ten years. Founded 2002.

Audible

email bizdev_uk@audible.co.uk
website www.audible.co.uk
Twitter @audibleuk

Producer and seller of digital audio entertainment, including fiction and non-fiction audiobooks for adults and children. Publishers keen to enquire about business opportunities with Audible may email the address above, or find out more about turning print books into audiobooks at www.acx.com. Founded 1995; acquired by Amazon 2008.

Audiobooks.com

website www.audiobooks.com
Twitter @audiobooks_com

Subscription audio book service, offering a wide range of fiction and non-fiction genres, as well as some children's titles.

Barrington Stoke – see page 22

BookBeat

email info@bookbeat.com
website www.bookbeat.com/uk
Twitter @BookBeatUK

Digital streaming service for adult and children's audiobooks across a variety of fiction and non-fiction genres. Monthly subscription model. Owned by Bonnier. Founded 2017.

Canongate Audio Books

14 High Street, Edinburgh EH1 1TE
tel 0131 557 5111
email support@canongate.co.uk
website www.canongate.co.uk
Twitter @canongatebooks

Classic children's literature such as *Just William*, *Billy Bunter* and *Black Beauty*; also adult, classic and contemporary literary authors. Founded 1991 as CSA Word; acquired by Canongate 2010.

Cló Iar-Chonnacht Teo

Indreabhán, Conamara, Co. Galway, Republic of Ireland
tel +353 (0)91 593307
email eolas@cic.ie
website www.cic.ie
Twitter @CloIarChonnacht
Ceo Micheál Ó Conghaile, *General Manager* Deirdre Ní Thuathail

Predominantly Irish-language children's books with accompanying audio of stories/folklore/poetry. Established 1985.

Dref Wen

28 Church Road, Whitchurch, Cardiff CF14 2EA
tel 029-2061 7860
website www.drefwren.com
Directors Roger Boore, Anne Boore, Gwilym Boore, Alun Boore, Rhys Boore

Welsh-language and dual-language children's books. Founded 1970.

The Educational Company of Ireland

Ballymount Road, Walkinstown, Dublin D12 R25C, Republic of Ireland
tel +353 (0)1 4500611
email info@edco.ie
website www.edco.ie
Chief Executive Martina Harford

Irish language CDs. Trading unit of Smurfit Kappa Group – Ireland. Founded 1910.

HarperCollins Publishers

The News Building, 1 London Bridge Street, London, SE1 9GF
tel 020-8285 4658
website www.harpercollins.co.uk
Twitter @HarperCollinsUK
Audio Director Rachel Mallender, *Creative Content Producer* Tanya Hougham, *Senior Audio Editor* Fionnuala Barrett, *Audio Editor* Jack Chalmers

Publishers of award-winning fiction and non-fiction audiobooks for adults and children. An imprint of HarperCollins. Founded 1990.

W. F. Howes Ltd

Unit 5, St George's House, Rearsby Business Park, Gaddesby Lane, Rearsby, Leicester LE7 4YH
tel (01664) 423000
email info@wfhowes.co.uk
website www.wfhowes.co.uk

Independent audiobook publisher. Also large-print publisher and digital-services provider to libraries.

Releases c. 80 new and unabridged audiobooks monthly. Works with authors/agents directly and a range of large UK publishers, including Penguin Random House and HarperCollins. Founded 1999; UK subsidiary of RBMedia.

Kobo

website www.kobo.com/gb/en
Twitter @kobo

Audiobook streaming service, for a monthly fee. Offers fiction, non-fiction, adult, children's and YA titles.

Macmillan Digital Audio

20 New Wharf Road, London N1 9RR
tel 020-7014 6000
email audiobooks@macmillan.co.uk
website www.panmacmillan.com
Publishing Director for Audio Rebecca Lloyd

Children's titles include *The Gruffalo* by Julia Donaldson and Axel Scheffler. Also adult fiction, non-fiction and autobiography. Founded 1995.

Naxos AudioBooks

5 Wyllyotts Place, Potters Bar, Herts. EN6 2JD
tel (01707) 653326
email info@naxosaudiobooks.com
website www.naxosaudiobooks.com
Twitter @NaxosAudioBooks
Managing Director Anthony Anderson

Classic literature, modern fiction, non-fiction, drama and poetry on CD. Also classical music. Founded 1994.

Penguin Random House UK Audio (Children's)

80 Strand, London WC2R 0RL
tel 020-7139 3000
website www.penguinrandomhouse.co.uk
Managing Director Hannah Telfer

Contemporary and classic literature for younger listeners. Authors include Malorie Blackman, Charlie Higson, Roald Dahl and Eoin Colfer.

Puffin Audiobooks – see Penguin Random House UK Audio

Children's book packagers

Many illustrated books are created by book packagers, whose particular skills are in the areas of book design and graphic content. In-house editors match up the expertise of specialist writers, artists and photographers who usually work on a freelance basis.

Aladdin Books Ltd

PO Box 53987, London SW15 2SF
tel 020-3174 3090
email sales@aladdinbooks.co.uk
website www.aladdinbooks.co.uk

Full design and book packaging facility specialising in children's non-fiction and reference. Founded 1980.

Nicola Baxter Ltd

16 Cathedral Street, Norwich NR1 1LX
tel (01603) 766585, 07778 285555
email nb@nicolabaxter.co.uk
website www.nicolabaxter.co.uk
Director Nicola Baxter

Full packaging service for children's books in both traditional and digital formats. Happy to take projects from concept to finished work or supply bespoke authorial, editorial, design, project management or commissioning services. Produces both fiction and non-fiction titles in a wide range of formats, for babies to young adults, and experienced in novelty books and licensed publishing. Founded 1990.

Bender Richardson White

PO Box 266, Uxbridge, Middlesex UB9 5NX
tel (01895) 832444
email brw@brw.co.uk
website www.brw.co.uk
Directors Lionel Bender (editorial), Kim Richardson (sales and production), Ben White (design)

Design, editorial and production of activity books, non-fiction and reference books. Specialises in non-fiction: natural history, science, history and educational. Writers should send a letter and synopsis of their proposal. Opportunities for freelancers. Founded 1990.

Brown Bear Books Ltd

1st Floor, 9–17 St Albans Place, London N1 0NX
tel 020-7424 5640
website www.windmillbooks.co.uk
Children's Publisher Anne O'Daly

Specialises in high-quality illustrated reference books and multi-volume sets for trade and educational markets. Opportunities for freelancers. Imprint of Windmill Books. Founded 1967.

John Brown Group – Children's Division

8 Baldwin Street, London EC1V 9NU
tel 020-7565 3000
email andrew.hirsch@johnbrownmedia.com
website www.johnbrownmedia.com
Directors Andrew Hirsch (operations), Sara Lynn (creative)

Creative development and packaging of children's products including books, magazines, teachers' resource packs, partworks, CDs and websites. Founded 2000.

Creative Plus Publishing Ltd

2nd Floor, 151 High Street, Billericay, Essex CM12 9AB
tel (01277) 633005
email enquiries@creative-plus.co.uk
website www.creative-plus.co.uk
Facebook www.facebook.com/CreativePlusPublishingLtd
Publishing Director Claire Coakley

Provides all editorial and design from concept to finished pages for books, partworks and magazines. Specialises in licensed characters, make-and-do, illustrated non-fiction and instructional video production. Opportunities for freelancers. Founded 1989.

Global Blended Learning Ltd

Singleton Court, Wonastow Road, Monmouth NP25 5JA
tel (01993) 706273
email info@hlstudios.eu.com
website www.globalblendedlearning.com

Primary, secondary academic education (geography, science, modern languages) and co-editions (travel guides, gardening, cookery). Multimedia (CD-Rom programming and animations). Opportunities for freelancers. Founded 1985.

Graham-Cameron Publishing & Illustration

59 Hertford Road, Brighton BN1 7GG
tel (01273) 385890
email enquiry@gciforillustration.com
Alternative address The Art House, Uplands Park, Sheringham, Norfolk NR26 8NE
tel (01263) 821333
website www.gciforillustration.com
Partners Helen Graham-Cameron, Duncan Graham-Cameron

Offers illustration and editorial services for picture books, information books, educational materials, activity books, non-fiction and reference books. Illustration agency with 37 artists. Do not send unsolicited MSS. Founded 1985.

Hart McLeod Ltd

14A Greenside, Waterbeach, Cambridge CB25 9HP
tel (01223) 861495
email jo@hartmcleod.co.uk
website www.hartmcleod.co.uk
Director Joanne Barker

Primarily educational and general non-fiction with particular expertise in reading books, school texts, ELT and electronic and audio content. Opportunities for freelances and work experience. Founded 1985.

Hawcock Books

242 Bloomfield Road, Bath BA2 2AX
tel (07976) 708720
website www.hawcockbooks.co.uk
Twitter @DavidHawcock

Designs and produces highly creative and original pop-up art and 3D paper-engineered concepts. Most experience is in developing, providing editorial assistance, printing and manufacturing pop-up books and novelty items for the publishing industry. Also undertakes demanding commissions from the advertising world for model-making, point-of-sale and all printed 3D aspects of major campaigns.

Hothouse Developments Ltd

The Old Truman Brewery, 91 Brick Lane,
London E1 6QL
tel 020-3384 2609, 07976 747338
email annemarie.ryan@hothousefiction.com
website www.hothousefiction.com
Director Reg Wright

Creative packager producing innovative partworks and commercial series fiction for children 5 years to teen. Genres include fantasy, horror, romance, magical, historical, animals, comedy and adventure. No unsolicited MSS. Supplies a full brief for all its projects. Selects writers for projects on the basis of unpaid writing samples, but successful writers paid an advance and royalty for published books. Welcomes new writers; visit website to register. Founded 2007.

Little People Books

The Home of BookBod, Knighton,
Radnorshire LD7 1UP
tel (01547) 520925
email littlepeoplebooks@thehobb.tv
website www.littlepeoplebooks.co.uk
Directors Grant Jessé (production and managing), Helen Wallis (rights and finance)

Packager of audio, children's educational and textbooks, digital publications. Parent company: Grant Jessé UK.

Orpheus Books Ltd

6 Church Green, Witney, Oxon OX28 4AW
tel (01993) 774949
email info@orpheusbooks.com
website www.orpheusbooks.com
website www.Q-files.com
Executive Directors Nicholas Harris, Sarah Hartley

Produces children's books and ebooks for the international co-editions market: non-fiction and reference. Orpheus Books are the creators of Q-files.com, the free online children's encyclopedia. Founded 1993.

The Puzzle House

Ivy Cottage, Battlesea Green, Stradbroke,
Suffolk IP21 5NE
tel (01379) 384656
email puzzlehouse@btinternet.com
website www.thepuzzlehouse.co.uk
Partners Roy Preston, Sue Preston

Editorial service creating crossword, quiz, puzzle and activity material for all ages. Founded 1988.

Toucan Books Ltd

The Old Fire Station, 140 Tabernacle Street,
London EC2A 4SD
tel 020-7250 3388
website www.toucanbooks.co.uk

International co-editions; editorial, design and production services. Founded 1985.

Umbrella Books

tel 07971 111256
email gary@allied-artists.net
website www.alliedartists-illustration.com
Contact Gary Mills

Packager of colourful and clever children's preschool novelty formats for generic and licensed books. Offers original formats, design, paper engineering and illustration. Is able to supply the complete 'package' through to supply of finished books.

David West Children's Books

11 Glebe Road, London SW13 0DR
tel 020-8876 1405
email dww@btinternet.com
website www.davidwestchildrensbooks.com
Proprietor David West, *Partner* Lynn Lockett

Packagers of children's illustrated reference books. Specialises in science, art, geography, history, sport and flight. Produces 50 titles each year. Opportunities for freelancers. Founded 1986.

Working Partners Ltd

9 Kingsway, 4th Floor, London WC2B 6XF
tel 020-7841 3939
email enquiries@workingpartnersltd.co.uk
website www.workingpartnersltd.co.uk

Managing Director Chris Snowdon, *Operations Director* Charles Nettleton

Children's and young adult fiction series: animal fiction, fantasy, horror, historical fiction, detective, magical, adventure. Recent successes include *Rainbow Magic, Beast Quest* and *Warriors*. Unable to accept any MSS or illustration submissions. Pays advance and royalty; retains copyright on all works. Selects writers from unpaid writing samples based on specific brief provided. Always looking to add writers to database: to register details visit website. Founded 1995.

Children's book clubs

Not all the companies listed here are 'clubs' in the true sense: some are mail order operations and others sell their books via book fairs.

Bibliophile

31 Riverside, 55 Trinity Buoy Wharf,
London E14 0FP
tel 020-7474 2474
email orders@bibliophilebooks.com
website www.bibliophilebooks.com
Proprietor Annie Quigley

Promotes value-for-money reading. Upmarket literature and classical music on CD available from mail order catalogue (10 p.a.). Over 3,000 titles covering art and fiction as well as travel, history and children's books. Founded 1978.

The Book People Ltd

Park Menai, Bangor LL57 4FB
tel 0845 602 4040
email marketing@thebookpeople.co.uk
website www.thebookpeople.co.uk

Popular general fiction and non-fiction, including children's and travel. Monthly.

Letterbox Library

Unit 151, Stratford Workshops, Burford Road,
London E15 2SP

tel 020-8534 7502
email info@letterboxlibrary.com
website www.letterboxlibrary.com
Twitter @LetterboxLib

Bookseller specialising in children's books that celebrate inclusion, equality and diversity, including multicultural and disability-related titles. Also provides pre-selected packs for early years settings and schools. Mail order catalogues and website. Well-established, not-for-profit, workers' co-operative and social enterprise. Orders taken online, by phone, fax (020-8503 4800) or by post.

Scholastic Book Fairs

Westfield Road, Southam, Warks. CV47 0RA
tel 0800 212281
email info@scholastic.co.uk
website https://bookfairs.scholastic.co.uk/
Twitter @scholasticuk

Sells directly to children, parents and teachers through 25,000 week-long events held in schools throughout the UK. See Scholastic Ltd.

Children's bookshops

The bookshops in the first part of this list specialise in selling new children's books and are good places for writers and illustrators to check out the marketplace. Most of them are members of the Booksellers Association and are well known to publishers. A list of secondhand and antiquarian children's bookshops follows. Independent Bookshop Week takes place each year in June or July.

The Alligator's Mouth
2a Church Court, Richmond, Surrey TW9 1JL
tel 020-8948 6775
email info@thealligatorsmouth.co.uk
website www.thealligatorsmouth.co.uk
Facebook www.facebook.com/alligatorsmouth
Twitter @alligatorsmouth

Independent children's bookshop stocking works for all ages from babies to teenagers. Runs regular story-time sessions, book clubs and author events. Nominated for Children's Bookseller of the Year in the *The Bookseller* Industry Awards 2018.

Bags-of-Books
1 South Street, Lewes BN7 2BT
tel (01273) 479320
email bagsofbooks@bags-of-books.co.uk
website http://bags-of-books.co.uk
Twitter @BagsofBooks
Proprietors Anna Morgan and Gavin Teasedale

Independent children's bookshop situated within a 16th-century building. Hosts author visits and runs a books for schools programme.

Bert's Books
email bert@bertsbooks.co.uk
website https://bertsbooks.co.uk/
Facebook www.facebook.com/BertsBooks/
Twitter @BertsBooks
Founder Alex Call

Online bookshop with a focus on diversity. Offers books in monthly bundles, including young adult titles. Founded 2019.

Blackwell's Children's Bookshop
Blackwell's Bookshop, 50 Broad Street, Oxford OX1 3BQ
tel (01865) 333694
email childrens@blackwell.co.uk
website http://bookshop.blackwell.co.uk/bookshop/home
Twitter @kidsblackwell

Stocks over 10,000 titles for children of all ages and holds a regular events programme including author visits to schools. The children's department is at the back of the ground floor of Blackwell's flagship bookshop in central Oxford.

The Book Burrow @ Aardvark Books & Café
The Bookery, Manor Farm, Brampton Bryan, Bucknell SY7 0DH
email aardvaark@btconnect.com
website www.aardvark-books.com
Twitter @AardvarkEthel
Proprietors Sheridan and Sarah Swinson

Book and play space with a castle, enchanted forest, pirate cabin and princess seat. Extensive range of books, mostly new but some secondhand and rare. Children's events throughout the year. BA member.

Book Corner
24 Milton Street, Saltburn-by-the-Sea, TS12 1DG
tel (01287) 348010
email jenna@bookcornershop.co.uk
website www.bookcornershop.co.uk
Facebook www.facebook.com/pages/category/Independent-Bookstore-Book-Corner-Saltburn-150632209595573/
Twitter @BookCornerShop
Proprietor Jenna Warren

Independent bookshop with dedicated children's section, stocking books for all ages from babies to young adults. Also stocks fiction and non-fiction for adults, and hosts author visits.

The Book House
93 High Street, Thame, Oxon OX9 3HJ
tel (01844) 213032
email office@thebookhousethame.co.uk
website www.thebookhousethame.co.uk
Twitter @the_book_house
Proprietor Brian Pattinson

Specialises in children's books alongside a wide range of titles for all ages. Established in the community for over 45 years, the Book House holds its own literary festival every October.

The Book Nook
First Avenue, Hove BN3 2FJ
tel (01273) 911988
email info@booknookuk.com
website www.booknookuk.com
Twitter @booknookhove
Proprietors Vanessa Lewis, Julie Ward

Specialist children's bookshop set in a child-friendly environment with author events, daily story-time, café and pirate ship. Named Children's Bookseller of the Year at *The Bookseller* Industry Awards 2015 and 2018.

Booka Bookshop and Café

26–28 Church Street, Oswestry, Shrops. SY11 2SP
tel (01691) 662244
email mail@bookabookshop.co.uk
website www.bookabookshop.co.uk
Facebook www.facebook.com/bookabookshop
Twitter @bookabookshop
Proprietors Carrie and Tim Morris

Independent bookshop and café offering a wide range of books, cards and gifts. Hosts a regular programme of author talks and signings, organises themed events, runs bookclubs and works with schools and the local library. Named Independent Bookshop of the Year at *The Bookseller* Industry Awards 2015.

Bookworm Ltd

1177 Finchley Road, London NW11 0AA
tel 020-8201 9811
email bookworm1@btconnect.com
website www.thebookworm.uk.com

Independent children's bookshop catering for all ages, from babies to young adults. Also supplies books to schools. Hosts author visits and holds regular story-time sessions.

The Broadway Bookshop

6 Broadway Market, London E8 4QJ
tel 020-7241 1626
email books@broadwaybookshophackney.com
website www.broadwaybookshophackney.com
Proprietor Jane Howe

General independent bookshop specialising in literary fiction with a strong selection of children's books for all ages.

Browns Books For Students

22–28 George Street, Hull HU1 3AP
tel (01482) 325413
email enquiries@brownsbfs.co.uk
website www.brownsbfs.co.uk
Twitter @BrownsBFS

Supplies any book in print to schools, colleges and international schools. Full school servicing of books on request.

Chicken & Frog

7 Security House, Ongar Road, Brentwood, Essex CM15 9AT
tel (01277) 230068
email info@chickenandfrog.co.uk
website http://chickenandfrog.com
Twitter @chickenandfrog
Proprietors Jim and Natasha Radford

Independent children's bookshop and tuition centre. Weekly rhythm and rhyme, creative writing and handwriting sessions. Organisers of the Brentwood Children's Literary Festival.

The Children's Bookshop – Hay-on-Wye

Toll Cottage, Pontvaen, Hay-on-Wye, Herefordshire HR3 5EW
tel (01497) 821083
email sales@childrensbookshop.com
website www.childrensbookshop.com
Twitter @childrnsbkshop
Proprietors Judith and Colin Gardner

Second-hand and antiquarian children's books.

Children's Bookshop (Huddersfield)

37–39 Lidget Street, Lindley, Huddersfield, West Yorkshire HD3 3JF
tel (01484) 658013
email hello@childrensbookshuddersfield.co.uk
website www.childrensbookshuddersfield.co.uk
Twitter @Lindley_Books
Contact Nicola Lee

Independent bookshop stocking a wide selection of titles for children, from picture books to YA. Also offers services to schools.

Children's Bookshop (Muswell Hill)

29 Fortis Green Road, London N10 3HP
tel 020-8444 5500
email admin@childrensbookshoplondon.co.uk
website www.childrensbookshoplondon.com

Specialist children's bookshop. Stocks approximately 12,000 titles and 25,000 books for children from babies to teenagers. Also offers services for schools and individuals. Founded 1974.

DRAKE The Bookshop

27 Silver Street, Stockton-on-Tees TS18 1SX
tel (01642) 909970
email books@drakethebookshop.co.uk
website www.drakethebookshop.co.uk
Twitter @drakebookshop
Proprietors Richard Drake, Melanie Greenwood

Independent bookshop with strong children's offering, as well as events and initiatives aimed at young readers and schools. The shop runs two children's book groups (Teen Readers and Young Bookworms) and offers a selection of dyslexia-friendly titles. Founded 2015.

ebb & flo bookshop

12 Gillibrand Street, Chorley, Lancs. PR7 2EJ
tel (01257) 262773
email info@ebbandflobookshop.co.uk
website www.ebbandflobookshop.co.uk
Facebook www.facebook.com/ebb & flo bookshop
Twitter @ebbandflobooks
Proprietor Diane Gunning

Small independent bookshop stocking books for children and adults, plus toys, cards and gifts. Supplies books to local schools, including library restocks and topic boxes. Organises author visits. Hosts a weekly story-time for preschool children as well as regular author events and holiday workshops.

The Edinburgh Bookshop
219 Bruntsfield Place, Edinburgh EH10 4DH
tel 0131 447 1917
email mail@edinburghbookshop.com
website www.edinburghbookshop.com
Twitter @EdinBookshop
Proprietor Marie Moser

Named UK Children's Bookseller of the Year at *The Bookseller* Industry Awards 2014. Events programme includes author visits, writers' workshops and a twice-weekly story-time for the under 5s. Founded 2007.

Far from the Madding Crowd
20 High Street, Linlithgow EH49 7AE
tel (01506) 845509
email sally@maddingcrowdlinlithgow.com
website www.maddingcrowdlinlithgow.com
Facebook www.facebook.com/Far From The Madding Crowd Linlithgow
Twitter @Furtherfrom

Independent bookshop with eclectic range of titles, including children's and preschool. Free story-telling every Saturday at 11am in the Bothy. Strong influence from Scottish publishers.

Glowworm Books & Gifts Ltd
Unit 2, 5 Youngs Road, East Mains Industrial Estate, Broxburn, West Lothian EH52 5LY
tel (01506) 857570
website www.glowwormbooks.co.uk

Specialises in supplying books for children, especially those who find reading difficult due to physical or special educational challenges.

Golden Hare Books
68 St Stephen Street, Edinburgh EH3 5AQ
tel 0131 629 1396
email mail@goldenharebooks.com
website www.goldenharebooks.com
Twitter @GoldenHareBooks
Manager Julie Danskin

Independent bookshop, nominated for Children's Bookseller of the Year in *The Bookseller* Industry Awards 2018. Events include regular Sunday story sessions for children aged between three and seven. Named Independent Bookshop of the Year at the British Book Awards 2019.

Harbour Bookshop
2 Mill Street, Kingsbridge, Devon TQ7 1ED
tel (01548) 857233
email hello@harbourbookshop.co.uk
website www.harbourbookshop.co.uk
Twitter @HarbourBookshop
Proprietor Jane Fincham, *Manager* Louise Sanders

Well-established independent bookshop with an extensive range of children's books for all ages. Next day delivery available. Also works with primary and secondary schools and holds children's book events and celebrations.

Heath Educational Books
Willow House, Willow Walk, Whittaker Road, Sutton, Surrey SM3 9QQ
tel 020-8644 7788
email orders@heathbooks.co.uk
website www.heathbooks.co.uk
Proprietor Richard Heath

Supplies books to schools and teachers throughout Europe. Large showroom.

Hunting Raven Books (Winstones UK)
10 Cheap Street, Frome, Somerset BA11 1BN
tel (01373) 473111
email winstonebooks3@gmail.com
Facebook www.facebook.com/HuntingRavenBooks
Twitter @HuntingRavenBks
Proprietor Wayne Winstone, *Manager* Tina Gaisford-Waller

Long-established independent bookshop with extensive range of books and gifts for all ages and a strong children's section. Holds events, signings and children's competitions regularly.
    Other Winstone's bookshops can be found in Sidmouth (http://winstonebooks.co.uk/sidmouth) and Sherborne (http://winstonebooks.co.uk/sherborne).

Madeleine Lindley Ltd
Book Centre, Broadgate, Broadway Business Park, Chadderton, Oldham OL9 9XA
tel 0161 683 4400
email books@madeleinelindley.com
website www.madeleinelindley.com
Twitter @teacher_books

Supplies books to schools and nurseries, provides information services and runs open days and training courses for teachers. Hosts author/publisher events for teachers and children.

The Mainstreet Trading Company
Main Street, St Boswells, Scottish Borders, TD6 0AT
tel (01835) 824087
email info@mainstreetbooks.co.uk
website www.mainstreetbooks.co.uk
Twitter @mainstreethare
Proprietors Rosamund and Bill de la Hay

General bookshop with a particular focus on children's books. Named Independent Bookseller of the Year at the *The Bookseller* Industry Awards 2012. Winner of Britain's Best Small Shop 2018.

Moon Lane Ink CIC

300 Stanstead Road, London SE23 1DE
tel 020-3489 7030
email info@moonlanebooks.co.uk
website www.moonlaneink.co.uk
Twitter @moonlaneink

Not-for-profit enterprise aiming to improve equality and diversity in children's books. In addition to a bookshop, runs enterprise workshops for children as well as a range of events. Founded 2018.

Nickel Books

9 Merlin Close, Sittingbourne ME10 4TY
07731 152089
email enquiries@nickelbooks.co.uk
website www.nickelbooks.co.uk
Twitter @NickelBooks
Instagram nickelbooks
Proprietor Andrea Don

Mail-order only. Specialises in children's books, from birth to teenage; also books for parents.

Norfolk Children's Book Centre

Church Lane, Alby, Norwich NR11 7HB
tel (01263) 761402
email marilyn@ncbc.co.uk
website www.ncbc.co.uk
Twitter @NorfolkCBC

Specialist children's bookshop for readers of all ages. Offers services to schools in East Anglia including storytelling, talks to children and parents, approval services and INSET for teachers. School library assessment and rejuvenation nationwide.

Octavia's Bookshop

24 Black Jack Street, Cirencester GL7 2AA
tel (01285) 650677
email info@octaviasbookshop.co.uk
website www.octaviasbookshop.co.uk
Twitter @octaviabookshop
Proprietor Octavia Karavla

Independent bookshop in which more than half the stock is dedicated to children's titles, from buggy books to teen fiction and classics. Book groups are available for children aged six upwards. Named Children's Independent Bookseller of the Year at the *The Bookseller* Industry Awards 2013.

The Oundle Bookshop

13 Market Place, Oundle, Peterborough PE8 4BA
tel (01832) 273523
email oundlebookshop@colemangroup.co.uk
website www.colemans-online.co.uk/oundle-bookshop.html

General bookshop with extensive children's selection.

Owl and Pyramid

10 Fore Street, Seaton EX12 2LA
tel (01297) 598030
email owl.pyramid@yahoo.com
website www.owlandpyramid.co.uk
Facebook www.facebook.com/owlpyramid
Twitter @OwlPyramid

Independent children's bookshop stocking fiction and non-fiction for young readers from babies to teenagers. Also runs three book groups: Fun Activity Book Club for 7–10 year-olds, 10+ Discussion Club and 12+ Discussion Club. Founded 2014.

Peters Ltd

120 Bromsgrove Street, Birmingham B5 6RJ
tel 0121 666 6646
website www.peters.co.uk
Facebook www.facebook.com/petersbooksandfurniture
Twitter @petersbooks

Specialist supplier of children's books and library furniture to schools, nurseries, academies and public libraries, with a book and furniture showroom, online ordering facilities and ten specialist children's librarians. Also provides a library design and installation service, ebook lending options for schools and public library authorities and book-related promotional material. Peters are sponsors of the CILIP Carnegie and Kate Greenaway Shadowing Awards, and also host regular professional development events for teachers and librarians, featuring speakers, authors and illustrators.

Pickled Pepper Books

10 Middle Lane, Crouch End, London N8 8PL
tel 020-3632 0823
email info@pickledpepperbooks.co.uk
website www.pickledpepperbooks.co.uk
Twitter @pickledbooks
Proprietors Urmi Merchant, Steven Pryse

Family-run specialist children's bookshop with a café and weekly programme of events for under 5s including story-times, art and craft, music groups, Spanish and French sing-alongs and NCT coffee mornings. After-school events include book groups for 9–12 year-olds and teens' creative writing and illustration clubs. The bookshop also hosts regular interactive author events, as well as innovative theatre and puppet shows. Founded 2012.

Rogan's Books

26 Castle Lane, Bedford MK40 3US
tel 07701 097361
email nowthen@rogansbooks.co.uk
website http://rogansbooks.co.uk
Twitter @RogansBooks
Proprietor Rachael Rogan

Specialist children's independent bookshop with a feminist twist: notable for issues-based titles including LGBTQ+, gender, families, activism, BSL, inclusion and mental health. Schools accounts, library consultation, author and illustrator events, family groups, book readings and signings. Independent Bookshop of the Year regional finalist 2017 and 2018 at the *The Bookseller* Industry Awards.

Round Table Books

97 2nd Avenue, Brixton Village, London SW9 8PR
website http://knightsof.media/
Twitter @BooksRound
Manager Khadija Osman

Inclusive children's bookshop, owned by the Knights Of... independent children's publisher, which champions authors and illustrators from diverse backgrounds. Founded 2019.

Seven Stories – see page 356

Seven Stories Bookshop

30 Lime Street, Ouseburn Valley, Newcastle upon Tyne NE1 2PQ
tel 0300 330 1095
email bookshop@sevenstories.org.uk
website www.sevenstories.org.uk
Twitter @7StoriesBooks
Manager Billiejo Carlisle

Independent children's bookshop and part of the National Centre for Children's Books. School accounts are available, as is advice on library stock.

Simply Books

228 Moss Lane, Bramhall, Cheshire SK7 1BD
tel 0161 439 1436
email enquiries@simplybooks.info
website www.simplybooks.info
Twitter @simplybooksNo1

Independent bookshop with strong children's selection, as well as regular events and reading groups for young readers.

Smallprint Books

37 Davids Road, London SE23 3EP
email hello@smallprint-online.com
website www.smallprint-online.com
Twitter @smallprintbks
Instagram smallprintbooks
Manager Jenny Thomas

Independent specialist children's bookshop, focusing on a curated collection of illustrated books for young readers from birth to 10. Events include regular weekday story and music sessions and author/illustrator craft workshops. Check website for details.

Storytellers, Inc.

7 The Crescent, St Anne's on Sea, Lytham St Anne's, Lancs. FY8 1SN
tel (01253) 781690
email info@storytellersinc.co.uk
website www.storytellersinc.co.uk
Twitter @storytellersinc
Proprietors Carolyn Clapham, Katie Clapham

Independent bookshop with dedicated children's section. Monthly book clubs for readers aged 6–7, 8–10, 11–13 and teens, as well as a range of events for adults. Supplies books to local schools. Regional winner (North) in the Independent Bookshop of the Year category at *The Bookseller* Industry Awards 2015.

Tales On Moon Lane

25 Half Moon Lane, London SE24 9JU
tel/fax 020-7274 5759
email info@talesonmoonlane.co.uk
website www.talesonmoonlane.co.uk
Twitter @talesonmoonlane
Proprietor Tamara Macfarlane

Specialist children's bookshop which runs yearly children's literature festivals in February and October, as well as weekly story-telling sessions for preschool children.

Through the Wardrobe Books

2 Nettleton Road, Mirfield, West Yorks. WF14 9AA
email hello@throughthewardrobebooks.co.uk
website www.throughthewardrobebooks.co.uk
Facebook www.facebook.com/throughthewardrobebooks
Twitter @WardrobeBooks
Founders Leanne Yeomans, Samantha Ward

Specialist children's and young adults bookshop. Open Monday to Saturday. Founded 2019.

West End Lane Books

277 West End Lane, London NW6 1QS
tel 020-7431 3770
email info@welbooks.co.uk
website www.welbooks.co.uk
Twitter @WELBooks

Independent family-owned bookshop, carrying fiction and non-fiction books and stationery. Offers twice-weekly story-time sessions for preschool children. Hosts regular author talks and book groups, and also offers a children's personal shopper service.

BOOKSELLERS FOR COLLECTORS

Blackwell's Rare Books

48–51 Broad Street, Oxford OX1 3BQ
tel (01865) 333555
email rarebooks@blackwell.co.uk
website www.blackwell.co.uk/rarebooks
Facebook www.facebook.com/rarebooks
Twitter @blackwellrare

Deals in early and modern first editions of children's books, among other subjects.

Bookmark Children's Books

Fortnight, Broad Hinton, Swindon, Wilts. SN4 9NR
tel (01793) 731693
email leonora-excell@btconnect.com
Contacts Leonora Smith, Anne Excell

Mail-order bookseller, specialising in books for collectors, ranging from antiquarian to modern. A wide range of first editions, novelty and picture books, chap-books, ABCs, annuals, etc. Also a selection of vintage toys, games, greetings cards and illustrated postcards, dolls and nursery china. Book-search service available within this specialist area. Member of PBFA, exhibiting at PBFA book fairs in London, Bristol, York, Bath and Oxford. Established 1973.

Plurabelle Books

Unit 8, Restwell House, Coldhams Road, Cambridge CB1 3EW
tel (01223) 415671
email books@plurabelle.co.uk
website www.plurabellebooks.com
Twitter @PlurabelleBooks

Second-hand bookseller specialising in academic books on literature, reading, history of education and children's literature. Free book search for out-of-print books. Visitors welcome by appointment.

Henry Sotheran Ltd

2–5 Sackville Street, Piccadilly, London W1S 3DP
tel 020-7439 6151

email rh@sotherans.co.uk
website www.sotherans.co.uk
website blog.sotherans.co.uk
Facebook www.facebook.com/sotherans
Twitter @Sotherans
Contact Rosie Hodge

Large showroom with hundreds of important children's books spanning two centuries, specialising in first editions and illustrated works by pivotal artists. Opening hours: Mon–Fri 9.30am–6pm; Sun 10am–4pm. Two specialist catalogues issued annually, available free on request.

Stella & Rose's Books

Monmouth Road, Tintern, Monmouthshire, NP16 6SE
tel (01291) 689755
email enquiry@stellabooks.com
website www.stellabooks.com
Twitter @stellarosebooks

Specialists in rare, out-of-print children's and illustrated books, also carrying a large and varied general stock (over 25,000 books in stock). Stock available for sale via website. Specialist lists issued regularly. Open 10.00am–5.00pm seven days a week. Single items or collections purchased. Founded 1991.

Books, sites and blogs about children's books

Caroline Horn selects some of the best print and online resources about children's books for readers, writers and illustrators.

There are many books written about children's books, offering practical advice on selecting books or invaluable research material for those pursuing degrees and diplomas in children's literature. For those who want to keep up to date with news and trends in picture books, middle-grade fiction and YA novels, there is also a host of blogs and websites sharing news and updates on a daily basis.

BOOKS

The Oxford Companion to Children's Literature
Edited by Daniel Hahn
Published by Oxford University Press (2015)
ISBN 978–0–19969514-0

An indispensable reference book for anyone interested in children's books. Over 900 biographical entries deal with authors, illustrators, printers, publishers, educationalists and others who have influenced the development of children's literature. Genres covered include myths and legends, fairy tales, adventure stories, school stories, fantasy, science fiction, crime and romance. This book is of particular interest to librarians, teachers, students, parents and collectors.

The Reading Bug – and how you can help your child to catch it
by Paul Jennings
Published by Penguin Books (2004)
ISBN 978–0–1413–18400

Paul Jennings is a well-known children's author. This book explains, in his unique humorous style, how readers can open up the world through a love of books. He cuts through the jargon and the controversies to reveal the simple truths, which should enable adults to infect children with the reading bug.

Sticks and Stones: The Troublesome Success of Children's Literature from Slovenly Peter to Harry Potter
by Jack Zipes
Published by Routledge (2002)
ISBN 978–0–4159–38808

Jack Zipes – translator of the Grimm tales, teacher, storyteller and scholar – questions whether children ever really had a literature of their own. He sees children's literature in many ways as being the 'grown-ups' version' – a story about childhood that

adults tell kids. He discusses children's literature from the 19th century moralism of Slovenly Peter (whose fingers get cut off) to the wildly successful *Harry Potter* books. Children's literature is a booming market but its success, this author says, is disguising its limitations. *Sticks and Stones* is a forthright and engaging book by someone who clearly cares deeply about what and how children read.

1001 Children's Books You Must Read Before You Grow Up
Edited by Julia Eccleshare
Published by Cassell Illustrated (2009)
ISBN 978–1–8440–36714

This aims to provide an introduction to the best of children's literature, ranging from international classics to contemporary writers. Reviews of each book are accompanied by line drawings and artwork from the books themselves. A number of authors including Michael Morpurgo and Jacqueline Wilson also write about their favourite books. The reviews are ordered according to the book's publication date, from past to present, and age range of the reader.

The Ultimate Book Guide
Edited by Leonie Flynn, Daniel Hahn and Susan Reuben
Published by A&C Black (2009)
ISBN 978–1–4081–04385

Over 600 entries covering the best books for children aged 8–12, from classics to more recently published titles. Funny, friendly and frank recommendations written for children by their favourite and best-known authors including Anthony Horowitz, Jacqueline Wilson, Celia Rees, Darren Shan, David Almond and Dick King-Smith. Plus features on the most popular genres.

The Ultimate First Book Guide
Edited by Leonie Flynn, Daniel Hahn and Susan Reuben
Published by A&C Black (2008)
ISBN 978–0–7136–73319

Comprehensive reference to help children aged 0–7 with their first steps into the world of books. Covers board books and novelty books, through to classic and contemporary picture books, chapter books and more challenging reads. It includes recommendations and features from top authors and experts in the field of children's books, including former Children's Laureate Michael Rosen, Tony Bradman, Malachy Doyle and Wendy Cooling. There are also special features on a variety of topics and themed lists, and a selection of cross-references to other titles children may enjoy.

The Ultimate Teen Book Guide

Edited by Daniel Hahn and Leonie Flynn
Published by A&C Black (2010, 2nd edn)
ISBN 978–1–4081–04378

Listings of over 700 books that might interest teenage readers, recommended and reviewed by authors such as Melvin Burgess, Anthony Horowitz, Meg Cabot, Eoin Colfer and Philip Pullman. Reviews cover the classics to cult fiction, and graphic novels to bestsellers, and each is cross-referenced to other titles as suggestions of what to read next. The book also contains essays on areas of teenage writing including *Race in Young Adult Fiction* by Bali Rai and *Off the Rails* by Kevin Brooks. There are also the results of a national teen readers' poll, plus reviews from teen readers.

ONLINE

Armadillo

www.armadillomagazine.co.uk

An online magazine about children's books, including reviews, interviews, features and profiles. New issues are posted at the end of March, June, September and December. It was founded in 1999 by author Mary Hoffman as a review publication for children's books.

BBC Bitesize

www.bbc.co.uk/bitesize

Information about UK schools' curriculum. Useful for those wishing to write for educational publishers but also for keeping abreast of curricular topics.

The Bookbag

www.thebookbag.co.uk

A UK-based website focused on great reviews about children's books, there are also booklists and information about book awards, as well as articles and author interviews.

Books for Keeps

http://booksforkeeps.co.uk

Featuring a quarterly online magazine for children's books including book reviews and features.

BookTrust

www.booktrust.org.uk

Dedicated children's reading charity, this is a useful site for professionals working with young readers. Information on events, prizes, books, authors, etc.

BookTrust Great Books Guide

www.booktrust.org.uk/books/great-books-guide/

BookTrust's independent annual 'pick of the best' in children's paperback fiction published in the previous calendar year. It is designed to help parents and those intersted in children's reading to select books for children, from babies to teenagers.

Branford Boase Award

www.branfordboaseaward.org.uk

The website for the annual children's book award dedicated to debut children's writers and their editor and includes a writing competition for young people.

CBBC

www.bbc.co.uk/cbbc

Website of the CBBC channel with games, activities and news for children.

The Children's Book Council

www.cbcbooks.org

The Children's Book Council in the USA is dedicated to encouraging literacy and the enjoyment of children's books. The website includes reviews of children's books published in the USA, forthcoming publications and author profiles. A good site for checking out the US marketplace.

Children's Laureate

www.booktrust.org.uk/what-we-do/childrens-laureate

Official website of the Children's Laureate with resources and activities for children.

Children's Literature

http://childrenslit.com/

US website of the Children's Literature Comprehensive Database (CLCD), a subscription database with over 400,000 reviews of children's books. Plus links to US author and illustrator websites.

CILIP Carnegie & Kate Greenaway Medals

http://carnegiegreenaway.org.uk

This website follows the only UK children's book award where the winners are selected by specialist children's librarians. The website includes a 'shadowing' area for schools to leave their comments about the books, plus interviews with shortlisted authors.

The Federation of Children's Book Groups

fcbg.org.uk/

The FCBG runs an annual children's book award, judged by children, and a network of local groups for those interested in finding out more about children's books and authors. See page 359.

Good Reads for Children

www.goodreads.com/genres/childrens

The Amazon-owned website supports consumer reviews about books for children that can be researched by categories including middle grade and picture books, etc.

The Horn Book

www.hbook.com

US website hosting *The Horn Book Guide Online*, a comprehensive, fully searchable database of over 80,000 book titles for children and young adults, and a monthly e-newsletter for parents, *Notes from the Horn Book*. Plus much more.

House of Illustration

www.houseofillustration.org.uk

The brainchild of author and illustrator Quentin Blake, the House of Illustration celebrates all forms of illustration, runs regular talks and events and supports schools-based activities.

National Literacy Trust

www.literacytrust.org.uk

The organisation is focused on developing literacy among adults and children and its website documents its activities. See page 361.

Picture Book Den

http://picturebookden.blogspot.co.uk

An independent website created by professional children's authors based in the UK and Ireland where they share their passion for picture books, with blogs on getting published, writing picture books, etc but not reviews.

ReadingZone.com

https://readingzone.com/home.php

A magazine-style website, created with Arts Council support, dedicated to children's books including monthly book reviews by teachers and librarians as well as children, chapters to download, author interviews, news, activities and a regular newsletter.

Caroline Horn is editor of www.ReadingZone.com

There are distinct areas for teachers, librarians, families, children and teenagers.

Scottish Book Trust

www.scottishbooktrust.com

Information on books for children of all ages in Scotland plus a national programme of events with children's writers: author tours, festivals, writing competitions and exciting activities.

Seven Stories

www.sevenstories.org.uk

The Seven Stories National Centre for Children's Books, based in Newcastle, provides regular events and exhibitions dedicated to children's literature which are highlighted on its website. See page 356.

The Story Museum

www.storymuseum.org.uk

Stories from around the world to watch, hear, read and tell.

Teen Reads

www.teenreads.com

US website with information, reviews, author links and features on teenage books. Part of The Book Report Network.

Toppsta

https://toppsta.com

A children's book review website that invites children and adults to review books for children and teenagers.

Who Next ... ?

www.whonextguide.com

Writers of children's fiction are listed with suggestions of other authors who write in a similar way, together with key book and series titles. There is a small annual subscription fee for accessing the information.

Words & Pictures

www.wordsandpics.org

The online magazine of SCBWI, a worldwide organisation of writers and illustrators of children's books, with advice on writing, news, blogs and activities. See page 353.

World Book Day

www.worldbookday.com

Providing a range of resources for children and teenagers, from writing and illustration mastercalsses to quizzes, activities and reading ideas.

Books

Making a writer

Sarah Crossan describes what led her to take her writing seriously, put her secret dream of being a writer into practice and – with time and resolve – achieve her goal.

I never thought a person like me could be a writer. I was an incredibly ordinary child, have become an even more ordinary adult, and believed many untruths about writing and writers. Firstly, I didn't come from a family connected to the literati, which I perceived as a major problem, though at the time I probably hadn't even come across the word 'literati'. Secondly, I wasn't privately educated and didn't have anything close to a BBC newsreader's accent – grand drawback. Finally, and perhaps most importantly, I didn't own a serious-looking scarf. You know the ones. All proper artists own them.

When I went to university, to study Philosophy and Literature, my fears about what went into making a writer were compounded as I carefully stalked the creative writing students: they all seemed aloof, important and occasionally sad, hanging out in the humanities building, wearing oversized jumpers and, yes, their scholarly scarves.

After my undergraduate degree, convinced writing wasn't for me (and secretly hating all those creative writing students who'd spent three years smugly impersonating Margaret Atwood), I went off to study teaching. It was a way to make books a part of my daily life. And I was actually really good at it. The students fell in love with words and sentences, with poems and novels. I even convinced a class of hardened Shakespeare haters (one of whom offered to steal my car for £50 so I could pick up the insurance money!) to perform scenes from *Romeo and Juliet*, as well as partake in some Renaissance dancing. I loved teaching – my job was about books and kids, words and relationships.

Then came an afternoon that changed everything – a lesson that had an outcome missing from my planning notes. I was teaching poetry, encouraging students to write about their dreams, their hopes, how they saw their lives developing. I believed in those kids. I knew they could be anything they wanted to be if they just puffed out their chests and did some hard work. They wrote wonderful poems. They wrote moving poems. And then, at the end of the lesson, one child put up his hand and asked a question: 'Have you always wanted to be an English teacher, Miss?'. Now, a more sensitive person might have read some subtext into this, namely *'Why are you a teacher, Miss? You're terrible at your job.'* But I don't think that's what he meant. He genuinely wanted to know whether or not I'd lived my dreams, so shyly I explained that, as well as being a teacher, I wanted to be a writer, a poet and a novelist, but that I didn't think I quite had what it took. The boy frowned, as did a few other students, and angrily replied, 'Well you have a bit of cheek then, don't you, telling us to live our dreams when you haven't even done it yourself. Have you even tried?'

Despite being young, I was a strict teacher; I never tolerated rudeness, but in that moment I was dumbstruck – because he was right. Who was I to lecture them on bravery and risk when I had never taken myself nor my own desires seriously? Instead of asking him to leave the room, where I could speak to him about his tone of voice, I quietly said, 'You're right. I've been too afraid to try.'

On the basis of that very bald conversation, I applied to go back to university and study creative writing – which I did the very next year, annoying the head teacher who had to find a replacement for the next academic year at short notice.

And so I began to write. And I began to take my writing seriously. Rather than going to the cinema when friends asked, I started to say, 'Sorry, I can't. I'm writing.' When they seemed irritated by my resolve, I didn't care. If I wanted to achieve my dream of writing for a living, I had to believe in myself, otherwise no one else would. I found a way out of my shame and into a pattern of work that I loved.

That doesn't mean a contract came quickly; it didn't. It was another ten years of graft and fine-tuning my skills before I found an agent, listed in the *Writers' & Artists' Yearbook* in the children's section, who seemed to fit the bill. I sent her my book and astonishingly she took me on within days. We are still together, for better or for worse, and when I start to flounder and find myself wondering if I should pack it all in, she reminds me that I don't need anything to succeed except a dash of self-belief and a bit of hard work. Oh, and my serious writerly scarf, of course. Everyone needs one of those!

Sarah Crossan is the award-winning author of the Young Adult novel *One* (Bloomsbury 2015) which won the CILIP Carnegie Medal, the YA Book Prize, the CBI Book of the Year award and the CLiPPA Poetry Award in 2016. Also published by Bloomsbury, her books *The Weight of Water* (2011) and *Apple and Rain* (2014) were both shortlisted for the CILIP Carnegie Medal. Sarah's other children's novels are *Breathe* (2012), its sequel *Resist* (2013), *We Come Apart* (co-authored with Brian Conaghan 2017) and the free verse novel *Moonrise* (2017), which was shortlisted for the Costa Children Book Award, the YA Book Prize and the CBI Book of the Year Award. Her latest book is *Toffee* (Bloomsbury 2019). In May 2018 Sarah was appointed Laureate na nÓg, the Irish Children's Laureate.

Notes from a Children's Laureate

Anthony Browne was the Children's Laureate 2009–11. Here he shares his passion for picture books and explains the importance of the Shape Game to develop the act of looking.

It was a long road to becoming the Children's Laureate but I believe it all started with the Shape Game, a simple drawing game that my brother and I thought we'd invented when we were young. I have spoken of this game to children all over the world, and they've made me realise that its prevalence in my own childhood was by no means unique. Children everywhere have invented their own versions of the Shape Game. It has certainly been a very important part of my career, for I have played it in every book I've made.

The rules are very simple: the first person draws an abstract shape; the second person, ideally using a different coloured pen, transforms it into something. It seems that all children love this game and are very good at it – far better than adults are. It is an unfortunate part of growing up that we lose a great deal of contact with our visual imagination. The wonder with which we look at the world diminishes, and this inhibits both our inclination to draw (most adults give up entirely) and also our ability to draw with any real creative value.

Even though the Shape Game is great fun to play, I believe it also has a serious aspect. Essentially, the game is about creativity itself. Every time we draw a picture, or write a story, or compose a piece of music, we are playing the Shape Game. When children ask me (and they always do) where I get my inspiration from, I tell them it's from the same place that they get theirs – from things that happened to me when I was a boy, or things that happened to my own children, from other people's stories, from films, from paintings, or from dreams. There are so many sources of inspiration. Everything comes from somewhere else, and when we create something we're transforming our own experience into a picture, a book, or perhaps a piece of music. We are playing our own Shape Game.

In my early years my father was the landlord of a pub near Bradford and apparently I used to stand on a table in the bar and tell stories to customers about a character called Big Dumb Tackle (whoever he was). I spent much of my childhood playing sport, fighting and drawing with my older brother and then studied graphic design in Leeds. While I was at art college my father died suddenly and horrifically in front of me, and this affected me hugely. I went through a rather dark period which didn't sit very happily with the world of graphic design. After leaving college I dabbled rather unsuccessfully in the advertising world then heard about a job as a medical artist and thought that it sounded interesting – it was. I worked at Manchester Royal Infirmary for three years painting delicate watercolours of grotesque operations. It taught me a lot more about drawing than I ever learned at art college, and I believe it taught me how to tell stories in pictures. I thought that it was probably time to move on when strange little figures started appearing in these paintings – and so began a career designing greetings cards. I continued to do this for many years working for the Gordon Fraser Gallery.

Gordon Fraser became a close friend and taught me a lot about card design which was to prove very useful when I started doing children's books. I experimented with many styles and many subjects, from snowmen to dogs with big eyes to gorillas. I sent some of my designs to various children's book publishers and it was through one of these that I met Julia MacRae who was to become my editor for the next 20 years. She taught me much of what I know about writing and illustrating children's books.

In 1976 I produced *Through the Magic Mirror*, a strange kind of book in which I painted many of the pictures before I wrote the story. I followed this with *A Walk in the Park*, a story I was to revisit 20 years later with *Voices in the Park*. Probably my most successful book is *Gorilla*, and it was around the time it was published in 1983 that I was badly bitten by a gorilla whilst being filmed for television at my local zoo.

I have published 50 books and been very lucky to win awards for some of these – the Kate Greenaway Medal twice (page 382) and the Kurt Maschler 'Emil' three times. In 2000 I was awarded the Hans Christian Andersen Medal (page 379), which is an international award and the highest honour a children's writer or illustrator can win, and I was the first British illustrator to receive it. My books have been translated into 28 languages. My illustrations have been exhibited in many countries – USA, Mexico, Venezuela, Colombia, France, Korea, Italy, Germany, Holland, Japan and Taiwan – and I've had the pleasure of visiting these places and working with local children and meeting other illustrators.

In 2001–02 I worked at Tate Britain with children using art as a stimulus to inspire visual literacy and creative writing activities. It was during this time that I conceived and produced *The Shape Game*.

In 2009 I was appointed Children's Laureate. In this capacity, my aim was to encourage more children to discover and love reading, focusing particularly on the appreciation of picture books, and the reading of both pictures *and* words. I strongly believe that picture books are special – they're not like anything else.

Sometimes I hear parents encouraging their children to read what they call 'proper' books (that's books without pictures) at an earlier and earlier age. This makes me sad, as picture books are perfect for sharing, and not just with the youngest children. As a father, I understand the importance of the bond that develops through reading and talking about picture books with your child. I believe the best picture books leave a tantalising gap between the pictures and the words, a gap that's filled by the reader's imagination, adding so much to the excitement of the book. Picture books are for everybody at any age, not books to be left behind as we grow older.

I also try to encourage the act of looking. Research has shown that visitors to art galleries spend an average of 30 seconds looking at each painting, and considerably more time reading the captions. It's an unfortunate element of growing up that we can lose a great deal of contact with our visual imagination, and by encouraging children – and adults – to play the Shape Game I hope this will change.

In the best picture books the pictures contain clues; they tell you what characters are thinking or how they're feeling. By reading these clues we get a far deeper understanding of the story. In the UK we have some of the best picture book makers in the world, and I want to see their books appreciated for what they are – works of art.

In spite of my concerns about the state of the market for picture books, I am optimistic about the future. I realise now more than ever that I am incredibly lucky to love what I do. Straight after finishing art college I was disheartened because it seemed inevitable that in order to make a living from art I would have to make massive compromises. The experience of doing those advertising jobs made any dreams I once had seem futile. I was getting paid, but the fun of drawing had been taken away. I retrieved some of the fun when

I was a medical illustrator, and I enjoyed making many of the card designs, but it wasn't until I discovered picture books that I learned it was possible to have as much fun with a paintbrush as I had done as a child *and* get paid for it. This is what I love most about my job. What I do now is exactly what I did then: tell stories and draw pictures. Nothing much has changed, not even my approach. Drawing was always my favourite thing to do, and you could say that my career is comparable to other little boys growing up and being paid to play with Lego or dress up as cowboys.

I am also extremely lucky that I have been able to continue 'playing' for a living for so long. I could never stop drawing. Even if I was to give up doing it for a living I would carry on drawing for pleasure. But doing it for a living *is* doing it for pleasure, so there really is no reason to stop!

Anthony Browne was the Children's Laureate 2009–11. His first book, *Through the Magic Mirror*, was published in 1976 and the classic, *Gorilla* (1983), won many awards, including the Kate Greenaway Medal and the Kurt Maschler Award. He has published a number of titles featuring the character Willy, the chimp. His other books include *Zoo, Alice's Adventures in Wonderland, Voices in the Park, Bear's Magic Pencil* and *Me and You*. In 2000 he was the first British illustrator to win the Hans Christian Andersen Award, for his services to children's literature. *The Shape Game* was based on his experiences as Illustrator in Residence at Tate Britain in London 2001–2. His most recent book, *Little Frida*, was published by Walker Books in 2019.

See also...
- *Notes from Jacqueline Wilson*, page 85
- *Who do children's authors write for?*, page 104
- *Writing books to read aloud*, page 109
- *Notes from the first Children's Laureate*, page 279

Notes from Jacqueline Wilson

Jacqueline Wilson shares her first experience of becoming a writing success.

I knew I wanted to be a writer ever since I was six years old. I thought it would be the most magical job in the world. You could stay at home by yourself and write stories all day long.

I loved making up stories. I had a serial story permanently playing in my head. I used to mutter the words, acting each imaginary character in turn, but I soon learnt that this made people stare or giggle. I mastered the art of saying the words silently, experiencing all sorts of extraordinary adventures internally, while I sat staring seemingly blankly into space. No wonder I was nicknamed Jacky Daydream at school. My Mum thought I wasn't all there, and was forever giving me a shake and telling me not to look so gormless. She laughed at me when I confided that I wanted to be a writer. 'Don't be so daft, Jac! Who on earth would want to read a book written by *you*?' she said.

She had a point. I was a totally unexceptional little girl, shy and anxious, barely able to say boo to a goose. My Mum wanted a daughter like Shirley Temple. She even permed my wispy hair to try to turn it into a cloud of golden ringlets. I ended up looking as if I'd been plugged into a light socket. I couldn't sing like Shirley, I couldn't tap dance like Shirley, and although I could recite long poems with dutiful expression I got so nervous performing I once wet myself on stage.

I didn't *want* to perform, well, certainly not in public. I would act out my stories enthusiastically whenever I was by myself, but I was a total shrinking violet in front of other people. I wasn't the life and soul of the party at school. I didn't clamour to have my friends round to play. I preferred playing elaborate imaginary games all by myself.

I saw a writing career as a wonderful grown-up version of these games. I suppose in a way it *is* – but I had no idea what it's *really* like to be a children's author. I don't think I've had a quiet day at home writing my book for weeks!

I suppose it used to be like that long ago. I've been writing children's books for nearly 50 years. For the first 20 years very few people had ever heard of me. I wrote several books a year for a whole variety of publishers. They were published, and if I hunted high and low I occasionally saw one title in a bookshop down at the end of the Ws. I got a few pleasant reviews, and I was stocked in libraries, but that was about it. I've got copies of my first 40 books and they're all first editions – because they didn't go into any other editions. Publishing was so different in those days. You were kept on lists even if your books barely covered their advances – although eventually my first publisher told me they didn't see the point in buying any more of my books because they were never ever going to be popular.

I was upset, of course, but I felt their remarks were justified. I wrote about lonely imaginative children, all of them odd ones out. I thought that only odd children themselves would want to read them. I was worried that I'd never find another publisher but very luckily for me I was taken on by Transworld (now Penguin Random House). I had the idea of writing a story about a fierce little kid in a children's home desperate to be fostered. I decided to tell it as if this child herself was writing her own life story. I wanted her to have a contemporary, quirky kind of name. Something like … Tracy Beaker.

I knew I wanted the book to have lots of black and white illustrations as if Tracy herself had drawn them. I wanted several to a page, even in the margins. David Fickling was my editor then and he's always been very open to suggestions. 'Brilliant!' he said, rubbing his hands. 'I think I know just the chap too. He's done some wonderful illustrations for poetry books. His name's Nick Sharratt. Let's all meet.'

So Nick and I met in the publishing offices. We were both very shy at first. Nick seemed lovely and very talented but I wasn't quite sure he was wacky enough for Tracy-type illustrations. Then I needed to bend down to get a pen out of my handbag on the floor. I saw Nick's socks peeping out from his trouser hem – astonishingly bright canary yellow socks. I knew everything was going to be fine the moment I saw those amazing socks. In fact it became a running joke between us and I'd buy him ever more zany spotty stripy socks all colours of the rainbow.

We've worked on so many books together now and it's been just as magical as I'd hoped – but not at all as I'd imagined. I don't stay home all by myself and write my books. I have a beautiful book-lined study but I'm hardly ever in it. Most days I do my writing on trains or in the back of cars, scribbling frantically in my notebook on my way to endless meetings and events. I'm lucky enough to be able to write happily in these rather distracting conditions, though it's sometimes embarrassing if the train is crowded. I write in the first person, and my lovely Italian notebooks look like private journals. If a business man glances from his *Daily Telegraph* to my notebook, God knows what he thinks if he reads my fictional teenage girl musing; *I so fancy the boy I saw on the bus. How will I ever get to go out with him?*

People often ask me why I think my books have been so successful. I think there are several reasons, apart from sheer luck. They look great, with Nick's fantastic covers, and his lively black and white illustrations inside break up the text and make it less forbidding for inexperienced readers. I care passionately about language and play little word games with my readers, though I try to write in an immediate colloquial style through my child narrators. My publishers promote my books with energy and commitment. However, I believe the *real* secret of my success is the fact that I started doing many school and library visits early on, talking about my books. In fact I don't think there's a single county in the UK where I haven't given a talk.

I vividly remember my very first talk to a small docile group of Year 7s in a secondary school. I was so nervous I could barely eat breakfast beforehand. I hoped I acted like a reasonably competent sociable adult but inside I was still that shy little girl, terrified of performing. However, I could see the whole point of giving talks to children. It was a wonderful way of introducing them to the delights of reading in general, and to my own books in particular! That was why I was willing to put myself through this torture.

I didn't really know what to talk *about*. It seemed like terrible showing off simply talking about myself and my own work. I ended up reading an extract from Daisy Ashford's *The Young Visiters* to show that children could very occasionally have their work published, and then reading an extract from *Jane Eyre*, which had been my favourite book when I was 12. I realised soon enough that this was completely the wrong approach. The children thought the Daisy Ashford bizarre and *Jane Eyre* boring. They only livened up when I changed tack and talked about what I'd been like when I was young. I started to relate to them properly, and found I could tell them funny stories about myself as an earnest teenager, my experiences as a very junior journalist, and then chat to them about my latest book and how it came to be written.

I learnt how to give a talk – but it was a long time before I actually *enjoyed* doing it. I still got very fussed and anxious about it, and I hated it if I couldn't win every child over. After a while you learn that there will be an occasional kid who will give everyone a hard time. You just have to do your best and try to interest all the others. I slogged round several schools and libraries up and down the country every single week – and I learnt so much. This is where children's authors are so lucky. We can meet so many of our readers and find out what they like – and what they don't.

I only go to individual schools and libraries now as special favours to friends, but I still do many talks at festivals. Once you do something enough times you get so used to it you simply can't find it scary. I never get the slightest bit nervous now, even if I've got an audience of hundreds. I had to perform in the garden of Buckingham Palace in front of the Queen and 3,000 children and even that wasn't too worrying. It's just part of my job and I find it great fun.

But I got it right when I was six years old. The *most* magical part of being a writer is staying at home by myself and writing stories all day long.

Jacqueline Wilson, DBE has sold over 40 million books in the UK, and has won many major awards. She was the Children's Laureate 2005–7 and was made a Dame for services to literature in 2008. *Jacky Daydream* (Random House 2007) is an account of her own childhood. Her children's books include *Wave Me Goodbye* (2017) and *Hetty Feather's Christmas* (2017), both illustrated by Nick Sharratt and published by Doubleday Children's Books. In 2018 she published a new title in her Tracy Beaker series, *My Mum Tracy Beaker*, which was shortlisted in the UK Author Category in the National Book Awards and listed as one of the *Observer's* Best Children's Books of 2018. Her most recent novel is *Dancing the Charleston* (Doubleday Children's 2019). Her website is www.jacquelinewilson.co.uk.

See also...

- *What makes a children's classic?*, page 4
- *Getting published*, page 93
- *Who do children's authors write for?*, page 104

A word from J.K. Rowling

J.K. Rowling shares her first experience of becoming a writing success.

I can remember writing *Harry Potter and the Philosopher's Stone* in a café in Oporto. I was employed as a teacher at the language institute three doors along the road at the time, and this café was a kind of unofficial staffroom. My friend and colleague joined me at my table. When I realised I was no longer alone I hastily shuffled worksheets over my notebook, but not before Paul had seen exactly what I was doing. 'Writing a novel, eh?' he asked wearily, as though he had seen this sort of behaviour in foolish young teachers only too often before. '*Writers' & Artists' Yearbook*, that's what you need,' he said. 'Lists all the publishers and … stuff', he advised before ordering a lager and starting to talk about the previous night's episode of *The Simpsons*.

I had almost no knowledge of the practical aspects of getting published; I knew nobody in the publishing world, I didn't even know anybody who knew anybody. It had never occurred to me that assistance might be available in book form.

Nearly three years later and a long way from Oporto, I had almost finished *Harry Potter and the Philosopher's Stone*. I felt oddly as though I was setting out on a blind date as I took a copy of the *Writers' & Artists' Yearbook* from the shelf in Edinburgh's Central Library. Paul had been right and the *Yearbook* answered my every question, and after I had read and reread the invaluable advice on preparing a manuscript, and noted the time-lapse between sending said manuscript and trying to get information back from the publisher, I made two lists: one of publishers, the other of agents.

The first agent on my list sent my sample three chapters and synopsis back by return of post. The first two publishers took slightly longer to return them, but the 'no' was just as firm. Oddly, these rejections didn't upset me much. I was braced to be turned down by the entire list, and in any case, these were real rejection letters – even real writers had got them. And then the second agent, who was high on the list purely because I liked his name, wrote back with the most magical words I have ever read: 'We would be pleased to read the balance of your manuscript on an exclusive basis … '.

This piece was written for the very first edition of the *Children's Writers' & Artists' Yearbook*, published in 2004.

J.K. Rowling, CH is the bestselling author of the *Harry Potter* books (Bloomsbury), published between 1997 and 2007, which have sold over 500 million copies worldwide, are distributed in more than 200 territories, translated into over 80 languages and have been turned into eight blockbuster films. J.K. Rowling has written a novel for adults: *The Casual Vacancy* (Little, Brown 2012), which was adapted for TV by the BBC in 2015. Her crime novels, written under the pseudonym Robert Galbraith, were published in 2013 (*The Cuckoo's Calling*), 2014 (*The Silkworm*), 2015 (*Career of Evil*) and 2018 (*Lethal White*). The books have been adapted for television, produced by Brontë Film and Television. J.K. Rowling has collaborated on a stage play, *Harry Potter and the Cursed Child Parts One and Two*, which opened in London's West End in 2016, on Broadway in 2018 and in Melbourne, Australia in 2019. *Harry Potter and the Cursed Child* is based on an original new story by J.K. Rowling, Jack Thorne and John Tiffany, written by Jack Thorne. In 2016 J.K. Rowling made her screenwriting debut and was a producer on the film *Fantastic Beasts and Where to Find Them*, a further extension of the wizarding world and the start of a new five-film series to be written by the author. The second film, *Fantastic Beasts: The Crimes of Grindelwald*, was released in November 2018.

If at first you don't succeed...

Frances Hardinge describes the steps she took, as a hopeful young writer, to brave rejection, persevere and grow in confidence, and the friends and resources that helped her find where her writing belonged and gain that first momentous book contract.

I was in my teens when I bought my first copy of the *Writers' & Artists' Yearbook*. Back then, the *Children's Writers' & Artists' Yearbook* didn't exist. But in those days I wasn't an adult writing children's fiction, I was a teenager trying my hand at adult fiction.

Buying the book felt significant – a little intimidating, in fact. I sensed that I was making a promise to myself. I wouldn't keep my stories safely hidden away. I would send them off to be judged, and expose my fragile, iridescent bubble-dreams to the jagged edges of the real world. In effect, I had *bought* some of my cowardly excuses into non-existence: '*I can't send my work off, I don't know where to start!*'; '*I don't know what to send, or where!*'. Well, now I did.

And whenever I let schoolwork or other commitments eat up all my time, I'd spot the *Yearbook* on my shelf, fire-engine red. A silent, insistent reminder of my promise to myself. A gentle but much-needed boot in the rear.

I meticulously typed out my stories on the roaring, ill-tempered electric typewriter I'd bought from my sister for five pounds. Every time I made an error and had to perform Tipp-Ex surgery, I agonised over it and considered typing the whole page again.

And all the while I was gripped by a crippling fear that my first submission might be my only chance, and that if I messed it up badly all would be lost. The submissions editor would look coldly at my clunkiest metaphor, or scowl at my Tipp-Ex, and then stride away to the dark chamber where the editor collective kept the Terrible Tome of Authors We Must Never Publish. They would add my name to the list, and from that moment all my other submissions would be doomed. Prospective editors would consult the book, see my name in blood-red letters, shake their heads and throw my manuscript in the bin.

Only after a few trembling submissions did I start to suspect that the Terrible Tome didn't actually exist. Rejection slips arrived in the post, but didn't bring the apocalypse with them. Occasionally there was an actual rejection letter. (My favourite of these effectively said: 'We rather liked your story, and we wish we knew what it was about.') Eventually I realised that I had nothing to lose but the cost of two stamps and a spoonful of pride. If I was turned down it didn't matter. All that mattered was that I kept trying.

By my twenties, I was subscribing to *Writers' News* and *Writing Magazine* to supplement the *Yearbook*. I now typed my stories on a little Franken-puter that my boyfriend had cobbled together from parts of discarded, elderly computers. My friends and I set up a small writers' group, which gave me a regular deadline to keep me writing. With their feedback I became more confident, and less precious about editing my work.

And one day, after sending a short story to a little independent magazine, I received an answer that wasn't a 'no'. This was the first in a series of 'not-no' responses. However, when I received my first book contract a few years later, it was thanks to my good friend Rhiannon Lassiter. She realised something I hadn't – that my peculiar dark fairy tales were actually children's fiction. Rhiannon persuaded me to try writing a children's novel, then wrested my first five chapters from my unwilling hands and marched off with them to her editor.

The *Children's Writers' & Artists' Yearbook* would have been invaluable to me as a young, aspiring children's writer, if I'd had the sense to realise that that was what I was. The latest editions of the *Yearbook* are even richer and more useful than those I bought in my teens and twenties, with more information on agents, prizes, courses, conferences, digital publishing and self-publishing, and a wealth of essays, articles and advice.

Even now, when I look at the *Writers' & Artists' Yearbook*, I still recall everything it symbolised for me. It looks too heavy for the shelf, packed to the binding with hunger, trepidation, determination and hope. It's still a little intimidating. Opportunities often are.

Frances Hardinge is the award-winning author of *Fly by Night* (Macmillan Children's Books 2005), winner of the 2006 Branford Boase award, and of *Twilight Robbery* (Macmillan 2011), shortlisted for the *Guardian* Children's Fiction Prize. Her other books include *Gullstruck Island* (Macmillan 2009), *A Face Like Glass* (Macmillan 2012), *Cuckoo Song* (Pan Macmillan 2014), which won the Robert Holdstock Award for Best Novel at the British Fantasy Awards 2015, and *The Lie Tree* (Macmillan 2015), which won the prestigious Costa Book of the Year 2015 award, the 2016 UKLA Book Award (12–16 category), the 2016 *Boston Globe* Horn Book Fiction Award, and the 2016 *Los Angeles Times* Young Adult Literature Prize. *The Lie Tree* was also shortlisted for the Independent Bookshop Week Award 2015, the *Guardian* Children's Fiction Prize 2015 and the 2016 Carnegie Medal. Her latest book is *A Skinful of Shadows* (Macmillan 2017).

See also...
- *Getting published*, page 93
- *From dream to reality*, page 95

My way into a different world

Sally Green describes how, in middle life, she found herself hooked on the creative process of writing and, by applying hard work and good advice, made her way into the world of the professional writer.

I remember the beginning of my writing career quite clearly. It was a sunny afternoon in June 2010, I was 48 years old and doing housework and I had an idea for a story. I'd never written anything before (no diary, no dabbling in short stories, no childhood dreams of being an author), but what did I have to lose other than a few hours of my time? Anything had to be more interesting than hoovering and no one would ever read the story but me, so I sat down and wrote.

At school I'd learnt the basics of grammar and punctuation, but I always felt inhibited about my writing and that I lacked imagination. Now I realize that everyone has imagination, but being brave and comfortable enough to risk expressing it is the hard thing. By June 2010 schoolgirl inhibitions were a distant memory, although learning wasn't as the previous year I'd begun to study Social Sciences with the Open University. Because of the OU course I had developed the habit of writing – I had to produce regular assignments and I enjoyed closing the door on the outside world and immersing myself in a new topic. I loved the process of putting ideas and words together and creating something, even if it was only a rather poor essay on politics.

So that June afternoon, with no more essays to write, I repeated the procedure but instead of an essay I began a short story about a girl who didn't know that she was a witch. I didn't have much of a plan – I just wrote, and I continued the next day and the next. After two weeks of this I had to admit to myself that the story wasn't that short; in fact I was probably writing a novel, and it was now taking up all my time. I was hooked. Possibly I was in love too – with my characters. I was obsessed with them, thinking about what they'd do and how, and why. I carried on writing and by September 2010 my story was complete and definitely not short (136,000 words). It wasn't atrocious but there were things wrong with it, though I wasn't even sure what those things were (the narrative point of view was jumping all over the place). I was desperate to improve and so I switched my OU course to Creative Writing, studying hard and all the while working on my manuscript.

I never really believed I'd be a published writer – it seemed less likely than winning the lottery – but I believed in my story. I wanted to try to get it published, but I had a problem: I didn't know a thing about the publishing world. However, I had heard about the *Writers' & Artists' Yearbook* and I found a rather battered copy at my local library. As soon as I started leafing through it I knew I'd found a book I could trust. I devoured its advice. It became my Bible, a source of knowledge and comfort. It was my way into a different world – the world of the professional writer.

I decided to try the traditional route of getting an agent who would then help me find a publisher, and so I listed the agents who accepted manuscripts for YA books, googled them and chose a few I thought might be interested in my story. I submitted to eight agents and within a few months received five brief replies saying 'No' (though the non-replies were fairly clear No's too). However, one reply was different: it was still a 'No', but the agent said she liked my writing style though the story 'didn't have the necessary edge for today's market'. I was delighted. OK – it was a rejection, but an agent from a prestigious London literary agency liked my writing style! I was over the moon. Better yet, I was fired up – I knew I could do edgy better than most people, and I knew that I could improve on the manuscript that I'd sent out. My mindset, once I decided I'd try to get published, was that I would write at least three novels before I'd give up, so starting again didn't daunt me. I gave myself a year to rewrite the story and immediately set to work. Best of all, I'd been released from the cage that I hadn't realised I was still in; I'd been told to be edgy, and to do that I had to let go of my writing inhibitions and make the story mine.

A year later I was back in the library with the *Writers' & Artists' Yearbook*, following its advice about covering letters and synopses (much better advice than the, often American, tips I'd seen online) for what turned out to be my first published novel.

I would have been lost without *Writers' & Artists' Yearbook* to guide me, and I'm delighted there is now this *Children's Writers' & Artists' Yearbook*. It's a wonderful resource – it's *the* resource for writers.

Sally Green is the author of an internationally acclaimed trilogy of young adult fantasy novels, published by Penguin, the first of which (her debut novel), *Half Bad* (2014), was named Waterstones Best Book for Teenagers 2015 and was shortlisted for the YA Book Prize 2015 and for the 2015 Branford Boase Award. The second title in the trilogy, *Half Wild*, was published in 2015, and the third and final book, *Half Lost*, came out in March 2016. The first book of her new fantasy series, *The Smoke Thieves*, was published by Penguin in May 2018 with the second title, *The Demon World*, published in August 2019.

See also...
- *Writing for the teenage market*, page 293
- *How to get an agent*, page 225

Getting published

Andy Stanton describes how he found his agent and his first publishing deal.

Good evening. You are holding in your hands one of two things. You are either holding one of the most powerful little books on the planet, a book which has the potential to CHANGE YOUR LIFE FOR EVER; or you are holding a cool little lifestyle accessory, a book which you can keep on your shelf to announce to yourself and others: 'Oh, I'm a writer-sort of person, I'm sure I'll use this book one day. But in the meantime, doesn't it look *professional*.' If you're holding the second version of the book, I'm not knocking you. For years before I got published I would frequently buy the latest copy of the *Writers' & Artists' Yearbook*, with the vague and magical idea that simply owning it was enough to effect an alchemical reaction in my life and turn me into a *writer*, with all the bunting, parades and adoring women that I imagined would naturally accompany such a position.

Well, the years wore on and I discovered something quite annoying: The *Writers' & Artists' Yearbook*, and indeed the *Children's Writers' & Artists' Yearbook*, won't actually turn you into a writer. Take another look at the book you are holding right now and know the dreadful truth. However much you stroke this book; however prominently you display it on your shelves; however much you pray to it at night – there is one component you have to bring along yourself. And (double-annoyingly, because I am very lazy and hate working) that extra component is this: You must write something. You must do some work. And only then will this book become something that could CHANGE YOUR LIFE FOR EVER. It certainly changed mine.

In 2002, I sat down and finally did the one thing I'd never done in all those years of wishing and longing and imagining all those adoring women. I wrote a story from start to finish. It was called *The Story of Mr Gum* and I wrote it partly to make my little cousins laugh, but mostly to see if I could actually finish a piece of work. Having written it, I promptly forgot about it for two years. When I rediscovered it, it was 2004 and I finally had a real and practical reason to buy the *Writers' & Artists' Yearbook*. But I found that fate had other, better plans for me, in the shape of the brand spanking new, first ever edition of the *Children's Writers' & Artists' Yearbook*. Just like its big brother, but so much easier! Now I wouldn't have to trawl through endless agents' listings, figuring out which ones accepted children's writers – no, every page of this publication was just for me. All the work had already been done. (Well, nearly all the work. I've already mentioned that one pesky component you'll have to provide yourself.)

Within a month, the book had found me an agent. She's great, by the way, and she's in this latest edition too. But no plugs, Eve White, no plugs. A month or so after I found [unnamed agent] I had a publishing deal. And in 2006, Egmont published my little story as *You're a Bad Man, Mr Gum!*. Well, folks, it's been a pretty amazing ride since then. There are now nine *Mr Gum* titles, which have sold over a million copies in this country alone. Additionally, I've written two books for Barrington Stoke and published a truly revolting picture book with Puffin. And it all started here, in these pages.

It's a shame it took me all that time to figure out how amazingly powerful this type of book can be. I hope it doesn't take you quite so long. See, it's a hard equation but it's fair. You get out what you put in. And if you put in something good, there's no book better qualified to help you reap your rewards (though a word of warning – the adoring women thing never really materialised). Well, that's enough from me. It's your turn now. You have here all the tools you need to CHANGE YOUR LIFE FOR EVER. So go to it! And the very best of luck.

Andy Stanton has been a medical secretary, a film script reader and a layabout, amongst other things. His favourite expression is 'good evening' and his favourite word is 'captain'. *You're a Bad Man, Mr Gum!* (2006) was his first book and is the first in the *Mr Gum* series (Egmont), for which he has won the Roald Dahl Funny Prize, the Red House Children's Book Award and two Blue Peter Book Awards. His other books include *Sterling and the Canary, Going to the Volcano*, illustrated by Miguel Ordóñez, *Natboff! One Million Years of Stupidity* and *The Paninis of Pompeii* (Egmont 2019).

See also...
- *Spotting talent*, page 1
- *What makes a children's classic?*, page 4
- *Who do children's authors write for?*, page 104
- *Writing humour for young children*, page 135

From dream to reality

Frank Cottrell Boyce provides his own winning formula for writing success.

Infallible spell for transforming yourself into a successful children's writer ... (it worked for me)

1. Acquire copy of current *Children's Writers' & Artists' Yearbook*.

2. Riffle pages. Inhale deeply of the fragrance of future fulfilment.

3. Place volume prominently on kitchen table or other work surface. You will remark an immediate alteration in the atmosphere. This alteration is caused by certain properties inhering in the vivid hues of its cover.

4. If working in a public space, insert Post-it notes and other bookmarks in profusion. Recall that the more attention the book attracts the more power it generates.

5. At certain intervals you may refresh the spirit by opening the book. Do not select the page. Allow the book to offer certain pages to your attention.

6. If the book offers you those pages on which are written the names of agents, consider all their descriptions to assay which ones reverberate most mellifluously in your heart. Seek out their addresses on Google Street View that you may see their doorways. Remember that each of these doorways is a portal to another, richer world. While you know not yet which doorway you will take, picture yourself walking through the doorway with your manuscript in hand (see note 1 below).

7. If the book offers you the pages describing festivals, then consider those festivals – the green rooms wherein great steaming buckets of latte stand next to towers of cupcakes, where the conversation is polished so that the very air doth seem to shine. See, in your imagination, yourself bedecked with lanyard and shepherded by volunteers to the tent where eager children wait to hear you speak (see note 2).

8. If the book offers you the pages describing literary awards then inscribe in your imagination the name of your book beneath those of past winners (see note 3).

9. Before closing the volume always riffle and inhale. The air thus imbibed is of a special type and potency. It is called Inspiration.

10. Maintain these habits and observe these practices until your ends are obtained.

Notes:

1. So you do have to write the book first.

2. Or you won't have anything to read out from.

3. And when you've written it, give it a title.

Before we walked on the Moon we had to spend hundreds of years imagining it. Before I became a writer I spent a lot of time pretending to be a writer. The ostentatious use of the *Writers' & Artists' Yearbook* (WAYB) in public places was a big part of that pretence. But it also helped me turn that pretence into a reality. I had never met a writer or indeed anyone who wanted to be one. The book showed me that it wasn't a 'dream' that somehow 'came true' but a job that involved work and meetings and word counts and layouts and invoices.

All the pragmatic guidance it offered helped crystallise my thoughts and turn the dream into an ambition. When you think about it, that is magic.

Frank Cottrell Boyce is an award-winning author and scriptwriter. His children's books include *Millions* (*New York Times* bestseller and winner of the CILIP Carnegie Medal 2004), *Framed* (2005), *Cosmic* (2008), *Chitty Chitty Bang Bang Flies Again* (2011), two further *Chitty Chitty Bang Bang* titles, and *The Astounding Broccoli Boy* (2015). All published by Macmillan Children's Book. In 2012 he won the *Guardian* Children's Fiction Prize for *The Unforgotten Coat* (Walker Books 2012). *Millions* was made into a movie by Oscar-winning director Danny Boyle. His latest book is *Runaway Robot* (Macmillan Children's Books 2019). Frank has written scripts for *Doctor Who* and for a number of feature films, and also the script for the opening ceremony of the 2012 London Olympics.

A jobbing writer's lot

Joanna Nadin describes the challenges, rewards, satisfaction and financial sense of taking on a variety of work, in different genres and for different ages, in order to make a successful and creative living from writing.

Seventeen years ago, I was called into the office of my soon-to-be agent, Sarah Molloy – an agent I'd found in the pages of the *Writers' & Artists' Yearbook*, a dog-eared and annotated copy from our local library. There, in a small, book-lined office, at the top of a skew-whiff staircase on St Martin's Lane in London, I was given two sage, salient pieces of advice: (1) don't cut off your hair, and (2) don't give up your day job until your advance is three times your salary.

The first I ignored and had my Shirley Temple curls shaved defiantly short. The second I have followed doggedly, and it has served me well. Firstly, it has kept me financially safe. I was working in politics at the time and, though hardly in the higher echelons, paid comfortably enough that no advance to this date has ever come close to one year's salary. Secondly, it denied me false hope, which I fear is all too prevalent in a world whose stock-in-trade is fiction and fairy tales.

What Sarah said made it patently clear to me that, if I wanted to make a living from writing, banking all my hopes on one big hitter was a fool's errand. For one thing, those deals are almost as rare as a ticket to a chocolate factory. For another, if they are laid on the table they may turn out to be a poisoned chalice, piling on pressure that a new and possibly novice writer doesn't need: if you don't earn your advance out, your publisher may view you as a disappointment. On top of which, the next advance, if you get one, is almost certain to be a lot smaller.

Debut novelists can be particularly prone to these 'golden hellos'; who wouldn't turn down a life-changing cheque, after all? But what I have found is that it can pay, in the long run, to work on building a reputation as a reliable freelancer. 'Be good, be nice, be on time,' I was once told by another clever fellow. And that is exactly what I try to be – working with both my agents (my style and savings adviser Sarah retired eventually) to find a variety of work that keeps me busy, and keeps the big, bad wolf from the door.

I write for all ages – from picture book up to adult – and across genres too. Alongside my own original trade fiction, I write for specialist publishers on school reading programmes, conjuring up exciting adventures for early readers, or retelling traditional tales with a contemporary twist. These deals are often arranged by the publishers directly with authors (usually those who have worked with them on trade titles) rather than through agents, but they are also something I ask to be actively put forward for by my agent. They do usually require working within strict subject guidelines and to strict word counts – sometimes as few as 50 words – and with limited lexicons as well. I see this not simply as a challenge, but also as an opportunity to help hone my storytelling and make it spare and succinct – a skill that can be put to excellent use elsewhere. On top of which, while initial advances for these deals are low, if there are royalties in the contract, these can mount up quickly as books are sold in class-size packs and around the world, meaning you earn out fast and earn several times your advance within five years.

Thanks to a Finnish publishing deal that brought me to the attention of a games company out there, I've written tie-in novels, under another name. These are on a flat fee basis, and were agreed after a synopsis and sample chapters met approval. But these hoops proved worth it for me, financially and creatively. While, again, this can mean your characters are already painted and your parameters set before you even begin to think about plot (since the people and world you're being paid to play with is likely to have featured in prequels, a film, a TV series, or, as in my case, a gaming app), I saw this as an opportunity to be freed of that part of the process.

I ghostwrite, too, working on a ten-book fiction series with the Olympian Sir Chris Hoy – a collaboration that has inspired and stretched my imagination, as I've helped to bring someone else's distinct vision and mission to life. Aimed at 5-8 year-olds, the *Flying Fergus* series (Piccadilly) has been a process of intense toing and froing between Chris and I as we conjure up the ideas, bringing our editor in once I've sketched them out on paper. Working in this way requires you to park your ego to an even greater extent than the usual editorial process, accepting that you may not even get your own darlings in the text in the first place to kill them off! But it is enormously rewarding, and having someone else come up with storylines in such a long-running series is almost a relief.

I also co-wrote the YA novel *Everybody Hurts* (Atom 2017) with Anthony McGowan, each of us taking one side of the story and playing ping-pong with chapters in a giant game of consequences. This requires patience – again, an effacing of one's own ego – as well as the ability to handle a complete curveball, when your partner decides to take the tale not just left-field but completely out of the park!

Finally, I've written three-minute-long TV scripts for puppet worms, presenting the links between programmes on the kids' TV channel Nickelodeon. The invention required to bring to life all-singing, all-dancing, but ultimately armless annelids is not to be underestimated.

I am, to all extents and purposes, a writer for hire, willing and able to turn my hand to most things. It helps, of course, that I have a background in journalism and politics. Not only did these worlds teach me to write tight copy to tighter deadlines, they also taught me never to work for nothing, and that writers' block is a luxury afforded only to those who don't use words to pay their bills. That's not to say writing isn't sometimes difficult, but it is never impossible.

The relative anonymity of my past employment has also served to satisfy me that these books aren't in some way worth less because they're series, or because my name isn't on the cover. They still allow me to flex my writing muscle, to show off (and, importantly, improve) my skills, and to plunder the soup of story that swirls in my head. This approach hasn't precluded commercial or critical success either. There have been awards, TV deals, places on bestseller lists, if only for a week or two.

Seventy-seven books later, and I'm still not J.K. Rowling or Jacqueline Wilson; you may not even have heard of me. But, do you know what? That's fine. Because, for the last decade, I've earned a living doing what I love – which is a rare privilege in itself.

Working like this does have its drawbacks – you have to be disciplined, organised, able to multitask, including switching between stories on a daily basis at times. And I still haven't entirely given up the day job, at least for one day a week. While I am passionate about publishing, it is a precarious profession and, besides, I am as happy writing scripts and speeches as I am short series or standalone thrillers. I also now hold a PhD in Creative Writing, I lecture on the acclaimed Masters course at Bath Spa University, I give workshops at festivals and events around the country, I visit schools. In other words, I have made words – rather than one or two books – my career. A career that allows me to spend days, weeks, months on end exploring new worlds, playing dress up and let's pretend, trying on new lives for size.

I am a jobbing writer, and I can't think of a better way to live.

Joanna Nadin worked as a journalist and in politics before becoming an award-winning writer. She has written more than 70 books for children, teenagers and adults including the Carnegie-nominated YA novel *Everybody Hurts* (Atom 2017) with Anthony McGowan, *Joe All Alone* (Little, Brown 2015) and *The Queen of Bloody Everything* (Mantle 2018). In 2018 the CBBC adapation of *Joe All Alone* won the BAFTA Children's Award for Best Drama. Joanna lectures in Creative Writing on the MA at Bath Spa University. For more information visit her website https://joannanadin.com. Find her on Facebook @joannanadinauthor and Twitter @joannanadin.

See also...
- *Writing for a variety of ages*, page 124

Books

Writing and translating children's fiction

Clémentine Beauvais explains the special satisfaction, pleasure and value to be found in translation, with its concentrated focus on language. She urges all writers to use translation to develop and re-energise their reading and writing skills.

This article is about writing children's fiction and translating children's fiction, and the peculiar kinds of pleasure and knowledge that arise when you do both. Let's start by stating the obvious: there shouldn't be any stark distinction between 'writing' and 'translating' children's fiction. Translating is an act of writing. Some translators actually prefer to call themselves 'writers of translations'. As Kate Briggs puts it beautifully, translated texts 'come to us twice-written'. Aren't we lucky, as readers of translations, that not just *one*, but *two* writers, gave their time and applied their talent to that text?

I was a children's writer long before I became a literary translator, and these days I spend roughly half of my time doing 'my' writing and half of my time translating – namely, redoing someone else's writing. Many people are surprised that I would choose to halve what they see as my 'real writing' time, a thought which you could well translate as: 'Surely translation is something you only do when you can't *really* write?'

My view, of course, is that you should translate only if you can *really* write. And only if you can *really* read. And the more you do it, the more it transforms your writing and reading. I want to convince you that if you wish to be a writer, you should *absolutely* write translations. Even if you don't speak another language fluently. Even though it will never bring you fame or money. Even if no one ever reads your translations. Translate. Do it for yourself, for your writing. Do it as a secret pleasure. Do it as a way of learning to write and read better. Here's why.

Translating is writing, rewriting and rewiring your writing

Translating forces you to focus on language, and only on language. I shiver to write this, because of course there's no such thing as 'only' language: it is literally the *only* stuff literature is made of. But when you write a whole novel, you need to keep a million things in mind at the same time: narrative structure, characterisation, audience considerations, chapter length, ideological aspects, the logistics of seriality. And that's even before the editorial dance starts.

When you're translating, you have one task: language. The story's in place, the characters are there; you have a global view of them, in their finished form. Your task is to focus on the words, and to make sure that, in the target language, each of them does the job of propping up this whole fictional world. By 'each of them' I do mean each word, and this is why translating is close to the purest kind of writing: rarely in one's writerly life does one get the luxury of 'angsting' so much over every single word. You think about every word at least twice – in the source language, and in the target one – when the equivalence is obvious. But it seldom is. So you think of each word many times. It is precision work, a series of micro-decisions, adjusting and tweaking language. That's your only job and it's a colossal one.

Doing so will show you two things that are crucial to developing your writing. Firstly: you are never an expert in your native language. All my qualms about writing in English collapsed when I realised I was working from an erroneous assumption – that I knew French. French fails me just as often as English does. We can never write perfectly in any language, nor even approach perfection. Those little failures of language, of any language, are literature.

Secondly: translating changes your writing by forcing you out of your writerly reflexes. My writerly self is lazy. There are certain character types, certain places, certain genres or certain voices it doesn't write because it can't be bothered to venture out of its comfort zone. And my writerly self is ignorant – it doesn't write about things it doesn't know. My translating self cannot afford such whimsicality. It needs to write a text full of those things my writerly self usually avoids or simply doesn't know about. When I translated Sarah Crossan's *Moonrise* (Bloomsbury Children's 2017), I had to write a whole novel about the American prison system; I ended up having, effectively, written it. I never knew anything about it before; I have now learnt not just facts but a way of writing them. Translating is one of the most enlightening acts of writing you can do, because it forces you into the writerly reflexes and comfort zones of someone else.

And it changes your writing, of course, because there's no way you can survive the experience and not acquire new practices, a new way of looking at structure, at character, at style. It inspires you and re-energises your writing. It gives you a glimpse of what your writing-from-scratch could be like if you tried out something entirely different.

Translating is reading, rereading, and learning to read

At the same time, translating is also an act of reading – arguably one of the most reverent, attentive and generous acts of reading. I was, so to speak, a professional reader before I became a translator – as an academic specialising in children's fiction – and those skills are evidently useful when reading-for-translation; it's helpful to be able to notice and name the literary devices, and know roughly what the equivalent ones would be in the other language. For instance, I know that an iambic pentameter in English is like the French twelve-footed alexandrin; both are the classic, solemn rhythms at which the hearts of those cultures beat.

Those reading skills, however, are activated not just for analysis and description, but in close relation with writerly decisions. If I'm looking for equivalence of *effect*, the TaDAM TaDAM TaDAM TaDAM TaDAM of my English iambic pentameter could become the tadadadadaDAM tadadadadaDAM of the French alexandrin. It is equivalently lulling, pleasant and familiar. But wait – perhaps I want my French reader to feel that English beat, to be slightly puzzled by that poetic rhythm from beyond the sea? And there I'll wrench my French into an awkward five-footed line.

I decide. I'm in charge. When you're reading-for-translation, you're exercising your critical reading skills and making that interpretation matter for writing. Thus translating teaches you a special kind of reading practice. You read with the eyes of a critic and a creator. Of course, all writers should read as widely as possible in their chosen genres and beyond, but when we say this we generally mean that they should do this for their own edification and/or for pleasure. Reading for translation adjusts a different kind of lens to your readerly eye; this is active reading, in the sense of reading activated by the writing that must come next.

So when I translated Meg Rosoff's minuscule novel *Moose Baby* (Barrington Stoke 2013), I needed to understand how she packed so much humour in so little space, and it was a free lesson in the mechanics of humour in literature. I learned to spot exactly where funny dwells, at the level of sentence, paragraph, page. But it was no academic exercise; none of this would have mattered unless I also thought about where to reinject that humour in the French rewriting. This is more than close reading – it's intimate reading: you reread the same sentence many times, holding in your head analytical considerations of literary devices, writerly considerations of effect, and your own sensitivity as a reader. In so doing, you learn to read better, and more precisely, as you start to develop a sense for the composition and aesthetics of even the tiniest units of text.

So go away and translate

So please: go away and translate. If you're lucky enough to have another language, use it for your writing. Write translations. Pick a book you love in the other language and translate it into your own. Not for money, not for networking, not for any kind of profitability as measured by normal standards. No one will thank you for it; you probably won't be paid for it. But it will teach you so much about reading and writing. It will teach you the amazing focus on language that only translating can afford – the aesthetic epiphanies brought about by the most minute of tweaks; the fact that so much in a good piece of literature depends on the right word; character, plot, and the way words pull them in this direction or that. The intense attention to words is a lesson you'll never learn better than when translating.

If you are unlucky enough to be monolingual, learn another language. I'm serious – do it. How can you claim to see what your own language can do if you can't watch it from the vantage point of another? All writers, if they really care about words and language – which is the stuff their work is made of, and therefore a professional requirement – should yearn to feel that estrangement, that distancing which brings understanding, knowledge and the destabilising sense that you can't say everything in your own language.

Careful – I'm not saying 'go away and become bilingual'. Fun fact: not all translators are fluent in the languages they translate *from*. Many can't actually hold a conversation. Translating is an act of writing and reading, not dazzling everyone with your perfect accent. Anyway, even bilinguals don't speak two languages perfectly. Even monolinguals don't speak their one language perfectly. Learn another language precisely, *because you'll never speak it perfectly.*

Start small. Pick up a picture book in whatever language you did at school, ages ago. Translate a few lines, painstakingly, using dictionaries and the internet. From that ugly literal translation, make a beautiful literary one. There you go. It's at the same time much more and much less difficult than it sounds.

People are awed by translators because they think 'they're really good at languages', whereas they should really be awed by thinking 'they're really good at writing'. You're good at writing, and that's all that matters: go and write translations. The more you do it, the more you'll develop that superpower and the better you'll write and the better you'll read. And one day you, too, will join that underground league of people who secretly think: 'Hey, writers. We know our stuff … *and* yours. Here we are, in your writing, taking your words, making them our words. No one's read you like we have. No one's rewritten you like we have. You are mine now.'

Clémentine Beauvais is a Senior Lecturer in English in Education at the University of York. She is also a writer for children and young adults in French, and a literary translator from English to French. Her books written in English include the *Sesame Seade Mysteries* series (Holiday House), *The Royal Babysitters* series (Bloomsbury Children's), *Piglettes* (Pushkin Press 2017, self-translated from the French) and *In Paris With You* (Wednesday Books 2019, translated by Sam Taylor). For more information visit www.clementinebeauvais.com/eng.

Books

Books

Who do children's authors write for?

When writing a children's book, who is an author really writing for? Michael Rosen shares his thoughts on this question and suggests what an author needs to take into account when writing.

People who can write for children don't come with a same format personality or a made-to-measure range of skills. We aren't people who can be easily categorised or lumped together. In part, this is because the world of children's books is constantly changing, starting out from a very diverse base in the first place. This derives from the fact that the world children inhabit is changing and indeed that there is a recognition within the children's books milieu that books are for everyone, not just one small section of the population.

In a way, this means that this is a great time to be writing or illustrating children's books. But that comes with a warning: diverse and changing – yes – but within a set of conventions (I won't say 'rules') and formats. Quite often, people who have written some stories or poems for children ask if I would take a look at them. Sometimes, the first problem that I can see with what they've written is that it doesn't 'fit in'. Or, another way of putting it, the writer hasn't taken a look at what's out there in the bookshops and schools and thought: how can I write something that could go alongside that book, or fit the same niche that that particular book occupies?

But what about artistic freedom? What about the rights of the writer to write about anything? Two things in response to that: nothing can stop you writing about anything you want to, however you want to. But there's no point in kidding ourselves that writing is really 'free'. We all write with our 'reading heads' on. That's to say, we write with the words, sentences, pages, chapters, plots, characters, scenes of the books we've read. If you say to yourself, 'I want to write a novel' or 'I want to write a picture book text', you're only doing so because your mind is full of novels or picture book texts. They are the 'already written' or the 'already read' material we write with. This affects everything we write, right down to the shape and structure of what we write, the tone we hit in the passages we write, the kinds of dialogue and thoughts we put into the writing. A crude analogy here is cooking. We cook with the ingredients that we are given. But more: if we say, we are going to make a cake, there is an understood outcome of what that will be (the cake), and an agreed set of ingredients that can arrive at that understood outcome. So, in a way, we not only cook with appropriate and given ingredients, we also cook with an understood outcome in mind. It has a shape, a smell and a taste that we expect the moment someone says, 'Here is a cake'. Our memory of past cakes prepares our mind and taste for what is to come. This set of memories of past writing and reading is what is in our mind as we write and indeed in the minds of the child readers as they sit down to something they can see is a book. These are what are known as the 'intertexts' we read and write with – memories of past texts.

Secondly, I would say that if you're interested in being published, then you have to look very, very closely at what publishers publish. This means looking at books not only from the point of view of what they say and how they say it. It also means looking at what kind of book it is and inquiring whether there are other books like it. How would you categorise it? This line of questioning puts into your mind a sense of format, of shape, of outcome to guide you as you write. Another analogy: an architect who is asked to design a house knows that he or she has to create rooms that are high enough and large enough for people to live in, that there is a basic minimum of kitchen and bathroom, there is a door to get in and out of, and so on. If it fulfils these conditions, we will call it a house – and not a factory, or a warehouse, say. It's a great help sometimes to look at books from an architect's point of view: what is particular to a book that makes it work? Ask yourself, how did the writer reveal what was coming next? Or, how did the writer hold back and conceal what was coming next? (Writing is a matter of revealing and concealing!) How did the writer arouse your interest? Was it an invitation to care about the people or creatures in the story? Or was it more to do with events or happenings? Or both? Did the book announce itself as being of a particular genre: thriller, historical fiction, comedy, etc? How did it do that? What are the requirements of that genre? Or is it a hybrid?

If all this sounds too technical let me introduce you to someone: the child. If you say to yourself, I'm going to write for children, then even as you say this, you're putting an imagined child (or children) into your mind. This is what literary theorists call 'the implied reader'. We do this in several ways. There might be a real child we know. Robert Louis Stevenson wrote *Treasure Island* largely as part of his relationship with his stepson, Lloyd. But even though we might say, 'RLS wrote it for Lloyd', this doesn't really explain things. What Stevenson was doing, possibly without knowing it, was keeping a mental map of Lloyd's speech and personality in his mind, so as he wrote, he had his version of Lloyd in his head monitoring, guiding and censoring what he was writing.

There is no single way of importing the implied child reader into your head. Some writers do it from memory, connecting with the child they once were and using that version of themselves to guide them in what they write and how they write it. They use memories of what they liked to read, how they themselves spoke and thought and perhaps wrote, when they were a child. Others immerse themselves in the company of children – their own, their grandchildren, nephews and nieces or children in playgroups, nurseries or schools. And some do it by immersing themselves so thoroughly in children's books that they pick up the implied child reader from the actual books. And of course, it's possible to work a combination of all of these ways. What I don't think you can do is ignore them all.

In fact, what you write can't avoid an implied reader. That may seem odd, because you might say that you had no one in mind when you wrote this or that. The reason you can't avoid it is because the language we use comes already loaded up with its audience. So, if I write, 'Capitalism is in crisis', this is a phrase that implies an audience that first of all understands English, then understands the words 'capitalism', 'crisis' and the phrase 'in crisis'. But more than that, it's an audience that wants to read something like that and is, in a sense, hungry or prepared and sufficiently 'read' to want to read such a sentence – or, more importantly, to go on wanting to read what comes next. If I write, 'My Dad was attacked by a banana …' then I'm already positioning the reader to think about someone who is a child and that child is telling something a bit absurd or possibly funny, perhaps the beginning of a family anecdote or family saga. It's also a 'tease', in that a reader who 'gets it', will know that bananas don't attack anyone. It implies a reader who knows that. In other words, the 'implied reader' is 'inscribed' into what we write. In a way, these implied readers are stuck to the words, phrases, sentences, plots and characters we write.

This means that as we write – and when we go back over what we've written – we need to think about the implied reader we've put there. Who is the child who is going to 'get it'? Who is the child who won't? What kind of children are we talking to? What aspects of those implied children's minds and childhoods are we talking to? The fearful person in the child? The envious one? The yearning one? The lonely one? The greedy one? And so on.

A last thought: we talk of 'writing for children'. To tell the truth, I don't think we do just write for children. I think we write as a way for adults to join the conversations that adults have with adults, adults have with children, children have with children – on the subject of what it means to be a child and live your life as a child. Because it's literature, this conversation often comes in code, with ideas and feelings embodied in symbols (teddy bears, giants, etc), it arouses expectations and hopes (what's coming next?) and because it's literature that children can and will read, it often comes along according to predictable outcomes (getting home, getting redeemed, being saved) that remove the obstacles to unhappiness and imperfection that the story began with, and so on. Nevertheless, children's literature has a magnificent history of saying important things to many people, often in a context where adults are caring for children. I think that's a good thing to attempt.

Michael Rosen has been writing since he was 16 and published his first book in 1969. As an author and by selecting other writers' works for anthologies he has been involved with over 200 books. His most recent books for children are *Who are Refugees and Migrants? What Makes People Leave Their Homes? And Other Big Questions* (Wayland 2019) and *Unexpected Twist, An Oliver Twist Tale* (Scholastic 2018). He was the Children's Laureate 2007–9 and has an MA and a PhD in Children's Literature. He is Professor of Children's Literature at Goldsmiths, University of London, where he co-devised and co-teaches the MA in Children's Literature. His website is www.michaelrosen.co.uk.

See also...
- *Spotting talent*, page 1
- *What makes a children's classic?*, page 4
- *A writer's ten commandments*, page 107

A writer's ten commandments

Michael Morpurgo offers a list of suggestions to help writers get the best out of their writing.

A writer's ten commandments … 'suggestions' may be a better word. Many of these I have not kept but know should be kept.

1. Read widely and often. It's how writers take exercise. Every book is a voyage of someone else's discovery. It is how you learn good and bad technique (useful to know both). It is how you explore the minds of other writers who have faced the blank page, stiffened their sinews, and done it. You can wonder at their achievement, at their mastery, and discover how it is done. Every book you read informs, builds confidence. With every book you read you are subconsciously finding your own voice. The more you read the more the music in words, the rhythm and cadence of a sentence becomes second nature. So read aloud sometimes – listen to literature, don't just read it.

2. Get the habit. Have a notebook handy, a writer's sketchbook – and jot down thoughts and ideas, memories, snatches of overheard conversations, moments of high drama, of quiet reflection. Frequency is important. The more you do it the less inhibited you become; the less you worry about words, the easier the flow comes. The habit takes the fear out of it. Writing becomes as natural a form of communication as speech. From these jottings will emerge the ideas for your stories and poems.

3. Live as full a life as possible, outside writing. Get out there, go places, meet people, experiment, take risks, move outside your comfort zone. Drink in the world around you, fill the well constantly, or else it will run dry. If that happens, then as a writer you are up a gumtree without a paddle – so to speak.

4. Take time, whacks of it, before you settle on the subject of the story you want to write. Read around it, dream around it, research around it, convince yourself you really want to spend months, possibly years of your life roaming around in this idea, developing it, loving it. Don't be in a hurry to decide. But once you've decided don't look back. Your story could turn to stone. And you could too.

5. Live in dreamtime for as long as it takes before you ever set pen to paper. Don't confront the blank page or screen till you've dreamed up the set design, till your players are walking live on your stage, strutting and fretting, till you can see them and hear them, till you know them intimately and the world they live in. You don't have to have decided where they will take you, what the denouement might be – remember that when it comes as a surprise to you, it'll be a surprise to the reader too.

6. Be comfortable when you write. You will be tense, and excited and anxious. So arrange yourself so that you don't hurt yourself. Wrists, shoulders, neck, the lower back bear the brunt of writing. Don't hunch over. Don't stay sitting too long. Get up and walk about every half hour. If you dry up, don't sit over it. Go for a walk, put it out of your mind and come back fresh. Do what I do, what Robert Louis Stevenson did, write on your bed, pillows piled up behind you, relaxed, at ease with yourself. Then you can go to sleep easily too – a very useful writing technique I find.

7. Once you begin, finish it. Go through with it to the final full stop. Every abandoned manuscript is a knockback, a huge dent in a writer's confidence. And confidence is the key to a writer's morale. Writers' block is simply a lack of confidence engendered by a lack of sufficient dreamtime.

8. Mean every word you write. What we are asking of a reader is to suspend disbelief. Our technique as writers, our writing voice, can help here. But most important is that we have to believe in the story we're writing. We mustn't pretend, we must mean it. Mean it and they'll read as you meant it and they'll listen. Mean it and they'll be moved to laughter and tears.

9. Rewrite, cut – if in doubt, cut it out! Edit yourself before anyone else does. You are your own best editor. Which is not to say that we don't need a good editor, we absolutely do. But never send it off half done, not right, not truly imagined and thought through. Read it out loud to yourself – feel the rhythm, listen to the music. It's fun and the best fault-finder I know.

10. Forget all about getting published, being famous, being rich. Abandon those dreams if you have them. Excise all such aspirations and ambitions. This is a prerequisite to becoming a writer of truth and integrity – I'm not sure if any other kind of writing is worth bothering about.

And one for luck: Don't sit around waiting for a publisher's or an agent's response to your book. You've done it, done your best. Simply get on with dreaming up your next one. If the reject letter comes, don't be downhearted. We've all been there. You pick yourself up, dust yourself down, and on you go …

This article first appeared in *Writing Children's Fiction: A Writers' & Artists' Companion* © Yvonne Coppard and Linda Newbery 2013.

Michael Morpurgo is one of Britain's best-loved writers for children. The author of more than 100 books, he was the Children's Laureate 2003–5. *War Horse* (Kaye & Ward 1982), reached wide audiences as a stage play at London's National Theatre and as a film, directed by Stephen Spielberg. Michael's many awards include the Blue Peter Book of the Year, the Whitbread Children's Book Award, the Nestlé Smarties Book Prize, the Red House Children's Book Award and (three times) the Prix Sorcières. With his wife, Clare, he set up Farms for City Children, a charity which enables urban children to experience country life and animal husbandry. He was knighted in the 2018 New Year's Honours. His latest books include *Flamingo Boy* (HarperCollins 2018), *Grandpa Christmas* (Egmont 2018), *In The Mouth of The Wolf* (Egmont 2018) and *Poppy Field* (Royal British Legion 2018).

See also...
● *Editing your work*, page 410

Writing books to read aloud

Bestselling author Anne Fine looks at why and how books are read aloud to children.

The first thing to say about writing books to read aloud is that they should be as much of a pleasure to read alone silently as any other story. Indeed, at first it's difficult to see where any differences might lie. Certainly when it comes to stories for the very young we tend to have a picture in our heads of the exhausted parent inviting the child to 'clean your teeth, hop into bed, and I'll read you a story'. And since all days are long for a parent, nobody wants their offspring to be worked into a frenzy all over again. So, in the classic bedtime stories for the younger child, there's very often a softer humour and a gentler tone, and a satisfactory and fulfilling ending.

And for the older child, there often isn't.

So, same old story really. No rules (or having to face the fact that rules appear to be there only for some other writer to irritate you intensely by making a fortune breaking them). But there are always the basic guidelines.

Keep things as simple as they can be for your particular story. With picture books you can of course assume that the child is propped up beside the reader, sharing each illustration as it comes along. But by the time the child is six, maybe they would prefer to snuggle down and shut their eyes to listen. So do you really have to take half a dozen sentences to describe the rigging, and the number and nature of the sails, and exactly how the ship was armed? Couldn't you just refer to it as 'the most magnificent galleon that ever sailed the seas' and leave it at that? After all, if those cannon ever come to be fired, we'll hear about it later.

Listeners are easily distracted. One minute they're all ears; the next, they're actually more interested in tracking the progress of a fly across the ceiling. Of course they're not going to admit they've lost the thread of the story, in case the parent snatches the opportunity to suggest they're too tired to listen and makes for the door, or the teacher decides it's time to move on to the workbooks. But their attention does stray. So it is best to try (as ever) to order your tale so you can start at the beginning and move on in sequence, steering clear of flashbacks.

On this matter of keeping things simple, does it sound mad to say that plots can be overrated? And never more so than in books designed to be read aloud to the young. In my own very short chapter book, *It Moved!*, Lily takes a stone in for Show and Tell and claims it sometimes moves, and we just get to see who in the class believes her and who doesn't, and how they all react over a day of watching it. In the *Stories of Jamie and Angus*, Jamie is an amiable child of about four in a perfectly normal household. His favourite soft toy is a little Aberdeen Angus bull. In the first story, Angus ends up in the washing machine when he's supposed to be 'dry clean only'. In another, the pair sort out the books in their bedroom according to their own rather strange shelving preferences. In yet another, they do little more than draw 'angry eggs'. The stories almost couldn't be more plain and domestic, and yet we still run through joy and misery, jealousy, anxiety, distress, fear, empathy, generosity, self-sacrifice, fury, resentment – the entire mercurial gamut of pre-school emotions. So do be confident that, especially for the very young, a tremendous amount can be forged from what seems, at first sight, not very much at all. With writing –

just as with practically everything else in life – it's not what you do but the way that you do it.

Children, like adults, have to *care* about what's being read. We adults tend to ask the 'Can I be *bothered* with these people?' question before returning a book, half-read, to the library. It's a test even harder to pass when you're writing for young ones. Remember Robert Browning:

If you want your songs to last
Base them on the human heart

because children love to identify with someone or something in the story – it doesn't really matter what. It could be another child, or a puppy, or even a lost pebble. But they do have to care. So perhaps it's best to make sure that, all the way through, your listener knows what your character (or puppy, or pebble) is feeling. And make sure that these are thoughts and emotions they will recognise. A child of six isn't 'disappointed that the weather is unpleasant'. It's all far more immediate. He feels the tears pricking because his socks are wet and his woolly hat is itching and his coat's too tight under his armpits. Ever heard them moan?

Joan Aiken once remarked that anyone who writes for the young 'should, ideally, be a dedicated semi-lunatic'. But you can go too far. The problem is one of differing – and shifting – levels of sophistication. What makes one child hoot with laughter will cause another to sneer, and there is in any case an entirely undefinable line between cashing in on a child's acceptance of the unlikely or the magical, and offering them something they think of as simply being 'stupid'. You might, for example, get away with the idea that the horse the child rescued from its cruel owner is being secretly kept in the garage, only to find your young readers baulking at the suggestion that Mum could walk in to fetch a screwdriver and not even notice it.

Avoid being arch. Of course there are differing levels at which many shared books can be read. The older reader often gets a sly chuckle out of things that sail right over the head of somebody smaller. But the joke does usually have to be at least potentially inclusive, so that, the tenth time around, out comes the thumb, down comes the chubby hand to stop you turning the page, and out comes the question: 'Daddy was just teasing them, really, wasn't he?' 'Mum *really* wanted to get back to reading the paper, didn't she?' In the benighted language of the National Curriculum, the child's already 'drawing inferences from text' (or, as we used to call it back in the good old days, 'reading').

Does it help to read your work aloud to children to see how it goes down? Not really, no. For one thing most children are notoriously polite and gentle with people they love, or strangers who come into class. And the sheer joy of having their opinions canvassed can send them haywire. One says, 'I liked this bit!' You beam, and all the other hands shoot up. 'I liked that bit!' 'And I liked that bit!' Everyone wants to have a go at the pleasure of shouting out to the visitor.

So trust your own judgement. You are the writer, after all. Try reading it aloud to an imaginary son or daughter or class. You'll soon notice which bits you're rushing through because they're tiresome, and which of the sentences you're tripping over because they're too clumsy or long. You'll realise that, yes, you *can* put that rather ambitious word into a story for four year-olds because the very context and the way in which it will be read out will make its meaning transparent.

Are there some subjects best avoided in books to be shared between adults and children? Again, it's hard to say. Some parents will read anything the child demands. Others, like teachers, will beach up on things like 'pottymouth' poetry ('Well, *you* just said bogey! And you just said poo *twice!*'). Or books that appear to encourage the child to relish – or, worse, be amused by – cruelty and the infliction of pain. I watched as at least 30 parents with small children trooped out of a book fair when one enthusiastic author read out a passage from one of his history books about red hot pokers being driven up people's bottoms. (I wondered, frankly, why the others stayed.) He may justifiably argue that he's sold hundreds of thousands of copies, but I would guess that few of them have been read aloud by squeamish parents to imaginative children before the lights go out. So use your sense.

What about *how* a book is read aloud? Should that make a difference to how you write it? I don't see how it can. After all, some readers treat the words in the old-fashioned way, and simply speak them with intelligence and inflections sympathetic to the meaning. They read, in short, as if it were a *book*. Others go half-mad, acting out every sentence, doing all the voices in different accents, shouting the yells and whispering the quiet bits. They treat the pages in front of them pretty well as a script for a stage performance. Like every other author whose work has been professionally recorded, I've shuddered through one actor's butchering of my work with his frantic showing off, and also been startled to find tears pricking as another has used her skills to mine a poignancy I had forgotten about or never even realised was there. It's their own voice that most writers hear in their head as they put down the words, so go along with that.

And that's the root of all writing, when it comes down to it. Your own voice. Children are strange. Ralph Waldo Emerson defined them as 'curly dimpled lunatics'. They assume that they're immortal. (Why else do adults have to step in so smartly and often, simply to keep them alive?) And children are at one with eternity. (When did you last see a nine-year-old glance at a clock and say, 'My God! It's three already! And I've got nothing done!') Their lives may change immeasurably. See how the language of their stories has moved so seamlessly over the centuries from tumbledown cottages in dark forests, through secret gardens and kind governesses, to the babysitter and the stepbrother. But in their essential nature – however individual and various those natures may be – children have barely changed at all.

So the successful children's authors will always be those who can best make their work chime in with the child's capacity to understand and enjoy it. And since, like Walt Whitman, all children 'contain multitudes', that gives the writer enormous scope to get it very, very wrong or very, very right.

Anne Fine OBE, FRSL is one of the best-known and most popular writers for children of all ages and was Children's Laureate 2001–3. She has twice won both the Carnegie Medal and the Whitbread Children's Book of the Year Award and at the Galaxy British Book Awards has twice been voted Children's Author of the Year. She has also won the *Guardian* Children's Fiction Prize and dozens of other awards in the UK and abroad. Her work is translated into more than 45 languages. Her latest book for older readers is *Blood Family* (Doubleday 2014) and for younger readers, *Sixteen Sisters* (OUP 2016). Anne also writes for adults. Her website is www.annefine.co.uk.

Writing for reluctant readers

Jon Mayhew describes some of the factors that discourage many children from reading and has some valuable rules and insights for writers on how to engage these young readers and inspire a passion for books.

Writing for reluctant readers … what does that even mean? Grouping readers into one huge category can be problematic. If you're writing for so-called 'reluctant readers', it is worth considering the reasons someone might be hesitant to read in the first place. There are some children who might actually want to read, but who find it so difficult to follow the text that they give up; there might be those who see reading as a waste of time; others may read slowly and fear failure when they feel pressured to get through a text quickly.

There are many books that readers such as these may enjoy: graphic novels, Manga, books with an even distribution and mix of image and text, but for the purposes of this article I'm talking about books specifically written with reluctant readers in mind. These books tend to have content that would be suitable for older readers but a lower reading age requirement to access them, and so are referred to as Hi-Lo books: in short, high interest age matched with low reading age.

I'm not sure if I was a reluctant reader as a child. I certainly wasn't a fast one. I never finished the school reading scheme, and there was something about the pressure of having to read a pile of books that sucked all the joy out of it. It made me not want to read. When I go into schools and talk to students who don't like reading, they identify strongly with that sentiment. A thick book can be off-putting in the same way; there's a point at which you have to put it down and then it sits there, awaiting your return, demanding your attention. What if you lose your page? What if you can't remember all the characters? What if it takes ages to read and you forget the beginning of the story or it turns out to have a disappointing ending? Won't that be a waste of time? Keeping books to a manageable length is important. Hi-Lo books can be anything from 250 words up to a maximum of 15,000.

I was a very visual child and I collected thousands of *Marvel* comics. These kept me in touch with storytelling; they moved fast, things happened, and I knew who was saying what to whom. Later in life, as a special needs teacher and a qualified dyslexia tutor, I found that children in my classes loved being read to. They loved short stories the most – something with a strong opening and a satisfying payoff at the end. I also had the joy of encouraging them to read for pleasure, on their own, without someone to interpret and explain each complex word or metaphor. Some of the Hi-Lo books we read were great, but many seemed to stop halfway through a story or just peter out, or they would include an endless stream of bum and poo jokes. So, when I was asked to write a book for reluctant readers a few years later, I had a fire in my belly and an eagerness to get it right.

The first thing you realise, when you start to write any kind of fiction, is that there are no hard and fast rules. Having said that, there probably *are* some rules when it comes to writing books for reluctant readers. Here are some:

1. Read and research the market

Just as in writing for any other genre, you should be familiar with what is already available. There's no point pitching a book to a publisher who already has that genre on their list.

Most publishers have an imprint that prints books for reluctant readers, but some only commission work from established authors. Some publishers produce books that are exclusively sold to schools: you can find out more about publishers and their submissions guidelines in the directory sections of this yearbook.

2. Find out what kinds of books reluctant readers like

Reluctant readers are individuals with their own tastes and preferences. They may read comics or enjoy stories through video games or film. Trying to find one kind of story that will appeal to all reluctant readers is doomed to failure. I often hear people suggest that the 'choose-your-own-ending' books are great for such readers. This is because, at each page, the reader has a choice to make and they 'control' the story. I know authors who tell me that these were the books that kept them reading when they were young. My son was a reluctant reader, but he hated such stories because, in his words, 'They never end, you don't know when they are going to finish.' Study of the current market shows that publishers are producing books that closely follow trends and tastes in the mainstream. You can find dystopia, thrillers, contemporary stories and books that reflect concerns that are relevant to a teenage reader today. Publishers are concerned that these books must look and feel like 'real books.'

3. Consider the structure, features and form

Structure

The general points about writing good commercial fiction also apply to books for reluctant readers; the story needs a strong structure, with a great beginning that will hook the reader and keep them turning the page, and an exciting middle that will carry them along to a satisfying conclusion. Books for reluctant readers usually differ in that they tend to rely on a linear narrative using a single point of view. Stories with multiple viewpoints, lots of flashbacks, or an unreliable narrator may make it difficult for some readers to follow the thread of a story. For the Hi-Lo book, storytelling should be paramount.

Characters

The rules for characters are much the same as for general fiction, but there shouldn't be too many or the reader may find it difficult to keep track of them all. Characters should be engaging and the reader should be able to connect with them in some way. I would argue, too, that the reader should be able to relate to the character's experiences. This isn't to say that you should only write about events that happen in a child's life, as stories don't have to be firmly anchored in the real world for a child to be able to relate to the character's experiences; a story on the theme of competition can be set on a pirate ship or on an alien planet and the reader will still recognize and connect with a competitive character. Characters can be multi-layered or nuanced, too; you just might have to explain a little more, and leave less to the reader's imagination.

Sentences and paragraphs

A story has to flow and sentences have to be varied. You can't tell an exciting story using nothing but short, simplistic sentences. Try to keep long sentences with sub-clauses to a minimum, though, without ruining the flow of the story. Short paragraphs will help the reader navigate their way through the story and this also breaks the page into manageable, bite-size chunks.

Books

Words

When I was a special needs teacher, I met quite a few children with profound dyslexia who could spell 'pterodactyl' but had trouble with simple three- or four-letter words. Sometimes it was the shape of the word that stuck in their minds, or that there was a striking visual image to go with the word; they were so interested and motivated by the subject of dinosaurs that the spelling of pterodactyl entered their brain and stayed there. Concrete nouns often have a clear visual image attached to them and so you can use these, even if they are difficult to spell, whereas abstract nouns with unusual spellings, such as 'fatigue', can present problems. Words with problematic letter blends, '-ough' words for example, should be avoided too.

Metaphor and imagery

We love a good metaphor; it wraps up a lot of description in one neat image, but if someone struggles with abstract concepts, then they might not understand why, all of a sudden, the main character is a pig when they're having their dinner. A simple simile might work in these cases, but always ask yourself – is this helping the story move along? If the answer is no, then cut it out.

Plain language

Keeping language straightforward is fine, but don't think for a moment that just because you are using simple words, your meaning won't be ambiguous or confusing. I remember reading a well-known children's fantasy novel that shall remain nameless and coming across the sentence: 'His breath came out in short pants.' Now, I knew what the writer meant, but another part of my brain created a completely different image and dragged me right out of the story!

Direct speech

If you have characters speaking to each other, it is important to make it clear who is speaking every time. Avoid overuse of pronouns that may cause the reader to lose track of who is speaking.

4. The writing process

The actual process of writing very much depends on what works for you. Generally, the advice is to write the story first; don't worry about sentence length or confusing words, just get the writing on the page. Once you have your story, then you can redraft it, change the sentence structure, eliminate confusing words or phrases and make sure your story is told as smoothly as possible. Read the story aloud and see if it flows.

Doing a road test

When your story is finished, you might ask: should I 'road test' my story with some reluctant readers? This is a fine thing to do – just so long as you ignore the praise and listen to the criticism. You should always be wary of a small group of children telling you that they loved your story; they may just be trying to flatter you, or they may feel flattered to have been consulted, making them biased in their response, or they may be simply giving you the answer they think you want to hear. Getting some brutal, honest feedback such as, 'I didn't understand why Joe did X' tells you more about your story than, 'We really loved it.' And please, please, please – never tell an agent or an editor that you read your story to some children and they loved it!

Jon Mayhew was a Writing Fellow for the Royal Literary Fund at the University of Chester. He was an English teacher for 25 years and is passionate about encouraging young writers and readers. He delivers writing workshops in schools and is a patron of reading for two high schools. His books, published by Bloomsbury, include *Mortlock* (2011), *The Demon Collector* (2012) and *The Bonehill Curse* (2012), and four titles in his *Monster Odyssey* series, including *The Curse of the Ice Serpent* (2015). His Hi-Lo books, published by Badger Learning, are *Death Road* (2014), *Death Wheels* (2016), *Have A Go* (2017) and *Dark Cove* (2019). He also writes Primary reading scheme books for OUP and Collins. His latest book, *Storycraft: How to Teach Creative Writing* is published in 2019 by Crown House Publishing. See more at www.jonmayhew.co.uk and follow him on Twitter @MayhewJ.

Finding new readers and markets

Tom Palmer shows how, by seeking out unexpected working partnerships, a children's author can open up mutually rewarding and productive markets and draw in new young readers.

I have managed to make a living as a full-time children's author for eight years. As everyone who has tried it knows, it is not easy to earn enough money to live on from being a writer. You're forever in fear. Forever asking yourself questions … How long will people want to buy your books? Will school events dry up as finances tighten and the political landscape changes? There is little respite, even if you are living the dream. Which I am.

That's why I spend a lot of time trying to think of ways I can attract interest to my books, so that people will continue to buy and borrow them. And so schools will keep paying me to visit. One of the most successful ways I have found to do this is to *give*.

Looking for partnerships

There are a lot of organisations, charities and companies who would benefit from working with a children's author. But who are they? What can you give them? And, what can they give you? I have developed relationships with several organisations – large and small – giving and taking. In partnership. As a result of those partnerships, I have boosted my longevity as a children's author.

Each partnership is different and each evolves in its own unpredictable way. But it usually starts with a series of questions that I ask myself, and which I suggest you ask *yourself*. Here is a plan of action:
• Think about what you've written. List subjects, settings, themes, ideas. And dig deep. Text your friends and family. Your readers. Ask them what *they* think you write about.
• Now look at your list. Are there natural partners for your work? (For instance, Beatrix Potter might have chosen the RSPCA, a pet shop chain or *Animals & You* magazine. Or she might not.)

> ### How to approach potential partners
> 1 The more you know about the possible partner the better. That includes researching the right person to contact.
> 2 Offer to do as much of the set-up and admin work as you can. They are likely to be under massive time-pressure with their job already.
> 3 When you meet for the first time, try to make it open and creative. Set it up as a thinking/sharing session, not just a blast of ideas from you.
> 4 You probably have to be willing to give first, to do stuff for free to demonstrate that your partnership could help them. Then, as your relationship evolves, the balance will tip back in your favour.

• Suss out one or more partners whose work is linked to what you write about. Again, stretch it. Brainstorm; be creative. Have ideas that are stupid. Cross them out. Have more. There might be one that fits.
• Think carefully about those potential partners. Go to their website. Watch them. What do they do? What do they want to achieve? Can you help them?
• Now think about what you could ask for from *them*. How can they help you to promote your books? Or, how can you link with them help you to promote your books?

Case studies

Over the last decade I have worked successfully with the RAF Museums, England Rugby, the Premier League, Divine Chocolate, Leeds Schools Library Service and many others.

Below are three different examples. They could help you see how to identify suitable partners that fit the writing and themes of your own books – ones you might approach as potential partners.

Fair trade chocolate

I was writing a book about football and fair trade for Puffin. It's called *Off Side* and includes storylines relating to the trafficking of young African footballers and to fair-trade cocoa bean farming. I needed help to write it. A lot of help. From people who knew about football and chocolate in Africa.

So I did a bit of research. In fact, my wife did. She came up with Divine Chocolate who work with fair-trade farmers so that the likes of us can give them a fair wage for what they farm. I identified the Right to Dream football academy in Ghana. They look after gifted young child footballers and help protect them from being exploited by corrupt football agents. I contacted both, suggesting that I could help raise awareness of what they do. Could they explain it to me? Could they help me research and write a meaningful book? They said they could.

I went to Ghana at my own expense. I saw everything I needed to see. It was amazing. When I got home I promoted Divine and Right to Dream and the great work they do through writing my story. And my book continues to sell well because it was properly researched and I knew what I was talking about. Job done.

But relationships evolve. When *Off Side* was published, Divine wanted me to tell the story of how fair trade makes a difference. They gave me a PowerPoint. I used it as part of my talk in schools. I did this for free, of course. But it enhanced my school events, made them more meaningful. As a result, more schools wanted to book me to go in and talk to their pupils, meaning my book became better known in schools with fair-trade status and beyond. More book sales. More paid school events. And the raising of awareness of very important issues.

Ask yourself:
– *Does my book deal with an issue or a cause?*
– *Which charity or campaign group might be interested in working with me?*
– *How can I help that cause through my book and events?*

The Royal Air Force

I was writing a series about children going back in time to fly famous RAF aeroplanes. I approached three organisations to ask if they'd like to work with me. Two did not reply. The RAF Museums did.

The RAF Museums have some amazing artefacts in their collections at Hendon and Cosford: tiny kite-like planes from the First World War; terrifying giants like the Vulcan bomber. But the RAF Museums are always looking for ways to bring those planes to life. For ways to tell the story behind them, and about the men and women who flew them. That was what they needed. A way of telling more stories. That's what I could give.

I volunteered to do a school event for them for free, to see if we could work together. It was a success, and they offered to pay me for the next one. Six months later, they had a new exhibition called 'First World War in the Air'. They asked me how we could work together to tell a story about the pilots. One of their exhibits is of the possessions of a 19-year-old pilot, Kevin Furniss, who was killed on his second sortie. His gloves. His shaving equipment. His Bible. His pipe. Letters home. These items were poignant enough on their own, but I suggested writing a story about Furniss using those objects before his fateful flight. The museum then used the story in schools to attract visitors. And I was paid for the story.

Now I am the museum's Children's Writer in Residence. I do four school and public events a year for them, based around the three important planes from their collections that I have since – with their help – written books about: the Sopwith Camel; the Spitfire; and the Eurofighter Typhoon. My book is on sale in their shops. They promote my events and books to the many RAF and aeroplane interest groups that they work with. We bring schools into their museum and run writing workshops based around their aircraft and artefacts.

Ask yourself:

– *Is there subject matter in my books that relates to a museum, gallery, festival, interest group?*

– *Which ones should I research and what might they be interested in from me?*

– *How could I or my book help them?*

– *Can we work together?*

England Rugby

I had a trilogy of rugby stories published in 2015 by Barrington Stoke (*Rugby Academy: Combat Zone*; *Rugby Academy: Dead Locked*; and *Rugby Academy: Surface to Air*). We timed their publication to tie in with the Rugby World Cup, hosted in the UK that year.

I contacted the education people at England Rugby, the RFU, in the hope that I could apply for money to create literacy interventions. With the RFU as a partners, I'd have a good chance. I suggested that the RFU and I apply for money to tour an event at the library near each of the 13 Rugby World Cup venues. I also suggested a set of literacy resources linking rugby to reading for pleasure and writing. And I said that I could write a live story to be read in schools as the Rugby World Cup was on. Would they be interested?

They were. My ideas met their needs because the RFU are keen to get into schools. They want to use the interest in the game to encourage children to read and write. They want to spread the culture of their five core values. And they want to start more rugby teams in schools to help create players for the future. So they offered to pay for it all direct, with no need to apply for funding.

I now work regularly with the RFU, performing events, creating resources and writing stories that they publish on their website. This has led to my *Rugby Academy* series becoming very well-known in rugby circles. Which goes a long way to explaining how all three sold out their advance within a year of publication.

Ask yourself:

– *Is there an activity or interest at the centre or on the margins of my book?*

– *Does a national or regional body administer that interest?*

– *Who can I work with? Who would be interested in my book?*

Working with partners has been a massive boon for my career. If I had not sought out those partners, I think that my full-time writing career may well have ground to a halt. In addition, I have been able to promote the joys of reading for pleasure to children and families I might not have reached without the help of those partners. And that is deeply satisfying and very much on my agenda. One downside could be that – in always working with partners – I am a slave to *their* agenda. I try to overcome that by making sure the books I write with partners always meet whatever my obsession of the moment is. Also, the good money I make from working with partners buys me time to write other work that is 100% what I want to do.

Tom Palmer is the author of three Puffin football series, *Football Academy*, *Foul Play* and *The Squad*. *Foul Play* was shortlisted for the 2008 Blue Peter Book Award. His other books include *Ghost Stadium* (2013), the *Rugby Academy* series (2015), and *Over the Line* (2014), all published by Barrington Stoke. His newest books include *Armistice Runner* (Barrington Stoke 2018), *D-Day Dog* (Barrington Stoke 2019) and three books in a rebooted *Roy of the Rovers* series published by Rebellion Graphic Novels (2018–19). Tom is Children's Writer in Residence at the RAF Museum. Find out more at http://tompalmer.co.uk, and follow him on Twitter @tompalmerauthor.

Writing adventures in the real world: children's non-fiction

Isabel Thomas explores the exciting world of children's non-fiction, and shares her tips for writing the perfect pitch.

Why write non-fiction?

Children's non-fiction is so much more than 'books with facts'. It's a different way for writers to reach young readers, to take them on a journey that makes them laugh, or cry, or bubble over with enthusiasm. It inspires children to explore their world – and to change it.

Recent years have seen an exciting renaissance in the genre. New children's non-fiction imprints have been launched, and publishers are investing in lavish illustrations and large formats. Bookshops and libraries have reconfigured their shelves to make space for titles big enough to dive into. Children's non-fiction titles appear in bestseller charts, award shortlists and festival programmes. Readers – and their families – are demonstrating a huge appetite for bold and beautiful adventures in the real world.

It's an exciting time to be writing and illustrating children's non-fiction, and the scope for creativity is huge. I've written picture books, graphic texts and biographies where text and illustrations play together on the page. I've created educational books for libraries and classrooms, activity books packed with paper engineering, and hands-on crafts and experiments.

A good children's non-fiction book is nothing like a textbook. It's an opportunity to tell a complete story that helps children connect bite-sized facts with the bigger picture.

Where do I begin?

Find something that excites YOU, and then work out the best way to pass that excitement on to young readers. For me, it's science and nature.

My first book was about blue and purple foods. Educational non-fiction is often published in series, and the mainstream colours had already been covered! As debuts go it was low key. But it gave me the confidence to offer my services as a science writer to other publishers. Finding your niche is useful in winning that first commission, but it's not enough to know your subject area in depth. To make a topic irresistible to children, you need to know your readers too.

Spend time with children and immerse yourself in their world. Not just literature, but TV, films, apps and playground trends. Children's non-fiction competes with all of these things. I volunteer as a school governor, a role that keeps me in touch with curriculum change, and the influences that shape children's lives. I also read at libraries and run school events. 130 books into my career, I've become an expert in thinking like an eight-year-old.

Finding your angle

The value of a non-fiction book lies not just in the information delivered – which must of course be accurate and up-to-date – but in the way it's presented. How will you hook your reader, so that your book educates *and* entertains? Play with ideas, make connections, and take your readers on a journey. It might be through humour, adventure, or quirky details. Or it might be by making a complex topic simple enough to give a child that 'wow' moment.

A strong angle helps a non-fiction book stand out on a crowded shelf. Instead of listing facts about space, weave them into an alien's guide to the solar system, or a book of rocket science for beginners. If you're writing about life cycles, how about a zookeeper's handbook, or a hypothetical battle of lion versus tiger?

Developing your idea

At this point, a fiction author would write the first draft, ready to polish to perfection. The advice for non-fiction is rather different: don't write the book!

Children's non-fiction is usually a team effort, combining the author's ideas with those of talented editors, illustrators and designers to create something extraordinary. Unless you are pitching a picture book, there is usually no need to write the entire manuscript up front. Instead, develop a proposal and a few sample spreads, and make these as polished as you can. Once your idea has been commissioned, the editor will work with you to refine the approach, perfect the pacing of content, and finalise the text features.

Don't forget to visit bookshops and libraries as you develop your idea. Holding the latest children's non-fiction books in your hands is much more revealing than looking at covers online. Get a feel for the typical extent and word count for each age group. How will you build knowledge and understanding over 48, 64 or 96 pages? Will you write a picture book with 20 words per page, or a reference book with 200? Read as many examples as you can to absorb the language level. Make a note of the page features that non-fiction writers use to break up the text into manageable chunks.

Writing a proposal – dos and don'ts

Children's non-fiction authors work with publishers in several different ways. The first will be familiar if you already write fiction. Pitch an original idea and negotiate an advance and royalty. Some non-fiction authors work with literary agents; others, like me, pitch directly to publishers and use the excellent Society of Authors (see page 349) for advice on contracts. When I worked as a non-fiction commissioning editor, I was equally happy to hear from both.

Editors also come to me with a subject in mind and ask for a text treatment – a fresh new approach that will work for their market. In this case, the remuneration may be a one-off fee, higher than the advance for a similar title. Either way, my first task for each new title is to write a concise and engaging proposal to make the case for my idea.

Begin with an **overview** that showcases your style and tone. It should be good enough to become the back-cover blurb (and it often does). Follow this attention-grabbing introduction with a longer **description**. Explain why the book is timely, perfect for the target age group, and why you are the best person to write it. There's no need to send the whole manuscript (unless you are writing a short picture book). Instead provide a **breakdown of the structure**, showing how will you build engagement and understanding. Finally, include two or three pages of **sample text** to bring the idea to life.

DO:

• **Explain why you are pitching to this publisher**. Visit bookshops and scour catalogues, including the rights catalogues that publishers produce for book fairs. Find out what makes their books special. Then show why your idea and their list are a perfect match.

Books

• **Come up with an attention-grabbing title** that hints at both subject matter and approach. Humorous and irreverent or lyrical and atmospheric? Hands-on activities or narrative adventure?

• **Point out anything that might drive sales**, such as anniversaries, curriculum links or exhibitions. Remember to work at least 18-24 months ahead – illustrated non-fiction takes around a year to journey from manuscript to shelf.

• **Showcase your voice.** Ten years ago, children's non-fiction often had a formal tone, edited to match house style. Today, a unique voice will help you stand out.

DON'T:

• **Claim that there is no competition**. More often than not, this points to a lack of research. Competition can prove that a topic is in demand. Publishers will always offer books on dinosaurs, space and animals and are hungry for creative new approaches to these popular themes. Compare your idea to existing titles – ideally successful ones! Explain why your approach will be different (and better).

• **Include illustrations**. Unless you're an author-illustrator, it's the publisher's role to find an illustrator that the audience will love (often, but not always, with your approval). Instead, note down ideas about the type of illustrations you think would work well, as part of your overall vision for the book.

• **Mention how much your family and friends like the idea**. Publishers get many proposals saying 'tested on my kids'. It's better to present the skills and experience that make you an expert in your subject area or target audience – or both!

Writing the book – three golden rules

1. Research is key

One of the best things about writing for a living is the chance to dive into a subject. You might be writing for ten-year-olds, but you'll need to understand your topic in much greater depth. To avoid introducing errors, track down original sources. If you read an interesting article, find the original research too. Better still, interview the author. Insist on two sources for every fact (and never make one of those sources Wikipedia). And be warned – when you're interviewing stuntwomen, scientists or astronauts, job envy is an occupational hazard!

2. Play on the page

Hooking the audience doesn't end with a creative angle. Every page, paragraph and sentence must work hard to weave in the information you'd like to cover, while keeping readers engaged.

Make good use of text features, such as infographics, charts, text boxes and quotes. They can help you to bring interesting facts to the fore, enticing a reader to explore the rest of the page. They also help to pace the flow of information, making complex topics or arguments easier to follow.

Resist the temptation to include everything. First drafts are often double the length of the final text, and the real work comes in deciding what to leave out.

3. Think visually

Illustrations are a key ingredient in children's non-fiction. Sourcing these illustrations (whether buying photographs, or commissioning illustrators) is the job of the publisher. But briefing them is the job of the author.

Think like an art director – how will information be broken up into chunks and displayed on the page? What diagrams will help you to explain a difficult concept? Will you include cartoons and visual jokes? An information book might need simple photo briefs, while a graphic text demands detailed descriptions of every panel. Create a wish list, to be realized by a talented illustrator and designer.

Building a writing career

Children's non-fiction authors develop valuable skills: the ability to carry out in-depth research, to write at just the right level for a certain age group, and to build a story that educates and entertains. These skills are in demand outside book publishing – by companies, charities and organisations that want to create outreach resources, by children's magazines, museums and science centres, and by producers of educational websites, blogs and vlogs. Writing other types of non-fiction content helps you keep your voice and ideas fresh. It can also be another way to reach your audience if you have an idea that's close to your heart, but find that there is no commercial demand for it in book form.

As a non-fiction author, you are well placed to **design and run events** linked to your writing. For example, pitch yourself to local schools, museums and festivals; run craft sessions in bookshops and libraries; help children unleash their own non-fiction writing power in an interactive workshop. Events are a direct way to keep in touch with your readers, and you'll come away with dozens of ideas for new books.

Nothing beats the feeling of discovering something wonderful for the first time. Whether I'm writing a biography, an activity book or a picture book, I aim to give readers the same feeling. If I can encourage children to pick up a book, think 'wow', and keep reading, I know I've done a good job. But if they read something that encourages them to close the book, head outside and explore the world ... well, then I know I've done a *great* job.

Where will your next non-fiction adventure take you?

Isabel Thomas has written more than 150 non-fiction and fiction books for children, published by Bloomsbury, Oxford University Press, Penguin Random House, Laurence King, Collins, Pearson, DK, Rising Stars, Raintree, QED, Curious Fox and Wren & Rook. Her titles have been shortlisted for the Royal Society Young People's Book Prize, the Association of Science Education's Book of the Year Award, and the Blue Peter Book Awards. She also writes for the children's science magazines *Whizz Pop Bang!*, *The Week Junior Science+Nature* and *STEM*. Isabel's most recent publications include *This Book is Not Rubbish* (Wren & Rook 2018), the *Little Guides to Great Lives* series (Laurence King 2018) and *Moth: An Evolution Story* (Bloomsbury 2018) which is illustrated by Daniel Egnéus and nominated for the CILIP Kate Greenaway Medal 2019. Find out more at www.isabelthomas.co.uk and follow her on Twitter @isabelwriting.

See also...
• *Finding new readers and markets*, page 116

Writing for a variety of ages

Geraldine McCaughrean has written for both babies and adults – and all ages in between. In this article she looks at the variety of writing forms she has been published in.

I spent my teenage years writing adult novels about things I knew nothing of, and (not surprisingly) having publishers turn them down. When I became an adult, I was published as an author of children's books, because at least I knew the world from a child's perspective: everyone has been a child. I was hugely prolific back then and, since each publication day felt like a fluke, constantly on the lookout for the chance to write more before my luck broke. It did not occur to me to specialise – in novels, in picture books, in educational or mainstream. Did you know that a baby's bath toy, if it has 25 words or more printed on it, becomes a book and exempt of VAT? I have reason to know this. I'm not proud, me.

Once my children's books started to win prizes, I was able to get adult novels published, too. Once, just once, I got paid the same for a 32-page picture book text that took a day to write as I got for a 600-page novel that had taken me two years. So which would I rather do? The answer is 'both', plus a few more titles for the ages in between, and a sprinkling of retellings for the fun of it. I have tried my hand at writing for almost every age, from toddler to adult. Three words are not enough to cover the many variants of Writing for Children. Each age range brings its own pleasures; each is as different from the others as crossword-puzzling is from writing a shopping list.

I confess that, when my daughter was small, I got very interested in writing picture books. As she grew older, my interest rose up in parallel with the pencil marks on the doorframe. Young children aren't much functional use to an author though, beyond their inspirational qualities. Horribly partisan, they love everything a parent or grandparent reads to them, regardless of merit. They only become really useful guinea-pigs and reviewers later. Be warned, though: they also grow up wanting to write.

Picture books

At the core of a successful picture book is a good visual idea that hasn't already been done. Unfortunately, such ideas don't come along to order. And a nice little story won't cut it as a picture book text. Since the text is not there to describe the pictures, it has to do something else. You have, essentially, to lay $14\frac{1}{2}$ visual opportunities in the lap of an artist, one for each spread plus the last verso.

The words mustn't vie with the pictures for room. The younger the age-pitch, the fewer the words – not just because the font size will be bigger, but because the child's concentration is shorter between page turns. A very young child's world does not extend far beyond home, parents, pets, toys and playschool, it's true. But within an astonishingly short time, nonsense, adventure, humour, delicious big words, sadness, bravery, magic, and wonder have all entered the child's ken. But whichever end of the scale you are writing for, there is always a third party to consider: the poor benighted soul who may be obliged to read this book over and over and over.

I once submitted a text almost sure it would fail. The young brain is slow to acquire the concept of Time, and this text was about a grandmother telling her granddaughter why she doesn't need a clock to tell her the time. It sold well because grandparents love it.

Children seem to love it too, but then they haven't read Piaget's work on conceptual development so they don't know any better.

I embark on a picture book as I would poetry rather than prose, piling on the word play and euphonious vocabulary, making the most of the aural splendour of words. It's almost sure to be read aloud, and small children love big language. After all, they have been acquiring new words every day without the aid of a dictionary, and are very good at it … which is why writing for the next age bracket is more depressing.

School readers

Gone is the invitation to roll in glistening language like a lamb in dew. Grim school gates have clanged behind us and there is literacy fodder on the lunch menu. Over and above the big, famous reading schemes, *a lot* of books are published for use with learner-readers; it's nice work if you can get it. Well, it's work.

Here, it is all simple vocabulary, simple syntax and a list of prohibitions: no pigs, knives, alcohol, guns, occult … From the fairy-tale world of stepsisters hacking off their heels, and pigs boiling water in readiness for the salivating wolf on the roof, the child moves forward into a bald landscape where female tractor drivers plough a furrow between capital and full stop, avoiding unpleasantness and pork products on the way. I'm generalising, of course, but it feels 'cabin'd, cribb'd and confin'd'. The design is functional, the illustration generally cheap – and the editors rewrite your words, leaving you wondering why they didn't just write it themselves in the first place.

Younger fiction for independent readers

So the next, independent-reading phase – for, say, 7–9 year-olds – ought to offer a merciful relief. The sector is horribly dominated by collectible series, of course, and since you won't beat them, you may want to join them in Pink-Pong land: pink prettiness for girls and naughty nasties for boys. Heigh-ho. Surely there must be a Middle Way between the female tractor driver and the pink sequin fairy? There is, of course. There are some wonderful books out there that reward close reading – just not enough.

I began writing for this age group after sitting on a few judging panels, where oddly few attractive entries had been submitted for the 7–9 year-old category. It's less neglected now – and it's fun to write for too, especially if your publisher can match you with a good sparky illustrator. Surely this is just the age when books should be covetable, tempting objects in themselves – miraculous little wedges of wonder with which to prop open new doors.

The best thing about writing for the primary age is that the school visits are more fun. Adult authors can be recluses if they choose, so long as they are interesting recluses who can hint at a dark and sensational past during their 'rare and long-awaited' interviews. But if you're a children's author you do school visits. It's useful, informative, punctures any illusion of achievement, and, for many authors, is a way of making ends meet. In primary and middle schools the audience is largely on your side and ready to join in (even those who hate books). Some authors can win over Year 9s and 10s and up as well. It's just that I've been trying for 40 years, and coming away exhausted from willing them to like me, speak to me, forgive my crime of polluting the world with books they don't want to read. With forethought – think! – I *could* have confined myself to writing for Years 1–8 and saved myself a lot of tears.

Myth, legend and retellings

The National Curriculum, restrictive as it is, has its advantages for a children's author. For instance, there are two 'Myth' slots (Years 5 and 7), which have brought the ancient gods out of their dingy library alcove and made them popular again. I keep going back to myth and legend, because they are an encounter with the Big Stuff: terror, love, creation, war, heroism, atonement, death, Fate and God ... It feels good to roam among the 'ageless' stories, where all narrative has its roots. And its juggernaut splendour crushes petty political correctness under its wheels without anyone even noticing.

I like to alternate original fiction with retellings of existing stories. After all, why incessantly create new beasts when there are magnificent old ones who have roamed the earth for centuries and should never be allowed to become extinct?

Teenage and young adult fiction

This is currently a thriving section of publishing. It is not very long since *Diary of a Wimpy Kid* - a junior-school book - was the most-read book among secondary school students. ("Remedial Literacy", with simple texts for older readers, is still, sadly, in demand.) But there would appear to be a healthy upturn in teen reading.

I tend to rely on my own experience of adolescene, but since that was 50 years ago, it may not be sound practice at all. There are many excellent authors currently writing who can connect with a much broader audience - teenage girls and boys from all manner of backgrounds, facing all kinds of problems.

'Problems' loom large in the realm of young adults. After a junior school stocked with sanitised books full of simplified language, secondary readers are hurled into a bleak landscape of war, suffering, abuse, bereavement, pollution, inhumanity, trauma, death, homelessness, sex, heartbreak and horror. As the theatre reviewer wrote of *Anthony and Cleopatra:* 'How different from the homelife of our own dear queen'.

Teenagers have always been drawn to the ghoulish, sexy, violent, supernatural, gory and tragic, but to that has been added 'eco-panic' about a world so ruined by adults that only the young are left to fend off extinction. There seems to be a requirement lately for every novel to tackle an issue of some kind. Perhaps this was always the case, but it feels more blatant of late. I do hope we are not burdening the young with too many wrongs to right. Are we sending them on a Children's Crusade, unarmed, against the Infidel? I know, if I had been told, when I was 15, to buckle-to and save the oceans from plastic, I would still be dragging the leaden guilt of failure behind me now, and suffering nightmares.

Literary fiction 11+

This is not a separate category from the one above. At least it shouldn't be. Research continues to show that the complex, linguistically challenging 12+ novel will be the first to go. Research still indicates that children's average reading age regresses in secondary school relative to their actual age: they favour simpler books than top juniors – or else don't read at all. And yet ... and yet ... the teenage market is holding up when other sectors are struggling. And 'literary' books still win prizes like the Carnegie, Guardian and Costa.

To my mind, the most pleasurable, diverse, gratifying field of all. The readers here have the skill and stamina to tackle a long book, can appreciate character, style and satire, tackle politics, philosophy, morality, and are open to new departures. They're still reading because they like books! They have worked out that, inside a book, they are free from the oppression of either teacher or parent.

At 12, there is no need to fan a libido or steer a path through bleak angsty fantasies. The author is free to revel in language and character, to experiment, to cultivate quirky plots.

Consequently, the field is hugely overcrowded. A lot of good authors have been 'let go'. The only books wanted are those likely to pay their way. Morale is low.

Annoyingly, books decide for themselves what they want to be, and there is no point in cutting them off at the knees to pretend they are younger, or standing them on a chair to pretend they are older. A book is only as old is it feels. However selfish it sounds, a book gains most from an author writing for the joy of it. It is simply a matter of writing the book that's in you.

And children's literature spans such a variety of forms – far more than for adults. When you consider the distance between babyhood and teenage years, it is hard not to relish the number of possibilities strewn along the way.

Geraldine McCaughrean has been a full-time writer for 40 years and has produced over 170 books and plays. Eight times shortlisted for the Carnegie Medal (which she won in 1989 and again in 2018), her novels do not fit readily into any one category, but tend towards adventure. She won the chance to write a sequel to J.M. Barrie's *Peter Pan and Wendy* for Great Ormond Street Hospital; *Peter Pan in Scarlet* was published in 2006 and has been translated into 50 languages. Her most recent novels are *The Middle of Nowhere* (2013) and *Where the World Ends* (2017), both published by Usborne. She is also the author of five novels for adults. Her website is www.geraldinemccaughrean.co.uk.

See also...
• *Children's books: genres and categorisation,* page 17

Overnight success

Lauren St John describes how she became an overnight success after 20 years of writing and being published.

I was ten when I first decided to become a novelist. At the time we were living on a farm in what was then Rhodesia and books were in short supply. When I did get a new *Famous Five*, Nancy Drew or Black Stallion novel, I'd devour it so quickly and feel so bereft when I reached the end that quite often I'd simply turn it over and start again.

One day, a visitor presented me with a box of secondhand books, among which was a novel written by a 13-year-old. The idea that a teenager could become a published author blew me away. I set to work at once writing a book about a sheep and a snake in a woodpile. I'd heard that it was important to write what you know and I had a string of adopted lambs. Added to which, the woodpile in our garden practically writhed with snakes – most of them poisonous.

The other thing I'd heard about publishers was that your manuscript needed to be typed. To this end, I had my mum take me to the nearest farm we could find that had a typewriter. There, I spent a busy afternoon working my way through a bottle of Tipp-Ex and filling a wastepaper basket with crumpled balls of paper. I never managed to type a single perfect page and that was the thing that defeated me. Publishers, I'd heard, were only interested in perfection.

By the time I turned 11, my principle goals were fame and saving animals. I didn't really care how I became famous and I didn't see lack of talent as a bar of any kind, especially if I achieved my number one ambition: becoming a pop star like Olivia Newton-John. Depending on the day of the week, I also wanted to become an Academy award-winning actress, an artist, an Olympic gold medal-winning eventer or a vet. English was my best subject but I didn't want to become a journalist like the career guidance counsellor advised because I thought journalists were quite horrible.

The funny thing was, I had a brief foray into most of these careers. Having left school at 16 (school, I'd decided, was interfering with my success) and had a couple of months at an art school in Cape Town, I announced to my parents that I wanted to move to the UK to become a pop singer. Until this point I'd led a fairly sheltered life on our farm and at a girl's boarding school (government, not private) and most sane adults would have fallen about laughing before saying a categorical: 'Are you out of your mind? Absolutely not!' End of story.

Fortunately, my parents are just the right side of crazy. My dad is a farmer and ex-soldier who's survived ambushes, snake bites, and being gored by a bull and attacked by a crocodile, so very little fazes him. He essentially shrugged and said it was fine if that's what I wanted to do. His main concern was that I didn't starve. My mum is a big believer in the following of dreams, so her response was: 'Here's an air ticket and a little pocket money. Bon voyage!'

By the age of 18 I'd spent a year working as a veterinary nurse in Maidenhead, Berkshire, waitressed and had a fleeting stint teaching horse-riding in Sussex. I'd also tried writing another novel. Having decided that songwriting was the way forward, I was back on the farm in Zimbabwe, riding my horse and working on my singing when my mum called (my parents were now divorced). 'There's a journalism course starting at Harare Polytechnic tomorrow,' she said, 'and you're going to be on it.'

My protests were in vain. When I was accepted onto the course, I grudgingly agreed to try it for two weeks. 'If I don't like it,' I told her, 'I'm quitting.'

In fact, I loved it. Few of our lecturers ever showed up, subjects such as sociology were started then aborted without explanation (I left college able to type only 25 words a minute because our typing teacher quit after two weeks and was never replaced), and our photography studies took place without cameras.

Once, we were taken on a rural reporting assignment where the only food available was goat curry. We slept on mud floors and the communal showers had no curtains. And yet I've never laughed more or learned more than I did that year. It remains one of the best experiences of my life. My diploma is not (in my opinion) worth the paper it's printed on, and yet my time at Harare Polytechnic taught me two things that I believe are critical for any writer:

• **Discipline.** You can write like Dostoevsky but if you can't deliver the goods when you're meant to deliver them, you're going to make a lot of people cross and mess up many production schedules.

• **The danger of preconceptions.** The ability to read people is a critical skill in a writer, as is psychological insight, but more important still is the capacity to have an open mind and the curiosity to look beneath the surface. The flashy, showy people, the beautiful ones, are rarely as interesting as the quiet ones sitting in the corner. As the *Desiderata* says, 'Listen to others, even the dull and the ignorant, for they too have their story.' The same applies to places and to stories.

It was while I was at college that I became obsessed with golf. By the time I graduated, three months later, I was so in love with it that I refused to get a real job. I spent the best part of a year working part-time for a shady promotions company. The director and I spent every available hour playing golf. The following March, with my 20-year-old brain turning slowly to mush, I decided that if I did have to work for a living I'd become a golf journalist. So I hopped on a plane with enough money for one month's rent and moved to London.

A white giraffe out of the blue

How I got from there to becoming a children's author is a long story. Suffice to say that it's taught me that no experience is ever wasted. Veterinary nursing, midnight feasts at boarding school, spending a decade on the PGA men's tour seeing the world and talking to Tiger, hanging out with musicians in Nashville, or childhood dreams of becoming a pop singer or winning the Badminton Horse Trials – it all comes in handy if you're an author, especially if you write for children.

People often ask me where I get my ideas, but the truth is that until I wrote *The White Giraffe* I'd never had a single decent plot idea for a novel in my life. Not one. And I'd been trying to dream one up since I was ten.

The White Giraffe itself came out of the blue. At the time I was struggling to find work. I'd spent eight years working as golf correspondent to *The Sunday Times*, as well as writing music features for other newspapers and eight well-received non-fiction books. Yet most of those books were out of print and when it came to convincing editors to take my stories, I couldn't get arrested. I knew I'd hit rock bottom when, desperate for money and fresh out of confidence, I wrote a piece on spec for *Your Cat* magazine and they turned it down. I call it my 'Your Cat' moment. I was forced to sell my flat because I couldn't pay the mortgage. I was fast coming to the conclusion that I'd have to give up writing and find a real job.

In 2005, I was on my way to do some Christmas shopping when, out of nowhere, an image of a girl riding a giraffe popped into my head. When I was a teenager we lived for six years on a farm and game reserve where we actually had a pet giraffe (along with warthogs, a goat, eight horses, eight cats, six dogs and the occasional python) and I thought, 'Wouldn't it be the coolest thing on earth if you could actually ride a giraffe?' And right there on the street the whole story came into my head, including the girl's name, Martine.

I envisioned *The White Giraffe* as a picture book and decided that one day, when I retired, I'd have a tinker with it. But I found I couldn't stop thinking about it. In January, I attempted the first chapter. To my astonishment, it was effortless. The images that poured into my mind were so vivid it was like watching a movie.

After that, I couldn't stop writing. The best part was that, throughout the whole process, I couldn't shake the feeling that the story was being gifted to me. Each day when I sat down to write, I had the strongest sensation that all I had to do was listen for the words. As a consequence, if a name or a plot twist came to me, I used it, no matter how bizarre.

I had the first draft completed in a month. It was 20,000 words long and, as numerous rejections testified, it needed more work done on it. I was prepared to accept that it was probably quite bad, but because of the way the story had come to me I was convinced that it had something special about it. I had a policy. If I disagreed with an editor's criticism of it, I ignored it. If I thought they had a valid point, I did my best to make the suggested changes. If more than two or more people disliked something in the book, I would concede that they might be right. Yet nothing I did seemed to make a difference. When my agent at the time told me the book was unpublishable, I was devastated.

Eighteen months, 20,000 more words and a change of agent later, four publishers wanted the book. In the meanwhile, I'd written a synopsis for my memoir, *Rainbow's End*, which was bid for by five publishers in the UK, three in the USA and two in the Netherlands. Hamish Hamilton in the UK and Simon & Schuster in the USA bought *Rainbow's End* and Orion gave me a four-book deal for the *White Giraffe* series. After nearly 20 years of trying, I was an 'overnight' success!

Ten children's books on, I'm still pinching myself. Every day I do the short distance commute from my bed to my computer and moments later I'm having an adventure. I might be escaping a volcano with Laura Marlin, saving the Amazon jungle with an ant named Anthony or riding at Badminton, but whatever it is it'll be fun.

I've learned to trust my imagination and the strange process by which stories come to me, out of nowhere and fully formed. *Dead Man's Cove*, the first Laura Marlin mystery, for instance, came to me after I read an article on the singer Laura Marling and thought that Laura Marlin would be a good name for a girl detective. At the time I was reading a book on modern day slavery and the two things coalesced in my imagination. The conservation themes in my *White Giraffe* series were inspired by my African childhood and my work rescuing leopards and dolphins with the wildlife charity, Born Free.

After decades without a solitary book idea, I now find enormous joy in thinking up plots. If you're stuck for ideas, remember that life is infinitely stranger than fiction. There is a wealth of potential bestsellers in every newspaper. A news story about a stowaway could be turned into a novel about a girl whose father works at the airport who rescues a boy. A story about a jungle plane crash could be turned into a girl's own adventure story about the lone survivor of a crash who has to cross the Amazon with a mongrel dog to make it to safety.

Finding *your* 'overnight' success

My number one piece of advice to would-be children's authors is to put the finding of an agent or publisher at the bottom of your priority list. I meet a staggering number of people who've barely written a chapter and yet are utterly obsessed with how to write a query letter and marketing strategies for their books. Trust me when I tell you that none of those things matter if you can't tell a good story.

Concentrate on writing the best book you can. Write from the heart, write for the love of it and write with passion. Contrary to popular belief, publishers and agents are desperate to find great novels. If you follow the advice above, there's no reason at all that yours can't be one of them. Remember that practice makes perfect. Write, write, write. If you value quality of plot and prose over marketing strategies and have faith and perseverance, chances are you will find your book a home.

Then, like me, you'll be an 'overnight' success!

Lauren St John is the author of the multi award-winning children's series published by Orion Children's that includes *The White Giraffe* (2007), *Dolphin Song* (2008), *The Last Leopard* (2009), *The Elephant's Tale* (2010) and *Operation Rhino* (2015). *Dead Man's Cove*, the first book in her *Laura Marlin Mysteries* series, won the 2011 Blue Peter Book of the Year Award and was shortlisted for the Children's Book of the Year. Her bestselling *The One Dollar Horse* series (Orion 2012) has been followed by *The Glory* (Orion 2015). Both *The White Giraffe* and *The Glory* have been optioned by Canyon Creek Films. She has also written eight non-fiction adult books, including *Rainbow's End*, a memoir of her childhood in Zimbabwe. *The Obituary Writer*, her first adult novel, was published by Orion in 2013. *The Snow Angel*, a standalone children's novel for Head of Zeus, was published in 2017. *Kat Wolfe Investigates*, the first in a new middle-grade mystery series, was launched by Macmillan Children's Books in 2018 followed by *Kat Wolfe Takes the Case* (2019).

See also...

- *Spotting talent*, page 1
- *What makes a children's classic?*, page 4

Keeping going: the ups and downs of being a published writer

Theresa Tomlinson shares the emotional and creative highs and lows, opportunities and hurdles an author may encounter during a long writing career. She tracks the course of her career – through finding and losing a trusted editor, writing fiction for children, adults and YA, and moving from traditional publishing to self-publishing.

As a child I had no ambitions to write, but I loved reading and delighted in magical escapes to Narnia. I failed the eleven-plus, and rather struggled at my convent boarding school, but discovered I had some facility for drawing and painting. I spent two years at Hull Art College but left without completing my graphic design course. Unsure of what to do next, I trained to be an infant teacher and it was in that role that I discovered the sheer joy of storytelling (in those days both children and teachers could look forward to a blissful story session at the end of each day).

Later, as the mother of three young children, I started to put together simple picture books, initially focusing on the artwork rather than the words. As time passed the stories grew longer; my interest in the artwork faded and I began to write somewhat obsessively. Visits to the local library provided huge inspiration as I discovered new and exciting children's writers; it was almost like finding a new version of Narnia. Discovering Jane Gardam was a revelation – not only did I love her humour, sensitivity and clear writing style, but I recognised many of the settings based on the part of the north-east coast where I grew up. I knew every street, garden and house in the background of *A Long Way from Verona* (Abacus 1997), heard familiar cadences in the dialogue and experienced once again the familiar tang of steelworks built close to the sea. I began to feel that I, too, had stories to tell.

Having discovered a local writers' workshop, tutored by Berlie Doherty, I settled to work more seriously as a writer; five years of hard work followed, including three inspiring Arvon courses. There were many rejections, but things started to look up when I was awarded a Yorkshire Arts Bursary to help me finish a book in progress – *The Flither Pickers* (1987) – stories of fishing families set on the north-east coast, along with an offer of publication from John Killick of the Littlewood Press, based at Hebden Bridge. Although it was a limited print run, it meant that I had a well-produced example of my work to send to publishers. Fairly soon after that I got my first (modest) offer from a London publisher – for a magical children's story set in the industrial seaside village that I had lived in as a child. The offer came from Julia MacRae, a highly respected publisher with her own imprint within Walker Books and – best of all – she was Jane Gardam's publisher! I was thrilled.

Over the next 20 years, with the support of Julia and my fabulous editor, Delia Huddy, I flourished. One book followed another. Historical themes appealed to me and were appreciated by schools. Julia MacRae moved to Random House and took me with her, though happily Walker Books continued to publish my younger-age 'time-slip' books, which allowed modern children to slip magically back through time to experience an earlier period. I was hugely encouraged when *Riding the Waves* (1990) a more modern novel, set on the north-east coast, was recommended for the Carnegie Medal and my young adult novels were translated into several languages and sold in the USA. I was regularly shortlisted for the Sheffield Children's Book Award (Michael Palin memorably turned his back on me and folded his arms when I was called up onto the stage twice in an award ceremony!); it was such good fun.

Publishing contracts were now becoming rather complicated for me to deal with, so I looked for an agent; persuading Caroline Walsh of David Higham to take me on turned out to be one of the best things I ever did. Educational publishers were asking for more historical time-slip stories and when again one of these, *Meet Me By The Steelmen* (1997), was shortlisted for the Carnegie Medal, I thought my future was secure ... But then gradually things started to change: schools became short of funds and invitations to visit grew scarce, ebooks appeared on the scene and time-slip stories seemed to fall out of favour. However, I still had the backing of my editor and a sympathetic agent.

For some time I had longed to use Anglo-Saxon Whitby as a setting for a story so, having moved to Whitby, I set out to write a trilogy of YA mystery/adventures with Hild's famous monastery as the setting. The research process was sheer pleasure and it was inspiring to be living in sight of the location. *Wolf Girl* (Corgi Children's 2006) was the first book completed and we had almost finished the editing process when my editor Delia suddenly died. The book was published but it didn't sell widely and Random House concluded that readers were not interested in Anglo-Saxon settings, but by then I had become passionately interested in the period; my bookshelves were filled with studies of food, clothing, language and crafts of the time – I'd persuaded my husband that our travels must include Sutton Hoo, West Stow Anglo-Saxon village, Durham, Bede's World (now Jarrow Hall), Yeavering, Bamburgh Castle and Lindisfarne.

By then, fortunately, trying to earn a living by writing had become less of a priority, but it was a depressing time; I almost considered giving up altogether. A few months of ignoring the computer, though, made me realise that it would be even more depressing not to write; for my own wellbeing, I needed to do it. Hearing that Whitby had a writers' group, I went to join them. It was like starting at the beginning again, and there was something rather exciting about that.

I couldn't let my Anglo-Saxon obsession go and began work on an adult murder mystery with the same setting as my YA book and with a theme somewhat similar to Ellis Peters' Cadfael series, but with a 7th-century half-pagan herb-wife, rather than a monk. Creating a much older protagonist was something I'd wanted to try for a while and the character of Fridgyth was already present in *Wolf Girl*, waiting to step forward into the limelight. Whitby Writers Group provided practical criticism and friendly encouragement and my pleasure in writing returned. A difficult decision had to be made when the manuscript was completed: whether to try to get it published traditionally or go down the self-publishing route. I talked it through with my agent and it became clear that, although I'd had some success as a children's writer, that wouldn't mean much when tackling the competitive, adult, historical crime fiction market. Even acceptance by a traditional publisher might mean waiting years for publication.

I was then in my 60s and felt time might be running out, so I decided to experiment with self-publishing. My agent negotiated a contract with Acorn Independent Press (www.acornselfpublishing.com). They provided discerning editing, and I enjoyed having lots of input into the cover design. The book was well produced as a print-on-demand

(POD) and ebook edition and Acorn helped with marketing and distribution. *A Swarming of Bees* (2012) was put forward for an Amazon promotion and within a few weeks it reached number three in the historical bestsellers chart – I was briefly placed between Hilary Mantel and C.J. Sansom and couldn't have been happier. I recovered my costs fairly quickly and local bookshops still sell copies at a steady pace, which I supply them with.

I set about writing a sequel and I also had a straightforward historical novel published, *The Tribute Bride* (2014), this time with a 6th-century setting. Self-publishing seemed to be working for me, so I began to look at my backlist of out-of-print titles. Two of my short novels, *The Flither Pickers* and *The Herring Girls*, focusing on the harsh lives of the fishing families of the north-east coast, were published in a paperback edition in 2017, illustrated with atmospheric Victorian/Edwardian photographs by Frank Meadow Sutcliffe. York Publishing Services (www.yps-publishing.co.uk) produced the book and it was a real benefit to be able to discuss the project face to face before agreeing to go ahead and at any point during the production process. YPS produced a Kindle version that displays the photographs beautifully and the books are selling steadily in local shops. YPS suggested an initial print run of 250 copies and I'm now into my second run.

However, self-publishing hasn't been all plain sailing. When the manuscript for my 'herb-wife' sequel was finished, Acorn were happy to put the book together but had decided to withdraw from providing marketing services. Once again, my agent came to the rescue: Caroline negotiated a rather different contract with Acorn, and David Higham Agency agreed to take on the setting up and management of a Kindle version and POD facility themselves. *Queen of a Distant Hive* (2017) was produced and has gathered positive reviews – not least from fellow historical writers. I sense that there is more interest in the Anglo-Saxon period now and I have discovered a good community of support out there, especially from those writing in a similar genre. Bloggers invite me to appear as their guest and provide reviews – Annie Whitehead (http://anniewhiteheadauthor.co.uk), Helen Hollick (https://discoveringdiamonds.blogspot.com) and Carla Nayland (http://carlanayland.blogspot.com) are three active examples.

I haven't entirely given up on traditional children's publishing and am working on a YA novel set in Victorian Whitby. At the age of 72 my ambitions are modest. I have a small pension, a supportive husband and a loyal agent – it's a privileged position to be in. I'm grateful simply to be able to sit down at my computer and still spend a few magical hours in Narnia – or any other time or place that I fancy.

Theresa Tomlinson is known for her YA and children's historical novels, particularly those set on the north-east coast of England. Her books include *The Flither Pickers* (1987), *Summer Witches* (1991), the *Forestwife* trilogy – *The Forestwife* (1993), *Child of the May* (1998) and *Path of the She-Wolf* (2000), five *Time Slip Adventures* including the republication of *Meet Me By the Steelmen* (Award Publications Ltd 2019), and the *Troy and the Warrior Women* series – *The Moon Riders* (2002) and *The Voyage of the Snake Lady* (2004). Theresa has been shortlisted twice for the Carnegie Medal and for the Sheffield Children's Book Award. For more information and Theresa's blog, see www.theresatomlinson.com.

See also...

• *Writing historical novels*, page 155

Writing humour for young children

Like most adults, children love humour. But in both cases the joke will fall flat unless it is aimed at the right audience. Jeremy Strong has ten rules for writing humour for young children.

The snappy bit: some simple rules

1. Never allow your bum to become gratuitous.
2. Write wrong.
3. Self mutilation is highly recommended.
4. Words are essential.
5. Pulchritude? No way.
6. Inside every 20-plus there's an eight year-old trying to get out.
7. You calling me a wozzer? Mankynora!
8. Just who do you think you're talking to?
9. Surprise!
10. Ha! I laugh at death.

The expansive bit. We begin at the beginning.

Rule Nine: Surprise!

Ha ha! That's pretty much self-explanatory.

Rule Six: Inside every 20-plus there's an eight year-old trying to get out.

Years ago, when I first began writing for children, I was often asked (by adults) why it was that the stories I wrote seemed to appeal to children. You have to imagine an adult asking this question, in a tone of voice that mixes one part admiration to nine parts complete bewilderment. I used to answer, fairly truthfully, that only my exterior had aged along with my chronological age, and that I was still aged about eight inside. The adult would usually laugh and would go away as bewildered as they were before they'd asked the question. The point here is, I think, that it isn't possible to really understand except from a child's viewpoint. If you have forgotten what it was like to be a child then you're unlikely to understand. No matter what you write you must keep your audience firmly in mind. You are writing specifically for them.

Rule One: Never allow your bum to become gratuitous.

To make matters worse, adults often think the things that make children laugh are puerile. To some extent this is true and it is easy to make a child laugh by playing 'lowest common denominator' jokes – jokes that refer to farts, snot, bums, knickers, etc. But whilst employing these guaranteed tickle-sticks it is easy to forget that children also like quite sophisticated jokes.

As for the bums and farts, it's okay to pop them in here and there but, for the sake of at least some self respect, keep them to a minimum and shun the gratuitous bum.

Rule Four: Words are essential.

Children love word play, and they love 'knowing' jokes – for example, jokes that are aware of how bad they are, or referential jokes that make use of things familiar to them, the things that mark out their lives, such as school, parents, family.

Books

Then there is the matter of what children can read and understand. Obviously, this is going to vary not only with age but with ability. There are children of six who can read like 11-year-olds, and vice versa, with all shades in between and quite frequently further beyond. Nevertheless, as a writer, you need to aim towards the centre. In this article I am going to concentrate on 6–11 year-olds because those are the ages I taught for 17 years.

Let's look at language. Things need to be fairly simple. Shorter, rather than longer sentences work best. But like all rules this one can be deliberately misused. For example, at some appropriate point in a story you might wish to hurl yourself into some ever-increasing sentence that just seems to plunge on and on at a relentless pace and with reckless abandon like a runaway car because that happens to be one of the best ways your writing can capture the manic activity that is going on in your story at that particular point. Maybe it is a description of a runaway car. You get the point. Children respond to this positively because, anchored as it is in a normally short and simple style of writing, the over-long sentence becomes not only a writing device, but also a source of humour.

Rule Ten: Ha! I laugh at death.

As with comedy for other age groups, nothing is held sacred. You will, however, have to obey the obvious rules that generally apply to writing for children, and also steer clear of the PC police. You can be smutty, but not dirty. You can be unkind to animals, but they mustn't be in a circus, unless you're a signed up freedom fighter for 'Say no! to performing dumb creatures'.

You can laugh about death. (It's an emotional release. Honest.) You can even have stereotypes and clichés – but in this instance don't expect to get published.

Rule Two: Write wrong.

Children love to recognise things that are wrong, and this is where word play often has great effect. Characters that get their words or spellings wrong are a good source of humour, not only because it is funny in its own right, but because children love the empowerment of recognising what's wrong. (You will, incidentally, lose brownie points for using words like 'empowerment'.)

Rule Seven: You calling me a wozzer? Mankynora!

Invented words can also be a terrific source of enjoyment for both writer and reader, especially when they are used as expletives – sort of coded (and therefore safe) swear words. Mankynora! Wozzer yourself! Let's also take a look at sophistication. You have to ask yourself, am I writing a joke for an adult or a child? I know for a fact that I am guilty of putting jokes for adults in some stories – jokes I know only an adult will understand. (Or sometimes a joke that a child will get on one level, but where the adult will see a second 'hidden' joke or implication.) The reason I do this is because I can't resist the temptation if it's a good one. Besides, many children's books are read to them by adults, and so I am putting in something to make it more enjoyable for them. Nevertheless, you need to make sure that the vast majority is firmly in the child's grasp.

Rule Five: Pulchritude? No way.

Whilst on the subject of sophistication it is worth thinking about the words you use. With each word you need to ask yourself: can a child of 'x' years read and understand this word? Apply a bit of common sense. There are some words a child might not understand but it might be worthwhile introducing such a word to them, allowing the context to help reveal its meaning.

The word 'sophistication' itself is a reasonable example. Many junior children would not understand it but, although it's long, it's not too difficult to work out what it says and you could argue that it's a good word for a child to know. On the other hand, the word 'pulchritudinous' is not only very hard for a child to work out but it is extremely unlikely you would need to use such a word when writing for junior children.

Rule Three: Self mutilation is highly recommended.

You have to be rigorously self disciplined about this. No matter how good a joke is, you have to cut it out if it's not actually funny to your audience. The humour also needs to arrive and leave quickly. Anything that takes pages to set up is not worth it and the longer it takes the more likely it is that your writing will become increasingly false and unnatural as you struggle with all the scaffolding you require to hold up the joke.

Rule Eight: Just who do you think you're talking to?

It is a mistake to think that the things adults laugh at in children make good material for children's books. They don't, for the simple reason that it's funny to the adult watching the child, and not the other way round. All of this points to one of the cardinal rules for writing anything: be aware of your audience. Keep that firmly in mind and you can't go far wrong. I was going to finish by writing: May the fart be with you. Then I realised that it would not only be out of place, but one fart too many.

Jeremy Strong writes humorous fiction for 7–11 year-olds. His books include *There's a Viking in My Bed*, which was made into a popular BBC television series; *The Hundred-Mile-an-Hour Dog*, for which he won the Federation of Children's Book Groups Children's Book Award; *Stuff*, which won the 2006 Manchester Book Award; and *Beware! Killer Tomatoes*, which won four book awards, including the Sheffield Children's Book Award. He also regularly writes titles, such as *Mad Iris* and *The Genius, Aged 8¼*, for Barrington Stoke who specialise in books for dyslexic readers. His most recent book is *Armadillo and Hare* (David Fickling Books 2018). He speaks regularly at festivals and in schools worldwide. His website is www.jeremystrong.co.uk.

See also...
• *Who do children's authors write for?*, page 104

How to write a picture book

Tessa Strickland highlights the enduring value of picture books, both educational and emotional, for young children in today's multimedia world, and offers advice for writers wishing to engage in the child's world on the process, practices, qualities and skills they will need to succeed.

A picture book is a child's first theatre. It's likely to be the first time a child experiences the drama of storytelling as the spoken word, accompanied by glorious illustration and skilful design. As on a theatre stage, several disciplines come together. The result is an art form whose impact on the imagination can extend well beyond childhood. I remain inspired by my favourite childhood picture books, among them Golden MacDonald's evocative Hebridean story *The Little Island* (Doubleday 1946), Kay Thompson's badass heroine *Eloise* (Simon & Schuster 1955), and Barbara Cooney's Caldecott-winning 1959 version of *Chanticleer and the Fox* (Crowell 1958). And on the shelves of my family library, the picture books that were my own children's favourites still take pride of place.

Picture books are not just about entertainment: they play a crucial role in establishing a child's basic literacy skills, emotional intelligence, acquisition of language, appetite for learning and enjoyment of art. Of course, the small child is not reading the text, it is being read to her. But as she listens, she knows that the adult reader is decoding those curious black marks that run along the page. She knows that these marks, these words, are the key to what is happening in the illustrations. So, the heart of the picture book is this marriage between the text and the illustration – each depends on the other. And the starting point is the story.

Where to start

Because most picture books are short (publishers typically require a text of less than 1,000 words), it's dangerously easy to think that they are easy to write. In fact, the opposite is the case. Writing a picture book text presents the same challenges as writing a poem. Your aim is to achieve a sense of balance and harmony between the story as music and the story as meaning. This is because small children won't necessarily be able to understand what all the words in the story are saying, but if the sound of the language is congruent with its meaning, they will happily let themselves be carried along by the emotional momentum of the narrative.

If you have not written for children before and you want to have a go, it is a very good idea to spend dedicated time with children under five. You may have children of your own; you may teach in an early-years setting; you may simply like the idea of storytelling for this enthusiastic and receptive age group. If you don't have children in your day-to-day life, and even if you do, volunteer to read aloud at your local pre-school, primary school or library. This will help you to get a sense of what stories the children enjoy listening to AND what kind of stories you most enjoy telling. Notice what the children are doing and saying when they play (children come into the world knowing instinctively that play is work; this is how they learn, and their interactions with each other reveal their major interests and preoccupations).

As well as engaging with the child's world, try to remember what you felt like as a child. Get these feelings into your storytelling. This will make your writing authentic. Children see straight through sentimentality, yet an alarming number of adults shy away from the intensities and terrors of childhood and try to sugar-coat it. This won't work.

Practice and peer groups

Write as often as you can and set aside time to practice. If it's not possible for you to write every day (for many of us, it isn't), then choose at least a couple of hours a week and make this your personal, uninterruptable writing time. Writing is a craft and like any craft, the more you practise it, the better you get. Look for a supportive writing group – the excellent Society of Children's Book Writers & Illustrators (see page 353) has many local chapters and there are also all kinds of courses online and masterclasses at literature festivals (see *Children's writing courses and conferences*, page 394). Peer support groups can be transformative and you will learn a lot, not only about your potential as a writer but also about how to give and receive feedback. Very few of us can write to please everyone. So, like any professional writer of any genre, one of your challenges will be how to decide what to retain because you instinctively believe that it works, and what to revise or discard based on other people's critical feedback.

Finding your thread

Aristotle got it right when he said that a story needs a beginning, a middle and an end. When you have an idea for a story, you may well be surprised by how difficult it is to start – to get a beginning that really *is* a beginning.

Once you *have* started, it can be harder than you first expected to tell the story you thought you were going to tell. Don't worry! This is a good sign. Writing is a creative act. Your characters may well take on lives of their own and decide they are going to get up to all kinds of antics you had not predicted. Be prepared to fool around for a good many drafts, to get to know the characters you are writing about, to give them a back story. The back story won't necessarily appear on the page, but by creating it you will ground your narrative and make it more convincing than it would otherwise be.

Some writers like to start with their characters and go from there. What ages are they? What are their strengths and weaknesses? What are their likes and dislikes? What do they need that they don't have? Try writing about two strongly contrasting characters: exaggerate their traits and explore the different ways in which they interact. You may be surprised at the results, and if you do this in a group, you will be fascinated by the different ways in which this primary one-to-one exchange can be unpacked.

Some writers prefer to start with a situation and then decide who they are going to conjure up to resolve it. This is also a sound and time-tested strategy. If your characters live in a trouble-free dream world or a happy-ever-after hedgerow, your readers are going to be bored and unconvinced, because life is not like this. So, to engage your young audience, you need a situation that becomes problematic. Then you need a way of resolving the problem that is transformative for your main characters. The problem may be internal (for example, your character may be afraid of something) or it may be external (for example, a storm is coming). And you may well find that solving one problem leads to another – learning how to find your thread AND hold onto it will require you to redraft and redraft.

Staying true to life

The infant's journey from birth to the age of five is the most formative passage in their entire life. As babies grow into toddlers and then into children, they find themselves among giants, with adults and perhaps older siblings looming above them and exerting tremendous power. This is why stories about larger-than-life characters resonate so powerfully in young children's minds. There is something of a trend in contemporary children's publishing to avoid scaring children. In my view, this is a mistake. Fear and rage, pain and sorrow are as familiar to small children as cornflakes at breakfast. They are often scared or infuriated in their everyday lives, and by hearing stories in which scary things happen and are successfully dealt with, they learn that there are ways of navigating and mastering their feelings. Often successful children's writers tackle these feelings through symbol and metaphor – territory in which most children are naturally at ease.

Using humour

One of the most valuable resources in the picture book writer's toolkit is humour. It is like medicine, and it can take many forms: it may be dry; it may be quiet; it may be outrageous. Understatement can go a long way with children. By contrast, irony and sarcasm tend to be too sophisticated for little ones. So, if you are using humour – and you probably are – keep it straightforward. It can be tempting, as the writer, to introduce layers of tongue-in-cheek humour that are evident to the adult (who is also, after all, the one who is likely to have paid for the book in the first place), and this can be wonderful. Just be careful that it is not at the expense of the child for whom you are writing.

Writing in verse

Aspiring writers can find themselves utterly bewildered by conflicting advice about whether or not to write in verse. My experience both as a publisher and as a writer is that verse is hugely popular. However, it's a common misperception among beginners that verse means no more than having a rhyme scheme. If you want to write in verse, you need to have an ear for metre and for the relationship between metre, tone and meaning. The rhyme is secondary. It is certainly valuable in all kinds of ways – children and adults alike take enormous pleasure in guessing and remembering the word that completes a rhyming couplet, and unexpected rhymes are particularly delightful. But without a convincing metre, verse becomes flat-footed. If you want to write in verse, read and decode the masters, and be prepared to do a lot of revision to get it right. One false note will kill your endeavour.

Going to market

You have been diligently writing for a year or two and you now have three or four manuscripts you are happy with. It is time to gird your loins and pitch your work to a publisher.

You don't need to find an illustrator; the publisher will do this. You just need to have a selection of short manuscripts that are skillfully crafted, that surprise and delight the editor who will read them first, and that show you have a distinctive voice. Before you make your submissions, check what is on the market and make sure someone else hasn't already had your idea (you will be surprised by how often this happens). Check the publisher's website in particular, so that you have a sense of what kind of taste its editors have and what its successes are.

Be professional. Follow the publisher's submission guidelines and keep your cover letter brief. You will not help your cause by saying that your children or grandchildren love your writing. Of course they do, but they are not the ones taking the commercial risk – and the commercial risk in picture book publishing is significant.

Persist. Many of the most successful picture book writers in the field have faced years of rejection. They have succeeded not only because they are talented but also because they have been prepared to work very hard and to persevere.

The international picture book market

Picture books are expensive to develop. This is one of the reasons why only a few new picture books appear on UK publishers' lists each year. The expense of sourcing and commissioning artwork, then paying for full-colour origination and printing, quickly runs well into five figures. To stand a chance of recovering this investment, UK publishers typically seek out publishing partners in other territories, from the USA to China. Economies of scale mean that the more copies a publisher prints, the lower the unit cost. Because the UK market is a small one, publishers here usually seek to sell co-edition licences to as many partners as possible before they go to press.

This process takes time. So, do not give up your day job! The period between having your manuscript accepted and seeing it in the world as a printed book can be anything from one to three years.

Writing in a multimedia world

The digital revolution has had and continues to have a major impact on publishing. This has brought many challenges – writers of picture books are now competing with developers of apps, for example – but it has also brought new opportunities. It is much easier nowadays for aspiring writers to find their way to writing courses, to research the market, to source potential publishers and to market themselves via social media. In early years and primary education, picture books are recognized as an essential springboard for both verbal and visual development in children. Research in recent years has made it evident that the adult-to-child interaction and the physical, tactile character of picture books gives them greater educational value than storytelling on digital devices – evidence that continues to be underlined by the insights of contemporary neuroscience. This growing awareness of the ways in which picture books contribute to children's emotional and mental wellbeing gives picture book writing continued relevance. As a writer of picture books, you may be sure that you are offering a precious gift to the children who come into contact with your work. So – if you are prepared to put in the graft – go for it!

Tessa Strickland is the co-founder and former Editor-in-Chief of independent children's publisher Barefoot Books. As Stella Blackstone, she has also written many bestselling picture books including *A Dragon on the Doorstep* (2005), *My Granny Went to Market* (2006) and *Walking through the Jungle* (2006), published by Barefoot Books. Under Tessa Strickland, she has published *Baby's First Words* (2017), *The Barefoot Book of Children 2017* (2017) and *Barefoot Books Children of the World* (2018), all published by Barefoot Books. She now runs a private psychotherapy and mentoring practice and leads the picture book writing programme for the Golden Egg Academy (www.goldeneggacademy.co.uk). For further information see www.challiscombe.com. Follow her on Twitter @Tessa_at_home.

Writing ghostly stories

Cornelia Funke describes the adventure of writing ghost stories for children. She highlights the questions writers can ask themselves when creating in this genre and considers how scary the stories can be for children.

I am not sure whether I liked ghost stories as a child. I know that at some point I loved Oscar Wilde's *Ghost of Canterville* (and now think it is the most touching ghost story ever told). But the first one I remember was written by a German, Otfried Preussler, whose *Satanic Mill* is an unforgettable tale: Preussler's ghosts were bowling with their own heads, as far as I recall.

Different types of ghosts

The funny ghosts who try to be scary and are not scary at all. We meet them in fairy tales, myths and Hollywood movies. They are slimy and loud, easily frightened by human heroes and of course are the most obvious choice for a ghost story written for children.

The first ghost I wrote about was that kind of ghost: Hugo, an ASG (Averagely Spooky Ghost), to be precise. I created him when an editor friend asked me many years ago to write a ghost story for 8–12 year-olds (don't we love it when publishers put our audience in cleanly separated boxes?). The story became a series of books, *Ghosthunters*, about a boy who is very afraid of ghosts but becomes a famous ghost hunter, with the assistance of the ASG. I had immense fun writing about COHAGs (Completely Harmless Ghosts), FOFIFOs (Foggy Fug Ghosts) and GHADAPs (Ghosts with a Dark Past). Interestingly, with every book my ghosts became darker and scarier.

My young readers became quite obsessed with the series and sent me lots of suggestions for ghost types. I heard from teachers that boys who despised reading had stolen *Ghosthunters* books from their tables to secretly devour them. My stories invited readers to play with fear – to make fun of it, hunt it, destroy it.

Ghosts are perfect for that. They are the impersonation of our greatest fears – the fear of the night, of death and what may await us on the other side. Not only that – they impersonate guilt, redemption, sadness that can't even be cured by death, they can bear witness to unspeakable crimes and of the inescapable heritage of the past.

Heavy themes.

Nothing suitable for children?

Oh yes, they are. All of them.

Children take life very seriously. Life, death, pain, loss … they still face the big questions, because they haven't learned to look away. We can develop quite a skill in that as grown-ups. Children want to look at the dark because they know that what they fear becomes even more frightening when they turn their back on it or lock it away.

Young readers often don't have emotional memories attached to the themes of death, loss and guilt, which makes them much tougher when they play with them. But they've heard about them, the great monsters waiting … and they love to encounter them on the safe grounds of a printed page. As for the children who do know – we so easily forget that many know quite a lot about death and loss, even guilt – they long for stories that help them to cope with the dark by asking questions about it or maybe even give meaning to it. For them, stories can be both shelter and comfort, without looking away, and ghosts can be the perfect travel companions into realms that know about pain and fear.

It was a long journey through life for me between *Ghosthunters* and *Ghost Knight*. During that period, I learned some things about death and loss, about human nature, good and evil – all this apart from the fact that I had always been completely obsessed with knights. (*The Once and Future King* by T.H. White is still my favourite book).

Serious ghosts

The ghosts I found for *Ghost Knight* were not funny. If you intend to write a ghost story that walks on the darker side of this genre I recommend that you find your heroes in real places. Children love the enchantment of fiction that makes them discover reality. The ghosts I found in Salisbury, Lacock and Kilmington were human, and shadows of ourselves. They take my young readers on a journey into their own future as grown ups, but they also tempt them to travel into the past, to Salisbury Cathedral, Lacock Abbey and Kilmington Graveyard. These are all places where they can touch and breathe times gone and lost and follow in the steps of those who have lived before them.

I will never forget the reading I did at Salisbury Cathedral late at night, surrounded by children and parents. It took place, of course, next to the tomb of William Longespee, the man who had inspired my ghostly hero and incarnated my dreams about knights, and who at the same time allowed me to bow to what Oscar Wilde taught me about the sadness of ghosts.

Writing a ghost story

So, as you see, a ghost story is not just a ghost story. Maybe that is especially true for one written for children. There are so many paths to take. A good story always starts with the right questions. Ghost stories like to hide from us, dress themselves in a dozen veils. In readings I always try to explain this by comparing them to a labyrinth. Each one is full of traps and surprises, full of characters that hide between the hedges and love to jump at the poor writer who is trying to find his way through. There are whispers. A story likes to keep its secrets, but it also likes to be chased, found out, hunted and tamed. So it teases you by giving you hints and wrong tracks. And there you are, a pen in your hand (well, as in my case, you may write using a computer), a Moleskine notebook under my arm (well, once again, you may just carry your laptop … be careful though, there's nowhere to plug in in the labyrinth). You are stumbling down the narrow paths, looking for the one that is exactly right – the one that won't be so long and windy that it bores your readers to death; the one that shows all the secrets, all the characters hiding and whispering … It is the greatest adventure to find the heart of a story. And it's true storyline. Of course this endeavour is especially scary when you are looking for a ghost story! You may only find out after turning several corners that you are dealing with a scary ghost. Did I give you the impression that you choose whether it will be funny or scary? I apologise. The story chooses, once you enter its labyrinth. So make sure you ask the right questions before you decide on the one you enter. What do you want the labyrinth to grow for you?

Do you want your readers to love the ghost whose story you'll tell? Do you want them to pity it? Or fear it? Once again – you may answer all these questions and then find that a completely different story emerges. It has happened to me. Many times.

What age group do you intend to tell your story for? Once again, this is a good question and it needs to be asked. But be ready to change your answer if the story demands it.

The setting. Once you've decided on where the story will be set it will be hard to change it, especially if you choose an existing location. With an imagined one you leave most decisions to the labyrinth (which can be interesting!). With a real place, you walk in with a map, with your research and knowledge guiding you. A real place, with all its history, can be like a bag of provisions for your writer's journey. It can be your main character, all the food you need. It will tell you about landscapes, weather, buildings – even characters – and your readers will be able to follow your tracks in their own world, making a wonderful adventure. I still receive photos showing children in Venice who have followed the tracks of my book, *The Thief Lord*. And I heard about a boy who knelt in front of Longespee's tomb in Salisbury Cathedral after meeting him in *Ghost Knight*.

Oh – one more question: who will you be? The hero? Somebody who watches him/her and all the others, a narrator who knows everything? The god of the story? (Well, ghosts don't accept these gods but try, if you want to.) Most likely, you will be all of them. That's the joy of being a writer. You can live a thousand lives and take a thousand shapes.

Yes, go and write ghost stories! And write them for children! Even the dark ones, soaked in tragedy and the shadows of death – maybe those especially. Children are the most magical audience. They slip into a story like a fish into water. Without hesitating. Without asking how deep it is and where you got it from. They will travel the past on their printed wings. They will face their fear of gravestones and shadows moving in the dark. They will consider the possibility that life may not end in death and wonder why it scares them to see proof of it. They'll remember those who came before them and may even get a glimpse at the never-ending circle of life. And if all that gets too scary, just let them chase the ghosts – to save the good ones and send the bad ones to hell.

Hurrah for ghost stories!

Cornelia Funke (pronounced Foon-kuh) is a multiple award-winning author of children's fiction and has sold over 20 million copies of her books worldwide. She was brought to the attention of Barry Cunningham at the Chicken House (see page 25) when a young German girl living in England asked him why her favourite author's books were not available in English. Chicken House published her latest title at that time in English translation, *The Thief Lord* (2006) and it stayed at No 2 on the *New York Times* bestseller list for 25 weeks. It was followed by the *Dragon Rider* series, the *Inkheart* trilogy, *Ghosthunter* series, and the *Reckless* series all published by Pushkin Press. Her most recent books are *The Glass of Lead and Gold* and *Behind the Water Curtain and other Tales from Around the World* (both Pushkin Press 2018). In July 2019, Bloomsbury published Cornelia's novelisation of Guillermo del Toro's *Pan's Labyrinth*.

See also...
- *Spotting talent*, page 1
- *Who do children's authors write for?*, page 104

Writing magic into fiction

Kiran Millwood Hargrave recommends the techniques she uses to feed and inspire her magical stories, and guides us through each stage of the process that allows a writer's fantastical ideas to come to fruition.

All fiction is a kind of magic: a conjuring. From your imagination, you are building whole people, whole worlds, making them so vivid and tangible your reader will be able to touch them, see them, wish they lived in your stories – but how do you layer magic upon magic and introduce a fantastical strand to your story? Perhaps you call it fabulism, perhaps magical realism, perhaps fantasy. They are all branches of the same enchanted tree, and here are my experiences of reading – and rooting my own stories in – magic.

Roots

My earliest love was the *His Dark Materials* trilogy by Philip Pullman. Read first when I was ten, much of it admittedly flew over my head, but I didn't mind because *how* it flew! Like witches on yew twigs, like swan daemons swirling, like angels stirring the clouds. I believe we all have 'books of power', as I term them, often discovered when we are young, that are keystones for the sort of stories we wish to write.

When I look at my own 'books of power', they largely fall into what I would call magical realism. Alongside Pullman's epic trilogy are: *Skellig* by David Almond, the *Chrestomanci* books by Diana Wynne Jones, *The Wolves of Willoughby Chase* by Joan Aiken, *Journey to the River Sea* by Eva Ibbotson, and the ubiquitous *Harry Potter* series by J.K. Rowling. All hold very different, varying systems and approaches to 'magic', and often my first task when writing a novel is to decide where I want my book to sit within that spectrum. My debut, *The Girl of Ink & Stars* (Chicken House 2016), plunges into fully-fledged fantasy; my second novel, *The Island at the End of Everything* (2017) finds magic in nature, and my most recent, *The Way Past Winter* (2018), is folkloric in its telling and so sits on the border of magical realism.

My first challenge to you is to ask: what are your 'books of power'? Do they tell you about the sort of books you love, and give you an insight, as I believe, into the sort of books you should probably be writing? Some of you will be fantasy fans, while others may prefer that world to be recognisable but knocked slightly ajar to let some magic in. I like to keep my 'books of power' on my desk throughout my current writing project (the books change from project to project). It's an excellent procrastination exercise, but also an inspiring one.

Shoots

Your books of power are on your desk; perhaps you're listening to a film soundtrack (Enya is my writing jam); maybe you have a scented candle wafting snatches of 'Mystical Forest' towards you – and now you're ready to write. It's all possibility … like new shoots of green life emerging in spring. Some of you will plunge straight in, others will plan your narrative to within an inch of its life, but as a self-confessed 'pantser' (as in by-the-seat-of-your-pants vs 'planner') I wholly condone the former. There is nothing more exciting to me than plunging into the adventure alongside your characters and, as they take on more life, letting them make the decisions.

That said, I started my writing life as a poet; a bit of structure has always helped me and I give this to myself in the form of a map. This piece of advice is probably most useful to those of you writing a quest narrative – something where the characters travel through landscape – but I've also worked on maps of houses, or schools, or streets. As soon as the perimeters of the places your characters will inhabit are solid, your imagination can run wild. Often these places also help to define the sort of magic you'll encounter in your world: if it's rife with mountains and dragons, you're probably reaching for an alternate universe, the rules of which you get to decide; if it's a secret door in an otherwise ordinary garden, you've got a beautiful set-up for magical realism. But my main advice at this stage is not to worry about labelling *what* sort of magic you're choosing. Let your story tell you what will work.

When I say 'draw a map', it does not need to be a work of art. My map for *The Girl of Ink & Stars* was a clumsily drawn circle with childish landmarks, with the routes of my characters plotted through the landscape in different colours for each. The plan for *The Way Past Winter* was even more basic: a house, some trees, some mountains, the sea, and an arrow pointing 'North'. Think of it as storyboarding, as they do for films. You have your whole story on one piece of paper – and you can always rip it up and start again.

Rings

I can only speak to describe my own experience of writing – and everyone is different – but I like to charge through my first draft, full pelt towards the conclusion. This results in very short, fast-paced first drafts, but it means that the fear of the blank page is conquered. Something is easier to improve than nothing, so I would encourage you to write your first draft quickly, too. Then, the real work begins.

A tree grows rings as it ages, and so too will your story. These next drafts are for firming up its core, and finding the confidence to set down more firmly what you perhaps only gestured at in first drafts. I would argue this is not the time for brutal editing. Rather, luxuriate in bringing your story more fully into being. If you've written a fantasy, full of mermaids and talking animals, give them their back stories. If you've written in magical objects that transport your character into parallel worlds, think about how they feel, smell, look, where they came from. Put in all those details you would want as a reader: colour your world in. Check that your characters' names suit them and the world they inhabit. Research any asides that observant readers will appreciate and think how clever you are. Enjoy playing around, giving credence to ideas that may not quite be working, but that you think *could* – with just one more draft (or three).

This stage takes the longest for me, but it is also the most fun. It's when I experiment and learn the most about myself as a writer, and about what I want this story to do, and what I want a reader to take from it.

Branches

This next stage may appear to be misleadingly titled, as it implies growth when actually it's very likely that your manuscript will shrink – but editing really *is* like growing branches; it's also a little bit about hacking off the weaker ones.

As a reformed poet, editing holds a special place in my heart. I love it, because finally I know what my story is, and editing will help me get it there. But I know not everyone shares my enthusiasm for hacking at sentences or scenes that took weeks/months/years to write. So my advice to you is this: look at it as *giving* your story something, not taking something away. Only by editing can you find the sub-plots worth growing, and those that need pruning. Only by editing can you find the heart of your story, and make it sing.

Buds

Now you're ready to submit (I hugely dislike this word: when I was on 'submission' to agents I made a spreadsheet to keep track of where/when/who and my husband changed all the headings to things like 'date soul delivered' to denote when I sent out the manuscript, and 'poop or not poop?' to indicate whether I got a full request or a meeting/rejection ... humour helps!). Speaking from experience, the waiting is possibly the worst bit of all. Even when you're waiting to hear from, and often being rejected by, publishers, at least you and your agent are in it together. So hang in there, and give yourself the best possible chance of success by taking special care when choosing which agents you send to.

I made a list from the *Children's Writers' & Artists' Yearbook* and thoroughly researched this shortlist, breaking it into a top-tier I wanted to send to first, and then a second to help me get straight back on the horse if those initial queries bore no fruit. Look at those who represent the writers of your 'books of power', and pop them on the list too. Aim high. I did, and I ended up with my first choice of agent. But there was something I did not do right, and that I would urge you to do – that is to classify what exactly I had written.

I've mentioned that one of my 'books of power' was *His Dark Materials* by Philip Pullman, but another was *One Hundred Years of Solitude* by Gabriel Garcia Marquez, and a third was *The Border Trilogy* by Cormac McCarthy. If that sounds like a confused list, it was, and it made for a confused manuscript. Fraught with long descriptions of landscape, and far too much pathetic fallacy, I wasn't sure what I had written. This showed in my query letter, which announced *The Girl of Ink & Stars* (then *The Cartographer's Daughter*) as a 'magical-realist YA/crossover adventure story'… Yes, I really did write all that down, and press 'send'. Luckily, my wonderful agent saw past it, but you can help yourself enormously by really pinning down what sort of book you've written. This is the only point at which this really matters, I would argue. Until you send your book to agents, just follow your instincts and write in whatever way your story needs you to write it. Once you have an agent, they can help you nail down what exactly you've written. We sent *The Girl of Ink & Stars* out as an adventure story and let the fantasy element come as a surprise.

That's why I've called this section 'buds' – it's about making your story look as appealing as possible, making it impossible for them *not* to want to represent you, and showing that you really know what you're talking about and are taking this seriously. So, finesse what you call your book. Perhaps it's a 'YA coming-of-age story with magic', like Harry Potter, or a 'fast-paced action adventure story' like Percy Jackson. Comparisons to other successful books on the market are always a good idea, but you should highlight how your book differentiates itself too.

Know that you are not alone in your fear and trepidation … or your big dreams. I look forward to reading your no-doubt magical stories.

Kiran Millwood Hargrave is an award-winning writer and poet. Her children's books include *The Girl of Ink & Stars* (2016) winner of the British Book Awards Children's Book of the Year and the Waterstones Children's Book Prize 2017, *The Island at the End of Everything* (2017), and *The Way Past Winter* (2018) winner of Blackwell's Children's Book of the Year 2018, all published by Chicken House. Her debut YA book, *The Deathless Girls* (Hachette Children's) was published in 2019. For more information see www.kiranmillwoodhargrave.co.uk. Follow her on Twitter @Kiran_MH.

Reinventing old stories for new readers

Deirdre Sullivan shares her fascination for retellings of fairy tales and the possibilities that arise from looking with fresh eyes at these stories, reworking their age-old power to inspire, influence and connect with young adult readers.

I think we all remember the first stories that spoke to us – however we encountered them, from the mouths of teachers or caregivers or by ourselves. Different voices speak to different readers, and Hans Christian Andersen's *The Little Mermaid* and Oscar Wilde's *The Nightingale and the Rose* spoke to me. I had learned to expect a 'happily ever after', in the way we all do, so these melancholy stories defied my expectations and lodged themselves in my heart, like a shard of the Devil's mirror.

In college I was introduced to the work of Jack Zipes and his anthology, *Don't Bet On The Prince* (Gower 1987) by a friend (to whom the book is dedicated), and I became acquainted with a greater breadth of fairy-tale retellings, in female voices. I had encountered feminist fairy tales before (a small Irish publisher, Attic Press, had published a children's series of these that I used to hunt for in libraries and secondhand bookshops), but revisiting them at the tail end of my adolescence was as potent as a poisoned comb to the skull. Fairy tales have always had what Marina Warner calls a 'suspect whiff of femininity', but I had been raised on stories told by men. Soon I was discovering Madame Leprince de Beaumont and Dortchen Wild. Female tellers had been there all along, it seemed, if you only took the care to look more closely. From then on, fairy-tale motifs wound themselves through my writing, both subtly and explicitly. I became hungry for more fairy-tale retellings, and devoured stories by the likes of Emma Donoghue, Robin McKinley, Neil Gaiman, Aimee Bender, Francesca Lia Block, Isabel Allende and Margaret Atwood.

In the summer of 2015 my publisher, Little Island, approached me about publishing a collection of my fairy-tale retellings. I was instantly excited about it. It felt right. I dusted off some old stories and began work on some new ones. As the collection progressed, though, I ended up writing 12 brand-new retellings, to ensure the themes and voice felt uniform. It wasn't a hardship. When I write, I feel like I am in conversation with myself and with the stories I have been told about the world around me. I run my hands over their edges, and I try to notice new details I am drawn to. I write what I know, but also what I fear and what I love.

Tangleweed and Brine (Little Island 2017) is a book that centres the female experience of the world within the fairy-tale realm. I wanted to write about bodies, and how terrifying and messy they can be. I wanted to talk about being a woman in a society built by and for men. I wanted to talk about fear, but also anger. I wanted to write about the lessons that the world teaches girls, drip by drip or all at once. I was 12 when the last Magdalene laundry closed, and I had lived my whole life in the shadow of the eighth amendment. My country was structured in a way that let me know, that let us all know – over and over again – how little women's lives mattered. That casts a shadow, and when I began to piece together the stories for the collection it was largely women in the shadows I was drawn to – women with bodies that didn't fit societal expectations, women used as pawns for political gain, women who try to find the right thing in a wrong world. It is a sad book, and an angry book, but there are moments of freedom there as well.

… Because there is a witchcraft to being female. From the whisper networks to tampons slipped underneath a cubicle by some kind hand, we find support in each other. There's a shared struggle that binds us. And no one knows that more than a teenage girl. Adolescence can be a very dangerous and lonely place, but there is a power in it, too, an alchemy: changing bodies, fluctuating emotions, the dawning realisations; it's a heady time, and an intense one. It's that mixture of dependence and independence, of forging your own path and being guided along the one envisioned for you. It is a time in my life I remember sharply, and a time that will continue to inspire me. I facilitate creative writing workshops for teenagers, and they are incisive and passionate readers who can enjoy books while recognising their faults. Recently someone asked me when I would write a book 'for adults'; this happens every now and then and is generally framed as a compliment. I brush it off quietly, saying things like 'Oh, you never know', but I'm fairly sure I do know. I write for young adults because I want to, and for the same reason that I tell the stories I do – because they inspire me.

I'm aware that *Tangleweed and Brine* came out at an opportune moment. There was something of a fairy-tale zeitgeist in the air, as well as increased discussion of feminism with the #MeToo movement started by Tarana Burke gaining traction in 2017, when the book had just been published. People, and young people in particular, were becoming increasingly comfortable confronting and unpacking previously unspoken things, looking at the way the world worked and articulating why that wasn't good enough. Whispers were becoming shouts. And my book was not alone – around that time Melissa Albert, Sarah Henning, Louise O' Neill and Daniel Ortberg also had books out that reworked or built on old stories and turned them into something of their own. There was something in the air that made writers look at the stories they had been told and hold them up to the light with fresh eyes. And each of us saw something different and built something that was our own from that. There may be a lot of talk about trends in YA but we are all living in the same world; we experience a lot of similar things, consume a lot of the same media, hear the same news headlines. The same inspiration can take two people on very different journeys … I love that.

My advice for someone who wants to rewrite fairy tales would be to be aware of what is out there – to read and reread to give you a sense of what can be done and has been done. Then to listen to yourself. In tarot readings, there are the prescribed meanings of the cards, but sometimes a reader will find themselves drawn to a detail or a symbol; they may not know why, but something about it draws the eyes. That sense of moving away from what a story is supposed to be towards what it could become for you in this moment – that little, precious space is inspiration. And it's worth worrying at those details like a dog, until you've chewed it into something that's yours alone. With old stories, the more familiar people are with them, the more of a shorthand you can use; a shoe, a wolf, an apple becomes symbolic. Whatever world you put it into, the old story will be humming underneath like a familiar tune. The reader will sense it pulling at them, making them remember when it first spoke to them and all the ways it has spoken to them since. When you retell a fairy tale, you are invoking something very old and very powerful; there's a responsibility to get it right, but a satisfaction when something clicks.

I had two big 'clicks' of this kind when writing *Tangleweed and Brine*. One of them came from years of trying and the other came to me in a dream. The second way was far easier, but I think the first was more satisfying. I had put a lot of 'Little Mermaids' into the collection at first, as it's a story I'm drawn to time and time again. As someone who feels like they spend a lot of time on the outside wondering how people work, I found the mermaid character spoke to me. I grew up beside the ocean, and the tang of salt air was never far away when I was small. The story of *The Little Mermaid* brought me my first sad ending and my first Disney princess, and both of those left small dents on my heart. I had to cull a fair few mermaids as I drafted *Tangleweed and Brine*, but I remember sitting in a café thinking that I could just have my mermaid kill the prince and return to the ocean, and feeling so happy for her. I'm not normally in favour of murder, but I wanted that little tongueless girl – who'd walked on glass for love – to choose herself. And so, in my story, I asked her to do that – and she did. The child I was when I first encountered that story wouldn't have been fond of it ending in a stabbing, but it made sense for me to follow the path not taken in the Andersen story ... and to send my mermaid home. The second magic click came with *Bluebeard*. I didn't know what to do; I'd written what was turning into a tender little love story, but the fairy tale demanded a roomful of murdered wives and I just didn't think the *Bluebeard* I had written would do that (#notallbluebeards). I worried and wondered about it for ages, tweaking other stories while I did (one of my favourite things to do when I get blocked on a project is to start something else, even a ridiculous thing; it provides the distance you need to stand back and see what must be done to set things right). It took a dream to point me in the right direction. I woke up with an image seared into my brain: a room full of dead men. And that gave me the key I needed to unlock my version of the story, where the secret is not the things that Bluebeard has done, but who he is and what he has survived.

I care a lot about these old stories. I have tried to inhabit them respectfully, but my experience is only one experience, and that's not enough for such an intricate world. The stories we tell matter. They can and should change. Your voices matter. I look forward to the next retelling and the next one – the same old story, through a different lens, a different heart.

Deirdre Sullivan is the author of the *Primrose Leary* trilogy: *Prim Improper* (2010), *Improper Order* (2013) and *Primperfect* (2014), the YA novel, *Needlework* (2016) which won the Honour Award for Fiction at the Children's Books Ireland Awards, three books in the *Nightmare Club* series under the name Annie Graves, and a collection of fairy-tale retellings, *Tangleweed and Brine* (2018), all published by Little Island. She also writes short fiction and poetry. Deirdre's latest book is *Perfectly Preventable Deaths* (Hot Key Books 2019). Her website is https://deirdresullivanbooks.com.

Plotting: how to keep your YA readers reading

Sarah Mussi spells out the function and importance of plot in driving your story along to a gripping climax, and provides a sure-fire plotting route-map you can follow to ensure your readers stay reading.

Books

When I was a child I loved playing chess. I loved the feel of the pieces and the way each one had its own character. My brother, four years my senior, used to challenge me to a daily best of three. I loved obscure openings and mad middles – all those heads that rolled! I adored setting the board up and the names of the pieces – rook and pawn, bishop and knight – but I hardly ever lasted long enough to experience endings. My brother wiped the board with me. At last, one day, he took pity on poor, beaten, eight-year-old me: he said, 'Thing is, sis, chess is a game of strategy – you've got to plot out your moves and, unless you learn how to do that, you're never ever going to win.'

I got a lot better at chess very quickly. I woke up from the dream of touch and name. Part of the magic was gone and I never really enjoyed the game in the same way. But now I won as often as I lost and, in time, the calculations of strategy brought their own pleasures.

Plotting a novel is much the same. In the good old days, I'd start at the beginning and meander through the story at whim, following errant characters and getting so excited about their lives. Somewhere around the middle, just as in those early games of chess, I'd come a cropper and do all I could to salvage the story. Then I'd send it out and cross my fingers … and get nowhere.

Now I plot. I plot to keep my YA readers thrilled, to keep my publishers coming back, and to succeed at the important craft of storytelling.

So what is a plot?

I think of plot as a journey, and very specific to the story I am setting out to tell. As for any successful journey, there are some basics I need to know, such as where I'm going, and the route; above all I need to know *why* I'm going at all. If the plot, then, is the journey, the structure is the *way* I tell you about it. Blow by blow, or after the event? Or perhaps framed by me sitting up in a hospital bed, in a way designed to raise your curiosity about how I ended up there? How I tell you about my journey is key to engaging your interest, manipulating your emotions, helping you and my teen readers relive the fun and feel the despair.

I believe every story is an emotional journey, and plot is therefore soul food, catharsis and relief from the seemingly random ravages of life. That is the true function of plot, and why it's so important to work hard at delivering it.

Setting the route

When considering any journey, it's a good idea to see who has made that journey before and whether they left a map. Luckily, since ancient Greek times, writers of story have charted many maps, among them the ubiquitous five-act structure of Shakespearean drama and Greek tragedy (six for comedy), which later inspired the three-act structure of modern storytelling and film. All share important features, but the key to delivering the story is in capturing causality. Without causality, the structure of the story starts to descend into happenstance, with random events taking over – a bit like in real life. One thing I have learned is: never let real life get in the way of a good story!

The key to causality lies in setting up a *character-driven plot*. The action can be driven by either the protagonist or the antagonist. The only difference is that in the former, a protagonist-driven narrative, the protagonist acts from his/her own desire to achieve a goal whereas in the latter, an antagonist-driven narrative, the protagonist reacts often in order to survive. The narrative equation in either case I like to establish before embarking on my story journey is:

character + goal (*desire/survival*) – obstacles + solutions = climax and catharsis

Therefore the key, in tying character and events together to form a balanced plot, is in *character motivation*. This drives the action and creates cause and effect. So one key question I ask both my protagonist and my antagonist is: what is motivating you?

Setting out on the journey

When I finally put fingers to keyboard, I want to know how the opening of my story will draw the reader in. The initial setting out (I prefer this term to 'setting', which risks being static) of the story must reveal the everyday life of my hero and establish reader identification with them. I check to make sure my hero is indeed heroic. I'd hate to go on a long car journey with a miserable moaning teenager – and I feel the same is true in story. I have to be selective about what to include about their backgrounds. Exposition is always clunky, so I work on a strictly need-to-know basis. If the reader doesn't need to know any bit of information, I don't tell them.

Being guided by the principal that every character needs a *purpose* (and a purpose in a story forms the foundations of plot), I try to always have my characters wanting something, even if it's just a glass of water. Then I make sure they don't get the water easily. Being mean to my characters is paramount.

The most useful story goal is one that is dramatic, for example your character receiving a gold medal as opposed to wanting to win. If I find my protagonist being driven to act by too much internalised feeling I stop and ask myself what would that look like? And jot the answer down under the section entitled: Planning the climax.

However, journeying towards a destination is not going to be momentous unless something is at stake. If the mission fails, there needs to be some consequence. Any journey could soon be aborted if nothing would be lost by doing so. I like to think of the stakes as the negative goals. Many a hero might have said, 'Oh heck to this, I'm going home,' when presented with the first obstacle – unless there was no home to go back to. The higher the stakes the better, too. If I can fix it so that the existence of the universe hinges on the achievement of the quest, then I know I've got a page-turner.

Understanding why the hero sets out to achieve their goal at all is key. Very early on I like to introduce the inciting incident – maybe even on the first page – sometimes even before that. I present my hero with an irresistible opportunity to start them on their journey.

I like to try and fill in a through line, just to be sure I'm staying on track, for example:

_____(*story title*)_____ is about _____ (*character/characters*)
_____who set(s) out to _____ (*the goal*) _____because _____ , but all
does not go smoothly because _____ (*the problem and
stakes*) _____so he/she/they end(s) up _____ (*the solution*).

Story beginnings are hard to get right. I personally like to be tutored by the ancients. I like to begin, as they did, *in medias res* (in the middle of things). Sometimes, of course, you have to work up to that and, like slicing the crust off a loaf to get to the yummy bit, you have to slice off your first few chapters. I console myself that my initial opening work will not be lost: after the story gets going and I head towards my first set piece, I can cut the characters enough slack to drip-feed in those key bits of background I had worked on initially.

Setting up the set piece

I consider a set piece to be a big scene and describe it as a set piece because it needs setting up. So, after 'setting out' comes 'setting up': I start by mentioning the event, then foreshadowing it. I remind the reader that 'something is coming'.

The set piece, like all set pieces when it arrives (Oh, that moment when Lucy and her siblings actually go through the wardrobe together …), should deliver a twist or a turning point. It should reverse the fortunes of the protagonist.

When it comes to a turning point, I love the word 'volte-face'. It reminds me to make sure my character comes out of the scene drastically changed by that experience. For example in *Snow White*, after the inciting incident (that unwelcome message from the mirror) the huntsman takes Snow White into the woods to be slaughtered. The fact that he spares her doesn't change the volte-face. She goes from being rich to penniless, from a princess to a beggar, from being alive to dead (in the reported sense).

So how do I deliver this? Well, I think it should be dramatic (i.e. a big scene) and pose a dilemma. It should leave the protagonist in a situation that is directly at odds with the one they were in when they entered the scene. The dilemma posed by the set piece needs to force the protagonist to act in a way that they had probably never considered before.

Middle or muddle?

Now the story has got punch. Each event can trigger the next and so on, upping the stakes as they occur, until the point of no return is reached.

And then what does your character do? Well, hopefully they make things a lot worse. Why so? Because no story is gripping without tension. So your character during Act Two must struggle onwards and fail, until nearly overcome by the challenges. For as Oscar Wilde said: 'The suspense is terrible, let's hope it will last.'

The setting (or the antagonist) can provide the challenges, as can the inner demons of the protagonist themselves. Like God testing Job on his rubbish tip, our job as gods in our narratives is to test our heroes by making things truly appalling.

But how do we deliver this? Well, plotting a downhill path for the hero means remembering that for every challenge the protagonist needs to formulate a solution. Each solution should not solve the problem, but instead *cause* the next problem. Inside every solution should be that built-in flaw. Each flawed solution might tap into the protagonist's main tragic flaw.

Using conflict in this way, I build until we reach the most serious volte-face, which reverses the fortunes for my hero so drastically that the darkest hour – the well of despond or last straw – is reached.

As the protagonist sits on his rubbish tip (à la Job) or feels despair in his cave (Robert the Bruce) or lies slaughtered upon the stone table (Aslan), it is worth considering the position of the antagonist and refreshing the readers' memory as to what the antagonist's motivations are, and especially what is their Achilles' heel. Think Smaug's loose scale or the White Witch's failure to study the Deep Magic. For therein lies the moment of truth, when the hero can search inside themselves and act from their inner essence to exploit their antagonist's vulnerability and reverse their own fortunes for the last time. Then they can go into the final set piece, the Act Three volte-face, the obligatory scene, the ordeal, the shoot-out at OK Corral, the climax of the plot, *and win*.

Setting the question

Several things must occur at the climax of the story: firstly, the hero must face their biggest obstacle or it will be an anticlimax. They must determine their own fate and the story goal must be resolved once and for all.

Hopefully during the climactic scene, as in a good pantomime, all of my key characters will appear. Hopefully I will have foreshadowed the setting, and visited it already early in the story, as this will avoid me engaging in any distracting description. I might have paired the scene with an earlier one as well, to mirror the action; I can't help thinking of Steinbeck when I plot out my climaxes – his so superbly plotted *Of Mice and Men* is a master class in how to deliver climaxes.

All that remains now is to enable my protagonist to: stay on a collision course with the antagonist; win by losing (to be kept heroic); undergo a 'seeming' death only to be reborn (without it all getting too B-movie). At the very end, I like to narrow things down to one simple action (the pull of a trigger as in *Of Mice and Men*; the dropping of a ring in *Lord of the Rings*); this focuses me and gives an elegance to the ending.

However, no story ends precisely with the resolution of the hero's objective. Readers want to know what happens afterwards; they want to know everyone gets their just deserts. I usually try to keep this as short as possible. Whilst readers do want to know, they don't want to know much. After a penalty shoot-out everyone wants to head home. So I keep it short and head home myself.

Writing a novel does indeed mean plotting out your moves. But I'll leave the last word on that to Wilkie Collins, a far greater master of it than myself:

'Make 'em laugh. Make 'em cry. Above all, make 'em wait.'

Sarah Mussi's first novel *The Lion Skin Rug* was shortlisted by the BBC Worldwide Children's Talent Fiction Award and her second novel, *The Door of No Return* (Hodder Children's 2007) won the Glen Dimplex & Irish Writers' Children's Book of the Year Award and was shortlisted for the Branford Boase Award. Later books include *The Last of the Warrior Kings* (Hodder 2009), *Angel Dust* (Hot Key Books 2012), *Siege* (Hodder 2013), *Breakdown* (Hot Key Books 2014), *Riot* (which won the Lancashire Book Award 2014) and *Bomb* (2014) both published by Hodder Children's. The first and second books of Sarah's *Snowdonia Chronicles* are, *Here Be Dragons* and *Here Be Witches* (Vertebrate Publishing 2015 & Shrine Bell Publishing 2017). Her most recent title, *You Can't Hide*, was published by Hodder Children's Books in 2019. Sarah is a regular tutor for the Winchester Writers' Conference, an editor for manuscriptfeedback.com and gives regular writing workshops. See her website www.sarahmussi.com or follow her on Twitter @sarahmussi.

Writing historical novels

Michelle Paver shares her thoughts on how to approach writing historical novels for children and the importance of focusing on the story.

Books about how to get published sometimes advise new writers to research the market thoroughly. Read the competition, see what sells – that sort of thing. If that appeals to you, fine, but I've never liked the idea and have never done it. In my view it isn't necessary, or even a good thing. You might just find it confusing and intimidating, and it could put you off what you really want to write.

I think it's better to concentrate on the story *you* want to write. The characters. The premise. The historical setting. You may not even know *why* you want to write it. But you do, and that's the main thing.

The period

Before you make a start, though, it's worth asking yourself why you want to set the story in your chosen historical period. Are you especially attracted to it? Did you daydream about it as a child; maybe you still do? Or does it simply have a vague appeal, perhaps based on having seen a few films or read some novels set in that time?

There's no harm in being drawn to a particular period for tenuous reasons. But if that is the case, I'd suggest that you become a little more familiar with it before deciding whether to use that time for your story. You'll need to know your chosen period pretty thoroughly; and if you decide halfway through writing your novel that it isn't quite as fascinating as you'd thought, then the chances are that the reader will think so too, and your story probably won't work. In short, you must be prepared to live and breathe it for months or even years.

The story is king

This would seem to be the logical point to talk about research, but I'm going to leave that for later because I don't think it's the most important thing. The most important thing is the story. Always. And particularly for children. In general, children don't read a book because it got a great review in *The Times*, or because they want to look impressive reading it on the train. They read it because they want to know what's going to happen next.

That might seem trite, but it's amazing how easy it is to forget, especially when you've done a ton of research on a particular period, and there are so many terrific things about it that you just can't wait to share with everybody else.

So it's worth reminding yourself that the basics of any good story need to be firmly in place: characters about whom you care passionately; a protagonist who wants or needs something desperately; perhaps a powerful villain or opposing force which poses a significant threat. Big emotions: anger, envy, pride, hate, loyalty, love, grief. And just because the book will be read by children, don't shy away from the bad stuff (although obviously, you'll need to handle it responsibly). Death, violence, neglect, loneliness. Children want to know. They're curious about everything.

The beginning

Everyone knows that the first page of a story is critical, but this is especially so for children. In fact, the first paragraph is even more critical. And the first sentence is the most critical of all.

This poses a special challenge if you're writing a historical novel. How do you root the story in the past without getting bogged down in clunky exposition?

There's no magic formula, but the idea of 'show, don't tell' is a good place to start. Perhaps you could begin with a situation that's specifically of that period, like a witch-burning. Or, as part of the story, weave in an object of the period, like a flint knife.

You might be tempted to write a 'prologue', like the ones they used to have at the beginning of old movies ('London, England. The Cavaliers and Roundheads are at war …'). By all means write one of these. I did, for the first draft of *Wolf Brother*. But you may well ditch it before you finish the final draft. You may find that by then it has done its work by helping to anchor you, the writer, in the period. If you leave it in, it might have a distancing effect for the reader, diminishing the immediacy of the story.

Telling the story

What I said about the beginning of the story goes for the rest of it, too. The challenge for the writer of historical novels is to make the reader 'live' the story along with the characters. Somehow you've got to make them see, feel, touch, taste that period – without resorting to wodges of boring description that might slow things down, or overdone 'period' dialogue which is tiring to read and may distance the reader.

Again, there's no formula, but a good guiding principle is to make the essential exposition an integral part of the story. Make this a story that couldn't really have happened at any other time in history – even though the emotions involved are universals with which the reader can readily identify.

If you do this, then it'll become fairly clear what needs to stay in and what should come out. And there will probably be a lot of cutting. Pare down the exposition to what's essential. For instance, you may not need to explain the background to the entire war; just the particular skirmish in which your heroine has been caught up.

And for the essential exposition, it can help to introduce it in a highly charged emotional way: perhaps an argument or a fight. 'Exposition as ammunition' was a favourite motto of the film-maker Ingmar Bergman and it's one that can serve you well. But don't get so hung up on explaining things that you lose sight of the emotional focus of the scene.

The same goes for 'period atmosphere'. I would think long and hard before including anything for this reason alone. Try to make your period details part of the story. Then cut them back, then cut them back some more. What you need is a swift, vivid, unforgettable image with *just* enough detail to bring it alive – but no more.

Research

Which brings me (finally) to research. Some novelists don't do any. If that works for them, that's great. But if you're setting your story in the past, I don't think you can get by without doing at least some. And probably rather a lot. You need to know, intimately, what it was like to live back then. It's the little everyday details which interest readers, particularly children. What did people eat, wear, live in? How did they fight, travel, work, entertain themselves? What did they *think*? How were they similar to us? How were they different? And the more you can actually experience some of this for yourself the better – for example, by location research, trying out the food of the period – because it will give you all sorts of intriguing ideas and insights that you couldn't have got in a library.

Bear in mind, too, that research isn't just a matter of getting the details right. It'll probably spark ideas for the story itself: incidents, twists, particular scenes. These are gold dust. Use them. (Provided, of course, that they work in the context of the story as a whole.)

Perhaps the hardest thing about research is that the vast bulk of what you've lovingly unearthed isn't going to make it into the final draft. Be ruthless about keeping *only* those details that you really need: either to move the story along, or to develop character, or to set the scene. And shun any whiff of teaching; this is a story, not a history lesson.

This means that you'll probably go through a rather painful process of cutting over the course of your first, second, and successive drafts. But don't grieve too deeply for your lost treasures. *You* know all that background, and your in-depth knowledge will give your writing an assurance that it wouldn't otherwise have.

Language and style

This can be especially tricky: a kind of balancing act between keeping the story and the characters accessible, while leaving the language with just enough special vocabulary or dialogue to remind us that we're in another time. All this without distancing us too much, or (just as bad) without obvious anachronisms.

I'm often asked if I write differently when I'm writing for children, as opposed to when I'm writing for adults. The answer is, no, not at all. For me, it's the nature of the story that dictates the language and the style. If you're writing a story set in a middle-class Victorian home, your vocabulary and style will be utterly different from that which you'd use if you were writing about a forest of the Stone Age.

Having said that, if children are going to be among your readers, one important thing to bear in mind is that lengthy flashbacks can weaken the force of a story by reducing its immediacy. Because children read to know what's going to happen next, it helps too, to have unexpected twists, surprises, action, high emotion, flashes of humour, and lots of dialogue, as well as the odd cliffhanger chapter ending. You've got to give them a reason to turn the page and to keep turning the pages, all the way to the end.

Who are you writing for?

'What age group are you "aiming" at?' is a frequently asked question. For myself, the answer is: none. Apart from a general idea that I'm not writing a picture book for six-year olds, I prefer to leave age groups to editors and publishers, and concentrate on the story.

Besides, once you start thinking in terms of 'aiming' a story at a particular group of people, where does it end? For instance, say you're 'aiming' a story at 9–12 year-olds. Well, what kind of 9–12 year-olds? They're not a homogeneous mass. Boys or girls, or both? And what kind? Middle-class or underprivileged? Immigrant or home-grown? Gifted, average, or special needs? If you start thinking like that, you run the risk of killing your story.

The same thing goes for the publisher's Holy Grail of the 'crossover' novel that's read by both adults and children. If you have this at the forefront of your mind when you're writing, it's unlikely that you'll do justice to the story. It may well end up being a mess which *nobody* will want to read.

Although this may sound a bit uncompromising, I have the same view when it comes to trying out your story on your own children – if you have them – or on others. In my view, this is risky and I prefer not to do it. (Well, in my case, I couldn't, because I don't have children, and don't know any very well.) In fact, quite a few children's writers don't have children of their own, but what many do have is a strong memory of what it was like to be a child and an ability to write from a child's perspective. That's what you need. Not market research.

Being true to your story, knowing your chosen period inside out but only including the most telling of details … Of course, none of this is going to guarantee success. But with luck, it'll improve your chances on the slush pile. *And* you'll have a lot more fun than if you'd been slavishly studying the market!

Michelle Paver is the author of the bestselling *Chronicles of Ancient Darkness* series, which has been published in 37 languages and the film rights sold to Sir Ridley Scott. *Ghost Hunter*, the final book in the series, won the 2010 *Guardian* Children's Fiction Prize. The series has also been recorded as audiobooks read by Sir Ian McKellen. Her first ghost story, *Dark Matter*, became an immediate bestseller and drew critical comparisons to the great M.R. James. Her second ghost story, *Thin Air*, was published in 2016 by Orion. Her most recent book *Wakenhyrst* was published by Head of Zeus in 2019. Her website is www.michellepaver.com.

See also...
- *Who do children's authors write for?*, page 104
- *Writing ghostly stories*, page 142

Writing for teenagers

Holly Smale discovered the importance and freedom of writing *for herself*, rather than for any imagined readership. She suggests that there are no limits and no rules to teen fiction but that, above all, in those exciting, terrifying teenage years, readers appreciate a story told with honesty, humour and empathy.

I never wanted to write for teenagers. Frankly, I didn't even know what they wanted when I *was* one. The vast majority of my adolescence was spent studying my peers, observing what they liked and did not like – which words they used, what brand of trainers they wore – and then getting it consistently wrong, with humiliating consequences.

By the age of 14, in fact, I hated teenagers so much I decided to skip being one entirely. Overnight, I replaced my beloved children's books with Hardy, Austen and Dickens; I studied obsessively and avoided social situations that might harbour lurking adolescents; I put my hair up like a grown-up Anne Shirley, with a kitchen sponge tucked underneath for volume. And I committed myself to a lifetime of writing *adult* books. That, I had already decided at the precocious age of five, was where my future lay. I adored words and stories, and I was going to write big, important novels for big, important people so that everyone would know that I, too, was big and important. There would be money, fame and awards, and grown-ups would flick with misty eyes through my hardback works and declare they had never seen such wisdom in anyone so young (or – I liked to think – with such lovely, puffy hair).

So I diligently set to work. With the *Writers' & Artists' Yearbook* by my side like a trusty steed I couldn't quite ride yet, I ploughed on, picturing exactly who would be reading my writing and what they would think of it, and of me. Until finally – in my early twenties – I started the Book That Would Change My Life. It was very long and very serious, it was for adults, it was about death and there were entire chapters about muffins and jam (unexplored metaphors about the transience of life, obviously). It took two solid years, then I packed it up optimistically and sent it off to agents as instructed: double-spaced, one-sided, Times New Roman. And I waited. I waited. I waited a little bit longer...

Finally (after about two days) I got bored of waiting. I grabbed my computer, and I started telling another story. Or, more specifically, the story started telling *me*. Because this time it was different. This time I didn't care about it being Big and Important, because my Real Book was on submission and nobody would want this one anyway. It was 2009, and there were no vampires; it was (I was told at various stages) 'niche', 'unfashionable' and 'unsellable' – which also freed me from hopes of money, success, awards, even any imagined *readers*.

This time it was just me and a 15 year-old girl, Harriet Manners: awkward, lonely, unpopular, insecure, trying to fit in at any cost. This time it was just me and a story I needed to tell, and I was going to unpack into this totally free therapy every raw emotion I could remember from my teenage years. As honestly as I could, I was going to tell the very story I had spent my entire life avoiding, about the very people I had gotten as far away from as possible.

And I was going to make it fiction, because otherwise it was no fun; and I was going to make it funny, because I was tired of writing about death and muffins; and I was going to enjoy it, because I was sick to the back teeth of jumping through imaginary hoops, trying to impress an audience I couldn't see. In short, I wrote the story for *me*.

Geek Girl (HarperCollins Children's 2013) became the biggest-selling teen book in the UK the year it came out. Nine books, a few awards and nearly a million sales in 30 different countries later, it has been kindly credited with 'changing the face of teen comedy'. The other book? It's still in a drawer, unpublished and unwanted. But *both* books changed my life, because they both taught me what I needed to finally be 'A Writer'.

The first and most important reader is yourself. You cannot write *for* anyone else; not for other adults, not for commissioning editors, and certainly not for teenagers. Those mystical approving or disapproving readers in your head don't exist, and even when they do exist, every single one of them will be different, have different interests and passions, and want something else from you. So stop worrying about them. Find the voice inside you that needs out, and let it out. Discover the story you really *want* to tell, and tell it.

And if that story just so happens to be about a teenager – even though you don't understand teenagers and you've avoided them your whole life and the story is about a teenager who doesn't understand other teenagers – go for it. The story will determine who you write for, not the other way around.

Teenagers haven't changed. That's what I've realised and had confirmed, over and over again – at schools, in festivals, over lunches, in workshops. They're the same now as they were when I was one. They don't *want* you to copy them. They don't want you to work out what's 'hot' and what's 'now', and to try and follow suit. They don't want to be patronised or talked-down to; they don't want to be second-guessed; and they *definitely* don't want you to attempt to keep up with them, because – and here's the secret – you never will.

The harder you chase your reader – the tighter you hold on, the more you try to impress them – the faster they will put your book down and sit as far away as possible. Readers (but especially teenage readers) don't want to read a story written *for them* – just as they didn't want my Green Flash trainers worn *for them* either. Take one glance at the bookshelf of a teenager and you'll find it stuffed with brilliant YA novels of every genre, every narrative style, every possible topic: comedy, horror, romance, dystopian, historical, tragedy, poetry. Told sensitively and with respect, there are no limits and there are no rules to teen fiction. You can forge your own path, and your readers will love you all the more for it. All a teenager wants is honesty – to read a good story, told with the story put first.

As for me, I came full circle. In accidentally writing about a teen, I finally realised what I should have realised at school: that being a teenager is the most glorious, raw and candid time in our lives, and that we are *all* just trying to find our way. In those few precious years, we blaze an exhilarating path between the safety of childhood and the freedom of adulthood, teetering and fumbling and flying as we go. Everything is new. Everything is fresh. Everything is exciting and terrifying, in equal measure. Channel that, and there are no boundaries to what you can write about, or how.

The truth I finally understood is this: there are no more 'important' books than those written about teenagers. Because if they can chart that heady journey truthfully, with empathy and understanding, teen novels have the power to change the lives of their readers; to help them work out who they are, what they want, how they see the world and other people, and who they want to be. They have the power to comfort, to inspire, to challenge, to provide escape, to amuse, encourage and support. Written honestly, these are the books we treasure even when our teenage years are over. *These* are the books that matter.

So here's my advice: find your inner teenager, tell your story and let your readers find you. Never, ever the other way round.

Holly Smale is the author of *Geek Girl*, the No. 1 bestselling young adult fiction title in the UK in 2013, which won the 2014 Waterstones Children's Book Prize and was shortlisted for the Roald Dahl Funny Prize. The *Geek Girl* series has now sold over 3.4 million copies in 32 languages worldwide. She is currently writing the critically acclaimed series, *The Valentines*, published by HarperCollins Children's Books. Holly has a BA in English Literature from Bristol University, as well as an MA in Shakespeare. Follow her on Twitter @HolSmale.

See also...
- *Writing crime fiction for teenagers*, page 162
- *Writing thrillers for teenagers*, page 165
- *Plotting: how to keep your YA readers reading*, page 151

Writing crime fiction for teenagers

Anne Cassidy is the author of more than 30 novels for teenagers and she explains here why she thinks the crime genre is perfect for teenage fiction.

I love crime fiction and that's why I write it for teenagers. In my first book, *Big Girls' Shoes* (1990), two teenage girls overhear a murder during a phone call. In *Dead Time*, a teenage girl sees a boy she hates get stabbed to death on a bridge over a railway line. The deaths are brutal and the books are dark. I make no apology for this. Crime fiction has to move the reader. The crimes have to be horrible so that the reader cares about the victim. I've locked up a victim in a container and left him to die. I've pushed a girl off a 16-storey block of flats, I've drowned several hapless teens and I've even poisoned one with arsenic pasta. I have no mercy.

I've written 30-plus novels for teenagers, all concerned with crime of one sort or another. I wrote a series in the 1990s called *The East End Murders* and three books in the *The Murder Notebooks* series. In between I've written a line of standalone thrillers, most of which have a murder at their core.

Characters and narrative

Writing for teenagers is not different in kind to writing for adults. You have a particular audience and you have a story to tell. In my case the audience is teenagers and the stories I tell fall into the crime genre.

In general terms, books for teenagers have two main features. Firstly, the main character is usually a teenager and the story centres round them. This teenager has to be completely and utterly believable. This is a writer's first challenge. What you don't do is focus on the external features of today's teenagers; the music, the fashions, the mobile phones and the 'teen' speak patois are ephemeral. What you're really looking for is the emotional core of your teenage protagonist and for that you have to go back and find your own teenage self again. When I wrote my first teen novel I dredged up as many memories as I could. I listened to lots of the music I'd liked at the time (much of it still among my favourites). I looked at family photographs. I spoke to family members and thought back to my own schooldays, writing down a rough journal of anything and everything that I remembered; names, places, books, lessons, clothes, shops. I revisited my own past and what I found, when I got there, was a teenager who'd spent her teen years feeling hard done by, where the tantalising promises of near adulthood had become mired in the day-to-day life of being a schoolgirl/daughter/sister. There I found the emotional core of my teenager: the struggle to move forward into adulthood while everything seemed to pull her back. I realised that contemporary teenagers are no different. The fashions, the temperament and the reliance on electronic gadgets are all modern but at heart today's teens are the same as I was 40 years ago. They have within them that essential contradiction of adolescence; negotiating the passage to adulthood, shrugging off the child they once were. So my teenage characters embody this struggle in one form or another.

The second feature of a teen book is that the story drives the novel. Novels for teenagers must have a strong narrative and this story has to move forward in every chapter. In general you cannot have pages and pages of musings about the meaning of life or overindulge in descriptive passages. But this doesn't mean that your story can't explore universal and important themes or that it cannot establish a sense of place. In my book *Looking for JJ,* a ten-year-old girl kills her friend and we meet her six years later when she is released from prison. The narrative follows her trying to live with a new identity. The theme of the book is forgiveness. Has she the right to expect a second chance in life after what she did?

The story of a crime teen novel should start when something dramatic is happening. *The Dead House* starts when the main character, Lauren, revisits the house in which her family were murdered ten years before. She alone survived. In *Forget Me Not* a child is abducted. In *Just Jealous* a girl is staring at the body of a boy who has been shot. The main character and others emerge through this early action and take shape quickly. By the end of the first chapter the reader should have a strong sense of story and character and an inkling of which direction the book is heading.

This is why I think the crime genre is so perfect for teenage fiction and why I have enjoyed writing it for so many years. A crime novel naturally starts with a dramatic event, often a murder. The main character is often involved in some aspect of the discovery of that murder. In a teen novel the main character will perhaps discover the body or be a friend of the victim, or perhaps he or she may be a murder suspect. The story will be told through his or her eyes whether it is in third- or first-person narrative. The rest of the novel will mirror an adult crime thriller in that there will be clues and red herrings, and secrets and lies will be exposed. There will be police involvement in some way and the tools of detection will be used – surveillance, research, interrogation. These things will happen whether the main character is a school student or a boy on the run. At the end of the book the killer will be exposed and the secrets revealed.

Language and savvy teenagers

Don't underestimate the teenage reader. Teenagers watch a lot of crime on television. When I visit schools I often ask them about it and they list anything from *CSI* to *Jonathan Creek* to *Morse* and *Poirot*. They are used to the complex narrative that a crime story necessarily needs. They like the twists and turns and the cliff-hangers and the secrets that emerge from the story. When teenagers are gripped by a story they will hold on to the various strands and read with gusto until they find out 'whodunnit'.

One of the main questions when writing for teenagers is 'How explicit can the content be?'. The writer is always writing with one eye on the reader and another on the 'gatekeeper': the librarian, teacher or parent. This is not just a matter of censorship. Teenagers as a group are not natural readers. They do not scour the review pages for new books and they do not haunt the shelves of Waterstones. They often find their books through librarians, teachers and parents and then from word of mouth via friends. So these 'gatekeepers' are not to be feared but rather to be seen as your most demanding reader. They will not 'promote' your book unless they think it is really good. I think how explicit the content can be is a matter of taste and style rather than censorship. In crime fiction the question is particularly relevant. Modern crime fiction encompasses some truly stomach-turning gore but, again, the question for me is whether its plot delivers the shocks and surprises needed to make a good crime novel. If it does, then the gore is window dressing for a particular audience. I do not have serial killer/torture violence in my books but this is an artistic decision rather than because of a fear of censorship. I think the taking of a small child or the murder of a mother and her baby or a teenage boy dying from a single punch is 'gore' enough. Who? Why? and How? are the questions that interest me.

My books are read by 12–14 year-olds onwards. The content is grown up and for this reason my characters are usually over 16. This is not a problem for the readers as teenagers like reading about older characters. It means, though, that my characters can do more grown-up stuff. A 17-year-old staying out all night or having a relationship is acceptable, whereas if the character was aged 14 it might cause added problems for the plot. My characters don't swear and I originally made this decision in part to avoid having my books kept out of school libraries just because of a couple of four-letter words. As time went on though and these four-letter words started to appear in other teen books it became a matter of choice. Conversation in novels is never realistic, it simply approximates to the way we think people speak; in sentences, cogently, without interruption. In reality speech is all over the place, fragmented and often incomprehensible. Likewise with swearing. If you stand near any group of teens you will be shocked at the range and frequency of swear words. If I were to try and replicate their speech the page would be peppered with four-letter words so I decided to leave them out altogether and let the reader supply them.

Series fiction and standalone novels

Crime fiction takes a number of forms but the most obvious two are series fiction and standalone novels. I have written both. The joy of a series is that it allows you to follow through on a group of characters and build a 'soap'-type plot from book to book. However, each book must stand up by itself and be a self-contained crime mystery. If a teenager picks book three of a series to read first they must have a satisfying plot and be informed of all the salient 'soap' developments without spoiling the enjoyment of reading books one or two. This is particularly relevant to me with my *Murder Notebook* series. These books are standalone murder mysteries but they all involve stepbrother Joshua and stepsister Rose who are both on a quest to find out about their parents' disappearance five years before. This disappearance is the continuing story of this series and each standalone murder mystery must in some way add to their knowledge of what happened to their parents. It's complicated but huge fun to do.

Standalone novels don't usually involve a 'detective' as such. They usually start with a teenager being drawn into some tricky situation and seeing how that teenager copes. In my book *Heart Burn*, Ashley owes a boy a favour. The favour he asks of her is illegal and dangerous. She agrees to help him and ends up fearing for her life. Standalone novels are often viewed as more 'literary' than series fiction. I think this is rubbish as series fiction has been written by many great writers. Patrick Ness has had his *Chaos Walking* series shortlisted for major awards and Kate Atkinson has given the adult crime novel a 'literary' feel with her *Case History* books.

What should you write – series or standalone novels? You should write the story that you want to write. If you have a good crime story to tell then decide which format it needs and write it. Don't underestimate your teenage audience. They are savvy and love a good murder mystery. Enough said!

Anne Cassidy is a full-time writer and has written more than 30 novels. Her most recent YA books are *No Virgin* (2016) and *No Shame* (2017) published by Hot Key Books. *Looking for JJ* (Scholastic 2013) was shortlisted for the Carnegie Medal 2005 and was the winner of the 2004 BookTrust Teenage Book Award; its sequel is *Finding Jennifer Jones* (Hot Key Books 2014).

See also...
• *Writing thrillers for teenagers,* page 165

Writing thrillers for teenagers

Sophie McKenzie considers the ingredients for writing a successful thriller for teenagers.

When people ask me what sort of books I write, I tend to reply that I write thrillers for teenagers and, more recently, for adults as well. But actually, I do no such thing – at least not deliberately … I just write the kind of stories I like to read, involving characters I care passionately about. And I write to please myself – not for a specific audience. So here's the only rule I'm going to suggest you stick to – always write what matters to you … not what you think other people want, need or expect. Everything else (i.e. the rest of this article) is just my opinion – a few thoughts and suggestions that helped me and might be useful to you.

A strong story

This is definitely my number one requirement in a top thriller – whatever the age of the audience. Remember that a story is *not* simply an interesting situation, though it may start with one. In a story, stuff happens. A good way to check if you have a really interesting story is to look at whether the scenario you've created gives your main character something they really want or need – *and* a big fat problem that gets in the way of that ambition. In my book, *Girl, Missing*, for instance, Lauren *really* wants to find out who her birth mother is and whether she was stolen from her original home as a toddler. Her main problem, at the start of the story, is that her parents refuse to talk about her adoption. This also means that Lauren can't look to her parents to sort out her problem, thus ensuring the story follows one of the basic principles of children's fiction and gets the adults out of the way as fast as possible! It also deepens the problem, as Lauren starts to suspect that her adoptive parents may have been the ones who stole her from her birth mother.

High stakes

Your character's needs and problems must be important to them. If they care and you care, chances are you'll get your reader to care too.

There are millions of things your character might want or need to find fulfilment and/ or salvation. And a top story will certainly need an original twist. But there are a few fundamental ambitions that almost everyone relates to. Most thrillers and adventure stories revolve around one or more of the following, though there are others:

• Coming home. This is a common desire, especially in children's stories – I'm talking here about characters who are trying to find their way back home – like Dorothy in *The Wizard of Oz* – and about characters trying to find a new home – like Harry in Robert Westall's marvellous *The Kingdom by the Sea*.

• Working out who you really are and/or finding your place in the world. This is another huge need shared by characters in identity/rites of passage stories as varied as *Being* by Kevin Brooks and the *Pretties* series by Scott Westerfeld. This 'goal' is particularly common in teenage fiction – identity issues seem to resonate strongly with adolescents aware they are no longer children but not yet sure how to be adults.

• Then there's love. Will the boy get the girl; will the child be reunited with the parents?

• And, of course, there's survival. Whether your character's goal is to save his own life, the lives of those he loves or the entire planet, survival stories usually involve plenty of action and interesting villains. In fact, baddies often provide stories with the best problems: imagine the Harry Potter books without Voldemort or *101 Dalmatians* without Cruella de Vil.

Not worrying about taboo subjects

Personally I don't think there's any subject that can't be tackled. What counts is how you treat the material. Teenagers, like the rest of us, want to read about subjects that matter to them. Families, friendships, loss, guilt, identity, ambitions in work and in love – are all relevant. Sometimes I think teens get a raw deal. Just because young people are aware of difficult topics doesn't necessarily mean they want to read about them in a heavy duty way. Beware of turning your thriller into an 'issues' book in which the main character only 'angsts' and 'never acts'. If you want to write a thriller around a challenging topic, that's great. Just make sure there's a strong story holding the whole thing together. In *Blood Ties*, I wanted to write about how it might feel to discover, aged 15, you'd been cloned as a replacement for your dead sister. That could easily have been the starting point for a much less pacy book than the one I ended up writing, which attempts to weave its thought-provoking subject material in and out of a fast-moving action story.

A central character to care about and identify with

A good story *has* to involve individuals we care about. And a teenage novel will usually feature one or more teenage protagonists. If memory (I was a teen), personality (I act like a teen) and research (I talk to teens) don't help you imagine yourself into the head of an adolescent, then you may struggle to write teenage books.

The stories I like best often incorporate a relationship drama that bubbles under the main action. From a writing point of view, focusing on the development of a romantic relationship – as well as a high-octane thriller plot – helps make your characters more interesting and your story more meaningful. *The Set-Up* is the first book in my *Medusa Project* series about a group of teens with psychic abilities. It begins with Nico, who narrates the story, discovering he has the gift of telekinesis. He uses this developing power on missions as well as trying to impress the girl he likes, Ketty. By the second book of the series, *The Hostage*, Nico and the other teens have been brought together to form a crime-fighting force. Much action and danger ensues from this, yet the story – this time narrated by Ketty herself – also focuses on what she really thinks about Nico.

Will boys read stories that contain an element of romance? Well, many won't, but I'm also certain that it's a complete myth to say that boys don't care about romantic relationships at all – they just don't want you to spend pages analysing them!

A clear sense of the point of view you're writing from

Whose story are you telling? Make sure you know, right from the start. Then try and keep that character at the centre of the action, moving the story along. In his commentary on the film adaptation of *The Lord of the Rings,* director Peter Jackson talks about the importance of turning the camera on the film's heroes at least every third shot. A useful tip – which translates in novel terms as follows: don't stray too far from what your main character can think, feel, see, touch, smell and hear. Writing from an omnipotent, narrator perspective is a perfectly valid choice but it does tend to distance the reader from the main character's mind. Almost all children love to identify with their heroes. And thrillers definitely benefit from the immediacy of a strong viewpoint. I wrote each book in the *Medusa*

Project series from a different character's point of view to explore each character's particular psychic power and personality.

Planning and plotting before you write

Some writers plan. Some don't. Personally, I like to plan the foundations – the outline of the story showing where the characters are going – before I start. But I save the fun stuff – showing how the characters are going to get there – for while I'm writing.

I came to the conclusion that planning was helpful after starting no fewer than 17 books in my first year of serious writing. Some of these had some merit – an interesting character here, an exciting scene there – but almost all of them fell apart by chapter five or so because the plots simply didn't pan out. Planning can feel like an overwhelming task. But unless you try and work through your story in advance, it's all too easy for the whole thing to crumble in your hands. This is, of course, particularly true for thrillers, which require suspenseful twists and turns in order to deliver their thrills.

Managing a plot is a bit like driving a chariot pulled by several huge, powerful horses. You have to concentrate on what you're doing – and be as fit and strong as possible – in order to hold together the reins and make sure that the various strands of the story you're weaving don't career down separate paths and send your chariot tumbling to the ground.

If you want to write thrillers, study thriller writers

I spent a lot of time studying other people's plots, working out how various authors whose plotting skills I admire handled that aspect of their writing. For instance, I read the first three books in Anthony Horowitz's *Alex Rider* series and wrote down everything that happened (literally, just the actions) that moved the story on.

That experience taught me many things – not least the value of breaking my plots into manageable amounts. When planning *The Set-Up*, I knew halfway through the story that Nico, the main character, would discover the man he had trusted up to that point was actually plotting to betray him. This enabled me to break the story down into two halves, making it less daunting to plan each one.

Have a laugh along the way

Just because you're writing a thriller doesn't mean your story can't have its lighter moments. An ironic narrative voice, a character with a great sense of humour or a funny situation do more than make the reader laugh – they provide a release for tension, allowing the next plunge into suspense to be even more powerful.

Creating suspense – hooks and hangers

The most important chapter is the first – get that right, drawing your reader in with a dramatic 'inciting incident' (as Robert McKee puts it in *Story*) and you will, hopefully, have set up your story in an interesting way and hooked the reader in. Some sort of conflict is usually necessary here, as exemplified by one of the best kids' thriller first chapters I've ever read – *Thief* by Malorie Blackman. And never forget the power of D.R.A.T. – that's the Desperate Race Against Time, guaranteed to inject a shot of excitement into any story!

Cliffhangers are great too – whenever I'm coming to the end of a scene, I try and work out what I need to write to give the reader a pay-off for sitting through that chapter – and what I can leave unexplained, as a hook to make them want to turn the next page.

And finally...

Here are my top three tips for producing a thrilling story: (1) Get into the story as fast as possible; (2) Make sure that every plot twist is unexpected but convincing; (3) Don't be indulgent ... if what you've written doesn't move the story on, cut it.

In the end, if all else fails, remember that so long as you're trying to write the best book you're capable of writing, nothing else really matters. So don't give up.

Sophie McKenzie is the award-winning author of *Girl, Missing*, *Blood Ties* and *Split Second*, all of which won the Red House Children's Book Award. Her thrillers include sequels in the series mentioned above, as well as the six-book *The Medusa Project* series and the suspense mystery *All My Secrets*. Sophie has also written two romance series: the *Luke & Eve* stories and the *Flynn* books, comprising *Falling Fast*, *Burning Bright*, *Casting Shadows* and *Defy the Stars*. Her latest teen novels are the psychological drama, *SweetFreak* (2017), which was nominated for the Crime Fest - Best Crime Novel for Young Adults Award 2018 and *Becoming Jo* (2019), a modern-day re-imagining of the children's classic *Little Women*. Sophie has also written four thrillers for adults, *Close My Eyes* (2013), *Trust in Me* (2014), *Here We Lie* (2015) and *The Black Sheep* (2017). Sophie's website is www.sophiemckenziebooks.com and she can be found on Twitter @sophiemckenzie_.

See also...

Dealing with tough issues in YA fiction

Holly Bourne shares advice for YA authors on how to deal with sensitive and difficult issues through fiction in a responsible, truthful and supportive way that provides 'a safe space for teenagers to explore the dark'.

The YA author has an undeniable influence on their readers, which is why it is vital that they write sensitively and responsibly. I believe that the right book given to a teenager at the right time can change – maybe even save – their life.

Puberty is a pretty ruthless stage in life; it is when weird things happen to your body, a time of first love and first heartache, of first-time sex, and maybe when bullying, loneliness, exam stress or mental illness cast a shadow over your life (75% of people who develop mental illness in their lifetime do so before the age of 18). In short, it is a period when you are grappling with your sense of identity, trying to figure out *who you are*. Being a teenager can be exhausting, exhilarating and terrifying, and I believe fiction can offer both refuge and respite during this time. The best stories don't only provide a gripping plot but also help young readers to make sense of their lives or to feel less alone.

As a YA writer, you must convey essential truths about the teen experience for your stories to have any hope of connecting with your readership. Teenagers are not naive about the hardships of their existence. I travel to schools all over the country to talk about books and mental health and I'm always blown away by how sensitive teenagers are to emerging social issues. There's not much darkness they're not already hugely aware of or personally wrestling with. They're hugely grateful to have books that shed light on the concerns that preoccupy them. Remember that teenagers are legally children and therefore, as a YA writer, you have a responsibility to tell the truth *safely*; you must ensure your story is truthful but not harmful. This delicate balancing act is something that can be tricky to get right.

Before I became a full-time author, I spent five years working as an advisor for young people at a charity called The Mix. This experience gave me a concrete understanding of teen issues and how to engage with young people about their problems within a rigorous safeguarding framework. This has provided me with an invaluable background to my fiction career, in which I feel able to tackle the darkest subject matter in a way I know is as safe for readers as possible. In my novels I've tackled suicide, self-harm, abusive relationships, rape and sexual assault, obsessive compulsive disorder, alcoholic and neglectful parents and many other 'tough issues'. If you research your topics intensively and remember any safeguarding training you have had and expert advice at all times, there are no limits to how dark you can go in your fiction. In fact, teenagers may be grateful that you have.

This safeguarding underpinning must be there at all times. Never let your writerly ego, or the thrill of writing the more dramatic bits on the page, seduce you away from your responsibility to provide a safe space for teenagers to explore the dark. Whatever issues you decide to tackle, you'll need to research them more vigorously than simply reading this article, but I hope the following guidelines will be a useful starting point. Now, where's the torch?

Writing suicide safely

I'm starting at the very darkest of where the dark can go. That's because it's a hugely common theme running through YA books and one that can have literally fatal consequences if tackled insensitively. Unfortunately, many YA books that have handled this topic dangerously have gone on to achieve huge publishing success. Rather than making it a free-for-all, we need to learn lessons from this – educating ourselves and trying to do better. Any author who wants to explore this issue should research its copycat nature and how getting it wrong can cost someone's life. For instance, Google searches for 'how to commit suicide' rose by 26% after Netflix released the first season of *13 Reasons Why*.

Strong starting-points for research include the Samaritans guidance for covering suicide, as well as the World Health Organisation's media guidelines for preventing suicide. Here are some of the most important guidelines:

• Try not to include any detailed suicide methodology

Leave out any technical details about how a character may take their own life, such as how many pills to take, and never discuss the 'success rate' of any method. Never imply there's any quick or painless way of completing suicide.

• Never show suicide as a solution to a problem

I once heard suicide described as 'a very permanent solution to a temporary problem.' Even if that is what's going on in a character's head, avoid glamorising the fatal notion that suicide is an 'answer' to life's hardships. Instead perhaps strive to show a character who overcomes this suicide idealisation, gets help and goes on to enjoy happiness. This is something I did in my novel *Are We All Lemmings and Snowflakes?* (Usborne Publishing 2018) which opened with my protagonist Olive in a suicidal state, but ended with her in a much better place. I was also careful to focus mostly on Olive's suicidal 'feelings' rather than showing her detailed thoughts.

• Avoid giving characters who have completed suicide 'notoriety'

The element of notoriety that may result when someone takes their own life is something that can glamorise it and cause copycat behaviours, which young people are particularly susceptible to.

• Suicide is never triggered by just one thing

It's is a hugely complicated behaviour, with no $a + b = c$ formula behind it, so it's important not to give a reason 'why' a character was triggered to take their own life.

The right book can save someone's life. Suicide is certainly not a subject to avoid; just ensure you take the time and consideration to write about it safely – there can be catastrophic consequences if you don't.

What is 'triggering'? And how to avoid it

Triggering is a word with a huge amount of misunderstanding and stigma attached to it. Currently we're seeing a backlash against so-called 'sensitive snowflakes' who demand 'trigger warnings' in art. To some extent it is true that you cannot produce any art that doesn't trigger someone, somewhere, somehow, but the term 'triggering' does actually relate to known psychological responses to trauma which it is important to write about safely. No, you can't keep every reader safe from being triggered, but the following guidelines will certainly minimise any unintentional harm in your writing:

• Self-harm
This is a behaviour that, like suicide, can have a copycat element to it, and reading descriptions of it can 'trigger' people to self-harm. Try to keep any description of self-harm off the page, focusing instead on the *feelings* rather than the behaviour itself. Certainly never describe the method a character uses to harm themselves, and avoid graphic descriptions of bleeding.

• Disordered eating
When writing about someone who overeats or under-eats, never actually state that character's specific weight or dress size. This can cause the reader to compare themselves with that character, triggering shame and further disordered eating. The same goes for calories consumed, and calories burned by a character's exercise regime – giving these specifics can be very unhelpful, especially as they're so easily avoided.

• PTSD
The phenomenon most commonly associated with the word 'trigger' is when something triggers a devastating flashback in somebody suffering with Post Traumatic Stress Disorder. A memory of trauma is not stored in the brain in the same way as other memories and therefore, for a PTSD sufferer, reading something similar to what they've been through can cause a flashback. A flashback is when the victim essentially feels like they're reliving their trauma in the present moment, which is obviously hugely upsetting. Although people may be triggered by many different things, I feel it's wise at least to try and minimise graphic descriptions of violence, and especially sexual violence, in your writing. Sadly, many young people are living with trauma and sexual trauma – one in thirteen young people have PTSD by the age of 18 – so keep that in mind when writing about these subjects. You don't need to explicitly 'go there' in order for your story to be powerful. If you get published, do flag the parts of the book you're worried about with your editor. They can then hire a sensitivity reader to check the manuscript, as well as putting a trigger warning on the cover. This is something we've decided to do in my book *The Places I've Cried in Public* (Usborne 2019) which has an off-page rape in it. My publisher hired a psychologist specialising in sexual violence triggers to go through the manuscript and the tweaks she suggested didn't impact the narrative in any way.

Remember mental illness does not exist in a vacuum
Recently there's been a welcome shift away from a simplistic biological explanation for mental illness. The World Health Organization has stated that it is inexplicably linked to human rights issues, and leading experts are campaigning for us to ask people 'What happened to you?' rather than 'What's wrong with you?'. The causes of mental illness might be environmental, socioeconomic or biological, so make sure your character's illness makes sense in the context of the wider world they live in. This is what I tried to explore in *Am I Normal Yet?* (Usborne 2015) about a girl called Evie who has OCD. The book explored both mental illness and gender inequality, making links between the two. I was careful to make sure Evie was never just characterised by her mental illness but was depicted as a fully rounded character who happened to have a mental illness.

An issue isn't a story

Just as a character is not merely representative of a single attribute or one defining feature, a single 'issue' is never a good substitute for an engaging, well-structured plot. It's completely natural that, when writing for and about teenagers, you should want to include tough issues, simply a realistic interpretation of a teenager's life, but the fundamentals of successful storytelling must not be lost.

Always offer hope

I feel a responsibility as a children's writer to ensure my novels have a hopeful tinge, especially when dealing with the tougher stuff. Though I'm careful never to perpetuate unhelpful fantasies such as *Love can cure mental illness*, I do want teen readers who see aspects of themselves in my characters to believe that light can emerge from the darkness. Whether that's through caring parents, the power of good friendships, or showing positive experiences of teenagers using mental health services, I believe a YA writer should always offer hope, and that your book should be a light that guides them towards it.

Holly Bourne is a bestselling author whose YA books, all published by Usborne Publishing, include the award-winning *Spinster Club* series: *Am I Normal Yet?* (2015), *How Hard Can Love Be?* (2016), *What's a Girl Gotta Do?* (2016) and *And a Happy New Year?* (2016). Her other books include *Soulmates* (2013), *It Only Happens in the Movies* (2017), *Are We All Lemmings & Snowflakes?* (2018) and *The Places I've Cried in Public* (2019). Holly has worked as a news journalist, an editor, relationship advisor and 'agony aunt' for The Mix, a youth charity which helps young people with their relationships and mental health. Follow her on Twitter @Holly_BourneYA.

See also...
- *Writing about love and loss for children*, page 173
- *Writing for teenagers*, page 159

Writing about love and loss for children

Natasha Farrant considers the responsibility shouldered by authors who write about love and loss for children and teenagers and how such novels can be a valuable opportunity for young readers to explore challenging emotions and life experiences.

Years ago, when I started out working in children's publishing and before I was published myself, I went to a lecture given by Anne Fine. A member of the audience asked her what the difference was between writing for children and writing for adults. She replied that you could write about all the same subjects, whatever the age of your readers, but that you would tell the story differently. It was all a question, she said, of the angle at which you shone the light. I want to explore that question here in relation to writing about loss and love, because these are subjects I have returned to again and again in my own books.

Even as I write this, I read in the *Bookseller* that authors John Boyne, Malorie Blackman and Sam Copeland, presenting their titles at the Penguin Random House Children's Showcase, 'spoke of transgender issues, experiences of psychosis and how to cope with anxiety as a small child'. And this focus on difficult themes is by no means new to children's literature. From *The Railway Children* to *The Secret Garden*, *Matilda* to *Journey to the River Sea* and *Harry Potter*, authors have dealt with parental imprisonment, poverty, bereavement, loneliness, persecution, child neglect – all huge issues; all, one way or another, connected with loss.

'Struggle and hardship are the essential ingredients of narrative', writes Trisha Lee, theatre director and founder of MakeBelieve Arts, in *Princesses, Dragons and Helicopter Stories* (Routledge 2015). She goes on to quote Kieran Egan in *Teaching as Storytelling* (University of Chicago Press 1989) who believes that it is our desire to explore global concerns with binary opposites – good and evil, fair and unfair, cruel and kind – that engages us with fiction. This is true whatever age the reader. It's up to us, the reader, to make that exploration as engaging, accessible and, dare I say it, as age-appropriate as possible.

My first book for young people, *The Things We Did For Love* (Faber 2012), is a Second World War love story based on the massacre which took place at Oradour-sur-Glane, near Limoges in South West France, in 1944. Years later, a friend still hasn't got over my writing this: 'A children's book! About a massacre!' Well, it wasn't a children's book, as was made clear by the cover. I have no desire to give it to a child – frankly, there are gentler ways for them to learn about man's brutality to man. But teenagers are a different matter. The novel deals with subjects most teens I know are familiar with: sex and desire, jealousy, shame, the awareness that although they long to do the right thing they often feel coerced by social pressure to do the opposite. Most teenagers, by dint of the online world we live in, do know about war. My book offers them a chance to reflect further on what it means.

What, though, makes it a book for teens, and not for adults? It's a tricky question. A book for young people doesn't mean adults can't enjoy it too. It doesn't mean it can't have adult characters. It doesn't mean, for example, that the characters can't have sex. Sex! How often have I heard book pitches along the lines of 'It's a love story, but don't worry, it's for teens so it doesn't have sex in it' – as if teenagers didn't have sex! In *The Things We Did For Love* my teenage protagonists Arianne and Luc have sex. In fact, Arianne uses sex, rather naively thinking that if she sleeps with Luc, he won't join the Resistance and leave her. I don't show them having sex. I show rose petals leading up to a door (corny, but I couldn't resist), and I show that door closing. But we know perfectly well what is happening, and it's the sort of device that's used in plenty of grown-up fiction.

So again, if I can show torture and I can (sort of) show sex, what makes this a book for teens rather than adults? How have I shone the light? Well, there's the characters, I guess – three of the main protagonists are teenagers; one is a child (and one is a fully-grown man, but we'll put that to one side). They have teen and childhood preoccupations, like falling in love and doing homework. Arianne is trying to fill the gap left by her dead mother and her imprisoned father. She believes she may have found her answer in Luc. She believes she can use her love for him to keep him from harm. And the unnamed teenage narrator, after the massacre, writes that the lovers will be together forever. As adults, we suspect that this is unlikely. As teenagers, it's important (I think) to believe that it is true. Maybe that is the key – that belief in the redemptive power of love.

One of my golden rules, when writing for young people, is this: do not leave the reader without hope. Do not destroy that belief that the world can do better. It's difficult, if you're writing about certain subjects. Climate change is a classic example. But I would suggest that if you see no future for humanity yourself, then perhaps writing for young people is not for you. There are various forms of redemption to be found in *The Things We Did For Love*. They were hard to find, in the bleakness of that event, but the focus of the book (and indeed its inspiration) is the small acts of heroism I discovered in the course of my research and which give the book its title. Because writing for children comes with a certain responsibility.

Scientific research has shown that 'when we connect with a story, parts of our brain related to a particular emotion or action light up, and our neurons start firing as if we were engaged in the activity ourselves' (Kieran Egan; *Princesses, Dragons and Helicopter Stories*). And what is true for us as adults is even more true for a child, during the plastic years of brain formation. Philip Pullman writes about his experiences of playing at Davy Crockett in the suburbs of Adelaide when he was growing up: 'When we children play at being characters we admire, doing things we value, we discover areas and depths of feeling it would be hard to reach otherwise. Exhilaration, heroism, despair, resolution, triumph, noble renunciation, sacrifice: in acting these out we experience them in miniature or, as it were, in safety' (*Daemon Voices: Essays on Storytelling*, David Fickling Books 2017). He goes on to write that, through play, he was 'building patterns of behaviour and expectation into my moral understanding'.

As children play, so they read. They *live* the books they love, and these books offer tremendous opportunity to learn about love and loss and everything in between. They will shape their young readers and make them who they are. And yet, remember this. When you are writing for children, know that you are writing for some of the toughest, most critical readers there are, who will not suffer unnecessary babble. Know that that babble includes you pontificating on love and loss, on how sad your heroine is, or how hard she is crying, or how slowly time is passing. Never forget that other golden rule: 'Show don't tell.' *Show* the loss. *Show* the emotion. *Show* the redemptive love. Use every writing trick at your disposal – metaphor, imagery, leitmotiv – to make them come to life. They're never going to live your book if they're bored.

My middle-grade book *The Children of Castle Rock* (Faber 2018) traces the grief of the main protagonist, Alice, as she mourns the death of her mother. The book opens as she prepares to leave her family home forever. Rather than linger on Alice's emotions, I choose to focus on her refusal to leave without taking her mother's commemorative rosebush, which is dug up and squished into the car. The rosebush then reappears periodically – on a balcony, as a watercolour and eventually in a new garden – in a way which shows the reader without spelling it out that Alice, without forgetting, is nevertheless learning to move on.

As I wrote the story, I asked myself these questions: What has Alice lost? What does she want? What does she need? These are the questions which drive the plot. Alice has lost her mum, her dad is completely unreliable, and her home is sold. She needs to rebuild a sense of family, she wants her dad to do this for her, and she needs to understand that he never will. These are the questions which give the novel emotional depth and a sense of purpose. They are not what make it an exciting read, though. The excitement comes from the fact that, in her pursuit of these needs, Alice runs away from boarding school, camps on a Scottish beach, almost drowns, breaks into a house and gets chased onto a stack of rocks by a bunch of Italian gangsters, where she gets cut off by the tide … and in the end conquers both her fear of losing her dad and her fear of heights by abseiling down a cliff.

Even as I write this, I'm aware how complex this question of responsibility is. It is absolutely not about watering down difficult subjects, but it's about rendering them in such a way that a child can explore them – as Pullman writes in the quote I cited earlier – in safety. Children, like all readers, will take what they can and what they need from a story. A child who has experienced severe loss will be alive to Alice's grief. A child with less experience of loss may simply enjoy the adventure. The story may lead to greater understanding; it may simply entertain. All forms of reading are valid.

In *The Children of Castle Rock*, as in all my other books, I have tried to acknowledge that bad things do happen, that the people you love are not always reliable, but that there are others who love you if you can open your eyes and heart to them. I have also tried to fulfil my other responsibility as a writer, which is to make my story as cohesive, exciting and as good as I possibly can. But there my task as a writer is finished. Alice's story is in the world, to be completed in as many ways as there are readers. Which is just as it should be.

Natasha Farrant is a writer and literary scout. Her books include *The Things We Did For Love* (2012) and *The Children of Castle Rock* (2018), as well as four titles in her popular children's series *The Diaries of Bluebell Gadsby: After Iris* (2013), *Flora in Love* (2014), *All About Pumpkin* (2015) and *Time for Jas* (2016), all published by Faber & Faber. She is also the author of two adult novels *Diving Into Light* (2008) and *Some Other Eden* (2009), published by Black Swan. For more information visit www.natashafarrant.com, and follow her on Twitter @NatashaFarrant1.

Including LGBT+ characters in children's fiction

Lauren James makes diversity the bedrock of her writing. She knows the importance of enabling children to grow up reading about and relating to LGBT+ characters, and has good advice for writers on how to promote inclusivity and avoid prejudices and stereotyping across all genres in fiction.

Looking back, the first and only character I can remember reading about as a child who was LGBT+ (Lesbian, Gay, Bisexual, Transgender or another queer identity) was Albus Dumbledore in *Harry Potter*. And even he barely counts – his character isn't explicitly written as gay. When I started writing, I realised that I wasn't the only one who'd grown up without LGBT+ role models. I decided that this dearth of LGBT+ representation in fiction was something I wanted to address in my work. I make no apologies for being a writer with an avowed agenda: telling stories that can change attitudes.

Children's and Young Adult writers have the ears of a whole generation; that comes with a huge responsibility beyond simply providing entertainment. Children read books to learn how the world works, and we have to make sure that the world they read about is as varied and diverse and representative as real life.

Before I was even sure whether I was going to be published, I had decided that the main character in my second novel, *The Last Beginning* (Walker Books 2016), would be gay. It would be clear from the very start that Clove was a lesbian, but the story would be about more than her sexual orientation. She would have clearly defined character traits – with flaws and positive qualities – and, like any well-drawn character, she would navigate her way through an enticing plot (and she'd 'get the girl' along the way too).

I knew that I might face negative consequences for this decision from the publishing industry; even today, publishers reject stories about LGBT+ characters, and give reduced exposure and publicity to those they do publish. Books are bought based on sales estimates, and in the case of LGBT+ titles it's only recently that there have been children's bestsellers, such as *Simon vs the Homo Sapiens Agenda* by Becky Albertalli (Penguin 2015) and *The Raven Cycle* series by Maggie Stiefvater (Scholastic), to prove that there is a huge market of readers searching for diverse titles.

Feedback from other authors in the YA online community who have written LGBT+-focused stories suggests a subdued reaction to LGBT+ fiction from bloggers and readers as well as from publishers. This is particularly true when a novel is female-focused and doesn't include a male main character, as in a novel with lesbian protagonists. In fact, when I started researching existing LGBT+ novels while writing my own, I was surprised by how many there *were* – but how few of them I had seen in bookshops or press reviews.

I knew that I ran the risk of not finding an agent – or not selling the novel at all. Despite this, I decided to write the book. I thought that if it was good enough, it would stand up on its own merits and find the audience it deserved. As I was writing, I kept thinking about the teenagers who would read the book – the ones who knew they were gay, the ones who had gay friends, the ones who hadn't yet realised they might be a member of the LGBT+ community. It has been proven that people who read have more empathy and social skills[1], so for children to grow up reading about and relating to LGBT+ characters can only help to reduce prejudice.

Even though I was braced for rejection, my agent, editors and publisher didn't miss a beat when I told them I was writing a story with an LGBT+ protagonist. I had only just secured a book deal for my debut novel *The Next Together* (Walker Books 2015), so I didn't have a track record to prove that the book would sell regardless of content – but it may have helped that *The Last Beginning* was the sequel to a heterosexual romance in *The Next Together*. This was an intentional decision on my part, as I wanted to get the LGBT+ book in the hands of readers who might not otherwise pick it up. This will have guaranteed the book an audience that a standalone LGBT+ novel from a debut author might not have found.

My publisher was happy to comply when I specifically requested that the cover and blurb clearly indicate that the novel contained an LGBT+ romance. I wanted the story to have a chance of getting to its audience of teenagers, especially those who were too afraid or confused to search out LGBT+ books for themselves. The publisher also made sure I was pitched for LGBT+-focused panels, festivals and articles. I wrote and released a bonus short story, *Another Beginning*, about my LGBT+ characters which was published free on Amazon Kindle for publicity. It was promoted at major YA conventions like YALC (Young Adult Literature Convention, www.londonfilmandcomiccon.com/index.php/zones/yalc) and Summer in the City (www.sitc-event.co.uk).

We're lucky enough that there are now enough LGBT+ books to keep a teenager very well supplied with reading matter – and the number is increasing every year[2].

I'm still learning about how to write

Recommended reads

Lesbian

We Are Okay by Nina La Cour (Dutton Books 2017);

Girlhood by Cat Clarke (Quercus Children's Books 2017)

Gay

I'll Give You the Sun by Jandy Nelson (Walker Books 2015);

More Than This by Patrick Ness (Walker Books 2013)

Bisexual

Grasshopper Jungle by Andrew Smith (Electric Monkey 2014);

The Pearl Thief by Elizabeth Wein (Bloomsbury Children's 2017)

Transgender

When the Moon Was Ours by Anna-Marie McLemore (Thomas Dunne 2016);

George by Alex Gino (Scholastic 2015)

Queer

The Prince and the Dressmaker by Jen Wang (First Second 2018);

Not Your Sidekick by C.B. Lee (Duet 2016)

Asexual

Radio Silence by Alice Oseman (HarperCollins 2016);

Clariel by Garth Nix (Hot Key Books 2015)

diversely and I'm sure I've made mistakes in the past. With that in mind, here are some of the most important things I've learnt about writing LGBT+ characters into my work:

1. Don't write books about the experience of being LGBT+ unless you are LGBT+ yourself

This doesn't mean that you should avoid writing stories containing LGBT+ characters, only that their identity should not be the main focus of the novel. For example, trans authors are best placed to write an authentic book about what it is like to transition genders.

1. Kidd, D., & Castano, E. (2017). *Different stories: How levels of familiarity with literary and genre fiction relate to mentalizing.* Psychology of Aesthetics, Creativity, and the Arts, 11(4), 474-486. http://psycnet.apa.org/record/2016-37488-001

2. www.malindalo.com/blog/2017/10/12/lgbtq-ya-by-the-numbers-2015-16

2. Do your research

Make sure that you read books written by people with the identities you want to include in your fiction (these books are known as 'own voices' fiction) and talk to anyone you know personally about their experiences; also reach out to people on social media or hire a sensitivity reader to check your manuscript for accuracy. You can find databases online of freelance editors who offer sensitivity services to help make sure that your writing isn't harmful to any readers; search for 'We Need Diverse Books' or 'Write in the Margins'. Some publishers will help with the costs of hiring sensitivity readers.

3. Avoid stereotypes

Not all gay men are fashionable, lesbians aren't always butch, and LGBT+ people don't all love Pride parades and nightclubs. There is no universal gay experience, just as there's no single straight experience. An easy way to avoid unintentional stereotyping is to make sure that your character's sexuality is not their only character trait. Avoid a sassy 'gay best friend' who has no real character development or plot involvement, or an LGBT+ antagonist whose terrible deeds are driven by their sexuality. Villains in children's media are often queer-coded (think of Hades, Ursula and Jafar in Disney films) and this can send the subliminal message that being LGBT+ is a negative trait.

Be intersectional with your characters too – don't be afraid to write disabled or BAME (Black, Asian and Minority Ethnic) LGBT+ characters. LGBT+ people are multi-faceted, just like anyone else.

4. Include LGBT+ characters in all genres

LGBT+ characters deserve complicated adventures where they get to save the world too. It is important to show teenagers that life continues beyond coming out, by giving them books to read in addition to contemporary coming-of-age novels. If you write historical fiction, remember that LGBT+ people have existed throughout all of history, even if at the time they weren't visible or their culture didn't have the words to describe them. If you are writing science fiction and fantasy, remember that the social prejudices you choose to include in your fictional world say more about you than anything else; there's no real reason for homophobia in a world of magic and dragons, and a futuristic novel with no diverse characters is more of a dystopia than anything else.

5. Don't bury your gays

It's so common for media featuring LGBT+ characters to end with their deaths that it even has a trope name – 'Bury Your Gays'. Try to flip convention and let your gay characters live at the end of your story. Remember that your young LGBT+ readers might not know about the historical or social context of prejudice against LGBT+ communities; all they will see is people like themselves being the focus of hate crimes. You're writing fiction, so feel free to take some liberty with the details.

6. Write LGBT+ characters of all ages

Including only teenage LGBT+ characters sends the unintentional message that LGBT+ people have no future. Sexuality is a spectrum, and people can discover they are LGBT+ at any age. You could include a newly transgender grandparent, a divorced dad in a relationship with a man for the first time, or a happily single bisexual aunt. Remember that children can realise they aren't straight very young too, often before puberty.

7. Don't be afraid of terminology

Demisexual, cisgender, aromantic – these all might sound like scary textbook terms that have no place in a children's book. However, think of a child reading your book and coming across the exact word they need to google to explain all the feelings they've never understood about themselves. Make your character's identity explicit by putting the word on the page. It's worth remembering that terminology is an ever-evolving science (consider the changing implications of 'transvestite' and 'queer' over the last few decades), so make sure that the words you choose to use are up to date and not considered a slur.

8. Don't shy away from representing physical intimacy

There's nothing more explicitly sexual about two boys kissing than a snogging boy and girl, and yet only occasionally is the former casually represented in children's fiction. At a time when sex education in schools around the world still fails to teach teenagers accurately about LGBT+ sexual health, books are often the only place where a confused teenager can find the information they need in a safe and reliable format.

9. Don't just have a token LGBT+ character

It is exceptionally rare for one LGBT+ person to be found alone in a group of straight friends. Having an isolated LGBT+ character sends the message to young LGBT+ readers that they will grow up to be the only person they know with their identity. To accurately reflect the real world, include multiple people of different LGBT+ identities in the same friendship group. LGBT+ people have deeply important platonic relationships with each other as well as romantic ones; not all gay characters exist to be shipped together.

10. Discuss LGBT+ issues

It isn't a sign of forward-thinking acceptance if LGBT+ characters never discuss their identity with anyone. Not all LGBT+ people are obvious (a trans man in a relationship with a woman will be straight-passing, for example), but if your characters never mention their sexuality, like Albus Dumbledore, it's an indication that they might not feel comfortable enough to discuss it, rather than a sign of a progressive social environment.

Including diversity of all kinds is now one of the first things I think about when starting a story. I believe it's an essential foundation for writing a novel in the 21st century. Deciding to write about LGBT+ protagonists may have been a risk, but it has opened so many doors for me – from speaking on LGBT+-focused panels at festivals and schools to writing for publications about sexuality. But nothing matches the time a young girl attending a signing with her mum told me that she had just come out, and my book was the first she'd ever read about a lesbian like her. Providing a role model for even one teenager made the whole thing worthwhile.

Lauren James is the Carnegie-nominated author of YA science fiction published by Walker Books, including *The Next Together* (2015), *The Last Beginning* (2016), *The Loneliest Girl in the Universe* (2017) and *The Quiet at the End of the World* (2019). *The Last Beginning* was named one of the best LGBT-inclusive works for kids and young adults by the *Independent*. Lauren is an Arts Council grant recipient and wrote the foreword to *The Bible: An Anthology of Personal Narratives and Essays about Bisexuality* (Monstrous Regiment 2017). Her website is www.laurenejames.co.uk.

Series fiction: writing as part of a team

Writer Lucy Courtenay spills the beans on the profitable world of series fiction, its fictional authors, the publishers and packagers, and skilled teams of editors and writers, that create and produce it.

Once upon a time, a group of editors sat around a table, brainstorming ideas for a new children's series for girls aged 6–9. It needed to be collectable with a strong series identity. One editor put up her hand. 'I had an idea for a series when I was seven years old,' she said. 'It was about seven fairies. One for each colour of the rainbow.'

The series, *Rainbow Magic* by Daisy Meadows, has since spawned over 200 titles. There are mini-series of four or seven interconnected titles within the overarching series which share common themes: the rainbow, the weather, the ocean, popstars and parties and animals, to give a few examples. Sales of the series currently stand at over ten million copies worldwide.

You might assume, on those statistics, that *Rainbow Magic* has made its author rich. It has, but not in the way you might imagine. If you remember, it was an editor's idea. Daisy Meadows herself doesn't exist. She is an amalgam of dozens of different writers and editors, all of whom have taken a share of her profits. She is successful because she is the product of professional, dedicated teams who know how to produce books that children love. The same is true of Lucy Daniels – whose *Animal Ark* series could be said to have started the whole series fiction phenomenon in the 1990s – and Adam Blade, more recently of the *Beast Quest* series. There are plenty of other examples, but these are perhaps the best known. When people first learn this, they are often surprised and baffled. What is the point? they want to know. Why do publishers produce books in this way? Shouldn't they be supporting original talent, promoting original authors?

A fictional author has no rights over a series, which makes that series more flexible and profitable for a publisher or a packager. A fictional author can also write six or more books at the same time, which does wonders for a publisher's production line and (you've guessed it) profits. A fictional author can be designed to fit a niche in the market. They can be given an alphabetically appropriate name to meet a browser's eye level or queue-barge on to the shelf ahead of the direct competition. They can be designed to fit as many commercial platforms as possible, should opportunity present: clothing, online games, stationery. They can also enjoy lives far more exotic than those of real authors. Adam Blade's biography charmingly gives him a pet capuchin monkey called Omar, while Lucy Daniels apparently lives in Yorkshire with Russian Blue cats.

If this seems hard-nosed and commercial, it is. Publishing is a business, and it has to think like a business in the current climate where books fight to be heard above the clamour of YouTube. And, as if the competition weren't tough enough, publishing is an industry with very low margins. A book is cheap compared to a games console; it's cheap compared to a pair of decent socks. In order to turn a profit these days, publishers need to sell a lot of books. A title ideally needs to shift around 10,000 copies a year. More if it's an expensive full-colour book.

Adam Blade, Daisy Meadows and friends sell in these quantities. Their success bankrolls the quieter titles, the books that publishers love but which won't set a financial spreadsheet alight: the standalones, the ones with sad endings and quirky illustrations and unusual production values, the literary prizewinners, and the poetry, and all the things which keep a publishing list energised and wide-ranging.

There are dozens of well-known authors now established in their own right who have written packaged series fiction at some point in their careers. Advances aren't high, but the steady stream of royalties and the great and glorious mysteries of PLR income (see *Public Lending Right*, page 400) often mean that the projects are worthwhile. It is a dependable source of income in an unreliable industry. Or 'gas-bill money', as literary agent Lesley Hadcroft once put it.

Publishers are wise to the series-fiction juggernaut and regularly design their own series, commissioning authors and illustrators. But series fiction also originates with packagers. Packagers are an intermediary business. They produce ideas and source writers. But they still have to pitch those ideas to publishers for publication and distribution. In that respect, they are in the same boat as the author rapping on doors to get a commissioning editor's attention. However, publishers take packagers with good track records more seriously than they might a first-time author. Working Partners, for example, has produced some of the biggest series in recent years, including *Rainbow Magic* and *Beast Quest*.

Packagers employ teams of highly experienced editors who have regular meetings to exchange ideas for series, like the meeting described in my opening paragraph. When an idea has been agreed, they will either find a publisher to take it on the strength of the idea (a rare Holy Grail) or, more often, they will ask writers to produce some sample material to fit the concept before presenting it to publishers. The writer is given character names, scenes and complete chapter breakdowns by the packager, with express instructions to fill out the characters and develop the scenes as energetically as possible. There is no fee for sample material, but writers are usually happy to oblige in the knowledge that a little free work can sometimes net a paid project. In terms of cold hard cash, there is usually a small advance if the project is accepted, with around one-third of the royalty charged by the packagers going to the writers.

And here's the good news. Commercial fiction packagers don't need established names to write for them. They simply need writers who can write, and who are able and happy to follow a detailed brief. What's more, they actively recruit them. Go to the website for Working Partners (www.workingpartnersltd.co.uk) and it's hard to miss the great big button shouting APPLY NOW! There are forms to fill in regarding experience and interests, and you are asked to submit some sample writing. Not everyone will make the cut, but if you can turn a phrase and hold a story together, you have as good a chance as anyone else.

It's important to note that packagers are not interested in your magnificent idea about a talking wombat. They are only interested in the mechanics of your writing. In the world of team fiction, it is up to them to produce the ideas. Your job is to fill in the gaps as fluently and excitingly as you can. As such, writing as part of a series team can be a humbling exercise. You might produce your best joke or most moving sentiment in years, but if it doesn't fit the flavour of the series you are writing for, it will be binned as swiftly and unthinkingly as old yoghurt. A successful team writer is the person who can produce writing that fits seamlessly into the whole, not the person with the individual edge.

If your ego can take it, writing series fiction is an incomparable crash course in how to write. I learned a vast amount at the coalface as Lucy Daniels/Adam Blade (yes, I'm both) about pacing, plotting, cliffhangers, world-building, character development, and all those other building blocks of successful storytelling. You work closely – often line by line – with expert industry editors, whose practical advice and guidance can feel like a creative writing course without the fee. Instead, miraculously, you are the one who gets paid. There's even a published book to show for your efforts at the end of it all. Writing in this way can be a valuable apprenticeship for the big bad world of author-led fiction that all writers hope lies in their future. Bring an open mind and a flexible pen to the process, and you will find that the craft of writing will lose several of its many mysterious layers.

You will note that producing series fiction in this way is about the writer, not the illustrator. Illustration and design for this type of series fiction lies strictly with the publisher who buys the concept. If you are an illustrator or author-illustrator, the series-fiction route probably isn't for you. If you are a writer: Hello, opportunity!

Lucy Courtenay has been writing children's fiction for 20 years, working as a team writer on series such as *Animal Ark, Dolphin Diaries, Beast Quest, The Pet Finders Club* and *Heartside Bay*. She has several series under her own name, including *Wild, Scarlet Silver* and *Space Penguins*, and the romantic teen comedies *The Kiss* (2015), *Movie Night* (2018) and *Girl at Sea* (2018) for Hodder Children's. She is the Managing Editor for Fiction at Egmont, a freelance editor of children's fiction for Cornerstones Literary Consultancy and the author of *Get Started in Writing; an Illustrated Children's Book* for the *Teach Yourself* series (John Murray 2016). She tweets @LucyCourtenay1.

The long and winding road to publication

Paul Stewart tells how he achieved his childhood dream of becoming a writer, championing illustrated books for children, and shares his experience of the submission process, rejection and success, and finding the ideal collaboration.

When I was at school, other boys in my class wanted to be footballers or train drivers. One wanted to be an astronomer. Me, I didn't have a clue. Possibly a singer in a band. Then, when I was eight, I was given a prize by a music teacher. Her husband worked for Collins and the prize was a book: *The Phantom Tollbooth* by Norton Juster, with illustrations by Jules Feiffer (Collins 1962). She apologized that it was an uncorrected proof, but thought I would love it. She was right. The novel took me to somewhere wonderful and, from that moment on, I knew I wanted to be a writer.

I started work on my own children's novel – as well as drawing the pictures to accompany it. I soon discovered two things: writing was more difficult than I'd thought, while illustrating was beyond me. I abandoned the project, but I never lost that new-found enthusiasm for my future career.

At university I studied English, choosing Lancaster because they offered a unit in Creative Writing. Then I applied for a (then almost unknown) writing MA at UEA, run by Malcolm Bradbury and Angela Carter. By the end of the course I had a folder of 20 short stories and an idea for a novel. One of those stories – a reimagining of Andersen's *The Snow Queen*, called *Ice* – was published in a literary magazine, *Bananas*. I still remember the thrill of reading their letter of acceptance: '… we'd like to use it in the next issue due out at the end of this month.' It was my first short story in print. I'd arrived.

I hadn't, of course. The other 19 stories – separately and as a collection – were not published, and the novel remained an idea. I decided that if it was indeed true that you should write about what you know, then I needed to know more. It was time to go travelling.

This was back before computers. Up until then I had been writing on an olive-green Olympia SM3 – allegedly a portable typewriter, but Charles Atlas would probably have had problems lugging it about. So I bought a lightweight Olivetti Lettera 32 and, following Malcolm's parting comment – 'I don't have the address but it is, like all the other addresses, in the *Writers' & Artists' Yearbook*' – got hold of a copy. Then I set off.

I lived in Greece, Germany and Sri Lanka; I travelled through Europe, India, parts of the Far East, Australia, the US, Kenya. I had numerous jobs – factory packer, security guard, fork-lift truck driver, bank operative, translator, EFL teacher, you name it – and I wrote something every day. The typewriter went everywhere I went, and each time I completed a piece of writing, I would search through the *Yearbook* for an appropriate publication. A growing number of magazines and publishers in the UK received examples of my work.

Most, to their credit, were kind in their rejections. Many offered advice. I always tried to match the manuscript to the publication, though not always successfully. A leading women's magazine responded to one story with the comment: 'The idea was ingenious but … we do try to keep death out of our stories.'

I also discovered that I was receiving letters from people I'd actually heard of: Robert McCrum, Bill Buford, Paul Samwell-Smith (ah, yes … still nurturing dreams of singing in a band, I'd also submitted a cassette of songs for appraisal). The thrill of communicating with famous people was tempered by the fact that they were sending me rejection letters – one after the other they arrived, enough to paper my walls, and I was feeling increasingly disheartened, though unable to stop writing.

It was this optimistic response from Tom Maschler of Jonathan Cape that set me back on track: 'The above said [i.e. the inevitable rejection], I don't like to lose sight of you because frankly I am convinced that you will make it as a serious writer, and think it likely that we would want to publish you in the future if we had the opportunity.'

I was in Sri Lanka in the '80s when civil war broke out. The school I'd been teaching in was closed, and I returned to England to find that the adult novel I'd almost completed over there suddenly seemed flippant and superficial. So I went back to the children's book I'd been musing over for more than two decades and, three months later, *The Thought Domain* was finished. Published by Viking in 1988, it was my first children's novel in print. For a second time, I'd arrived.

Largely on the strength of that published book, I was taken on by a literary agent. This took a lot of the hard work – and inevitable heartache – out of the process of trying to find a home for my scribblings. I now had someone to do it for me. Three years later, a deal was secured for a book I'd been researching. Based on a true story I'd stumbled upon in Kenya, it was accepted by – yes – Jonathan Cape. In 1991, my first adult book, *Trek*, was duly published. I'd *arrived* …

Apart from that one book (and even *Trek* itself reads like a *Boy's Own* tale of gung-ho misadventure), it was children's literature that I pursued. I liked the discipline of writing for a younger audience, as well as the rigour, clarity and sincerity it demands. My early books were our-world-but-with-a-twist fantasies, often starting with a simple What if…? premise. What if there was a dimension where our thoughts were stored? What if a child was born able to communicate with animals? What if a video machine could record our nightmares?

After the publication of *The Thought Domain*, I submitted fresh proposals in the form of the first three chapters of the new work, a rough outline of the entire novel and a working title, in order to gauge whether my primary editor thought it had legs. If he didn't, my agent would send it to other publishers. I had, by this time, given up teaching EFL to devote myself to writing full time. I did not intend to return to the classroom. Not only did I generate my own stories, but I also started taking on commissions – writing to order, following briefs. I wrote football stories, puzzle adventures books, graded readers, horror and fantasy novels; I had short stories published in themed anthologies.

All these pieces of work, even the ones for older children, were illustrated. I considered this a good thing; I still do. There is, I believe, something perverse about using pictures to lure children into the world of books and then, when they've cracked reading, to remove them. It feels almost like a punishment. If I'd been able to I would have illustrated my own texts but, since I wasn't good enough, the next best thing was to find an illustrator I could work closely with.

This proved far from easy. Publishers often keep authors and illustrators apart. An American editor once explained that this was company policy, as authors 'tend to bully illustrators'. A likely story! Had there been closer cooperation between me and my various illustrators, however, maybe a scene I'd written about a boy on a bike being attacked by a slavering dog wouldn't have been depicted by an old bicycle leaning up against a wall. I mentioned my disappointment to my editor and was given a new illustrator – based in Tasmania …

It was at a publisher's party in London that I first got talking to Chris Riddell. Beforehand, we had seen each other at the nursery our two sons went to, but we'd never spoken. On our train journey home that evening we talked about working together and, after a couple of false starts, produced a picture book about a rabbit and a hedgehog: *A Little Bit of Winter* (Andersen Press). It was my first picture book and my first collaboration.

The year was 1998, and that wasn't the only work we had published … Working together on *Rabbit and Hedgehog*, we'd both realized how much we enjoyed the collaborative process. Chris drew me a fantasy map entitled The Edge: 'Here's the world,' he said. 'What happens in it?'. It was at this stage that we tested our ability to work together to the max. This wasn't a 12-page spread picture book; it would be a long novel for 11-year-olds, illustrated throughout. There were times when we both wondered whether it would ever be completed, but finally, 15 months later, *Beyond the Deepwoods* (Doubleday 1998) – the first of what would become a 13-part fantasy series, *The Edge Chronicles* – was on the shelves. I'd arrived. Again!

Oddly, the series nearly didn't happen. I'd spoken to my editor at the time about the idea. She thought pictures would make the fantasy look too young. 'Not Chris's pictures', I assured her and, though unconvinced, she suggested I send in the proposal. In the usual way, I printed up the three chapters we'd completed, plus a rough synopsis of the book and outline of the world, and included a wad of Chris's pictures. The envelope came back return of post. Being a writer with a string of rejections under his belt, I naturally assumed they'd dismissed it out of hand as a rubbish idea. It was two days later when a tentative phone enquiry revealed that a youngster on a Youth Opportunities scheme had decided to tidy up the office and sent back all the manuscripts that were lying around – ours included. I've often fantasized about other novels that might have been rejected in the same batch …

Chris and I have written and illustrated more than 40 books together to date. One of us will come up with a very general idea, then we talk, talk, talk. If that initial idea starts to fly, we set about building a self-contained world – with maps, characters, names, back histories – for the two of us to immerse ourselves in; a place where we discover the stories that will turn into books. A flying box containing an ominous warning became the first *Far-Flung Adventure* – *Fergus Crane* (Doubleday 2004); a Victorian delivery lad with an insight into the supernatural became the *Barnaby Grimes* novels; a trio of aliens on a spurious mission to Earth became *The Blobheads*; humans versus killer robots – *Scavenger*; cowboys and dragons – *Wyrmeweald*.

Since Chris and I come to a piece of work from different perspectives, the text itself goes through many revisions. Although it is immensely enjoyable working with someone else – the writing, the events, the festivals, plus the fact that 'writer's block' is impossible if two of you are working together on a piece – collaboration is never easy. If we had tried working together when we'd first left college, it might not have worked. By the time we did start, I think we were both old enough to realize that the finished item was of far more importance than our individual egos. And certainly, none of the books we produced together could have been done by either of us alone.

Looking back on my writing career, it seems to have been so arbitrary. I kept thinking I'd arrived, only to discover that it was not my final destination – that there was always somewhere else to go to. All I know is that, ever since first realizing that 'I wanted to be a writer', everything has been geared towards making that a possibility. Publishing is currently changing. It is interesting to see that in the latest *Children's Writers' & Artists' Yearbook* there is a section on 'Digital and self-publishing'. I wonder where I will arrive at next …

Paul Stewart is the bestselling author of children's and adult books, co-creator (with Chris Riddell) of the *Edge Chronicles* series, the *Far-Flung Adventures* series including *Fergus Crane* (Gold Smarties Prize winner), *Corby Flood* and *Hugo Pepper* (both Silver Nestlé Prize winners), as well as the *Barnaby Grimes* series, the *Wyrmeweald* and *Scavenger* trilogies, all originally published by Doubleday. His other books include two *Muddle Earth* adventures and the *Blobheads* series (for younger readers), published by Macmillan Children's, and the *Rabbit and Hedgehog* picture books (Andersen Press). Paul travelled and taught EFL in Germany and Sri Lanka, then upon his return to England, he taught EFL at a language school before becoming a full-time writer. His latest book is *Wings* (Otter-Barry Books 2017), illustrated by Jane Porter. For more information see www.edgechronicles.co.uk.

See also…
• *Writing for a variety of ages*, page 124

Murderous inventions

Robin Stevens reveals how her murder mystery books, written for her 12-year-old self, have tapped into children's fascination for the nasty parts of life. When so much of a writer's career depends on chance, she stresses the value of following your instinct and of finding exactly the right agent and editor to share one's vision and passion.

It's probably not surprising that I'm an author. I grew up in a family that believed in books, and there's never been a moment of my life that I haven't told stories. I have always known with absolute determination that I wanted to have those stories published – but as a child I also wanted to own a zoo, be a wizard and live inside an Eva Ibbotson novel, and all of those ambitions seemed about as likely as each other. So no, it's not surprising that I'm an author – but all the same, I still wake up delighted every single morning by my bewildering good fortune, because *Murder Most Unladylike* (Corgi 2014) was not supposed to be the book that got me published.

I wrote the first draft of it in 2010, during NaNoWriMo (National Novel Writing Month). I really want to stress that I did not have even smallest insight into the children's book market at the time. The simple fact was that there was no story that made more sense to me. I had discovered Agatha Christie's murder mysteries aged 12 and was then sent to Cheltenham Ladies' College aged 13. Detective stories and boarding schools are in my blood, and so deciding to write a murder mystery set at a boarding school was as obvious as falling in love – a feeling of: ... *Oh, of course it's you.*

Murder Most Unladylike let me work through all my confused memories of a boarding-school life that was neither as good nor as bad as Enid Blyton had promised it would be. The structure of its detective story felt like a reassuring arm around my shoulders in an adult world which was turning out to be far less organised that I had been expecting. I knew no one else would want this story, but I realised that I really needed it.

That sounds like a fairy tale, but of course the truth of writing an actual book is not a fairy tale at all. I wrote the first 50,000 words in a wild rush unlike anything I'd done before. I had a full-time job at the time, and so I had to hammer out my word count during lunch breaks, early in the morning and late at night. Daisy and Hazel were the only characters who had names, and they spent long scenes just chatting emptily to each other because I didn't know what was supposed to happen next. I wrote that first draft in 30 days, but I spent two years heavily working and reworking my text before I felt confident enough to actually send the book out to agents.

Once I'd decided to do that, though, I truly realised that I had no idea how to go about it. How did people find agents for their books? And, for that matter, what was my book? It was about children who solved a murder – so did that make it for children, or for adults? The only thing I did know was that when I thought about my favourite authors, they wrote for children. So off I marched to a bookshop, bought a copy of the *Writers & Artists' Yearbook 2012* (I still own it) and began to randomly pick children's agents from its pages.

I know now that this was a terrible idea. I should not have just been looking for an agent who works on children's books. I should have looked for children's agents who had specific experience in the type of book I had written. I *should* have been seeking out agents with a specialty in adventurous crime stories that centre on female characters. Hindsight is obviously a wonderful thing, but I wish I could take my younger self by the hand and gently explain to her that genres are important, that picture books are not the same as children's fiction which is not the same as YA fiction, that there are differences between commercial books and prize winners.

Of course, I got a lot of rejections – partly because what I was pitching was a murder mystery for kids, but mostly because I was approaching the wrong people. I have learned since that this is really the cause of almost every 'No' you'll ever get: the people rejecting you are not stupid, or cruel, or wicked – they are simply not obsessed with what you have written. An agent doesn't just need to *like* your book, they need to *love* it with every fibre of their being. They need to be able to spend five, or ten, or twenty years of their lives so wild about it that they will collar random strangers at parties to tell them how brilliant it is. As an author, you shouldn't want an agent that isn't perfect for you – and I was lucky enough (it really was the most incredible luck) to find the perfect agent in Gemma Cooper.

One day I stumbled on a blog post Gemma had written about how much she loved shows like *Murder She Wrote* and *Poirot*, and how she'd love to find a book like that for children – and I suddenly realised where I'd been going wrong. I sent my manuscript to her, not as a random children's agent but as a lover of murder mysteries who understood the children's book market. And it worked. Gemma met me and bowled me over with her enthusiasm for my book and her keen business sense. I signed with her a week later and she helped me trim my flabby and chaotic 80,000-word manuscript (this word count makes me wince to remember it) into a 60,000-word crime novel squarely aimed at children. We sent the book out to UK publishers in the spring of 2013.

Again, we got a lot of rejections. I want to stress that if any author tells you no one ever rejected them, they are either lying or the luckiest human on the planet. *Everyone gets rejected.* J.K. Rowling got rejected *repeatedly*, and the publishers who rejected J.K. Rowling were not idiots. They were just *not the right publishers* for J.K. Rowling. If one of them had bought *Harry Potter*, they would not have cared about it with enough passion to propel it higher into the bestseller charts with every title. It would not have become the global phenomenon that it is, and other authors would not have to spend so much time explaining to their friends and family why they are not as rich as J.K. Rowling.

Only Random House offered for *Murder Most Unladylike*, because only my editor Natalie Doherty was right for my book. She was besotted with it six years ago, and she's still wild about it today, which is how I know this is true. She believed so passionately that a children's book about murder would sell that she convinced her publicity team and sales team, and they convinced booksellers, and then … the book sold.

I need to be very honest here and say that I was not expecting *Murder Most Unladylike* to do this well. By the time it came out, in June 2014, I was working in children's publishing myself. I knew the size of the market, and I was realistic about a debut author's chances. Most books – and aspiring authors should prepare themselves for this – sell about 1,000 copies. If you are selling more than 100 books a week you are doing very well indeed. If you sell more than 300 copies a week your publishers will have a small party at their desks in your honour. There are a lot of books on the market, and most of them get lost in the noise. And that was what I was prepared for. I'm still pinching myself that this is not what happened.

I was helped by a lot of things that I had nothing to do with: I had a great cover; I got a few nice reviews; my second book was chosen as the Waterstones Children's Book of the

Month in February 2015; and then I won the Waterstones Prize for Younger Fiction in March. I could not have influenced those events, but I'm not sure I would be writing the ninth book in the series today if even one of them had not occurred. A lot of what happens to an author happens outside their orbit – all you can do is react as calmly as possible to the news in your inbox every morning. This lack of control is slightly horrific, and it's a lot to take on board. In fact, what I have realised is that there is only one aspect of my writing career that is within my control – as it is in the control of every writer in the world: the books I write. And I think the content of those books certainly helped me, because the truth is that children *love* thinking about murder.

As adults (or at least, as the good sort of adults), we work very hard to keep children safe. The world is a horrible, stressful place that we struggle to deal with ourselves, and so we put a lot of effort into making sure children do not realise how awful it is until they are grown up and it is too late. Children, on the other hand, spend pretty much every waking hour trying to work out everything they can about the nastiest parts of life. Children are *desperate* to know what adults do to each other, why they behave the way they do, why bad things happen and what those bad things look like.

When you write for children, you have to stop being an adult and remember what it's like to be a child. Children want to understand and explore the darkest places in the universe, and as authors we can let them do that. (We always make sure that we leave behind invisible safety trails, of course, but they're more for us than for our audience). And children also want to be shown that sometimes small is powerful; that kids can be strong and brave and save the day, even when they feel weak and scared; that sometimes adults are good, and sometimes adults are bad; and that it's possible to work out the difference.

I didn't consciously know I was doing all of this when I wrote *Murder Most Unladylike*, of course I didn't. I'm not that clever. But watching how children respond to my series, I've realised this is the key to its success, and to the success of every good children's book ever written. I thought I didn't know who I was writing for, but of course I was lying to myself. I wrote for that 12-year-old Robin who was very grown up but also not grown up at all, who wanted life to be okay and worried that it wasn't, who cared very deeply about crime and justice. This is the only key to success as a children's author that I can pass on to you. *So* much is down to chance and circumstance. You can't hope to give the market what it wants. All you can do is write the book that would have set your younger self's world on fire, and trust that we're all very similar underneath.

Robin Stevens is the author of eight *Murder Most Unladylike Mysteries*, including *Murder Most Unladylike* (2014), *First Class Murder* (2016) and most recently *Top Marks for Murder* (2019), published by Puffin, and five *Wells and Wong Mysteries*, reissued by Simon & Schuster. She is also the author of *The Guggenheim Mystery* (Puffin 2017), from an idea and characters by Siobhan Dowd. Born in California, Robin came to live in England at the age of three. She worked as an editor in children's publishing before becoming a full-time writer. For more information see https://robin-stevens.co.uk, and follow her on Twitter @redbreastedbird.

See also...
- *Writing crime fiction for teenagers,* page 162
- *Writing thrillers for teenagers,* page 165

Who am I today? Writing under multiple pseudonyms

A prolific author who prefers not to be pigeonholed, Julia Golding (or is that Joss Stirling, or Eve Edwards?) explains the creative, practical and commercial advantages of writing under different names.

Time for a rethink

Here are some things I believed before I started on the writer's career path.

1. Getting published was the finish line.
2. Having, say, six books published in my lifetime would constitute a career.
3. Somehow points 1 + 2 would add up to an income.

I can now tell you, 13 years after my first book was published, that all three are way off target. I aimed at my future career with no Robin Hood accuracy; I was pretty much firing my arrows straight up into the air and was just lucky they didn't hit me on the way down. So to help you think through the realities of what it's like to make a living as a writer and what strategies you might use, here are a few arrows more precisely directed.

Once you get your work onto the bookshelf, the challenge then becomes *staying* published. You are at the beginning rather than at the end of a very long march. How can you achieve more than a brief passage across the literary stage? It is really difficult to do, so don't let anyone tell you otherwise. We all have to find our own way and mine recently has been simply to multiply myself.

One for all, and all for one

In an essay from 2011 in the *New York Times*, Carmela Ciuraru, author of *Nom de Plume: A (Secret) History of Pseudonyms* (HarperCollins 2011), lists the three traditional reasons for adopting a name: 'Women writing as men. Writers with dirty secrets to hide. Highbrow writers slumming it in trashy genres.' She then goes on to suggest some others which include: a sign of mental disorder; to adopt a name that sounds like a great author rather than ordinary Joe Bloggs; to be freed up to imagine yourself as someone else; to cope with the modern day online world where multiple identities are normal – a practice she calls 'self promotion under the pretence of hiding'. Oddly, for someone who has written a book on the subject, she has missed in her essay *all* the reasons I do it – and these are the very ones that might come in useful for an aspiring writer. This is best explained by telling my own story.

Looking back, I now see that I was incredibly fortunate with my debut year. I won a couple of major prizes with *The Diamond of Drury Lane* (Egmont Books 2006) and had three other books published with two publishers. This meant that my publishers, my agent and I already knew I had the ability to be prolific. Thirteen years on, I have had 50 books published. When people ask me how I can possibly 'write so much!' (and it is always said with an implied exclamation mark) I find it very hard to answer. It is just what I do. I suppose I am something of a dynamo, powered by the desire to tell stories, so the novel ideas do not stop. Like Dory in *Finding Nemo*, I just keep swimming. I am greatly helped by the fact that writing is my idea of fun. It isn't my intention to terrorise my editors with my fiendish efficiency, honest – though it is amusing to reverse the usual expectation and have the publishers apologising for missing deadlines. If you do not already know, this is not industry standard.

My creative productivity was definitely a plus at the beginning of my career but, a few years in, it did start to become a problem. Reviews began to discuss the amount I was writing rather than the actual book in question and I had a vague sense that I was breaking some kind of rule within the author world. I wasn't supposed to do this – though no one quite said it to my face. The second hitch was more practical: I was competing against myself on my own bookshelf. There is only so much room and attention that the trade will give a writer and it was being spread too thin.

Famous noms de plume	
Author name	**Pen name**
Eric Blair	George Orwell
Anne Brontë	Acton Bell
Charlotte Brontë	Currer Bell
Agatha Christie	Mary Westmacott
David Cornwell	John le Carré
Charles Dodgson	Lewis Carroll
Mary Ann Evans	George Eliot
Daniel Handler	Lemony Snicket
Ruth Rendell	Barbara Vine
J.K. Rowling	Robert Galbraith

So what was my solution? I decided to learn from writers such as Nora Roberts/J.D. Robb, Jayne Ann Krentz/Amanda Quick/Jane Castle and Iain Banks/Iain M. Banks. These internationally successful authors handle their books in different genres by publishing them under different names. The variation is minor for Banks – the middle initial goes on his science fiction. American romance writer, Nora Roberts, adopts J.D. Robb as a name more suited to her futuristic detective stories and is incredibly prolific under both. Krentz uses her three different names for books set in the past, present and future. That gave me the idea of splitting my middle grade fiction (age 9–12) from my teen books, and so Joss Stirling came into being.

And just like buses, after waiting a while, the offers started coming along in twos and threes. At the same time as I was writing my first Joss, I was approached by Puffin to write a historical YA book. How to handle? OK, why not spin off another name?, I thought. Rather than launch Joss as doing two different things for teens, I decided to keep the brands straight and have contemporary romance as Joss and historical YA as (… scratches head …) Eve Edwards!

The advantages

I soon saw that the multiple names brought advantages. Creatively I found it fed something in me, rather like an actor landing a variety of good roles. It was greatly liberating. My family ask me 'Who have you been today?' when we gather at supper. Have I been darkly romantic as Joss, or grappling with the serious issues of World War I as Eve, or running with monsters and mythical creatures as Julia? No one can pigeonhole me as a writer.

There are commercial advantages too. I get three spots in most bookshops, hopefully increasing the chance someone will pick one up while browsing. Writing as Julia Golding, I have in mind a mixed audience up to the age of about 13 and I cover a wide range of genres from fantasy to thriller. Both Joss and Eve write romances when writing teen fiction, something only a few boys will read or admit to reading. By keeping the hearts-and-flowers out of Golding books, I have not alienated a swathe of readers. The flipside of this is that

Eve and Joss both write with teens (and more recently adults) as their target audience, so the situations, dilemmas and language suit that older group. There does not have to be an age warning on the jacket, which might be the case if, known for writing for the pre-teens, I suddenly branch off into more mature material.

And the final advantage is that, in a difficult book market, I can easily keep on reinventing myself so I always have something to offer that a publisher wants (at least I hope so). If one genre is flagging and publishers have stopped contracting in that area, I can put it aside and return to it when the market is ready for that kind of book again. For example, I retired Eve Edwards for a while but am bringing her back with an adult 'UpLit' novel (HarperCollins) very soon.

And the disadvantages? So far I've not come across any serious ones but I suppose there is a dilution of identity. I am happy with that because my motivation for writing is to entertain and inspire readers while making enough money to live on. If I get fan mail to Joss, Eve or Julia saying how much a particular book was enjoyed, I'm content. It is not about seeing my name up in lights but whether my books are in stock.

Three names are also more work for the author. I run three online identities and answer three lots of fan mail. I toyed with the idea of amalgamating everything under one roof (I have done so for my website which, with changing online habits, was getting less traffic than social media) but decided that diminished the value of branding for difference, which was my aim in the first place, so I have had to knuckle down and put in the hours to make a success of the pen names.

When is it time to change hats?

So when might you want to consider doing a quick swap in the literary equivalent of Mr Benn's changing room? Is your old hat looking a bit tired and do you need a new one? Should you put aside the beret for a Stetson, or a spaceman's helmet for a wizard's hat? Here are some times in your career when that might be a good idea:

Scenario 1

Publishers love debut authors but they no longer (or very rarely) stay around to help you make your reputation if you do not do reasonably well as a first timer. This is not because they are cruel and callous, even if it feels that way; it is because they are commercial entities. If your debut does not win the prizes and only sells a few thousand copies, what can you do next? I have heard some new writers speak as if it is the end of the road, but it really does not have to be. If you think you will not get a hearing as you have already shot your bolt, why not submit a new book under a different name? The book should be the only thing by which you are judged. You do not need to drag around a sense of unfulfilled promise like the ghost of Jacob Marley and his cash boxes.

Scenario 2

Do you have too many stories for one name to bear? For example, maybe you have a high fantasy series in mind and a contemporary real life story to offer to publishers. Thinking commercially, a chocolate bar manufacturer does not put Mars and Twix out under the same name, so why should you put your different 'tastes' out together? Remember Iain M. Banks and Roberts/Robb. You do not have to go the whole way to a new identity but you could differentiate with two versions of your pen name.

Who am I today? Writing under multiple pseudonyms 193

Books

Scenario 3

So you have made a name for yourself writing mermaid and animal stories for the younger end of the market and now want to deal with some challenging YA subjects, such as suicide, drugs, bullying, sex and violence. You probably do not want to bring your readers with you – not for a few years anyway. Being known as a writer for the littlest readers might also stand in your way for getting the new departure taken seriously. To keep your audiences straight, a pseudonym removes the need for book jacket explanations and keeps publishers happy.

Final thought

When I started out on the pseudonym route, I kept it quiet. It wasn't a secret but neither did I want too many people to know. Like J.K. Rowling (but without the millions), I didn't want my Robert Galbraith equivalent to be reviewed through the lens of my existing reputation.

Yet since the books took off in their own right, I have become extremely relaxed and open about the fact that I write under three names. I have linked them on one website and include a YouTube video explaining why I do it (*One Author, Three Names!* www.youtube.com/watch?v=Fl4OMud5594/). Really keen readers feed across to the other names. It works best with Julia Golding readers growing up because they will find teen books waiting for them when they are ready, but there is plenty of cross-fertilisation all three ways. This benefits me, of course, but it also means that a child or young person who would never dream of reading a different genre might just have their horizons expanded by taking that small step into the world of a different pseudonym. And I find that a very pleasing thought.

Julia Golding is an award-winning writer for children, young adults and adults, who also writes under the pen names of Joss Stirling and Eve Edwards. She has now published over 50 books in genres ranging from historical adventure to fantasy. Her latest book as Joss Stirling is an adult psychological thriller, *The Silence* (HarperCollins 2019). As Julia Golding she published two new children's books in 2019 in The *Curious Science Quest* series: *Victorian Voyages: Where Did We Come From?* and *Modern Flights, Where Next?* (Lion Children's Books 2019). Visit her website, www.goldinggateway.com or follow Julia on Twitter @jgoldingauthor or @jossstirling.

See also...

From self-publishing to contract

Janey Louise Jones shares her tale of how she successfully self-published her first *Princess Poppy* book, which led to a contract with Random House and huge sales.

My journey to self-publishing

For some children, a bookshop has more delicious flavours than a sweetshop. I was one of those children. When I was a little girl, I wanted to be a writer *and* a princess. So, with my *Princess Poppy* books now selling in their millions around the world, I find myself reflecting on the life experiences which have led to me realising my childhood dreams.

People often say that the story of Princess Poppy, going from a childhood notion, to kitchen table, to self-published success, then on to a Random House contract, is a fairy tale in itself. Perhaps so, but even fairy tales are laced with problems and trials, and self-publishing has been a very challenging experience. I highly recommend starting alone as a way of presenting a vision, proving strong sales and learning the full craft of producing a book – but it is not an easy process.

As a child, I saw witches at my window, and fairies in the moonlight. I loved ballet and the flower fairies, and made petal perfume. I was idealistic and romantic and although I was very loved, I never felt special enough. So I developed a perfectionist streak – always driven to do my very best. I began to express my feelings and identity through words. Like so many book lovers, I loved the physical look and texture of a book as much as what it said to me.

Growing up in the 1970s, it wasn't fashionable to be gender specific for children. Being ultra-feminine was frowned upon as frothy in a way that it isn't now. Did any other girls of the 1970s have a dark brown, checked, floor-length party dress, or was I especially unlucky? I felt a conflict between wanting to be educated, well read and serious on the one hand, and wanting to be a pretty fairy princess, on the other. Could I possibly be 'Fairy Blue Stocking'?

My favourite childhood books included *The Secret Garden, Little House on the Prairie, Little Women, The Children of the New Forest* and *The Diary of Anne Frank.* Later on, at Edinburgh University in the late 1980s, I became intrigued with the concept of 'the novel' and through my love of Victorian and early 20th century authors, I was asked to contribute to *Chambers Dictionary of Literary Characters.* This was my first formal writing experience, which taught me the valuable lesson that when it comes to writing, effort and remuneration are not always commensurate.

Somehow, during my degree course, the wistful child within me resurfaced and I produced a storyboard for a magical, mythical character – Princess Poppy. People often ask me: 'Is she your child, your daughter?' (I have three boys). But no, she isn't my child, she is *me* as a child. I found it difficult to enter adulthood and Poppy beckoned me back to my childish dreams. So, the cliché that one's first and best work is autobiographical is certainly true for me.

Back at this early stage, I lacked confidence and direction, my ideas blowing in the wind – all too easily blown away. (It is so important to hold with your vision at this stage.) In fact, I was convinced by someone that there was no chance of such a character coming to life and so I actually put Poppy to one side for many years. I also heard the well-rehearsed adages that you can't write well until you're at an age when you've experienced life, and also that if you're a proper writer, it will just happen. There might be a bit of truth in these notions.

I became an English teacher, in an Edinburgh girls' school akin to that of Miss Jean Brodie. Then like any self-respecting princess in an ivory tower, I needed to be rescued by a dashing knight. Or, to put it another way, teaching wasn't much fun, and domesticity seemed more appealing. Conveniently, I fell in love with a Royal Marine Commando. This fitted neatly into my script. After a fairy tale wedding, I settled into the real 'grown-up' world of motherhood.

My main writing outlet in this period was a mother's answer to *Bridget Jones's Diary* – Jane Jones's Dairy – a kitchen sink drama of the daily intrigues of the 'stay-at-home-mum' with three infants under four years of age. My years of 'extreme mothering' definitely prepared me for the world of publishing and made my writing much more real and touching.

Curiously, Poppy re-emerged with great vibrancy when my grandmother died in 2000. I wrote about my wonderful granny, Emma Brown, in a eulogy entitled *Pale Pink, Lace and Pearls*. This piece of writing was so well received in my family, that I felt a burst of confidence, which is very elusive when little children take over your world. I finally left behind my own childishness and began to write as an adult, looking into childhood.

I found that Poppy was becoming an 'every girl' princess, instead of a traditional or mythical princess as she had been before. The theme of my Poppy stories is that through family love, every girl is a true princess. I don't like the idea of so-called 'alpha females' – lucky girls who are richer, prettier or smarter – every child has a right to feel equally special. Poppy is innocent, but not old-fashioned. Although I am nostalgic in some ways in my writing, I often think there is something rather brutal about girl stories of the 1950s, as if children were somehow less cherished then, so my books do not hark back. I prefer to reach the children who are growing up, right now, in the 21st century. Childhood is so precious and I want to prolong it, as most mothers do, so I attempt to evoke a world which is both contemporary and yet aspires towards a sweeter way of life.

Self-publishing Princess Poppy

As the Poppy book idea gathered energy, the story became quite focused. The decision to focus on one clear plot was a breakthrough after months of endless bright ideas. I plumped for a birthday party to introduce the heroine, her world and the cast of additional characters. The biggest challenge was with the visual, illustration side of my first book. I collected a roomful of reference materials: wild flowers, books, cards, magazines, fairies, photographs, butterflies, bridesmaids, princesses, tiaras and ballerinas. Slowly and almost imperceptibly, my own sketches became good enough for the trial book. Asking artists to sketch Poppy was potentially tricky. What if the publisher liked the pictures, but not the words, or vice versa? Arrangements between authors and illustrators at pitching stage have to be very clear cut.

I decided to self-publish when I became frustrated with the slow ways of the publishing world. I had sent off a few versions of Poppy, as well as some other ideas, and I'd had one helpful phone call from a publisher and some other words of encouragement – but no deal was in sight. I was in the Lake District when I realised that Beatrix Potter had self-published, along with many other stars such as Virginia Woolf, John Grisham and James

Joyce. I decided there and then to speed up my career by producing the book as I imagined it. I had every confidence of it selling well. I dismissed the idea of using a firm specialising in self-publishing, even though some are perfectly respectable because I believed, and still do, that you can project manage it yourself and use your budget on strong production values instead of a middle-person.

There is something about making the financial investment which proves one's serious intentions: you can produce your book with plenty of trial copies for the cost of a holiday. I broke the self-publishing process down into the following ten-point battle plan:

1. Write a good, fast-paced story of the right length for your audience. (Ask for a few objective opinions. If there is not one common criticism, ignore all negative comments.) Remember: theme, character, plot and dialogue are the building blocks of any story.

2. Edit it objectively. (Ask a friend if necessary.) Know when to let go of words. Ask yourself if it is truly original. Innovate, don't imitate.

3. Illustrate it if it's a picture book. (Ask an artist to do this, either for a fee or as part of the pitch.)

4. Think of a wonderful jacket design, explore fonts, imagery and message.

5. Design and lay out the pages. (Use a professional designer who will also advise on a printer.)

6. Have it printed in sensible quantities. Use a printer who has produced 'perfect bound' books before, i.e. *not* those stapled down the spine, which would look amateurish. Test the market with a few hundred copies.

7. Hand-sell it to bookshops, both chains and independents.

8. Have it distributed. Ensure that the distributor has relationships with all the national chains.

9. Promote it to get it noticed (radio, television, articles).

10. Offer to do events and festivals to ensure ongoing sales.

After self-publishing: getting the deal and beyond

The first Princess Poppy book sold 40,000 copies in six months, which meant that the concept was noticed in the trade. All the main bookseller chains, as well as independents, were incredibly supportive. I was invited to visit headquarters of booksellers and soon the chains were distributing the book to their branches. All of this relied on good distribution, which is hard to find with only one title, but persistence is the key.

I paid for professional public relations which helped a lot, but is not essential. I began to be invited to book parties across Edinburgh and found that the publishing reps from large publishing houses were very willing to help. They took news of my book to London offices and soon I was being invited to these for meetings. At this point, I produced a second book, and a doll, which showed the series potential of the Princess Poppy concept. But it was all getting too much for one person. I was running a business now, with printers to liaise with as well as the press, the distributors and events co-ordinators. When two offers for Poppy came in on my newly set up email, I didn't have to think twice about accepting.

I have been lucky enough to have a great relationship with my editor and publisher. Working with a major publisher requires the right amount of compromise, without losing personal direction and control. I believe in professional standards and feel that being part of an arts-based work cycle is no excuse for being chaotic. I always deliver texts on time and try not to be needlessly awkward or diva-ish. The author is simply a bit-part player in the successful production of a book. If you are incredibly hung up on ownership of rights, trademarks and the like, then self-publishing really might be best for you. Ironically, once you are published by a traditional publisher, you have to let all of that go.

I wouldn't change the way I did it, as I understand the whole world of publishing much more than I would have done otherwise. And I may never have got the deal at all, without self-publishing first. For those who say it is vain to self-publish, I would say, yes it is, as is the whole idea of wanting others to pay for your written words. But when one's main pleasure in life is reading, it makes perfect sense to create stories for others to enjoy. I can think of no better career, and when fan letters drop through the door, the whole process is complete.

Janey Louise Jones continues to write the *Princess Poppy* series with two new books for 2019 published by Eden Cooper: *Please, Please Save the Bees* and *Fantastic, No Plastic* where Poppy is now a junior conservationist. Her *Superfairies* series was published in the USA (Capstone Books) and in the UK. Follow Janey on Twitter @janeypoppyjones.

See also...
- *Notes from Jacqueline Wilson*, page 85
- *An indie's journey to award-winning success*, page 198
- *What do self-publishing providers offer?*, page 201
- *Editorial services and self-publishing providers*, page 208

An indie's journey to award-winning success

Setting aside the idea of her novel being published traditionally, Griselda Heppel found the high standards and professionalism of a self-publishing company gave her the best of both worlds.

It used to be so simple. Aspiring writers had two options: to land a contract with a traditional publishing house or, failing that, pay for publication themselves, thus earning the undying scorn of the literary world for anyone resorting to the so-called 'vanity press'. A book not published in the usual way must, the argument went, by definition be badly written, poorly edited and have no appeal to anyone but the writer and their own loyal family.

Well, if that was true once it isn't anymore. In today's competitive publishing world it is extremely hard for unknown authors to be taken on by traditional firms. Where once an editor might have had time to nurture a new talent, now financial realities demand strong projected sales that makes such slow-burn methods increasingly unlikely. The new book and the new author have to be winners from the word go and that is a big ask, especially if your book does something no one has ever tried before.

Like creating a children's version of Dante's *Inferno*, for instance.

I've always loved stories that draw on great myths and epics: *The Iliad* and *The Odyssey*, Greek and Roman legends, Norse sagas, King Arthur and Robin Hood. Classical works provide rich narrative material and form the basis for many of the best books ever written for children. Yet the *Inferno*, in which Dante imagines himself descending into ever darker circles of Hades, having to deal with Cerberus, Harpies, Minotaur, Furies – a gold mine of fantasy and adventure if ever there was one – seems to have been neglected in this respect, and I was determined to put that right. Dante became 12-year-old Ante (Antonia) who finds herself plunged on this hellish journey, accompanied by her arch enemy, Florence, and a mysterious 13-year-old boy called Gil (Virgil – a reference to the Roman poet who is Dante's guide).

When I sent the completed manuscript to publishers and agents, it attracted some interest but ultimately no offers. Some of the rejection letters contained useful feedback, for which I was grateful. Others told me my story was too complicated for children; they'd be confused by the combined themes of Hell, mythical creatures and the First World War (an important element in *Ante's Inferno*). I knew they were wrong about this. My book had already been read by 40 or so children, aged 9–16 years, not one of whom had any difficulty in understanding it, and the fact that young people's abilities can still be so underestimated frankly puzzled me.

It struck me that however much I rewrote *Ante's Inferno*, as an unknown author I'd never get past this conservative view from mainstream publishing companies. I realised that if I wanted to see my book in print, I'd have to get on with it myself. I knew it would be hard but there were advantages: how and when the book was published would be up to me, I could commission my own cover illustration and I'd have the final say on design, print and production. I'd be in control.

The rapid growth in recent years of ways in which to self-publish has opened up a number of choices to authors. I was determined that *Ante's Inferno* should be a top-quality book, well-designed with high production values. There'd be an ebook version, of course, but for children the act of holding, feeling, smelling a book is a vital part of their enjoyment (actually, it is for me too); *Ante's Inferno* should be a pleasure to pick up in bookshops, where it wouldn't look out of place among all the traditionally published titles, and retailers should be able to order it from their wholesalers in the usual way. In short, what I needed was an established publishing company that would do a professional job.

Google 'self-publishing' and you'll come up with a bewildering array of companies offering services. Some of these are very basic and very cheap and, not surprisingly, their books look it. But there are others whose high standards mean their products can compete with the best of any published books. I settled on Matador, which, as an imprint of trade publishing company Troubador, offers partnership services to authors supported by professional expertise in copy-editing, design, production, marketing and distribution fields. 'For authors whose work we are happy to publish,' says Matador on its home page, 'we will undertake as much or as little of the publishing process as required.'

And there you have it: the gulf between self-publishing and the low quality control associated with the vanity press. Submitting your manuscript to Matador does not guarantee publication. Matador may offer partnerships in which authors take on financial risk, but they will only do so if they consider the books to be of a high enough standard. If not, an author will be advised to rework the manuscript, perhaps after undergoing a critical assessment from a literary consultancy or a professional editor. A significant proportion of all books offered to Matador are rejected in this way.

This brings me to the heart of getting your book published by whatever method, traditional or independent: the quality of the book itself. I rewrote *Ante's Inferno* many times, responding to feedback from literary agents, editors and writing mentors, before sending it to Cornerstones Literary Consultancy for a critique. Their editorial report was tough and hard-hitting. It was difficult criticism to take on board but it proved invaluable, enabling me to resolve structural issues and tighten up the writing. By the time I submitted *Ante's Inferno* to Matador, it had already gone through a rigorous editorial process and was a much better book as a result.

Once taken on by Matador, I could have left it all to them but I didn't want to. For the cover, I commissioned Hilary Paynter, a top wood engraver, to create a dark and menacing image of the path down to Hell, reminiscent of the atmospheric illustrations of Dante's *Inferno* by Gustave Doré. I had input on jacket and page design but was glad for my publisher to take charge of production, printing, distribution and marketing. I had no illusions that bookshops throughout the UK would instantly stock *Ante's Inferno* – the thousands of new children's titles that appear every year are all fighting for the same space, after all – but Matador would present them with every opportunity to do so.

Next came the hard bit: promotion. Unless you have the full weight – and budget – of a large firm's publicity department, it is extremely difficult to get your book noticed by the media. Even authors signed by traditional publishing companies can be disappointed to find the funds allocated to publicising their book are relatively small. Increasingly they are expected to promote themselves, in a way not demanded before (and often contrary to their nature – not all authors are confident extroverts!). It's not enough just to write books, it seems; you need to establish an online presence by blogging, tweeting and updating Facebook and website pages with amusing snippets (not just sales pitches) to charm and entertain potential readers. All this can be fun, but it's also time-consuming, not to mention stressful (am I tweeting/blogging/facebooking enough?).

I entered this world of social media with some trepidation but found it a great way of connecting with other writers, readers, agents and editors and making new friends, as well as spreading the word about *Ante's Inferno* and garnering a good number of reviews. In addition, my publishers ran a publicity campaign which achieved a decent amount of press coverage – local, mainly, but also some on a national level – on radio programmes, in newspapers and magazines. Eager to share my interest in Dante with children, I put together an illustrated talk about the themes that inspired *Ante's Inferno*. This goes down extremely well in schools (Years 5–8) and I fit in a few school visits every term.

It was a wonderful feeling when *Ante's Inferno* won a Silver in the Wishing Shelf Awards (www.thewsa.co.uk), swiftly followed by – even more exciting – the Children's category of the People's Book Prize (www.peoplesbookprize.com). Both competitions are judged exclusively by readers: the Wishing Shelf Awards by schoolchildren alone, and the People's Book Prize by any member of the public, either online or through their local library. For me it was a solid endorsement, not just of *Ante's Inferno*, but of the independent publishing method I'd gone for.

There are downsides, however. Partnership publishing has been a terrific experience but there's no disguising the amount of time and effort it takes up, arguably leaving less of both for the writing itself. A well-known, mainstream firm can inevitably give a book wider exposure than *Ante's Inferno* has achieved (though selling out its first 1,000 copy print run in eight months isn't bad).

Still, I have a tried and trusted model that works and a growing fan base for my next book, *The Tragickall History of Henry Fowst*, which came out in August 2015. For this tale of an ordinary 13-year-old boy who, somewhat unwisely, calls up a demon to help him with his problems, Hilary Paynter and Pete Lawrence have created another brilliantly spooky cover. While the design process – both for the jacket and pages inside – took longer this time, leading to some panicky moments over deadlines (something familiar to all publishers!), the thrill of seeing my vision for the book translated into reality remains as strong as ever. So strong in fact that, while as a writer I'll always be open to the possibility of mainstream publishing, it would take a very good offer to tempt me.

Perhaps even a Faustian pact.

Hm, now there's an idea …

Griselda Heppel read English at Cambridge and worked in publishing before moving to Oxford with her husband to bring up their four children. Her first book, *Ante's Inferno* (Matador 2012) won the People's Book Prize and a Silver Wishing Shelf Award. In 2017 it underwent a special reprint for the Passchendaele Centenary 1917– 2017. Her second children's novel, *The Tragickall History of Henry Fowst*, was published by Matador in 2015. Find out more at www.griseldaheppel.com.

See also...
- *From self-publishing to contract*, page 194
- *What do self-publishing providers offer?*, page 201
- *Editorial services and self-publishing providers*, page 208

What do self-publishing providers offer?

Jeremy Thompson presents the options for engaging an author services company.

Now that self-publishing is widely accepted and it is easier to do it than ever before, authors are presented with a broader range of opportunities to deliver their book or ebook to readers. This brings with it a greater responsibility to you, the author and publisher, to make the right choices for your publishing project. The various options for self-publishing may seem bewildering at first, and each has their pros and cons. But some relatively simple research will prove invaluable in ensuring you make the right choices for your book.

Motivation influences method

There are many reasons why authors choose to self-publish, and contrary to popular belief, the decision to do so is not always motivated by the aspiration to be a bestselling novelist! That is only one reason; others include the wish to impart knowledge to a wider audience; the desire to publish a specialist book with a relatively small target audience; the fulfilment of a hobby; publishing as part of a business or charity; and yes, vanity (a wish to see one's name on a book cover is fine, as long as you have realistic expectations of your work).

Understanding why you are self-publishing is important, as the reasons for doing so can help point to the best way in which to go about it. For example, if you are publishing simply for pleasure, and have few expectations that your book will 'set the world alight', then you'd be wise not to invest in a large number of copies; using 'print on demand' (POD) or producing an ebook could be a good way forward. If you have a book that you're publishing to give away or sell as part of your business to a relatively captive audience, then a short print run of a few hundred copies might be wise. If you want your novel to reach as many readers as possible and to sell it widely, you'll need to have physical copies to get into the retail supply chain and in front of potential readers, so opt for a longer print run of perhaps 500 or more. The more copies you print, the greater the economies of scale.

Decisions on how to self-publish are often influenced by the money you are prepared to invest in (and risk on) your project. Making a decision on what self-publishing route to take based on financial grounds alone is fine, as long as you understand the implications of that decision. For example, as the name implies, print-on-demand (POD) books are only printed when someone actually places an order for a copy; there are no physical copies available to sell. As POD books are largely sold on a 'firm sale' basis, bookshops will rarely stock them, so most POD sales will be made through online retailers. In addition, as the POD unit cost is higher than if a quantity of books are printed in one go, the retail price of a book is likely to be fairly high in order to cover the print cost and retailer's discount, and make you, the publisher, some profit. Authors often assume that POD is some miracle form of low-cost book publishing but, if that were so, why aren't all the major commercial publishers distributing all of their books in this way? The disadvantages of POD include limited distribution and high print cost; these can work for many types of book, like specialist non-fiction titles or academic books that command high cover prices, but it can be difficult to make it cost-effective for mass market books.

At the other end of the scale, printing 3,000 copies of a novel will only pay off if you can get that book onto the retailers' shelves and in front of potential readers, or if you have some other form of 'captive' readership that you can reach with your marketing. Distribution to retailers works largely on the 'sale or return' model, using distribution companies and sales teams to sell new books to bookshops (and whatever you may have heard to the contrary, bookshops are still the largest sellers of books in the UK). If you can't get your book into that distribution chain, you are limiting the prospect of selling your 3,000 copies, and money tied up in unsaleable stock is money wasted.

Publishing an ebook is also an increasingly popular method of self-publishing, but it too has its pros and cons. On the up side, it can be done very cheaply and quickly; the flip side is that, as hundreds of new ebooks are published each day, how do you get yours noticed? Making your ebook available through one retailer (e.g. Kobo) effectively limits your potential readership … what about readers with a Kindle, an iPad or a Nook? How and where should you market your ebook?

As a self-publisher, you need to make sure you understand the limitations of each form of publishing method before you decide on the best route for your book(s). It can make the difference between success or failure for your book before it's even produced.

Choosing an author services company

In its truest sense, self-publishing means that you as author undertake all the processes undertaken by a commercial publisher to bring a book to market: editing, design, production, marketing, promotion and distribution. If you're multi-talented and have a lot of spare time, then you may want to do all of these things yourself, but for most authors it's a question of contracting an author services company to carry out some or all of the tasks required. From the start it should be understood that most author services companies make their money by selling their services to you as the author; very few have a lot of market knowledge and even fewer offer any real form of active marketing or have a retail distribution set-up. Choosing the right company to work with is crucial in ensuring that your self-publishing expectations stand a chance of being met. Author services companies come in various guises, but they can broadly be broken into three categories:

• **DIY POD services.** You upload your manuscript and cover design, and your book (or ebook) is simply published 'as is'. It's relatively cheap, and great if you are not too concerned about the design quality and POD or electronic distribution is what you want.

• **Assisted services companies.** These companies offer typesetting and cover design, and perhaps some limited distribution and marketing options. If you're looking for a better product and some basic help in selling your book then this could be right for you.

• **Full service companies.** These suppliers tend to work at the higher quality end of the self-publishing market, offering authoritative advice, bespoke design, active trade and media marketing and, in a couple of cases, real bookshop distribution options.

In addition, there is a plethora of companies and individuals offering component parts of the book production and marketing process, such as copy-editing, proofreading, cover design, public relations, etc.

The key for any self-publisher in choosing a company to work with is research. Having decided why you are self-publishing and set your expectations from doing so, the next step is to see who offers what, and at what cost, and to match the right company with what you are seeking. A search on the internet for 'self-publishing' will present you with many choices, so explore the company websites, compare what is being offered, and generally get a feel for what each says they do. Are they just selling services to authors, or are they selling their authors' books? Do they offer active marketing or just 'marketing advice'? Don't take their word for it, though: seek independent advice from other authors or independent industry commentators – there are three sources of reliable, independent information on self-publishing service providers: this *Yearbook* and associated website (www.writersandartists.co.uk); ALLi (see page 352); and the Independent Publishing Magazine (www.theindependentpublishingmagazine.com), which gives authoritative reviews of self-publishing companies and a monthly ranking of the best (and worst) based upon author feedback.

Having identified some companies that look as if they will help you meet your publishing expectations, you need to establish how much it will cost. Get detailed quotations from companies and compare like-for-like. Ask questions of those companies if anything is in doubt: ask to see a contract; ask for a sample of their product (many companies still produce terrible quality books!). Time spent at this stage will ensure that you get a good feel for the company you're considering working with, and that can be the difference between a happy self-publishing experience and a disastrous one.

Marketing and distribution

Authors often concentrate on producing a book or ebook and ignore the part of the equation that actually sells the book. Examine carefully what author services companies offer. Distribution includes all the processes involved in getting a book or ebook in front of potential readers, but many companies offer only a limited, online-only service. Marketing is the process of alerting both the media (whether in print, on air or online) and potential readers that a book is available. Similarly, very few companies spend much effort to actively market their authors' work. The right choice of marketing and distribution service can make or break a book even before production has started.

As the author and self-publisher, you must decide how the world will find out about your book, and how to get it into the hands of readers. You will need to make decisions on whether POD distribution or wider retail distribution is required; whether the marketing services offered by an author services company are enough for your book; or if a public relations company might be the way forward. And, of course, all of this has a cost implication.

A brave new world

Self-publishing offers authors a host of opportunities to make their work available to readers. Making the right decisions to meet your expectations for your book or ebook in the early stages of the publishing process will pay dividends. Understand your motivations; research the production options well; understand distribution choices; give marketing the importance it requires; and above all, enjoy your self-publishing experience.

Jeremy Thompson founded Troubador Publishing (www.troubador.co.uk) in 1996 and started the Matador (www.troubador.co.uk/matador) self-publishing imprint in 1999, which has since helped over 9,000 authors to self-publish. Troubador also runs the annual Self-Publishing Conference (in its seventh year in 2019) and holds a 'Self-Publishing Experience' Day three times a year at its offices near Leicester. Troubador also runs Indie-Go (www.indie-go.co.uk), offering component author services, and in 2015 it acquired The Book Guild Ltd, an independent partnership publisher.

The hybrid author: you can do it all – your way!

Shelli R. Johannes explains what it is to be a hybrid author, explores the pros and cons of traditional publishing and self-publishing, and describes how an author can enjoy the best of both worlds.

My journey

When I was a little girl, I never believed there was only one way of doing things. So I grew up trying to accomplish things in a different way. As you can imagine, my parents weren't always thrilled about me 'thinking outside the box'. Years later, nothing has changed. I feel the same way about publishing. As a writer, I was always told there was a right way and a wrong way to break down walls in the secret society of publishing. Like many writers, I stood outside the closed doors to publishing, banging my head against invisible barriers. If I couldn't find my way in, I decided I would carve my own passage.

In 2011, when I first decided to self-publish, this was still considered to be 'taboo' in the industry. To many, taking that route meant I was cheating the system – that maybe I wasn't good enough to barge through the front door of traditional publishing. In my heart, I knew that wasn't true. I had an agent who loved my writing. My books had made it to acquisitions at several publishing houses. But as many of you know, writing is like any art – it's subjective and it's competitive. At any given time, there are hundreds of other manuscripts vying for that same opening at a publishing house. So I thought maybe self-publishing was my way.

Eventually, I ended up selling over 150,000 ebooks of my *Nature of Grace* series. I have self-published five books to date and plan to continue. Not only did I sell well, but I also loved the whole process – the control in creating my own covers, the excitement of watching my sales numbers, choosing where and when I wanted to publish. It was like nurturing my own books. However, although I loved it, I still wanted to publish in the traditional way because I wanted the experience of working with a big publisher. Again, I was told I had to choose – it was one way or the other.

At that time, there wasn't a word or even a title for authors who straddled both sides of the great divide. Now, we call it *hybrid publishing*.

Self-publishing: pros and cons

PROS
- control over process
- retain rights
- higher royalties
- digital printing options
- fast to market
- timely topics

CONS
- minimal distribution
- stigma
- tough marketing
- publishing expense
- author handles business end-to-end
- hard to find direct readers

What is a hybrid author?

A hybrid author is someone who publishes through many different media. For example, hybrid authors can self-publish some books while selling other books to a traditional publisher. I realized publishing doesn't have to be one way or the other. For a long time, I wavered between playing them all at once or deciding which one to play first. With so many pros and cons to each channel, everything was exciting and new.

So, what are the pros and cons of being a hybrid author? In general, a hybrid author gets the benefits of the traditional advance, professional editing, distribution and marketing. But they also get the self-publishing benefit of creative control, flexible pricing, and the opportunity to write and publish timely titles for immediate earnings (see boxes: *Self-publishing/Traditional publishing: pros and cons* boxes).

How to be a successful hybrid author

As authors, we have no reason to stay in one lane. We can do it all. But it's important for an author to understand what he or she is getting into and how to do it right. Before you dive into hybrid publishing, it's important to research – do your homework and seek advice. Here are a few points to keep in mind when preparing your action plan:

1. Write an amazing book

Always have a book in your queue. I like to write for my agent first because the traditional path tends to be much slower than the self-publishing channel. Once my

> ### Traditional publishing: pros and cons
>
> **PROS**
> - advance
> - team makes book
> - mass print distribution
> - validated
> - access to TV, film, etc
> - access to reviewers
>
> **CONS**
> - sells rights
> - little marketing
> - lower royalty
> - slower to market
> - risk averse in type of book published
> - decreasing revenue

book is on submission or in my agent's hands, I work on developing my own novels for self-publishing. This way, I'm always working on something that can move my career forward. It's also critical to 'go for high-quality' in all your writing. Every piece of work should be your absolute best. Being a hybrid author isn't a short cut to writing, it's a short cut to market. So write the best book possible and *then* figure out how to publish it. Bad writing doesn't sell in *any* market or in any channel – no matter how you publish.

2. Be prepared to run a business

To be a successful hybrid author, you have to be prepared to manage your writing as a business. You will have to juggle many different processes at the same time. Traditional publishing will include the basics in editing and marketing; in self-publishing, you have to do those things too, but self-publishing also demands a business acumen and an entrepreneurial spirit to keep everything moving forward. You will be expected to learn about and manage the production of the book (covers, editing, jacket copy, etc), plus the business side of publishing such as inventory, sales, distribution, finances, marketing and much more. Some people don't mind this part – but it can be overwhelming at times. It also takes away from your writing time, so you need to be efficient and organised. Find out what works for you. Being a hybrid author requires a different business mindset from traditional publishing because you have to juggle simultaneous processes across multiple channels. Don't be scared – it can be done, but it is a tough process. You will have to try new things, not be afraid of failing, and take risks. It's all part of the process.

3. Do yourself a favour and get an agent!
If you think you are going to be a hybrid author, I believe you need to get an agent. Agents can help you figure out which books are best for each publishing path. They know the market. They can also help you navigate some of the other tasks, like contract negotiation and managing other rights – foreign, subsidiary, etc. Of course, you need an agent who believes in the hybrid model. You must find the right agent/agency that truly believes there are viable sales on both publishing paths. Make sure they are experienced in digital publishing and open to any and all opportunities that arise. I was lucky enough to find my agent Lara Perkins at Andrea Brown Literary Agency at a conference; she understood and valued the possibilities of the self-publishing model. You need someone on your side, and someone who has your best interest and career in mind. Trust me, agents are worth their 15%, and then some! (see box *How an agent can help you succeed*).

> **How an agent can help you succeed:**
>
> • **Channel management** – Helps decide which path is best for your books.
>
> • **Contract negotiation** – Reviews any issues that might surface.
>
> • **Editorial advice** – Provides manuscript revisions and edits.
>
> • **Market knowledge** – Gives insight into the various markets/channels.
>
> • **Networking** – Has access to a variety of resources.
>
> • **Rights management** – Can facilitate the sale of other rights.
>
> • **Trusted partner** – Offers advice on whole career and portfolio.

4. Make a book plan
Decide which books you want to publish traditionally and which ones you want to keep for yourself. My agent helps me choose the best path for each book idea we discuss. Because, let's face it, self-publishing doesn't work for all books, and traditional publishing doesn't work for everything either. For example, my picture books (such as *Ceca Loves Science*) and chapter books on submission are better suited for traditional publishing currently, whereas some of my YA material based on a timely topic (such as *ReWired*) or that may target a leaner audience (such as the *Nature of Grace* wilderness thriller series), may be better geared toward self-publishing. So decide what you want to write and then figure out what the best channel to market may be; consider time, topic and level of control.

5. Always keep writing
The indie world is very fast paced while the traditional model is much slower. Doing both can bog you down in tasks, project management and marketing. But it's important to always keep writing. This is the best way to build a portfolio. When one book is in edits, work on a new idea. When one manuscript is in your agent's or critique partner's hands, outline your next book. Never sit and wait for something to happen. Make something happen. It's all worth it in the end!

I want to continue with my hybrid career because I love both the traditional and self-publishing options for very different reasons. I value the flexibility and control that self-publishing offers. BUT I also enjoy the collaborative process of working with an editor at a publishing house. As I develop as a writer, I want to remain open to ANY writing opportunity or path available. I want to pave my own way in this exciting, frustrating, wonderful and challenging industry. Because at the end of the day, I just want to write great books and reach people across all ages with my words. I'm proud to be a hybrid author – one who publishes my work, my way.

Remember, there is no right way to make this journey, there's only *your* way!

Shelli R. Johannes is the co-author of a new science picture book series, *Cece Loves Science* (HarperCollins/Greenwillow 2018) and author of the award-winning *Nature of Grace* teen thriller series. Her new YA novel is *ReWired* (Coleman and Stott 2017). After earning a Masters in Marketing and working in corporate America as a Senior Vice President, Shelli traded in her heels and suits for flip-flops and jeans to follow her passion of writing. She lives in Atlanta with her husband, two kids, one bird, one fish, and two crazy-haired goldendoodles. For more information see www.srjohannes.com and follow her on Twitter @srjohannes.

See also...

Books

Editorial services and self-publishing providers

This is a selection of the rapidly expanding list of companies that offer editorial, production, marketing and distribution support predominantly for authors who want to self-publish. As with all the organisations mentioned in the *Yearbook*, we recommend that you check carefully what companies offer and precisely what they would charge. Note that in the entries below, 'POD' refers to 'print on demand'.

Albury Books

Albury Court, Albury, Thame, Oxon OX9 2LP
tel (01844) 337000
email hannah@alburybooks.com
website www.alburybooks.com
Twitter @AlburyBooks

Collaborates with writers and illustrators to publish and/or re-publish their work through the Albury BookShelf platform. Provides POD and/or short print runs and co-edition deals to small publishers, agents, and individuals. Rights management also available. Focuses on re-publishing picture books that have had rights reverted. Each book published is listed for sale in the Albury online store and made available to major booksellers. Founded 2013.

Amolibros

Loundshay Manor Cottage, Preston Bowyer,
Milverton, Somerset TA4 1QF
tel (01823) 401527
email amolibros@aol.com
website www.amolibros.com
Director Jane Tatam

Offers print and ebook design, production, copy-editing and distribution through online retailers. Sales and marketing services include design and production of adverts, leaflets, author websites, distribution of press releases and direct mail campaigns.

Blue Falcon Publishing

The Mill, Pury Hill Business Park, Alderton Road,
Towcester, Northants NN12 7LS
tel 07955 002040
email books@bluefalconpublishing.co.uk
website www.bluefalconpublishing.co.uk
Facebook www.facebook.com/bluefalconpublishing
Twitter @bluefalconpub
Instagram bluefalconpub

Small independent company publishing children's fiction books with a focus on high-quality, personal service. Services include: editing; illustrating; typesetting; publishing; ebook production, marketing; social media and screenwriting. Partnership and self-publishing contracts available, starting from £600.

Book Create Service Ltd

22 Coleman Ave, Teignmouth, Devon TQ14 9DU
email enquiries@bookcreateservice.com
website www.bookcreateservice.com

Book layout and cover design services for new and experienced authors, as well as ebook conversion. Price information available on the website.

Bookollective

email hello@bookollective.com
website www.bookollective.com
Facebook www.facebook.com/bookollective
Twitter @bookollective
Contacts Esther Harris (editorial), Aimee Coveney (design), Helen McCusker (publicity)

Award-winning team offering a range of publicity, promotion and marketing options, editing services, book-cover design and website creation. Works alongside publishers, industry professionals and direct with writers. Also hosts regular networking events and literary areas within festivals.

BookPrinting UK

Remus House, Coltsfoot Drive, Woodston,
Peterborough PE2 9BF
tel (01733) 898102
email info@bookprintinguk.com
website www.bookprintinguk.com
Twitter @BookPrintingUK
Contact Naz Stewart

Offers colour and b&w printing and POD books in a range of bindings. Can provide custom illustration and interior layout options, as well as typesetting. Supplies templates for formatting manuscript files before sending. Can also distribute print books direct to customers. Prints bookmarks, posters and flyers.

Clink Street Publishing

71–75 Shelton Street, London WC2H 9JQ
tel 020-7993 8225
email info@clinkstreetpublishing.com
website www.bookpublishing.co.uk

Boutique self-publishing imprint from Authoright, with an experienced team of editors, project managers, designers and publicists publishing and promoting writers across all genres. Also has links with literary scouts with a view to securing foreign translation rights and Amazon's Audible service for audio rights. Case studies and testimonials available on request.

CompletelyNovel

website http://completelynovel.com
Twitter @completelynovel

Provides simple online publishing tools for authors to upload their manuscripts to create and distribute POD paperbacks. A number of sales and distribution options are available. Website also offers a cover-creator option, as well as self-publishing advice on topics including editing, cover design and social media marketing.

eBook Versions

27 Old Gloucester Street, London WC1N 3AX
website www.ebookversions.com

Offers ebook and paperback self-publishing and distribution through online retailers and trade wholesalers including Amazon Kindle Direct Publishing, Apple iBookstores, Kobo Books, Gardners Books and more than 300 independent high street booksellers. Fees begin at £95 for ebook conversion of a manuscript of up to 100,000 words. POD paperback and hardback pre-press production is available from £295. OCR scanning of hardbacks, paperbacks and typescripts is also offered.

Frank Fahy Publishing Services

5 Barna Village Centre, Barna, Galway, Republic of Ireland
tel +353 (0)86 2269330
email frank.fahy0@gmail.com
website www.frank-fahy.com

Specialises in preparing manuscripts for book production, either as printed books or digital ebooks. This can include, as required, copy-editing and/or proofreading, or preparing presentations for submission to publishers. Estimates are free of charge and authors' individual requirements discussed. Publishing projects of all kinds considered, from individuals, institutions or businesses. Founded 2007.

The Golden Egg Academy

The Wool House, 6 Cork Street, Frome, Somerset BA11 1BL
email info@goldeneggacademy.co.uk
website www.goldeneggacademy.co.uk
Twitter @TheGEAcademy
Founder & Managing Director Imogen Cooper

Experienced children's publishing and creative writing professionals who aim to provide guidance, industry-led direction and networking opportunities to talented writers for children.

Led by Imogen Cooper, previously Editorial Director and Editor at Chicken House Publishing,

winner of the Branford Boase Award and one of *The Bookseller's* Rising Stars 2016, Golden Egg offers talks, workshops, online classes and one-to-one editorial support, and caters for writers who wish to submit their work to agents and publishers. Golden Egg works closely with Chicken House Publishing, The Viney Shaw Agency, Andersen Press and Peters Fraser and Dunlop, and has strong links with other companies. Please check the website for submission guidance, events and workshop listings.

Grosvenor House Publishing

Link House, 140 The Broadway, Tolworth, Surrey KT6 7HT
tel 020-8339 6060
website www.grosvenorhousepublishing.co.uk
Founder Kim Cross

Publishes across a range of genres including children's and non-fiction in colour, b&w, POD, paperback, hardback and ebook formats. Offers a £795 publishing package which includes typesetting and five free print copies as well as an ISBN, and print and ebook distribution via online retailers. Authors can design covers online. Marketing services include producing posters and postcards, and website set-up from template with two years' hosting. Ebook publishing costs £195 if the print edition of the book has been produced by the company and £495 otherwise. Print costs and royalties depend on book specification. A proofreading service is offered at a rate of £5 per 1,000 words. See website for full list of costs.

I AM Self-Publishing

TMRW, 75–77 High Street, Croydon CR0 1QE
tel 020-3488 0565
email hello@iamselfpublishing.com
website www.iamselfpublishing.com
Facebook www.facebook.com/iamselfpub
Twitter @iamselfpub

Offers a range of professional publishing services, including: cover design; typesetting; editing; proofreading; POD and short-run printing; ebook conversion; author branding and marketing; and backlist republication. Paperback, hardback and ebook formats covered. Assistance available for authors at all stages of the process. No royalty taken: authors retain 100% of earnings.

Jelly Bean Self-Publishing

Candy Jar Ltd, Mackintosh House, 136 Newport Road, Cardiff, CF24 1DJ
tel 029-211 57202
email submissions@jellybeanselfpublishing.co.uk
website www.jellybeanselfpublishing.com
Twitter @Jelly_BeanUK
Director Shaun Russell

Self-publishing imprint of Candy Jar Books. Offers a bespoke service for new and experienced authors at all stages of the process, including but not limited to editing and typesetting, illustration, cover design, website design and other marketing services. Submissions are welcomed, and face-to-face meetings are available on request. Founded 2012.

Kids Active Media Ltd

PO Box 12567, Epping, Essex CM16 9EZ
tel 020-3633 3761
email contact@kidsactivemedia.com
website www.kidsactivemedia.com

Offers a range of bespoke services for children's authors, including copy-editing, proofreading and typesetting; also provides marketing, promotional and PR packages. In-house literary agents assist with contracts, distribution and translation rights. Online members' portal contains information for new and established authors: initial membership is free, but upgrades offering more detailed advice are available for a fee.

Produces print books (paperback, board books, perfect bound and activity colouring books), as well as ebooks, audiobooks and iBooks. All titles published though KAMedia are available for sale through its online shops, with the option to sell on other major platforms also.

Kindle Direct Publishing

website https://kdp.amazon.com
Facebook www.facebook.com/KindleDirectPublishing
Twitter @AmazonKDP

Ebook self-publishing and distribution platform for Kindle and Kindle Apps. Its business model offers up to a 70% royalty (on certain retail prices between $2.99–$9.99) in many countries and availability in Amazon stores worldwide. POD options are also available. Note that KDP Select makes books exclusive to Amazon (which means they cannot be sold through an author's personal website, for example), but authors can share in the Global Fund amount every time the book is borrowed from the Kindle Owners' Lending Library.

Kobo Writing Life

email writinglife@kobo.com
website www.kobo.com/gb/en/p/writinglife
Facebook www.facebook.com/KoboWritingLife
Twitter @kobo

Ebook self-publishing platform where authors can upload manuscripts and cover images. These files are then converted into ebooks before being distributed through the Kobo ebookstore. Authors are able to set pricing and DRM territories, as well as track sales. Royalty rates vary depending on price or territory; enquire directly. Free to join.

Manuscripts & Mentoring

25 Corinne Road, London N19 5EZ
tel 020-7700 4472

email manuscriptmentoring@gmail.com
website www.genevievefox.com
Twitter @genevievefox21
Contact Genevieve Fox

Helps both fledgling and experienced writers of fiction, non-fiction and YA fiction get from first draft to finished manuscript. Primary services: editing; manuscript overviews; advice on structure, plot, themes and characterisation; submission to agents; and self-publishing. Also available: mentoring; writing plans; ghost-writing; media coaching. Genevieve Fox is a published author, journalist and creative writing tutor.

Matador

Troubador Publishing Ltd, 9 Priory Business Park, Wistow Road, Kibworth Beauchamp, Leicester LE8 0RX
tel 0116 279 2299
email matador@troubador.co.uk
website www.troubador.co.uk/matador
Facebook www.facebook.com/matadorbooks
Twitter @matadorbooks
Managing Director Jeremy Thompson,
Operations Director Jane Rowland

The self-publishing imprint of Troubador Publishing. Offers POD, short-run digital- and litho-printed books as well as audiobooks and ebook production, with distribution through high-street bookshops and online retailers. Also worldwide ebook distribution. Author services include all book, ebook and audiobook production, trade and retail marketing, plus bookshop distribution via Orca Book Services and Sales Representation by Star Book Sales. Founded 1999.

MJV Literary Author Services

71–75 Shelton Street, London WC2H 9JQ
email authors@mjvliterary.com
website www.mjvliterary.com
Contact Matt McAvoy

Offers copy-editing and promotion services for book authors of all genres, including fiction, non-fiction and children's books, as well as a popular download podcast course 'Fiction Writing Basics'.

Services include translation into English, proofreading, complete copy-editing, formatting for e-book creation and print-ready typesetting for paperback. Senior Editor Matt McAvoy also carries out book-review and beta-reading services, and is a member of the Society for Editors and Proofreaders.

Editing services start from £4.50 per 1,000 words; promotion services include Twitter campaigns, reviewer submissions and interview requests. Clients include self-published and traditionally published authors, as well as publishers.

M-Y Books Ltd

187 Ware Road Hertford Herts. SG13 7EQ
tel (01992) 586279

email jonathan@m-ybooks.co.uk
website www.m-ybooks.co.uk
Facebook www.facebook.com/
MYBookspublishingandmarketing
Twitter @jonathanbooks
Editorial Director Jonathan Miller

Self-publishing service provider for authors at all stages of their careers. Offers a concierge-style service aimed at authors who are either new to self-publishing or who require a bespoke package. Author visits welcome. Online marketing also available. Audio book production specialists. Clients include international bestselling authors. Founded 2002.

Peahen Publishing

tel 0117 427 0126
email info@peahenpublishing.com
website www.peahenpublishing.com
Twitter @peahenbooks
Contact Carly Corlett

Independent publisher specialising in children's books, from storybooks to rhyming books, memoirs and novels to short story collections. Guides authors through the publishing process, from initial manuscript consultation to illustration, from paper and font selection to print. Founded 2015.

PublishNation

Suite 544, Kemp House, 152 City Road,
London EC1V 2NX
email david@publishnation.co.uk
website www.publishnation.co.uk
Publisher David Morrison

Offers POD paperback and Kindle format ebooks, available through Amazon. Publication in both print and digital formats costs £250 or £150 for Kindle format. Images may be included from £2.95 each. A range of book sizes is available, as are free template book covers. Enhanced cover design costs £40. Marketing services include creation of a press release, social media accounts and author website. Standard proofreading is £7 per 1,000 words, while an 'express' option from £125 focuses on the beginning of the manuscript. Editorial critique reports range in price from £99 for manuscripts of up to 15,000 words to £219 for manuscripts of up to 120,000 words.

SilverWood Books

14 Small Street, Bristol BS1 1DE
tel 0117 910 5829
email info@silverwoodbooks.co.uk
website www.silverwoodbooks.co.uk
Twitter @SilverWoodBooks
Publishing Director Helen Hart

Offers bespoke author services tailored to individual projects, as well as three comprehensive publishing packages, with prices dependent on specification. Services include professional cover and page design, typesetting, ebook hand-formatting and conversion, b&w and colour POD, short-run and lithographic printing, one-to-one support and coaching. Distributes to bookshops via wholesalers and to online retailers including Amazon.

Also provides the Amazon Look Inside feature, and lists books in its own SilverWood online bookstore. UK wholesale distribution via Central Books. Nielsen Enhanced Data Listing. Marketing services include author websites, social media set-up, online book trailer campaign and blog tours. Editorial services include an initial assessment and manuscript appraisal. VAT at the standard rate added to services but not print. See www.silverwoodbooks.co.uk/packages for guidance on prices and packages.

WRITERSWORLD

2 Bear Close Flats, Bear Close, Woodstock,
Oxon OX20 1JX
tel (01993) 812500
email enquiries@writersworld.co.uk
website www.writersworld.co.uk
Founder & Owner Graham Cook

Specialises in self-publishing, POD books and book reprints. Also issues ISBNs on behalf of authors, pays them 100% of the royalties and supplies them with copies of their books at print cost. Founded 2000.

Xlibris

Victory Way, Admirals Park, Crossways, Dartford,
Kent DA2 6QD
tel 0800 056 3182
email info@xlibrispublishing.co.uk
website www.xlibrispublishing.co.uk
Twitter @XlibrisUK

Established POD publisher, offering b&w, colour and speciality publishing packages (such as poetry and children's). Services range from design and editorial to ebook creation and distribution with online booksellers, website creation and marketing materials including a press release and book video. A subsidiary of Author Solutions LLC.

York Publishing Services

64 Hallfield Road, Layerthorpe, York YO1 7ZQ
tel (01904) 431213
email enqs@yps-publishing.co.uk
website www.yps-publishing.co.uk
Twitter @ypspublishing

Offers print and ebook publishing options, as well as distribution to bookshops and online retailers including Amazon. Services include copy-editing, proofreading, page and cover design, and printing. Provides page proofs and sample bound copy before main print run. Marketing services include compiling a press pack with press release sent to media; social media set-up (£250 plus VAT); posters; and direct mail campaigns. Book is also listed on the YPS online bookstore. Printing and editing price dependent on specification.

Poetry
Flying the poetry flag

Poet and anthologist John Foster explains the difficulties faced by aspiring children's poets and offers practical advice on writing poetry for children.

Once upon a time, there was a teacher who enjoyed sharing poems with the children she taught. As well as reading them poems from books in the class library, she read some of the poems she had written herself. She was encouraged by their response and decided to see if she could get the poems published. She looked in publishers' catalogues and found that there were numerous anthologies of poetry for children, as well as a number of single author collections.

She chose a publisher and sent them her poems. The publisher liked the poems. But as she was unknown they did not think they could risk a single author collection. However, they thought her poems showed promise, so they forwarded them to one of their anthologists. Although the anthologist liked the poems too, they did not fit into the anthology that he was currently working on. But he added her to the list of contacts to whom he sent details of new anthologies, specifying the subject of the collection and the types of poem he was looking for. When he next did an anthology, she submitted a number of poems for consideration and the anthologist chose three of them to be included.

She managed to track down other anthologists and they sent her details of the anthologies they were compiling. She became a regular contributor to anthologies and an established name in the children's poetry world, and gave up full-time teaching so that she could accept invitations to visit schools to read her poems and run poetry workshops. She struggled to find a publisher to do a single author collection. But eventually she managed to get a collection published and it sold well on her school visits. She didn't make a fortune from writing children's poetry, but her success and the obvious enjoyment children got from her poems was gratifying.

That was how it was in the late 1980s, throughout the 1990s and in the early 2000s, when children's poetry was in fine fettle. How lucky she and the rest of us children's poets were then and how times have changed. Whereas in those days there were plenty of poetry books for children published annually, now there are only a few and new anthologies are a rarity.

Briefly, in 2010/11 it looked as if children's poetry might be making a comeback. Writing in the summer 2011 *Carousel* magazine (see page 305), Brian Moses heralded what he hoped was a new spring for children's poetry, spearheaded by the launch of a new poetry list by Salt Publishing and a new imprint from Frances Lincoln. However, the Salt Children's Poetry Library has failed to make an impact and, despite the best efforts of Macmillan, A&C Black and Frances Lincoln, children's poetry publishing remains in the doldrums.

What explains the dearth of new children's poetry books? There are a number of factors involved. But it has nothing to do with children's attitudes towards poetry. Children enjoy reading poetry as much as they did in the boom years of the 1990s. Children's poets are as much in demand at Book Weeks in schools as they have always been. They perform their poems to rapt audiences, who go on to get their parents to buy whatever poetry books they have managed to get publishers to publish or, in desperation, have self-published.

So why has children's poetry publishing declined? It is partly due to the attitude of booksellers. They argue that poetry books don't sell. Of course they don't, if they don't stock them. Walk into the children's section of a bookshop today and you'll find a handful of poetry books, often hidden away on the bottom shelf, alongside the joke books. In the past, you'd find a shelf full of poetry books at eye-level.

In the eyes of the book buyers, who control what is stocked in bookshops, children's poetry isn't fashionable at present. This has a knock-on effect. The publisher's sales team report back that poetry books don't sell, despite the evidence to the contrary from the travelling poets, who sell hundreds of pounds' worth of their books during their school visits. So the publishers only publish a fraction of the poetry books that they used to. It's a vicious circle.

And the economic climate doesn't help. A full-colour poetry book aimed at younger children is like a picture book in terms of how much it costs to produce. But poetry doesn't translate in the way that stories do, so it isn't possible to sell foreign rights as a way of recouping the costs of production. It can be hard for a commissioning editor to convince the publishing committee to back a poetry project that will not make much money on the first printing.

Nevertheless, while many of the mainstream children's book publishers still shy away from publishing poetry, smaller independent publishers, such as Martin West at Troika and Janetta Otter-Barry at Otter-Barry Books, are producing an increasing number of poetry books. But the number remains very small when compared to the number of children's novels that are published annually.

Consequently, the aspiring children's poet faces a daunting task. There aren't the anthologies that it was possible to contribute to in the past and it is even harder these days to get a single author collection accepted. But if you are determined to write children's poetry, here are a few tips.

Get inspired by children

Starting with the most obvious, get to know children's language. If you are writing about an experience from a child's point of view, you must get the language right. It is, perhaps, not surprising that many of the most successful children's poets are from a teaching background – for example, Tony Mitton, Wes Magee, Judith Nicholls, Paul Cookson and Brian Moses. Teachers not only know what children's interests are, but they also know how children think and how they express themselves. Steep yourself in children's language, not just the language of your children and those of your friends, but of children from all sorts of backgrounds and cultures.

Try to arrange to visit schools in different areas. But always go through the correct channels with a letter to the literacy coordinator, copied to the headteacher, explaining the reasons you would like to visit. Schools these days are, quite rightly, very security-conscious.

If you are visiting a school, you can offer to run a writing workshop. You have the opportunity to try out your poems too. There's nothing like a deafening wall of silence greeting that punchline which you thought they would find so amusing to let you know that, in fact, the poem doesn't work!

Visiting schools is also worthwhile because you can bring yourself up to date with how poetry is being used in the classroom. For example, the new curriculum requires that pupils learn poems by heart. Literacy co-ordinators will therefore be on the lookout for new performance poems. There is an educational as well as a trade market for children's poems and it is worth knowing what the educational publishers might be looking for.

Schools are also a good source of ideas. Many a poem comes from a child's tale or a teacher's comment. In one school, I met a girl called Alison, who told me what had happened when she tried to pull a loose tooth out with a piece of string. So I went home and wrote this poem, 'When Allie Had a Loose Tooth':

When Allie had a loose tooth
She did as her dad said.
She went into the kitchen
And found a piece of thread.
She tied it round the tooth.
She tied it to the door.
But when she slammed the door shut,
The knob fell on the floor.

Appealing to the reader

Visiting schools will also give you an idea of what interests children have and what subjects to write about. Then it's up to you to think of something that will appeal to them. But a word of warning: be careful of being risqué just to appeal to the reader. Avoid being rude for the sake of it, and especially don't be crude. Besides, you could easily get yourself labelled! During a performance in Glasgow, I included two poems which made references to 'bottoms' and 'knickers', getting the usual delighted response from the audience. However, I was taken aback when I asked them to suggest why publishers won't allow me to illustrate my poetry books. Instead of giving me the expected – and correct – answer that my drawings are no good, the first boy that I asked said: 'Because your poems are dirty!'

You want your poems to stand out for some reason, so try to come up with something that is different. One way of making your poem stand out is to write it in a more unusual form. For example, say you are going to write a poem about St George and the dragon, instead of writing it in couplets, you could write it in the form of an encyclopedia entry, as a series of entries in St George's diary or even as a text message. Try experimenting with forms, not just haiku and cinquains but triolets, villanelles and univolics. You can find examples in *The Works 8 – Every shape, style and form of poem that you could ever need for the Literacy Hour* (Macmillan 2009).

Children enjoy the ridiculous and the bizarre, but getting an idea can be hard. If you are stuck for a humorous idea, one way of trying to find one is to look through a book of jokes. I was racking my brains to think of an idea for a new poem to include in a book of magic poems, when I came across this joke: Why are the ghosts of magicians no good at conjuring? Because you can see right through their tricks! This led to:

The ghost of the magician said:
'I'm really in a fix.
The trouble is the audience
Sees right through all my tricks!'

I learned a great deal about how to write children's poetry by being an anthologist. So study the work of established children's poets and learn, for example, about how to play with words by reading Roger McGough's poems and about how to write story-poems as dramatic monologues by reading Michael Rosen's poems. You can get ideas, too, from researching what established poets have written. Two of my nonsense poems, both of which are well received in schools, 'The Land of the Flibbertigibbets' and 'On the Clip, Clop Clap' were inspired by Spike Milligan poems – 'The Land of the Bumbly Boo' and 'On the Ning Nang Nong'.

If you get the opportunity, go along to a school, library or festival at which a children's poet is performing. In addition to listening to what they have to say, you may be able to talk to them afterwards. But don't expect them necessarily to be prepared to look at your poems and to give you a free tutorial on how to write children's poetry.

It's also worth looking at the websites of established writers. One particularly useful website is The Poetry Zone (http://poetryzone.co.uk), set up by the poet Roger Stevens. It consists of articles about writing children's poetry, as well as reviews and interviews with children's poets. The children's section of the Poetry Archive (www.poetryarchive.org) is worth visiting too.

Getting into print

So how does the aspiring children's poet get published? As I've explained, it's far harder now than it used to be, in the days when there were lots of anthologies being published. One way is to do it yourself. Self-publishing is not as expensive as it used to be. You can get 500 copies of an A5 booklet printed for around £500 and, if you get onto the school circuit, you can sell them directly yourself and more than cover your costs.

Then, there's the internet. You can post your poems on a website. You won't, of course, make any money from doing so and once the poems are out there, then there's the danger that someone else will copy them and claim to have written them. But at least they'll be there for people to read.

You can also consider publishing your poems as an ebook. But there are so many other books available as ebooks that you probably won't sell many copies.

It's not easy for the aspiring children's poet to get recognised at present and you certainly won't make a fortune. But children's poetry is far from dead, as the enthusiastic audiences that greet visiting poets in schools show. So good luck! Keep writing. Visit schools and fly the poetry flag. Join the campaign for a national poetry month, such as exists in the USA. Children's poetry may not be as fashionable as it once was, but it's far from finished!

John Foster's collected poems *The Poetry Chest* (2007) is published by Oxford University Press. His latest book, *Eggs with Legs*, illustrated by Korky Paul, was published in 2018 by Troika. His anthologies *Fantastic Football Poems*, *Dragon Poems* and *Dinosaur Poems*, also illustrated by Korky Paul, have recently been reissued by Oxford University Press.

See also...
- *An interview with my shadow*, page 217
- *Poetry organisations*, page 219

An interview with my shadow

Brian Patten talks about writing poetry.

Who are you?

I'm your shadow.

What's that you're eating?

It's the shadow of an apple.

Surely shadows can't detach themselves from walls and eat shadow-apples?

They can if they are writers' and poets' shadows.

Why do you write for children as well as for adults?

I don't know, it just happened that way. But I really do believe that writing for one is no easier than writing for the other. If somebody tries to write for adults and finds they aren't any good at it, then they will very likely be even worse at writing for children.

Can you really appreciate poetry at seven or even 11 years old?

Of course you can! Adults have no monopoly on feelings. I suspect that many adults never feel as intensely about things as they did when they were younger.

What are the best kinds of things to write about?

You can write about anything you want. Sometimes the weirder the better. At ten you will probably write very different poems than when you're 14 and when you are 40 you'll write different poems again.

How about telling stories through poems?

Very short stories, yes. But not long stories. For long stories children prefer prose, and quite rightly I think. Part of poetry is to do with condensing, not expanding. It is different if you are writing a series of poems about the same character or about a particular situation or unusual creatures, or seeing certain themes from different angles. Then snapshots can build up into a story. But there have been very few successful long story-poems written for children.

I thought poets were supposed to be daydreamers. Some people think poetry is a bit soft.

Modern poetry for children is usually anarchic – anything but soft. Having said this, there is an awful lot of bad so-called 'children's poetry' about. Almost as much as bad 'adult poetry'.

How so?

Well, there is more rhyme and word play in contemporary children's poetry than in contemporary adult poetry. People can make things rhyme, but they either don't or can't work on the scansion, and then the whole metrical structure falls apart. People who think they can get away with writing sloppy verse simply because it's for children are deluding themselves. No matter how good an idea, it is the execution of the work that brings it to life.

Did you intend that last sentence to be ironic?

Yes. And it is true. Would-be writers forget it at their peril! Children won't be fobbed off with lazy work.

Why did you begin writing poetry? Did anyone teach you?

No, one day I just started writing things down. You see, as a child I lived in this tiny house with three adults. They were all unhappy people. My mother was young and couldn't afford a place of her own, so we lived with my grandmother. My grandmother wore callipers and she dragged herself round the house by her hands. I remember thinking they were like talons.

What has this got to do with poetry and beginning to write it?

Everybody in that little house was miserable and they didn't talk to each other, and although they knew they were miserable and why they were miserable, they couldn't explain why.

You mean they could not express themselves?

Yes, and because they could not express themselves they kept everything walled up inside them, where it hurt and festered for want of light.

Were you like this as well?

To begin with. I don't know how it happened, or why, but I realised the only way I could express my feelings was by writing them down. I think that is how I started to become a poet. I began writing down what I felt. So really, I began writing poetry before I even began reading it. I needed to express my feelings and writing poetry was like writing a very intense diary.

Would you say you were a 'real' poet at that age? I mean, when you began writing did you think that you would ever become a professional poet?

No. That happened when I began changing words and moving lines around. When you begin to *make* something out of the words is when the professional element comes into play. A good poem is something that carries your feelings and ideas inside it. People remember a good poem because of the way it is written, just as much as because of what it says.

Would you like a bit of my apple?

I'm not sure. What does a shadow-apple taste like?

Brian Patten was born in Liverpool and writes poetry for adults and children. His publications for adults are *Collected Love Poems* (Harper Perennial 2007) and *Selected Poems* (Penguin 2007), and for children, *The Big Snuggle-Up* (2011) and *Can I Come Too?* (2013), both illustrated by Nicola Bayley and published by Andersen Press, plus *The Monster Slayer* (Barrington Stoke 2016), with illustrations by Chris Riddell. His most recent book, *The Book of Upside Down Thinking*, is a collection of humorous and thought-provoking verse inspired by traditional folk stories from the Near and Middle East and published by From You to Me Limited in 2018. His website is www.brianpatten.co.uk.

See also...

- *Flying the poetry flag*, page 213
- *Poetry organisations*, page 219

Poetry organisations

Poetry is one of the easiest writing art forms to begin with, though the hardest to excel at or earn any money from. Below are some organisations which can help poets take their poetry further.

WHERE TO GET INVOLVED

A range of organisations – from local groups to larger professional bodies – exists at which emerging and established poets can access support or learn more about others' work. A concise selection appears below.

Literature Wales

Glyn Jones Centre, Wales Millennium Centre, Bute Place, Cardiff CF10 5AL
tel 029-2047 2266
email post@literaturewales.org
website www.literaturewales.org

Champions the development of literature in Wales. Working collaboratively, bilingually, and in a wide range of communities, Literature Wales ensures that literature is a voice for all. The organisation's many projects and activities include Wales Book of the Year, the National Poet of Wales, Bardd Plant Cymru and Young People's Laureate Wales, Literary Tourism initiatives, Writers on Tour funding scheme, creative writing courses at Tŷ Newydd Writing Centre, Services for Writers (including bursaries and mentoring) and Young People's Writing Squads. Literature Wales is a registered charity (no. 1146560) and works with the support of the Arts Council of Wales and the Welsh Government.

The Poetry Book Society

c/o Inpress Ltd, Churchill House, 12 Mosley Street, Newcastle upon Tyne NE1 1DE
tel 0191 230 8100
email pbs@inpressbooks.co.uk
website www.poetrybooks.co.uk
Facebook www.facebook.com/poetrybooksoc
Twitter @poetrybooksoc

Book club for readers of poetry founded in 1953 by T.S. Eliot. Every quarter, expert poet selectors choose one outstanding publication (the PBS Choice), and recommend four other titles; these are sent to members, who are also offered discounts on other poetry books. The PBS also produces the quarterly membership magazine, the *Bulletin* (available to all members), which contains the poet selectors' reviews of the Choice and Recommendations, interviews with international poets, reviews and listings.

The Poetry Business

Campo House, 54 Campo Lane, Sheffield S1 2EG
tel 0114 438 4074
email office@poetrybusiness.co.uk
website www.poetrybusiness.co.uk

Publishes pamphlets by young poets between the ages of 17 and 24 under The New Poets List imprint; runs the literary magazine, *The North*. Also organises a national pamphlet competition for young poets between the ages of 17 and 24, writing days, and residential courses.

Poetry Ireland

11 Parnell Square East, Dublin D01 ND60, Republic of Ireland
tel +353 (0)1 6789815
email info@poetryireland.ie
website www.poetryireland.ie

Organisation committed to achieving excellence in the reading, writing and performance of poetry throughout the island of Ireland. Poetry Ireland receives support from The Arts Council / An Chomhairle Ealaíon and The Arts Council of Northern Ireland and enjoys partnerships with arts centres, festivals, schools, colleges and bookshops at home and abroad. Its commitment to creating performance and publication opportunities for poets at all stages of their careers helps ensure that the best work is made available to the widest possible audience. Poetry Ireland publishes the well-regarded poetry journal, *Poetry Ireland Review*.

The Poetry Society

22 Betterton Street, London WC2H 9BX
tel 020-7420 9880
email info@poetrysociety.org.uk
website www.poetrysociety.org.uk

The Poetry Society is Britain's leading voice for poets and poetry. Founded in 1909 to promote a more general recognition and appreciation of poetry, the Society has nearly 4,000 members. With innovative education, commissioning and publishing programmes, and a packed calendar of performances, readings and competitions, the Society champions poetry in its many forms.

The Society also publishes education resources for teachers and educators; organises high-profile events including an Annual Lecture and National Poetry Day celebrations; runs Poetry Prescription, a critical appraisal service; and provides an education advisory service, INSET packages for schools and networks of schools, a poets in schools service, school membership, youth membership and a website.

A diverse range of events and readings take place at the Poetry Café beneath the Society's headquarters in

London's Covent Garden. The Society also programmes events and readings throughout the UK.

Competitions run by the Society include the annual National Poetry Competition, with a first prize of £5,000; the biennial Popescu European Poetry Translation Prize; the Ted Hughes Award for New Work in Poetry; and the Foyle Young Poets of the Year Award.

Tower Poetry

Christ Church, Oxford OX1 1DP
tel (01865) 276156
email info@towerpoetry.org.uk
website www.towerpoetry.org.uk

Exists to encourage and challenge everyone who reads or writes poetry. Funded by a generous bequest to Christ Church, Oxford, by the late Christopher Tower, the aims of Tower Poetry are to stimulate an enjoyment and critical appreciation of poetry, particularly among young people in education, and to challenge people to write their own poetry.

WHERE TO GET INFORMATION

Your local library is a good first port of call, and should have information about the poetry scene in the area. Many libraries are actively involved in speading the word about poetry as well as having modern poetry available for loan.

Alliance of Literary Societies (ALS)

email ljc1049@gmail.com
website www.allianceofliterarysocieties.org.uk
President Claire Harman

Umbrella organisation for literary societies and groups in the UK. It provides support and advice on a variety of literary subjects, as well as promoting cooperation between member societies. Its publications include a twice-yearly members' newsletter, *Not Only But…*, and an annual journal, *ALSo*. ALS holds an AGM weekend which is hosted by a different member society each year, moving around the UK. Founded 1973.

Arts Council England

Arts Council England, 21 Bloomsbury Street, London WC1B 3HF
tel 0161 934 4317
email enquiries@artscouncil.org.uk
website www.artscouncil.org.uk

National development agency for the arts in England, providing funding for a range of arts and cultural activities. It supports creative writing including poetry, fiction, storytelling, spoken word, digital work, writing for children and literary translation. It funds a range of publishers and magazines as well as providing grants to individual writers. Contact the enquiries team for more information on funding support and advice.

Arts Council of Wales

Bute Place, Cardiff CF10 5AL
tel 0845 8734 900
email information@arts.wales
website www.arts.wales

Independent charity, established by Royal Charter in 1994. It has three regional offices and its principal sponsor is the Welsh Government. It is the country's funding and development agency for the arts, supporting and developing high-quality arts activities. Its funding schemes offer opportunities for arts organisations and individuals in Wales to apply, through a competitive process, for funding towards a clearly defined arts-related project.

National Association of Writers' Groups

Old Vicarage, Scammonden, Huddersfield HD3 3FT
email info@nawg.co.uk
website www.nawg.co.uk

Aims to bring cohesion and fellowship to isolated writers' groups and individuals, promoting the study and art of writing in all its aspects. There are many affiliated groups and associate (individual) members across the UK.

The National Poetry Library (Children's Collection)

Level 5, Royal Festival Hall, Southbank Centre, London SE1 8XX
tel 020-7921 0943
email info@poetrylibrary.org.uk
website www.nationalpoetrylibrary.org.uk
Facebook www.facebook.com/NationalPoetryLibrary
Twitter @natpoetrylib
Instagram @nationalpoetrylibrary

Comprises thousands of items for young poets of all ages, including poetry on CD and DVD. The library has an education service for teachers and writing groups, with a separate collection of books and materials for teachers and poets who work with children in schools. Group visits can be organised, allowing children to interact with the collection in various ways, from taking a Poetry Word Trail across Southbank Centre, to exploring how the worlds of science and poetry interact, engaging with war poetry via the Letters Home booklet, or becoming a Poetry Library Poetry Explorer. Nursery schools can also book a Rug Rhymes session for under-5s. Children of all ages can join for free and borrow books and other materials. A special membership scheme is available for teachers to borrow books for the classroom. Contact the library for membership details. Open Tuesday to Sunday, 11am to 8pm.

The Northern Poetry Library

The Chantry, Bridge Street, Morpeth, Northumberland NE61 1PD

tel (01670) 620391
email mylibrary@activenorthumberland.org.uk
website www.northernpoetrylibrary.org.uk
Twitter @nplpoetry

Largest collection of contemporary poetry outside London, housing over 15,000 titles and magazines covering poetry published since 1945. Founded 1968.

The Scottish Poetry Library

5 Crichton's Close, Canongate, Edinburgh EH8 8DT
tel 0131 557 2876
email reception@spl.org.uk
website www.scottishpoetrylibrary.org.uk

Houses over 45,000 items: books, magazines, pamphlets, recordings and the Edwin Morgan Archive of his published works. The core of the collection is contemporary poetry written in Scotland, in Scots, Gaelic and English, but historic Scottish poetry as well as contemporary works from almost every part of the world are also available. All resources, advice and information are readily accessible, free of charge. The SPL holds regular poetry events, including reading and writing groups, details of which are available on the library website. Closed Sunday and Monday. Founded 1984.

ONLINE RESOURCES

There is a wealth of information available for poets at the click of a mouse: the suggestions below are a good starting point.

The Children's Poetry Archive

website http://childrenspoetryarchive.org

World's premier online collection of recordings of children's poets reading their work. Visitors to the website may listen, free of charge, to the voices of contemporary English-language poets and of poets from the past. Featured poets include Allan Ahlberg, Michael Rosen and Valerie Bloom, but the Archive is added to regularly.

LoveReading4Kids.co.uk

website www.lovereading4kids.co.uk

Independent literature recommendation site designed to inspire and inform parents about the best new reads in children's publishing from toddlers to YA, including poetry. Features include: categories broken down by age range and theme; downloadable opening extracts of featured books; like-for-like recommendations for discovering new authors; exclusive online book reviews by children's books experts including Julia Eccleshare, Andrea Reece and Joanne Owen; and authentic reader reviews from children across all relevant age groups. Includes book price comparison to a wide range of affiliates.

The Poetry Kit

email info@poetrykit.org
website www.poetrykit.org

Collates a wide variety of poetry-related information, including events, competitions, courses and more for an international readership.

Poetry Space

email susan@poetryspace.co.uk
website www.poetryspace.co.uk

Specialist publisher of poetry and short stories, as well as news and features, edited by Susan Jane Sims. Operates as a social enterprise with all profits being used to publish online and in print, and to hold events to widen participation in poetry. Submissions of poems, stories, novel extracts, photographs and artwork accepted all year for Young Writers' and Artists' Space (18s and under).

Seven Stories – National Centre for Children's Books

email info@sevenstories.org.uk
website www.sevenstories.org.uk
Twitter @7Stories

Seven Stories is the only place in the United Kingdom dedicated to the art of children's books. Its website features a blog and online catalogue that may be of use to researchers and authors.

Teachit: English Teaching Resources

website www.teachit.co.uk
Twitter @TeachitEnglish

Resource website for teachers, with over 20,000 pages of classroom worksheets, PowerPoint presentations and activities that have been written and edited by experienced English teachers. The website offers free pdfs as well as teaching packs, classroom posters and books designed for Key Stages 3, 4 and 5. Teachit English is part of AQA Education.

Write Out Loud

email info@writeoutloud.net
website www.writeoutloud.net

Poetry news, features and reviews, with comprehensive listings of poetry events, publications, festivals and competitions. Members may post poems, join discussions, add their profile, etc. 50,000+ monthly users.

WHERE TO CELEBRATE POETRY

Festival information should be available from Arts Council England offices (see page 362). See also *Children's literature festivals and trade fairs* on page 390.

The British Council

10 Spring Gardens, London SW1A 2BN
tel 020-7389 4385

email uk-literature@britishcouncil.org
website https://literature.britishcouncil.org
Twitter @litbritish

Visit the website for a list of forthcoming festivals.

Imagine: Writers and Writing for Children

Southbank Centre, London SE1 8XX
tel 020-7960 4200
website www.southbankcentre.co.uk/whatson/
festivals-series/imagine-childrens-festival
Takes place February

An annual festival celebrating writing for children featuring a selection of poets, storytellers and illustrators.

Ledbury Poetry Festival

The Master's House, St Katherine's, Bye Street, Ledbury HR8 1EA
tel (01531) 636232
email manager@poetry-festival.co.uk
website www.poetry-festival.co.uk
Festival Director Chloe Garner, *Festival Manager* Phillippa Slinger
Takes place July and throughout the year

Ledbury Poetry Festival runs a year-round programme during which it sends poets into primary and secondary schools in the region. It also runs poetry events for children during the ten-day summer festival. An International Poetry Competition, with £1,000 prize money and winners' reading event during the Festival, launches every February; see website for details.

StAnza: Scotland's International Poetry Festival

email stanza@stanzapoetry.org
website www.stanzapoetry.org

StAnza is international in outlook and aims to celebrate poetry in all its forms. It is held each March in St Andrews, Scotland's oldest university town. The festival is an opportunity to engage with a wide variety of poetry, to hear world-class poets reading in atmospheric venues, to experience a range of performances where music, film, dance and poetry work in harmony, to view exhibitions linking poetry with visual art and to discover the part poetry has played in the lives of a diverse range of writers, musicians and media personalities. Founded 1988.

WHERE TO WRITE POETRY

Arvon

Lumb Bank – The Ted Hughes Arvon Centre, Heptonstall, Hebden Bridge, West Yorkshire HX7 6DF
tel (01422) 843714

email lumbbank@arvon.org
Totleigh Barton, Sheepwash, Beaworthy, Devon EX21 5NS
tel (01409) 231338
email totleighbarton@arvon.org
The Hurst – The John Osborne Arvon Centre, Clunton, Craven Arms, Shrops. SY7 0JA
tel (01588) 640658
email thehurst@arvon.org
website www.arvon.org

Arvon's three centres run five-day residential courses throughout the year for anyone over the age of 16, providing the opportunity to live and work with professional writers. Writing genres explored include poetry, narrative, drama, writing for children, song-writing and the performing arts. Bursaries are available to those receiving benefits. Founded 1968.

City Lit

1–10 Keeley Street, London WC2B 4BA
tel 020-7831 7831
email infoline@citylit.ac.uk
website www.citylit.ac.uk
Twitter @citylit

Offers classes on poetry appreciation as well as practical workshops.

The Poetry School

1 Dock Offices, Surrey Quays Road, Canada Water, London SE16 2XU
tel 020-7582 1679
website www.poetryschool.com

Teaches the art and craft of writing poetry, with courses in London and around the UK, ranging from evening classes, small seminars and individual tutorials, to one-day workshops, year-long courses and an accredited MA. Activities for beginners to advanced writers, with classes happening face-to-face and online. Three termly programmes a year, plus professional skills development projects and CAMPUS, a social network for poets.

Tŷ Newydd Writing Centre

Llanystumdwy, Cricieth, Gwynedd LL52 0LW
tel (01766) 522811
email tynewydd@literaturewales.org
website www.tynewydd.wales

Tŷ Newydd, the former home of Prime Minister David Lloyd George, has hosted residential creative writing courses for writers of all abilities for over 25 years. Whether you're interested in a poetry masterclass, writing for the theatre, developing a novel for young adults or conquering the popular fiction market, there'll be a course in the programme suitable for you. Courses are open to everyone over the age of 16 and no qualifications are necessary. Staff can advise on the suitability of courses, and further details about each individual course can be obtained by visiting the website, or contacting the team by phone or email. Tŷ Newydd also offers courses for schools, corporate courses and away days for companies. Tŷ Newydd Writing Centre is run by Literature Wales, the national company for the development of literature in Wales.

HELP FOR YOUNG POETS AND TEACHERS

National Association of Writers in Education (NAWE)

Tower House, Mill Lane, off Askham Fields Lane, Askham Bryan, York, YO23 3FS
tel 0330 3335 909
email admin@nawe.co.uk
website www.nawe.co.uk

National membership organisation which aims to further knowledge, understanding and enjoyment of creative writing and to support good practice in its teaching and learning at all levels. NAWE promotes creative writing as both a distinct discipline and an essential element in education generally. Its membership includes those working in Higher Education, the many freelance writers working in schools and community contexts, and the teachers and other professionals who work with them. It runs a national database of writers, produces a weekly opportunities bulletin, publishes two journals – *Writing in Education* and *Writing in Practice* – and holds a national conference. Professional membership includes public liability insurance cover.

Poetry Society Education

The Poetry Society, 22 Betterton Street, London WC2H 9BX
tel 020-7420 9880
email educationadmin@poetrysociety.org.uk
website www.poetrysociety.org.uk

An arm of The Poetry Society aiming to facilitate exciting and innovative education work. For over 30 years it has been introducing poets into classrooms, providing comprehensive teachers' resources and producing accessible publications for pupils. It develops projects and schemes to keep poetry flourishing in schools, libraries and workplaces, giving work to hundreds of poets and allowing thousands of children and adults to experience poetry for themselves.

Through projects such as the Foyle Young Poets of the Year Award and Young Poets Network, The Poetry Society gives valuable encouragement and exposure to young writers and performers.

Schools membership offers a range of benefits, including quarterly Poetry Society publications, books and posters, and free access to the Poets in Schools placement service. Youth membership is also available (for ages 11–18; from £20 p.a.) and offers discounts, publications, poetry books and posters.

Young Poets Network

email educationadmin@poetrysociety.org.uk
website https://ypn.poetrysociety.org.uk
Twitter @youngpoetsnet

Online resource from The Poetry Society comprising features about reading, writing and performing poetry, plus new work by young poets and regular writing challenges. Aimed at young people up to the age of 25.

YOUNG POETRY COMPETITIONS

Children's competitions are included in the competition list provided by the Poetry Library: this is free online at www.nationalpoetrylibrary.org.uk/write-publish/competitions. Further information on literary prizes can be found on the Book Trust website (www.booktrust.org.uk/prizes).

Foyle Young Poets of the Year Award

The Poetry Society, 22 Betterton Street, London WC2H 9BX
tel 020-7420 9880
email fyp@poetrysociety.org.uk
website www.foyleyoungpoets.org
Twitter @PoetrySociety

Annual competition for writers aged 11–17. Prizes include publication, mentoring and a residential writing course. Deadline 31 July. Free to enter. Founded 2001.

Christopher Tower Poetry Prize

Christ Church, Oxford OX1 1DP
tel (01865) 276156
email info@towerpoetry.org.uk
website www.towerpoetry.org.uk/prize
Twitter @TowerPoetry

Annual poetry competition (open from November to March) from Christ Church, Oxford, aimed at students aged between 16 and 18 in UK schools and colleges. The poems should be no longer than 48 lines, on a different chosen theme each year. Prizes: £3,000 (1st), £1,000 (2nd), £500 (3rd). Every winner also receives a prize for his or her school.

FURTHER READING

Addonizio, Kim, *Ordinary Genius: A Guide for the Poet Within* (W.W. Norton and Co. 2012)

Bell, Jo, and Jane Commane, *How to Be a Poet: A 21st Century Guide to Writing Well* (Nine Arches Press 2017)

Bell, Jo, and guests: *52: Write a Poem a Week – Start Now, Keep Going* (Nine Arches Press 2015)

Chisholm, Alison, *A Practical Guide to Poetry Forms* (Compass Books 2014)

Fairfax, John, and John Moat, *The Way to Write* (Penguin Books, 2nd edn revised 1998)

Greene, Roland, *et al.*, *Princeton Encyclopedia of Poetry and Poetics* (Princeton University Press, 4th edn 2012)

Hamilton, Ian, and Jeremy Noel-Tod, *The Oxford Companion to Modern Poetry in English* (Oxford University Press, 2nd edn 2013)

Kowit, Steve, *In the Palm of Your Hand: A Poet's Portable Workshop* (Tilbury House, 2nd edn 2017)

Maxwell, Glyn, *On Poetry* (Oberon Books 2012)

Oliver, Mary, *Rules for the Dance: Handbook for Writing and Reading Metrical Verse* (Houghton Mifflin 1998)

Padel, Ruth, *52 Ways of Looking at a Poem: A Poem for Every Week of the Year* (Vintage 2004)

Padel, Ruth, *The Poem and the Journey: 60 Poems for the Journey of Life* (Vintage 2008)

Roberts, Philip Davies, *How Poetry Works* (Penguin Books, 2nd edn 2000)

Sampson, Fiona, *Poetry Writing: The Expert Guide* (Robert Hale 2009)

Sansom, Peter, *Writing Poems* (Bloodaxe 1993, repr. 1997)

Whitworth, John, *Writing Poetry* (A&C Black, 2nd edn 2006)

See also...
- *Flying the poetry flag*, page 213
- *Interview with my shadow*, page 217

Literary agents
How to get an agent

Because children's publishing is highly competitive, in this article Philippa Milnes-Smith explains that finding an agent isn't child's play.

If you have ambitions to be a children's writer or illustrator, do not think that the process of getting published will be any easier than for the adult market. It's just as tough, if not tougher, partly because writing for children can be seen as an easy option. It can't be that difficult to write a kid's book, can it? After all, it is just for kids …

Nowadays, too, there is extra competition in the children's field. Adult writers have found a new area for their talents, comedians have found new audiences for their humour, celebrities from every field, from soap to sport to YouTube vloggers, have also entered the fray. The children's market is crowded, global and highly competitive. And the competition is often very experienced and very market savvy.

So, what is a literary agent and why would I want one?

See if you can answer a confident 'yes' to all the questions below:
• Do you have a thorough understanding of the publishing market and its dynamics?
• Do you know who are the best publishers for your book and why? Can you evaluate the pros and cons of each? Do you know the best editors within these publishers?
• Are you up to navigating the fast-changing – and fast growing – world of digital publishing? And evaluating self-publishing versus traditional publishing?
• Are you financially numerate and confident of being able to negotiate the best commercial deal available in current market conditions?
• Are you confident of being able to understand fully and negotiate a publishing or other media contract?
• Do you know the other opportunities for your work beyond publishing and how these might be exploited? Could you deal with the complexities of a franchise? Or ongoing development of intellectual property?
• Do you enjoy the process of selling yourself and your work, and dealing with business affairs?
An agent's job is to deal with all of the above on your behalf. A good agent will do all of these well – and let you get on with the important creative work of being an author. They should be able to see the long-term strategy as well as the best deal opportunities for you.

What else do agents do?

Some agents play a more editorial role; all should involve themselves more on marketing, promotion and social media; all should provide efficient business support and process contracts and money promptly and efficiently; all should work in the best interests of their clients; all should understand their clients' work, needs and objectives.

Do I need a specialist children's agent?

Most specialist children's agents would probably say you definitely need a specialist; many general agents will say you don't. In the end you will have to make up your own mind about whether an individual agent is right for your work and for you as an individual. Knowledge, experience and excellent industry contacts (in the right companies and the right categories) are essential qualities in an agent who is going to represent you. If you are writing younger fiction, an agent whose expertise is in adult books with a few forays into young adult fiction probably won't have a full grasp of its potential. If your project is something specifically for the schools and education market it may well require different representation than for the consumer market (projects for educational publishers usually need to be tailored to the education syllabus). If your work reaches beyond traditional publishing, again you will need an agent who can deal with this.

If you are interested only in illustrating work by other people rather than developing your own projects and would like to try illustration work across a broad range of genres and formats, you may be best served by an artists' agent rather than a literary agent (see *Illustrators' agents* on page 289).

I am writing a text for an illustrated book – do I need to send some illustrations for an agent to consider it?

No, not unless you are an accomplished illustrator and intend to do the illustrations yourself. The wrong illustrations will put off an agent as they will a publisher. A good text should speak for itself. And never, in any case, put original artwork at risk: always send copies.

What if I have a brilliant novelty proposal, like a pop-up book? Do I need to show how it is going to look?

If you can do it competently and it helps demonstrate how different and exciting your project is, yes. But be prepared for the fact that you may need to make more than one working model, as the original runs the risk of getting damaged or, at worst, getting lost.

I definitely do want an agent. Where do I begin?

Firstly, using this *Yearbook* (see page 247) and the internet, identify the agents to whom your work will appeal. Then think about whether you are ready to see your children's book as a commercial proposition. An agent will only take someone on if they can see how and why they are going to make money for the client and themselves (and, of course, a client who is making no money tends quickly to become an unhappy client). Then do some further research online and perhaps see if there are any festivals, book fairs, events and/or local writers' groups in which agents are taking part and which you can attend. More agents are doing this kind of outreach work to reach new and prospective authors.

Do agents just think about deals and money?

Good agents do care about deals and money but also care about the quality of work and the clients they take on. They are professional, committed people. They also know that good working relationships count. This means that, if and when you get as far as talking to a prospective agent, you should ask yourself the questions: 'Do I have a good rapport with this person? Do I think we will get along? Do I understand and trust what they are saying?' Follow your instinct – more often than not it will be right.

So how do I convince them that I'm worth taking on?

Make sure you only approach an appropriate agent who deals with the category of book you are writing/illustrating. Check to whom you should send your work and whether there are any specific ways your submission should be made: some agents enjoy an initial exchange on Twitter and others don't. Some only accept electronic submissions. Include a short covering letter with your project explaining what it is, what the intended audience is and providing any other *relevant* context. Always say if and why you are uniquely placed and qualified to write a particular book. Provide a brief, relevant autobiographical paragraph, something that gives a sense of who you are. Prepare as you would for a job application. Above all, make your approach personal, individual and interesting.

You might only get one go at making your big sales pitch to an agent. Don't mess it up by being anything less than thorough.

And if I get to meet the agent?

Treat it like a job interview (although hopefully it will be more relaxed than this). Be prepared to talk about your work and yourself. An agent knows that a prepossessing personality in an author is a great asset for a publisher in terms of publicity and marketing – they will be looking to see how well you communicate. Do also take the chance to find out, if you are discussing children's projects in particular, how and where they submit their clients' work and how well they understand the children's market themselves. Also check that they have good relationships with the sort of publishers/media companies with whom you think your work belongs. Don't be afraid to question them on their credentials and track record. If you have personal recommendations and referrals from other writers, publishers and other industry contacts, do follow these up. Ask, too, about representation in digital and other media, as well as overseas. Is this agent going to get their clients' work noticed by the right people in the right places and win them the best deals? Check if they are a member of the Association of Authors' Agents.

Will they expect me to be an expert on children and the children's market?

Not as such, but they might reasonably expect you to have an interest in what children like and enjoy and show an understanding of a child's eye view of the world. Basically, an agent will be looking for a writer/illustrator who is in sympathy with the target audience. However, it won't do any harm if you spend time at your local bookshop and/or library and befriend your local librarian or specialist children's bookseller to find out what books and authors are working well and if anyone is doing exactly what you plan to do. It's good, basic market research, as is browsing what else is available through internet retailers and reading other good children's books. There is no shortage of information available online.

And if they turn my work down? Should I ask them to look again? People say you should not accept rejection.

No means no. Don't pester. It won't make an agent change his or her mind. Instead, move on to the next agency who might feel more positive towards your work. The agents who reject you may be wrong. But the loss is theirs.

Even if they turn my work down, isn't it worth asking for help with my creative direction?

No. Agents will often provide editorial advice for clients (some go as far as running their own creative groups) but are under no obligation to do so for non-clients. Submissions are usually sorted into two piles of 'yes, worth seeing more' and 'rejections'. To get teaching and advice, creative writing courses and events (see page 395) and writers' and artists' groups are better options to pursue. However you do it, it is vital to practise and develop your creative skills. If you are looking to get your work published, you will be competing with professionals who have spent years perfecting their craft. There are also particular considerations that need to be given to the creation of children's books. In a picture book, the text needs to work specifically with the illustrations: the fewer words there are, the more they matter. In writing fiction for a young age group, where language and sentence construction have to be simple enough for a seven year-old child, the writer often has to work much harder to generate emotion and excitement and give the story personality. Like the business of children's books, the creative challenge is never child's play.

Philippa Milnes-Smith is a literary agent and children's and YA specialist at the Soho Agency (formerly Lucas Alexander Whitley; see page 252). She was previously Managing Director of Puffin Books and is a past president of the Association of Authors' Agents.

See also...
- *What do agents do for their commission?*, page 229
- *How to sell your book to an agent*, page 232
- *Choosing the right agent*, page 234
- *Meet the parents: agent, author and the birth of a book*, page 240
- *Do you have to have an agent to succeed?*, page 243
- *Children's literary agents UK and Ireland*, page 247
- *Children's literary agents overseas*, page 258
- *The Society of Authors*, page 349
- *Illustrators' agents*, page 289

Matador® Serious Self-Publishing

Reliable and realistic advice on self-publishing from the UK's most widely recommended author services company

Whether it be writers' services like Jericho Writers, high street or online retailers, literary agents, other publishers – not to mention the *Writers' & Artists' Yearbook...* time and again Matador is recommended to authors wishing to self-publish a book, ebook or audiobook for pleasure or profit.

"A new breed of self-publishing companies offer authors a kind of halfway house between conventional self-publishing and the commercial kind. Of these, the company that has gone the furthest is Matador..." Writers' & Artists' Yearbook Guide to Getting Published

We produce books for authors to their specifications at a realistic price, as print on demand, or as a short or longer print run book. As well as a high quality of production, we insist on a high quality of content, and place great emphasis on the marketing and distribution of our books to high street retailers. We also offer great customer service.

Matador is ranked as the best self-publishing services supplier in the world by *The Independent Publishing Magazine* (November 2018)

But publishing a book is the easy part... getting it into the shops is harder. We offer a full sales representation and distribution service through our distributor and dedicated sales team. We also offer a full ebook and/or audiobook creation and distribution option to our authors, distributing ebooks and audiobooks worldwide.

"We've always liked Matador because they have the best values in their industry. Apart from anything else, they actually try to sell books. It sounds crazy, but most of their rivals don't. They print 'em, but don't care about selling 'em. Matador do." Jericho Writers

Ask for a free copy of our guide to self-publishing, or download a copy from our website. Or call us if you want to speak to a human being!

www.troubador.co.uk/matador

Matador, Troubador Publishing Ltd,
9 Priory Business Park, Kibworth, Leics LE8 0RX

Tel: 0116 279 2299
Email: matador@troubador.co.uk

Matador
exhibiting at
the 2019
London
Book Fair

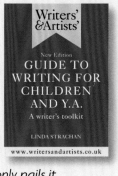

MASTER YOUR CREATIVE WRITING CRAFT

The Manchester Writing School

Join our MFA/MA Creative Writing programme and one of the UK's largest and most successful literary centres.

- Study on campus or from anywhere in the world via online distance learning (September or January entry).

- Follow a specialist route in Novel, Poetry, Writing for Children & Young Adults, Scriptwriting or Creative Non-fiction.

- Complete your own full-length manuscript with editorial input from one of our world-leading writers.

- Campus or online PhD, short writing courses, two-day Summer School and MA English

£10k Poetry and Fiction Prizes

Every year the Manchester Writing Competition offers the chance to win £10,000 for Poetry or Fiction, the UK's biggest literary awards for unpublished work.

Find out more:
manchesterwritingcompetition.co.uk

What do agents *do* for their commission?

Generally, literary agents take 15% of their clients' earnings as their commission. Julia Churchill explains what she does in her role of literary agent in return for that percentage.

My role as a literary agent is to help my authors have successful careers. I endeavour to make money in as many rights streams as possible (with an eye on the long term), and enable an easier professional life for my clients so that they can focus on writing. My job involves spotting talent, helping to develop it and selling it.

Some of my clients came to me as established authors wanting to take their careers up a gear, but most have come via my slush pile, as debut writers. I get well over 100 submissions a week, and I may take on a new writer every few months (if I'm lucky). Spotting talent is often where my job starts. I think I have good taste, and I know that my taste isn't unique. If I love a book, it is likely that there are others who will love it too.

I tend not to follow trends, but I am aware of them. There are two markets to consider, and a good agent will have a clear understanding of both. The first is what I focus on when I sell books to publishers. The editor is the buyer and I need to think about their enthusiasms and needs for their list. Then there's the real market, which is reflected in what people are buying from booksellers right now. Both these markets change constantly and part of my job is to keep up to date with trends, and the preferences of individual editors. This knowledge feeds into my decision-making when considering new authors and guidance for my existing clients, although there are also many opportunities outside of obvious trends. To some extent I'm looking for what's fashionable, but more than anything I'm looking for what may be evergreen.

What I am looking for

When I read a manuscript, I'm looking to connect with a voice, a concept, a character and a story, a book with something to say. I'm looking for clarity and intent in the storytelling, and to be taken somewhere new.

Most debut manuscripts that arrive in my office are not yet ready to sell to a publisher, and I may work with the author to focus on what's best about the character(s) and story. Every edit is different. We may sit down together with a cup of tea and talk through the book, exploring such questions as: What does the writer do best? Where does the story lose focus? How can we keep raising the stakes? Why does this section not work? Is it needed? Is the story pulling in too many directions? What is the book about, in the small ways and the big ways?

Before I offer to represent an author, I'll talk them through the work that I think their manuscript needs. I want to be sure, for the author's sake as well as my own, that we're pointed in the same direction and in sync with our ambitions. It's my job to help the author bring out what is best in the manuscript. Sometimes these conversations are about the architecture of the book, and at other times just the interior design. I don't always work on my clients' books. I simply do what's necessary to maximise the chance of achieving a book deal and the value of that deal.

When I'm satisfied that the book is ready, I submit it to editors. On occasion, I may approach just one editor, and one publishing house, if there is a very specific reason why this would be the best possible outcome for the author. This is matchmaking. More often, I send out the manuscript widely in order to find the publisher with the most passion for the book and the best plan for it.

Selling the book

My favourite aspect of being a literary agent is seeing talent before the rest of the world does. The publishing business relies on having champions for books and an agent is the first professional champion. The agent shares their passion about a book with editors, who in turn pass it on to sales and marketing experts, publicists, reviewers, bloggers, librarians, booksellers, and then finally readers.

Sometimes it takes just a few days to sell a book and for other books it can take months – on occasion it has taken years. An auction is lively, but more than anything it's a logistical challenge and requires being organised and systematic. Auctions provide an opportunity for the agent and author to see each publisher's vision, and they give maximum leverage for the best possible deal. Although the idea of an auction may sound exciting, I probably get as much professional satisfaction from humbly selling a book that's been very tough to place as I do from an eight-publisher auction that takes days to tie up.

Looking at contracts

Being a literary agent is not all about passionate pitches, editorial chats over cups of tea, and champagne celebrations. There is some glamour to our business, but in many ways an agent's job is quite mundane and is taken up with working on contracts between publishers and authors. A contract has a long life and it requires rigour and experience to convert a publisher-friendly contract into one that is author-friendly. Negotiating contracts is not confined to increasing the advance and pushing for the best royalty and high discount rates, although that is where an agent is likely to show the most immediate value. It's also about ensuring that the author gets their rights back if the book stops selling above a certain level, that the pay-out is staggered in a way that favours the author, that certain sub-rights revert if they are unexploited, that the delivery and acceptance terms are favourable, that in a multi-book deal the books are accounted separately, that the split of sub-rights are as good as they possibly can be, that there is total clarity on what electronic rights the publisher has and that they don't cut across the author's reserved rights. The list of considerations is long: there is a lot to cover in a contract.

An agency will often sell translation rights, and television and film rights. Some of my clients make more money in Brazil or Norway than they do in the USA or UK. And while some markets shrink, others thrive, so for books with reach, it's important to have a strong international team and relationships with film scouts and production companies.

As in any career, a writer is faced with opportunities and decisions to make. Some are small and possibly of little consequence, and some are big and important to get right. Every now and then, there are huge forks in the road which require bravery, clear-minded counsel and an ally. The role of an agent is to be informed and to guide each of their authors to make the best decisions. On behalf of the author, an agent is responsible for talking through grievances, ensuring that publishers deliver what has been promised, feeding into conversations about strategy regarding their work, saying 'no' when it's appropriate, finding work, and pushing back.

While everyone concerned in the publishing process wants a book to succeed, my interests as an agent are the same as those of my client. Publishers' interests obviously dovetail with those of the author, but they aren't identical. This is why we generally find ourselves harmonious and in accord with the process, but occasionally in conflict with it. It's my job to have the necessary conversations to look after my authors, to do everything I can to ensure they have the career they want. We are in it together.

Julia Churchill is the Children's Agent at A.M. Heath Ltd (see page 251). She is always on the lookout for new writing talent and considers the slush pile to be the greatest place on earth. She is looking for debut and established authors with storytelling magic, from picture book texts through to young adult fiction. Follow her on Twitter @JuliaChurchill.

See also...
- *A writer's ten commandments*, page 107
- *How to sell your book to an agent*, page 232
- *Meet the parents: agent, author and the birth of a book*, page 240
- *Choosing the right agent*, page 234
- *Do you have to have an agent to succeed?*, page 243
- *Children's literary agents UK and Ireland*, page 247
- *Children's literary agents overseas*, page 258
- *The Society of Authors*, page 349

How to sell your book to an agent

Literary agents wade through slush piles to find a manuscript that shines out and entices them to read more. Madeleine Milburn offers some helpful tips on how to get your submission noticed.

Submission packages for agencies are usually of a similar format. Most require you to send a covering letter, synopsis and the all-important first three chapters. When you feel that your manuscript is as good as it can be and you are ready to submit to an agent, here are some key tips to consider.

The title

Use a strong and compelling title that grabs an agent's attention. Bestselling titles resonate with a reader before they open a book, for instance *Bad Dad*, *Oi Cat!*, *The Book of Dust*, *The Hate U Give*, *The Upside of Unrequited* or *I Want My Hat Back*. Don't use a title that only makes sense to a reader once they have read the story. Think of how you, as a reader, approach books in bookshops. What grabs your attention?

The covering letter

A covering letter should include a brief introduction, for example, 'I am currently seeking representation for my debut novel …', followed by an intriguing sentence that will draw the reader into your story; a slightly longer, enticing blurb; a reason why you have chosen the agent you are submitting to; a short profile; and a brief sentence or two about what you are/will be working on next.

Pitch your book in your letter, *not* in your synopsis. The letter is the place to get an agent excited about your opening chapters and where you need to 'sell' your book. Read the back cover blurb of books in the genre you are writing in, and study why they rouse your attention and interest. Practise pitching your book in a single sentence to get to the core of your story. You need to position your book straight away and make it evident to the agent what genre you are writing in.

Imagine your book on the shelves of a bookshop. Where would it sit? Next to Suzanne Collins or John Green? I want to see that a writer has researched the market and knows that there is a readership for their work. An editor who loves your book will need to persuade the rest of the publishing team that there is a market for it. But when comparing yourself to another author, please don't say you are 'the next' J.K. Rowling; instead express the hope that your work will appeal to 'readers of' J.K. Rowling.

Only mention your achievements that are relevant to the book you are submitting. I applaud Duke of Edinburgh adventurers, dirt road bikers, members of Save the Whale foundations and other wonderfully colourful hobbyists, but unless the activity is specifically relevant to your book, for now, please keep the information short and sweet. Use the covering letter to sell the story, not yourself. I'd love to hear everything about you later, over a coffee, if I ask you to meet up.

Pitch just one book in your letter. If you have written more than one book, choose the one you'd like to launch your writing career with. If an agent loves the book you are submitting, he or she will be interested in all of your work. If you write both adult and children's stories, pick one (for now). A prospective editor will want your next book to appeal to the same readers as your first book – and I like to do two- or even three-book deals with publishers to ensure that they are committed to developing an author's career.

The synopsis

A synopsis is a straightforward chronological account of the *most important* things that happen in a story. A lot of agents read this last, or only read it if they want to see more chapters. Don't include every single detail; try to stick to one A4 page. If there are any twists or plot revelations, don't keep them hidden like you would in a blurb. An agent needs spoilers to see how original your plotting is compared to what is currently on the market, so this aspect can be crucial to deciding whether your manuscript is requested.

The opening chapters

Your first three chapters are extremely important as, together with your covering letter, they are what an agent judges your work by. They need to be strong, enticing and compelling. There must be a strong sense of atmosphere, empathy or intrigue. Be wary of including irrelevant background information or context at this stage: it never grips readers' attention when they are not yet familiar with the characters. At worst, it can also slow the pace and be boring.

Strong characters are so important. Everyone remembers characters rather than the intricate details of a plot – just think James Bond, Sherlock Holmes and Harry Potter. Let your readers do the work. Create suspense and hook us in with a central character so that we are desperate to know more about them and read on.

Don't make your chapters too long to get around the three-chapter limit. I sometimes get asked whether I'd like to see more than three chapters because theirs are relatively short and the answer is 'no thank you'. I don't count a Prologue as a chapter though.

I personally read everything that comes into my 'slush pile'. I represent a wide range of adult, young adult and children's fiction, and would be delighted to look at your work.

Checklist for submitting to an agent

- Make sure your book has a strong title.
- Research the market and check that the length of your novel is appropriate for the genre you are writing in.
- Print out the manuscript and check that all spelling is correct. You will be surprised at how many errors you find.
- Take care to follow the instructions that are specific to each agency. For instance, I like to see 1.5 line spacing for the opening chapters and a one-page synopsis.
- Create a strong and attention-grabbing one-line hook that captures the heart of your story and will entice people to buy and read your book.
- Write a compelling back cover blurb.
- Consider all the selling points for your book. Write a summary of the book's appeal: be clear who the audience is and confident that they will identify with the book. Know the strengths of your manuscript and why it is unique. Think about what previous experience you have that could help promote your book.
- Tailor your profile to be relevant to your writing career. State if you are on a creative writing course, are a member of any writing clubs or societies and if you have won any writing competitions.
- If you have been published before, it is important to be upfront about it. Provide any writing history and say whether you have had an agent in the past.
- Write a synopsis that summarises your book's plot in chronological order with the ending included.

Madeleine Milburn represents award-winning and bestselling authors of adult and children's fiction and non-fiction who consistently feature on the *Sunday Times*, *New York Times* and international bestseller lists. Milburn was awarded Literary Agent of the Year at the British Book Awards 2018 where she was praised for her 'prolific deal-making' and 'long-term vision for her authors'. She is known by editors as a 'tenacious negotiator and an excellent collaborator with a nose for commercial success'. She is also one of a small handful of agents to be included in the *Bookseller*'s list of the 100 Most Influential People in the book trade, alongside the likes of J.K. Rowling, Jamie Oliver and the Ceos of the major publishing houses. Since its formation in 2012, Madeleine Milburn Ltd has become a leading global literary agency run from its London office with co-director Giles Milburn (see page 253). Follow her on Twitter @agentmilburn.

Literary agents

Choosing the right agent

Literary agent Gill McLay describes some of the differences between big and small agencies, and identifies some of the ways you can discover which might be the right one for you to approach and to sign up with if you are offered representation.

After completing my marketing and publishing degree I moved to London and went straight into my first publishing job. Over 20 years later I am still in publishing. I have worked for small, independent publishers and large global publishers, always on the publicity, marketing and sales side of the business. Then, about ten years ago, I decided I wanted to work for myself. One of the many things I did was to set up the Bath Festival of Children's Literature (http://bathfestivals.org.uk/childrens-literature), which is now the largest festival in Europe devoted exclusively to books, authors, illustrators and readers of children's books – from picture books right up to YA. I knew it had to start big if it was to compete in the already vibrant and well-developed literary festivals calendar. Now in its 12th year, it is an integral part of the wider Bath Festivals, which are run throughout the year and cover a broad spectrum of creativity, from visual arts, music and drama. I remain its artistic director alongside my husband and business partner, John McLay.

It was while I was working more closely with authors, through the festival, that I started to be asked for publishing advice. I would frequently recommend agents that fledging writers could approach and was repeatedly asked why I didn't offer an agent service myself. Being an agent is an all-encompassing job and I knew it would need me to be full-time, so I decided that when my son started school I would do it!

At the time, I was running media training courses for authors and was always surprised by the questions they asked (or hadn't dared or thought to ask). I decided that if I was to be an agent, I would manage careers rather than projects and I would allow authors to become a fully engaged part of my agency. For me, part of surviving in this tough and competitive business is to help my clients be prepared, and to share my knowledge of why decisions are made and how. As well as showing respect for my authors' writing and other creative work, I set out to establish working relationships based on mutual respect, understanding and gratitude for the respective skills of both author and agent; from such close links, greater successes emerge. *Teams* of people create books, and I wanted to put this team spirit right at the heart of my agency.

The Bath Literary Agency is a relatively small company that offers a very hands-on style of management for writers of children's books. We are one of many small literary agencies based outside London, the main publishing metropolis, and we like to think that we offer authors something different to what a larger agency provides. The agency is now eight years old and continues to go from strength to strength, due to my clients who work incredibly hard to deliver saleable books. Together we are always working on our next project.

How can *you* find the right agent?

I believe that having an agent is essential. Once you are lucky enough to find your publishing home, it makes a big difference if you can focus on the creative side and let your agent focus on the business aspects of your writing.

This doesn't mean you don't get involved. You *must* be involved. It does, however, mean that you can talk through things with your agent and ask all the questions you like without fear of asking the wrong thing – which might not be the case if you were talking directly to a publisher. It also gives you a greater understanding of which things to challenge and which to accept, both contractually and creatively. There is a huge difference between writing for yourself and writing to be published; an agent can help you navigate this fine line.

What are the differences between small and large agencies?

Bigger agencies, London-based agencies, multimedia agencies and small boutique agencies (with only one or two agents, say) all offer different things. They each have their strengths and weaknesses; the most important thing for you, as a new author, is to get the right agent for *your* books and *your* needs.

The size of the agency is actually irrelevant in many ways, because everything comes down to the relationship you have with one person, your own agent.

That relationship should be symbiotic, with writer and agent coming together to make the strongest possible offering to a publisher, and thus ultimately to your readership or market. Your respective strengths and weaknesses should complement each other.

This is why you need to know your agent's experience. Agents come from all sorts of different backgrounds, which can make a huge difference to their individual approach. Many have been editors, some move over from selling rights in publishing houses to agenting, and others have come from the sales and book-buying side of publishing. Each set of skills and experience has its own strengths.

> **In a nutshell**
>
> **Know what you want:**
> • Do you want to be a big fish in a small pond?
> • Do you write across several genres; if so, does the agent represent them all?
> • Do you want an agent with editorial skills to help shape your writing?
> • Do you want personal support or purely business/commercial help?

My background is in sales and marketing. As a result, I approach things from a very commercial angle and spend almost as much time scouting for new opportunities as I do creating them. When I advise my clients, we talk about long-term objectives and career progression. The individual books are important, but I am always keen to find out what else an author can do and where they want to be.

An agent with an editorial background, however, may focus more on the individual manuscript. For some authors this is essential and they need this support, but others may already have confidence and feel secure in their writing, but they may need help to understand the market and publishing process and to pitch their story to the right audience and gatekeepers (i.e. publishers).

Part of this writer-development process, fostering authors of tomorrow, comes from the other professional hats I wear. Media training for authors and for the children's festival has given me a real insight into the life of a successful author today. Gone are the days of being able to write, send your script to an agent, sell your book and then start writing again. An author needs to promote and reach their audience. The first book you sell to a publisher will be the last before you add the role of juggler to your CV, as you tackle the balancing act of writing *and* promoting!

Literary agents

A larger agency will often have staff who specialise in rights, contract, legal, accounts and admin support. A smaller agency is more likely to have only a couple of these specialists, and sometimes they will have none; the agent may co-ordinate all aspects of the process. Which you prefer and works best for you is completely personal. Do you want to work with one person who answers everything, or do you wish to work with a team? Larger agencies may also be able to offer you other focused advice. For example, if you wish to write for adults, write plays or film scripts, they may have people on hand to advise or represent you beyond, for example, your initial work in YA fiction. Smaller agencies can sometimes do this too, but tend to be more specialised.

Ideally, you should meet agents from both large and smaller agencies – that's if you are lucky enough to be offered representation by more than one agency. This will help you make an informed decision. It is in no one's interest for you to be with the wrong agent. Choosing the right agent is a balance of gut instinct and information; do your research before you contact them with your initial submission, and then again when they have shown interest in representing you.

One thing that everyone needs is an agent who is nice to work with, but also one who is an effective and strong dealmaker. When selecting your agent, there are some **key things to consider**:

1. How many clients do they have and who are they? If you feel that you will need and want a lot of hands-on support with your writing, a large agency may not be for you. If you are a confident writer and want someone who has big agency presence, then maybe the children's agent in a bigger agency would suit you.

2. Do they have clients that write in the same genre as you? This is a great indicator that they have strong contacts with the right commissioning editors and can sell this genre. But if they have lots of authors in this field, will you be competing with other clients within their agency? The balance needs to be right. So do look at their client list.

3. Where are they based? These days this seems to matter less and less but, if they are not near you, how often could you and they travel to a mutually sensible location (e.g. London)?

4. What sort of agent are they? Do you want an editor or commercial management? Do you have one book that you need an agent to sell, or do you have multiple ideas that you want someone to help you develop?

5. Can you relax and feel comfortable with them? You need to be able to communicate well with your agent. Is this someone you can work with? The relationship will become really important as you set off on the rollercoaster ride of getting published; you need to be yourself and have complete trust in your agent.

Always trust your gut instinct. If this is the agency and person you can imagine working with, then take the next step and sign up. Getting published is a long process, success doesn't come overnight, so who you share your journey with is important. Big agency or small agency, it's all about best fit and only you can decide which is right for you.

Gill McLay runs the Bath Literary Agency which specialises in children's books and is the founder and artistic director of the annual Bath Festival of Children's Literature.

See also...
- *How to get an agent*, page 225
- *How to sell your book to an agent*, page 232

A message for under-represented writers: We Want You

Davinia Andrew-Lynch knows that, as well as a good story, agents and editors are also on the lookout for talented writers from groups and communities currently under-represented in the world of children's publishing. She has advice for marginalised writers on how to find the representation, confidence and support they need.

Despite the increasing number of children's books published each year, many budding authors find the world of publishing daunting. And, for those of you from under-represented groups (including, but not limited to, minority ethnic/religious, LGBTQ+ and working-class communities), this London-centric industry can seem wholly unwelcoming.

Things are changing, however. The vital importance of youngsters seeing themselves reflected in the books they read has become an issue more frequently recognised by 'gatekeepers' across the industry. The inclusion of these different narratives is not only good for society; it is also good for the health of our business. So, let's get practical. Whilst this book contains a plethora of information to get you on your way, the advice offered highlights how you, as an under-represented writer, can kick-start your career and get noticed.

When submitting to agents, always *do your research*. Does the agent you're looking at represent picture books, middle grade, YA or all of these? What genres do they favour? Are they newer agents actively on the hunt for talent? Studying an agent's existing list will answer many of your questions, but Twitter can also provide you with extra up-to-date information. You never know, an agent's simple #MSWL (Manuscript Wish List) alert may just equate to the very book you've written. And check out #DVpit (strapline 'A Twitter Pitching Event for Marginalized Voices'); it's a great *free* opportunity.

At the same time, do not be deterred from approaching an agent whose list *doesn't* seem obviously inclusive. Time and time again I have met authors who have not submitted work to an agency because they didn't feel that they were reflected by an agent's existing clientele. And, do you know what? Often agents will say that they're just not hearing from marginalised writers, and that they don't understand *why*. Clearly there's a bit of a catch-22 situation going on here, because I for one know that you exist. Remember that agents are essentially looking for a good story and, granted, it is their job to look for talent in (and from) all forms and places; by not submitting your work, you are limiting your chance of discovery. If your story has the elements of a potential success, then the right agent will give you that chance of representation. So, if you like the look of an agent and think your work may appeal, type that email and hit Send!

If you are not yet ready to submit your manuscript, an extensive satellite industry of advice and support has developed to provide authors with the tools to navigate the world of publishing. And, now more than ever, many of these programmes are actively looking to reach out to those who may not have previously believed or found publishing to be a welcoming space. Often you will find events giving you access to many of the individuals on the 'inside', and these insiders (including agents and editors) want to hear from *you*. Understand, these gatekeepers are not wanting to pay lip service to a fad; they are driven by the satisfaction of finding and supporting genuine talent.

Literary agents

Writers' conferences and festivals can often be a good place to start. Yes, they can be an expense, but they can also be a worthwhile investment. Not only are they a vast source of information but, by giving you a couple of days to immerse yourself in a space which celebrates and encourages your writing, they can be the perfect boost for your confidence. You will have the opportunity to attend specific workshops, panel events, hear keynote speeches and often you can book a one-to-one appointment with an agent or editor. For many authors, these one-to-ones can be particularly valuable, and in fact I met one of my current clients at the Winchester Writers' Festival in this way (and 2020 is certainly shaping up to be an excellent year for her!). One of the most prominent such events, focusing on children's content, is hosted by SCBWI, a worldwide members network (see page 353). Their conference offers all of the above, but it also gives you access to a community of like-minded authors, and this can be a particular draw and comfort.

Do check the conference listings in this *Yearbook* (which start on page 395). As you will see, there are a number of them taking place around the country, at different times of the year and sometimes focusing on a specific area of publishing. But do understand, it is not about attending as many as possible. Assess your situation; consider what it is that you want to know about the industry and then do your research. If you are making the choice to spend your money in this way, then you should ensure that it is cash well spent – you want to leave that conference feeling better equipped to deal with what will, hopefully, be a future career. If the idea of a conference feels too much, then consider the many evening salons, day workshops, and afternoon panel sessions offering more tailored advice. There really are events aplenty, and sometimes these are more affordable financially and timewise.

How do you find out about these events? Check out your local regional literary organisations, for instance, New Writing North/South, Writing West/East Midlands and Spread the Word (London) are a few of the most prominent (see *Societies, associations and organisations* section, starting on page 362). Each of these bodies work tirelessly to support new writers – and particularly those who may have to overcome varying barriers due to a, frankly, institutional bias (however unintentional). Not only do these organisations host their own events but they will often highlight and promote worthwhile external opportunities. A good example of this is the Free Reads Scheme organised by The Literary Consultancy (one of the largest editorial services companies in the country). In conjunction with the Arts Council, the scheme works with local literary organisations to find authors who may require and appreciate a subsidised manuscript assessment service. It is a brilliant opportunity which acknowledges that the choice to write is not necessarily an affordable one – a fact which in itself makes publishing seem as though it should only be for the privileged few. And, on the issue of expense, you may find that some of these services will offer bursaries for specific groups of people. They are there to help, not isolate. Do not hesitate to get in touch with those who are organising such events and ask whether there is anything you can apply for.

Do also keep an eye out for upcoming competitions; industry magazine the *Bookseller* often announces the most notable of these. While many are open to all writers, it is also worth investigating the increasing number which specifically target under-represented groups. These competitions may not land you with the hallowed publishing deal or representation but, depending on the scheme, they may offer the opportunity for you to get a foot in the door. For instance (and please excuse the personal plug here, ahem ahem …):

the FAB Prize (see page 383) was set up by Faber Children's and Andlyn, looking specifically for un-agented and un-published BAME writing/illustrating talent. The individual category winners were awarded with mentoring, and an anthology of their work and the work of the runners-up was circulated around children's literary agents. Since the Prize's inception, a number of entrants have gone on to gain representation and get published. The prize was a *platform*, but these writers reached their goal off the back of their own merit. Be sure to use these opportunities – that is what they are there for.

I would be remiss not to mention the Arts Council (see page 362) in this context. Easily forgotten, but open to all, it has a number of grant schemes which provide writers with the time and space to focus on their writing. It has to be said that, particularly within children's publishing, the body is incredibly keen to help address the imbalance of marginalised voices. As mentioned, the financial implications of wanting to be a writer stretch far and wide; if this applies to you, see whether there is a grant for which you may qualify.

Having dealt with the practical side of pursuing your writing career, here's my take on how our identities can enrich the stories we tell. Children's publishing has always been synonymous with the idea that its stories and literature can teach children about the society in which they live. Yet statistics (most recently those led by BookTrust and CLPE – the Centre for Literacy in Primary Education – on multicultural diversity) show that there is a serious dearth of stories featuring characters from under-represented backgrounds. In my conversations with authors, the word 'diversity' seems to have inadvertently given way to the suggestion and/or impression that diverse stories should be 'issue'-led, that they should highlight the barriers or difficulties of 'other' lives. And, because there are so few novels in the market featuring minority groups and/or marginalised characters within a British context, it has become all too easy to associate particular kinds of stories with the different under-represented groups.

This means that, to some extent, an element of stereotyping has come in to play. But why? We can learn about each other within the framework of a simply entertaining and *mainstream* story. Your idea, *not* your identity, should be your USP. Remember you want (and deserve) to be measured on the same scale as any other author and, with that, there should be a freedom to write any kind of story. If you want to create an epic 'through the wardrobe'-style adventure, a YA rom-com, or a rather left-of-centre comedy, then you must. Saying that, if you want to write a gritty issue-led tale, feel free to do that too! For those working within the industry, your ability to produce an excellent narrative is the attraction, but when your stories reflect you, your community, your *rarely seen world* – that is refreshing, and frankly a bonus.

There are many individuals within children's publishing who actively want to change the landscape so that its output is more inclusive. It cannot be denied, however, that our intentions are often left rattling around an echo chamber and that this message of inclusivity isn't necessarily being received on the 'outside'. So I am saying this very clearly now: as an industry we need your stories but, more importantly, we want you … *all of you, not just your demographic.* We look forward to hearing from you soon!

Davinia Andrew-Lynch founded the literary agency Andlyn in 2015, and specialises in children's and YA fiction and content. She had previously worked as an associate agent at the Dench Arnold Agency, a film/TV agency, and as a freelance children's fiction editor and reader. For more information see www.andlyn.co.uk. Follow Davinia on Twitter @nocturnalreader.

Literary agents

Meet the parents: agent, author and the birth of a book

Stephanie Thwaites describes the agent's role in the route to a happy marriage between author and publisher.

Before I started work experience at Curtis Brown I had no idea what a literary agent did. Within my first year as an assistant I had tackled mountains of filing, collected dry cleaning, responded to fan mail, received a gift from Penhaligons, and drawn up my first audio rights contract. While my daily duties have certainly changed since then, the variety and excitement of the job still keeps my pulse racing and I never know what exactly will await me each morning.

As a children's agent, it amazes me that we haven't yet quashed the idea that writing for children is easy, or somehow easier than writing for adults. Shorter doesn't mean simpler. In fact, writing for children can be more difficult than writing for adults because of the very specific demands of the market. Quality writing alone won't work – a strong idea and engaging plot is vital. Then there's the challenge of finding the right voice, avoiding being patronising and keeping an energetic pace throughout. Thanks to a couple of high-profile success stories, new writers can start with inflated and unrealistic expectations. Part of our job as agents is to explain the business to new clients and to encourage them to have reasonable and achievable goals. While it is crucial to be positive and aim high, it is also worth remembering that there's really no such thing as an overnight success and children's authors often work incredibly hard for years before seeing the fruits of their labour. Young readers' taste evolves rapidly and writers and their representatives cannot afford to rely too heavily on 'author loyalty' when it comes to building a career and body of work. This is a readership with an ever-changing face as new child readers discover new authors, and existing readers are continually moving on too. A lot of children's authors and illustrators have other jobs and don't rely solely on writing for their income. Many work tirelessly visiting schools, speaking to children, teachers and librarians, appearing at literary festivals and running workshops. More recently, writers have been encouraged to develop new skills – to create their own websites, use social networking, join Twitter, try blogging and even make Skype appearances. It's not enough for authors just to write and deliver their books – they are expected to promote them ever more energetically too.

The role of the agent

An agent is involved throughout the life of a book, and aims to support an author by acting as a sounding board for ideas, giving feedback on material before it reaches an editor, liaising with editors at different publishing houses, guiding the author, providing specialist industry knowledge and enabling them to find the right home for their book and to strike the best deal. An agent negotiates the terms, and often sells the translation, US, audio and film rights (collectively known as subsidiary rights), which can sometimes be as important as the original publishing deal. Agencies manage the accounting side – invoicing, chasing payments and checking royalty statements – together with handling miscellaneous requests.

Enormous changes are currently taking place in the publishing world and it is an agent's responsibility to keep abreast of new developments and to consider how their clients will be affected by these changes. A good agent will ensure their authors are in a position to seize new opportunities; and where a 'traditional' approach is not effective, the agent should be able to try other approaches and work with their authors to devise new strategies. Ideally, the relationship will be career-long for both agent and author. When the road is bumpy, the agent feels keenly the successes and disappointments of their authors. The unfortunate reality is that most authors will not become instant bestsellers and it can take years and a great deal of patience and determination for an author to build a strong foundation.

Manuscript submissions

It is natural to assume that agents spend all of their working day reading manuscripts but in fact the majority of reading takes place outside of office hours. With limited time to focus on new submissions, we have to be very selective about the material we read in full and unfortunately we often have to make decisions based on just three chapters. However, even before we reach the opening page, we will already have formed a first impression from the covering letter. A letter which is poorly executed, sloppy, riddled with spelling mistakes or addressed to 'Mr Curtis Brown' or 'Dear Editor' will not pique our interest. The letter should be arresting but not gimmicky; informative but brief. Writing the perfect letter is an art in itself. I prefer to receive just one page with an overview of the story, the age range of the target readership, an idea of where it could be positioned and a line or two about the author. It is important to remember that this may be your only opportunity to communicate with an agent and it's worth bearing in mind how many times a book will be pitched beyond this initial letter – to editors (in the UK, USA and translation markets), to their teams in-house, to buyers and to customers. Asserting that your own children have enjoyed it probably isn't the most persuasive argument to advance.

To give you the best chance at securing an agent it is worth starting your research well before submitting your manuscript. If you're reading this, no doubt you are already doing just that. Check that you are approaching the right agents – look at their interests and consider the writers and genres they represent. Make sure you follow submission guidelines and try to resist chasing up your manuscript too soon. It is not unheard of now for approaches to be made via Twitter. Writing is, to an extent, a job like any other job. Just as you would research a company or industry before an interview, so you should do your homework before writing a covering letter. Reading other titles and reviewing what else is being published successfully will help give you a sense of the area you are writing in and of what might appeal to your target readership. If there's a gap in the market, sometimes there's a reason for that – it could be due to a lack of demand or just that it's the wrong moment for the subject. The style of books we might have enjoyed as children may not make it through an acquisitions meeting where publishers have to assess costs and sales potential. However, while awareness of what is commercially viable is important, a great story will always be irresistible. Writers should follow their instincts and inspiration and write what comes naturally.

The most satisfying success stories are the small, unlikely, unexpected ones. There's no substitute for a book that wins your heart. We've all heard reports of 22 publishers turning down a manuscript before one publisher takes a chance with it, offering a tiny advance and subsequently retiring on the profits as it becomes a blockbuster. The subjectivity and

Literary agents

unpredictability of publishing is simultaneously frustrating and thrilling and there's no feeling quite like reading a manuscript then witnessing it go on to make waves and inspire young readers.

As a new writer, sharing your work with others can be a terrifying experience, but inviting feedback is a good form of preparation. An editor I know came up with a brilliantly simple but useful phrase: 'The end is not the end' – you might think you've finished a manuscript but usually this is just the beginning. Publishing is a collaborative process and compromise is often necessary if you are to succeed. Publishing a book involves many different parties and while you won't agree with all of them at all times it is important to be able to work as part of a team – albeit with the author as the star player.

Arranging a happy marriage

Just as an author might need to develop different skills and wear a number of hats, not just that of writer, so the agent will adopt a range of roles. Our strategies and activities might differ from client to client, project to project and day to day. To sum this up it might help to adopt a matrimonial analogy for the role of the agent in relation to author, and editor and publishing house. The agent can be seen as a bizarre hybrid of marriage broker, ceremony officiator, marriage counsellor and sometimes mother of the bride! How exactly? Well, we're responsible for helping the author to choose their publishing partner, introducing them to the right match – an editor who they will really connect with and a publishing house where they can thrive. Sometimes we might find there are several suitors and the agent will help the author weigh up the options and select the most suitable partner. So the agent acts as matchmaker for the 'author-bride', the principal player on the wedding day. Next we conduct the negotiations and handle the contractual side of the arrangement, outlining each side's obligations. The agent, at this juncture, is a cross between cleric and the pre-nup lawyer. Combining two families is never easy, and the extended publishing family can include marketing and publicity departments, production, sales and accounting and rights teams. Ensuring good relations can sometimes be a challenge. The agent will keep a close eye on these areas and promote good communication and, hopefully, marital bliss. Ultimately, however, like the proud and loving mother of the bride we remain firmly on the side of the bride, representing her best interests and advising and guiding her, sharing her disappointments and rejoicing in her triumphs.

Stephanie Thwaites is a literary agent at Curtis Brown (see page 250) where she has worked for more than a decade. She represents children's fiction, commercial fiction for adults and narrative non-fiction. Her clients range from debut authors and illustrators to established names, bestsellers, prize winners and Literary Estates.

See also...
- *How to get an agent,* page 225
- *What do agents do for their commission?,* page 229
- *How to sell your book to an agent,* page 232
- *Do you have to have an agent to succeed?,* page 243
- *Choosing the right agent,* page 234
- *Children's literary agents UK and Ireland,* page 247
- *Children's literary agents overseas,* page 258
- *The Society of Authors,* page 349

Do you *have* to have an agent to succeed?

Bestselling children's author Philip Ardagh has over 100 titles to his credit but chooses not to have a literary agent to represent him. In this article he tells us why.

There are a lot of people out there who think that they're children's writers ('I was a child myself once, you know') and who send unsolicited manuscripts directly to publishers in their hundreds – possibly thousands – every year. These manuscripts usually end up on what is called the 'slush pile'. Some publishers won't even read them. Some do but, usually, only after a very long time. Many manuscripts are very badly written or very badly presented. Some are perfectly good but a little too much like something already out there in the bookshops, or they lack that indefinable something that makes them stand out from the crowd. Others are perfectly good but are sent to completely the wrong publisher. The best children's fantasy novel ever isn't going to appeal to a publisher specialising in adult DIY manuals, is it? Getting an agent cuts through this process.

Having an agent

Firstly, if an agent submits a manuscript it will go to the publisher they think that it's best suited to, and probably to the most suitable editor within that company – more often than not someone they know or have had dealings with in the past. So your manuscript is being seen by the right people at the right place. It's also neatly bypassed the slush pile. It will actually get read. Hurrah! The agent has acted as a filter. The publisher knows that, if you've been taken on by a reputable agent, your words are probably *worth* reading. You're ahead of the game.

An agent knows the ins and outs of advances, royalties, escalators, foreign rights, and a million and one other things that make the humble writer's head spin. Agents know the 'going rates' and will get you the very best deal they can if a publisher wants to publish your work. And, should there be problems further down the line, your agent can play the bad guy on your behalf – renegotiating contracts and doing the number crunching – whilst you only deal with the nice fluffy creative side with your editor.

That's the theory, of course, and much of it is true. They take their 10–15% share but they're not a charity and, if they're on a percentage of your earnings, it's generally in their interest to make you as much money as possible, isn't it?

The question is: is it possible to be a successful children's author without an agent? Of course it is. Anything's possible. I'm an agentless author and I'm doing fine, but not without help, advice, common sense, good luck and, as time has passed, experience.

So what are the disadvantages of having an agent? If you've got the right agent, the answer is probably very few, if any. Sure, you're not earning the full advance or royalty because you're giving them a percentage but your manuscript may never have become a book (or the advance and royalty may have been much lower) if they didn't represent you in the first place. If you have an agent you don't get directly involved in every aspect of negotiation and discussion with your publisher because you've handed that role over. And

Literary agents

if you like the on-hands approach (for that read 'are a control freak'), you may miss out on that but, overall, the pros seem to outweigh the cons.

If you're *not* happy with your agent, though, it can be a very different story. You're not your agent's only client and you may feel – rightly or wrongly – that they're not giving you enough attention. Many is the writer and illustrator I know who has said, 'I find more work for myself than my agent does', or who isn't happy with the advance they've received and said, 'I'm not sure why my agent was so keen for me to agree to this deal.' Another familiar lament is, 'She seemed so enthusiastic when I first signed up, but now she's gone really quiet.' Your filter has become a barrier.

There may also be jobs which your agent is reluctant for you to take. In children's non-fiction, many authors are still paid flat fees, and small ones at that. Many agents will tell you not to touch them with a barge pole but – if you are at the beginning of your career – who knows what that little job might lead to? I once wrote the text to a book that owed its subsequent international success not to the beauty of my prose but to the illustrations and brilliant paper engineering. My fee was peanuts and, in immediate financial terms, it made no difference if the book sold three copies or 300,000. But it did my writing career the power of good. My name was associated with a successful title, I got known by various people within that particular publishing house, I went on to write many more books for them *with* royalties, and added to my reputation, generating interest from other publishers.

Going it alone

I enjoy that getting-to-know aspect of developing a relationship with publishers and, when it comes to contracts, I have a very useful not-so-secret secret weapon. I may not have an agent but I can call on the contracts experts at the Society of Authors (see page 349). As a member of the Society, they'll go through a contract line by line for me, free and for nothing, offering comments, suggestions and advice. They also publish excellent easy-to-understand pamphlets on various aspects of publishing. If you're not already a member, rush out and join immediately! If you don't understand something, don't be afraid to ask.

Remember, whatever impression a publisher might give, there is very rarely such a thing as a standard contract, written in stone, that can't be altered; sometimes significantly. Be prepared to concede some minor points, maybe, in return for sticking to your guns over a point which may really matter to you. (Different things matter to different writers.)

My big break came by luck, but luck borne out of developing contacts and making real friendships in the course of my agentless foray into the children's publishing world. The bulk of my 100 or so titles are non-fiction, but the bulk of my income and 95% of my recognition comes from my fiction, but one grew from the other. Because I was involved and enthusiastic, I was invited to promote one of my non-fiction titles at a sales conference. As a result of how I ad-libbed at the conference, following a mighty cock-up, I was asked if I wrote fiction. *Awful End* (my first Eddie Dickens book) was pulled out of the drawer and a deal was done. One thing had, indeed, led to another. Eddie's adventures are in over 30 languages and read around the world, and have picked up a few literary awards along the way.

Your rights

Publishers love to have world rights to books. Agents love to sell the rights separately. You can see why. An agent will argue that they can get more for you (and therefore more for them) by selling foreign rights separately to foreign publishers – perhaps creating a US auction for your fabulous book, for example – rather than your signing everything over to your UK publisher in one fell swoop. If, however, you sell the world rights to the publisher, and you have a good relationship with them, they're in effect acting as your agent on foreign deals and can still negotiate some excellent ones *in consultation with you*. And, having your world rights, they can share in your international success when it comes, so may be more keen to nurture you (and your money-generating, recognition-building world rights) in the future than, possibly, another writer whom they only publish in the UK.

And remember, an advance is an advance of royalties. If the advance is small and the book is a success, it simply means that the advance is earned out sooner and the cheques start rolling in. My advance for *Awful End* was just a four figure sum, but the money I've earned from additional royalties has been very-nice-thank-you-very-much. And my advances for the later Eddie Dickens books and other fiction were significantly larger.

Making the right decision

I know from friends and colleagues that, when you're starting out, you can find it as hard to get an agent as a publisher, which is why some people choose to go straight for the publishing houses. My advice – and this may surprise some of you – is to stick at trying to get an agent. If I was starting out now, I'd do that. Having an agent from the beginning makes sense.

If you're dead against the idea, feeling convinced that you can do a great job (see Philippa Milnes-Smith's checklist on page 225) or are exhausted trying, there are a few obvious things you can do. Even now, I sometimes ask myself 'Am I getting the very best deal?' and 'Could an agent do better for me?' Financially, the answers to these are probably 'Maybe not' and 'Yes', but are these the right questions? Surely what I need to ask is: 'Am I happy with this deal?' and 'Is it a reasonable sum reflecting what I think I'm worth and showing the commitment and understanding of the publisher?' And the answer to that is, more often than not, 'Yes'. And remember, money ain't the be-all and end-all. A good working relationship with an editor and publisher who understand you, consult with you, nurture you and your writing, promote and market you in a way you're happy with is beyond price.

Approaching a publisher

But let's not get ahead of ourselves. One of the most important, important, *important* – it's important, get it? – things you need to be sure of before sending a manuscript to an agent *or* a publisher is that it's ready to be seen. Some unpublished writers are so keen to show their work to others in the hope of getting it published as soon as possible that it's still in a very raw state. They're not doing themselves any favours. In fact, they could be ruining their chances. Sure, there is such a thing as overworking a piece, but you really need to be confident that it's about as good as it's going to get, especially if you're bypassing the agent route and going direct to the publisher. With no agent 'filter', you've got to be sure that you're representing yourself, through your work, in the very best possible light.

Look in bookshops to find out who publishes what. Once you've chosen a publisher, look them up in this *Yearbook*, find out their submissions procedure and ring them up. Ask the receptionist the name of the person you should send your manuscript or sample chapters to. This way you can address and write a letter to a particular person, rather than taking the 'Dear Sir/Madam' approach.

Literary agents

The covering letter you should write to the publisher is almost identical to the one for writing to a prospective agent (see *How to get an agent* on page 225 and *How to sell your book to an agent* on page 232) except, of course, that you should also include the reason why you think they'd be the right people to publish your work.

Finally, do treat the business side of selling yourself as a business. It's not simply that 'the writing's the important bit' and that it'll 'sell itself'. Network, send in invoices on time, get in touch when you say you'll get in touch and be contactable (there's no excuse for dropping off the radar in this age of emails and mobile phones). If you're shy or don't like parties, still go to the ones you're invited to by your publisher. You never know what that chance meeting with that rather scruffy bloke by the chilli dips might lead to. He could end up turning your book into a 24-part television series.

Oh, and one last thing: never admit that, secretly, you enjoy writing so much that you'd happily be published for nothing. Oops. Me and my big mouth!

Agented or agentless, good luck.

Philip Ardagh is an award-winning children's author, reviewer and commentator, whose prizes include the Roald Dahl Funny Prize and the prestigious Deutscher Jugendliteraturpreis from Germany. He is a patron of the Stratford Literary Festival and an ambassador for the Northern Children's Book Festival. He has collaborated with illustrators such as Axel Scheffler and David Roberts, and with Sir Paul McCartney on his children's book, *High in the Clouds*. He is currently working with writer/illustrator Elissa Elwick on their *Stick & Fetch* and the *Little Adventurers* series; with illustrator Jamie Littler on the *Secret Diary* series for the National Trust, in which 'only the facts are true'; and with illustrator Tom Morgan-Jones on their *Norman the Norman* series. A lifelong Moomin fan, he wrote *The World of Moominvalley*, a 300-plus page definitive guide to Tove Jansson's Moomins. With works such as *The Eddie Dickens Trilogy* and *The Grunts*, he has been translated into over 40 languages. Follow Philip on Facebook or on Twitter @PhilipArdagh.

See also...

Children's literary agents UK and Ireland

The *Children's Writers' & Artists' Yearbook*, along with the Association of Authors' Agents and the Society of Authors, takes a dim view of any literary agent who asks potential clients for a fee prior to a manuscript being placed with a publisher. We advise you to treat any such request with caution and to let us know if that agent appears in the listings below. However, agents may charge additional costs later in the process but these should only arise once a book has been accepted by a publisher and the author is earning an income. We urge authors to make the distinction between upfront and additional charges. Authors should also check agents' websites before making an enquiry and should familiarise themselves with submission guidelines.

*Member of the Association of Authors' Agents

The Agency (London) Ltd*
24 Pottery Lane, London W11 4LZ
tel 020-7727 1346
email hd-office@theagency.co.uk
website www.theagency.co.uk
Children's Book Agent Hilary Delamere

Works in conjunction with overseas agents. The Agency also represents screenwriters, directors, playwrights and composers; for more information check the agency's website. Represents picture books, including novelty books, fiction for all ages including teenage fiction and series fiction. *Commission* Home 15%, overseas 20%. Submission guidelines on website. *Founded* 1995.

Aitken Alexander Associates Ltd*
291 Gray's Inn Road, London WC1X 8QJ
tel 020-7373 8672
email reception@aitkenalexander.co.uk
website www.aitkenalexander.co.uk
Twitter @AitkenAlexander
Instagram @AitkenAlexander
Agent Gillie Russell

Children's and young adult fiction. Handles fiction for 9+ to YA. *Commission* Home 15%, overseas 20%. Email preliminary letter with half-page synopsis and first 30 pages of sample material via agency website or to submissions@aitkenalexander.co.uk. No picture books.
   Clients include Sue Durrant, Jane Hardstaff, Emma Hill, Rhian Ivory, Mark Lowery, Nicola Penfold, Benjamin Scott, Emily Thomas, Moira Young. Client estates: Paul Gallico, Mary Norton, Louise Rennison. *Founded* 1977.

Darley Anderson Children's Book Agency Ltd*
Suite LG4, New Kings House,
136–144 New Kings Road, London SW6 4LZ
tel 020-7736 1438
email childrens@darleyanderson.com
website www.darleyandersonchildrens.com
Twitter @DA_Childrens
Instagram @da_childrens
Contacts Darley Anderson (Managing Director), Camilla Bolton (Director), Clare Wallace (Senior Agent), Lydia Silver (Agent), Peter Colegrove (Financial Director)

Children's fiction (for all ages from picture book to middle grade through to young adult and crossover), non-fiction and illustrators. *Commission* Home 15%, illustration/USA/translation 20%. Send covering letter, short synopsis and first three chapters/ illustration samples by email. No scripts or screenplays.
   Clients include Cathy Cassidy, John Connolly, Caroline Crowe, Martyn Ford, Stewart Foster, A.M. Howell, Polly Ho-Yen, Rachel Ip, Claire Powell, Beth Reekles, Dave Rudden, Lorna Scobie, Rashmi Sirdeshpande, Kim Slater, Deirdre Sullivan.

ANDLYN
tel 020-3290 5638
email submissions@andlyn.co.uk
website www.andlyn.co.uk
Twitter @andlynlit
Founder and Agent Davinia Andrew-Lynch
Represents authors of picture books, middle grade, YA and crossover fiction – all genres. Also represents adult fiction and non-fiction. Actively looking for new clients. *Commission* Home and audio 15%, USA, foreign/translation, film/TV, multi-platform and online media rights 20%. See website for submission guidelines.
   Clients include Malcolm Duffy, Bex Hogan, Julie Middleton, Annabelle Sami. *Founded* 2015.

Bath Literary Agency
5 Gloucester Road, Bath BA1 7BH
tel (01225) 317894

email submissions@bathliteraryagency.com
website www.bathliteraryagency.com
Twitter @BathLitAgency
Instagram @bathlitagency
Contact Gill McLay

Specialist in fiction for children and young adults. Also accepts submissions in picture books, non-fiction and author illustrators. *Commission* UK 15%, overseas 20%, film/TV 20%. For full submission details, refer to the website.

Clients include Lou Abercrombie, Fox Benwell, Conor Busuttil, Philippa Forrester, Dr Jess French, Nell Gifford, Joe Haddow, Demelsa Haughton, Harry Heape, Laura James, Pippa Pixley, Dr Shini Somara, Tessa Strickland, Anna Terreros Martin, Chris Wakling. *Founded* 2011.

The Bell Lomax Moreton Agency*
Suite C, 131 Queensway, Petts Wood, Kent BR5 1DG
tel 020-7930 4447
email agency@bell-lomax.co.uk
website www.belllomaxmoreton.co.uk
Twitter @BLM_Agency
Executives Eddie Bell, Pat Lomax, Paul Moreton, June Bell, Lauren Gardner, Sarah McDonnell, Jo Bell

Will consider most fiction, non-fiction and children's (including picture books, middle grade and young adult) book proposals. Submission guidelines on website. Physical submissions should be accompanied by an sae for return and an email address for correspondence. Does not represent poetry, short stories or novellas, education textbooks, film scripts or stage plays, or science fiction. *Founded* 2000.

The Bent Agency*
21 Melliss Avenue, Richmond TW9 4BQ
email info@thebentagency.com
website www.thebentagency.com
Agents Molly Ker Hawn, Nicola Barr, Gemma Cooper, Sarah Hornsley, Zoe Plant (UK); Jenny Bent, Heather Flaherty, Louise Fury, John Silbersack, Laurel Symonds (US)

Full service literary agency with offices in the UK and US. Represents authors of fiction and non-fiction for adults, children and teenagers. Unsolicited submissions welcome by email only: query and first ten pages pasted into body of email. See complete guidelines on the website.

Clients include Sophie Anderson, P.G. Bell, Stephanie Garber, Alwyn Hamilton, Anstey Harris, Hilary McKay, Peadar O'Guilin, Mo O'Hara, Sibeal Pounder, Jo Spain, Robin Stevens, Jessica Townsend. *Founded* 2009.

The Blair Partnership*
PO Box 7828, London W1A 4GE
tel 020-7504 2520
email info@theblairpartnership.com
email submissions@theblairpartnership.com

website www.theblairpartnership.com
Twitter @TBP_agency
Founding Partner Neil Blair, *Agency Director* Rory Scarfe, *Agent* Josephine Hayes

Represents a range of people internationally from debut and established writers to broader talent across business, politics, sport and lifestyle. Range of work spans fiction, non-fiction, digital, TV and film production. Considers all genres of fiction and non-fiction for adults, young readers and children. Will consider unsolicited MSS. Email a covering letter, a one-page synopsis and the first three chapters.

Clients include Bana Alabed, Claire Barker, Michael Byrne, Dawn Coulter-Cruttenden, Helena Duggan, Emma Farrarons, Sir Chris Hoy, Inbali Iserles, Frank Lampard, Virginia Clay, Kieran Larwood, Zoom Rockman, J.K. Rowling and Nicki Thornton. *Founded* 2011.

The Bright Agency
103–105 St John's Hill, London SW11 1SY
tel 020-7326 9140
50 West Street, C12, New York, NY 10006
tel +1 656 604 0992
website www.thebrightagency.com
Twitter @BrightAgencyUK
Contacts UK: Vicki Willden-Lebrecht (Founder and MD), Arabella Stein (Director), Hanna Curtis (Director), Courtney Arumugam (Senior Creative Executive for Film & TV; US: James Burns (Managing Agent, Anne Moore Armstrong (Managing Agent)

A collective of specialist agents representing the best in global talent across all areas of children's publishing, art, licensing, illustration, film, theatre and TV. Picture books, children's fiction and non-fiction, activity, novel and pre-school. See website for up-to-date submission requirements. No submissions by post.

Authors include Sue Hendra and Paul Linnet, Benji Davies, David Litchfield, Jarvis, Petr Horácek, Yasmeen Ismail, Fiona Woodcock, Galia Benstein, Maddie Frost, Zoe Persico, Aura Lewis, Merchal Roe. *Founded* 2002.

Jenny Brown Associates*
31 Marchmont Road, Edinburgh EH9 1HU
tel 0131 229 5334
email childrens@jennybrownassociates.com
website www.jennybrownassociates.com
Contact Lucy Juckes

Writing and illustration for children, fiction and non fiction. Has a preference for working with writers or illustrators based in Scotland. *Commission* Home 15%, overseas/translation 20%. A small agency which only reads submissions at certain points in the year; check website before sending work.

Clients include Sam Angus, Christopher Edge, Keith Gray, Emily MacKenzie, Jonathan Meres, Alison Murray. *Founded* 2002.

Felicity Bryan Associates*

2A North Parade, Banbury Road, Oxford OX2 6LX
tel (01865) 513816
email agency@felicitybryan.com
website www.felicitybryan.com

Translation rights handled by Andrew Nurnberg Associates; works in conjunction with US agents. Fiction for children aged 8–14 and young adult, and adult fiction and general non-fiction. *Commission* Home 15%, overseas 20%. No scripts for TV, radio or theatre, no crafts, how-to, science fiction, light romance or poetry.

Children's authors include David Almond, Irena Brignull, Jenny Downham, Sally Gardner, Natasha Farrant, Clare Furniss, Liz Kessler, Annabel Pitcher, Meg Rosoff, Lauren St John, Chris Vick, Lisa Williamson, Jeanne Willis, Lucy Worsley. *Founded* 1988.

C&W*

(previously Conville & Walsh)
Haymarket House, 28–29 Haymarket, London SW1Y 4SP
tel 020-7393 4200
website www.cwagency.co.uk

Fiction for 5–8 and 9–12 year-olds, teenage fiction, series fiction and film/TV tie-ins. Also handles adult literary and commercial fiction and non-fiction. *Commission* Home 15%, overseas 20%. Submissions welcome: first three chapters, cover letter, synopsis by email. Part of the Curtis Brown Group of Companies; simultaneous submission accepted. Not taking on picture books.

Children's authors include the estate of John Burningham, Kate Cann, Katie Davies, Connie Glynn, Rebecca James, Astrid Lindgren estate, P.J. Lynch, Joshua Mowll, Paula Rawsthorne, Niamh Sharkey, Nicky Singer, Piers Torday, Steve Voake. *Founded* 2000.

Georgina Capel Associates Ltd*

29 Wardour Street, London W1D 6PS
tel 020-7734 2414
email firstname@georginacapel.com
website www.georginacapel.com
Agents Georgina Capel, Rachel Conway

Literary and commercial fiction, history, biography; film and TV; also writers for children and young adults. *Commission* Home/overseas 15%. See website for submission guidelines. *Founded* 1999.

The Catchpole Agency

53 Cranham Street, Oxford OX2 6DD
tel 07789 588070
email james@thecatchpoleagency.co.uk
website www.thecatchpoleagency.co.uk
Proprietor James Catchpole

Agents for authors and illustrators of children's books from picture books through to young adult novels. See website for contact and submissions details. *Founded* 1996.

Anne Clark Literary Agency

email submissions@anneclarkliteraryagency.co.uk
website www.anneclarkliteraryagency.co.uk
Facebook www.facebook.com/anneclarkliterary
Twitter @AnneClarkLit
Contact Anne Clark

Specialist in fiction, picture books and non-fiction for children and young adults. *Commission* Home 15%, overseas 20%. Submissions by email only. See website for submission guidelines.

Clients include Mike Barfield, Anne Booth, Moira Butterfield, Lou Carter, Tamsin Cooke, Patricia Forde, Pippa Goodhart, Greg Gormley, Miriam Halahmy, Cath Howe, Penny Joelson, Anna Mainwaring, Rebecca Patterson, Lucy Rowland. *Founded* 2012.

Coombs Moylett Maclean Literary Agency

120 New Kings Road, London SW6 4LZ
tel 020-8740 0454
website www.cmm.agency
Contacts Lisa Moylett, Jamie Maclean, Zoe Apostolides

Looking for oustanding voices and for writing that's fresh, original and effective. Will accept the following submissions: picture book author/illustrators with texts of less than 1,000 words; high-concept/character-led chapter book series; middle-grade novels; YA books. *Commission* Home 15%, overseas 20%, film/TV 20%. Works with foreign agents. Does not handle poetry, plays or scripts for film and TV.

Authors include Sam Haysom, Murray Lachlan Young, Amy Tipper. *Founded* 1997.

Creative Authors Ltd

11A Woodlawn Street, Whitstable, Kent CT5 1HQ
email write@creativeauthors.co.uk
website www.creativeauthors.co.uk
Twitter @creativeauthors
Director Isabel Atherton

Fiction, women's fiction, literary fiction, non-fiction, humour, history, science, autobiography, biography, business, memoir, health, cookery, arts and crafts, crime, children's fiction, picture books, young adult, graphic novels and illustrators. *Commission* Home 15%, overseas 20%. Only accepts email submissions.

Authors and illustrators include Guojing, Ged Adamson, Coll Muir, Bethany Straker, Lucy Scott, Colleen Kosinski, Jules Miller, Grace Sandford, Megan Tadden, Cassie Liversidge. *Founded* 2008.

Rupert Crew Ltd*

6 Windsor Road, London N3 3SS
tel 020-8346 3000

email info@rupertcrew.co.uk
website www.rupertcrew.co.uk
Managing Director Caroline Montgomery

International representation, handling accessible literary and commercial fiction and non-fiction for adult and children's (8+) markets. *Commission* Home 15%; overseas, TV/film and radio 20%. No unsolicited MSS: see website for current submission guidelines. No picture books, plays, screenplays, poetry, journalism, science fiction, fantasy or short stories. *Founded* 1927.

Curtis Brown Group Ltd*

Haymarket House, 28–29 Haymarket, London SW1Y 4SP
tel 020-7393 4400
email cb@curtisbrown.co.uk
website www.curtisbrown.co.uk
website www.curtisbrowncreative.co.uk
Twitter @CBGBooks
Twitter @cbcreative
Children's Agent Stephanie Thwaites

Children's fiction ranges from picture books to young adult novels across all genres. Represents prominent writers, from debut authors to established prize winners and bestsellers. Actively seeking talented new writers, particularly for books aimed at 8–12 year olds, adventure, fantasy, gothic stories and humour. Curtis Brown manages the international careers of authors with strong relationships in translation and US markets.

Clients include exciting debuts and established brands, and a number of well-known personalities, from world-renowned politicians to business leaders and comedians. *Founded* 1899.

DHH Literary Agency*

23–27 Cecil Court, London WC2N 4EZ
tel 020-7836 7376
email enquiries@dhhliteraryagency.com
website www.dhhliteraryagency.com
Facebook www.facebook.com/dhhliteraryagency
Twitter @dhhlitagency
Agents David H. Headley, Broo Doherty, Hannah Sheppard, Harry Illingworth, Natalie Galustian

Children's fiction and YA fiction. Also adult fiction, women's commercial fiction, crime, literary fiction, science fiction and fantasy; and non-fiction including history, cookery and humour. *Commission* UK 15%, overseas 20%. Send informative preliminary email with first three chapters and synopsis. New authors welcome. No picture books, plays or scripts, poetry or short stories.

Authors include Matthew Crow, Phyllida Shrimpton, James Goodhand, Abi Elphinstone, Keris Stainton, Gabrielle Kent, Kate Mallinder, Faridah Àbíké-Íyímídé. *Founded* 2008.

Diamond Kahn & Woods Literary Agency*

Top Floor, 66 Onslow Gardens, London N10 3JX
tel 020-3514 6544

email info@dkwlitagency.co.uk
email submissions.ella@dkwlitagency.co.uk
email submissions.bryony@dkwlitagency.co.uk
website www.dkwlitagency.co.uk
Twitter @DKWLitAgency
Agents Ella Diamond Kahn, Bryony Woods

Children's, young adult and crossover fiction; literary and commercial fiction (including all major genres) and non-fiction. Interested in new writers. *Commission* Home 15%, USA/translation 20%. Email submissions only. Send three chapters and synopsis to one agent only. See website for further details on agents, their areas of interest and submission guidelines.

Clients include Vanessa Curtis, Virginia Macgregor, Nicole Burstein, David Owen, Sharon Gosling, Sylvia Bishop, Sarah Baker, Katherine Orton, Dan Smith, Emma Pass, Tom Huddleston. *Founded* 2012.

Eddison Pearson Ltd*

West Hill House, 6 Swains Lane, London N6 6QS
tel 020-7700 7763
email enquiries@eddisonpearson.com
website www.eddisonpearson.com
Contact Clare Pearson

Small, personally run agency. Children's and young adult books, fiction and non-fiction, poetry. *Commission* Home 10–15%, overseas 15–20%. Enquiries and submissions by email only; email for up-to-date submission guidelines by return. May suggest revision where appropriate.

Authors include Valerie Bloom, Sue Heap, Caroline Lawrence, Robert Muchamore, Mary Murphy, Megan Rix. *Founded* 1997.

Fraser Ross Associates

6 Wellington Place, Edinburgh EH6 7EQ
tel 0131 553 2759, 0131 657 4412
email agentlmfraser@gmail.com
email kjross@tiscali.co.uk
website www.fraserross.co.uk
Facebook www.facebook.com/fraserrossassociates
Twitter @FraserRossLA
Instagram @fraserrossassociates
Partners Lindsey Fraser, Kathryn Ross

Represents writers and illustrators. See website for submission guidelines.

Clients include Gill Arbuthnott, Tim Archbold, Barroux, Emily Dodd, Lari Don, Ciara Flood, Vivian French, Chris Higgins, Barry Hutchison, Tanya Landman, Kasia Matyjaszek, Eilidh Muldoon, Sue Purkiss, Sarah Rubin, Chae Strathie. *Founded* 2002.

The Good Literary Agency

email info@thegoodliteraryagency.org
website www.thegoodliteraryagency.org
Twitter @thegoodagencyuk

Represents non-fiction (including personal memoirs, biographies, essay collections and ideas from journalists, academics, experts and professionals writing in their field); fiction (all genres, short story collections and graphic novels); and children's and young adult. For detailed submission guidelines, visit the website.

Annette Green Authors' Agency

5 Henwoods Mount, Pembury,
Tunbridge Wells TN2 4BH
tel (01892) 263252
website www.annettegreenagency.co.uk
Partners Annette Green, David Smith

Literary and general fiction and non-fiction, popular culture, history, science, teenage fiction. *Commission* Full-length MSS: home 15%, overseas 20/25%. Preliminary letter, synopsis, sample chapter and sae essential. No picture books, dramatic scripts, poetry, science fiction or fantasy.

The Greenhouse Literary Agency

4th Floor, 9 Kingsway, London WC2B 6XF
email submissions@greenhouseliterary.com
website www.greenhouseliterary.com
Twitter @sarahgreenhouse
Twitter @nolanpolly
Director Sarah Davies, *UK and US Agent* Polly Nolan

Specialist children's book agency with a reputation for impressive transatlantic deals. Represents picture book author-illustrators through to writers for teens/young adults. Represents European and Commonwealth authors writing in English as well as North American authors. *Commission* USA/UK 15%, elsewhere 25%. No postal submissions. Queries by email only. Strict submission criteria (see website for details). No non-fiction. No adult fiction. No picture book texts unless also illustrated by author.

Authors include Jennifer Bell, Julie Bertagna, Sarwat Chadda/Joshua Khan, Chloe Coles, Lindsey Eagar, Juliette Forrest, Tae Keller, Dawn Kurtagich, Megan Miranda, Sinéad O'Hart, Ali Standish, Louie Stowell, Matilda Woods. *Founded* 2008.

Marianne Gunn O'Connor Literary Agency

Morrison Chambers, Suites 52 & 53,
32 Nassau Street, Dublin D02 RX59,
Republic of Ireland
email mgoclitagency@eircom.net
Contact Marianne Gunn O'Connor

Literary fiction, upmarket fiction including book club and psychological suspense. Also handles children's books, middle grade, young adult, new adult and crossover fiction, as well as exciting new non-fiction authors with a focus on narrative non-fiction, health, some memoir and biography. No screenplays. *Founded* 1996.

Hardman & Swainson*

S86 Somerset House, London WC2R 1LA
tel 020-3701 7449
website www.hardmanswanson.com
Facebook www.facebook.com/Hardman-Swainson-262825420515276/
Twitter @hardmanswainson
Directors Caroline Hardman, Joanna Swainson

Literary and commercial fiction, crime and thriller, women's, accessible literary, YA and middle-grade children's fiction. Non-fiction, including memoir, biography, popular science, history, philosophy. *Commission* Home 15%, USA/translation/film/TV 20%. Will work editorially with the author where appropriate. Submissions by email only to submissions@hardmanswainson.com. No poetry or screenplays.

Clients include Alex Bell, Justin Davies, Lauren Price, Fiona Sandiford, Maria Kuzniar. *Founded* 2012.

Antony Harwood Ltd

103 Walton Street, Oxford OX2 6EB
tel (01865) 559615
email mail@antonyharwood.com
website www.antonyharwood.com
Contacts Antony Harwood, James Macdonald, Jo Williamson (children's)

General and genre fiction; general non-fiction. *Commission* Home 15%, overseas 20%. Will suggest revision.

Children's authors include Tamsyn Murray, Jennifer Gray, Peter Bunzl. *Founded* 2000.

A.M. Heath & Co. Ltd*

6 Warwick Court, London WC1R 5DJ
tel 020-7242 2811
website www.amheath.com
Twitter @amheathltd
Contact Julia Churchill

Children's fiction and non-fiction from picture books to young adult. Also handles adult literary and commercial fiction and non-fiction. *Commission* Full-length MSS: home 15%, USA/translation 20%. Film/TV 15–20% by agreement. Digital submission via website. No screenplays, poetry or short stories except for collections.

Children's authors include Nicholas Allan, Cat Clarke, Sam Copeland, Sarah Crossan, Conn Iggulden, Pip Jones, Michelle Harrison, Sarah Lean, Jenny McLachlan, Joanna Nadin, Amy Sparkes, Patricia Toht, Jason Wallace, Holly Webb and the estates of Noel Streatfeild and Christianna Brand. *Founded* 1919.

Sophie Hicks Agency*

email info@sophiehicksagency.com
website www.sophiehicksagency.com
Twitter @SophieHicksAg
Agents Sophie Hicks, Sarah Williams

Fiction for 9+. Also handles adult fiction and non-fiction. *Commission* UK/USA 15%, translation 20%. Email submissions only, see website for guidelines.

No poetry or scripts.

Children's authors include: Herbie Brennan, Anne Cassidy, Lucy Coats, Eoin Colfer, Andrew Donkin, Kathryn Evans, Emerald Fennell, Padraig Kenny, Will Kostakis, Sarah Mussi, Siobhan Parkinson, Alexander Gordon Smith, Kate Thompson, Shamim Sarif, Mark Walden. Founded 2014.

David Higham Associates Ltd*

6th Floor, Waverley House, 7–12 Noel Street, London W1F 8GQ
tel 020-7434 5900
email dha@davidhigham.co.uk
website www.davidhigham.co.uk
Managing Director Anthony Goff, Books Veronique Baxter, Anthony Goff, Caroline Walsh, Foreign Rights Alice Howe, Allison Cole, Emma Jamison, Emily Randle, Film/TV/Theatre Nicky Lund, Georgina Ruffhead, Clare Israel, Penelope Killick

Children's fiction, picture books and non-fiction. 35% of the agency's list is for the children's market. Represented in all foreign markets. Also represents illustrators for children's book publishing (home 15%). Submit colour copies of artwork by post or via email. Include samples that show children 'in action' and animals. Handles novelty books, picture books, fiction for 5–8 and 9–12 year-olds, teenage and YA fiction, series fiction, poetry, plays, film/TV tie-ins, non-fiction and audio. Also handles adult fiction, general non-fiction, plays, film and TV scripts. Commission Home 15%, USA/translation 20%, scripts 10%. See website for submissions policy.

Clients (children's market) include Martin Brown, Emma Chichester Clark, Cressida Cowell, Nicola Davies, Anna Kemp, Geraldine McCaughrean, Tom McLaughlin, Michael Morpurgo, Kate O'Hearn, Liz Pichon, Catherine Rayner, Nick Sharratt, Jonathan Stroud, Jenny Valentine and Jacqueline Wilson. Founded 1935.

Johnson & Alcock Ltd*

Bloomsbury House, 74–77 Great Russell Street, London WC1B 3DA
tel 020-7251 0125
website www.johnsonandalcock.co.uk
Contact Anna Power, Ed Wilson, Liz Dennis

All types of children's fiction and non-fiction (ages 9+), young adult and teenage fiction.
Commission Home 15%, USA/translation/film 20%. Send first three chapters (or 50 pages), full synopsis, and brief covering letter with details of writing experience. For submission guidelines see website. Return postage essential. No short stories, poetry or board/picture books. Founded 1956.

Kane Literary Agency

2 Dukes Avenue, London N10 2PT
tel 020-8351 9680
website www.kaneliteraryagency.com
Twitter @YasminKane3

Director Yasmin Kane

Interested in discovering new writers and launching the careers of first-time writers. Also handles literary and commercial fiction for adults. Children's fiction – middle grade and up, all YA, no picture books. Commission Home 15%, overseas 20%. Send submissions by email only; no submissions by post. Send first three chapters and synopsis (one side of A4) with a covering letter, all double-line spaced. No picture books.

Authors include Sarah Harris, Emily Nagle, Louise Cliffe-Minns, Farah Cook, Andrew Murray. Founded 2004.

LAW (Lucas Alexander Whitley Ltd)*

2nd Floor, 16–17 Wardour Mews, London W1F 8AT
tel 020-7471 7900
website www.lawagency.co.uk
Contacts Philippa Milnes-Smith

Represented in all markets. Novelty books, picture books, fiction for 5–8 and 9–12 year-olds, including series, young adult, film/TV and non-fiction. Commission Home 15%, overseas 20%. Unsolicited and debut work considered. See website for further information about the clients and genres represented and essential information on submissions.

Clients include Chris Judge, Sophie Kinsella, Gillian Cross, Emily Gravett, Philip Reeve, Chris Riddell, Andy McNab, Ian Livingstone and Steve Jackson, Stephen Cole, Linda Chapman, Sarah Webb. Founded 1996.

LBA Books*

91 Great Russell Street, London WC1B 3PS
tel 020-7637 1234
email info@lbabooks.com
website www.lbabooks.com
Twitter @LBABooks
Agents Luigi Bonomi, Amanda Preston, Louise Lamont

Fiction and non-fiction. Keen to find new authors and help them develop their careers. Works with foreign agencies and has links with film and TV production companies including Endemol, Tiger Aspect, BBC Radio, HatTrick, Plum Pictures, Zodiak and Sega. Fiction: young adult and children's, commercial and literary fiction, thrillers, crime, psychological suspense, women's fiction, fantasy. Non-fiction: history, science, parenting, lifestyle, cookery, memoir, TV tie-in. Commission Home 15%, overseas 20%. Send preliminary letter, synopsis and first three chapters. No poetry, short stories or screenplays.

Authors for children and young adults include Sarah Alderson, Virginia Bergin, Joanna Boyle, Rebecca Cobb, Julia Gray, Rachel Hamilton, Helen Hancocks, Rachael Lucas, Julie Mayhew, S.A. Patrick, Lucy Strange, Tamsin Winter, Laura Wood, Katherine Woodfine, Emma Yarlett. Founded 2005.

Lindsay Literary Agency
East Worldham House, Alton, Hants GU34 3AT
tel (01420) 831430
email info@lindsayliteraryagency.co.uk
website www.lindsayliteraryagency.co.uk
Twitter @LindsayLit
Director Becky Bagnell

Specialists in children's fiction, teen/YA, middle grade, picture books. *Commission* Home 15%, translation 20%. Send first three chapters, synopsis and covering letter by email to address above. No submissions by post. No reading fee. Will suggest revision.
   Authors include Pamela Butchart, Christina Collins, Donna David, Sam Gayton, Ruth Hatfield, Mike Lancaster, Giles Paley-Phillips, Sharon Tregenza, Rachel Valentine, Sue Wallman, Joe Wilson. *Founded* 2008.

Christopher Little Literary Agency LLP*
(in association with Curtis Brown Group Ltd)
48 Walham Grove, London SW6 1QR
tel 020-7736 4455
email info@christopherlittle.net
website www.christopherlittle.net
Contact Christopher Little

Fiction for 9–12 year-olds and teenage fiction. Also handles adult fiction and non-fiction. *Commission* Home 15%, overseas 20%, digital 20%. No unsolicited submissions. No poetry, plays, science fiction, fantasy, textbooks, illustrated children's or short stories. No illustrated children's or short stories.
   Children's authors include Cathy Hopkins and Darren Shan. *Founded* 1979.

Luithlen Agency
88 Holmfield Road, Leicester LE2 1SB
tel 0116 273 8863
website www.luithlenagency.com
Agents Jennifer Luithlen, Penny Luithlen

Children's fiction, all ages to YA. *Commission* Home 15%, overseas 20%, performance rights 15%. See website for submission information. *Founded* 1986.

Eunice McMullen Ltd
Low Ibbotsholme Cottage, Off Bridge Lane, Troutbeck Bridge, Windermere, Cumbria LA23 1HU
tel (01539) 448551
email eunicemcmullen@totalise.co.uk
website www.eunicemcmullen.co.uk
Director Eunice McMullen

Specialises exclusively in children's books, especially picture books and older fiction. Handles novelty books, picture books, fiction for all ages including teenage, series fiction and audio. *Commission* Home 15%, overseas 15%. No unsolicited scripts. Telephone or email enquiries only.
   Authors include Caroline Jayne Church, Ross Collins, Emma Dodd, Alison Friend, Charles Fuge,

Cally Johnson Isaacs, Sarah Massini, David Melling, Angela McAllister, Angie Sage, Gillian Shields. *Founded* 1992.

Andrew Mann Ltd*
email info@andrewmann.co.uk
website www.andrewmann.co.uk
Twitter @AML_Literary
Contacts Tina Betts, Louise Burns

Currently closed to new submissions. *Founded* 1968.

Marjacq Scripts Ltd*
Box 412, 19–21 Crawford Street, London W1H 1PJ
tel 020-7935 9499
email catherine@marjacq.com
website www.marjacq.com
Twitter @MarjacqScripts
Contact Catherine Pellegrino (children's and YA); Sandra Sawicka (YA only)

Handles all rights. In-house legal, foreign rights and book-to-film support. All genres represented. *Commission* All full-length MSS: home 15%, overseas/film 20%. See website for submission guidelines.
   Clients include James Campbell, Rose Edwards, Roopa Farooki, Steve Feasey, Gemma Fowler, Nick Garlick, T.C. Shelley, Claire Waller, Harriet Whitehorn. *Founded* 1973.

MBA Literary and Script Agents Ltd*
62 Grafton Way, London W1T 5DW
tel 020-7387 2076
website www.mbalit.co.uk
Twitter @mbaagents
Children's book agent Sophie Gorell Barnes, *Film & TV agent* Diana Tyler

Fiction and non-fiction, children's books. Foreign rights handled by Louisa Pritchard Associates. *Commission* Home 15%, overseas 20%, TV/theatre/radio 10%, films 15%. See website for submission guidelines.
   Clients include Sita Brahmachari, Christopher William Hill, Mimi Thebo, Mark Wheeller. *Founded* 1971.

Madeleine Milburn Literary, TV & Film Agency*
10 Shepherd Market, London W1J 7QF
tel 020-7499 7550
email submissions@madeleinemilburn.com
website www.madeleinemilburn.co.uk
Facebook www.facebook.com/MadeleineMilburnLiteraryAgency
Twitter @agentmilburn
Directors Madeleine Milburn, Giles Milburn, *Rights Director* Liane-Louise Smith, *Children's and YA Agents* Alice Sutherland-Hawes, Chloe Seager, *Associate Agent and TV & Film Coordinator* Hayley Steed (overseas associates CAA for film (LA/

Hollywood), *In-house Editor* Anna Hogarty, *Assistant* Georgia McVeigh

Special interest in launching the careers of debut authors and illustrators. Represents a dynamic and prize-winning range of children's and young adult fiction and non-fiction. Award-winning and popular fiction including fantasy, real life/contemporary, YA thrillers, mystery, action, historical, science fiction, romance, coming of age, and film/TV tie-ins.

Represents British, American and international authors. Handles all rights in the UK, US and foreign markets including film/TV/theatre/radio (for clients with book deal in place only) and digital. Areas include picture books, 6–8 years, 9–12 years, 12+, teen, YA, new adult and books appealing to both children and adults. *Commission* Home 15%, USA/translation/film 20%. No longer accepts submissions by post. See submission guidelines and agency news on website. Works editorially with all clients.

Authors and illustrators include Holly Bourne, Samuel Pollen, C.J. Daugherty, Poonam Mistry, Katie Cottle, Caleb Krisp, Dave Lowe, Lara Williamson, Hayley Barker, Damaris Young, Matt Ralphs, Rupert Wallis, Kate Ling, Danielle Jawando. *Founded* 2012.

Miles Stott Children's Literary Agency Ltd*

East Hook Farm, Lower Quay Road, Hook, Haverfordwest, Pembrokeshire SA62 4LR
tel (01437) 890570
email nancy@milesstottagency.co.uk
email mandy@milesstottagency.co.uk
email victoria@milesstottagency.co.uk
website www.milesstottagency.co.uk
Twitter @milesstott
Director Nancy Miles, *Associate Agents* Victoria Birkett, Mandy Suhr

Specialist in children's novelty books, picture books, fiction for 6–9 and 10–12 year-olds, young adult fiction and series fiction. *Commission* Home 15%, film, tv & overseas 20%. Fiction submissions by email only to fictionsubs@milesstottagency.co.uk including covering letter, brief synopsis and first three chapters. Picture book submissions by email only to picturebooksubs@milesstottagency.co.uk including covering letter, complete text and/or pdfs of sample artwork.

Authors include Rachel Bright, Stacy Gregg, Frances Hardinge, Gill Lewis, Zoe Marriot and Mark Sperring. *Founded* 2003.

Kate Nash Literary Agency*

1 Swift Way, Brackley, Northants NN13 6PY
tel 0844 415 7844
email submissions@katenashlit.co.uk
website www.katenashlit.co.uk
Facebook www.facebook.com/KateNashLiteraryAgency
Twitter @katenashagent

Twitter @linalanglee
Contacts Kate Nash, Lina Langlee

Represents general and genre fiction, popular non-fiction and children's and YA fiction. Open to approaches from both new and established authors. General fiction, literary fiction, crime and thriller, historical fiction, romantic fiction, middle grade, YA, popular non-fiction. *Commission* UK and Ireland 15%, USA 15% (direct) and 20% (sub-agented), overseas 20%, book to screen 15% (20% if sub-agented). See website for full submission guidelines. No poetry or drama. No children's picture books.

Clients Christie Barlow, Deborah Carr, Rachel Dove, Pia Fenton, Naomi Joy, Jane Lovering, Faith Martin, Bella Osborne, Glynis Peters, Maggie Sullivan, Gill Stewart, Helen Watts. *Founded* 2009.

Northbank Talent Management*

email info@northbanktalent.com
email childrens@northbanktalent.com
website www.northbanktalent.com
Twitter @northbanktalent

Commercial fiction, non-fiction and children's books. Fiction: women's, crime, thrillers, literary fiction with a strong storyline, science fiction, fantasy, young adult, middle grade, children's. Non-fiction: politics, current affairs, memoir, real-life stories, celebrity, autobiography, biography, business, popular history, popular science, self-help, popular psychology, fashion, health and beauty, children's. *Commission* Home 15%, overseas and rights in other media 20%. Send cover letter, synopsis and first three chapters as Word or Open Document attachments. Aims to give initial response within two weeks. No poetry, academic books, plays, scripts or short stories.

Authors include Brian Cox, Jon Butterworth, Anthony Seldon, Camilla Cavendish, Damian Collins, Carla Valentine, Christopher Harding, Marisa Merico, Shelina Janmohamed, Kate Thompson, Katerina Diamond, Rachel Wells. *Founded* 2006.

Paper Lion Ltd

13 Grayham Road, New Malden, Surrey KT3 5HR
tel (07748) 786199 / (01276) 61322
email katyloffman@paperlion.co.uk
email lesleypollinger@paperlion.co.uk
website www.paperlion.co.uk
Agents Katy Loffman, Lesley Pollinger

Paper Lion is a cross-media literary agency which brings together the digital publishing expertise of Katy Loffman and Lesley Pollinger's extensive experience as a literary agent. Represents a prestigious list of clients including authors, literary estates, archives, film producers, virtual reality developers and online publishers. Paper Lion has a strong focus on the exploration of digital opportunities and solving complex copyright, dramatic rights and literary issues from the present and past.

Clients include Max Allen, Michael Coleman, Vince Cross, Fiction Express, Catherine Fisher, Dave

Gatward, Bruce Hobson, Saviour Pirotta, Summersdale Publishers Ltd and the estates of authors including Gene Kemp, Gwynedd Rae and H.E. Bates. *Founded* 2017.

Redhammer Management Ltd
website www.redhammer.info
Vice President Peter Cox

A boutique literary agency providing in-depth management for a restricted number of clients. Specialises in works with international book, film and television potential. Submissions must follow the guidelines given on the website. Do not send unsolicited MSS by post. No radio or theatre scripts.

Rogers, Coleridge & White Ltd*
20 Powis Mews, London W11 1JN
tel 020-7221 3717
email info@rcwlitagency.com
website www.rcwlitagency.com
Twitter @RCWLitAgency
Instagram @rcwliteraryagency
Chairman Gill Coleridge, *Managing Director* Peter Straus, *Finance Director* Nelka Bell, *Directors* Sam Copeland, Stephen Edwards, Natasha Fairweather, Georgia Garrett, Laurence Laluyaux, Peter Robinson, Zoe Waldie, Claire Wilson (Head of Children's Books), *Agents* Jennifer Hewson, Cara Jones, Jon Wood

International representation for all genres of fiction, non-fiction, children's and YA. *Commission* Home 15%, USA 20%, translation 20%. See website for submissions information.

Clients include David Baddiel, Frank Cottrell Boyce, Cerrie Burnell, Catherine Doyle, Lissa Evans, Moira Fowey-Doyle, Sally Green, Anna James, Michelle Magorian, Ross Montgomery, Alice Oseman, Katherine Rundell, Katie and Kevin Tsang, Mary Watson. *Founded* 1967 as Deborah Rogers Ltd, 1989 as Rogers, Coleridge and White Ltd.

Steph Roundsmith Literary Agent
7 Stubbs Close, Billingham,
Stockton-on-Tees TS23 3GH
email submissions@stephroundsmith.co.uk
website www.stephroundsmith.co.uk
Facebook www.facebook.com/stephroundsmith
Twitter @stephroundsmith
Contact Steph Roundsmith

Specialises exclusively in fiction for children. Accepts picture books and fiction to age 12. Send synopsis and first three chapters for longer works, and the full MS for picture books. Email submissions only. Include a short biography.

Elizabeth Roy Literary Agency
White Cottage, Greatford, Nr Stamford,
Lincs. PE9 4PR
tel (01778) 560672

website www.elizabethroy.co.uk

Children's fiction, picture books and non-fiction – writers and illustrators. *Commission* Home 15%, overseas 20%. Send preliminary letter, synopsis and sample chapters with names of publishers and agents previously contacted. Return postage essential. *Founded* 1990.

Uli Rushby-Smith Literary Agency
72 Plimsoll Road, London N4 2EE
tel 020-7354 2718
email uli.rushby-smith@btconnect.com
Director Uli Rushby-Smith

Fiction and non-fiction, literary and commercial. *Commission* Home 15%, USA/overseas 20%. Send outline, sample chapters and return postage. No poetry, picture books, plays or film scripts. *Founded* 1993.

Caroline Sheldon Literary Agency Ltd*
71 Hillgate Place, London W8 7SS
tel 020-7727 9102
email carolinesheldon@carolinesheldon.co.uk
email felicitytrew@carolinesheldon.co.uk
website www.carolinesheldon.co.uk
Twitter @CarolineAgent
Twitter @FelicityTrew
Contacts Caroline Sheldon, Felicity Trew

Represents in all areas of children's fiction, whether picture book, middle grade or YA. Looks for strong concepts, wonderful characterisation and excellent story-telling. Also represents leading illustrators of children's books. All genres of children's writing including fantasy, humour, contemporary life, thriller, stories set in schools, and non-fiction. *Commission* Home 15%, USA/translation 20%, film/ TV 20%. Authors – send an introductory email with the first three chapters or equivalent length attached. In the subject line write 'Proposal' and title of the work. At head of the email include a three-line synopsis of the work and give further full information in the email about the work and about yourself. Illustrators – send an introductory email with work attached or a link to your work. In the subject line write 'Proposal from Illustrator', and include information about yourself and your work in the email.

Represents prominent, award-winning and bestselling clients in all fields including books, audio, digital and theatre. Works closely with a media agent on film, TV and other opportunities. *Founded* 1985.

Dorie Simmonds Agency Ltd*
tel 020-7736 0002
email info@doriesimmonds.com
Twitter @Dorie_Simmonds
Contact Dorie Simmonds

Children's fiction. *Commission* Home 15%, USA 15%, translation 20%. Send a short synopsis, two to three sample chapters and a CV with writing/publishing background; sae required. *Founded* 1997.

Skylark Literary Limited

19 Parkway, Weybridge, Surrey KT13 9HD
tel 020-8144 7440
email info@skylark-literary.com
email submissions@skylark-literary.com
website www.skylark-literary.com
Facebook www.facebook.com/SkylarkLiteraryLtd
Twitter @skylarklit
Directors Joanna Moult, Amber Caraveo

Specialists in children's and young adult fiction. All genres considered. *Commission* Home 15%, overseas 20%. Keen to support new and established authors. Will consider unsolicited submissions. Agents have editorial backgrounds and will work closely with clients on their manuscripts to increase chances of publication. Submissions by email only. Will suggest revision where appropriate. No adult fiction/non-fiction.
   Clients include Amy Wilson, Simon James Green, Alyssa Hollingsworth. *Founded* 2014.

Abner Stein*

Southbank House, Suite 137, Black Prince Road, London SE1 7SJ
tel 020-7373 0456
website www.abnerstein.co.uk
Contacts Caspian Dennis, Sandy Violette

Fiction, general non-fiction and children's. *Commission* Home 15%, overseas 20%. Not taking on any new clients at present.

Rochelle Stevens & Co

2 Terretts Place, Upper Street, London N1 1QZ
tel 020-7359 3900
email info@rochellestevens.com
website www.rochellestevens.com
Directors Rochelle Stevens, Frances Arnold

Adult drama scripts for TV, theatre and radio. Children's drama scripts for TV, film and theatre. *Commission* 10%. Send preliminary letter, CV, short synopsis and opening ten pages of a drama script by post (sae essential for return of material). See website for full submission guidelines. *Founded* 1984.

Sarah Such Literary Agency

81 Arabella Drive, London SW15 5LL
tel 020-8876 4228
email info@sarah-such.com
website sarahsuchliteraryagency.tumblr.com
Twitter @sarahsuch
Director Sarah Such

High-quality literary and commercial non-fiction and fiction for adults and children. Always looking for original children's and YA writers and projects. Translation representation: The Buckman Agency, The English Agency (Japan) Ltd. Film/TV

representation: Lesley Thorne, Aitken Alexander Associates Ltd. Particular focus on debut young adult novels, children's series, picture books and graphic novels. *Commission* Home 15%, TV/film 20%, overseas 20%. Will suggest revision. Submit synopsis and a sample chapter (as a Word attachment by email) plus author biography. No postal submissions unless requested. No unsolicited MSS or telephone enquiries. TV/film scripts for established clients only. No radio or theatre scripts, poetry, fantasy, self-help or short stories.
   Authors include Matthew De Abaitua, Jeffrey Boakye, Kit Caless, Maxim Jakubowski, Antony Johnston, Amy Lankester-Owen, Louisa Leaman, Vesna Maric, Benjamin J. Myers QC, Rachel Pashley, John Rowley, Caroline Sanderson, Tony De Saulles, Nikhil Singh, Sara Starbuck. *Founded* 2007.

United Agents LLP*

12–26 Lexington Street, London W1F 0LE
tel 020-3214 0800
email info@unitedagents.co.uk
website www.unitedagents.co.uk
Agent Jodie Hodges (children's/young adult writers and illustrators), Emily Talbot (children's/young adult writers and illustrators). Other agents also represent children's writers. See website for individual lists.

Fiction and non-fiction. *Commission* Home 15%, USA/translation 20%. See website for submission details. *Founded* 2008.

Jo Unwin Literary Agency*

West Wing, Somerset House, London WC2R 1LA
email submissions@jounwin.co.uk
website www.jounwin.co.uk
Twitter @jounwin
Agents Jo Unwin, Rachel Mann

Represents authors of literary fiction, commercial women's fiction, memoir, YA fiction and fiction for children aged 5+ (picture books only accepted if written by established clients).
   Authors include Marianne Levy, Sarah Moore Fitzgerald, Hayley Scott, Nadia Shireen, Emma-Jane Smith-Barton. *Founded* 2016.

Watson, Little Ltd*

Suite 315, ScreenWorks, 22 Highbury Grove, London N5 2ER
tel 020-7388 7529
email office@watsonlittle.com
email submissions@watsonlittle.com
website www.watsonlittle.com
Twitter @watsonlittle
Contacts James Wills (Managing Director), Laetitia Rutherford (Agent), Megan Carroll (Agent), Rachel Richardson (Rights Director)

Film and TV Associates: Ki Agency and The Sharland Agency; US Associates: Howard Morhaim Literary

Agency and The Gersh Agency. YA and middle-grade fiction, picture books and children's non-fiction in all genres. *Commission* Home 15%, USA/translation 20%. Send informative preliminary letter, synopsis and sample chapters by email only. No poetry, TV, play or filmscripts. *Founded* 1970.

Whispering Buffalo Literary Agency Ltd

97 Chesson Road, London W14 9QS
tel 020-7565 4737
email info@whisperingbuffalo.com
website www.whisperingbuffalo.com
Director Mariam Keen

Commercial/literary fiction and non-fiction, children's and young adult fiction. Special interest in book-to-screen adaptations; TV and film rights in novels and non-fiction handled in-house. *Commission* Home 15%, overseas 20%. Only accepts submissions by email. Will suggest revision. *Founded* 2008.

Eve White Literary Agency Limited*

54 Gloucester Street, London SW1V 4EG
tel 020-7630 1155
email eve@evewhite.co.uk
email ludo@evewhite.co.uk
website www.evewhite.co.uk
Twitter @EveWhiteAgency

Contact Eve White, Ludo Cinelli

Boutique agency representing young, middle grade, teenage and young adult fiction, picture books and film/TV tie-ins. Also handles adult commercial and literary fiction and non-fiction; 35% of the list is for the children's market. *Commission* Home 15%, overseas 20%. Will suggest revision where appropriate. See website for up-to-date submission requirements. No submissions by post.

   Children's clients include Andy Stanton, Rae Earl, Tracey Corderoy, Abie Longstaff, Elli Woollard, Ruth Warburton, Sarah Naughton, Michaela Morgan, Simon Nicholson, Kate Scott, Kate Maryon. *Founded* 2003.

Susan Yearwood Agency

2 Knebworth House, Londesborough Road, London N16 8RL
tel 020-7503 0954
email submissions@susanyearwood.com
website www.susanyearwood.com
Twitter @SYA_Susan
Contact Susan Yearwood

Children's fiction 9+ and YA. *Commission* Home 15%, overseas 20%. Send submission with covering letter and brief synopsis via email. Submissions not accepted by hand or post. *Founded* 2007.

Children's literary agents overseas

This list includes only a selection of agents across the English-speaking world. Selected lists of agents in non-English speaking territories can be found at www.writersandartists.co.uk/listings. Before submitting material, writers are advised to visit agents' websites for detailed submission guidelines and to ascertain terms.

AUSTRALIA

ALM: Australian Literary Management
tel +61 (0)9 818 8557
email alphaalm8@gmail.com
website www.austlit.com

For full details of genres represented and submission guidelines, see website. Does not consider scripts of any kind or books for children by unpublished authors. Does not accept self-published work or writing by non-Australian authors.

The Authors' Agent
PO Box 577, Terrigal, NSW 2260
email briancook@theauthorsagent.com.au
website www.theauthorsagent.com.au

Specialises in adult fiction, narrative non-fiction and children's books. Accepts submissions by email. For detailed guidelines, see website.

Golvan Arts Management
website www.golvanarts.com.au

Represents a wide range of writers including writers of both adult and children's fiction and non-fiction, poetry, screenwriters and writers of plays. Also represents visual artists and composers. See the General Information section on the website before making contact.

CANADA

CookeMcDermid
email admin@cookemcdermid.com
website www.cookemcdermid.com
Agents Dean Cooke, Sally Harding, Martha Webb, Chris Bucci, Suzanne Brandreth, Ron Eckel, Rachel Letofsky, Paige Sisley

CookeMcDermid was formed when two pre-eminent literary agencies, The Cooke Agency and The McDermid Agency, amalgamated, combining over 47 years of experience. CMD represents authors of literary, commercial and sci-fi/fantasy fiction; a broad range of narrative non-fiction; health and wellness resources; and middle grade and young adult books. See https://cookemcdermid.com/submissions for submissions guidelines and form. Sells Canadian and American rights directly. Cooke International

represents UK and translation rights, in conjunction with a network of co-agents around the world. CMD also works with associates to sell film and television rights in Canada and abroad. *Founded* 2017.

Carolyn Swayze Literary Agency Ltd
7360-137th Street, Suite 319, Surrey, BC V3W 1A3
email reception@swayzeagency.com
website www.swayzeagency.com
Proprietor Carolyn Swayze

Fiction and non-fiction for teens and middle-grade readers. No science fiction, poetry, screenplays or children's picture books. Eager to discover strong voices writing contemporary, historical or supernatural stories if the metaphor reflects relevant themes. No telephone calls: make contact by email. Send query including synopsis and short sample. Provide résumé, publication credits, writing awards, education and experience relevant to the book project. Allow six weeks for a reply. *Founded* 1994.

Transatlantic Agency
2 Bloor Street East, Suite 3500, Toronto, Ontario M4W 1A8
tel +1 416-488-9214
website www.transatlanticagency.com
Facebook www.facebook.com/TransLitAgency
Twitter @TransLitAgency

Represents adult and children's authors of all genres, including illustrators. Refer to the website for submission guidelines. *Founded* 1993.

NEW ZEALAND

Glenys Bean Writer's Agent
198A Opito Bay Road, Kerikeri 0294
email glenys@glenysbean.com
Directors Fay Weldon, Glenys Bean

Adult and children's fiction, educational, non-fiction, film, TV, radio (10–20%). Send preliminary letter, synopsis and sae. No reading fee. *Founded* 1989.

Total Fiction Services
PO Box 6292 Dunedin North, Dunedin 9059
email tfs@elseware.co.nz
website www.elseware.co.nz

General fiction, non-fiction, children's books. No poetry, individual short stories or articles. Enquiries from New Zealand authors only. Email queries but no attachments. Hard copy preferred. No reading fee. Also offers assessment reports, mentoring and courses.

USA

Member of the Association of Authors' Representatives

Adams Literary*

7845 Colony Road, C4 #215, Charlotte, NC 28226
email info@adamsliterary.com
website www.adamsliterary.com
Facebook www.facebook.com/adamsliterary
Twitter @adamsliterary
Agents Tracey Adams, Josh Adams

Exclusively children's from picture books to teenage novels (home 15%, overseas 25%). Submissions through website. See website for guidelines. *Founded* 2004.

Bradford Literary Agency*

5694 Mission Center Road, Suite 347, San Diego, CA 92108
email queries@bradfordlit.com
website www.bradfordlit.com

Currently looking for picture books, chapter books, middle grade, young adult in both fiction and non-fiction categories. Query by email only. For detailed submission guidelines, see website. No reading fee.

Andrea Brown Literary Agency

email andrea@andreabrownlit.com
website www.andreabrownlit.com
President Andrea Brown, *Agents* Laura Rennert, Kelly Sonnack, Caryn Wiseman, Jennifer Rofe, Jennifer Laughran, Jamie Weiss Chilton, Jennifer Mattson, Lara Perkins, Kathleen Rushall, Jennifer March Soloway

Exclusively all kinds of children's books. Represents both authors and illustrators. Email submissions only. See website for guidelines. *Founded* 1981.

Maria Carvainis Agency Inc.*

Rockefeller Center, 1270 Avenue of the Americas, Suite 2915, New York, NY 10020
tel +1 212-245-6365
email mca@mariacarvainisagency.com
website www.mariacarvainisagency.com
President and Literary Agent Maria Carvainis

Young adult fiction (home 15%, overseas 20%). Also handles adult fiction and non-fiction. No reading fee. See website for full submission guidelines.

The Chudney Agency

72 North State Road, Suite 501, Briarcliff Manor, NY 10510
tel +1 201-758-8739

email steven@thechudneyagency.com
website www.thechudneyagency.com
Contact Steven Chudney

See website for full guidelines for queries and submissions, and for details of genres represented. *Founded* 2002.

Curtis Brown Ltd*

10 Astor Place, New York, NY 10003
tel +1 212-473-5400
email info@cbltd.com
website www.curtisbrown.com
Twitter @CurtisBrownLtd
Instagram @curtisbrown.ltd
Ceo Timothy Knowlton, *President* Peter Ginsberg, *Contacts* Katherine Fausset, Sarah Gerton, Elizabeth Harding (*Vice President*), Ginger Knowlton (*Executive Vice President*), Jonathan Lyons, Steven Salpeter, *Translation rights* Jonathan Lyons and Sarah Perillo

Fiction and non-fiction, juvenile (see Agent page on website as not all agents handle juvenile), film and TV rights. No unsolicited MSS. See individual agent's entry on the Agents page of the website for specific query and submission information. No reading fee; no handling fees. *Founded* 1914.

Liza Dawson Associates*

121 West 27th Street, Suite 1201, New York, NY 10001
website www.lizadawsonassociates.com
Twitter @LizaDawsonAssoc
Ceo Liza Dawson

A full-service agency which draws on expertise as former publishers. Young adult, middle grade: thrillers, mysteries, romance, historical fiction, science fiction and fantasy, contemporary. See website for submission guidelines and email contacts.

Sandra Dijkstra & Associates*

PMB 515, 1155 Camino Del Mar, Del Mar, CA 92014
tel +1 858-755-3115
website www.dijkstraagency.com
Contacts Sandra Dijkstra, Elise Capron, Jill Marr, Roz Foster, Thao Le, Andrea Cavallaro, Jessica Watterson, Suzy Evans, Jennifer Kim, Haneen Oriqat

Young adult science fiction, fantasy and contemporary, middle-grade fiction and non-fiction and picture books by author/illustrators only (home 15%, overseas 20%). Works in conjunction with foreign and film agents. Email submissions only. Please see website for the most up-to-date guidelines. No reading fee. *Founded* 1981.

Dunham Literary Inc.*

110 William Street, Suite 2202, New York, NY 10038
email dunhamlit@gmail.com
website www.dunhamlit.com
Contact Jennie Dunham, Bridget Smith

Children's books (home 15%, overseas 20%). Handles picture books, fiction for 5–8 and 9–12 year-olds and teenage fiction. Also handles adult literary fiction and non-fiction; 50% of list is for the children's market. Send query by post or to query@dunhamlit.com. Do not send full MS. No reading fee. *Founded* 2000.

Dystel, Goderich & Bourret LLC*
1 Union Square West, New York, NY 10003
tel +1 212-627-9100
website www.dystel.com
Contacts Michael Bourret, Jim McCarthy, Stacey Glick, John Rudolph, Eric Myers, Lauren Abramo, Mike Hoogland

Children's fiction (home 15%, overseas 19%). Handles picture books, fiction for 5–8 and 9–12 year-olds, teenage fiction and series fiction. Looking for quality young adult fiction. Also handles adult fiction and non-fiction. Send a query letter with a synopsis and up to 50 pages of sample MS. Will accept email queries. No reading fee. Will suggest revision.
  Children's authors include James Dashner, Gayle Forman, Richelle Mead, Sara Zarr, Morgan Rhodes, Lisa McMann, Geoff Herbach, A.S. King, James Riley. *Founded* 1994.

The Ethan Ellenberg Literary Agency*
155 Suffolk Street, Suite 2R, New York, NY 10002
tel +1 212-431-4554
email agent@ethanellenberg.com
website www.ethanellenberg.com
President and Agent Ethan Ellenberg, *Senior Agent* Evan Gregory, *Associate Agent* Bibi Lewis

Fiction and non-fiction (home 15%, overseas 20%). Interested in all types of children's fiction: new adult, young adult, middle grade, chapter books, picture books. Will consider all genres: literary, mystery, romance, fantasy, sci-fi, humorous. Will consider other illustrated works. No scholarly works, poetry, short stories or screenplays.
  Will accept unsolicited MSS and seriously consider all submissions, including first-time writers. For fiction, submit synopsis and first three chapters. For shorter children's works, send complete MS. Illustrators should send a representative selection of colour copies (no original artwork). Unable to return any material from overseas. See website for full submission guidelines. *Founded* 1983.

Flannery Literary
email jennifer@flanneryliterary.com
website www.flanneryliterary.com
Contact Jennifer Flannery

Specialises in children's and young adult, juvenile fiction and non-fiction (home 15%, overseas 20%). *Founded* 1992.

Folio Literary Management*
The Film Center Building, 630 9th Avenue, Suite 1101, New York, NY 10036

website www.foliolit.com

Represents both first-time and established authors. Seeks upmarket adult fiction, literary fiction, commercial fiction that features fresh voices and/or memorable characters, and narrative non-fiction. Folio Jr is devoted exclusively to representing children's book authors and artists. Consult agents' submission guidelines on the website before making contact. In 2018, Folio Literary Management purchased Harold Ober Associates Inc.

Barry Goldblatt Literary LLC*
594 Dean Street, Brooklyn, NY11238
tel +1 718-832-8787
email query@bgliterary.com
website www.bgliterary.com
Contact Barry Goldblatt

Represents young adult and middle-grade fiction, as well as adult science fiction and fantasy. No non-fiction. Has a preference for quirky, offbeat work. Query only. See website for full submission guidelines.

The Greenhouse Literary Agency
4035 Ridge Top Road, Suite 550, Fairfax, VA 22030
tel +1 571-758-5615
email submissions@greenhouseliterary.com
website www.greenhouseliterary.com
Director Sarah Davies (North American submissions only), *Agent* Polly Nolan (US, UK, Irish submissions)

Children's fiction from chapter books through to teen/young adult (USA/UK 15%, elsewhere 25%). Occasional non-fiction projects will also be considered. Represents both US and UK authors. No poetry, film scripts or material for adults. No reading fee. Will suggest revision. Queries by email only, see website for details.
  Authors include Sarah Aronson, Tami Lewis Brown, Caroline Carlson, Sarwat Chadda, Donna Cooner, Elle Cosimano, Bill Doyle, Jan Gangsei, Tae Keller, Lindsey Leavitt, Megan Miranda, Mae Respicio, Tricia Springstubb, Blythe Woolston, Brenna Yovanoff. *Founded* 2008.

John Hawkins & Associates Inc.*
80 Maiden Lane, Suite 1503, New York, NY 10038
tel +1 212-807-7040
email jha@jhalit.com
website www.jhalit.com
Agents Moses Cardona (President), Warren Frazier, Anne Hawkins, Annie Kronenberg

Fiction, non-fiction, young adult. No reading fee. *Founded* 1893.

kt literary*
9249 S. Broadway 200–543, Highlands Ranch, CO 80129
tel +1 720-344-4728
email contact@ktliterary.com
website www.ktliterary.com

Contact Kate Schafer Testerman, Sara Megibow, Hannah Fergesen

Primarily middle grade and young adult fiction. No picture books. Some select narrative non-fiction for children. Email a query letter and the first three pages of manuscript in the body of the email (no attachments) as per website instructions. No snail mail.

Clients include Maureen Johnson, Stephanie Perkins, Matthew Cody, Ellen Booraem, Trish Doller, Amy Spalding, Jaleigh Johnson, Stefan Bachmann. *Founded* 2008.

Gina Maccoby Literary Agency*
PO Box 60, Chappaqua, NY 10514
tel +1 914-238-5630
email gm@maccobylit.com
website www.publishersmarketplace.com/members/
GinaMaccoby/
Contact Gina Maccoby

Looking for high-quality upmarket fiction and non-fiction for adults and children. A compelling and engaging voice is most important; across all forms the agency is looking for strong storytelling and fresh perspectives. Children's, YA, middle grade, picture books; writers/illustrators only. Non-fiction areas of interest include history, biography, popular science and narrative journalism. No unsolicited submissions. Query first: query@maccobylit.com. Due to the volume of submissions received, will only reply if interested.

McIntosh & Otis Inc.*
207 E. 37th Street, Suite BG, New York, NY 10016
tel +1 212-687-7400
email info@mcintoshandotis.com
website www.mcintoshandotis.com
Head of Children's Department Christa Heschke

Board books, picture books (fiction and non-fiction), fiction for 5–8 and 9–12 year-olds, teenage fiction, series fiction, poetry and non-fiction for children. No unsolicited MSS for novels; query first via email, see website for instructions. No reading fee. *Founded* 1928.

Erin Murphy Literary Agency
824 Roosevelt Trail 290, Windham, ME
tel +1 928-525-2056
website http://emliterary.com
President Erin Murphy, *Senior Agent* Ammi-Joan Paquette, *Agents* Tricia Lawrence, Kevin Lewis, *Associate Agent* Tara Gonzalez

Children's books: fiction, non-fiction, picture books, middle grade, young adult (home 15%, overseas 20–30%). No unsolicited queries or submissions; considers material only by referral or through personal contact such as at conferences. *Founded* 1999.

Olswanger Literary LLC*
email anna@olswangerliterary.com
website www.olswanger.com
Contact Anna Olswanger

Specialises in representing author-illustrators. Clients have won the Newbery Honour, Asian Pacific American Award for Literature Honour, Flora Stieglitz Strauss Award for Non-fiction, Orbis Pictus Honour, PEN/Steven Kroll Award for Picture Book Writing, Parents Choice Gold Award, Bank Street College of Education Best Children's Book, Sibert Award Honour, Ezra Jack Keats Book Award Honour, and have been on the *New York Times* bestseller list. A member of SCBWI.

Alison Picard, Literary Agent
PO Box 2000, Cotuit, MA 02635
tel +1 508-477-7192
email ajpicard@aol.com

Adult fiction and non-fiction, children's and young adult (15%). No short stories, poetry, plays, screenplays or sci-fi/fantasy. Please send query via email (no attachments). No reading fee. *Founded* 1985.

Pippin Properties Inc.
110 West 40th Street, Suite 1704, New York, NY 10018, USA
tel +1 212-338-9310
email info@pippinproperties.com
website www.pippinproperties.com
Facebook www.facebook.com/pippinproperties
Twitter @LovethePippins
Contact Holly McGhee, Elena Giovinazzo, Sara Crowe, Larissa Helena, Ashley Valentine

Focuses on children's book authors and artists (home 15%, overseas 25%), from picture books to middle grade, graphic novels and young adult novels, and adult trade books on occasion. Query by email. *Founded* 1998.

Susan Schulman Literary Agency LLC*
454 West 44th Street, New York, NY 10036
tel +1 212-713-1633
email susan@schulmanagency.com
website www.schulmanagency.com

Agents for negotiation in all markets (with co-agents) of fiction, general non-fiction, for picture books, middle grade and young adult markets, and associated subsidiary rights including plays, television adaptation and film (home 15%, UK 7.5%, overseas 20%). No reading fee. Return postage required. Email enquiries to queries@schulmanagency.com.

Stimola Literary Studio, Inc.*
308 Livingston Court, Edgewater, NJ 07020
tel +1 201-945-9353
website www.stimolaliterarystudio.com
President and Founder Rosemary B. Stimola, *Senior*

Agent Erica Rand Silverman, *Agent* Adriana Stimola, *Associate Agent* Allison Remcheck, *Director of Operations and Graphic Novels Agent* Peter K. Ryan

Children's fiction and non-fiction, from preschool to young adult (home 15%, overseas 20%). Most clients come via referral. *Founded* 1997.

S©ott Treimel NY*
434 Lafayette Street, New York, NY 10003
tel +1 212-505-8353
email general@scotttreimelny.com
website www.scotttreimelny.com
Twitter @scotttreimel

Exclusively children's books: picture books for author/illustrators, illustrators, middle grade and young adult novels (home 15%, overseas 25%). Interested in seeing picture books, first chapter books, series, middle grade and teenage fiction, commercial non-fiction for all ages. No religious books. Periodicially open to submissions: presently closed unless personally recommended by writer and editor associates. *Founded* 1995.

WME
11 Madison Avenue, 18th Floor, New York, NY 10010
tel +1 212-586-5100
website www.wmeentertainment.com

Represents bestselling authors, critically acclaimed literary writers, award-winning thought leaders and up-and-coming talent.

Writers House LLC*
21 West 26th Street, New York, NY 10010
tel +1 212-685-2400
website www.writershouse.com

Fiction and non-fiction, including all rights; film and TV rights. See website for submission guidelines and contact details for agents. *Founded* 1974.

Illustration

Notes from a successful children's author and illustrator

Lauren Child describes how *Clarice Bean, That's Me* came to be published and shares her experiences of taking advice from publishers and editors.

My first attempt at writing a children's book was when I was 18 – my friend Bridget and I had an idea. Everything seemed simple – we were going to write a book, get it published and get on with something else. Almost immediately, and by sheer fluke, we had an interested publisher. We were invited along for a 'working lunch' to discuss the story development. The editor made some suggestions for improvement which we were quite happy about – we really had no objection to rewriting; we were happier still with the business lunch and were fuelled by the confidence of youth that life would always be this easy. We did nothing, of course, and the whole thing fell through which, with hindsight, was a relief – I think we would both be squirming now. It was a number of years later before I even thought to write anything else.

Please yourself

The next time I learnt the hard way, by trekking around uninterested publishers with my portfolio – something it would be almost impossible to do now, as no one wants to see unsolicited work. I used any contacts I had, however distant. I forced myself to phone complete strangers in order to get appointments and advice, which I hated doing. When I met with publishers they seemed to have very set views on what a children's book should be. I listened to their advice and always tried to write the book they wanted me to write. But, whenever I went back to them with my work, there was always something missing – I could never write the book they had in mind.

So, unable to interest publishers, no matter how hard I tried to give them what they said they wanted, I forgot about the whole project and got on with other things. One day, having reached a rather low point in my life, and having looked at every possible career path, a friend suggested that I leave my portfolio of designs, drawings and ideas with her so she could show it to her business manager who had created and managed various successful companies. When I met with this woman, I mentioned I had an interest in film and animation and also designing products for children. Although I had no relevant training, she suggested that I try to write a children's book because, hopefully, it would prove I could create characters and invent a world for them. I think that I was just at a point where I was ready to listen – perhaps because she was very successful, perhaps because it made sense, perhaps because she was a complete stranger.

I started to write the odd sentence, then draw a character, then write a bit more … there was no order to it, no plot structure. I wasn't even sure what I was writing, all I knew was that I was interested when I hadn't been before. I think it helped enormously that I wasn't fixated on creating the perfect children's book – it was merely a means to an end, a way to get into something else. I stopped being self-conscious about what I was doing and stopped trying to please everyone else. When I took this book – *Clarice Bean, That's Me* – to publishers, the difference was very obvious – they were all interested! However, no one was willing to take it on – they all thought it was unpublishable and told me so. But I had written something that had at least got their attention.

Listening to publishers

Nearly every publisher made suggestions of what I should change in order for this book to be published, some of them quite fundamental. I was told to drop the illustrations and simplify the text. I was told that varying fonts and integrating text and pictures was too complicated, that it would confuse young readers. I listened to them all; I considered what they had to say, but I knew they were all wrong – I knew they were wrong because I knew I wouldn't be happy with the end result. Because I had written something which felt right to me, it seemed better not to be published at all than to publish a book that wasn't really mine. After four or so long years, I eventually found a publisher who was willing to take the book on pretty much as it was.

And I think this is one of the most important things to know – how far will you go, how far *should* you go to be published? When it comes to this you have to follow your gut instinct. Despite my experience, I do think it is important to listen to what publishers have to say – it is always wise to listen, but it is not always right to take it on board. In the end, they can give you the benefit of their experience, but they cannot write the book for you, and you cannot write the book for them. As the writer, the book has to come from you. Of course, if more than one or two people pick up on the same thing then it may be worth following that advice, but for me it is never worth making a change when, after much consideration, it still feels wrong.

Know who you are writing for

When it comes to the question of writing for the 6–9 year-old market, I would say there is no formula. I don't write for 6–9 year-olds, I write for myself. My books are for anyone who wants to read them. For me, writing young fiction is less about writing for a particular audience or age group and more about telling a story that interests me. I have never thought 'Is this a book for 6–9 year-olds?' or 'Is this a book for 8–12 year-olds?'. I feel the same when writing picture books; they are there to be enjoyed by both adults *and* children because while the child looks at the pictures, it is the adult who usually reads the story.

How does a writer come up with the interesting ideas in the first place? As an adult writing a children's book, is it helpful – even necessary – to have children of your own? My own view is that it is simply irrelevant. First, we have all been children and anyone who wants to write for children must have strong feelings from his or her own childhood to draw upon. But more importantly, good fiction writing is not about imitation – it is about imagination. Just as having children does not mean you have anything to say to them in book form, so not having children is no bar to writing in a manner to which they will respond. Writing for anyone is about having something to say – a point of view. Writing for children is no different. When it comes to writing fiction, I think that any good writer will see children as people first, and as children second. Of course the context of childhood experiences is different from those of adults, but there is no emotion experienced as a child which is not felt equally in adult life.

At the more practical level, I do not believe that there are any fixed rules. I know that many writers plot a book out before they start, and I had always been told that I needed to plot my books and understand where they were going if I was to write successfully. But

I never begin writing a book knowing how it is going to end. I never normally know how it is going to start either. I generally just begin with a sentence taken at random. For me, it is all about an idea taking hold, and the writing tends to be more about a feeling than anything. *Clarice Bean, Don't Look Now* began as a book about love and ended up being a book more about loss than anything else. I wrote a few sentences about Clarice's inability to sleep and from that the whole mood of the book was determined. I started to write about insomnia and then wondered why Clarice might experience this, which led to thinking about her worries, which in turn led to the idea that she might be feeling very insecure and start questioning things around her. So, in a way, a few sentences shaped the whole plot because they reflected something that I felt personally at the time. I didn't try to force a story that I wasn't interested in writing; instead it became a book about Clarice's anxieties, her inability to explain the world to herself, and some recognition on her part that not only is life something which cannot be controlled, but it's also something which can only be imperfectly understood.

I write a lot of material and read it over and over, until I see what themes are emerging and then I look for a way to hang it all together. Once it has a solid plot, I start to cut. Writing picture books is a very good discipline for writing novels because with just 800 or so words to play with, you have to decide what is important and what isn't: what exactly is this book *about*? Writing picture books makes you much less frightened of editing out the bits that you love. You really can't be indulgent, and have to pare your writing down to the essence of what that story is about. Although of course a novel gives you much more freedom – *Don't Look Now* was 42,000 words – I still consciously try to make sure that every chapter is pushing the story forward and has something to say.

A good editor

That brings me on to another important part – your editor. I really have to trust who I am working with. I rely so much on my editor because of the patchwork way I work. A good editor will let you debate back and forth until you've finally reached a point where you know that you can't make something any better. You do have to trust them because it is so easy to lose your perspective about your own work. You may think it's great and not listen to criticism, but more often than not you will get doubtful and think it's all rubbish, and that's where an editor can keep you believing in your work.

If there's a single piece of advice I could offer for writing fiction, it would be to write from the heart. When I wrote *Clarice Bean, That's Me*, I became passionate about what I was writing and found it exciting. If you're bored when you're writing, you will write a boring book. And no matter how hard you find the early stages, keep going. You just need to write and write until you've written the imitation stuff out of you. It is hard but it is very rewarding too. Writing is one of the best things in the world – a licence to discuss ideas – even if it's just with yourself.

Lauren Child's picture books have won many awards, including the Kate Greenaway Medal in 2000 for *I Will Not Ever Never Eat a Tomato* (2000); the Smarties Gold Award in 2002 for *That Pesky Rat* (2002); and the Smarties Bronze Award for *Clarice Bean, That's Me* (1999); *Beware of the Storybook Wolves* (2000); and *What Planet Are You From, Clarice Bean?* (2001). In 2002 she published *Utterly Me, Clarice Bean*, the first of three Clarice Bean novels. In 2007 she illustrated a new edition of Astrid Lindgren's *Pippi Longstocking*. Three animated TV series of *Charlie & Lola* have been shown on CBBC and on channels around the world, and the series has won four BAFTAs. Her latest books are *Hubert Horatio: How to Raise Your Grown Ups* (Harper Collins Children's Books 2018) and the newest addition to her Ruby Redfort series, *Ruby Redfort Blink and You Die* (Candlewick Press 2018). Lauren has written and/or illustrated over 40 books and was made Children's Laureate in 2017. She is a trustee of the House of Illustration. Her website is www.milkmonitor.com.

The craft of the illustrator

Salvatore Rubbino describes how he finds inspiration by looking at the world around him with curiosity and wonder, and explains the exciting creative and collaborative process by which sketches and ideas are woven together into finished picture books.

Looking is a wonderful thing

As a picture book illustrator, I spend my day drawing and thinking about stories. I love words – the music they make and the taste they leave behind in my mouth – but above all I think in pictures. My task is to shape a tangible graphic world where story events and characters can thrive, a world that the reader can believe in. Pictures are a perfect story-telling tool and stories help to give a context to experience and our lives. We simply can't live without them!

Looking at the world around me is where my ideas come from. Drawing roots me to the spot and turns an initial glance into a long hard stare. It connects me to my surroundings and reminds me how interesting and varied life can be. Looking and drawing is a process of discovery; it helps me to notice the 'overlooked' and feeds my imagination.

We live a good deal of our lives in the humdrum (punctuated every now and then, perhaps, with something extraordinary) but I find the 'everyday' and the tiniest events inspiring and full of poetry. I carry a notebook with me wherever I go, ready to capture those special moments; I have little books for drawing on crowded trains should I see a compelling face, and larger paper that I might lay out on the pavement for more sustained work. I like to collect characters – we are all interesting and everyone comes with a story, and I have certain themes that I often return to. Musicians give the city a rhythm; they perform to be noticed and I have pages full of expressive players, particularly accordionists, so I hope one day to weave my musical drawings into a tale.

I've overheard some astonishing phone conversations whilst out walking – albeit only one half of the exchange (if you're an illustrator you're allowed to be nosey!). We continue to be expressive, pulling faces and gesturing vigorously, even when we can't see the other person on the line, and this gives me the chance to record some wonderfully animated behaviour. I can never pass a group of gossiping ladies without straining to hear what they're talking about and capture them in a picture. To be an illustrator, it's also necessary to cultivate a sense of wonder. This starts with a willingness to look with curiosity and to train the eye to find meaning in everything around you. I'm still learning.

From observation to imagination

City life has always inspired me – almost any street corner will do, although the busier the better, a spot where I can watch little everyday dramas unfold. My first picture book was set in New York (*A Walk in New York*; Candlewick Press 2009) and describes a walk over the course of a day. It follows a real route that a family might attempt (importantly no more than 3km), with stops for lunch and cheesecake – and no doubt the loo, too. It was quite a rigorous process to join up landmarks and beautiful views to form a satisfying sequence. When I was thinking about the characters, I asked myself, 'Well, who do you know?'. In the end I decided to have a dad based on me (more dapper and taller, why not? – after all, anything is possible in a story) and the boy who was a version of my son. At the time my son was only six months old, but I imagined him as a boy aged about seven, in a striped T-shirt and occasionally dragging his tired feet, even though in real life he had not yet learned to walk. I showed both of us craning our necks to look up at the skyscrapers, just as I did on my visit to the Big Apple when collecting ingredients for the book.

As a Londoner, I was excited when asked to make my next walk and subsequent book, *A Walk in London* (Candlewick Press 2011), about 'my' city. When you've lived somewhere all your life it's easy to feel you know it, the challenge was to see the city with fresh eyes. So, I bought a very large sketchbook and set out to audition locations and landmarks for a role in the book. One of my favourite places is Trafalgar Square. There's something quite joyful about a spurting fountain, especially on a hot day when you can put your hand in the water to cool down. I can't think of many national landmarks that you're allowed to climb, but, as long as you're careful, no one actually tells you off if you decide to sit on one of the lions guarding Nelson's column at the heart of the Square.

I am a little embarrassed to admit that I had never seen the Changing of the Guard ceremony in front of Buckingham Palace until I chose to include it in my story. It's a spectacle of synchronised walking accompanied by an orchestra and a cheerful tune. It begins with military precision at 11.27 a.m., and I made sure I had a place in front of the palace in good time, as I knew it would get crowded. And then it happened – an elegant lady wearing a wide-brimmed hat walked out of a side door, accompanied by her entourage; she got into her car and drove away – it was, of course, the Queen! I was astonished, but the encounter triggered an idea. I introduced a 'spot the royals' game, with the royal car weaving its way through the book; it's not mentioned explicitly, but the characters (a girl and her mother this time) receive a royal wave on the last page. I doubt if I would have thought of the idea without this experience of 'meeting the Queen'.

My early visual thinking for all pages in the London book was a flat plan. It records a conversation I had with my publisher when we made decisions about what to include, what to say about London, and how to organize everything into a coherent whole. There are crossing outs and several blank pages, so it is still a work in progress. Your publisher or editor may have different opinions, and – whilst it's important to have an honest discussion – it's worth remembering that they want to find the best treatment for the story too. Trust your creative instinct, but also be prepared to listen.

Marshalling your creativity

The text for a story arrives, via the publisher rather than directly from an author, in a compact form – usually a couple of sides of A4, accompanied by a few notes from the publisher ending with 'Please let me know if you're interested' (I'm always very interested!). By the time it reaches me the text has already undergone a rigorous process of rewriting, and has a well-crafted plot and clear point of view. Being invited to illustrate someone else's words is like collaborating with someone else's imagination – it's extremely exciting. I may sometimes meet the author and discuss the project, but our paths don't cross very often. Our relationship is via the publisher, who realises that I need to respond to the text in my own way.

I tend to start with a slow read-through of the story and then I re-read it whilst busily scribbling first impressions all over the manuscript. These notes might be about mood, a sense of place, character, or anything that's particularly vivid. I don't start work straight away. Instead I let the story sink in over the next few days. I will try to visit places or find aspects of the story that I can see and draw. I don't want to illustrate the text word for word (like a list) but instead I slide up to the story … sideways. I'm trying to find a way into the heart of the story. I'm looking for interesting things to describe, dramatic moments full of visual friction with the potential for mark-making, or moments that might allow me to draw the things that I like and a chance to celebrate beauty.

My first drawing attempts for a book are usually quite unrefined. There is no process or formula an illustrator has to follow, or indeed that I follow, for each new project. In every case, I'm meeting the book's characters for the first time, getting to know them and the world they inhabit. I might simply respond to one line or phrase to begin with, until eventually I feel confident enough to start mapping a composition on the page. A book takes time.

I tend to approach a new book rather like a method actor learning a role. *A Book of Feelings* (Walker Books 2015) allowed me to be expressive and play with character in a way I had not tried before. I purchased a mirror so that I could practice a grimace or gesture, in order to draw myself and understand the way in which the child characters in the story might feel and behave and look – even doing a range of voices to help inhabit each emotional state I was depicting. The face has over 40 muscles, which makes it a fantastically elastic communication tool. I try to think about situations in my own life that relate to those described in a story, to provide me with creative inspiration.

What else can illustrators do?

If you are a commissioning editor reading this, I'd like to remind you that illustrators are resourceful people and good problem-solvers. Support them and help to celebrate images together. If you're an author, it's worth adding that illustrators make keen collaborators and will relish the chance to draw your story. And if you're an illustrator, why not consider sharing your appetite for creating pictures? Illustration can be a solitary business, but talking about pictures, running workshops or teaching can be very rewarding, as well as another way to support yourself financially. I'm often invited to take part in festivals and events and I like to cultivate this (time permitting). I also teach, as a visiting tutor, and regularly deliver activities at schools and museums.

I always find watching other people draw or demonstrate a technique quite magical. From humble beginnings something takes shape until it becomes more substantial, to form a face, an animal or a landscape full of life. We all seek to express ourselves, and drawing and creating is a perfect vehicle. People are keen to know 'how it's done' and as an illustrator you can take them on a behind-the-scenes tour.

The picture books I make often have a family at the heart of the story, doing things together; there's friction sometimes, but a good deal of understanding too. Running family activities allows me to observe how children and adults collaborate and eventually find a solution by working together, feeling proud of their achievements by the end of the task. One child might be busy cutting whilst their dad holds the card; another sibling is gluing, untroubled about sticky fingers, and at the same time mum or a grandparent may be helping to colour in. Explaining to others what I do, and thinking about pictures with others, makes me deeply aware of my own creative practice; at the same time it exposes me to lots of refreshingly different points of view – and so, whilst sharing, you never stop learning.

Salvatore Rubbino graduated from the Royal College of Art in 2005. His first picture book, *A Walk in New York*, was published in 2009 by Candlewick Press, followed by *A Walk in London* in 2011. His other books, all published by Walker Books, include *Just Ducks!* (2012) written by Nicola Davies, *A Walk in Paris* (2014), *A Book of Feelings* (2015) and *Our Very Own Dog* (2016) written by Amanda McCardie, and *Harry Miller's Run* (2015) by David Almond. His latest book, *We're Getting a Cat!*, written by Vivian French will be published in August 2019 by Walker Books. Salvatore teaches at the Cambridge School of Art and at Southampton Solent University. He received a BookTrust Best New Illustrators Award in 2011.

See also...

• *On being a storyteller: the illustrator's story,* page 272

Illustration

Being an illustrator *and* a writer

Writer and illustrator of children's books, Liz Pichon, tells how persistence, hard work – and following the urge to create the kind of books *you* would have enjoyed as a child – can bring successful and very enjoyable results.

I always loved drawing and writing stories, but it wasn't something I ever thought I could do for a living. I was a bit hopeless at spelling (and still am). My route to becoming an author came through being asked to work on other people's stories as an illustrator. I found it too stressful sitting around waiting for someone else to give me a job, so I had a go at writing my own picture book ideas to illustrate as well. I already had an agent for my illustration work in books (Caroline Walsh at David Higham Associates), who was very encouraging (and has stuck by me for over 16 years).

My first picture book, *Square Eyed Pat*, was published in 2004. This was followed by *My Big Brother, Boris*, which won the Smarties Book Prize Silver Award (0–5 Years) and gave me more confidence to keep writing and drawing.

The *Tom Gates* series started life as a picture book idea. Publishers said they liked the format but didn't think there was sufficient story. So eventually, after rewriting it in different formats, I sat down and wrote afresh the first pages in a school exercise book. I imagined Tom writing about a rotten camping holiday he'd had with his family which included his teacher's comments as well as lots of drawings and doodles.

This was about the third (or fourth) go I'd had at it. But when Caroline sent out this version we got seven offers from seven different publishers within two weeks – which of course had NEVER happened to me before.

Here's my advice to anyone who wants to write or illustrate children's books:
• Be persistent. I know lots of people who have had their first efforts turned down or ideas rejected. But if the comments from publishers are positive, keep going and don't give up. Take feedback on board, especially if you're being told the same thing from different publishers. (However, some of my best ideas have lingered around for a while.)
• Think about what kind of books YOU really enjoyed reading when you were a child. I was crazy about a series about a bear called Mary Plain. Looking at them now, I realise that the quality of those books wasn't amazing, but Mary used to write letters with lots of drawings and doodles as part of them. I loved these bits so much that I would skip through the whole book to devour her letters. This is exactly why the *Tom Gates* books have so many doodles and drawings in them: I wanted to write a book that I would have enjoyed as a child.

The *Children's Writers' & Artists' Yearbook* is a fantastic source of information, STUFFED full of useful FACTS to help you get writing (and drawing). So be sure to make good use of it. And if you're lucky enough to get a book published – ENJOY it! Put together an event and do anything you can to help it along the way. I love going to schools and doing events now, although I found it tricky at first. It's really fantastic to be invited to talk about your books and meet the children and other people who are reading them. I often get ideas from going out and about.

The *Tom Gates* series is now published in 33 different languages and I've recently completed book ten. And I can honestly say I've never worked so hard on anything or enjoyed myself so much. So keep going and don't give up!

Here's my feet　　　　　　　　　　　not touching the ground

– because that's what has happened to me since *The Brilliant World of Tom Gates* was published in April 2011.

Liz Pichon is a writer and illustrator of children's books, including *A Tale of Two Kitties*, *Bored Bill*, *My Big Brother, Boris* (winner of the Smarties Book Prize Silver Award in 2004), *The Very Ugly Bug*, *Spinderella*, *Square Eyed Pat*, *Penguins*, *My Little Sister, Doris* and *The Three Horrid Pigs and the Big Friendly Wolf*. The newest edition of her *Tom Gates* series, *Extra Special Treats (Not)* was published in May 2019 and *Tom Gates: The Music Box* is due to be published Autumn 2019, both by Scholastic. *The Brilliant World of Tom Gates* won the 2011 Roald Dahl Funny Prize (7–14 Years), the 2012 Red House Children's Book Award (Younger Readers) and the 2012 Waterstones Children's Book Prize (Best Fiction for 5–12s); and *Tom Gates – Genius Ideas (Mostly)* won the 2013 Blue Peter Book Awards (Best Story). The *Tom Gates* series has been a multiple No 1 children's bestseller and has been translated into 43 languages. Find out more on her website http://lizpichon.com/ and follow her on Twitter @LizPichon.

See also...
● *Notes from a successful children's author and illustrator*, page 263

On being a storyteller: the illustrator's story

Korky Paul describes his craft and role as an illustrator, what inspires and unlocks his visual concept of the writer's story, and the steps involved in creating the final artwork.

I am an illustrator. I am not a writer. I seldom meet the authors of the books I illustrate. For me a picture book always begins with someone else's manuscript. I prefer not to have a brief, giving me descriptions of place or character. A good writer should include these in the manuscript, and that is where I glean inspiration – finding stimulation on how to tell the story visually.

A good writer entrusts the illustrator, the image-maker, to interpret their work. But both writer and illustrator are equally important to the success of a picture book.

The early years

I studied Fine Arts at Durban Art School, South Africa and landed a job as a junior visualiser at a glitzy advertising agency De Villiers & Schonveldt in Cape Town. They called me 'the new drawer'. No personal statement required – no showing of qualifications, no listing of hobbies, just a presentation of me and my portfolio … and a vague introduction from an old school friend.

It was the best thing that happened to me and definitely helped my future as an illustrator. I learnt to take ideas and concepts to pencil rough stage. I learnt layout, design, composition, typography and the importance of promotion and advertising. But most of all, I learnt that craft and skill are essential to any creative endeavour.

'Drawer' is a fair job description of what I did then but, I realize, not an accurate description of what I do now. Now I am a drawer *and* a storyteller – not verbally, but through my illustrations.

Becoming an illustrator

In the '70s I fled apartheid South Africa for Europe and continued to work in advertising while trying to crack the children's book world as an illustrator. My brother, Donald, worked for Oxford University Press. He wrangled a meeting for me with the then Children's Books editor, Ron Heapy, who was wary. You can imagine – some bloke working at OUP Africa Sales Division has an older brother who draws …

He looked at my portfolio, then photocopied a few illustrations. 'We'll put these on file', he intoned, followed by the usual 'Don't phone us, we'll phone …'.

Then, as I slunk out feeling depressed, Ron handed me a manuscript: 'Do me three drawings. It's an A4 format, paperback, double staple bound and part of an Oxford reading programme. It's about a witch who lives in a black house with a black cat. Written by an Australian, Valerie Thomas.'

A few weeks later, I returned with three full-colour illustrations in a large picture book format.

'That's not what I asked for,' he muttered.

'I know. But it's a great story', I replied. 'Pity to publish it as an A4 staple bound …'.

Winnie the Witch has since appeared in 16 picture books, has been translated into 30 languages and sold nearly 6 million copies. I am amazed and delighted.

Working from the manuscript

I liken illustrating picture books to making a movie. As the drawer, you are the cinematographer, director, casting agent, costume designer, set designer *and* are responsible for locations, camera, lighting, props and continuity! The text is the soundtrack and that special combination between words and pictures makes for good storytelling. As in a movie, neither text nor illustration can exist comfortably on its own.

What do I look for in a story? The subject matter is unimportant; I will draw anything. What appeals to me are stories with an unexpected ending or a neat, clever twist. If on the first reading the story inspires me, filling my head with images, I feel confident I can do it justice.

I may discuss themes or ideas with a writer, but I choose not to be involved in the writing of drafts or final manuscripts. I leave this to the author and editor. I prefer to work from an A4 clean-typed, double-spaced text of a final manuscript approved by author and editor.

Creating the flatplan

The next stage is to divide the manuscript into 12 double-page spreads. This is known as 'doing the flatplan' and this all-important process should always be assigned to the illustrator. It is the key factor in determining the pace and rhythm of the story. I always urge writers to concentrate on writing the story and not to concern themselves with the flatplan. At this stage, it distracts the illustrator.

The majority of picture books contain 32 pages:
• Page 01 glues to the inside front cover
• Page 32 glues to the inside back
• Pages 02+03 are the front end papers
• Page 30+31 are the back end papers
• Page 04 is the copyright details + dedication page
• Page 05 is the title page
• Pages 06+07 are Spread 1
• Pages 08+09 are Spread 2, etc
• Pages 28+29 are Spread 12
This makes a total of 8 pages allocating 24 pages, or 12 'double-page spreads' for the text and the illustrations.

Now you begin the process of visual storytelling while decoding someone else's written imagination. I read the finished manuscript several times, scribbling scenes or characters that drift into my mind's eye. I look for key words or phrases to prompt an image. Returning to the movie analogy, the flatplan is the shooting script. There are no fixed rules, but a good tip is to treat each spread as a chapter.

Generally the first task I do is to pencil in the following:
• Spreads 1+2 — the beginning
• Spreads 6+7 — the middle
• Spreads 11+12 — the surprise ending

Illustration

• Spreads 3, 4, 5 — for build-up to the middle part
• Spreads 8, 9, 10 — for build-up to the 'neat twist'.
Then I look for cues for the remaining spreads:
• An introduction of a new character (or new characters)
• Passage of time, i.e. day/night scenes
• Change of scene
• A 'cliffhanger' sequence needing a page-turn to discover the outcome.
I have to be aware of the pace, rhythm and drama of the story, and the writing style when breaking down the text.

Preparatory sketches and ideas

In most of the picture books I've illustrated the writer offers little or no description of the characters' appearance or the environment they inhabit. In a picture book this is redundant as I will imagine and draw these aspects, unless the writer offers significant keys to the action or plot.

Some characters require hours of doodling before I feel they're right. It's difficult to articulate how you decide on a look or a face, as it's something that develops within you. For each spread, I select incidents I feel will visually expand the story, the drawing adding imaginative layers as the tale unfolds. This process requires endless scribbles, preparatory sketches and oodles of time – but it's such fun!

In *Winnie the Witch*, the writer Valerie Thomas used only one adjective to describe our heroine's home: 'black'. My initial sketches showed a picturesque cottage with thatched roof and timber beams. The results were dull and commonplace.

'What's the opposite of cottage?' I asked myself. Answer: 'stately home'. This opened the story for me. The rooms and paraphernalia of a stately home would serve as a dramatic backdrop for Winnie's antics with her cat, Wilbur. The real challenge lay in illustrating it all in black! This is where my training as a fine artist mattered. Our classical art training taught us that, when painting black, add reds for warm and blues for cold black.

The grid template

This is the skeleton of the book. The roughs and the finished art are done 25% larger than the printed size. Using InDesign or Quark I prepare the grid template for the left-hand page (verso) and the right-hand page (recto) on A3 photocopy paper at 125% showing:
• *Trim* (page edge)
• *Bleed* (extra 5mm on all outside edges)
• *Spine* (the centre of the spread using a dotted line)
• *Live picture area* (by showing the margins on the verso and recto pages using a dotted line)
• *20mm margin* top and left and right sides of the pages
• *25mm margin* on the bottom of both pages.
• Any other layout info, which is common to all pages
• 15 copies at least of verso and recto are printed.

The pencil roughs

Each A3 verso and recto page are glued together to make a single spread, thus becoming A2 size. On a separate piece of paper I print out the text for that spread with typesetting at 125%. With a pencil I sketch in my ideas, moving the text around to fit with the illustration. It is very important that text and pictures work together.

Many of my spreads are dense with detail, enticing reluctant readers to have fun, to explore the illustrations, talk about them, even stimulate their own stories. The backgrounds or environments contain layer upon layer of detail, tales within tales connected to the story or elaborating on its themes. I try to create a world with many imaginary creatures, inhabiting a world festooned with stuff.

When I am satisfied with the pencil sketch and position of the typesetting, I redraw over the pencil lines using pen and ink, making alterations and improvements to the pencil where necessary. Often, the roughs cover many pieces of paper; I arrange and glue these into 'collage' drawings. Sometimes a preparatory drawing is exactly what I want but is the wrong size; I'll enlarge or reduce it on a photocopier, then collage it into position on the rough.

The finished art

The finished artwork is done on a 190gm^2 Saunders's Waterford CP/NOT Surface watercolour paper. I tape the completed rough onto a light box (a drawing board with a glass worktop and strip lights beneath the glass; an essential drawing aid).

Over the rough I tape down the watercolour paper, flick on the lights so the rough sketch underneath shows through. With a very sharp HB pencil I lightly trace in the illustration, again altering and improving. The primary reason for tracing the rough onto the watercolour paper is to position the illustration exactly where I want it. Also, it helps avoid drawing too close to the edge of the page, or into areas reserved for text, or drawing crucial details over the spine or gutter.

> ### How to present your idea for a picture book
>
> Below are four items you need to include in your presentation:
> 1. **Story** (written by you or someone else).
>   Divide the manuscript into a flatplan of 12 spreads. Text should be clean typed, double-line spaced, with each spread numbered and printed on separate sheets of A4.
> 2. The **first three spreads** worked out as roughs AND finished art.
> 3. The **subsequent three roughs** worked out.
> 4. **Preparatory drawings, sketch books and reference material.**

I remove the watercolour paper from the light box and start drawing – not tracing! There's a great difference between the two. I don't slavishly follow the pencil lines, as this would produce a dull, lifeless work. They are merely guides. The trick is to recapture the fresh spontaneity so often found in the rough drawings. I draw mainly with a dip-pen using black Kandahar ink or waterproof coloured inks, but toothbrushes, porcupine quills, goose feathers have all been used achieve certain effects. Once the line work is complete, I paint with Schmincke Horadam Aquarell watercolours.

Masking fluid. Masking fluid is applied over complex objects in the foreground. Background colours and washes can be painted broadly and effortlessly over the masked objects, which is simpler than painting around them. Colourless masking fluid is best applied with silicone brushes (colour shaper) or, for fine details, a dip-pen.

Do you need an agent?

Publishers seem to insist on authors having agents but not so with illustrators. My problem is that agents claim a percentage of your earnings in perpetuity. I do not have an agent.

After nearly 40 years I still love what I do. My aim is always to entice reluctant readers to enjoy the world of books through my illustrations. When I experience this, it's a real pleasure.

'That's a magic moment!', as Winnie the Witch would say…

Korky Paul is an award-winning illustrator of picture books, pop-up books, chapter books, educational books and poetry books for children. His bestselling *Winnie the Witch* series began with *Winnie the Witch* (Oxford University Press 1987) which won the Children's Book Award in 1988. Other publications include *Dinner with Fox* (Dial Books for Young Readers 1990), *Professor Puffendorf's Secret Potions* (Checkerboard Press 1992), *The Rascally Cake* (Andersen Press 1994) and *The Fish Who Could Wish* (OUP 2008). The latest in his *Sir Scallywag* series (written by Giles Andreae) is *Sir Scallywag and the Battle for Stinky Bottom* (Puffin 2015). Whilst the latest in his Winnie and Wilbur series are *Winnie and Wilbur: The Santa Surprise* (OUP 2018) and *Winnie and Wilbur: The Bug Safari* (OUP 2019), and for 2020, *Winnie and Wilbur at Chinese New Year*. New poetry books with John Foster include *Eggs With Legs* (Troika Books 2018) and a re-issue of *Dinosaur Poems*, *Dragon Poems* and *Football Poems*. An animated TV series, *Winnie and Wilbur*, based on the multimillion-selling *Winnie the Witch* books, produced with UK-based Winduna Enterprises and Channel 5's 'Milkshake' is now going into production as a 52-part series. See more at http://www.korkypaul.com/ and www.winnieandwilbur.com.

Creating graphic novels

Raymond Briggs has created many graphic novels and here he describes his method.

Book writers have such an easy time of it. They sit down, write their book and when they come to the end they send it off to the publisher. It might be long, it might be short, the publisher doesn't mind.

The writer needs no materials or equipment. He can do it all with a pencil and a note pad. Even the typing may be done for him. Unlike the illustrator, he needs no paints, crayons, T-squares, set squares, brushes, dividers, spray cans, handmade paper and mounting boards, light boxes, cutting tables, guillotines, type scales, magnifier lamps, wall-to-wall display boards and masses of space. The writer can scribble it all in bed. (They often do.)

Drawing the book

For the picture book illustrator, when he has finished the writing, that is the easy bit done. His true task then begins.

First he has to design the book. Picture books have to be exactly 32 pages, not 33 or 31. This includes prelims. So the text has to be divided into fewer than 16 spreads. On rare occasions, the publisher may allow 40 pages, or on even rarer occasions 48, though this allowance may contain 'self-ends' which take up eight pages. (This is too technical to explain to book writers.)

Then, the illustrator becomes a typographer. He casts off the manuscript, chooses a suitable font, decides on the type size, the measure and the leading, and has it set. Surprisingly, some writers I have met know nothing about typography. Some don't even know the name of the font their own book is set in! Some have never even set foot in a printer's.

If the book is strip cartoon with speech bubbles, the task is even greater as each speech bubble has to be individually designed. The size and shape of it is part of its expressive quality and once the bubble is finalised the illustrator becomes a hand-lettering expert and letters in, possibly many hundreds of words, trying to maintain a consistent style over many days' work. In America, strip cartoon work is divided amongst several people: writer, pencilling-in artist, inker-in, and letterer. In England we are made of sterner stuff – 'blood, toil, tears and sweat' and we 'graphic novelists' do it all.

The illustrator then makes a dummy (a blank book) with the correct number of pages and of the exact size. If he is well established and commands respect from the publisher, the publisher may have a dummy made for him – but you need to be at least 60 years old to be granted this privilege (you might have to show them your bus pass). He then cuts up the type proofs (which used to be called 'galleys') and sticks them onto the dummy, imagining the pictures on the page as he does so. Again, for strip cartoons it is much more complicated – you have to consider not just what text goes on each spread but how many frames the text is to be divided amongst, and what size and shape the frames are to be.

This brings us to the next stage: designing the 'grid', i.e. how many rows of frames per page and the number of frames in each row there are to be. Places where small frames give way to a big picture, either vignetted or bled off, will be determined by the text itself, not only in terms of space but also by the feeling the text is trying to express.

Illustration

Creating the action

When all this is done, it is time to stop book designing and start making the 'film'. You become the director. Who comes on from the left and who from the right? A slight nuisance is that the character on the left is the one who has to speak first. What are the characters doing and thinking and feeling? We have their words, but is there a subtext? Can this be expressed by body language? Is one of them angrily scrubbing the floor, whilst the other gazes moodily out of the window?

You then become the art director, designing the sets. Where does the scene take place? Indoors or outdoors? In the garden or in the street? What does a 1930s kitchen look like? How big is the room? What is the view from the window?

You also have to be the costume designer and the lighting designer. What would they be wearing at the time? Is it winter or summer? What were overcoats and hats like then? What did they wear on the beach? Should it be daylight or artificial light in this scene? What exactly was the look of gaslight? Does it need a dark ominous light or a happy morning light?

Then as the cameraman you have to decide where to shoot from. Close-up, long shot, or middle distance? Both characters in shot or one off-screen? Perhaps a speech bubble stays in the frame but the speaker is unseen, through a doorway or simply out of shot. Shall it be a high view looking down on the scene or a low angle looking up? It all depends on what the action is trying to convey.

Finally, you have to become the actor and feel yourself inside the character when you're drawing it. This is the essence of good narrative illustration. It is an odd bit of psychology. You have to be mentally in two places at once. One part of you is inside character, feeling what it is like to be huddled and running in the pouring rain, the other part of your brain is detachedly looking at this figure from a certain point of view, taking note of perspective. 'Ah yes, the lower leg will be foreshortened from this angle; we're looking down on the thigh and on the back; we can't see his face as his head is down and his arm is up. Will we see the sole of the shoe that is raised or is it edge on?'

The lucky writer need know nothing about human and animal anatomy, perspective, drawing, line tone or colour. All they have to do is write down some words! It's a doddle.

I wish I could do it.

Raymond Briggs CBE is creator of *The Snowman, Fungus the Bogeyman, Father Christmas* and many other characters and stories for children, and *When the Wind Blows* and *Ethel and Ernest* for adults. His long-awaited collection, *Time For Lights Out,* will be published by Jonathan Cape in November 2019. Since leaving art school in 1957 he has been a writer and illustrator, mainly of children's books. He has written plays for the stage and radio and a few 'adult' books. In 2004 he designed the Christmas stamps for the Royal Mail, and was made a Fellow of the Royal Society of Literature, but his proudest achievement is going on the radio programme *Desert Island Discs,* twice. In 2017 he was awarded the prestigious BookTrust Lifetime Achievement Award and in the same year he was awarded the CBE in the Queen's Birthday Honours. His fansite is www.toonhound.com/briggs.htm.

See also...

- *Notes from a successful children's author and illustrator,* page 263
- *Eight great tips to get your picture book published,* page 281
- *Writing and illustrating picture books,* page 285

Notes from the first Children's Laureate

Quentin Blake was the first Children's Laureate (1999–2001).

I started life – my life as someone who does pictures to appear in print, that is – by doing illustrations and cartoons for magazines. It wasn't so long, however, before I got the idea that I would like to be on my own between two covers; or at least on my own with an author. There were various reasons. One was that I wanted to organise a sequence of images that would follow a narrative; another was to get into a wider range of subject matter, a wider range of mood and atmosphere than was supplied by humorous commentary on current everyday life. I had been trained as a teacher, and I thought it was possible that, as the humour I had to offer was mainly visual, children might appreciate it as much as adults. The prospect of children's books was an attractive one, but I had no idea at all about how to begin. In the event I asked a friend, John Yeoman, if he would write something for me to illustrate. He could read Russian and it was a sample Russian folk-tale that he offered to me, which I illustrated, and which we submitted to Faber and Faber. We fell on our feet. I think perhaps we had hoped for a picture book, but Faber said that if we could find another handful of stories they would publish them – and in due course they became a book called *A Drink of Water*.

So we were very lucky. We were spared the frustrating (and generally unavoidable) round of submissions, and we had something printed. And there is nothing, I suspect, so reassuring to a prospective commissioning editor as seeing drawings actually in print.

Now (50 years later), holding the *Children's Writers' & Artists' Yearbook* in my hand, it's clear to me that, if we hadn't been as lucky as we were, how useful such a volume as this would have been. It has two great virtues. One, of course, is the wealth of information it contains. From their listing in 'Children's book publishers UK and Ireland', for example, we discover that Faber and Faber won't look at unsolicited manuscripts – so we wouldn't have got far with them nowadays.

The other is an impressive raft of notes, comments and advice from practitioners in every aspect of the business. It's as good as a correspondence course in the creation of children's books. And as well as the sage advice of such examples as Raymond Briggs and Tony Ross, there are more recent personal reactions. I was fascinated to read accounts of self-discovery from Lauren Child and David Lucas. The great advantage of such a personal approach is that the advice you find there is not merely prescriptive. In fact, though there is useful advice to be had, nothing is certain. Conventional wisdom would no doubt say that a readership of eight- and nine-year-olds wouldn't want to be given a heroine years younger than themselves, nor would that age group want to read about a middle-aged bachelor trying to persuade a middle-aged woman to marry him. But Matilda is a huge success, and *Esio Trot* does pretty well too. The book that you now hold in your hand is a wonderful guidebook, but it's still nice to think that none of us know quite where we may be going.

Illustration

Quentin Blake CBE has always made his living as an illustrator, as well as teaching for over 20 years at the Royal College of Art, where he was Head of Illustration 1978–86. His first drawings were published in *Punch* when he was 16 and he continued to draw for *Punch*, the *Spectator* and other magazines over many years. He entered the world of children's books with *A Drink of Water* by John Yeoman in 1960 and has since collaborated with other writers such as Russell Hoban, Joan Aiken, Michael Rosen and, most famously, Roald Dahl. He has also illustrated classics such as *Don Quixote* and *Candide*, and created much-loved characters of his own, including Mister Magnolia and Mrs Armitage. Since the 1990s Quentin Blake has curated shows in, among other places, the National Gallery, the British Library and the Musée du Petit Palais in Paris. His work can be seen in the wards and public spaces of several London hospitals and mental health units in England and France. He has been very involved in setting up the House of Illustration. His books have won numerous major prizes and awards. In 1999 he was appointed the first ever Children's Laureate. In 2012 he won the Prince Philip Designers Prize. He was knighted in 2013 and in 2014 was appointed a Chevalier of the Légion d'Honneur.

See also...
- *Notes from a Children's Laureate*, page 82
- *Creating graphic novels*, page 277
- *Eight great tips to get your picture book published*, page 281
- *Writing and illustrating picture books*, page 285

Eight great tips to get your picture book published

Tony Ross gives some sound advice for illustrators and writers of children's picture books.

I have always had the uncomfortable feeling that if I can get published, anyone can. A belief that being published is something that only happens to other people, holds some very good writers and illustrators back.

Assuming you have drawings – or a story – to offer, there are several ways to go about it. Probably the best way is to have a publishing house in the family! Failing that, all is not lost.

Work can be sent directly to a publisher's office. Most editors receive a good amount of unsolicited work, so be patient with them for a reply. A stamped addressed envelope for the return of postal submissions is always appreciated, bearing in mind that the majority of work submitted is refused. At the beginning of a career, refusal is quite normal and a great deal about yourself and your talent can be gleaned from this experience. Sometimes, advice gained at this stage can change your future.

Starting on a drawing career is an exciting time and I think it's a good idea to get yourself in perspective. Visit the library and some bookshops to look at all the styles that are around. Get a sense for what's out there: you don't want to regurgitate it, but to get a feel for the parameters. You can learn a lot, maybe more than you learned at art school, from looking at great artists such as Edward Ardizzone, E.H. Shepard, Maurice Sendak and Chris Van Allsburg.

Great Tip No. 1: Use black and white

There is great appeal in working in full colour but it's good to remember black and white. Sometimes a publisher may have a black and white project waiting for an illustrator, while all of the big interest is going into the colour picture book list. Some of the greatest children's books are illustrated in black and white – A.A. Milne and E.H. Shepard made one of the greatest partnerships with those tiny black ink drawings contributing so much to a great classic. Not a bad place to start, eh?

Ink drawing is simple in the hands of a master but not easy. That unforgiving fluid! Wonder at the uncomplicated, straightforwardness of the Pooh drawings. Consider Toad in *The Wind in the Willows*. When he applied to do the illustrations, Kenneth Graham said to Shepard: 'I have seen many artists who can draw better than you, but you make the animals live.' Can you learn anything from that? Look at Ardizzone's ability to draw mood. He can show both a summer afternoon and a cold November morning simply by using black ink. There is so much to look at, so much to learn from.

Try to include black and white work in your folder. Also include a series of perhaps 30 drawings, such as a fully illustrated story, where you show your ability to be consistent with the characters and the style, without repetition or irrelevance (like the radio programme *Just a Minute*).

It is a duty of an illustrator to be able to read, i.e. to try and understand the writer's aims, and to help them rather than to inflict a totally different angle onto the book (again, think of the Milne and Shepard partnership). Much of this comes down to being sensitive enough to recognise the tone of the writing, and skilful enough to draw in the same tone. So the importance of really taking an interest in the story cannot be overstressed. In the text, there will be either clues, or blatant instructions to help the drawings gel. Be very aware.

Great Tip No. 2: Experiment

I have known illustrators who convinced themselves that they couldn't use black ink. Mostly this was because they were using the wrong ink, the wrong pen, and/or the wrong paper. Types of black ink vary: waterproof behaves differently from water soluble. Fine nibs and broad nibs each give a totally different result, as does an old fountain pen or a sharpened stick. Try ten different inks, 50 different nibs, odd sticks and all the papers you can find: tracing, layout, calendered, five different cartridges, smooth and rough water-colour, handmade, wrapping paper, anything at all. It's a case of finding the combination that suits your hand and your intention. Your own genius, unrecognised at art school, could surprise you.

Many of the points I've made about black and white work also apply to colour. The marriage of image to text will be in your hands, but it must work.

Great Tip No. 3: Choose the right words

I am hesitant to give advice to writers. After all, there are few rules, and the next J.K. Rowling may read this. My own view is really quite simple, and rather obvious. I write mainly for under eight year-olds, so my stories are as short as I can make them. I feel that it is good to have a magnetic first sentence, and an ending that EXPLODES WITH SURPRISE. I think that the ending is the most important part of the story. The bit in the middle should waft the reader along, remembering that the *sound* of words and sentences can be a useful tool.

I like stories to be either funny or scary. *Very* funny, or *very* scary. To be dull is the worst thing in the world! That sounds so obvious, but it gets overlooked. If you are not excited with your work, maybe nobody else will be either.

A picture book has about 23 pages of text (but this can be flexible). I think those pages should have fewer than 2,000 words; 1,000–1,500 is good. One word per page would be great, if the one word was brilliant. As brilliant as the story. Don't be frightened of editing out surplus words. One brilliant one will work better than a dozen mundane ones.

Don't fall into the mindset that writing for children is easy. It has all the disciplines of writing for adults, with the added problem of understanding a child's mind and world. The great writers have a passport to a child's world – think of Roald Dahl. I have seen many brilliant ideas, with less than brilliant pictures, make wonderful books. I have seen a bad idea saved by wonderful illustrations. So, writing style apart, be your own concept's greatest critic. It is quite natural to be protective of your baby, of your story. But try to remember that there are a lot of good editors out there and it will be in your own interest to consider their advice. So don't be a young fogey: be flexible, listen, understand experi-enced points of view. This can be a good time to change for the better, and to start a relationship with one publishing house that may serve you for a lifetime.

Great Tip No. 4: Choose what you draw

Don't plan huge drawing problems into your submitted roughs. They may be accepted, and the editor will expect the final art to be better than the roughs.

I illustrate my own writing. This appeals to me for all sorts of reasons, few of them noble. Firstly, I get all of the available fee or/and royalty because I don't have to let half or more go to a writer. Secondly, if there is something I don't like to draw, I don't write about it. For instance, most of my stories take place in the summer, because I prefer to handle trees with their leaves on.

Illustrations being worked on to be published is not the place to practise your drawing. *Practise, change, experiment* all the time, but not in a publishing project. Your finished illustrations must be as good as you can make them. I know an illustrator who won't draw feet, always hiding the ends of legs in grass, water, behind rocks, etc. This is okay if the text will allow; a well-drawn puddle is better than a badly drawn foot any day. It is better to think around a drawing problem, than just to go along with it.

Great Tip No. 5: Experiment with your main character
Before you start, try drawing your main character (the most important visual element of the story) in all sorts of ways. A day spent doing this can be so valuable. Getting the main character right can indicate ways to proceed with the whole book.

Great Tip No. 6: Think global
Remember that editors react well to stories with wide appeal, rather than minority groups. Foreign sales are in everyone's interest, so try to allow your work to travel. Rhyme is sometimes difficult to translate, as are unusual plays on words.

Great Tip No. 7: Plan the whole book
Do little mock-up books for yourself to plan what text goes on which page. This helps to get the story right throughout the book. A 32-page children's book (the most common extent for a picture book) includes covers, end papers, title and half-title pages. This leaves you 23–25 pages to play with. These little mock-ups are for your own use, not to be presented as roughs, so they can be quite workaday.

By working out what text goes on which page you will get some sort of an idea of which illustrations go where. Just as the drawings are creative, so is their use on the page. If you use a full double-page spread, another can be expected to follow it. But imagine the effect if the next page explodes with huge typography, and tiny pictures? I am not suggesting you do this, only reminding you that pages of a book are there to be turned, and the turning can be unpredictable and adventurous. Book design is important, along with everything else.

Great Tip No. 8: Persevere
So much to do, so much to remember. The main thing is, every children's illustrator and writer I know who has kept trying has got there in the end and been published. But I've also seen great talents give up far too early. Remember that rejection is normal: it's only someone's point of view. Some great books have had long hunts for a publisher. Be open to change and always bear in mind that editors have the experience that you may lack and an editor's advice is meant to help you, not choke you off. However, not all of their advice may apply in your case, so try to recognise what applies to you. When I worked in advertising, I had an art director who said: 'Half of what I say is rubbish. Trouble is, I don't know which half.'

Illustration

And a reminder

Don't waste time by sending work to publishers who don't publish material like yours. Libraries and bookshops are worth exploring to familiarise yourself with which publishing houses favour what types of work. Research of this kind is time well spent.

Try to show your work in person so that you get a chance to talk, and learn. Do not, however, just drop in. Make an appointment first and hope that these busy people have some time available.

There are also agents prepared to represent new talent (see *Illustrators' agents* on page 289). Of course, an agent will take a percentage of the fee for work sold, but as my dad used to say, '75% of something is better than 100% of nothing.'

I am troubled by giving advice. I can't help thinking of the young composer who approached the slightly older Mozart and asked, 'Maestro, how should I compose a concerto?' to which Mozart replied, 'You are very young, perhaps you should start with a simple tune'.

The young composer frowned and argued: 'But, Maestro, *you* composed a concerto when you were still a child!'

'Ah yes,' said Mozart, 'but I didn't have to ask how'.

Tony Ross is a renowned illustrator of international repute and the creator of such classics as *The Little Princess* and *I Want My Potty*. His first book was published in 1976 and since then he has illustrated around 3,000 books including titles by David Walliams, Astrid Lindgren, Francesca Simon, Roald Dahl and Jeanne Willis. His most recent books are *An Anty-War Story* (2018) and *Silly Mr Wolf* (2019) both published by Andersen Press.

See also...

Writing and illustrating picture books

Debi Gliori tells the story of how she started writing and illustrating children's books.

The prospect of spending your life making children's books has a great deal to recommend it, not least the fact that you will never have to buy those nasty big itchy rolls of rockwool to insulate the walls of your home ever again. Twelve thousand or so volumes will do the job far better. Following the children's books career path will ensure that books will pour into your home, year after year, yours and other people's; foreign editions and large-print versions; pop-ups and boards; collections and anthologies; so many that you might think about studying 'Elementary Bookshelf Building for Beginners and Fumblethumbs' before your piles of books reach to the ceiling. You will also be forced to develop a pronounced and sincerely apologetic grovel each time your postman staggers laden to your door – after all, his sciatica/lower back pain/slipped disc is *entirely your fault*.

Tottering heaps of hardbacks notwithstanding, I can say, with hand-on-heart, that being a children's author and illustrator is the best job in the world. I'm not alone in this opinion. Some years ago, a midwife visited me in the studio I work from in my garden and said, apropos of nothing: 'Eee lass, you've landed with your bum in the butter'.

Unsurprisingly, I looked suitably horrified. (What *was* this, pray? Surely not more indignities to be visited upon my person in the name of childbirth?) Seeing my expression, she hastily explained that what she had *meant* was that I was exceedingly fortunate to be paid to do what I love best. 'Bum in the butter' huh? Takes all sorts. But hey, Gentle Reader, it was not always thus. Back in the mists of that ghastly period of human history known as the Eighties when I set off on this Quest for Publication, I recall that I underwent a long period of major struggle during which many lentils were consumed. This was a lengthy phase which also involved dressing in the morning *in* bed, serious layering of woolly jumpers and, I kid you not, bathrooms so cold that one's toothbrush *froze*.

After graduation from Edinburgh College of Art, I trawled round London publishers with my too-big portfolio and quickly realised that good picture book texts were as rare as talking bears. While illustrators, such as I'd been studying to become, were everywhere in abundance. Encouraging, *not*.

Stubborn is my middle name. That's right, Debi Stubborn Gliori – I know it's weird, but parents ... pffff, what can I say? Anyway, stubbornly I decided that there was no way that I was going to take on a badly paid job to 'support' my unpaid non-existent career in children's books. That would be *two* jobs. I mean, get real. Nor did I much fancy the kind of grinding-noble-poverty-consumption-in-a-garret artist's lifestyle afforded by a complete lack of cash. Mercenary little beast that I was, I picked up as many well-paid advertising jobs as possible (illustrating whisky labels and smoked salmon packaging, mainly) and in my spare time hauled myself off to libraries and bookshops and did my research. Who was publishing what? Why were these books published rather than, say, *mine*? What was fashionable and why? Did retellings work? Were books for babies no-brainers? Trust me, it wasn't all that hard for me to see what was required from a good picture book. I won't insult your intelligence by telling you. You know this stuff. Or if you don't, you'll pick it up quickly.

So, armed with a rough idea of what first publishers, then parents and finally, children might want (the order is, sadly, significant), I holed myself up in a 1.2 square metre cupboard and wrote a book which, joy of joys, was picked off the Walker Books slush pile and published. Read my lips: at that point, I had no 'in' in publishing – no contacts, no money and no influence. I was a single parent living in a freezing cold, damp cottage waaaaay out in the sticks in Scotland. And yet, and yet, and yet, I managed to get my book published. The message here is Take Heart. It *can* be done.

Making a picture book the Gliori way

How I go about starting to make a book from scratch is another matter. All of us approach the process of creating picture books from a multitude of different directions. For what it's worth, here's how I go about it. Although I always start with the text, nine times out of ten the initial idea for a book arrives in my head as a couple of images that I know I'd love to paint. Unsurprisingly, I never experience a burning desire to make a book that involves cars or horses, mainly because I cannot draw either. On the other hand, I love landscapes. So, for example, there's a scene in one of my early books called *Mr Bear Babysits* in which Mr Bear is walking home by moonlight through trees, and all around him are baby animals, birds and insects being tucked in for the night. Immediately that image sparks off a series of questions. What season would this be set in? Answer – summer, because then I can draw golden moonlit fields and haystacks. What time is it? Probably after midnight. Why is Mr Bear out so late? Maybe he's having a *liaison dangereux* with Mrs Grizzle-Bear ... or then again, perhaps not. Let's imagine he's been babysitting for the Grizzle-Bear cubs. How many? Three. Heavens, poor Grizzle-Bears, they must *really* need a night off. What are the cubs like? Rumbustious. Has Mr Bear got kids of his own? Is he going home? Is this the end or is it the beginning? You can see the process, can't you? By trying to supply answers to my own questions, I am effortlessly beginning to build a framework round which I could start to construct a narrative.

I wouldn't like you to think that it's easy though. Frequently, the entire framework begins to assume the tensile properties of overcooked tagliatelle, at which point I will decide that this is an idea that's not ready to be written yet. I have several of these raw and palely loitering things tucked away in various notebooks, and once in a while I'll drag them out into the unforgiving daylight; poke, prod and play with them until they turn to mush at which point, with deep regret, I'll put them back and try a different tack. Sometimes, to my delight, the poking and prodding succeeds and a picture book text emerges, oozing and flubby in parts, but with a decent story at its heart. Over the course of the next month, I'll return to that text and read it out loud until my ears bleed, because reading out loud is the single best way for me to expose flaws, glitches and bumpy bits before I self-edit in what I blithely imagine to be a ruthlessly incisive fashion.

Afterwards, breathless and pink with the unaccustomed exertion, I type it out and email it to my editor. When I was a beginner, I would assemble a thick envelope in which I included the following items for editor-seduction purposes: one lovingly typed covering letter on headed stationery, one double-spaced (with Tipp-Ex blobs) manuscript (both typed and corrected on an ancient manual typewriter bought in a junk shop), a set of thumbnail sketches showing how I anticipated pacing the text and pictures over 32 pages, two hideously expensive colour photocopies of two spreads of artwork and one sae for the return of said hideously expensive samples. And then I would wait ... and wait ... and wait.

These days, it varies. Depending on which publishing house I'm working with, if an editor likes my initial idea, she or he usually lets me know within a month of my email.

This is only the first of many stages, however. An editor has still to pass the idea round his or her colleagues and garner feedback from fellow editors, sales, marketing, bean counters, that talented bloke down in the post room and Melissa who is *terrifically* good at spotting a dud but is invariably off on sick leave on the day of the week when these meetings happen. These days, I'm beginning to wonder if actually being published has anything to do with talent, and has more to do with simple good fortune. Several books ago, my editor knew my work and trusted me. I suspect she was the human equivalent of a Sherman tank and simply swept all objections out of the way in order to publish what she believed to be the holy grail of publishing; an evergreen that would go on selling in the multiple thousands for many decades. However, we're living and publishing in *interesting* times nowadays. The business of books has changed beyond recognition. We grizzled veterans meet at book festivals and nod meaningfully at each other over the heads of the bright and shiny debut authors. *You'll learn*, we mutter balefully. *Once, I was just like you, but look at me now.*

Supposing my text actually does pass this first winnowing process (or *round* as they are known – as in a boxing round) there's a little back and forth and text tweaking between the editor and myself followed by my drafting out very detailed black-and-white pencil roughs showing how I intend each spread to look. Back these go to round two.

Months pass, depending on where in the calendar my initial submission has fallen. The pre-Christmas period is a bad time to expect anything to happen, January is full of norovirus and flu, February and March aren't too good because of the run-up to the Bologna book fair, as is May because there's the post-Bologna and London Book Fair catch-up and meeting-fest and then there's the Silly Season of summer vacations which seems to span July through to the end of September. So I've realised that it might be expedient to start something entirely new while I wait. My editor may leave the company for pastures new, leaving me with a slightly different team working on my book than before. This also slows things down as the new addition(s) need to get bedded in before they can make any decisions on anything much other than which colour of chair they'd like and their password for the office database.

Finally, my roughs make their way back, no longer peppered with post-it notes (*o tempora, o mores*) but sent by cyberpost with a liberal drizzling of yellow digital notebook comments. Only *suggestions*, Debi. Put that axe down. And back we go for round three. More roughs. More meetings. Another round (four) by which time I can barely remember what it was I was trying to say. I peer at the text, wondering if it bears any relation to me. Like – who wrote this thing? I struggle with redoing roughs, mainly because they're so very hard to do (pulling images out of the ether? that's a pretty good job description for an illustrator) and the more I tweak and discard and redo, the more overworked the whole project begins to feel. I don't work on a computer, so all my roughs are drawn by hand, over and over and over again. Back they go for what one sincerely hopes is the final round (five) and then I wait. Regardless of how long I wait at this stage, I can guarantee that five months after being given the final go-ahead, I will deliver camera-ready artwork.

Proofs and publication

Back when I was starting out, nothing much happened after I delivered a book. There was a lull and then the first proofs arrived – a stage I loved, and still love, because suddenly the whole book appears to fall into focus – it looks like a real book at last and it's one of many identical copies, thus saving me from my illustrator's artwork-related paranoia about someone accidentally dropping a slice of raw tomato onto it. Before you dismiss me as neurotic, Gentle Reader, let me say that this tomato-on-watercolour-artwork-falling-in-cident really happened. He'll never walk again without a limp, though. After the heady rush of seeing my work in proof form, came the not-so heady rush of publication day, which came … and went, unremarked. Sometimes there would be a wee card in the post, signed by everyone who'd had anything to do with the book; sometimes I'd cook something special for my family, or bake a cake or just sit in my studio and gnaw my fingernails off one by one, wondering just how far we could make 10% of not a lot stretch.

These days, I'm so involved with my next project that I'll have achieved a measure of distance from the book just published. If my publishers think that the book is worth spending a large chunk of the publicity budget on, then I'll be out on tour, talking about my new book to lots of small children in various locations around the UK. This helps to get the book 'out there' and hopefully enables me to attend some of the more prestigious book festivals around the UK, and possibly sell some copies of the book in order to justify the publicity budget. Then I return home, sleep for 14 hours straight, and get back to writing and illustrating again.

What happens to your book from now on is, by and large, out of your hands. Publication date is the one that unpublished authors dream of: the day you see *your* book in print. Perhaps I'm just an old cynic, but seeing my book in mint condition in bookshops doesn't press any of my buttons whatsoever. No, what *I* want to see is *my* book being read till it *falls to bits*. I want to see the date-stamp page at the front of a library copy of one of my books full to the brim with the inky evidence of many withdrawals. *That's* the whole point. Being *read* – not being published.

But first you have to get published, and that's why we're here; you reading and me attempting to spout wisdom like an illustrator's version of the Delphic Oracle. Problem is, I'm not an oracle, and nor am I a teacher. All that I know is based on my own experience of the business. Your experience will be significantly different. Without sitting down beside you and looking over your text or your portfolio, the best advice I can give is *keep going*. Be stubborn – if you want to be published, you're going to have to be rhinoceros-like in your determination as well as acquiring a rhino-hide to shrug off those slings and arrows of unkind comment. Follow your own star, even if it's a redundant Russian satellite. Er, learn how to put up bookshelves and develop a series of nifty recipes for lentils. And good luck: like all the best things in life, the process of learning how to make picture books is well worth the effort.

Debi Gliori has written and illustrated numerous picture books and her best-loved titles include *No Matter What* (Bloomsbury Children's 1999) and *What's the Time, Mr Wolf?* (Bloomsbury 2012). She is also the author of the *Pure Dead…* series of novels for older children and the *Witch Baby and Me* series of books for in-between-picture-books-and-novels children. Her most recent books include *The Bookworm* (Bloomsbury Children's 2019), *Night Shift* (Hot Key Books 2017), a book about depression for YA and adults shortlisted for the 2018 Greenaway Award, and the picture book, *All the Way Home* (Bloomsbury 2017). She lives in Scotland and works from her International Shedquarters at the bottom of her garden. Her website is www.debiglioribooks.com.

See also...
• *Notes from a successful children's author and illustrator*, page 263

Illustrators' agents

Before submitting work, artists are advised to make preliminary enquiries and to ascertain terms of work. Commission varies but averages 25–30%. The Association of Illustrators (see page 364) provides a valuable service for illustrators, agents and clients.

*Member of the Society of Artists Agents
†Member of the Association of Illustrators

Illustration

Advocate Art Ltd

Suite 7, The Sanctuary, 23 Oakhill Grove, Surbiton, Surrey KT6 6DU
tel 020-8390 6293
email mail@advocate-art.com
website www.advocate-art.com
Director Edward Burns

Has seven agents representing 300 artists and illustrators. Bespoke illustration for children's books, greeting cards and fine art publishers, gift and ceramic manufacturers. For illustrators' submission guidelines see website. New: animation, design and original content represented through LaB – Writers and Artists colLaBorate. Also original art gallery, stock library and website in German, Spanish and French. Founded 1996.

Allied Artists/Artistic License

tel 07971 111256
email info@allied-artists.net
website www.alliedartists-illustration.com
Contact Gary Mills

Represents over 90 illustrators ranging in styles from realistic, through stylised to cute for all types of publishing but particularly children's illustration. Commission: 33%. Founded 1983.

Arena Illustration Ltd*†

Arena Illustration Ltd, 31 Eleanor Road, London E15 4AB
tel 020-8555 9827
website www.arenaillustration.com
Contact Tamlyn Francis

Represents 25 artists illustrating mostly for book covers, children's books and design groups. Average commission: 25%. Founded 1970.

The Art Agency

21 Morris Street, Sheringham, Norfolk NR26 8JY
tel (01263) 823424
email artagency@me.com
website www.the-art-agency.co.uk
Facebook www.facebook.com/illustrationagency

Provides non-fiction, reference and children's book illustration. Specialises in non-fiction illustrations across a wide variety of subjects and age groups. Submit by email up to six samples along with a link to your website. Founded 1990.

The Artworks†

12–18 Hoxton Street, London N1 6NG
tel 020-7729 1973
email mail@theartworksinc.com
website www.theartworksinc.com
Contacts Lucy Scherer, Stephanie Alexander-Jinks, Alex Gardner

Represents 35 illustrators for design and advertising work as well as for non-fiction children's books, book jackets, illustrated gift books and children's picture books. Commission: 25% advances, 15% royalties, 25% book jackets. Founded 1983.

Beehive Illustration

42A Cricklade Street, Cirencester, Glos. GL7 1JH
tel (01285) 644001
email enquiries@beehiveillustration.co.uk
website www.beehiveillustration.co.uk
Contact Paul Beebee

Represents 200 artists specialising in ELT, education and general children's publishing illustration. Commission: 25%. Founded 1989.

The Big Red Illustration Agency

tel 0808 120 0996
email enquiries@bigredillustrationagency.com
website www.bigredillustrationagency.com
Director Adam Rushton

Presents portfolios of over 50 artists creating work for children's book publishers, design agencies, greeting cards and toy companies. Founded 2012.

The Bright Agency

103–105 St John's Hill, London SW11 1SY
tel 020-7326 9140
US Office 50 West Street, C12, New York, NY 10006
tel +1 646-604-0992
email mail@thebrightagency.com
website www.thebrightagency.com
Managing Director & Founder (UK) Vicki Willden-Lebrecht, *Publishing Agent (UK)* Arabella Stein, *Publishing Agent (US)* Anne Moore Armstrong, *Publishing Agent (US)* James Burns, *Senior Agent, Educational Illustration (UK)* Lucie Luddington, *Senior Agent for Children's & Fiction (UK)* Nicky Lander, *Senior Agent for Art Licensing & Illustration (UK)* Hannah Curtis, *Senior Creative Executive, Children's Content (UK)* Courtney Arumugam

Represents artists who work in children's publishing covering all ages.

Jenny Brown Associates – see page 248

The Catchpole Agency
53 Cranham Street, Oxford OX2 6DD
tel 07789 588070
email james@thecatchpoleagency.co.uk
email celia@thecatchpoleagency.co.uk
website www.thecatchpoleagency.co.uk
Proprietors James Catchpole, Celia Catchpole

Agents for authors and illustrators of children's books from picture books through to young adult novels. Commission from 12.5% to 15%. See website for contact and submissions details. See also page 249. Founded 1996.

The Copyrights Group Ltd
6th Floor, 4 Pancras Square, London N1C 4AG
tel 020-880 0134
email enquiries@copyrights.co.uk
website www.copyrights.co.uk
SVP Licensing UK Rachel Clarke, *SVP Brand and International Licensing* Polly Emery, *VP Creative Services* Demi Patel

A Vivendi company, a full-service international brand licensing company offering strategic worldwide brand development, licensing and retail expertise. Focuses on the long-term development of quality merchandise programmes around the world. Properties include *Paddington Bear*, *The Country Diary of an Edwardian Lady*, *Father Christmas*, *Fungus The Bogey Man* and *Greenwich Polo Club*. Founded 1984.

David Lewis Agency
3 Somali Road, London NW2 3RN
tel 020-7435 7762, 07931 824674
email davidlewis34@hotmail.com
Director David Lewis

All kinds of material for all areas of children's publishing, including educational, merchandising and toys. Represents approx. 25 artists, half of whom produce children's material. Also considers complete picture books with text. Send A4 colour or b&w copies of samples with return postage. Commission: 30%. Founded 1974.

Good Illustration Ltd
11–15 Betterton Street, Covent Garden, London WC2H 9BP
tel 020-8123 0243 (UK), +1 347-627-0243 (US)
email draw@goodillustration.com
website www.goodillustration.com
Directors Doreen Thorogood, Kate Webber, Tom Thorogood

Represents 50+ artists for advertising, design, publishing, animation. Send return postage and samples. Commission: 25% publishing, 30% advertising. Founded 1977.

Graham-Cameron Illustration
59 Hertford Road, Brighton BN1 7GG
tel (01273) 385890
email enquiry@gciforillustration.com
Alternative address The Art House, Uplands Park, Sheringham, Norfolk NR26 8NE
tel (01263) 821333
website www.gciforillustration.com
Partners Helen Graham-Cameron, Duncan Graham-Cameron

Represents 37+ artists and undertakes illustration for publishing and communications. Specialises in educational, children's and information books. Phone before sending A4 samples with sae or email samples or link to a website. No MSS. Founded 1985.

David Higham Associates Ltd – see page 252

Inky Illustration
32 Brook House, Brook Street, Tipton DY4 9DD
(0121) 330 1312
email info@inkyillustration.com
website https://inkyillustration.com/
Facebook www.facebook.com/inkyillustration/
Twitter @inkyillo

The agency showcases the work of talented artists from across the globe. Their range of illustrators have experience working with clients, including working on international advertising campaigns, publications and editorials, as well as commissions for smaller companies. The agency is always pleased to receive new work. New artists should fill out the application form on the website or email to: submissions@inkyillustration.com. Hard copies of work are accepted with a self-addressed envelope if the work is to be returned.

B.L. Kearley Ltd
16 Chiltern Street, London W1U 7PZ
tel 020-7935 9550
email christine.kearley@kearley.co.uk
website www.kearley.co.uk
Agent C.R. Kearley

Represents over 30 artists and has been supplying top-quality illustrations for over 60 years. Mainly specialises in children's book and educational illustration for the domestic market and overseas. Known for realistic figurative work. Specialises in the sale of original book illustration artwork. Commission: 25%. Founded 1948.

Kids Corner
The Old Candlemakers, West Street, Lewes BN7 2NZ
tel 020-7593 0506

email claire@meiklejohn.co.uk
website www.kidscornerillustration.co.uk
Managing Director Claire Meiklejohn

Represents illustrators, from award-winning to emerging artists for children's publishing. Styles include fun, cute, stylised, picture book, young fiction, reference, graphic, traditional, painterly and digital. Founded 2015.

LAW (Lucas Alexander Whitley Ltd)
2nd Floor, 16–17 Wardour Mews, London W1F 8AT
tel 020-7471 7900
website www.lawagency.co.uk
Contacts Philippa Milnes-Smith

Illustrations for children's publishing for children 0–16 years. See website for submission requirements. Particular interest in authors/artists creating their own projects. Clients include Chris Judge, Philip Reeve, Chris Riddell, Emily Gravet, Steve McCarthy and Jane Porter. Commission: 15% (20% overseas). See also page 252. Founded 1996.

Frances McKay Illustration
17 Church Road, West Mersea, Essex CO5 8QH
tel (01206) 383286
email frances@francesmckay.com
website www.francesmckay.com
Proprietor Frances McKay

Represents 15–20 artists for illustration mainly for children's books. For information on submissions please look at website. Submit email with low-res scans or colour copies of recent work; sae essential for return of all unsolicited samples sent by post. Commission: 25%. Founded 1999.

NB Illustration
40 Bowling Green Lane, London EC1R 0NE
tel 07720 827328
email info@nbillustration.co.uk
website www.nbillustration.co.uk
Directors Joe Najman, Charlotte Dowson

Represents over 50 artists, 40% of whom produce children's material for picture books and educational publishing. For submission details see website. Submissions by email only. Commission: 30%. Founded 2000.

The Organisation
6 Manor Wood, Chepstow, Gwent NP16 6DS
tel 07973 172902
email info@organisart.co.uk
website www.organisart.co.uk
Contact Lorraine Owen

Represents 60 artists, 75% of whom produce children's material for all ages. Can supply both traditional and digital illustration for all markets. Also produces illustrations for other print markets, advertising, packaging and editorial. Before submitting samples research the website. New artists

must not have a similar style to one already represented. Send samples by email no larger than 8mb. Average commission: 30%. Founded 1987.

Plum Pudding Illustration
Chapel House, St. Lawrences Way, Reigate, Surrey RH2 7AF
tel (01737) 244095
email letterbox@plumpuddingillustration.com
website www.plumpuddingillustration.com
Director Mark Mills *Associate Director* Hannah Whitty

Represents 100+ artists, producing illustrations for children's publishing, advertising, editorial, greeting cards and packaging. See website for submission procedure. Commission: 30%. Founded 2006.

Sylvie Poggio Artists Agency
36 Haslemere Road, London N8 9RB
tel 020-8341 2722
email sylviepoggio@blueyonder.co.uk
website www.sylviepoggio.com
Directors Sylvie Poggio, Bruno Caurat

Represents 40 artists producing illustrations for publishing and advertising. Founded 1996.

Elizabeth Roy Literary Agency
White Cottage, Greatford, Nr Stamford, Lincs. PE9 4PR
tel (01778) 560672
website http://elizabethroy.co.uk

Handles illustrations for children's books. Only interested in exceptional material. Illustrators should research the children's book market before sending samples, which must include figure work. Send by post with return postage; no CD, disk or email submissions. See also page 255. Founded 1990.

Caroline Sheldon Literary Agency Ltd
71 Hillgate Place, London W8 7SS
tel 020-727 9102
email carolinesheldon@carolinesheldon.co.uk
email felicitytrew@carolinesheldon.co.uk
website www.carolinesheldon.co.uk
Twitter @CarolineAgent
Twitter @FelicityTrew
Contacts Caroline Sheldon, Felicity Trew

Represents leading illustrators of children's books working in a broad range of styles, selling their work throughout the world and in all media. All genres of illustration including humour, cartoon, realism, avant-garde and unusual. Commission: UK 15%, USA/translation 20%, film/TV 20%. Submission guidelines: Illustrators – send an introductory email with work attached or a link to your work. In the subject line write 'Proposal from Illustrator', and include information about yourself and your work in the email. Clients: represents prominent, award-winning and bestselling clients in all fields including books, illustration, audio, digital and theatre. Works closely with a media agent on Film, TV and other opportunities. Exclusions: None. See also page 255. Founded 1985.

Vicki Thomas Associates

195 Tollgate Road, London E6 5JY
tel 020-7511 5767
email vickithomasassociates@yahoo.co.uk
website www.vickithomasassociates.com
Facebook www.facebook.com/vickithomasassociates
Twitter @VickiThomasA
Consultant Vicki Thomas

Represents approx. 50 artists, 75% of whom produce children's material for all ages. Specialises in gift products and considers images for publishing, toys, stationery, clothing, decorative accessories. Email sample images, covering letter and CV. Commission: 30%. Founded 1985.

United Agents LLP

12–26 Lexington Street, London W1F 0LE
tel 020-3214 0800
email info@unitedagents.co.uk
website www.unitedagents.co.uk
Agent Jodie Hodges (née Marsh)

Represents illustrators of children's books for all ages (home 15%, USA/translation 20%). See website for submission details. Founded 2008.

Magazines and newspapers
Writing for the teenage market

How can a writer try to please today's teenage audience, who have so many added distractions, demands and pressures on their time? Michelle Garnett sets out some important guidelines, advising you to jettison any preconceptions and to respect the individuality, intelligence and concerns of this complex and fascinating age group.

There's no denying that the reading habits of teenagers have changed dramatically in recent years. Rewind to the 1990s and most likely your average adolescent reader would be sitting quietly, turning the pages of a book or a magazine. Fast forward to the present day and they're scouring their iPhone on the move, or devouring information on their tablet or laptop in bite-sized chunks. It's not surprising, considering 83% of 12–15 year-olds now own smartphones and 99% go online for nearly 21 hours a week (Ofcom – *Children and Parents: Media Use and Attitudes Report* 2017).

But enough of the stats. Times might be a-changing, but teenagers are still the same complex – and fascinating – individuals they ever were. Adolescence is an intense time. Just starting out in the world, teens are attempting to navigate the transition from child-hood to adulthood, walking the fine line between feeling invincible and feeling totally lost, while ticking off a rapid succession of firsts: first love, first car, first job, first holiday with their mates ... the list goes on.

They're breaking away from their parents and making their own decisions – and con-sequently notching up a fair few mistakes along the way. They're also starting to look outward, finding their place in the world and figuring out how their actions affect others. And with the advent of the internet and the rise of social media they're having to grow up faster than ever, with so many distractions and demands on their time.

So with all this in mind, how does a writer even begin to try to please these (demanding, streetwise and fickle) customers?

1. Get to know your readers

If you're going to write for a teen audience you've got to get into their mindset and suss out what makes them tick. Young people are too often made to feel inconsequential and their views are commonly ignored. Talk to them, ask their opinion, find out what their priorities are, what fires their passions, what dreams and ambitions they have. They'll appreciate your interest – and, given the chance to talk, they'll be searingly honest.

You also need to discover how much they already know about your proposed subject, whether you're likely to be challenging any prejudices and what kind of questions your feature might prompt. By painting a clear picture of your reader in your mind you'll find it so much easier to define your motive. They'll only care how much you know when you show how much you care – and that means showing that you're aware of who they are and what they're about.

2. Lay off the teen slang

If you're talking to teens, you need to use their lingo, right? Wrong. Forget about any attempts to sound cool. Put down that 'yoof' dictionary. You'll struggle to keep up with their ever-evolving language and your efforts will reek of 'trying too hard' – a trait that's a total no-no when it comes to appealing to young people.

'*When adults use text talk or slang it's annoying and embarrassing*', confirms Emily (16). '*Teenagers don't actually say LOL when they're talking.*'

Instead, be direct and informative. Adopt an authoritative tone, but keep it chatty.

3. Offer reassurance

Puberty is a confusing, and sometimes lonely, time. Reach out to your readers by talking about their worries and insecurities. Sure, not all of them are necking vodka in their school lunch break, risking unprotected sex or having panic attacks over their exams, but for many, it's their reality. Whether it's bullying, unwanted pregnancy, peer pressure, drugs, abusive relationships or an uncertain future, it's happening out there all around them and even if your readers aren't directly experiencing these issues, you can bet a classmate, a teen neighbour or a 'friend of a friend' will be.

Teen magazines historically adopted the guiding tone of an older sister. It's a good starting point. Build trust by being frank with your facts and crystal clear with your message. And be sure to let your readers know that they're not alone.

4. Celebrate individuality

The teen years are full of contradictions. Most young people yearn to belong and be part of a community while also testing out their emerging individual attributes and attitudes, and pinpointing what makes them unique. Big up that uniqueness. Let them know it's good to be different.

And avoid making assumptions about what motivates them. They don't all aspire to being permatanned, WAG-wannabes or football fanatics with chiselled six-packs. Goth girl, tech geek, eco-warrior, skater boy ... they're all guises teens adopt as they seek out their true identities.

Jack (14) points out that teens' interests are as far-reaching and diverse as those of adults: '*We don't all listen to R&B, you know. One of my friends listens to opera music!*'

Carla (16) agrees: '*I can't bear it when all teens get tarred with the same brush. Adults assume we're all the same, but very few teenagers are 'yobs', hanging around in parks causing trouble, and we're not all 100% obsessed with social media. We have other interests too.*'

And get this: some teens are well-rounded, untroubled, rational individuals who, contrary to the navel-gazing, introspective stereotype, are (gasp!) capable of showing interest in and empathy for others.

5. Don't underestimate teens ... ever

Today's teens are far savvier than previous generations. They have the world with all its gritty realism at the swipe of a finger. What's more, having come to the realisation that their parents don't actually know as much as they initially made out, they have a tendency to mistrust 'adults telling them how it is'.

So don't lecture them or come across as 'preachy' and condescending. Most teens have a finely tuned, built-in radar that hones in on an author who believes themselves to be superior simply because of their more advanced years. After all, the majority of young people soak up the same TV programmes and websites as adults, and those nearing the end of their teen years are only a short amble from adulthood itself.

As 16 year-old Sam points out, '*I don't think there always needs to be much deviation when writing for teens from how you would write for adults. I'm obviously not speaking for all of teen-kind, but there's so many mind-numbing reality shows and celebrity magazines out there, I actually enjoy having my intellect challenged now and then.*'

Respect their intelligence and integrity.

6. Find your inner teen

You were an adolescent yourself once upon a time (maybe not that long ago in fact), so dredge the deep recesses of your mind for memories of your youth. One word of caution: beware when making references to popular teen culture. Raving on about the finer points of NSYNC's first album or discussing the complex love triangles on *Dawson's Creek* will blow your cover. Remember, most of your readers were still in nappies when Busted bounced onto the pop scene. Gulp …

7. Consider the where and when

Think about where and when your teen readers are likely to be reading your copy. Will you have their full concentration or will they be interacting with other media at the same time (listening to music on their iPod or phone, watching TV, messaging their mates)?

Keep the flow of your writing fast-paced. Use shorter, to-the-point sentences and split up long copy with frequent paragraph breaks. Your article will appear less daunting and your readers will have more opportunity to dip in and out as desired. With so many distractions threatening to steal their attention, there's an even greater need than normal to write a punchy opener, use bullet points, lists, sub-heads and box features to create an easily digestible format and create a clear, logical structure.

'*It's easier to read features when they're broken up into chunks. Then you can just choose the bits that are more interesting or apply to you,*' says Clara (16). But as Jack (14) rightly points out, '*It's important to get the correct balance. You want some detail in there so the feature is useful, but if it's too long, it just becomes plain dull.*'

8. Think about your tone

The success of books like *The Hunger Games*, with its themes of warfare, betrayal and sacrifice, and the *Twilight* series, which explores vampire-slaying and the old standby of Good versus Evil, is proof of teenagers' craving to read about the deeper, darker side of reality.

What attracts them? Well, adult and teen brains work differently. Adults think with the rational area of their noggins, while teens use the emotional part and they're hungry for gritty, thought-provoking material.

They also have a thirst for humour. With exams, emotional upheavals and friendship issues to contend with, life can be tense. '*Even when I'm reading about a serious subject, I don't want it to be written in a long-winded, serious way,*' says Jack (14).

Entertain them. Make them laugh. Play up to their love of sarcasm and dry wit.

9. Relax the rules of grammar

I'm not suggesting you take an anarchic approach to grammar, dropping punctuation and scrimping on your syntax with every tap of your keyboard, but remember: this is one audience who might appreciate you being a little more informal with your writing. Feel free to allow sentences to end abruptly and prematurely or to double back on themselves.

Magazines and newspapers

As long as you put your point across clearly, a casual regard of the rules will give your text a more youthful, friendlier feel.

10. Give them what they want

Avoid topics that your audience have had more than enough of from teachers, parents and other scholarly types. '*I like reading things that we don't learn in school – advice that's useful to my age group, like how to travel safely alone,*' says Emily (16).

Put simply, yet another 'How To' guide to studying will provoke immediate boredom. Sure there's already a plethora of features online exploring drugs, self-harm, sexism, eating disorders – but that's why it's your challenge to take on an old issue that affects your audience directly, and to find a new angle to tackle it from. Reading about other teens' lives is also a winner, nine times out of ten, but the stories don't have to be overwhelmingly traumatic and depressing. Choose ones that show the wonderful variety amongst the young individuals out there.

To sum up

Shake off those preconceptions of the stereotypical teen; recognise the demands being placed on their rapidly eroding free time; give young people the respect they deserve – and the credit to handle weighty issues with intelligence and empathy, and offer them reading matter that doesn't just dish out the same old lazy messages, but ignites their enthusiasm, seeks to reassure them, and empowers them to greater thoughts and actions.

Michelle Garnett is an ex-teen magazine editor who now divides her time between copy-writing and subbing for various B2B publications, and writing, interviewing and editing at weekly celebrity titles including *OK!* magazine. Her website is www.michellegarnett.co.uk.

See also...
- *Writing for a variety of ages,* page 124
- *Writing for teenagers,* page 159
- *Writing crime fiction for teenagers,* page 162
- *Writing thrillers for teenagers,* page 165

Creating a children's comic

Tom Fickling shares his passion and enthusiasm for the weekly comic, no longer a thing of the past but an exciting, cutting-edge technology with the ability to inspire a love of reading. He describes the reader-focused philosophy which drives the creativity of his team at *The Phoenix*.

Just as my deadline for this article was looming we found out that our printer had gone into administration. Not a nice thing to hear when you have the relentless *Phoenix* schedule perched on your shoulder, but also not an enormous surprise. The print business is a tough one, with ridiculously tight margins and expensive machinery that takes years to earn out.

But though it wasn't much of a shock, it was panic stations at *Phoenix* HQ. Because when you make a comic that comes out every week of the year, usually on the same day (it's called 'Phoenix Friday'), not having a printer can really throw a spanner in the works!

Everyone in the team shared the same immediate thought: 'We have to ensure the readers get their comic next week!'. It doesn't matter what you make – be it book or comic or something else – the reader should come first. That is perhaps brought into starker relief with a weekly publication because you have to make a lot of decisions on a very tight timescale, with the impact of those decisions being felt only a few days later. But it's true across the board.

We often get asked why we started *The Phoenix*, and of course there are lots of reasons, but ultimately the answer is: for the readers. But what does that really mean? And why do these readers (or in this case, children) need a weekly comic? After all, common sense tells us that weekly comics are a thing of the past and that's where they should stay.

People say we need to move forward, that we need new and exciting things. You know, tablets and gadgets and VR headsets and the like. (Alright, we definitely need the headsets). Comics may have been around for a while but I want to tell you that, far from being outdated, comics are a *cutting-edge technology*. A cutting-edge *reading* technology.

That's the thing about *common sense* – it never really leads anywhere interesting. And while *The Phoenix* may be a weekly comic, we prefer to think of it as a medium that has been honed and crafted over the years until it has become the most incredible story-delivery device known to adult or child. And it's one that goes right to the homes of children across the country. Wham! What a delight! What a wonder! It's a story-jack that feeds straight into the brains of children every week.

Our aim at *The Phoenix* is simple: to delight, to inspire, to fill minds with awe and wonder. Above all *The Phoenix* is *for* its readers. We want to make them go 'wow' when they tear open that envelope. We want their hearts pounding with excitement. We want them hooked on story, totally mesmerised by fascinating non-fiction, and their minds blown to smithereens by awesome puzzles.

We try desperately hard to inhabit the minds of those reading the comic. We don't always get it right, of course. But this celebration of the reader was instilled in me by my father. He's a publisher and he's published some stone-cold classics. In fact, of the 2016 World Book Day top 10 list of future children's book classics, he had published three of them. And commissioned a fourth that was on the list. So on these matters I take his advice quite seriously. (See *What makes a children's classic?* on page 4.)

That cherishing of the reader and how they feel has been drummed into me. It is one of the most valuable pieces of advice I have ever received. And it applies to writers and artists as much as it does to publishers. It goes right to the heart of what I believe to be one of the key skills of a great storyteller. And I use the term 'storyteller' to mean anyone who is trying to convey a story via some creative medium. It's not just about writing – which seems a frequent misconception. That great skill is the ability to hold what *you* want as the creator side by side with what you think the *reader* wants: being able to satisfy your own creative urges while not disappointing the person consuming your story. It's hard. It means holding doubt and confidence hand in hand, both of which can be damaging in their own way.

At *The Phoenix* this means publishing things we know for a fact that children will love, alongside things that we *think* they will love. Because often the reader doesn't *know* what they want. And asking them what they want rarely produces the right answer. As Henry Ford said, if he'd asked people what they wanted before he mass-produced the first car they'd have just asked for a faster horse. It's the same with books. It took J.K. Rowling, not a focus group, to introduce us to Harry Potter. Philip Pullman conjured *His Dark Materials* from a lifetime of thinking and the words of Milton, not from a feedback form.

All this focus on the reader is not entirely altruistic. The thinking goes like this: make an awesome comic that a child and their family will love. Not *like*, but *love*. And love so much they want to tell people about it. The more they love it, the more people they will tell, and the more readers we will have. We do think of them first, not what they can do for us (though, of course, we think of that too).

So back to the question; why start *The Phoenix*? Well, a weekly comic is a great way to inspire love. Love of stories and, importantly, love of reading. Think about it – has a better hook for reading been invented? Regular exciting stories, the anticipation of its arrival, the cliffhanger, the enormous array of content, and lots more. There are other magazines for children that care about things like this. *Okido*, *Anorak*, *Aquila* and so on. But these are all independent companies, just like *The Phoenix*. Most other publications for children seem to spend little on storytelling and much more on marketing, plastic cover mounted toys and promotion. That's why *The Phoenix* is a subscription-focused comic that relies on word of mouth to really drive it. And word of mouth comes from love and passion and trust in something – which all originates from the reader.

But to inspire love you need amazing content. We are tremendously lucky to work with some incredible story creators at *The Phoenix*. Some are writers, some artists, many are both. Some are novelists, some are practised comic creators, and some complete novices. All are welcome. Of course, working with such a varied group presents us with an editorial problem of tone, but our approach to that is again rooted in the experience of the reader. *The Phoenix* readership is aged roughly 6–12 years. That's a much broader range than most book publishers have to consider for specific titles.

We want excitement and adventure and scares and all the rest of it, but we also want six and seven year-olds to love it. There are plenty of examples of stories that can be enjoyed by all ages. Anyone heard of *Star Wars*? That's the kind of cross-generation appeal we ultimately aim for. It's a great target audience. Some might say it means dumbing things down, but I think that actually it means cutting straight to the heart of what a story is about. You can't hide behind gratuitous violence or gore or other salacious details. You just have to nail the story. It's tough, and rarely done, of course, but amazing when someone hits it out of the park and grandparents can enjoy it side by side with their grandkids.

So all you storytellers out there, no matter what medium you choose to tell your stories in, remember the reader. Or the watcher or the puzzler or whatever else they might be. And perhaps you might consider comics. It is a gloriously visceral medium to work in. For you writers it's a true joy to send off a script and have it returned beautifully illustrated by an amazing artist. And I know many brilliant illustrators who really enjoy bringing a writer's ideas to life. And for you publishers, consider the comic. And by comic we mean anything that is of the comic art form. There is no real difference between a graphic novel and a comic beyond the format. The methods of storytelling are essentially the same. Because kids love comics; they love them all over the world and it's time we recognised that again in the UK.

People are always talking about the need to raise literacy levels, to encourage 'reading for pleasure'. Comics are immediate and accessible and exciting. Children like reading comics because they like reading them. Not because someone told them to. I like the way Art Spiegelman put it (have you read *Maus* by the way? If not, you should!): 'Comics are the gateway drug to reading.' What an appropriately inappropriate way of putting it. And that fits comics perfectly.

P.S. If you've got a great idea for a comic story or non-fiction series, send it in to us! Apologies in advance if we are slow to respond. We're a tiny team. You can check out our submission guidelines at www.thephoenixcomic.co.uk/submissions. To find out what sort of thing we are looking for, the best thing to do is to grab a copy of *The Phoenix*. Or even better, find a child you know and stick one in their hand to see what items they respond to best. But don't discount your own view because remember – it's all about the reader. And that means you too.

Tom Fickling worked in film production for a number of years on a range of films, from small British productions to large Hollywood blockbusters. He was part of the core team that published *The DFC*, the precursor to *The Phoenix*. He joined *The Phoenix* full time in 2012 and was appointed Editor in May 2015 and managing director in 2016. In 2019, Tom was appointed managing director of David Fickling Books.

See also...
- *Magazines and newspapers for children*, page 300
- *Creating graphic novels*, page 277

Magazines and newspapers for children

Listings of magazines about children's literature and education start on page 305.

AdventureBox

Bayard, PO Box 61269, London N17 1DF
tel 0800 055 6686
email contact@bayard-magazines.co.uk
website www.bayard-magazines.co.uk
Facebook www.facebook.com/Bayard Children's Magazines
Twitter @BayardKidsMags
Editor-in-Chief Simona Sideri
10 p.a. £5.50

Aimed at 6–9 year-old children starting to read on their own. Each issue contains a 44pp illustrated story plus games, a nature/science feature and comic strips. Specially commissions most material. Founded 1996.

Animals and You

D.C. Thomson & Co. Ltd., Albert Square, Dundee DD1 1DD
tel (01382) 575863
email animalsandyou@dcthomson.co.uk
website www.animalsandyou.co.uk
Twitter @animalsandyou
Every 4 weeks £62 p.a.

Features, stories and posters for readers who love animals. Founded 1998.

Anorak

Unit L/M, Reliance Wharf, 2–10 Hertford Road, London N1 5EW
email anorakmagazine@gmail.com
website www.anorakmagazine.com
Twitter @AnorakMagazine
Editor Cathy Olmedillas
4 p.a. £6.50

Aimed at children aged 6+, and designed to encourage creativity. Founded 2006.

Aquila

Studio 2, 67a Willowfield Road, Eastbourne, East Sussex BN22 8AP
tel (01323) 431313
email office@aquila.co.uk
website www.aquila.co.uk
Facebook www.facebook.com/AquilaChildrensMagazine
Twitter @AquilaMag
Editorial Director Freya Hardy
Monthly £55 p.a.

Dedicated to encouraging children aged 8–13 to reason and create, and to develop a caring nature.

Short stories and serials of up to three parts. Occasional features commissioned from writers with specialist knowledge. Approach in writing with ideas and sample of writing style, along with sae. Length: 700–800 words (features), 1,000–1,100 words (stories or per episode of a serial). Payment: by arrangement. Founded 1993.

The Astonishing Spider-Man

Panini UK, Brockbourne House, 77 Mount Ephraim, Tunbridge Wells TN4 8AR
tel (01892) 500100
email astonspid@panini.co.uk
website https://comics.panini.co.uk
Facebook www.facebook.com/MarvelCollectorsEditions
Editor Brady Webb
Every 2 weeks £3.99

76pp of comic strips, including both contemporary and classic stories.

BBC Doctor Who Magazine

Panini UK, Brockbourne House, 77 Mount Ephraim, Tunbridge Wells TN4 8AR
tel (01892) 500100
email dwa@panini.co.uk
website https://doctorwhomagazine.com/
Twitter @DWtweets
Editor Marcus Hearn
Monthly £5.99

Magazine for 6–12 year-old fans of *Doctor Who*. Readers are immersed into the world of the Doctor, taking them on an adventure into time and space, with monsters and creatures, excitement, action, adventure and humour. Founded 2006.

Beano

D.C. Thomson & Co. Ltd, 2 Albert Square, Dundee DD1 1DD
email beano@dcthomson.co.uk
website www.beano.com
Facebook www.facebook.com/BeanoOfficial
Twitter @BeanoOfficial
50 p.a. £2.75

Comic strips for children aged 6–12. Series, 8–20 pictures. Artwork and scripts. Payment: on acceptance.

The Caterpillar

Ardan Grange, Milltown, Belturbet, Co. Cavan, Republic of Ireland

tel +353 (0) 49 9522995
email editor@thecaterpillarmagazine.com
website www.thecaterpillarmagazine.com
Facebook www.facebook.com/thecaterpillarmagazine
Founders Rebecca O'Connor and Will Govan, *Editor* Rebecca O'Connor
Quarterly €7, €28 p.a. (UK and Republic of Ireland), €32 p.a. (RoW), including postage

Features original poetry and short stories written by adults for children aged 7–11, alongside full-colour artwork. Submissions from adults welcome, but contributors should familiarise themselves with magazine content first. Send no more than six poems or two short stories (max. 1,500 words) by email or post (sae). Also publishes *The Moth* and runs The Caterpillar Poetry Prize (€1,000 for best poem written for children by an adult) and The Caterpillar Story for Children Prize (€1,000 for best story written for children by an adult). Founded 2013.

CBeebies Art
Immediate Media Co. Ltd, Vineyard House, 44 Brook Green, London W6 7BT
tel 020-7150 5021
email hello@cbeebiesart.com
Twitter @CBArtmag
Editor Stephanie Cooper
Every 4 weeks £3.99

Aimed at young children who like art. Linked to popular CBeebies art brands including Mister Maker and Get Squiggling.

CBeebies Magazine
Immediate Media Co. Ltd, Vineyard House, 44 Brook Green, London W6 7BT
tel 020-7150 5119
email hello@cbeebiesweekly.com
website www.bbc.co.uk/cbeebies
Twitter @cbeebiesmag
Editor Stephanie Cooper
Weekly £2.99

Preschool magazine with educational content targeted at 3½-year-olds. Actively promotes learning through play. Showcases new characters, presenters and programmes as they appear on the CBeebies channel. Founded 2006.

Commando
email generalenquiries@commandomag.com
website www.commandocomics.com
Facebook www.facebook.com/pages/Commando-Comics/168688426504994
Twitter @CommandoComic
4 per fortnight £2

Fictional stories set in time of war told in pictures. Scripts: about 135 pictures. Synopsis required as an opener. Submissions information can be found at www.commandocomics.com/submissions. Payment: on acceptance. Founded 1961.

DiscoveryBox
Bayard, PO Box 61269, London N17 1DF
tel (0800) 055 6686
email contact@bayard-magazines.co.uk
website www.bayard-magazines.co.uk
Facebook www.facebook.com/Bayard Kids Mags
Twitter @BayardKidsMags
Editor Simona Sideri
10 p.a. £5.50

Voyage of discovery through nature, science and history for children aged 9–12. Every issue contains: animal topics, information about important historical events, articles about the world, DIY activities, comic strips, games and more. Founded 1996.

DOT
Unit L/M, Reliance Wharf, 2–10 Hertford Road, London N1 5EW
email anorakmagazine@gmail.com
website www.anorakmagazine.com/dot
Editor Cathy Olmedillas
4 p.a. £6

Ad-free magazine aimed at encouraging creativity and learning in the under-5s.

Eco Kids Planet
Eco Kids Planet, 41 Claremont Road, Barnet EN4 0HR
tel 0800 639 1365
email hello@ecokidsplanet.co.uk
website www.ecokidsplanet.co.uk
Twitter @EcoKidsPlanet
Editor Anya Dimelow
11 p.a. £3.90

Aimed at 7–11 year-old children. Each issue is dedicated to a different ecosystem and contains facts, photographs, puzzles and projects. The magazine uses fun, fictional characters in a story format to convey facts about nature and the environment. It also provides children with real-world examples of how they can make a difference on the planet. Length: 500–1,200 words (themed articles). Requirements: well-researched, up-to-date, informative articles, creative approach, interesting language. Specially commissions most material. Payment: by arrangement. Founded 2014.

Essential X-Men
Panini UK, Brockbourne House, 77 Mount Ephraim, Tunbridge Wells TN4 8AR
tel (01892) 500100
email paninicomics@panini.co.uk
website https://comics.panini.co.uk
Every 4 weeks £44 p.a.

76pp of graphic stories centred around the Marvel X-Men characters.

FirstNews

Dennis Publishing Ltd, 31–32 Alfred Place,
London WC1E 7DP
tel 020-3890 3890
email anna_bassi@dennis.co.uk
website http://theweekjunior.co.uk
Twitter @First_News
Editor Anna Bassi
Weekly Fri £1.99

Covers news and events in the UK and
internationally for children aged 8–14. Founded 2006.

Girl Talk

Immediate Media Co. Ltd, Vineyard House,
44 Brook Green, London W6 7BT
tel 020-7150 5000
email hello@girltalkmagazine.com
Editor Kelly Wilks
Fortnightly £2.99

Magazine for children aged 7–12. Contains pop, TV
and film celebrity features, personality features,
quizzes, fashion, competitions, stories. Length: 500
words (fiction). Payment: £75. All material is specially
commissioned. Founded 1997.

guiding Magazine

17–19 Buckingham Palace Road, London SW1W 0PT
tel 020-7834 6242
email guiding@girlguiding.co.uk
website www.girlguiding.co.uk
3 p.a. Free download

Official magazine of Girlguiding. Articles of interest
to women of all ages, with special emphasis on youth
work and the Guide Movement. Illustrations: line,
half-tone, colour. Payment: £300 per 1,000 words.
Please email with proposal in the first instance.

Headliners

49–51 East Road, London N1 6AH
tel 020-7749 9360
email enquiries@headliners.org
website www.headliners.org
Twitter @HeadlinersUK
Director Fiona Wyton

Award-winning news agency charity (does not
publish a magazine or newspaper) offering young
people aged 8–18 the opportunity to write on issues
of importance to them, for newspapers, radio and
TV. Founded 1995.

Kick!

Kennedy Publishing, Greenway Farm, Bath Road,
Wick, Bristol BS30 5RL
tel 0117 937300
email info@kennedypublishing.co.uk
Twitter @KiCKmagazine
Editor Ash Rose
Monthly £3.99

Football magazine for boys and girls aged 7–14.
Reports on leading players and teams from a variety
of divisions, including the Premier League; also
includes puzzles, competitions and interviews.

Kids Alive! (The Young Soldier)

The Salvation Army, 101 Newington Causeway,
London SE1 6BN
tel 020-7367 4911
email kidsalive@salvationarmy.org.uk
website www.salvationarmy.org.uk/kidsalive
Editor Justin Reeves, *Deputy Editor* Cara Mott
Weekly £23.49 p.a.

Children's magazine: scripts and artwork for cartoon
strips, puzzles, etc; Christian-based articles with
emphasis on education and lifestyle issues.
Illustrations: half-tone, line and four-colour line,
cartoons. Payment: by arrangement. Founded 1881.

Kookie

Missprint Media, PO Box 2410, LL11 0NY
email hello@kookiemagazine.com
website www.kookiemagazine.com
Twitter @kookiemagazine
Founders Vivien Jones, Nicky Shortridge
4 p.a. £6.50

Ad-free magazine for girls aged 8–12. Features
interviews with inspiring women and girls, original
fiction, information on key science, sports and IT
topics as well as craft, book reviews and a problem
page. Founded 2018.

Marvel Legends

Panini UK, Brockbourne House, 77 Mount Ephraim,
Tunbridge Wells TN4 8AR
tel (01892) 500100
email astonspid@panini.co.uk
website www.paninicomics.co.uk
Facebook www.facebook.com/
MarvelCollectorsEditions
Editor Brady Webb
Every 4 weeks £4.99

76pp of comic strips, including both contemporary
and classic stories.

Match!

Kelsey Media, Cudham Tithe Barn, Berry's Hill,
Cudham, Kent TN16 3AG
tel 01733 353358
email match.magazine@kelsey.co.uk
website www.matchfootball.co.uk
Editor Stephen Fishlock
Monthly £2.40

Aimed at teenage football fans. News, statistics and
information on leading Premier League, Football
League and Scottish Premier League teams.

Match of the Day

Immediate Media Co. Ltd, Vineyard House,
44 Brook Green, London W6 7BT
tel 020-7150 5000
email shout@motdmag.com
website www.motdmag.com
Editor Ian Foster
Weekly £2.60

Aimed at football-mad children with star interviews, match results, gossip and quizzes. Also includes 8pp pull-out football skills guide.

National Geographic Kids

12–14 Berry Street, London EC1V 0AU
email kids@ngkids.co.uk
website www.ngkids.co.uk
Facebook www.facebook.com/ngkids
Twitter @ngkidsuk
Editor Tim Herbert
Monthly £3.99

Facts and figures about the environment, different cultures, animals and history for children aged 8–12.

The Official Jacqueline Wilson Mag

D.C. Thomson & Co. Ltd, 2 Albert Square,
Dundee DD1 1DD
tel (01382) 223131
email contact@jw-mag.com
website www.jw-mag.com
Every 3 weeks £4.25

Based on the books and characters of award-winning author, Dame Jacqueline Wilson. Aimed at readers aged 7–12, content is tailored to encourage literacy and creativity across a range of reading abilities. Contains interactive features, art and writing projects, recipes and crafts; for less confident readers, educational benefits are presented in a fun and interesting format – e.g. story-starter games and writing prompts, design challenges and word puzzles. Dame Jacqueline contributes photos, stories and writing tips and her illustrator, Nick Sharratt, supplies drawings and art secrets.

Okido

1–5 Vyner Street, London E2 9DG
email sophie@okido.co.uk
website www.okido.co.uk
Twitter @okidomagazine
Monthly £5

48pp arts and science magazine for children aged 3–8 and their families. Designed to engage young children in the scientific world around them in the most creative manner. Contains stories, characters, games, experiments, doodles, recipes, poems and a fan page. Produced in-house and with regular guest artists; fully illustrated on heavyweight FSC paper using biodegradable vegetable inks. Advertisement-free. Founded 2007.

The Phoenix

29 Beaumont Street, Oxford OX1 2NP
email theeditor@thephoenixcomic.co.uk
website www.thephoenixcomic.co.uk
Twitter @phoenixcomicuk
Editor Tom Fickling
Weekly £3.25

32pp weekly anthology comic for boys and girls aged 6-12. Features serialised stories and one-off stories as well as non-fiction. Encourages reading for pleasure and children's critical thinking, creative writing and drawing skills. Contributors include Jamie Smart and Neill Cameron. Founded 2011.

PONY Magazine

Marlborough House, Headley Road, Grayshott,
Surrey GU26 6LG
tel (01428) 601020
email pony@djmurphy.co.uk
website www.ponymag.com
Twitter @PONY_mag
Editor Jo Browne
13 p.a. from £3.99

Lively articles and short stories with a horsey theme aimed at readers aged 8–16. Technical accuracy and young, fresh writing essential. Length: up to 800 words. Payment: by arrangement. Illustrations: drawings (commissioned), photos, cartoons. Founded 1949.

Scoop

Curious Publishing, Suite 101, 9 Jerdan Place,
Fulham, London SW6 1BE
email hello@scoopthemag.co.uk
email illustration@scoopthemag.co.uk
website www.scoopthemag.co.uk
Twitter @scoop_the_mag
Director Clementine Macmillan-Scott, *Editor-in-Chief*
Sarah Odedina
Bi-monthly 10 p.a. £6.50

48pp monthly magazine for boys and girls aged 7–12. Features fiction, non-fiction, illustration, comics and competitions, and invites readers to think for themselves through many different types of story-telling. Contributors include Raymond Briggs, Laura Dockrill and Chris Riddell. Founded 2015.

Shout

2 Albert Square, Dundee DD1 1DD
tel (01382) 223131
email shout@dctmedia.co.uk
website www.shoutmag.co.uk
Facebook www.facebook.com/shoutmag
Twitter @shoutmag
Monthly £4.25

Magazine for 11–15 year-old girls. Includes fashion and beauty; celebrity gossip and interviews; TV and pop content; real-life stories; emotional and advice features with a teen focus. Length of article accepted:

up to 1,000 words. Illustrations: links to online portfolios or websites welcome, but illustrations are commissioned on a feature-by-feature basis only. Payment: on acceptance. Founded 1993.

Storybox

Bayard, PO Box 61269, London N17 1DF
tel (0800) 055 6686
email contact@bayard-magazines.co.uk
website www.bayard-magazines.co.uk
Editor-in-Chief Simona Sideri
10 p.a. £5.50

Aimed at 3–6 year-old children. Each issue presents a new, full-colour, 24pp story created by teams of writers and illustrators for laptime reading. A non-fiction section linked to a theme in the story follows, together with pages of games and craft ideas. Also includes games, an animal feature, science and a cartoon. Length: 500–1,000 words (stories). Requirements: rhyme, repetition, interesting language. Specially commissions most material. Payment: by arrangement. Founded 1996.

Storytime

Luma Creative Ltd, Studio 2B18,
South Bank Technopark, 90 London Rd,
London SE1 6LN
email hello@storytimemagazine.com
website www.storytimemagazine.com
Twitter @StorytimeMag
Monthly From £36.99 p.a.

Illustrated bedtime story magazine for children aged 3–8. Accepting submissions from illustrators: see website for full submission guidelines. Calls for submissions from short-story writers also occur periodically; check online for details.

Teen Breathe

GMC Publications, 86 High Street, Lewes BN7 1XN
tel (01273) 477373
email hello@breathemagazine.com
website www.teenbreathe.co.uk
Publisher Jonathan Grogan
Bi-monthly £3.99

Tips, exercises and ideas on how to make mindfulness part of teenagers' lives so that they can stay positive and improve their wellbeing. Submissions welcomed from experienced or new writers, and from illustrators. See www.teenbreathe.co.uk/submissions for specific requirements for each type of potential contributor.

Top of the Pops

Immediate Media Co. Ltd, Vineyard House,
44 Brook Green, London W6 7BT
tel 020-7150 5123
email totpmag@totpmag.com
Editor Peter Hart
Monthly £3.99

Celebrity gossip and news, primarily aimed at girls aged 10–14. Founded 1995.

Toxic Magazine

Egmont UK Ltd, The Yellow Building,
1 Nicholas Road, London W11 4AN
website www.toxicmag.co.uk
Twitter @ToxicMagUK
Editor Matt Pratt
Every 3 weeks £3.99

Topical lifestyle magazine for 8–12 year-old boys. Includes competitions, pull-out posters, reviews and jokes. Covers boys' entertainment, sports, video games, films, TV, music, fashion and toys. Slapstick humour. Showcases latest products, events and trends. Payment: by arrangement. Founded 2002.

2000 AD

Rebellion Publishing, Riverside House, Osney Mead,
Oxford OX2 0ES
website www.2000adonline.com
Twitter @2000AD
Weekly Wed £2.85

Cult science fiction and fantasy comic. Submissions accepted by post only. Founded 1977.

The Week Junior

Dennis Publishing Ltd, 31–32 Alfred Place,
London WC1E 7DP
tel 020-3890 3890
email hello@theweekjunior.co.uk
website http://theweekjunior.co.uk
Editor-in-Chief Anna Bassi
Weekly £2.25

Covers news and events in the UK and internationally for children aged 8–14.

Wolverine and Deadpool

Panini UK, Brockbourne House, 77 Mount Ephraim,
Tunbridge Wells TN4 8AR
tel (01892) 500100
email paninicomics@panini.co.uk
website https://comics.panini.co.uk
Every 4 weeks £4.50

76pp comic based around the exploits of the eponymous Marvel heroes.

Magazines about children's literature and education

Listings of magazines and newspapers for children start on page 300.

Armadillo

Louise Ellis-Barrett, 62 Horton Hill, Epsom,
Surrey KT19 8ST
tel (01372) 745876
email armadilloeditor@gmail.com
website www.armadillomagazine.co.uk
Facebook www.facebook.com/Armadillomag
Twitter @Armadillomag
Instagram ArmadilloMagazine
Editor Louise Ellis-Barrett
4 p.a. Free

Online children's book review magazine including
reviews, interviews, features, competitions and
profiles. Linked to a blog for weekly children's book
news updates; issues posted March, June, September
and December. New reviewers and writers always
welcome. Founded 1999.

Books for Keeps

Books for Keeps c/o Helen Swinyard, Library,
Heartlands High School, Station Road, London
N22 7ST
tel 020-8889 1292
email andrea@booksforkeeps.co.uk
website www.booksforkeeps.co.uk
Twitter @booksforkeeps
Editor Andrea Reece
Bi-monthly Free

Features, reviews and news on children's books.
Readership is both professionals and parents.
Founded 1980.

The Bookseller

Floor 10, Westminster Tower,
3 Albert Embankment, London SE1 7SP
tel 020-3358 0369
email katie.mansfield@thebookseller.com
website www.thebookseller.com
Twitter @thebookseller
Editor Philip Jones, *Features and Insight Editor*
Tom Tivnan
Weekly £4.95

Journal of the UK publishing and bookselling trades.
The *Children's Bookseller* supplement is published
regularly and there is news on the children's book
business in the main magazine. Produces the
Children's Buyer's Guide, which previews children's
books to be published in the following six months.
The website features news on children's books,
comment on the children's sector, author interviews
and children's bestseller charts. Founded 1858.

Carousel – The Guide to Children's Books

Unit 1, West Court, Saxon Business Park,
Stoke Prior, Worcestershire, B60 4AD
tel 07413 980203
email office@carouselguide.co.uk
website www.carouselguide.co.uk
Twitter @CarouselDave
Editors Elaine and David Chant
3 p.a. along with a free Christmas supplement £13
p.a. (UK), £19 p.a. (Europe), £22 p.a. (RoW)

Independent reviews of the best new books for
children of all ages from babies to adults. Also a
variety of articles and interviews from and about the
world of children's books and to inspire a love of
reading. Recent features/interviews include Chris
Riddell, Helen Oxenbury, David Almond and
EmpathyLab. Website features news, reviews, index
to past interviews, sample articles and subscription
form. Founded 1995.

Children's Bookshelf

Publishers Weekly, 71 West 23 Street, Suite 1608,
New York, NY 10010, USA
tel +1 212-377-5500
email childrensbooks@publishersweekly.com
email DRoback@publishersweekly.com
website www.publishersweekly.com
Facebook www.facebook.com/pubweekly
Twitter @PWKidsBookshelf
Chiildren's Books Editor Diane Roback
Semi-weekly Free

E-newsletter about children's and young adult books.
Published under the auspices of *Publishers Weekly*,
which was founded in 1872. Children's book news,
feature story ideas, new trends and pitches for author
or illustrator interviews should be sent to the Editor.
Visit website for PW's submission guidelines.

Educate

National Education Union, Hamilton House,
Mabledon Place, London WC1H 9BD
tel 020-7380 4708
email educate@neu.org.uk
website https://neu.org.uk/educate
Editor Helen Watson
6 p.a. Free to NEU members

Articles, features and news of interest to all those involved in the education sector. Email outline in the first instance. Length: 500 words (single page), 1,000 (double page). Payment: NUJ rates to NUJ members.

Inis – The Children's Books Ireland Magazine

Children's Books Ireland,
17 North Great George Street, Dublin D01 R2F1,
Republic of Ireland
tel +353 (0)1 8727475
email jenny@childrensbooksireland.ie
website www.childrensbooksireland.ie
Editor Jenny Murray
3 p.a. €5

Wide variety of children's literature articles and features, as well as in-depth reviews of new titles for young people of all ages, from babies to teenagers. Published by Children's Books Ireland. Founded 1989.

Literacy

UK Literacy Association, 9 Newarke Street,
Leicester LE1 5SN
tel 0116 254 4116
website www.ukla.org
Editors Diane R. Collier, Natalia Kucirkova
3 p.a. (subscription only)

Official journal of the United Kingdom Literacy Association (see page 377), aimed at those interested in the study and development of literacy. Readership comprises practitioners, teachers, educators, researchers, undergraduate and graduate students. It offers educators a forum for debate through scrutinising research evidence, reflecting on analysed accounts of innovative practice and examining recent policy developments. Length: 2,000–6,000 words (articles). Illustrations: b&w prints and artwork. Formerly known as *Reading – Literacy and Language*. Published by Blackwell Publishing. Founded 1966.

Nursery World

MA Education, St Jude's Church, Dulwich Road,
London SE24 0PB
tel 020-8501 6693
email liz.roberts@markallengroup.com
website www.nurseryworld.co.uk
Editor Liz Roberts
Fortnightly £102 p.a.

For all grades of primary school, nursery and childcare staff, nannies, foster parents and all concerned with the care of expectant mothers, babies and young children. Authoritative and informative articles, 800 or 1,300 words, and photos, on all aspects of child welfare and early education, from 0–8 years, in the UK. Practical ideas, policy news and career advice. No short stories. Illustrations: line, half-tone, colour. Payment: by arrangement.

Publishers Weekly

71 West 23 Street, Suite 1608, New York, NY 10010,
USA
tel +1 212-377-5500
email childrensbooks@publishersweekly.com
email DRoback@publishersweekly.com
website www.publishersweekly.com
Facebook www.facebook.com/pubweekly
Twitter @PWKidsBookshelf
Children's Books Editor Diane Roback

International news magazine for the book industry. Covers all segments involved in the creation, production, marketing and sale of the written word in book, audio, video and electronic formats. In addition to reaching publishers worldwide, it influences all media dealing with the acquisition, sale, distribution and rights of intellectual and cultural properties.

Children's books for review, from preschool to young adult, should be sent to Diane Roback, Children's Books Editor; note that all reviews are pre-publication. Also send to her story suggestions on children's publishing, new trends, author or illustrator interviews, etc for the semi-weekly *Children's Bookshelf* e-newsletter. Founded 1872.

The School Librarian

School Library Association, 1 Pine Court,
Kembrey Park, Swindon SN2 8AD
tel (01793) 530166
email sleditor@sla.org.uk
website www.sla.org.uk
Features Editor Barbara Band, *Reviews Editor* Joy Court
Quarterly Free to SLA members

Official journal of the School Library Association. Articles on school library management, use and skills, and on authors and illustrators, literacy, publishing. Reviews of books, websites and other library resources from preschool to adult. Length: 1,800–2,500 words (articles). Payment: by arrangement. Founded 1937.

TES (The Times Educational Supplement)

26 Red Lion Square, London WC1R 4HQ
tel 020-3194 3000
email newsdesk@tes.com
email features@tes.com
website www.tes.com
Twitter @tes
Editor Ann Mroz
Weekly £30 per quarter print and digital; £15 per quarter digital only

Education magazine and website. Articles on education written with special knowledge or experience; news items; features; book reviews. Outlines of feature ideas should be emailed. Illustrations: suitable photos and drawings of educational interest, cartoons. Payment: by arrangement.

TESS (The Times Educational Supplement Scotland)
email scoted@tess.co.uk
website www.tes.com
Twitter @TESScotland

Contact Henry Hepburn
Weekly £30 per quarter print and digital

Education newspaper. Articles on education, preferably 800–1,000 words, written with special knowledge or experience. News items about Scottish educational affairs. Illustrations: by arrangement. Payment: by arrangement. Founded 1965.

Television, film and radio
Adapting children's books for stage and screen

Emma Reeves offers her experience of the challenges and rewards of adapting other people's literary creations for the television or stage, with practical advice on securing rights and successfully reimagining and reshaping a story you love in a way that works for the new medium.

If you are a working writer for stage, screen or radio, whether you're writing for children, adults or both, it's highly likely that adaptations will form a regular part of your work – and income. Audio drama, film, TV and theatre have a voracious appetite for valuable IP (intellectual property) and the rights to successful books are fought over ruthlessly. TV companies working in children's television are constantly reading and keeping up with the latest events in children's publishing.

CBBC's two biggest home-grown brands are probably *Horrible Histories* (based on the books by Terry Deary) and *The Dumping Ground*, evolved from *Tracy Beaker Returns* (created by Elly Brewer and Ben Ward), an original TV series which continued the story of Jacqueline Wilson's popular protagonist, Tracy Beaker, and introduced a whole new set of characters and problems. Tracy and her world have now been a vital part of the CBBC landscape for nearly 20 years – yet the CBBC development exec who initially championed Tracy's cause admits that it was an uphill struggle to get the powers that be to buy into the realistic story of a brutally neglected child who experiences bed-wetting, meltdowns, rages and attachment issues as an all-too-plausible result of a heartbreaking upbringing. In the end, Tracy's inimitable spirit – and 20 years of fierce audience loyalty – won the day; but it's worth keeping in mind that, when it comes to commissioning, nothing is ever really a 'no-brainer' – and if you truly believe in an idea, it's probably worth fighting for.

Book adaptations have a strong appeal for TV and theatre producers, who like to have a tangible idea of what they're getting before commissioning a new series or play. This can be frustrating for new writers who are desperate to get their own big new idea out there. It does mean, though, that producers are often looking for the 'right' writer to match with a project, which can be a shortcut to a paid commission. And artistically, it can give you the chance to experience the joy, fear and pain of taking control of a group of beloved characters in a rich, well-realised world.

Riding the highs and lows
The highs and lows of adaptation are dizzying. It's certainly not easier than original work. If you do happen to find it easier, I will sincerely try to be happy for you, but I enviously suspect that you're doing it wrong. In my personal experience, it doesn't hurt any less to fail as an adapter than as an originator – in fact, it's worse. You haven't just let yourself down, you've betrayed your original author, your guide, your travelling companion, maybe even your hero.

Of course, when things *do* work and people profess to love the resulting show, the Bad Voices in every writer's head lose no time in pointing out that *everything good is because of the original author ... everything bad is* your *fault*. And if those voices should ever abandon you (unlikely), there's always the internet ...

Which brings me to Rule One of adapting – no, Rule One of everything, ever: Never, *ever* search the internet. Just don't do it.

Rule Two: when you inevitably ignore my advice and search the internet – remember, they're just people, like you; maybe too much like you. As a child, I was an obsessive reader, and I still suffer from very strong 'fannish' tendencies. I know very well that there are certain books and authors of which no adaptation will ever satisfy me. The people who are hardest to please are the most devoted. If someone comes down hard on your adaptation, console yourself by imagining the review you'd give to any adaptation of *your* favourite book of all time.

The real high of adaptation is that you get to play inside someone else's incredible creation. And what could be better than that? As a stage adapter, I've been privileged to reimagine childhood favourites – *Little Women, Carrie's War, Anne of Green Gables, Sherlock Holmes, Cool Hand Luke, Doctor Jekyll and Mr Hyde* – and also to discover the work of a new generation of children's writers. I've written for *The Story of Tracy Beaker, Tracy Beaker Returns* and *The Dumping Ground* – all based on Jacqueline Wilson's work – and also worked on both the stage and TV versions of her *Hetty Feather*.

Every experience is different and brings its own challenges. Even within the same medium, there are different types of show. On TV, for example, at one end of the scale is the straight, closed-ended adaptation, where you are expected to more or less follow the story of the book. At the other end of the spectrum is the open-ended drama which may take nothing more from its source material than a few names and a situation, relying on the ingenuity of the script writers to come up with episodic plots. Most TV shows are somewhere in between – perhaps a novel may provide the protagonist's journey for series one, but then it's up to the writers to come up with new material.

Check out the rights

A lot of my adaptation work has come about through people approaching me. But what if you've fallen in love with an original work and you just have to adapt it or write a sequel? What should you do? Before you type your first words, make sure the rights are available and that you've got a realistic chance of getting them. The only exception is for out-of-copyright material (where the author has been dead for 70 years or more). Otherwise, anything you write without the blessing of the author or their estate is basically fan fiction; you may enjoy it, your friends may enjoy it, but you can never reach a mass audience, and certainly never make any money, unless you want a lawsuit on your hands. So, if you're serious about sharing your vision with the world, check out the rights before doing anything else.

If you have an agent, or an interested production company, they will be able to help you approach the rights-holders. If not, you can search online for the writer's agent or go through the publisher. Bear in mind that the latest hot properties and surprise hits will almost always be optioned already – but options lapse, so it's worth enquiring about the length of the option and trying again at the appropriate time. Read more obscure work in the hope of finding an un-optioned gem.

Despite all this, securing book rights is comparatively easy compared to getting the rights to adapt film or TV shows. This is particularly tricky for lone writers, as TV and film properties tend to have multiple owners and sorting out the various claims requires an army of showbiz lawyers. As a general rule, it's only worth pursuing if you have a major producing force on your side (both to give you credibility and to pay those lawyers' fees!), but there are always exceptions. If you're really passionate about a project and you think you can persuade the rights-holders, go for it. Our business is built on stories of those few lucky people whose tenacity and love for their project enabled them to break all the rules and succeed.

Reimagining the story

What happens next? A producer friend regularly chides me that he doesn't know why my scripts take so long, when all I have to do is copy down the book and cross out the description. Although I generally laugh bitterly at such comments, adaptation is a broad church and there are some gigs which are perhaps better described as abridging – such as when I worked out a three-hander version of *King Lear* and a four-hander version of *The Importance of Being Earnest* for a small touring company. Although you have to be a bit creative in situations like that, you're working within the intended medium and almost exclusively using the author's original text. At the other end of the scale of fidelity to the original work, I once worked on a children's TV show for two years before anyone informed me that it was actually based on a novel!

These two extremes aside, the job of the adapter is usually to reimagine the story in a way which works for the medium. For example, when I worked on the stage version of *Hetty Feather*, we started with Jacqueline's book and created the show in the rehearsal room with six actors. Using the wealth of material in the book, and even more which was generated by the actors, my job was to steer the story into a coherent structure which would fit into two hours' stage time, streamlining plot moments and making some tough calls about which brilliant bits to jettison. When I wrote episodes of the TV show, I had to come up with self-contained plots lasting half an hour. In the first case I had an overabundance of other people's material to deal with; in the second, it was up to me to tell new stories. People asked if I found it confusing but, to me, the worlds of *Hetty* the book, *Hetty* the stage show, and *Hetty* the TV show were so different that I never struggled in that way. In some respects, the medium informs the writing experience possibly more than the original material does.

When you start to adapt a book, you are entering somebody else's world, and meeting their characters. In order to feel comfortable in that world, I always try to read as much of the writer's other work as I can. This may seem like obvious advice, but the benefits are so great that it's worth emphasizing. If the author writes a lot about a specific time and place, that's useful for research and background colour. If they are preoccupied with certain ideas or social issues, you can get a greater understanding of where they were coming from when they wrote the book. I have actually transposed scenes from (out-of-copyright!) lesser-known works of authors, in order to illuminate important moments which I felt were glossed over somewhat in the work I was adapting. Cheeky perhaps, but it worked for me.

Creating the shape

So, you've got a handle on the world and the characters. Everything may be clearly set out for you, or you may need to fill the gaps – or change certain elements. You may discover what you need to change as you go along. At this stage, you take a step back from the source material (and its potentially seductive prose) and ask the normal questions of dramatic writing: Whose story is it? What do they want? Who is trying to stop them getting it?

A specific problem I have encountered is that many beloved books are episodic in nature: this happens, then that happens, then this happens … In drama, stories tend to need ongoing hooks: this happens, SO that happens, SO that happens … I find I need to work hard to create a sense of building drama and inevitability. Also, coincidence feels much harder to mask in drama than in novels. I find myself investigating plot conveniences – are they really just happenstance? Or did someone plan it? If you can decide that the events are the result of someone's plan, it immediately feels easier to dramatise plausibly.

You have to keep your characters active and keep your hooks dangling. Keep your protagonist pushing through to the end. When you're watching previews, or in the edit, try to resist the temptation to keep a 'good bit' in if your gut is screaming at you that it's slowing down the story and risks letting the audience's interest drop. Sometimes that comedy interlude just sits too awkwardly at a moment when the hero has to make a life-or-death choice and risk everything. Sometimes, it's time to stop piling torture, misery and despair on a character and let the audience know that they're ready to fight back. As an adapter, you need to take responsibility for the work as a whole – the shape is now up to you. And you may have to keep a mediocre bit at the expense of a good bit if, after a lot of consideration (and discussion with the director, editor or whoever), you realise that that's what the shape of the story needs.

Interestingly, not a word of the paragraph above couldn't also be usefully applied to original drama scripts.

So in summary: enjoy the highs, the fun and the privilege; appreciate the work that other people have done so you don't have to; but if something's not working, don't shrug it off as the original author's problem – look at it from all angles until you find a way to make it work for you. It's the very least that the author deserves. After all, it's probably their name that got you the gig.

Emma Reeves is an award-winning writer whose TV credits include *The Dumping Ground, Tracy Beaker Returns* (winner of the Royal Television Society award for Best Children's Drama, 2012), *Young Dracula, The Worst Witch, The Story of Tracy Beaker* and *The Demon Headmaster*. Her stage adaptations include *Carrie's War, Anne of Green Gables, Little Women, Hetty Feather, Cool Hand Luke* and *The Worst Witch*. *Hetty Feather* (the stage show) was nominated for an Olivier Award and won the first ever Cameo award for best page-to-stage adaptation. In 2016 Emma received the Writers' Guild Award for Best Children's TV Episode for *Eve: Final Episode – Control, Alter, Delete*. She is currently Chair of the Writers' Guild TV Committee. Follow her on Twitter @emmajanereeves.

See also...
● *Adapting books for the stage*, page 337

Children's literature on radio and audio

The technologies for transmitting the spoken word to children are developing rapidly. Neville Teller describes the fast-changing world of radio and audio, and explores what a writer for the microphone needs to know to break into this market.

'Read me a story' – one of childhood's perennial cries. Until radio arrived, parents found little relief from it (palming it off on grandma or auntie was perhaps the best bet). But from its very beginning, radio included in its schedules stories read aloud for children. So, for part of the time at least, the loudspeaker was able to provide a fair substitute for mummy or daddy by providing literature, specially prepared for performance at the microphone, read by professional actors.

Very early on, actors learned that performing at the microphone was a new skill – the techniques were specialised and quite different from those required on the stage. Writers, too, had to acquire a whole range of new skills in preparing material for radio. Two things quickly became apparent. First, the time taken to read a complete book on the air would be far too long to be acceptable, and in consequence most books would need to be abridged. Secondly, literature simply read aloud from the printed page often failed to 'come across' to a listening audience, because material produced to be scanned by the eye is often basically unsuited to the requirements of the microphone.

Today there are two main outlets in this country for aspiring writers for children in the radio/audio sphere: online radio/audio and audiobook publishers. How has this market reached its present position?

Radio

Children's radio in the UK came into existence in December 1922, just a few weeks after the BBC itself was born, and for some 40 years the daily 'Children's Hour' became an established and much-cherished feature of life.

However, in the 1960s the imminent death of radio was a generally accepted prognostication. Starting in 1961, in the belief that television was children's preferred medium, children's radio was slowly but surely strangled. First the much-loved title 'Children's Hour' was dropped, then the time allotted to 'For the Young' (as the programme was subsequently called) was cut back. Finally, in March 1964, it was put out of its agony.

The demise of children's radio naturally evoked a massive groundswell of protest. In response the BBC of the day did grant some sort of reprieve. *Story Time* – a programme of abridged radio readings – started life in the old Children's Hour slot with a strong bias towards children's literature. It was not long, however, before more general literature began to be selected, and finally, in 1982, that programme too was dropped. For the next 20 years the only regular children's programme left on BBC radio was *Listen with Mother*, the 15-minute slot for the under-fives.

Early in the new millennium the BBC – moved, doubtless, by mounting evidence of the undiminished popularity of radio – decided to reintroduce a regular programme for children. All they could offer at the time was a 30-minute programme each Sunday evening on Radio 4 called *Go4It*, a magazine-type show which included a ten-minute reading, and I found myself abridging books for it like *The Lion, the Witch and the Wardrobe* by C.S. Lewis and *The Wolves of Willoughby Chase* by Joan Aiken. Unfortunately, this renaissance was typically short-lived. *Go4It* was axed on 24 May 2009.

But the door had been pushed ajar, and in the autumn of 2002, when the BBC launched its new digital radio channel, BBC7, its schedules included, as a basic ingredient, daily programmes for children incorporating readings from children's literature, both current and classic. I prepared a considerable number of books for these programmes, including not only classical children's literature like *Robinson Crusoe* and *The Prince and the Pauper*, but also more general classics like *20,000 Leagues Under the Sea* and *Oliver Twist*. The programme for older children also featured up-to-the-moment favourites such as Anthony Horowitz's series about his boy secret agent, Alex Rider, the *Artemis Fowl* novels by Eoin Colfer, Terry Pratchett's *A Hat Full of Sky* and *The Amazing Maurice*, and Jackie French's *Callisto* series. For younger listeners, I abridged books like the *Whizziwig* series by Malorie Blackman, the *Lily Quench* books by Natalie Jane Prior, and Kaye Umansky's *The Silver Spoon of Solomon Snow*.

Children's radio had been re-established and all seemed set fair. But towards the end of 2006 came news of major changes. The programme for younger listeners was converted into a radio extension of CBeebies, the BBC's digital television channel for the youngest children, while the BBC7 schedule included readings drawn from the programme's extensive archive, including my own abridgements of, among many others, *Bootleg* by Alex Shearer, *Stop the Train* by Geraldine McCaughrean, *Huckleberry Finn* by Mark Twain, *Slaves of the Mastery* and *Firesong* by William Nicholson, *Stig of the Dump* by Clive King, *The BGF* by Roald Dahl, *The Little House on the Prairie* by Laura Ingalls Wilder, *Dream Master* by Theresa Breslin, and *Point Blanc* by Anthony Horowitz.

Nothing lasts for ever, and 2011 saw BBC7 transformed into BBC Radio 4 Extra. With the transformation came a new shape to children's radio – almost a return to the Children's Hour concept of yesteryear, *The Four O'Clock Show* always including abridged readings of children's literature. Among the specially commissioned readings I abridged Frank Cottrell Boyce's *Chitty Chitty Bang Bang Flies Again*, *Wonder* by R.J. Palacio and *Maggot Moon* by Sally Gardner.

Sadly, *The Four O'Clock Show* too succumbed to the rapidly changing technological needs of its audience. 30 April 2015 saw its final transmission. By then only around 5,900 children were listening to the programme each week, and the BBC Trust concluded 'few children would be affected' by its closure. The axing of this hour of dedicated children's radio meant that there is no longer any children's programming on Radio 4 Extra, and its service licence has been amended to remove its commitment to the content.

However, the BBC is providing three online streams of children's programmes. CBeebies Radio is a daily web-based radio show for preschool children. They can either listen online through the CBeebies Radio Player or download and keep the podcast, choosing when and where is best for them to listen. Meanwhile the BBC iPlayer has built up an impressive selection of radio programmes under its genre category 'Children', including readings and drama. It can be found at www.bbc.co.uk/radio/categories/childrens. In addition, the BBC provides a dedicated online service for 3-5 year-olds via its School Radio programme. The range of podcasts available for download can be found at: www.bbc.co.uk/schoolradio/subjects/earlylearning.

In addition to the BBC, February 2016 saw the launch of a national digital radio station dedicated entirely to children aged 6–12. Fun Kids is a nationwide 18-station digital multiplex whose content is also available via its website (www.funkidslive.com). Its programmes include stories, drama and educational material.

All these outlets require dedicated writers for children, prepared to adapt existing, or provide new, material in audio format specifically for young listeners.

Audiobooks

Audiobooks are literary works of all types, read by actors and available as CDs or as downloads from the internet. Audiobooks have become the fastest growing area of consumer publishing in the UK. Ahead of the 'Love Audio Week', which ran in June 2018, the industry published figures showing that spending on audiobooks had more than doubled in the previous five years. Booming sales accelerated into the first quarter of 2018, which registered year-on-year growth of 32%. Audible dominates the audiobook market, but faces growing competition from newcomers such as Audiobooks.com, Kobo and Bookbeat, as well as Google and Apple. Current estimates put the children's share of the market at 40% of the total.

The BBC's audio output, including the large and flourishing children's backlist, is now marketed through outlets such as Audible and Random House.

Nowadays, it is common for major publishers to launch a fair number of their new books, including books for older children, in printed and audiobook form simultaneously. Publishers of books for younger children often adopt the 'twin pack' concept – packaging book and audiobook together – so that children can read and listen at the same time. This development has mushroomed since 2003, when HM Revenue & Customs decided that such products could be zero-rated for VAT.

In March 2009 ECOFIN (the EU's Economic and Financial Affairs Council) agreed to reduce VAT on audiobooks to 5%. As a result, it was expected that within a reasonable period of time UK audiobook publishers would be able to charge significantly less for both their physical and digital products. However, so far no intention to apply a reduced rate to audiobooks in the UK has been announced, although following Brexit lobbying to do so will no doubt increase.

How children listen

The ways in which children listen to the readings intended especially for them are multiplying at what seems an ever-increasing rate. Younger children can either listen online to their special CBeebies radio show through the CBeebies Radio Player or download and keep the podcast. Fun Kids radio can be heard via digital radio sets, computers, smartphones and tablets. Primary school teachers download BBC School podcasts and play them back in class.

Downloads are a growing method for children to access audiobooks especially for them. There are a range of online outlets, including Audible and Apple iTunes, whose HomePod went on the market in February 2018. Taken together, these DTO (Download to Own) providers have available an enormous and expanding list of children's books, and stories are proving a popular second-best to music for many children. Subscribers pay either a monthly fee for the right to download a specific number of titles or pay for downloads book by book. However, these days a surprising number of websites are offering free downloads of children's stories. One US website lists no less than 62 online sites from which children can download stories at no cost. The UK also has a fair number of such sites, including those run by the *Independent*, Storynory, Mashable, Oxford University Press and OpenCulture.

Amazon has some 30,000 children's audiobooks available to be purchased and downloaded. Users can start listening within seconds, transfer the audiobook to a Kindle, computer, tablet, iPod or other device, or burn it to a CD. Other specialist providers of audiobooks for children include KidsAudioBooks (www.kidsaudiobooks.co.uk), Children's Storybooks Online (www.magickeys.com/books) and the Story Home (www.thestoryhome.com). All commission new stories for children.

Young people are increasingly accessing not only their social networks via their smartphones, but also audiobooks. Google, Amazon and Audible are providing access to audiobooks via the mobile phone, and other providers are crowding into the marketplace.

Amazon's ebook reader, the Kindle, and its younger brother, Kindle Fire, which offers a colour touch-screen, have been runaway successes. The Kindle can download a book in about 30 seconds, either to be read on its 6-inch wide screen or to be read aloud to you (albeit in a somewhat robot-like voice).

Other brands of ebook readers (such as the Sony and Kobo) are available, but the Kindle's biggest rival as a non-print reading device is Apple's iPad and iPad Mini, and its growing number of tablet competitors. All tablets include an ebook application (or app), through which an enormous selection of books can be downloaded speedily.

In-car MP3 playback, via the car radio, now widely available, is becoming increasingly popular as a means of keeping children happy on long journeys. Children's audiobooks are also now part of in-flight entertainment on long-haul flights.

A recent phenomenon is 'podiobooks', or podcast audiobook novels, released on the internet in instalments, and free. They are commonly offered together with a range of stickers, ringtones and wallpapers – all designed to appeal to the younger market. The pioneer is Scott Sigler, whose website (https://scottsigler.com) offers free audio fiction, together with videos, ebooks and blog posts via social media. The whole concept is aimed particularly at teenagers and young people.

The message of all this for writers is that the radio/audio market is mushrooming, and that burgeoning technological developments and innovations seem designed to appeal particularly to the internet-savvy younger generations. If you are keen to break into the rapidly changing world of children's literature on radio and audio, this seems as favourable and opportune a time to succeed as ever. For contact details for children's radio, see *Children's television and radio* (page 326) or search online for children's audiobook publishers, and offer your services. Do not be discouraged by initial rejection – that is often a writer's early experience. Persevere. As in all professional fields, the tyro is faced with the classic catch-22 situation: radio producers and audio publishers are reluctant to offer commissions to people without a track record, while it is of course impossible to gain a track record without having won a commission or two. The only advice is to keep plugging away, hoping for that elusive lucky break – and the only consolation on offer is that even the most experienced of today's professionals was once a complete novice.

Writing for the microphone

What of the techniques that need to be applied in converting material produced for the printed page into a script that can be performed by an actor with ease at the microphone, and bring real listening pleasure to the child at the other end?

Getting to grips with abridging books for the microphone requires, in the first instance, the application of some simple arithmetic. Take a book of around 70,000 words. CDs can accommodate some 70 minutes of airtime, which translates to about 10,500 words. So a 140-minute abridgement presented in the form of two CDs will allow the abridger about 21,000 words. Where the writer is called on to abridge specifically for download, the audiobook publishers will specify the length either in terms of time or wordage. Remember, an actor can normally get through about 2,200 words in 15 minutes.

What makes a good abridgement? To reproduce the sense of an original in fewer words while, in addition and quite as important, to retain the character of the original writing. That demands the capacity to respond sympathetically to the feel of an author's style and to be able to preserve it, even when large chunks of the original are being cut away.

How much liberty is the abridger allowed in translating the printed to the spoken word, while reducing the wordage? Some audiobook producers ask for the minimum of interference with the published text; some radio producers are content for the abridger to adapt the original freely, so as to enhance the actor's performance at the microphone. The different approaches reflect the fact that, in acquiring radio reading rights, the BBC retains editorial independence over the final product, while the granting of abridged audio rights is often conditional on the original writer's approval of the abridged text. So audio producers, reluctant to run the risk of rejection, sometimes allow the abridger very little freedom.

Nevertheless it is an undoubted fact that the requirements of eye and of ear do not always coincide, and that a message easily absorbed from the printed page can become surprisingly garbled if transmitted unamended at the microphone.

In crafting a radio/audio script, the needs of the listener must be one of the prime considerations. The needs of the actor who will read it at the microphone are another. The writer must keep in the forefront of their mind the fact that the script has to be performed. The words must 'flow trippingly off the tongue'. With audio the listener is in control, and can switch on or off whenever convenient.

Principles, principles – what about practice? Let me offer a modest illustration, assuming I'm abridging for radio or podcast.

'How are you going?' Harriet said, stifling a yawn.

'The Oxford bus,' returned Pam.

Nothing wrong with that – on the printed page. If faced with it, though, the experienced radio abridger would feel it necessary to present it somewhat along the following lines:

Harriet stifled a yawn.

'How are you going?'

'The Oxford bus,' said Pam.

Why? Let's take the points in order.

Harriet said.

If the speaker's name instantly follows a piece of reported speech, and especially a question, a moment of confusion can arise in the listener's mind. In this instance, it could be unclear for a second whether 'Harriet' is included in, or excluded from, the question. It might be: *'How are you going, Harriet…?'*

The meaning is soon resolved, of course, but impediments to understanding are best eliminated.

'Stifling a yawn' is an indication of the way in which the words were said. If the actor is to provide that indication, he or she needs to know ahead of the speech how it is to be delivered. Moreover, taking the original version, if the actor stifles a yawn while saying Harriet's speech, and then reads 'said Harriet, stifling a yawn,' the passage becomes tautologous.

For this reason it is best to cut back to a bare minimum all indications in the text of how speeches are delivered – 'grimly', 'lugubriously', 'chuckling merrily', and so on. It is better to leave it to the actor and the producer to interpret most of them.

There are no apostrophes on the air. By and large, 'said' is the best radio indicator of speech. An alternative is to precede speech by some description of the speaker, and to insert the words spoken with no further indication of who is speaking. Thus:

Harriet stifled a yawn.

'How are you going?'

It is clearly Harriet speaking.

'The Oxford bus,' returned Pamela.

Two points here. Almost all the literary variants of 'said' ring false through the loudspeaker or headphones – 'cried', 'riposted', 'remarked', 'answered', and so on. For reading purposes, most are best replaced with 'said' (or better, wherever possible, omitted altogether) and the speech in question left to the actor to interpret. In this instance, 'returned' is particularly difficult for the listener – again, for no more than a moment – but is 're-turned' part of the speech? *'The Oxford bus returned...?'* It is surely best to eliminate obstacles to understanding.

This peek into the radio/audio abridger's toolbox might leave one thinking that the business is all gimmick and no heart – noses pressed up so hard against tree trunks that there is no time for the wood. It is certainly necessary in this field, as in any other, for basic techniques to be acquired and then absorbed to the point where they become second nature. Only then can they be applied to ensure that the radio and audio media are used to interpret a writer's intentions as fully and as honestly as possible.

It is, though, equally essential that the abridger of children's books reproduces, as far as possible, the plot, atmosphere and character of the original. The aim must be to leave the listener with as complete a feeling of the original book as possible, given the technical limitations of time and wordage. It is, in short, an essential aspect of the radio/audio writer's craft to keep faith with the author.

Neville Teller MBE has been contributing to BBC radio for over 50 years. He has well over 250 abridgements for radio readings to his credit, some 50 radio dramatisations and some 300 audiobook abridgements. His most recent children's abridgements include *Silver* by Andrew Motion and Michael Morpurgo's *A Medal for Leroy*. His most recent radio dramatisation was *Ozma of Oz* by Frank Baum, for broadcast across the USA. That script, together with nine others, is included in his new book *Audio Drama: 10 Plays for Radio and Audio* (2019) published by Troubador. Neville Teller is a past chairman of the Society of Authors' Broadcasting Committee and of the Audiobook Publishing Association's Contributors' Committee. He was made an MBE in 2006 'for services to broadcasting and to drama'.

See also...

Writing for visual broadcast media

Jayne Kirkham shares her experience of writing for the ever-changing world of children's broadcast media, confident that the writer's role remains essentially unchanged: the writer needs to tell a story with characters and concepts that their audience will remember and love all their lives.

'Writing for kids' telly? Easy! I mean … how hard can it be?'

So says someone who doesn't write for children. If you watch much children's content (and, if you're interested in writing for children, you should) you may be inclined to think the same. But what looks so simple has been put through a furnace of development: an idea will have been shaped, moulded, reshaped, possibly with a good deal of firing, before it is finally hammered into something that perfectly suits a broadcaster's particular audience. And that audience is very particular; children have all the myriad tastes and genre preferences of adults but with the different stages of a child's personal, social and physical development thrown in. Furthermore, the content has to be fun or, as kids in a recent report put it, 'amazing/cool/excellent' (*Social Media, Television and Children Report 2019: University of Sheffield, BBC Children's and Dubit*). Even the serious stuff must engage or children simply won't watch.

When I started writing for children's TV, it was a hugely competitive but fairly straightforward world to navigate, with only a handful of broadcasters and producers that commissioned shows. If you went to the Children's Media Conference (or Showcomotion, as it was called then), you could fit everyone you needed to meet into one room. Nowadays, if you go to the Children's Media Conference (and if you're interested in writing for children, you should), everyone you need to meet will still be there – but that 'everyone' covers not just TV but online, games, books, apps and toys! Changes in children's media policy, and advances in technology, mean that children and young people have grown accustomed to accessing content (what used to be called 'programmes') whenever and wherever they like, and in all sorts of formats. They might watch something on TV while accessing extra information about it on their tablet and simultaneously playing along on their phone; what's more, they are now able to make and broadcast their own content!

So it looks like a much harder world, and a bewildering world, for a writer to get into. But actually, whatever innovations arise and throw the industry into flux, for a writer the basics remain the same: know your audience and know how to tell a story, with characters and concepts that kids will remember and love all their lives. If you know your audience, you will know what they are watching and where. You will understand that they may prefer to watch their content on YouTube rather than CBBC, and you will be aware of the growth of Netflix, the Sky Kids app, smart speakers, and whatever new players are on the scene by the time you read this.

For a writer, things haven't changed as much as everyone would have us believe; children still enjoy drama, comedy, animation, game shows, documentaries and news made by professional media companies. Those companies need writers like you and me, but getting in touch with them can take a bit of detective work – and a decent pause button, so that you can read a programme's credits properly. Another source of information is the programme's entry on www.imdb.com (International Movie Database) and, once you know the name of the production company, you can do an online search for their website where you can generally find contact details for particular producers and/or development departments. Before you contact anyone about writing for them, however, find out as much as you can about the producers, production companies, and their intellectual properties (IP). What have they made in the past? What are they developing now? What do they want to develop?

Similarly, the children's channels or platforms have websites you can explore. By 'platforms', I'm referring to online providers such as Netflix, Amazon, Azoomee and Hopster, as well as the public service broadcasters (BBC, ITV, Channel 4 and Five) and the subscription channels (Nickelodeon, Pop, Cartoon Network, Disney, etc). To get beyond the shiny, public pages of games and fan chat, enter words like 'producer guidelines' or 'commissioning' into your search engine; you need to find the broadcasters' business pages which show what they are looking for. Remember, each channel/platform has its own brand identity, catering for a specific audience. Make sure you know the difference between a Nickelodeon and a Netflix show.

An easy way to compare and contrast the different platforms is to attend a trade event, such as the Children's Media Conference held in Sheffield every July (www.thechildrensmediaconference.com). There are other conferences and festivals, but I think the CMC is the best for children's media professionals; all the broadcasters attend and hold commissioning sessions where they explain what they want to produce in the next few years. It's also a great opportunity to meet producers and other professionals you may want to collaborate with or work for, with lots of time in the conference schedule for networking.

Children's media has been through some very troubled times in recent years but, thanks to some hard-fought campaigning by organisations such as the Children's Media Foundation and the WGGB (Writers' Guild of Great Britain; see page 377), there are many reasons to be cheerful; tax incentives for children's content, along with the new BFI Young Audience Content Fund (see www.bfi.org.uk/supporting-uk-film/production-development-funding/young-audiences-content-fund), have done much to boost the production sector. If you've been watching the credits carefully (and if you're interested in writing for children, you should), you will have noticed that very few shows are the product of one producer and one broadcaster. International co-production is the norm; this may mean that some of the writing will be given to overseas writers but, rather than despair, let this open your eyes to other markets and territories. Countries like China, Brazil, India and many others have looked to the UK for writing talent in recent years. Annual international conferences, such as the Children's Media Conference here in the UK, Mipcom Junior in Cannes (www.mipjunior.com) and Kidscreen in Miami (http://kidscreen.com), are great places to meet international companies face to face. But that can be costly and time-consuming – it's easier and cheaper to subscribe to their regular newsletters for excellent insider information that you can follow up.

I feel that working for an overseas company is one of the few reasons why a screenwriter might need an agent. I know a good number of non-agented writers working in the UK on existing shows; the contracts are generally straightforward and many follow WGGB guidelines. But when I have had overseas commissions, I've been grateful to have an agent used to dealing with other territories – not least getting the exchange rate and tax implications right.

It surely must be the dream of every screenwriter to get their own show produced. When the traditional broadcasters were the only players in town, new shows were generally commissioned from writers who had already proven themselves on other series. To get their ideas on screen, writers were dependent on the broadcaster's own producers or independent production companies and they often lost much creative control. The internet has created many more routes by which you can now reach your intended audience and writers can be much more entrepreneurial, using YouTube, creating games, crowdfunding or working with schools. For example, *Night Zookeeper* – now available on Sky Kids – started as a web-based teaching aid to encourage children to start writing their own stories.

However, no matter how you intend to get your idea in front of your audience, it needs to go through the same rigorous development process: interrogating the concept and the characters to make sure that it is age-appropriate and will engage the audience utterly, not just in its main format but also in different 'transmedia' guises (as an app, books, in social media, video game). And don't forget to consider toys and other merchandising, as appropriate. Different genres will, of course, have different opportunities and limitations. A drama like *The Dumping Ground* is unlikely to sell as many lunchboxes as, say, preschool animation *Paw Patrol*, but that doesn't mean it shouldn't get made. Just remember to allow the potential revenue returns to determine the budget. Rather confusingly, industry people tend to bandy the term 'genre' in their own special way, using it to describe animation, drama, preschool or comedy. If you watch enough kids' content, you will know that nearly all dramas have a lot of comedy, that animation covers everything from wacky shorts to sitcom to intense re-enactments for documentaries, and that preschool covers everything but in a way that's appropriate for the under-sixes. As I've mentioned, the specific requirements for each broadcaster/platform brand should be available on their websites.

Once you have sufficiently developed your idea – and in that development I would include writing some sample scripts to fully prove whether your idea works or not – and have researched the market, it is time to get it out there. Does your intended recipient give guidelines on submitting your intellectual property (IP)? They may ask you to use an online submission portal. If there are no guidelines, write a brief email introducing yourself and your project as succinctly as possible. Can you pitch it in one sentence? Can you explain the series on a single sheet of A4 paper? Do you have a decent sample script to show off your writing talents? Some producers are wary of unsolicited attachments, so you may want to start with just the email and then follow up when they have responded. Again, be led by their specific guidelines.

If you have the opportunity to pitch in person, practise! These are very busy people, so clarity and passion are essential for you and your idea to stand out. Show that you know your audience and any business or creative constraints: how easy would it be to animate your idea? Would young actors be able to deliver your stunts? The first time I pitched in person, I was a quivering jelly and just about as coherent. But – you know what? – I wasn't eaten, and the world didn't end. It sounds silly, but producers and commissioners are people and, in this industry, they're usually lovely people at that.

Being realistic, it is unlikely that your first project will get picked up. There is a lot to learn, so learn it; take feedback when it is offered and get better. It can feel galling to take what feels like a barrage of criticism from a 12 year-old 'executive', but that '12-year-old' will know better than you do what works on their platform. And they may well be in a position to offer you work on another show. That does often happen. There can be many reasons why an executive doesn't like your project, but that doesn't mean they don't like you or your style of writing. They may not get back to you for a while … I was once called out of the blue by a producer who had rejected an idea of mine several years before; I ended up writing an animation series and a feature film (and, while the feature is in interminable 'pre-production', I still enjoy the residual fees from the international sales of the TV series).

The best advice I was ever given as a new writer was that you only fail when you give up. So keep on writing; keep on submitting; keep on keeping on.

Jayne Kirkham is a screenwriter and a script and development consultant. With over 30 years' experience working with and writing for children and young people, Jayne has written for a wide range of theatre, film, TV, radio and online projects, ranging in size from small conservation films in Africa to international feature films. Her most recent credits in the UK include BBC's CBeebies' *Bing Bunny* and *Treasure Champs* and original stories and poems for radio and online. Jayne taught at the Northern Film School for 14 years, and is a member of the board of directors of the Children's Media Foundation. See her website https://jaynekirkham.com for more information.

See also...
● *Children's literature on radio and audio,* page 313

Writing to a brief

In the exacting process of writing to a brief, the writer has to produce work to satisfy others as opposed to exploring their own project ideas. The writer may work with others as part of a team when script writing or collaborate with an artistic director when adapting a play. Di Redmond looks at three aspects of writing to a brief for children.

Writing to a brief is enormously varied. I never know what's going to land on my desk – it could be an animation, a series of books, a live action drama script or a stage play. When writing to a brief, you need to have the ability to absorb material very quickly and be disciplined enough to put your own ideas on the back burner. If you twist the commissioner's brief in order to accommodate what you want to write you'll very soon be out of a job!

Animation
The writing team
An animation series is usually commissioned in blocks of 26 or 52 ten-minute episodes. US companies like to have commissioning meetings with large numbers of writers brainstorming for two or three days. UK companies generally prefer smaller groups of writers brainstorming for a day at most. You might be invited to meetings through your agent or through your own personal contact with the animation house or broadcaster. At the initial meeting you will be told the content of the show, after which you'll pitch ideas – or 'thumbnails' as they are often called. If they are approved, you will become one of the writing team.

On a financial note, every stage of the writing process should be covered in your writer's contract, from the writers' meeting where you should receive a full day's fee plus travelling expenses, to separate payments for the Treatment, Draft 1, Draft 2, and the Final Polish Draft. If a contract along these lines isn't offered in advance I'd be extremely wary of attending any meeting.

The writing process
Working from the 'Bible', a document which contains everything the writer needs to know, from character descriptions to locations and props, the writing process begins in earnest. It's a real bonus if the 'Bible' contains a fully executed script as it is the best template to work from: an added bonus would be a promo tape to give you the chance to see the characters and hopefully hear their 'speak'. Hearing Neil Morrissey as Bob the Builder on a promo CD crystalised Bob's character for me and made the writing process so much fun and a lot easier too. Your writing will be hugely affected by the animators' criteria. CGI (computer-generated image) animations like Disney's *Zou* and *Wanda and the Alien* are vastly different from stop frame puppetry animation like *Timmy Time* and *Postman Pat*. Discuss the practical problems with the animators at an early stage so you don't waste time writing scripts that are impossible to execute. For example, if your plot line is about bubbles, make sure the studio can do bubbles; if it's about little boats bobbing in a harbour, check that the animators can do different kinds of water – stormy, misty, calm and choppy. There's nothing more frustrating than getting to Draft 1 stage only to discover that one of

the main elements in the story can't be animated. Be bold and ask the practical questions right from the start.

When you finally get the green light to go to Draft 1, remember that behind the dialogue other things are happening simultaneously: action on the set, facial expressions, sound effects and music all have to be written alongside the script.

Storylines

To kick-start a series, storylines might be developed when the writing team meet for the first time. Writers may be invited to choose a storyline that grabs them and develop it into a three- or four-page treatment, which is a detailed scene-by-scene breakdown of a ten-minute episode. The first script is without doubt the hardest because no matter how thorough the 'Bible' is you've still got to familiarise yourself with the characters and their locations, and balance out the A and the B plot. If the script is too long it will be edited down before it's recorded, so make sure that it's the right length before you send it off to the broadcaster. A ten-minute script with opening and closing credits is around 13–15 pages, depending on the font size you use. The commissioners will be looking for scripts that contain humour, warmth, clarity and an understanding of the target audience. If the show is about a builder then a building job will be essential to every plot line; if it's about a postman then he has to do his post round. Most scripts, even if they're only ten minutes long, have an A and a B plot, both of which have to be reconciled by the end of the episode. Some commissioners prefer a three-act structure, with three underpinning questions – What's the goal? What's the risk? What does the character learn? It's a challenging writing process which highlights the dramatic peaks in the story.

The script editor

A good script editor coordinates the scripts and makes sure the series has one voice, whether it's a ballerina, an alien, a runaway train or a sailing boat. Writers have different styles, which is why they've been chosen to do the job. The script editor with her overall view of the show has the sensitive task of liaising with the commissioner and the producer on the writers' behalf. Sometimes you *don't* want to see the notes the producer has made: they may be too abrupt or confusing. A good script editor will work on the notes before handing them on to the writing team; they'll also be rigorous about timing.

Stage plays

As well as writing my own stage plays, I've also adapted stage plays from the classics such as *Hard Times* by Charles Dickens and Homer's *The Odyssey*. *Hard Times* was commissioned for the Edinburgh Festival with a cast of 30, whilst *The Odyssey* was staged at the Polka Theatre in London with a cast of six. Writers should listen hard to the artistic director's requirements and take on board the limitations of the theatre's budget. If too much is spent on props and costumes it may be at the cost of funding an actor, so be prepared to adapt and compromise.

Adapting from the classics

The two books I adapted couldn't have been more different although the writing process was exactly the same. I read both books until I knew them backwards, after which I felt confident about dramatising them for a young modern audience.

The brief for *The Odyssey* was to write a 90-minute play with a ten-minute interval for 8–12 year-olds. But *The Odyssey* is full of sex and the language of Homer, though hauntingly beautiful, is certainly not pitched at children. The greatest challenge was making the story come alive for a very young audience without destroying the nobility of the original piece. Working closely with the artistic director, I wrote three drafts of the play before I felt I'd got it right, by which time I felt like the gods and heroes of Ancient Greece were part of my extended family! It's a knowledge I've never lost and have since written four books based on classical Greek heroes. That's another great thing about writing: you can transpose a story from one art form to another.

Book series

A book series may be commissioned as a result of a writer pitching an idea to a publisher, or a publisher may have spotted a gap in the market that a writer has been invited to fill. The books vary in length – 2,000–40,000 words – depending on the age range.

I've written series on football, show jumping, theatre school, a veterinary practice, a drama queen, and a dog. No matter what target age group you're writing for, you have to thoroughly research the subject. For my show-jumping series I virtually lived at the livery yard, trailing the head groom and asking questions. I've been lucky finding professionals who have allowed me into their lives and let me watch them at work, though I have had a few nasty shocks in the process. Once I found myself masked and gloved in an equine operating theatre watching a Newmarket racehorse under the scalpel. You *really* do have to know your subject when you're writing this kind of specialist book. The readers will be highly critical of any inaccuracies, so be careful what you write otherwise you'll get letters of complaint.

Di Redmond is a prolific writer for children's television. She has worked for Disney, Aardman, CBBC, CITV, HIT Entertainment NYC, Milkshake Channel 5, Nikelodeon and Nick Jr. Her credits include *Zou, Timmy Time, Duckport, Wanda and the Alien, Elias, Bob the Builder, Postman Pat, Roary the Racing Car, Tweenies, Fifi Forget-me-Not* and *Angelina Ballerina*. She also writes for screen, stage and radio and has published over 100 books, and is a ghostwriter. Di also writes under the pen name Daisy Styles.

See also...

- *Children's literature on radio and audio,* page 313
- *Writing for children's theatre,* page 331
- *Adapting books for the stage,* page 337

Children's television and radio

The information in this section has been compiled as a general guide for writers, artists, agents and publishers to the major companies and key contacts operating within the children's broadcasting industry. As personnel, corporate structures and commissioning guidelines can change frequently, please check the relevant websites for the most up-to-date information.

REGULATION

Ofcom

Riverside House, 2A Southwark Bridge Road, London SE1 9HA
tel 020-7981 3000, 0300 123 3000
website www.ofcom.org.uk
Ceo Sharon White

Ofcom is required to report annually to parliament and exists to: further the interests of consumers by balancing choice and competition with the duty to encourage plurality, protect viewers and listeners, promote diversity in the media and ensure full and fair competition between communications providers.

Advertising Standards Authority

Mid City Place, 71 High Holborn, London WC1V 6QT
tel 020-7492 2222
website www.asa.org.uk
Ceo Guy Parker

The Advertising Standards Authority is the UK's independent regulator of advertising across all media. Its work includes acting on complaints and taking action against misleading, harmful or offensive advertisements.

TELEVISION

BabyTV

Baby Network Ltd, 10 Hammersmith Grove, London W6 7AP
email info@babytvchannel.com
website www.babytv.com
Channel Manager Debbie Pattinson

BabyTV is the world's leading baby and toddler network, for children under five and their parents, airing 24 hours a day and completely commercial-free. BabyTV features top quality shows that are created by child development experts and are designed for child and parent to enjoy together. Each hour on BabyTV is an enriching journey full of stories, songs, rhymes and loveable characters.

The BBC

BBC Broadcasting House, Portland Place, London W1A 1AA
website www.bbc.co.uk
Director, Children's Alice Webb

The BBC is the world's largest broadcasting organisation, with a remit to provide programmes that inform, educate and entertain. Established by Royal Charter, the BBC is a public service broadcaster funded by a licence fee. The Director, Children's is responsible for the overall direction and management of all of the BBC's services for children, including CBeebies and CBBC channels and their websites.

Commissioning

CBeebies and CBBC are self-commissioning and self-scheduling, and proposals may be submitted at any time throughout the year. All submissions for TV and online should be made via Pitch. For further details and commissioning guidelines visit:
www.bbc.co.uk/commissioning/tv/childrens-discovery
www.bbc.co.uk/commissioning/tv/articles/cbeebies
www.bbc.co.uk/commissioning/tv/articles/cbbc
www.bbc.co.uk/commissioning/tv/articles/pitch

CBeebies

website www.bbc.co.uk/cbeebies
Head of Content, BBC Children's Cheryl Taylor,
Commissioning Michael Towner, Julia Bond, Joel Wilenius

CBeebies offers mixed genre output for TV, online and radio and is specifically produced for a young audience using a variety of formats including live action and animation. Content covers drama, comedy, entertainment and factual, and the target audience is children aged 0–6 years. CBeebies is on air daily from 6am–7pm.

CBBC

website www.bbc.co.uk/cbbc
Commissioning Melissa Hardinge, Kez Margrie, Hugh Lawton, Amy Buscombe, Julia Bond, Mario Dubois

CBBC offers mixed genre output for TV and online. Content covers drama, factual, comedy, entertainment, animation and news, and the target audience is children aged 6–12 years. CBBC plans to include more content for teenagers aged 13–16 via the iPlayer service. CBBC is on air daily from 7am–9pm.

BBC writersroom

website www.bbc.co.uk/writersroom

BBC Writersroom is the first port of call at the BBC

for unsolicited scripts and new writers. It champions writing talent across a range of genres, including children's drama and comedy. Visit the website to discover:

- how and when to submit a script;
- new opportunities for writers;
- writing tips and success stories;
- interviews and top tips from writers;
- competitions and events.

The BBC Writersroom blog provides a wealth of behind-the-scenes commentary from writers and producers who have worked on BBC TV and radio programmes: www.bbc.co.uk/blogs/writersroom.

Boomerang
email contact@cartoonnetwork.co.uk
website www.boomerangtv.co.uk

Boomerang was developed by Cartoon Network to provide fun, entertaining and light educational viewing for children aged 4–7 years. Online, children can experience a range of games and activities including adventure, sports, puzzles and fun educational games.

Cartoon Network
email contact@cartoonnetwork.co.uk
website www.cartoonnetwork.co.uk

Cartoon entertainment broadcast 24 hours a day. Sister channel Cartoonito (www.cartoonito.co.uk) provides fun, entertaining and light educational viewing for preschoolers.

Channel 4
124–126 Horseferry Road, London SW1P 2TX
tel 020-7396 4444
website www.channel4.com/commissioning/
Ceo Alex Mahon
Director of Programmes Ian Katz

Channel 4 is a publicly owned, commercially-funded, not-for-profit public service broadcaster and has a remit to be innovative, experimental and distinctive. Its public ownership and not-for-profit status ensure all profit generated by its commercial activity is directly reinvested back into the delivery of its public service remit. As a publisher-broadcaster, Channel 4 is also required to commission UK content from the independent production sector and currently works with over 400 creative companies across the UK every year. In addition to the main Channel 4 service, its portfolio includes E4, More4, Film4, 4Music, 4Seven, channel4.com and digital service All 4 which presents all of C4's on-demand content, digital innovations and live linear channel streams in one place online for the first time.

4Talent supports people to build their careers in the media industry across a range of disciplines. Visit http://4talent.channel4.com

Commissioning
Information about commissioning and related processes and guidelines can be found at www.channel4.com/info/commissioning.

Channel 5
17–29 Hawley Crescent, Camden Town, London NW1 8TT
tel 020-3580 3600
email viewerenquiries@channel5.com
website www.channel5.com
Director of Progamming Ben Frow

Channel 5 brands include Channel 5, 5Star and 5USA, and an on-demand service, My5. Channel 5 broadcasts over 24 hours of children's programmes every week under the Milkshake brand, which is aimed at children aged 2–7 years and airs daily from 6–9.15am (10am at weekends). Channel 5 commissions, co-produces and acquires preschool programming through a wide range of deals and arrangements.

Commissioning
email milkshakeprogramming@channel5.com
website www.channel5.com/commissions
website www.channel5.com/childrens-programming

CITV
The London Television Centre, Upper Ground, London SE1 9LT
website www.itv.com/citv
Ceo Carolyn McCall

ITV is the UK's largest commercial TV network. In addition to TV broadcasting services, ITV also delivers programming via a number of platforms, including ITV Player. The ITV network is responsible for the commissioning, scheduling and marketing of network programmes on ITV1 and its digital channel portfolio including ITV2, ITV3, ITV4, ITVBe, ITV Encore and CITV, the commercial free-to-air children's channel. CITV commissions and acquires a variety of programmes aimed at children up to age 11 years.

Commissioning
website www.itv.com/commissioning

See website for information about commissioning and how to submit an idea.

Disney Channel UK
3 Queen Caroline Street, London W6 9PE
tel 020-8222 1000
email help@disney.co.uk
website www.disney.co.uk/disney-channel

A cable and satellite network run by the Walt Disney Company specialising in programming for children from preschoolers to teens. There are three channels: Disney Channel, Disney Junior and Disney XD.

Television, film and radio

Nickelodeon UK

17–29 Hawley Crescent, London NW1 8TT
email letterbox@nick.co.uk
website www.nick.co.uk

Nickelodeon UK comprises three channels with a target audience spanning children aged approximately 2–12 years: Nickelodeon, NickToons (www.nicktoons.co.uk) aimed at children aged 6–9 years and NickJr (www.nickjr.co.uk) aimed at children aged 2–5 years.

POP

Columbia Pictures Corporation Ltd, 25 Golden Square, London W1F 9LU
email info@popfun.co.uk
website www.popfun.co.uk

Cartoons and live action series for boys and girls aged 4–9 years with two sister channels:

Tiny Pop

website www.tinypop.com

Cartoons and live action series for children aged 3–7 years.

Pop Max

website www.popmax.co.uk

Animated and live action series aimed at boys aged 7–12 years.

Radió Telefís Éireann (RTÉ)

Donnybrook, Dublin 4, Republic of Ireland
email info@rte.ie
website www.rte.ie

RTÉ offers a comprehensive range of programmes for children and young people. RTÉjr is aimed at children under 7 years and delivers a mix of original and acquired live action and animated content. RTÉ Two offers preschool programming in the mornings. Mixed programming for older children is available on TRTÉ.

Commissioning

website https://about.rte.ie/commissioning/commissioning-briefs/rte-young-peoples/

See website for information about commissioning and submitting proposals for children and young people.

S4C

Parc Ty Glas, Llanishen, Cardiff CF14 5DU
tel 0370 600 4141
website www.s4c.co.uk
Ceo Owen Evans

S4C is the world's only Welsh language TV channel, broadcasting programmes on sport, drama, music, factual, entertainment and culture. S4C also provides services for children including: Cyw, for younger viewers and Stwnsh for older children and teenagers. See website for full details of commissioning and production guidelines and personnel.

RADIO

CBeebies Radio

website www.bbc.co.uk/cbeebies/radio

CBeebies Radio is aimed at encouraging preschool children to develop their listening skills. Over 70 shows are available and in addition to radio output, the website contains games, songs, make & colour and story-time activities.

BBC School Radio

website www.bbc.co.uk/schoolradio

BBC School Radio provides audio resources for primary schools including podcasts, downloads, audio and video clips, learning resources and teachers' notes that are curriculum-linked to Key Stages 1, 2, 3 and 4. Some Early Years Foundation Stage (EYFS) resources are also available.

Fun Kids

website www.funkidslive.com

A British children's digital radio station (not national) providing programming to entertain children aged 7–12 years with a mixture of songs, stories, competitions and news. Available to listen via the website or on DAB Digital Radio across London and south east England.

ORGANISATIONS CONNECTED TO BROADCASTING

BARB

20 Orange Street, London WC2H 7EF
tel 020-7024 8100
email enquiries@barb.co.uk
website www.barb.co.uk
Ceo Justin Sampson

The Broadcasters' Audience Research Board is the official source of viewing figures in the UK.

Ipsos MORI

3 Thomas More Square, London E1W 1YW
tel 020-3059 5000
website www.ipsos-mori.com/ipsos-mori/en-uk
Ceo Ipsos MORI Ben Page
Audience Measurement and Media Development Liz Landy

One of the UK's leading research companies, involved in the work of BARB and RAJAR.

Media.info

website http://media.info/uk

Maintains detailed listings of UK TV and radio

providers, newspapers, magazines and media ownership.

Pact (Producers Alliance for Cinema and Television)

3rd Floor, Fitzrovia House, 153–157 Cleveland Street, London W1T 6QW
tel 020-7380 8230
website www.pact.co.uk

Pact is the trade association representing the commercial interests of UK independent TV, film, digital, children's and animation media companies. For details of children's independent TV and film production companies, see the website.

Public Media Alliance

Arts 1.80, DEV, University of East Anglia, Norwich NR4 7TJ
email info@publicmediaalliance.org
website www.publicmediaalliance.org
Ceo Sally-Ann Wilson

World's largest association of public broadcasters.

The Radio Academy

Suite 9A, Crown House, 94 Armley Road, Leeds LS12 2EJ
website www.radioacademy.org
Managing Director Sean Childerley

The Radio Academy is a registered charity dedicated to the promotion of excellence in UK radio broadcasting and production. For over 30 years the Radio Academy has run the annual Radio Academy Awards, which celebrate content and creativity in the industry.

RadioCentre

6th Floor, 55 New Oxford Street, London WC1A 1BS
tel 020-7010 0600
email info@radiocentre.org
website www.radiocentre.org
Ceo Siobhan Kenny

RadioCentre is the voice of UK commercial radio and works with government, policy makers and regulators, and provides a forum for industry-wide debate and discussion.

RAJAR

6th Floor, 55 New Oxford Street, London WC1A 1BS
tel 020-7395 0630
website www.rajar.co.uk
Ceo Jerry Hill

RAJAR – Radio Joint Audience Research – is the official body in charge of measuring radio audiences in the UK. It is jointly owned by the BBC and the RadioCentre on behalf of the commercial sector.

Television, film and radio

Theatre
Writing for children's theatre

Writing plays for children is not a soft option. David Wood considers children to be the most difficult audience to write for and shares his thoughts here about this challenge.

'Would you write the Christmas play?' These six words, uttered by John Hole, Director of the Swan Theatre, Worcester, unwittingly changed my life, setting me off on a trail I'm still treading over 40 years later. It wasn't a totally mad question, even though I was then cutting my teeth as an 'adult' actor/director – and indeed I have managed to continue these so-called mainstream activities to a limited degree ever since. No, it had already struck me that children's audiences were important and, by doing magic at birthday parties since my teens, I had already developed an aptitude for and delight in entertaining children.

At Worcester I had organised Saturday morning children's theatre, inveigling my fellow repertory actors into helping me tell stories, lead participation songs and perform crazy sketches. And I was still haunted by the memory of seeing, a couple of years earlier, a big commercial panto in

Further information

TYA (Theatre for Young Audiences)
website www.tya-uk.org
TYA is the UK Centre of ASSITEJ (International Association of Theatre for Children and Young People). The website lists most of the companies currently in production. In association with Aurora Metro Press, it publishes *Theatre for Children and Young People* (see 'Further reading'), a comprehensive collection of articles about the development of children's theatre and theatre-in-education in the UK over the last 50 years.

National Theatre Bookshop
National Theatre, South Bank, London SE1 9PX
tel 020-7452 3456
email bookshop@nationaltheatre.org.uk
website www.shop.nationaltheatre.org.uk

Samuel French
tel 020-7387 9373
email submissions@samuelfrench.co.uk
website www.samuelfrench.co.uk
Online shop for playscripts and books about theatre, details of licensing and performance rights for plays and musicals, and publisher of new plays. Launched Abbott, their play reading app, in 2017.

which the star comedian cracked an off-colour joke to a matinee house virtually full of children, got an appreciative cackle from a small party of ladies in the stalls, then advanced to the footlights and said, 'Let's get the kids out of here, then we can get started!'. In the dark I blushed and my hackles rose. How dare this man show such disdain for the young audience whose parents' hard-earned cash had contributed towards his doubtless considerable salary? It set me thinking about how few proper plays were then written and performed for children. There were traditional favourites like *Peter Pan* in London, the occasional *Wizard of Oz*, *Toad of Toad Hall* and *Alice in Wonderland* in the regions but that was about it. Nothing new. Later I discovered my assessment had been too sweeping. There were several pioneers out there presenting proper plays for children, including Brian Way (Theatre Centre), Caryl Jenner (Unicorn), John Allen (Glyndebourne Children's Theatre) and John English (Midlands Arts Centre), but their work was not then widely recognised. Their contribution to the development of children's theatre in the UK cannot be overestimated. Also, in 1965, the Belgrade Theatre, Coventry, had created the first theatre-in-education company, touring innovative work into schools; and early in 1967, I had acted in the first production of the TIE Company at the Palace Theatre, Watford.

So writing *The Tinder Box* for Christmas 1967 seemed a natural opportunity and, although I don't think it was very good, it paved the way for me to write around 75 (so far) plays that try to trigger the imagination, make children laugh, cry and think, and hopefully lead them towards a love of theatre. The journey hasn't always been easy. It is frustrating that children's theatre is still often perceived as third division theatre; funding for it is less than for its adult counterpart, even though it often costs as much, sometimes more, to put on, and always commands a lower seat price; critics generally ignore it; and most theatre folk seem to think it is only for beginners or failures, a ridiculous belief, since children are the most difficult and honest audience of all – and yet the most rewarding when we get it right.

Let's pause briefly to talk terminology. The phrase 'children's theatre' means different things to different people. Whereas 'youth theatre' clearly implies that young people are taking part in the play, 'children's theatre' can mean not only children performing but also (more correctly, in my view) theatre produced by adults for children to watch. And, although I have occasionally, and enjoyably, written plays for children to perform (*Lady Lollipop*, from Dick King-Smith's book) or for children to take part in alongside adults (*The Lighthouse Keeper's Lunch*, from Ronda and David Armitage's book and *Dinosaurs and All That Rubbish*, from Michael Foreman's book), the vast majority of my plays have been written for professional actors to perform for children. Don't get me wrong. Participation by children is hugely beneficial and worthwhile, but I like to feel my plays might provide the inspiration to encourage them to want to do it themselves. I believe that children respond to exciting examples that inspire them. I also believe that children are more likely to, say, want to learn to play a musical instrument if they see and hear the best professional musicians playing in a concert. They are more likely to want to excel at football if they see – live or on television – the best professional teams displaying dazzling skills.

So any advice I can offer about children's theatre is mainly aimed towards writers who would like to create plays for grown-ups to perform for children. Having said that, it has always surprised me that several of my professionally performed plays have been subsequently put on by schools and youth groups who cope, showing tremendous flair and imagination, with tricky technical demands. I sometimes wish I could write more plays specifically for schools and youth groups, but I think I might be tempted to oversimplify (which would be patronising) or to try to write enough roles for a very large cast, which might dilute the content and fail to provide a satisfying structure.

Encouragingly, the professional children's theatre scene today is much healthier than when I started. There are many more touring companies (see page 344) large and small, producing high-quality work for all ages. There has been an exciting explosion in the amount of work for under-fives. And at last, we have two full-time children's theatre buildings – Unicorn and Polka – who put on their own plays as well as receive other companies' work. They are both in London, and the big hope is that there will in the future be many more such beacons in other cities and towns. Children are entitled to their own theatre, and creating theatre buildings especially for them, run by committed professionals, is the best way to improve the quantity, quality and status of the work. Alongside that, our major theatres, including the National and the Royal Shakespeare Company, should be setting an example by making children's theatre an integral part of their programming, rather than occasionally mounting a children's play as an optional extra. And this means more than coming up with an annual Christmas show.

Study the market

Go to see shows. Which companies are doing what? How many cast members can they afford? Are they looking for original plays as well as adaptations of successful books with big titles and box office appeal? Try to meet the artistic directors, to discuss what they might be looking for. What size spaces are the companies playing in? Studios? Large theatres? Do they have facilities for scene changes? Is there flying? Incidentally, restrictions on cast size and staging possibilities are not necessarily a bad thing. Well-defined parameters within which to work can be a help not a hindrance. I was asked to write a play for the Towngate, Basildon, a theatre that had no flying, not much stage depth and virtually no wing space. And I was allowed a cast of only six. At first I despaired but then managed to think positively and wrote *The Gingerbread Man*, which ended up paying the rent for 30 years! The play is set on a giant Welsh dresser. No props or scenery come on or off stage during the show – the basic set is self-contained. And the six characters are joined by the off-stage voices (recorded) of the 'Big Ones', the human owners of the dresser.

It may be putting the cart before the horse to worry about where and how your play might be performed – before you've written it! But it really is foolish to start before finding out what might be practical and realistic. Quite frankly, a cast of 20, or even a dozen, is going to be out of the question for most professional companies, so if your idea demands such numbers, maybe you should approach a school, a youth drama group or an amateur dramatic society instead.

Rather than rely on others, might you be in a position to create your own openings? Many children's theatre practitioners, including myself, have had to start by 'doing it themselves'. I, like Richard Gill, Vicky Ireland and Annie Wood (former artistic directors of the Polka Theatre) not only write but also direct. And Richard Gill, Tim Webb (Oily Cart), Guy Holland (Quicksilver) and I (Whirligig), went as far as to create companies to produce our own work, because we knew we were unlikely to get other companies to put it on. The TYA (Theatre for Young Audiences) website (see box) lists most of the companies currently in production, and is a useful first port of call to see the scope of the work.

What 'works' for children?

A good, satisfying story makes a helpful start, told with theatrical flair. By that I mean that we should use theatrical techniques to spark the imagination of the audience – scenery, costume, sound, lighting, puppetry, magic, circus skills, masks, mime, dancing and music. The physical as well as the verbal can help to retain the attention and interest of children. Page after page of two characters sitting talking are likely to prove a turn-off. It's better to see them do something rather than just talk about it. I try to introduce lots of 'suddenlies' to help keep the audience riveted to their seats, wanting to know what happens next. I've often said that my life's work has been dedicated to stopping children going to the lavatory. Suddenlies – a new character appearing, a sound effect, a lighting change, a surprise twist, a musical sting – can be a huge help. Compare it to the page-turning appeal of a successful children's book.

Theatre

Play ideas can be found in fairy tales, myths and legends, traditional rhymes and popular stories. Be careful, however, not to waste time adapting books in copyright, unless you have got the necessary permission – no public performances, paid or unpaid, can be given without this. Approach the publisher or the author's agent to discover if the stage rights are available and, if they are, how much it might cost to acquire them for a year or two. Or you might use an incident from history, a pertinent modern social issue, such as conservation, or the real life of an inspirational or controversial person. Or you could explore a social problem especially relevant to children, like single-parent families or bullying.

In my book *Theatre for Children: A Guide to Writing, Adapting, Directing and Acting*, I identify useful ingredients for children's plays. They are really fairly obvious – things that we know children respond to. They include animals, toys, fantasy, a quest, goodies and baddies, humour, scale (small characters in large environments and vice versa), a child at the centre of the story. And justice – think *Cinderella*. Children, like adults, have a strong sense of fairness and will root for the underdog. Roald Dahl's stories, eight of which I have been lucky enough to adapt, all use this. Sophie (in *The BFG*), James (in *James and the Giant Peach*) and Boy (in *The Witches*) are all disadvantaged orphans whose strength of character leads them through immense difficulties to eventual triumph. They are empowered to succeed in an adult-dominated world, and children identify with them.

The use of audience participation is an option much argued about by children's theatre practitioners. Many hate it. For some plays, it would, indeed, be totally inappropriate. But for others it can be exciting and fun. I'm not talking about basic panto participation – 'he's behind you!' – though even this can be used on occasion with integrity. I'm talking about what I call 'positive participation', in which the audience contribute to the action by helping or hindering, by having ideas or by taking part in a 'set piece'. In *The Selfish Shellfish* they create a storm to fool an oil slick. In *The Meg and Mog Show* (for very small children), they make springtime noises and movements to encourage Meg's garden to grow. In *The See-Saw Tree* they vote on whether to save an ancient oak or allow it to be cut down to make way for a children's playground. In *The Gingerbread Man* they help catch the scavenging Sleek the Mouse under an upturned mug. Their contribution is crucial to the development and resolution of the plot. In *The Twits* the audience fools Mr and Mrs Twit by making them think that they, the audience, are upside down. They all remove their shoes, put them on their hands and stretch their arms up while lowering their heads! The sight of a thousand children all doing this, with joy and not a shred of cynicism, is pure magic to me.

I don't believe that a children's play has to have a moral, a self-improving message for the audience. But I do believe a children's play should *be* moral, presenting a positive attitude and an uplifting, hopeful conclusion. And I resent the notion that children's plays should always be written to tie in with the National Curriculum. Many do, but the educationalists shouldn't dictate our agenda – the tail shouldn't wag the dog.

Before you start

I strongly recommend that you create a synopsis, outlining the events in story order. This leads to clarity of storytelling, to the disciplined pursuit of a through-line, with not too many subplots that could end up as time-wasting, irrelevant cul-de-sacs. For myself, it would be foolish to think I had the brilliance to start a play with only an initial idea and just let my imagination lead me through uncharted waters. I find it far better to let the juices flow during the synopsis stage and, when it comes to writing the play, to conscientiously follow through my original instincts with not too many diversions.

Good luck with getting your first play produced. Getting it published may need determination. It was a very special day for me when Samuel French accepted (after initial rejections) *The Owl and the Pussycat Went to See…*, my second play, co-written with Sheila Ruskin. After its first production at Worcester, I beavered away to get it on stage in London and, thanks to several friends helping financially, managed to produce it at the Jeannetta Cochrane Theatre. To save money I directed it myself. We were lucky enough to get two rave reviews. I approached Samuel French again. They came to see it and, hallelujah, offered to publish it. Since then their loyalty has been more than gratifying – they still publish most of my efforts. There are now several specialist children's play publishers, many of whom also act as licensees of amateur performances. The National Theatre Bookshop and French's Theatre Bookshop stock a fair number of plays and, when searching for a publisher, it is worth checking out their shelves. The internet can help too. Tap in the names of successful children's playwrights, like Mike Kenny, Charles Way, Brendan Murray or the late Adrian Mitchell and see what comes up.

I find that the challenge of writing a play for children never gets easier, however many times I go through the process. It certainly isn't a soft option, i.e. easier than writing a play for adults. And it carries, I believe, a big responsibility. I always worry that I haven't the right to fail: the last thing I want to do is write something that might put children off theatre for life. I'm aware that many in the audience will be first-time theatre-goers, some of whom never asked to come! It's so important to get it right, to enthuse them so much they can't wait to return. And this is where the passion comes in. Most children's theatre practitioners are passionate about what they do, with an almost missionary zeal to stimulate and delight their audience. Also, we all know that, unlike adult audiences who tend to sit quietly and clap at the end, even if they've hated the play, our children's audiences won't be (and shouldn't be) so polite. It is palpably obvious when we 'lose' them. We are dedicated to using our experience and instinct to 'hold' them, to help them enjoy the communal experience of a theatre visit and willingly enter the spirit of the performance. The buzz I get from being in an auditorium of children overtly having a great time – listening hard, watching intently, reacting, feeling, letting the play take them on a special, magical, unique journey – is a buzz I constantly strive for. I suppose that's really why I do it.

David Wood OBE has been dubbed 'the national children's dramatist' by *The Times*. His plays are performed regularly on tour, in the West End and all over the world. In 2006, for the Queen's 80th birthday party celebrations, he wrote *The Queen's Handbag*, which was broadcast live from Buckingham Palace Gardens and watched by eight million viewers on BBC1. Since 2008, his adaptation of Judith Kerr's *The Tiger Who Came to Tea* has toured the UK and abroad and played five West End seasons. The production was nominated for an Olivier Award in 2012. David's grown-up musical, *The Go-Between* (co-written with Richard Taylor, adapted from L.P. Hartley's novel), won Best Musical Production in the Theatre Awards UK 2012 and in 2016 opened in the West End at the Apollo Theatre starring Michael Crawford. His adaptation of Michelle Magorian's novel *Goodnight Mister Tom* won the 2013 Olivier Award for Best Entertainment and Family, following its season at the Phoenix Theatre. It returned to the West End (Duke of York's Theatre) and toured in 2015/16. He has adapted the following Roald Dahl novels for the stage: *The BFG*, *The Witches*, *Fantastic Mr Fox*, *James and the Giant Peach*, *The Twits*, *George's Marvellous Medicine*, *Danny the Champion of the World* and *The Magic Finger*. In 2017 there were tours of David's adaptations of *The Twits*, *Babe*, *The Sheep-Pig* and *The Tiger Who Came to Tea*, which returned to the West End in 2018. And *The See-Saw Tree* opened at the China National Theatre for Children in Beijing. His website is www.davidwood.org.uk.

Further reading

Bennett, Stuart (ed.), *Theatre for Children and Young People: 50 Years of Professional Theatre in the UK* (Aurora Metro Press 2005)

Ireland, Vicky and Paul Harman (eds), *50 Best Plays for Young Audiences* (Aurora Metro 2016)

Maguire, Tom and Karian Schuitema (eds) with foreword by David Wood, *Theatre for Young Audiences: A Critical Handbook* (Institute of Education Press 2013)

Wood, David, with Janet Grant, *Theatre for Children: A Guide to Writing, Adapting, Directing and Acting* (Faber and Faber 1997)

See also...

• *Adapting books for the stage*, page 337

Adapting books for the stage

Stephen Briggs ponders the challenges and rewards of dramatising other people's novels.

Why me?

Stephen Briggs? Stephen Briggs? Who on earth is Stephen Briggs to write about adapting novels for the stage?

Well, many years ago I wrote a stage version of *A Christmas Carol* for my amdram group … no, stick with me on this…. *Then*, a few years later I adapted two Tom Sharpe novels (these were for one-off productions and the scripts are now long gone). *However*, my overwhelming – and more recent – experience has been with dramatising the novels of the late Sir Terry Pratchett. I've now adapted 22 of Terry's books – four for Transworld/Doubleday, three for Samuel French, three for Oxford University Press, six for Methuen Drama (now at Bloomsbury) and three for Oberon Books, with three more being contracted as I type. These have been staged by amateur groups in over 20 countries from Zimbabwe to Antarctica (yes, really, Antarctica) and by professional groups in France and the Czech Republic. I also co-scripted the mini-dramatisations used by Sky One to promote their big budget television films of Terry's *Hogfather* and *Colour of Magic*.

I have been involved in amateur theatre since I left school. Not just acting, but also directing, choreography, set design/construction, costume design/construction – even including brewing mulled wine for the audiences in our chilly medieval theatre. None of this makes me an expert, not by any interpretation of the word, but I was the one who had to make my scripts work on stage since I also directed them. I was also able to get useful and honest feedback from the original author. Hopefully I've learned a few lessons along the way, which I'm happy to pass on.

Dialogue

When you watch a film, a lot of screen time is taken up by fancy stuff – Imperial star cruisers roaring through space, ill-fated liners ploughing the waves, swooping pan shots over raddled pirate ships. In a play, you don't get any of that stuff. The dialogue has to drive the action.

The methods used to adapt a novel for the stage are as varied as the authors you try to adapt. Terry Pratchett, like Charles Dickens, wrote very good dialogue and the scenes already leap from the page. Other authors make greater use of narrative which the adapter has to weave into the play as well, if they are to keep to the spirit of the original work. Terry was well known for his use of footnotes and, for some of the plays, I even included the Footnote as a 'character' – a Brechtian alienation device, for those who want a more literary justification.

Keep it simple

Terry Pratchett wrote 'filmically' – his scenes cross-cut and swoop like a screenplay. On the silver screen, you can set a scene visually in a second. On the stage it can take longer, and you have to give the audience a chance to realise where they are if they are to have any possibility of keeping up with the – often quite complex – plot.

It's important to remember that a theatre audience doesn't have the luxury of being able to reread a page, or skip back to check a plot point – they (usually) get to see the play only once. It's vital, therefore, to ensure that important plot points are not lost along the way while one is tempted to keep in other favoured scenes from the much longer novel.

Keep it moving

Novelists are not constrained by budget – they can destroy cities, have characters who are 60-foot long dragons, write vital scenes involving time travel and other difficult concepts. These can initially appear to be a challenge for anyone without the budget of Industrial Light and Magic (www.ilm.com).

When I write, I have the good fortune to be writing for a theatre which has very limited space – on and off stage – and virtually no capacity for scenic effects. This makes staging the plays a nightma…, ahem… a challenge, but the benefit is that my adaptations can be staged virtually anywhere. I don't write them with essential big effects or big set changes. Of course, drama groups with huge budgets can go wild with all that – but the plays can work without it.

Plays which demand massive set changes or pose huge scenic problems are likely to put off many directors working to a tight budget. It's different if you're Alan Ayckbourn, of course … onstage swimming pool, floating river cruiser … no problem.

People say that radio has the best scenery. Allowing the audience to fill in the gaps can not only save on costly wood and canvas, but on occasions, can even be more effective than an expensive but stagey scenic effect. After all, Shakespeare's *Antony and Cleopatra* includes a sea battle between two great navies – all seen by two blokes standing on a hill.

The plays – like the books – have to keep moving. Scenes need to flow fairly seamlessly into one another. Set changes slow things down. I get to see large numbers of productions of my plays and the general rule is that the ones with frequent set-changes are the ones which plod.

Writing for schools

Three of my plays were written specifically for classroom use. I had to bear in mind that the plays were as likely to be used for reading in a classroom as for production on a stage. So I tried to keep the number of stage directions to a minimum because I know all too well from reading plays with my own amateur drama group that the need to read through huge chunks of explanatory stuff in italics, interspersed with snippets of uninformative dialogue, is very tedious. Here is an example (not, I hasten to add, an extract from a real play):

> (*As Smithers looks out of the window, Bert rushes downstairs, carrying an aspidistra in a brass bowl. He passes, but fails to notice, the gorilla. He trips and falls, dropping the plant and pot on Smithers' head*)
> SMITHERS: Oof!
> (*Smithers picks up a broom from the floor and chases after Bert. They run into the kitchen and out again, up the stairs and across the landing. Bert takes a wad of banknotes out of his pocket and throws them at Smithers*)
> BERT: Take that!

It was also important to avoid characters with just 'one line and a cough'. Nothing is worse in a read-through than to be given the role of 'King of France' only to find that the character speaks one line on page one and then is silent for the rest of the play. Except, perhaps, being allocated a role meant for someone of the opposite sex and then finding it contains dialogue that will invite ridicule from the rest of the class: 'I fink I've got a beard coming through' or 'Oh la, I feel so pretty; I do love wearing frilly pink underwear'.

I also try to ensure that whatever special effects are mentioned should be either easily achievable or not essential and again, that the plays can be performed with the minimum amount of scenery.

Two of the three plays I wrote for OUP I would not be staging myself. It was really fascinating (and quite gratifying) to see the plays staged by schools and to find that they *worked*.

How do I start?
• **I read the book.** Then I read the book again. I then put it down, leave it for a week and write down all the main plot points I can recall, and a rough list of scenes. That should give me a rough shape for the play. Anything I've forgotten to include can probably go high up on the list of potential material to cut.

• **I write it.** I sit down and write the script. At this stage I don't try to keep to a specific length; I just adapt the book, making mental notes of any scenes that show potential for trimming, cutting or pasting into another as I go along. My overall plan is to keep the play to around two hours. If, when I get to the end, the play is too long, I then go back and look again at each scene and character to ensure they can justify their place in the script.

• **I dump it.** Reducing a 95,000-word novel into a 20,000-word play means that there will have to be an element of trimming. The trick, I suppose, is to ensure that the cuts will not be too glaring to the paying audience ('I reckon if we cut out the Prince of Denmark, we can get *Hamlet* down to an hour and a half, no problem'). Hopefully, there will be subplots, not vital to the main story, which can be excised to keep it all flowing. But even so, occasionally tough decisions have to be made once all the fat's been removed and one is forced to cut into muscle and bone (as it were). It's important to let stuff go – even if it's a favourite scene in the book, or a favourite character.

• **I share it.** It's good then to let someone else read it. It's all too easy to get so far into the wood that you can no longer see the trees. Being challenged on the decisions you made in adapting the book is a very good thing. I'd certainly recommend anyone adapting a book to have the script read by someone who knows the book well, and who can point out any important plot omissions. It is also good to have your script read by someone who does *not* know the book and who can ask the 'what on earth does that mean?' questions.

It's useful for me that many of my drama club are not *Discworld* 'fans'. Their outsider's view of the script is extremely useful. I also then have the luxury of amending the script in rehearsal to tidy up scenes, add in bits and take bits out. This means that the script which is submitted to the publisher is then fully tried and tested.

Some golden rules
It's difficult to be hard and fast about 'rules' for adapting books, but here are a few useful guidelines that I try to stick to:

• **Don't change the principle plot** – there's no point in calling a play *Bram Stoker's Dracula* if you're then going to have Dracula surviving at the end and starting up a flourishing law firm in Whitby.

• **Never sacrifice 'real' scenes in order to add in some of your own** – after all, you've chosen to adapt the author's work because, presumably, you admire their writing. If you

Theatre

think you can improve on their humour/drama/characterisation you should really be writing your own plots and not torturing theirs.

• **Use the author's dialogue whenever possible** – same as the above, really. Also try to attribute it to the right character whenever practicable.

• **Don't add characters** – stick to the ones the author has given you.

• **Don't be afraid to cut material** – after all, you're trying to squeeze a 300-page novel into a two-hour play; you just can't fit everything in, so don't try. Anything which does not advance the main plot should be on your list for potential dumping if your play overruns.

• **If it doesn't *need* changing – don't change it.**

As well as the 22 plays he mentions in his article, **Stephen Briggs** is the co-author, with Terry Pratchett, and illustrator, of *Turtle Recall: The Discworld Companion, The Streets of Ankh-Morpork, The Wit & Wisdom of Discworld* and a small raft of other publications emanating from Terry Pratchett's *Discworld* books. He read the unabridged audio versions of Terry's books for Isis, HarperCollins and for Random House (in the USA). In 2005 he won an Audie Award (Audio Publishers Association, USA) for his reading of Terry's *Monstrous Regiment* and in 2013 was nominated for his reading of *Dodger*. He also won the Audible Audio Download Book of the Year 2008 for *Good Omens* and in 2009 received an Odyssey Award for his recording of Terry's *Nation* for Harper Audio. In 2010 he won two awards from *AudioFile* magazine for his recording of *Unseen Academicals*, and in 2014 he won two more for *Raising Steam* and for *The Science of Discworld*. He was also a member of the cast of Dirk Maggs' audio drama of Terry's *Unseen Academicals* for Audible.

See also...

• *Writing to a brief*, page 323
• *Writing for children's theatre*, page 331
• *Theatre for children*, page 341
• *Adapting children's books for stage and screen*, page 309

Theatre for children

London and regional theatres are listed below; listings of touring companies start on page 344.

LONDON

Chickenshed Theatre

Chase Side, Southgate, London N14 4PE
tel 020-8292 9222
email info@chickenshed.org.uk
website www.chickenshed.org.uk
Twitter @CHICKENSHED_UK
Artistic Director Lou Stein

Produces theatre for all ages as well as running successful education courses, outreach projects and membership programmes.

Colour House Theatre

Merton Abbey Mills, Watermill Way,
London SW19 2RD
tel 020-7542 5511
email info@colourhousetheatre.co.uk
website www.colourhousetheatre.co.uk
Twitter @ColourHouseThtr
Founder and Chief Executive Peter Wallder,
Artistic Director Charlie Shakespeare

Grade II-listed building seating 50–70 people. The resident children's theatre has now staged over 100 original musical adaptations of famous fairy tales, such as Little Red Riding Hood, and achieved charitable status in 2008. The one-hour shows run for 10 weeks each (July and August excepted) on Saturdays and Sundays at 2pm and 4pm.

Polka Theatre

240 The Broadway, London SW19 1SB
tel 020-8543 8320
email stephen@polkatheatre.com
website www.polkatheatre.com
Twitter @polkatheatre
Artistic Director Peter Glanville

Theatre of new work, with targeted commissions. Temporarily closed for extensive redevelopment; due to reopen summer 2020. Founded 1967.

The Questors Theatre

12 Mattock Lane, London W5 5BQ
tel 020-8567 0011
email enquiries@questors.org.uk
website www.questors.org.uk
Twitter @questorstheatre
Executive Director and Chief Executive Andrea Bath

Largest independent community theatre in Europe. Produces 15–20 shows a year, specialising in modern and classical world drama. Also hosts visiting productions. No unsolicited scripts. Also runs a youth theatre for young people aged between 6–18, as well as summer workshops.

Theatre-Rites

Unit 206, E1 Studios, 7 Whitechapel Road,
London E1 1DU
tel 020-7164 6196
email info@theatre-rites.co.uk
website www.theatre-rites.co.uk
Facebook www.facebook.com/TheatreRites
Twitter @TheatreRites
Artistic Director Sue Buckmaster

Creates devised theatre for family audiences and young people using a mix of performance, installation, puppetry, dance and sound. Working within the UK and internationally, the company creates site-specific and touring productions. Founded 1995.

Unicorn Theatre

147 Tooley Street, London SE1 2HZ
tel 020-7645 0560
email hello@unicorntheatre.com
website www.unicorntheatre.com
Facebook www.facebook.com/unicorntheatre
Twitter @unicorn_theatre
Artistic Director Justin Audibert, *Executive Director* Anneliese Davidsen

Produces a year-round programme of theatre for children and young people under 21. In-house productions of full-length plays with professional casts are staged across two auditoria, alongside visiting companies and education work. Unicorn rarely commissions plays from writers who are new to it, but it is keen to hear from writers who are interested in working with the theatre in the future.
Do not send unsolicited MSS, but rather a short statement describing why you would like to write for Unicorn along with a CV or a summary of your relevant experience.

Young Vic Theatre Company

66 The Cut, London SE1 8LZ
tel 020-7922 2922
email info@youngvic.org
website www.youngvic.org
Facebook www.facebook.com/youngvictheatre
Twitter @youngvictheatre
Artistic Director Kwame Kwei-Armah

Leading London producing theatre. Founded 1969.

A Younger Theatre

website www.ayoungertheatre.com
Facebook www.facebook.com/AYoungerTheatre

Twitter @ayoungertheatre
Managing Editor Samuel Sims

Voluntary project with teams of reviewers, feature-writers and bloggers who write for free in return for seeing a show or in order to build a portfolio of interviews or promote their own performance work. Content is generally aimed at those aged 26 and under.

REGIONAL

Chichester Festival Theatre

Oaklands Park, Chichester, West Sussex PO19 6AP
tel (01243) 784437
website www.cft.org.uk
Twitter @chichesterFT
Artistic Director Daniel Evans

Stages annual Summer Festival Season April–Oct in Festival and Minerva Theatres together with a year-round education programme, winter touring programme and youth theatre Christmas show. See website for unsolicited scripts policy.

Contact Theatre Company

Oxford Road, Manchester M15 6JA
tel 0161 274 0600
website www.contactmcr.com
Twitter @ContactMcr
Artistic Director Matt Fenton, *Head of Creative Development* Suzie Henderson

Multidisciplinary arts organisation focused on working with and for young people aged 13 and above.

Creation Theatre Company

tel (01865) 766266
email boxoffice@creationtheatre.co.uk
website www.creationtheatre.co.uk
Facebook www.facebook.co.uk/CreationTheatre
Twitter @creationtheatre
Chief Executive Lucy Askew, *Producer* Crissy O'Donovan, *Education Manager* Jess Braviner

Produces site-specific adaptations of classic texts all over Oxford in unusual spaces, from castles to antique mirror tents, college gardens, bookshops and factories. Also stages summer productions of Shakespeare and eccentric family shows at Christmas, as well as a wide range of education events and workshops. No unsolicited manuscripts.

The Dukes

Moor Lane, Lancaster LA1 1QE
tel (01524) 598505
email info@dukes-lancaster.org
website https://dukes-lancaster.org/
Twitter @TheDukesTheatre
Artistic Director Sarah Punshon

Producing theatre and cultural centre. Its Young Writers scheme was launched in January 2017. See

website for up-to-date information about the theatre's productions and programming approach.

The Edge Theatre and Arts Centre

Manchester Road, Chorlton, Manchester M21 9JG
tel 0161 282 9776
email info@edgetheatre.co.uk
website www.edgetheatre.co.uk
Twitter @TheEdgeMcr
Artistic Director and Chief Executive Janine Waters, *Musical Director* Simon Waters

Produces and presents theatre for all ages, including families and children. Musical and children's theatre specialities. 70-seat flexible theatre space and studio spaces. Also runs classes, courses and workshops in theatre, dance, music, writing and other creative genres, including: Theatre Club for ages 6–8; Edge Youth Theatre for ages 9–12; Aspire for young people with learning difficulties aged between 13–17; and Edge Youth Dance. Founded 2011.

The Egg

Sawclose, Bath BA1 1ET
tel (01225) 823409 (reception and administration)
email egg.reception@theatreroyal.org.uk
website www.theatreroyal.org.uk/the-egg
Twitter @theeggbath

Part of the Theatre Royal Bath. Purpose-built theatre for young people and their families. Hosts and produces shows for children and young people alongside a year-round participation and outreach programme for people aged 0–21. Opened 2005.

Everyman Theatre Cheltenham

7 Regent Street, Cheltenham, Glos. GL50 1HQ
tel (01242) 512515
email admin@everymantheatre.org.uk
website www.everymantheatre.org.uk
Twitter @Everymanchelt
Creative Director Paul Milton

Regional presenting and producing theatre promoting a wide range of plays. Small-scale experimental, youth and educational work encouraged in The Studio Theatre. Contact the Creative Director before submitting material.

Leeds Children's Theatre

c/o The Carriageworks Theatre, The Electric Press, 3 Millennium Square, Leeds LS2 3AD
email enquiry@leeds-childrens-theatre.co.uk
website www.leeds-childrens-theatre.co.uk
Twitter @LeedsCT

One of the many amateur dramatic societies based at The Carriageworks Theatre. A member of the National Operatic and Dramatic Association (NODA) and the Leeds Civic Arts Guild, Leeds Children's Theatre stages two productions each year. The society is dedicated to the principle of quality, affordable entertainment in order to introduce the theatrical experience to young children, and covers most aspects of theatrical production. Membership is open to all young people aged seven and above (adult membership is available as well). It also facilitates a weekly drama workshop for younger members. Founded 1935.

Leeds Playhouse

Playhouse Square, Quarry Hill, Leeds LS2 7UP
tel 0113 213 7700
website https://leedsplayhouse.org.uk
Twitter @LeedsPlayhouse
Artistic Director James Brining, *Executive Director* Robin Hawkes, *Literary Associate* Jacqui Honess-Martin, *Youth Theatre Director* Gemma Woffinden

Twin auditoria complex; community theatre. Has a policy of encouraging new writing from Yorkshire and Humberside region. Its Furnace programme for artistic development allows writers at different stages of their professional journey to test out new ideas. See website for full details. The Playhouse Youth Theatre runs weekly sessions for young people aged from 5 to 25, commissions new plays for young audiences, and helps them develop a range of performance skills. A programme for older people is under development, while outreach work is under way to local communities whose engagement with the arts has been low to date. Formerly the West Yorkshire Playhouse.

Norwich Puppet Theatre

St James, Whitefriars, Norwich NR3 1TN
tel (01603) 629921 (box office), (01603) 615564 (admin.)
email info@puppettheatre.co.uk
website www.puppettheatre.co.uk
Facebook www.facebook.com/Norwich-Puppet-Theatre
Twitter @norwich_puppet
General Manager Ian Woods

Norwich Puppet Theatre is the base for a professional company which creates and presents its own productions at the theatre, as well as touring to schools and venues throughout the UK and to international venues and festivals. Founded 1979.

Nottingham Playhouse

Nottingham Playhouse Trust Ltd, Wellington Circus, Nottingham NG1 5AF
tel 0115 941 9419
website www.nottinghamplayhouse.co.uk
Twitter @NottmPlayhouse
Artistic Director Adam Penford

Works closely with communities of Nottingham and Nottinghamshire. Seeks to nurture new writers from the East Midlands primarily through its Artist Development programme, Amplify. Will accept two submissions a year per writer but asks that the second one is not sent until feedback has been received on the first. See website for information on submissions.

The Playhouse offers a range of groups and youth theatres for young people aged two and above. See www.nottinghamplayhouse.co.uk/participation/younger-people for more details.

Queen's Theatre, Hornchurch

(Havering Theatre Trust Ltd)
Billet Lane, Hornchurch, Essex RM11 1QT
tel (01708) 443333
email info@queens-theatre.co.uk
website www.queens-theatre.co.uk
Twitter @QueensTheatreH
Artistic Director Douglas Rintoul, *Executive Director* Mathew Russell

Regional theatre with a rich heritage, working in Outer East London, Essex and beyond, which celebrated its 65th birthday in 2018. Each annual programme includes home-grown theatre, visiting live entertainment and inspiring learning and participation projects.

The Queen's Youth Theatre Programme provides the opportunity for young people aged 6–18 to develop creativity, confidence and teamwork, as well as offering valuable opportunities to perform on the Queen's Theatre stage and elsewhere. Younger members start their journey with the QSteps Programme whilst older members graduate into the Young Company Programme, which offers performance, technical and dance opportunities for those who wish to develop further a range of theatre techniques. See the 'Get Involved' section of the website for further details.

Royal Shakespeare Company

The Royal Shakespeare Theatre, Waterside, Stratford-upon-Avon, Warks. CV37 6BB
tel (01789) 296655
email literary@rsc.org.uk
website www.rsc.org.uk
Twitter @TheRSC
Artistic Director Gregory Doran, *Deputy Artistic Director* Erica Whyman, *Head of Literary* Pippa Hill

On its two main stages in Stratford-upon-Avon, the RST and the Swan Theatre, the Company produces a core repertoire of Shakespeare alongside new plays and the work of Shakespeare's contemporaries. In addition, its studio theatre, The Other Place, produces festivals of cutting-edge new work. For all its stages, the Company commissions new plays, new translations and new adaptations that illuminate the themes and concerns of Shakespeare and his contemporaries for a modern audience. The Literary department does not accept unsolicited work but rather seeks out writers it wishes to work with or commission, and monitors the work of writers in production in the UK and internationally. Writers are welcome to invite the Literary department to readings, showcases or productions by emailing the address above.

Sherman Theatre

Senghennydd Road, Cardiff CF24 4YE
tel 029-2064 6900
website www.shermantheatre.co.uk
Twitter @shermantheatre
Executive Director Julia Barry

Produces two Christmas productions (for ages 3–6 in English and Welsh and an actor/musician-led production for ages 7+) and actively seeks high-quality work for children and young people as part of its programming. Participatory work with youth theatres for those aged from 5 to 25. Founded 2007.

Theatr Clwyd

Mold, Flintshire CH7 1YA
tel (01352) 701521
email gwennan.mair@theatrclwyd.com
website www.theatrclwyd.com
Twitter @clwydtweets
Artistic Director Tamara Harvey, *Executive Director* Liam Evans-Ford, *Director of Creative Engagement* Gwennan Mair Jones

Aims to be a leading force in developing projects, nurturing writers, offering compelling revivals and the best new writing. The Creative Engagement team produces work for children, young people and their communities.

Visible Fictions

Suite 325/327, 4th Floor, 11 Bothwell Street, Glasgow G2 6LY
email office@visiblefictions.co.uk
website https://visiblefictions.co.uk
Twitter @visiblefictions
Artistic Director Dougie Irvine, *Producer* Laura Penny

Accessible theatre for young people and adults. Also works in creative learning settings – community, educational, institutional and professional – to create bespoke and immersive projects.

TOURING COMPANIES

Arad Goch

Stryd y Baddon, Aberystwyth, Ceredigion SY23 2NN
tel (01970) 617998
email post@aradgoch.org
website www.aradgoch.org
Twitter @AradGoch
Artistic Director Jeremy Turner

Performs in Welsh and English and tours nationally throughout Wales, and occasionally abroad. The company is particularly interested in enabling children and young people to recognise and appreciate their own unique cultural identity though theatre. Some of the company's work is based on traditional material and children's literature but it also commissions new work from experienced dramatists and new writers. Arad Goch performs in theatres and other locations, including schools, and also offers seminars/workshops for students and teachers. The company has its own production house in Aberystwyth which is used by other arts and community organisations and where it programmes a variety of participatory activities for young people. It organises the biennial 'Agor Drysau–Opening Doors' Wales International Festival of Performing Arts for Young Audiences (www.agordrysau-openingdoors.org). Founded 1989.

Booster Cushion Theatre

75 How Wood, Park Street, St Albans, Herts. AL2 2RW
tel (01727) 873874
email admin@booster-cushion.co.uk
website www.booster-cushion.co.uk
Facebook www.facebook.com/boostercushiontheatre
Twitter @BoosterCushion
Director Philip Sherman

Comical theatre company formed especially to re-tell traditional tales to primary-school pupils and their families using surprising Big Books. BCT has performed to over 500,000 people in schools, libraries, museums and theatres across the UK using pop-up books up to 3m tall and concertina books over 5m wide.

All productions are solo performing shows using mime, voice and some sign language. They involve a high level of audience participation. Each show is completely portable and can be performed inside or outside; technical requirements are minimal. Founded 1989.

Boundless Theatre

Unit A207, The Biscuit Factory, 100 Clements Road, London SE16 4DG
tel 020-7928 2811
email admin@boundlesstheatre.org.uk
website www.boundlesstheatre.org.uk
Instagram boundlessabound
Artistic Director and CEO Rob Drummer

Creates new plays with and for audiences aged 15 to 25. Tours the UK and internationally. Also runs a variety of projects to help young people develop their creativity; these focus on performance, writing and digital innovation. Founded 2001 (as Company of Angels).

Cahoots NI

109–113 Royal Avenue, Belfast BT1 1FF
tel 028-9043 4349
email info@cahootsni.com
website www.cahootsni.com
Facebook www.facebook.com/Cahoots NI
Twitter @CahootsNI
Artistic Director Paul Bosco McEneaney, *Company Administrator* Matthew Bradley, *Creative Engagement Manager* Emma Wilson, *Development Manager* Paula Cardiff

Professional children's touring theatre company which concentrates on the visual potential of theatre and capitalises upon the age-old popularity of magic and illusion as an essential ingredient in the art of entertaining. It aims to provide inspiring theatrical experiences for children and to encourage appreciation of the arts in young audiences from all sections of society via outreach work. The company has performed in Ireland, the UK, the US and Asia in theatres, schools and healthcare settings. Founded 2001.

Catherine Wheels Theatre Company
Brunton Theatre, Ladywell Way,
Musselburgh EH21 6AF
tel 0131 653 5255
email admin@catherinewheels.co.uk
website www.catherinewheels.co.uk
Twitter @cwheelstheatre
Artistic Director Gill Robertson

Producing company that tours the UK and internationally, performing for children and young people. One of the founders of the Theatre in Schools Scotland initiative.

Fevered Sleep
Shoreditch Town Hall, 380 Old Street,
London EC1V 9LT
tel 020-3815 6430
email admin@feveredsleep.co.uk
website www.feveredsleep.co.uk
Artistic Directors Sam Butler, David Harradine

Creates performances, installations and digital art for children and adults that the company describes as 'collaborative, participatory, research-led art'. Founded 1996.

Kazzum Arts
Oxford House, Derbyshire Street, London E2 6HG
tel 020-7749 1123
email hello@kazzum.org
website www.kazzum.org
Twitter @KazzumArts
Artistic Director Alex Evans

Creates playful theatrical experiences in unusual places that involve the imaginations of diverse young audiences. A theatre and participative arts company which applies an innovative approach to producing theatre that allows young people to become part of a captivating experience in a safe environment. Founded 1989.

Konflux Theatre in Education
4100 Park Approach, Thorpe Park, Leeds LS15 8GB
tel (01937) 832740
email info@konfluxtheatre.com
website www.konfluxtheatre.com
Twitter @KonfluxTheatre
Artistic Director Anthony Koncsol

Theatre in Education company, accredited Gifted & Talented provider and Arts Award Supporter. Works with approx. 700 schools each year, building close working relationships with teachers and other education professionals and ensuring its programmes and their delivery are tailored to the needs of the organisation. Konflux offers over 70 curriculum-based Play in a Day® workshops designed to build confidence and promote team work. They give pupils the opportunity to learn through drama, increase their acting skills and present a performance back to peers and parents. Founded 1998.

The Little Angel Theatre
14 Dagmar Passage, London N1 2DN
tel 020-7226 1787
email info@littleangeltheatre.com
website www.littleangeltheatre.com
Twitter @LittleATheatre
Artistic Director Samantha Lane

Committed to working with children and families through schools, the local community and the wider community through its extensive touring programme. Little Angel Theatre develops innovative projects, implements improved access to their creative work, increases opportunities for participation and provides stimulating learning and creativity for all using puppetry. Termly activities are run for children, families and schools, including INSET training for teachers. Regular introductory and professional development courses are held throughout the year for teenagers and adults.

Productions last approximately an hour and many are toured to theatres, arts centres and festivals around the UK. Little Angel Theatre is committed to its education programme and continues to work with schools, youth groups and education authorities.

Little Blue Monster Productions
Peter House, Station Road, Ollerton, Newark,
Notts. NG22 9BN
tel 0330 133 2000
email hello@littlebluemonster.co.uk
website www.littlebluemonster.co.uk

Professional touring theatre company offering productions for children and their families across the UK and abroad. Stages adaptations of original work and popular children's books, including *Giraffes Can't Dance* and *The Owl Who Was Afraid of the Dark*.

The London Bubble
(Bubble Theatre Company)
5 Elephant Lane, London SE16 4JD
tel 020-7237 4434
email admin@londonbubble.org.uk
website www.londonbubble.org.uk
Twitter @LBubble
Creative Director Jonathan Petherbridge

Aims to provide the artistic direction, skills, environment and resources to create inspirational, inclusive and involving theatre for the local community and beyond. Also runs a number of groups for children and young people as well as an adult drama group, a Creative Elders group and the Rotherhithe Shed initiative.

M6 Theatre Company
Studio Theatre, Hamer C.P. School,
Albert Royds Street, Rochdale, Lancs. OL16 2SU
tel (01706) 355898
email admin@m6theatre.co.uk
website www.m6theatre.co.uk
Twitter @M6Theatre
Artistic Director Gilly Baskeyfield

Touring theatre company specialising in creating and delivering innovative theatre for young audiences.

Oily Cart
Smallwood School Annexe, Smallwood Road,
London SW17 0TW
tel 020-8672 6329
email oilies@oilycart.org.uk
website www.oilycart.org.uk
Twitter @oilycart
Artistic Director Ellie Griffiths

Touring company staging at least two children's productions per year. Multisensory, highly interactive work is produced, often in specially constructed installations for three specific audiences: very young children aged 6 months–2 years; children aged 3–6 years; and young people (3–19) with profound and multiple learning disabilities or autism. Considers scripts from new writers, but at present all work is generated from within the company. Founded 1981.

The Pied Piper Theatre Company
1 Lilian Place, Coxcombe Lane, Chiddingfold,
Surrey GU8 4QA
tel (01428) 684022
email info@piedpipertheatre.co.uk
website www.piedpipertheatre.co.uk
Twitter @PiedPiperLive
Artistic Director Tina Williams

Specialises in bringing new writing for children to the stage. Typically tours one show a year in the UK, sometimes two, and occasionally tours in Europe and Asia. Pied Piper is an ethical ITC member. Founded 1984.

Prime Theatre
(formerly Sixth Sense Theatre for Young People)
c/o The Wyvern Theatre, Theatre Square,
Swindon SN1 1QN
tel (01793) 614864
email info@primetheatre.co.uk
website www.primetheatre.co.uk
Twitter @PrimeTheatreUK

Artistic Director Mark Powell

Professional theatre company prioritising work with young people. Prime Theatre produces both issue-based and creative theatre productions and performs in schools, theatres and arts centres in the South-West region and beyond. These productions are supported by additional young people-led work, workshops, training sessions and other projects.

Proteus Theatre Company
Proteus Creation Space, Council Road, Basingstoke,
Hants RG21 3DH
tel (01256) 354541
email info@proteustheatre.com
website www.proteustheatre.com
Twitter @proteustheatre
Artistic Director and Chief Executive Mary Swan

Small-scale touring company particularly committed to new writing and new work, education and community collaborations. Produces up to three touring shows per year plus community projects. Founded 1981.

Replay Theatre Company
East Belfast Network Centre,
55 Templemore Avenue, Belfast BT5 4FP
tel 028-9045 4562
email info@replaytheatreco.org
website www.replaytheatreco.org
Twitter @ReplayTheatreCo
Artistic Director Janice Kernoghan-Reid, *Chief Executive Officer* Brian Mullan, *Finance and Operations Manager* Hayley McBride, *Lead Artist Inclusion* Andrew Stanford, *Communications Officer* Andrew Moore

Innovative, high-quality work for audiences under the age of 19, including school groups, disabled children and young people, and families. Each show is shaped through creative consultation with its intended audience, and those who live and work with them. Tours locally, nationally and internationally. Founded 1988.

Scamp Theatre
42 Church Lane, Arlesey, Beds. SG15 6UX
tel (01462) 734843
email admin@scamptheatre.com
website www.scamptheatre.com
Twitter @scamptheatre
Director Louise Callow

Produces high-quality theatre for audiences of all ages, with an increased focus on the adaptation of children's literature, including works by Julia Donaldson. With productions constantly touring, Scamp has operated in London, on tour and at international venues and festivals. Does not accept unsolicited manuscripts. Founded 2003.

Tell Tale Hearts

c/o 4 Oxspring Road, Penistone, Sheffield, S36 8AB
email info@telltalehearts.co.uk
website www.telltalehearts.co.uk
Twitter @TellTaleHeart
Artistic Director Natasha Holmes

Produces participatory theatre for primary-school pupils and younger years in a range of settings, from theatres to schools and other community venues. Also runs workshops, INSET training and offers other consultancy services. Note that the Tell Tale Hearts rarely produces theatre from written work; it is a devising company and actively seeks out collaborations with contributing artists. Occasionally works with a writer as part of its collaborative team, but this is to produce new work. Contact the Artistic Director before sending any work in order to gauge interest. Founded 2003.

Theatr Iolo

Chapter, Market Road, Canton, Cardiff CF14 3HS
tel 029-2061 3782
email hello@theatriolo.com
website www.theatriolo.com
Twitter @theatriolo
Artistic Director Lee Lyford

Aims to produce and programme the best of live theatre, making it widely accessible to children and young people across Wales and beyond.

Theatr Spectacle Theatre

c/o The Factory, Jenkin Street, Porth CF39 9PP
tel (01443) 430700
email info@spectacletheatre.co.uk
website www.spectacletheatre.co.uk
Facebook www.facebook.com/Theatr-Spectacle-Theatre
Twitter @SpectacleTheat1
Manager/Creative Director Steve Davis

Community theatre company. Performance, workshops, training and mentoring.

Theatre Centre

Shoreditch Town Hall, 380 Old Street, London EC1V 9LT
tel 020-7729 3066
email admin@theatre-centre.co.uk
website www.theatre-centre.co.uk
Facebook www.facebook.com/TheatreCentreUK
Twitter @TClive
Artistic Director Natalie Wilson

Young people's theatre company producing plays and workshops which tour nationally across the UK. Productions are staged in primary and secondary schools, arts centres and other venues. Keen to nurture new and established talent, encouraging all writers to consider writing for young audiences. Also runs creative projects and manages writing awards: see website for details. Founded 1953.

Theatre Hullabaloo

The Hullabaloo, Borough Road, Darlington DL1 1SG
tel (01325) 405681
email info@theatrehullabaloo.org.uk
website www.theatrehullabaloo.org.uk
Twitter @hullabalootweet
Artistic Producer Miranda Thain

Specialist theatre company that creates and tours work for young audiences. Promotes greater awareness of the value of theatre to children and young people by working with academic researchers, teachers and others through courses, events and publications. Tours professional theatre productions to schools and venues across the North East and nationally. Organiser of the annual Take Off Festival since 1994. Theatre Hullabaloo opened The Hullabaloo, a new purpose-designed theatre venue for children and families, in 2017.

Travelling Light Theatre Company

Barton Hill Settlement, 43 Ducie Road, Lawrence Hill, Bristol BS5 0AX
tel 0117 377 3166
email info@travellinglighttheatre.org.uk
website www.travellinglighttheatre.org.uk
Facebook www.facebook.com/Travelling Light Theatre Company
Twitter @tl_theatre
Artistic Producer Heidi Vaughan

Professional theatre company producing work for young audiences. Collaborates with many different arts organisations to create original, cross-artform productions that inspire and engage young people. Tours to theatres and festivals throughout the UK and abroad as well as to local schools. Also runs an extensive participation programme engaging with 0–25 year-olds through youth theatre groups, holiday and school projects, work experience, placements and mentoring. Founded 1984.

Tutti Frutti Productions

Shine, Harehills Road, Harehills, Leeds LS8 5DR
tel 0113 388 0027
email emma@tutti-frutti.org.uk
website www.tutti-frutti.org.uk
Twitter @tuttifruttiprod
Artistic Director Wendy Harris

Professional theatre aimed specifically at family audiences (age 3+ and accompanying adults). Productions are adaptations of children's books and stories or specially commissioned new shows, and include original music together with different art forms, i.e. puppetry, dance, movement. Tours nationally and internationally and performs in a host of different small- and middle-scale venues, including theatres, arts centres, village halls, rural touring schemes and schools, undertaking approx. 200 performances a year. Founded 1991.

Theatre

Societies, prizes and festivals

Society of Authors

The SoA is the UK trade union for all types of writers, illustrators and literary translators at every stage of their careers.

Members

SoA members include household names, such as J.K. Rowling, Philip Pullman and Joanne Harris, but they also include authors right at the start of their careers. Amongst the SoA membership are academic writers, biographers, broadcasters, children's writers, crime writers, dramatists, educational writers, ELT writers, health writers, ghostwriters, graphic novelists, historians, illustrators, journalists, medical writers, non-fiction writers, novelists, poets, playwrights, radio writers, scriptwriters, short story writers, translators, spoken word artists, YA writers, and more.

The benefits available to all SoA members include:
• assistance with contracts, from negotiation and assessment of terms to clause-by-clause, confidential vetting;
• unlimited advice on queries, covering any aspect of the business of authorship;

Membership

The Society of Authors
24 Bedford Row, London WC1R 4TQ
tel 020-7373 6642
email info@societyofauthors.org
website www.societyofauthors.org
Chief Executive Nicola Solomon
President Philip Pullman

We have two membership bands: Full and Associate membership.

Full membership is available to professional writers, poets, translators and illustrators working in any genre or medium. This includes those who have: had a full-length work traditionally published, broadcast or performed commercially; self-published or been published on a print-on-demand or ebook-only basis and who meet sales criteria; published or had broadcast or performed an equivalent body of professional work; or administrators of a deceased author's estate.

Authors at the start of their careers are invited to join as Associates.

Associate membership is available to anyone actively working to launch a career as an author. This includes: authors who are starting out in self-publishing but who are not yet making a profit; authors who have been offered a contract for publication or agent representation but who are not yet published; students engaged on a course of at least one academic year's duration that will help them develop a career as an author, as well as other activities that mark the early stages of an author's career. Associate members enjoy all the same services and benefits as Full members. Full eligibility details can be found at www.societyofauthors.org/join.

Membership is subject to election and payment of subscription fees.

The subscription fee (tax deductible) starts at £25.50 per quarter, or £18 for those aged 35 or under. From the second year of subscription there are concessionary rates for over 65s who are no longer earning a significant amount of income from writing. Annual payment schedules are also available.

- taking up complaints on behalf of members on any issue concerned with the business of authorship;
- pursuing legal actions for breach of contract, copyright infringement, and the non-payment of royalties and fees, when the risk and cost preclude individual action by a member and issues of general concern to the profession are at stake;
- conferences, seminars, meetings and other opportunities to network and learn from other authors;
- regular communications and a comprehensive range of publications, including the SoA's quarterly journal, the *Author*;
- discounts on books, exclusive rates on specialist insurance, special offers on products and services, and free membership of the Authors' Licensing and Collecting Society (ALCS; see page 425);
- Academic and Medical Writers Groups – investigating and highlighting the issues faced by these authors, including confusion and concern around Open Access requirements and Creative Commons licensing.
- Broadcasting Group – representing members working in radio, TV and film;

> 'It does no harm to repeat, as often as you can, "Without me the literary industry would not exist: the publishers, the agents, the sub-agents, the accountants, the libel lawyers, the departments of literature, the professors, the theses, the books of criticism, the reviewers, the book pages – all this vast and proliferating edifice is because of this small, patronised, put-down and underpaid person."' – *Doris Lessing*

- Children's Writers and Illustrators Group – a professional community of writers and illustrators who create content for the children's publishing market;
- Educational Writers Group – protecting the interests of educational authors in professional matters, especially contracts, rates of pay, digitalisation and copyright;
- Poetry and Spoken Word Group – a new, increasingly active group to which all new member poets are subscribed on joining SoA;
- Society of Authors in Scotland – organises a varied and busy calendar of activities in Scotland through a committee of volunteers;
- Translators Association – a source of expert advice for individual literary translators and a collective voice representing the profession;
- Writers as Carers Group – a new group designed to help keep writers writing when they take on caring responsibilities for someone with an illness or disability.

The SoA also facilitates many local groups across the UK.

Campaigning and lobbying

The SoA is a voice for authors and works at a national and international level to improve terms and treatment of authors, negotiating with all parties including publishers, broadcasters, agents and governments. Current areas of campaigning include contract terms, copyright, freedom of expression, tax and benefits arrangements and Public Lending Right (PLR, see page 400) – which the SoA played a key role in establishing. It also campaigns on wider matters which affect authors, such as libraries, literacy and a fair playing field for publishing.

In the UK the SoA lobbies parliament, ministers and departments and makes submissions on relevant issues, working closely with the Department for Culture, Media and Sport and the All Party Parliamentary Writers Group. The SoA is a member of the British Copyright Council and was instrumental in setting up ALCS. It is recognised by the BBC in the negotiation of rates for authors' contributions to radio drama, as well as for the broadcasting of published material.

The SoA is highly active and influential at a European level and is a member of the European Writers' Council and applies pressure globally, working with sister organisations as part of the international Authors' Foundation.

The SoA also works closely with other professional bodies, including the Association of Authors' Agents, the Booksellers Association, the Publishers Association, the Independent Publishers Guild, the British Council, the National Union of Journalists and the Writers' Guild of Great Britain.

Awards and grants

The SoA supports authors through a wide range of awards and grants. Over £100,000 is given in prizes each year and more than £230,000 is distributed in grants.

As of 2019, the SoA administers:

• the Authors' Foundation and K Blundell Trust, which give grants to assist authors working on their next book;

• the Francis Head Bequest and the Authors' Contingency Fund, which assist authors who, through physical mishap, are temporarily unable to maintain themselves or their families;

• the Women's Prize for Fiction;

• the *Sunday Times*/University of Warwick Young Writer of the Year Award;

• the *Sunday Times* EFG Short Story Award;

• Travelling Scholarships, which give honorary awards;

• three prizes for first novels: the Betty Trask Awards, the McKitterick Prize and inaugural Paul Torday Memorial Prize;

• the Somerset Maugham Awards for a full-length published work;

• two poetry awards: the Eric Gregory Awards and the Cholmondeley Awards;

• the ALCS Tom-Gallon Award for short story writers;

• two audio drama prizes: the Imison Award for a writer new to radio drama and the Tinniswood Award;

• awards for translations from Arabic, Dutch/Flemish, French, German, Greek, Italian, Spanish and Swedish into English;

• the ALCS Educational Writers' Awards.

Alliance of Independent Authors

The ALLi is a professional association of self-publishing writers and advisors.

Alliance of Independent Authors

Membership

The Alliance of Independent Authors
Free Word Centre, 60 Farringdon Road,
London EC1G 2RA
email info@allianceindependentauthors.org
website http://allianceindependentauthors.org,
www.selfpublishingadvice.org

The Alliance of Independent Authors (ALLi) is a global organisation with a mission of fostering ethics and excellence in self-publishing and advocation for author-publishers globally.

Founded in 2012 at the London Book Fair by author, poet and creative entrepreneur, Orna Ross, ALLi is headquarted in London but with members all over the world. In addition to its member services, the organisation offers outreach education to the self-publishing community through its popular online Self-Publishing Advice Center, which features a blog, podcast, bi-annual online conference and series of guidebooks.

ALLi has an Advisory Board of successful author-publishers, educators, and service providers, and an active Watchdog desk which runs a publicly available ratings board of the best and worst self-publishing services. It also publishes an annual Directory of its Partner Members: vetted self-publishing services, from large global players like Amazon KDP and Ingram Spark to local freelance editors and designers. Many of these offer discounted services to ALLi author members.

ALLi advocates for the interests of independent, self-publishing authors within and outside the literary, publishing and bookselling industries. Its campaigns includes 'Open Up To Indie Authors', which urges booksellers, festivals, prize-giving committess, libraries, book clubs and corporate media to include author-publishers in their programmes; 'Self-Publishing 3.0', which calls on government and creative industry bodies to support authors' digital business development; and 'Blockchain for Books', which urges authors to consider how new technologies could foster a creator-led payment model for authors.

ALLi offers community, advice, education, professional and business development to independent ('indie') authors everywhere and fosters an empowered, engaged and entrepreneurial attitute to authorship.

Society of Children's Book Writers & Illustrators

The Society of Children's Book Writers & Illustrators (SCBWI) is the only international professional organisation dedicated to serving people who share a vital interest in children's literature, magazines, film, television and/or multimedia.

Whether you are a professional children's writer or illustrator, or a newcomer to the field, SCBWI has plenty to offer you, from local to national to international events, from advice on getting your first deal to help in navigating your career as a writer or illustrator. Established in 1971, SCBWI now has over 22,000 members in 70 regional chapters worldwide. Membership benefits include professional development and networking opportunities, marketing information, events, publications, online profiles, grants and awards.

What does SCBWI British Isles do?

SCBWI British Isles is a dynamic and friendly chapter of 1000 members, which aims to support aspiring and published writers and illustrators and provide opportunities for them to network, hone their craft and develop their careers. Events include an annual two-day conference, a fiction and picture book retreat, an annual Agents' Party, the Industry Insiders series (six talks a year in London aimed at professional development on a variety of topics), the Illustrators' series (Saturday workshops with a hands-on craft element), sketch and scrawl crawls, author masterclasses and PULSE events (SCBWI PULSE provides professional development opportunities for published members). A network of regional organisers run local critique groups, workshops and social events across the British Isles.

> **Further information**
>
> **Society of Children's Book Writers & Illustrators (SCBWI)**
> *website* www.scbwi.org, www.britishisles.scbwi.org
> *Co-Regional Advisors (Co-chairs)* Natascha Biebow and Kathy Evans
> *email* ra@britishscbwi.org
> *email* finance@britishscbwi.org*Membership Coordinator* Anita Loughrey
> *email* membership@britishscbwi.org
> *Membership* £75 p.a. and £50 for students

What SCBWI does for its members

• SCBWI is a professional guild. It speaks as a consolidated global voice for professional children's writers and illustrators. In recent years, SCBWI has successfully lobbied for such issues as new copyright legislation, equitable treatment of authors and artists, and fair contract terms.

• It keeps members up to date with industry developments through the SCBWI PULSE series of events, with opportunities to learn more about the 'business' of writing and illustrating, including maretking, school and festival visits, and exclusive networking events with librarians and booksellers.

• It offers members invaluable exposure to editors, art directors and agents through one-to-one manuscript or portfolio reviews at the annual conference and retreats, the members-only Agents' Party, and the Slush Pile Challenge and biennial SCBWI Undiscovered Voices (www.undiscoveredvoices.com) competitions.

• It supports professional development for members to hone their craft through the Masterclass series, conference workshops and highly-successful critique groups.

• It gives members increased visibility online with a free profile on its website, which is a point of call for agents, art directors and editors.

• It provides support and a network of like-minded people, helping to answer members' queries through a variety of online resources, including a popular social networking site.

• It facilitates networking opportunities with professionals worldwide.

• Publications include the *Bulletin*, the SCBWI international magazine, *Insight* e-newletter, weekly *Words & Pictures* newsletter blog with daily content (www.wordsandpics.org), and resources including the annual publications and market guide.

• Website resources include book launch parties, members' bookshop, discussion boards, illustrator gallery, find-a-speaker search facility, webinars and podcasts.

Awards and grants

The SCBWI administers a number of awards and grants:

• The Golden and Crystal Kite Awards are for the most outstanding books published by SCBWI members each year, voted for by SCBWI peers.

• The Sid Fleischman Humour Award is presented to authors whose work exemplifies the excellence of writing in the genre of humour.

• The annual Spark Award recognises excellence in a children's book published through a non-traditional publishing route.

• The Book Launch Award provides authors or illustrators with $2,000 in funds to help the promotion of their newly published work and take the marketing strategy into their own creative hands.

• The Emerging Voices Award fosters the emergence of diverse voices in children's books.

• For Translators: Work-in-Progress Grants to assist children's book writers and illustrators in the completion of a specific project currently not under contract.

• Ann Whitford Paul - Writer's Digest Manuscript Award is an annual award given to the Most Promising Picture Book manuscript.

• SCBWI PJ Library Jewish Stories Award is an award sponsored by the PJ Library to encourage the creation of more high-quality Jewish children's literature.

• Bologna Illustrators Gallery (BIG) is given bi-annually to an illustrator of promise. The winner is announced at the New York Conference, and the winning art is displayed prominently at the SCWBI Bologna Book Fair booth.

• The Multi-Cultural Work-in-Progress Grant assists writers in the completion of a manuscript featuring a voice traditionally underrepresented in children's books.

• The Magazine Merit Awards are presented for outstanding original magazine work for young people.

• The Sue Alexander Most Promising New Work Award is for the best manuscript submitted for individual critique at the LA conference.

• The Martha Weston Grant encourages authors and illustrators to nurture their creativity in a different genre of children's books.

• The Lee Bennett Hopkins Poetry Award recognises and encourages the publication of an excellent book of poetry or anthology for children or young adults (given every three years).
• The Jane Yolen Mid-List Author Grant honours the contribution of mid-list authors.
• Several Work-in-progress Grants are available each year.
• Don Freeman Work-in-Progress Grant is to assist illustrators in the completion of a book dummy or portfolio.
• The Portfolio Award is presented to the best art portfolio on view at the Juried Portfolio Display at the LA conference.
• There are four Student Illustrator Scholarships for full-time graduate and undergraduate students of children's book illustration.
• There are two Student Writer Scholarships to the Summer and Winter conferences for full-time university students in an English or Creative Writing programme.
• There are three Annual Conference Scholarships to attend the annual SCBWI-BI conference.

See also...

● *Seven Stories – The National Centre for Children's Books*, page 356
● *The Children's Book Circle*, page 358
● *Federation of Children's Book Groups*, page 359

Societies, prizes and festivals

Seven Stories – The National Centre for Children's Books

At Seven Stories the rich heritage of British children's books is collected, explored and celebrated.

seven stories
National Centre for Children's Books

Once upon a time an idea was born on the banks of the Tyne to create a national home for children's literature – a place where the original work of authors and illustrators could be collected, treasured and celebrated. After ten years of pioneering work by founding directors Elizabeth Hammill and Mary Briggs, that dream became a reality. In August 2005 Seven Stories, the Centre for Children's Books, opened in an award-winning converted seven storey Victorian granary in the Ouseburn Valley, a stone's throw from Newcastle's vibrant quayside. Seven Stories is now officially known as The National Centre for Children's Books, following approval by Arts Council England in 2012. It is the only accredited museum in the UK that specialises in children's books.

The collection

At the heart of Seven Stories is a unique and growing collection of manuscripts, artwork and other pre-publication materials. These treasures record the creative process involved in making a children's book and provide illuminating insights into the working lives of modern authors and illustrators. The collection focuses on work created in modern Britain. It already contains thousands of items by authors such as Peter Dickinson, Michael Morpurgo, Enid Blyton, Berlie Doherty, Jan Mark, Philip Pullman, Michael Rosen, Robert Westall and Ursula Moray Williams; illustrators like Edward Ardizzone, Faith Jaques, Harold Jones, Anthony Maitland, Pat Hutchins, Helen Cooper, Jan Ormerod and Jane Ray; and editors and other practitioners such as Kaye Webb. Many more bodies of work are pledged. A catalogue of the collection is available via the Seven Stories website and Seven Stories first book *Drawn from the Archive* (Walker Books 2015) is now available.

Exhibitions

A celebration of creativity underpins the Seven Stories project: its collection documents the creative act, and its exhibitions and programmes interpret this original material in unconventional but meaningful ways. The aim is to cultivate an appreciation of books and their making, and inspire creativity in its audience.

Seven Stories, known during its development as the Centre for the Children's Book, has been mounting exhibitions since 1998 – first in borrowed venues and now in its own home. Here it provides the only exhibition space in the UK wholly dedicated to showcasing the incomparable legacy of British writing and illustrating for children. With exhibitions changing every year, Seven Stories have showcased the impressive work of children's authors such as Judith Kerr, Michael Morpurgo and David Almond. Their latest exhibition, *Elmer and Friends: the Colourful World of David McKee*, is running Feb 2019–Feb 2020, bringing well-known characters such as Mr Benn and of course Elmer the Patchwork Elephant to life for all generations.

Throughout its seven storeys – from the Studio to the bookshop and café to the Artist's Attic, visitors of all ages are invited to engage in a unique, interactive exploration of creativity, literature and art. In this ever changing literary playground and landscape for the imagination, they can become writers, artists, explorers, designers, storytellers, readers or collectors, in the company of storytellers, authors, illustrators and Seven Stories' own facilitators and learning team.

Seven Stories aims to place children, young people and their books at the heart of the UK's national literary culture. An independent educational charity, it is committed to access for all and has initiated several innovative participation projects. The centre has developed close links with the Newcastle and regional communities, and is working with the Children's Literature Unit in the Department of English Literature, Language and Linguistics at Newcastle University to develop the Seven Stories collection and maximise its potential for research and display.

Seven Stories is dedicated to the celebration of children's literature. It is supported by Arts Council England and Community Foundation Newcastle Culture Investment Fund.

Further information

Seven Stories – The National Centre for Children's Books
30 Lime Street, Ouseburn Valley,
Newcastle upon Tyne NE1 2PQ
tel 0300 330 1095
email info@sevenstories.org.uk
website www.sevenstories.org.uk
Registered Charity No 1056812.

Public opening hours Tues–Sat 10am–5pm, Sun 10am–4pm, Open Daily during school holidays.

Admission charges Adult (17 and over) £7.70; child (4–16)/concession £6.60; toddler (1–3) £2.50; family £23.10; under 12 months free. Annual passes available.

See also...
- *Society of Children's Book Writers & Illustrators*, page 353
- *The Children's Book Circle*, page 358
- *Federation of Children's Book Groups*, page 359

Societies, prizes and festivals

The Children's Book Circle

The Children's Book Circle is open to anyone who has a passion for children's books; the activities of the organisation are introduced here.

Are you passionate about children's books? Since 1962, the Children's Book Circle (CBC) has provided an exciting forum for lively debate on important issues in the children's book world, as well as opportunities to socialise and build a network within the industry. Membership is open to publishers, librarians, authors, illustrators, agents, teachers, booksellers and anyone with an active interest in the field. The CBC caters to both creators and consumers of children's books and holds events throughout the year for aspiring authors and illustrators alongside industry-led panels, talks and meet-ups. It's not a route into getting published, but it will give you opportunities to engage with people from the industry in an informal and enjoyable context.

> **Further information**
>
> **The Children's Book Circle**
> *website* www.childrensbookcircle.org.uk
> *Facebook* @childrensbookcircle
> *Twitter* @ChildBookCircle
> *Membership* £25 p.a.; students £20 p.a.; corporate membership (up to five staff covered) £100 p.a. Includes free or discounted entry to all events. Non-member tickets can also be purchased for individual events from the website.

The CBC meets regularly at venues in central London and frequently invites guest speakers to debate key issues relating to the world of children's books. Upcoming events include panel discussions on the importance of diversity and the rise of licensing in children's books, and 'Meet and Critique' evenings for aspiring authors and illustrators to discuss their projects with industry experts. Social drinks and the ever-popular Pub Quiz are fast becoming part of the CBC calendar and are a great chance to catch up with industry contacts and make new ones.

The CBC is also the proud host of the annual **Eleanor Farjeon Award** (sponsored by the estate of Eleanor Farjeon) and the **Patrick Hardy Lecture**. The Eleanor Farjeon Award recognises an outstanding contribution to the world of children's books. Recent winners include Michael Morpurgo, John Agard, Keats Community Library and Terry Pratchett (posthumously). The Patrick Hardy Lecture is delivered each year at the same event by a distinguished speaker and has previously been presented by Nicola Davies, Lauren St John, Lauren Child, Verna Wilkins (founder of Tamarind Books) and Michael Rosen.

A yearly membership gives you discounted access to all CBC events and keeps you up to date via the newsletter. CBC welcome enthusiasts of children's books from all backgrounds and aims to be as widely representative as possible.

See also...
- *Society of Children's Book Writers & Illustrators*, page 353
- *Seven Stories – The National Centre for Children's Books*, page 356
- *Federation of Children's Book Groups*, page 359

Federation of Children's Book Groups

'The Federation of Children's Book Groups, has, in its own quiet, single-minded way, done more for reading than almost anyone else.'
— Anthony Horowitz

The achievements of the Federation of Children's Book Groups were publicly recognised in 2011 when it was nominated for and subsequently won the Eleanor Farjeon Award (see page 383). Its aim is simple: to bring children and books together, promote children's books and inspire a love of reading through its national and local events. If you are a parent, carer, author, illustrator or professional with a passion for encouraging children to read, the Federation will be of interest to you.

Federation history

The Federation of Children's Book Groups was formed in 1968 by Anne Wood to coordinate the work of the many different children's book groups already in existence across the country and in 2018, it celebrated 50 years of bringing children and books together.

In 1981 they inaugurated the Children's Book Award, the only national award voted for entirely by children. Throughout the year Federation Testing Groups read and vote on new fiction supplied by publishers. Each year 150,000 votes are cast involving nearly 250 schools and families across the UK. A shortlist (Top Ten) is drawn up with four picture books in the Younger Children category, three shorter novels for Younger Readers, and three novels for Older Readers, with children from all over the UK voting in their groups or online. You do not have to be a member to vote in the Top Ten. The Award has a track record of identifying future bestsellers: the first Overall Winner was *Mr Magnolia* by Quentin Blake; other winners include *The Hunger Games*, and the *Harry Potter* and *Percy Jackson* books. For over ten years the Award was supported by Red House, with award ceremonies held at a number of prestigious venues, including the Queen Elizabeth Hall in London as part of the Imagine Children's Festival (see page 222). The 2019 Award is sponsored by BookLife Publishing.

In 1976 National Tell-A-Story-Week was established and it has now grown into National Share-A-Story-Month (NSSM), which takes place each May. It enables groups to focus on the power of story and to hold events which celebrate all forms of storytelling. The theme in 2019 was 'Travelling tales'.

The website hosts the NSSM pack, full of ideas and activities, which is sent to each book group and can also be downloaded by non-members. In 1977, the first Federation anthology was published, and since then we have compiled booklists covering the whole age range from picture books to the latest teen and young adult novels; these are available on request free of charge via the website. 2019 saw the publication of our *Wordless Picture Books list*, which covers a wide age range.

In 2010 the Federation created National Non-Fiction Day to celebrate the quality and variety of information books available for children; this takes place on the first Thursday of each November, with a host of events focused on non-fiction. It has expanded to be National Non-Fiction November and further details can be found on the website (www.fcbg.org.uk). The theme changes each year and there are always resources to download for free.

Each year the Federation holds a conference: three days of author and illustrator events, panel discussions and seminars enable group and individual members, publishers, authors, illustrators, teachers, librarians and booksellers to meet and exchange ideas. Delegates are inspired by meeting others who share their passion. Venues range across the country: in 2019, Lewes and Oxted hosted the conference, with the theme 'Opening Doors' and a wide range of speakers including Frank Cottrell Boyce, Nick Sharratt, Jane Ray, Francesca Simon, Guy Puzey, Holly Smale and a whole crowd of poets. See www.fcbg.org.uk/conference for more details.

The Children's Book Groups

Federation Book Groups exist throughout the UK: from Plymouth to Dundee, from Ipswich to St David's and from Harrogate to Lewes. Their activities are as varied and diverse as the groups themselves, serving their own community's needs, including author and illustrator visits, bonfire parties, museum and library events and book swaps. But, above all, we are passionate about children's books, bringing together ordinary book-loving families, empowering parents, grandparents, carers and children to become enthusiastic and excited about all kinds of good books. Some book groups are based around schools run by enthusiastic librarians and teachers. You can still be a member of the Federation if there is no book group near you. Individual and professional membership enables everyone to participate in sharing their passion for children's books.

Further information

Federation of Children's Book Groups
1 Oakwell Close, Bragbury End, Stevenage, Herts. SG2 8UG
tel 0300 102 1559
email info@fcbg.org.uk
website www.fcbg.org.uk
Registered Charity No 268289

See also...
- *Society of Children's Book Writers & Illustrators*, page 353
- *Seven Stories – The National Centre for Children's Books*, page 356
- *The Children's Book Circle*, page 358

National Literacy Trust

The Trust is an independent charity that transforms lives through literacy.

The National Literacy Trust focuses on working with children in disadvantaged areas where they can have the biggest impact. The charity believes that literacy is a vital element of action against poverty, and that improving reading, writing, speaking and listening skills boosts life chances and increases employability and earning potential. It runs literacy projects in deprived communities and supports schools and early years settings to deliver outstanding literacy provision. Its research and analysis makes it the leading authority on literacy and drives its interventions. The National Literacy Trust campaigns to make literacy a priority for politicians and parents. Early action on literacy can turn around a child's future and the Trust's work is focused on those critical moments in literacy development where it can make the greatest impact. Its mission is to equip disadvantaged young people with the literacy skills they need to get a job and to be successful in life.

The Trust's impact in 2017/18:
• it directly supported the literacy of 116,290 children through its programmes;
• it supported literacy in 5,529 schools and 184 early years settings;
• it launched Hubs in Swindon and Nottingham;
• work in its National Literacy Trust Hubs in Middlesbrough, Bradford, Peterborough and Stoke went from strength to strength;
• it engaged 63 businesses with the literacy challenge through its Vision for Literacy Business Pledge;
• 47,786 children and young people took part in its annual literacy survey and it released four research reports with the findings;
• its campaigning had a media reach of 262m and an equivalent advertising value of £5.2m;
• its Twitter followers reached 61K and its Facebook likes rose to 10,500.

Further information

National Literacy Trust
68 South Lambeth Road, London SW8 1RL
tel 020-7587 1842
email contact@literacytrust.org.uk
website https://literacytrust.org.uk

Societies, prizes and festivals

Societies, associations and organisations

The societies and associations listed here include appreciation societies devoted to specific authors, professional bodies and national institutions. Some also offer prizes and awards (see page 379).

AccessArt

6 West Street, Comberton, Cambridge CB23 7DS
tel (01223) 262134
website www.accessart.org.uk

AccessArt is a UK Charity which aims to inspire and enable high-quality visual arts teaching, learning and practice. The AccessArt website features over 500 unique resources to inspire practice, plus online courses in drawing and sketchbooks.

Action for Children's Arts

PO Box 169, Ashtead, KT21 9BY
email admin@childrensarts.org.uk
website www.childrensarts.org.uk
Membership See website for rates or contact membership@childrensarts.org.uk

A membership charity organisation that values children, childhood and the arts. It embraces the UN Convention on the Rights of the Child:

• by campaigning for the right of all children in the UK to experience high-quality arts experiences as an integral part of their childhood;
• by connecting people within and across the cultural and education sectors, across art forms and across the regions and nations of the UK;
• by celebrating achievement, dedication and best practice in artistic activity for and with children. The J.M. Barrie Award is given annually to a children's arts practitioner or organisation whose work, in the view of ACA, will stand the test of time. Winners: Dick King-Smith (2005), Judith Kerr (2006), Oliver Postgate and Peter Firmin (2007), Quentin Blake (2008), Roger McGough (2009), Shirley Hughes (2010), Lyndie Wright (2011), Baroness Floella Benjamin (2012), Lynne Reid Banks (2013), Bernard Cribbins (2014), Dame Jacqueline Wilson (2015), Michael Morpurgo, OBE (2016), David Wood, OBE (2017), Stuart and Kadie Kanneh-Mason (2018). Founded 1998.

Louisa May Alcott Memorial Association

Orchard House, 399 Lexington Road, PO Box 343, Concord, MA 01742–0343, USA
email admin@louisamayalcott.org
website www.louisamayalcott.org

A private, not-for-profit association that provides the financial and human resources required to conduct public tours, special programmes, exhibitions and the curatorial work which continues the tradition of the Alcotts, a unique 19th-century family. Founded 1911.

Alliance of Independent Authors – see page 352

American Society of Composers, Authors and Publishers

website www.ascap.com

An organisation owned and run by its members, it is the leading performance rights organisation representing over 600,000 songwriters, composers and music publishers.

Arts Council/An Chomhairle Ealaíon

70 Merrion Square, Dublin D02 NY52, Republic of Ireland
tel +353 (0)1 618 0200
website www.artscouncil.ie

The national development agency for the arts in Ireland. Founded 1951.

Arts Council England

tel 0161 934 4317
website www.artscouncil.org.uk

The national development agency for the arts in England, distributing public money from the Government and the National Lottery. Arts Council England's main funding programme is Grants for the Arts, which is open to individuals, arts organisations, national touring companies and other people who use the arts in their work. Founded 1946.

Cambridge
24 Brooklands Avenue, Cambridge CB2 8BU

Nottingham
Room 005-005A, Arkwright Building, Nottingham Trent University, Burton Street, Nottingham NG1 4BU

London
Bloomsbury Street, London WC1B 3HF

Newcastle
Central Square, Forth Street, Newcastle upon Tyne NE1 3PJ

Manchester
49 Lever Street, Manchester M1 1FN

Brighton
New England House, New England Street, Brighton
BN1 4GH

Bristol
4th Floor, 66 Queen Square, Thomas Lane, Bristol
BS1 4JP

Birmingham
The Foundry, 82 Granville Street, Birmingham
B1 2LH

Leeds
1st Floor South, Marshall's Mill, Marshall Street,
Leeds LS11 9YJ

Arts Council of Northern Ireland

1 The Sidings, Antrim Road, Lisburn BT28 3AJ
tel 028-9262 3555
email info@artscouncil-ni.org
website www.artscouncil-ni.org
Chief Executive Roisín McDonough

Promotes and encourages the arts throughout
Northern Ireland. Artists in drama, dance, music and
jazz, literature, the visual arts, traditional arts and
community arts can apply for support for specific
schemes and projects. The value of the grant will be
set according to the aims of the programme. Artists
of all disciplines and in all types of working practice,
who have made a contribution to artistic activities in
Northern Ireland for a minimum period of one year
within the last five years, are eligible.

Arts Council of Wales

Bute Place, Cardiff CF10 5AL
tel 0845 873 4900
email info@arts.wales
website www.arts.wales

National organisation with specific responsibility for
the funding and development of the arts in Wales;
operates in both English and Welsh languages. Arts
Council of Wales receives funding from the Welsh
Government and also distributes National Lottery
funds for the arts in Wales. Makes grants to support
arts activities and facilities, including annual revenue
grants to full-time arts organisations such as
Literature Wales and to individual artists or projects.
Wales Arts International is the international arm of
the Arts Council of Wales and works in partnership
with the British Council, which works to promote
knowledge about contemporary arts and culture from
Wales and encourages international exchange and
collaboration.

North Wales Regional Office
Princes Park II, Princes Drive, Colwyn Bay LL29 8PL
tel (01492) 533440

Mid and West Wales Regional Office
The Mount, 18 Queen Street, Carmarthen SA31 1JT
tel 0845 873 4900

Association for Library Service to Children

American Library Association, 50 East Huron Street,
Chicago, IL 60611–2795
tel +1 800-545-2433
website www.ala.org/alsc

Develops and supports the profession of children's
librarianship by enabling and encouraging its
practitioners to provide the best library service to US
children.

Association for Scottish Literary Studies

c/o Dept of Scottish Literature,
University of Glasgow, 7 University Gardens,
Glasgow G12 8QH
tel 0141 330 5309
email office@asls.org.uk
website www.asls.org.uk
President Alison Lumsden, *Secretary* Craig Lamont,
Director Duncan Jones
Membership £60 p.a. individuals; £15 p.a. UK
students; £90 p.a. corporate

ASLS promotes the study, teaching and writing of
Scottish literature and furthers the study of the
languages of Scotland. Publishes annually *New
Writing Scotland*, an anthology of new Scottish
writing; an edited text of Scottish literature; a series of
academic journals; the e-zine *The Bottle Imp*; and a
bi-annual newsletter. Also publishes *Scotnotes*
(comprehensive study guides to major Scottish
writers), literary texts and commentaries designed to
assist the classroom teacher, and a series of occasional
papers. Organises three conferences a year. Founded
1970.

Association of American Publishers

email info@publishers.org
website www.publishers.org
Twitter @AmericanPublish

AAP is the largest trade association for US books and
journal publishers, providing advocacy and
communications on behalf of the industry and its
priorities nationally and worldwide. Founded 1970.

Association of Authors' Representatives Inc.

302A West 12th Street, #122, New York, NY 10014
email administrator@aaronline.org
website www.aaronline.org

A professional organisation of over 400 agents who
work with book authors and playwrights. Founded
1991.

Association of Canadian Publishers

174 Spadina Avenue, Suite 306, Toronto,
Ontario M5T 2C2
tel +1 416-487-6116

email admin@canbook.org
website www.publishers.ca
Executive Director Kate Edwards

Represents approximately 120 Canadian-owned and controlled book publishers from across the country. Founded 1976.

The Association of Illustrators

Somerset House, Strand, London WC2R 1LA
tel 020-7759 1010
email info@theaoi.com
website www.theaoi.com
Facebook www.facebook.com/theaoi
Twitter @theaoi

Trade association which supports illustrators, promotes illustration and encourages professional standards in the industry. Publishes *Varoom* magazine (two p.a.); presents an annual programme of events; holds annual competition, exhibition and tour of the World Illustration Awards in partnership with the *Directory of Illustration* (www.theaoi.com/awards). Founded 1973.

Australia Council

PO Box 788, Strawberry Hills, NSW 2012
tel +61 (0)2 9215 9000
website www.australiacouncil.gov.au
Ceo Adrian Collette

Provides a broad range of support for the arts in Australia, embracing music, theatre, literature, visual arts and crafts, dance, indigenous arts, community and new media arts.

Australian Copyright Council

PO Box 1986, Strawberry Hills, NSW 2012
tel +61 (0)2 9101 2377
email info@copyright.org.au
website www.copyright.org.au
Facebook www.facebook.com/AustralianCopyrightCouncil
Twitter @AusCopyright
Chief Executive Officer Grant McAvaney

Provides easily accessible and affordable practical information, legal advice, education and forums on Australian copyright law for content creators and consumers. It represents the peak bodies for professional artists and content creators working in Australia's creative industries and Australia's major copyright collecting societies, including the Australian Society of Authors, the Australian Writers' Guild and the Australian Publishers Association.

The Council advocates for the contribution of creators to Australia's culture and economy; the importance of copyright for the common good. It works to promote understanding of copyright law and its application, lobby for appropriate law reform and foster collaboration between content creators and consumers. Founded 1968.

Australian Publishers Association

60–89 Jones Street, Ultimo, NSW 2007
website www.publishers.asn.au
Twitter @AusPublish

The APA is the peak industry body for Australian book, journal and electronic publishers. Founded 1948.

Australian Writers' Guild

Level 4, 70 Pitt Street, Sydney, NSW 2000
tel +61 (0)2 9319 0339
email admin@awg.com.au
website www.awg.com.au

The professional association representing writers for stage, screen, radio and online and has protected and promoted their creative and professional interests for more than 50 years. Founded 1962.

Authors Aloud UK

72 Castle Road, St Albans, Herts. AL1 5DG
tel (01727) 893992
email info@authorsalouduk.co.uk
website www.authorsalouduk.co.uk
Facebook www.facebook.com/Authors-Aloud-UK-497942623573822/
Twitter @AuthorsAloudUK
Directors Naomi Cooper, Annie Everall

An author booking agency which brings together authors, illustrators, poets, storytellers and trainers with schools, libraries and festivals to promote enthusiasm for reading, both for enjoyment and information. Happy to take on new speakers published by mainstream children's publishers, who meet the relevant criteria and guidelines. Keen to work with children's authors who wish to visit schools and libraries. Also organises tours and events for publishers and other organisations.

Authors' Licensing and Collecting Society Ltd – see page 425

Enid Blyton Society

email tony@enidblytonsociety.co.uk
website www.enidblytonsociety.co.uk

Provides a focal point for collectors and enthusiasts of Enid Blyton through its magazine *The Enid Blyton Society Journal* (three p.a.) and the website. Founded 1995.

Book Marketing Society

email admin@bookmarketingsociety.co.uk
website www.bookmarketingsociety.co.uk

The Book Marketing Society was launched with the objective of becoming the representative body of marketing within the book industry. It provides a forum for sharing best practice, inspiration and creativity across the sector through regular awards and a lively programme of member meetings, development workshops, masterclasses and social events. Anyone who works for a book publisher, book retailer or book wholesaler is eligible for membership, including those working in associated areas of the publishing and book retailing industry.

The Booksellers Association of the United Kingdom & Ireland Ltd
6 Bell Yard, London WC2A 2JR
tel 020-7421 4640
email mail@booksellers.org.uk
website www.booksellers.org.uk
Managing Director Meryl Halls

A membership organisation for all booksellers in the UK and Ireland, representing over 95% of bookshops. Key services include National Book Tokens and World Book Day. Founded 1895.

BookTrust
G8 Battersea Studios, 80 Silverthorne Road, London SW8 3HE
tel 020-7801 8800
email query@booktrust.org.uk
website www.booktrust.org.uk
Ceo Diana Gerald, *Chair of Trustees* John Coughlan

BookTrust is the UK's largest children's reading charity, dedicated to getting children reading because children who read are happier, healthier, more empathetic and more creative; they also do better at school. BookTrust gets children reading in lots of different ways, but its priority is to get children excited about books and stories.

BookTrust reviews at least one children's book each day and runs the Blue Peter Book Awards, Waterstones Children's Laureate, BookTrust Storytime Prize and BookTrust Lifetime Achievement Award. In 2019, it launched BookTrust Represents, a project to promote authors and illustrators of colour. See the website to find out more about BookTrust's work.

BookTrust Represents
BookTrust, G8 Battersea Studios, 80 Silverthorne Road, London SW8 3HE
tel 020-7801 8826
email booktrust.represents@booktrust.org.uk
website www.booktrust.org.uk/booktrustrepresents

A project to support and subsidise authors and illustrators of colour to promote their work and to reach more readers through events in bookshops, festivals and schools, including training and mentoring for less experienced creators. For more details and to get involved, see the website.

The British Council
British Council Customer Service UK, Bridgewater House, 58 Whitworth Street, Manchester M1 6BB
tel 0161 957 7755
email general.enquiries@britishcouncil.org
website www.britishcouncil.org
Twitter @BritishCouncil
Chief Executive Ciarán Devane, *Director of Arts* Kate Arthurs

Connects people worldwide with learning opportunities and creative ideas from the UK. It has staff in offices, teaching centres, libraries and information and resource centres in the UK and over 100 countries and territories worldwide. Working in close collaboration with book trade associations, British Council offices participate in major international book fairs.

Works with hundreds of writers and literature partners in the UK and collaborates with offices overseas to broker relationships and create activities which link artists and cultural institutions around the world. The Department works with writers, publishers, producers, translators and other sector professionals across literature, publishing and education.

Promotes the UK's visual arts sector internationally. It stages and supports contemporary art projects in areas of the developing world via exhibitions, training and development, professional study visits and the management of the British Pavilion at the Venice Biennale and an expansive collection of British art.

Canadian Authors Association
192 Spadina Avenue, Suite 107, Toronto, Ontario M5T 2C2
tel +1 416-975-1756
website www.canadianauthors.org
National Chair Margaret A. Hume, *Executive Director* Anita Purcell

Provides writers with a wide variety of programmes, services and resources to help them develop their skills in both the craft and the business of writing. A membership-based organisation for writers in all areas of the profession. Branches across Canada. Founded 1921.

The Canadian Children's Book Centre
Suite 217, 40 Orchard View Blvd, Toronto, ON M4R 1B9
tel +1 416-975-0010
email info@bookcentre.ca
website www.bookcentre.ca

A national, not-for-profit organisation, founded in 1976, that is dedicated to encouraging, promoting and supporting the reading, writing, illustrating and publishing of Canadian books for young readers.

CCBC programmes, publications and resources help teachers, librarians, booksellers and parents select the very best for young readers.

Canadian Publishers' Council
3080 Yonge Street, Toronto, Ontario M4N 3N1
email dswail@pubcouncil.ca
website www.pubcouncil.ca
Executive Director David Swail

Represents the interests of Canadian publishing companies that publish books and other media for schools, colleges and universities, professional and reference markets, the retail and library sectors. Founded 1910.

Canadian Society of Children's Authors, Illustrators & Performers

720 Bathurst Street, Suite 503, Toronto, Ontario M5S 2R4
tel +1 416-515-1559
email office@canscaip.org
website www.canscaip.org
Administrative Director Helena Aalto
Membership $85 p.a.

A non-profit support network for Canadian children's artists. CANSCAIP promotes children's literature and performances throughout Canada and internationally. Founded 1977.

The Lewis Carroll Society

email membership@lewiscarrollsociety.org.uk
website www.lewiscarrollsociety.org.uk
Facebook www.facebook.com/groups/68678994062/
Twitter @LewisCarrollSoc
Membership £25 p.a. UK; £30 p.a. Europe; £35 p.a elsewhere; special rates for students and institutions

Promotes interest in the life and works of Lewis Carroll (Revd Charles Lutwidge Dodgson, 1832–98) and to encourage research. Activities include regular meetings, exhibitions, and a publishing programme that includes the first annotated, unexpurgated edition of his diaries in nine volumes, the Society's journal *The Carrollian* (two p.a.), a newsletter, *Bandersnatch* (quarterly) and the *Lewis Carroll Review* (occasional). Founded 1969.

Lewis Carroll Society of North America

email secretary@lewiscarroll.org
website www.lewiscarroll.org
President Linda Cassidy, *Secretary* Sandra Lee Parker
Membership $35 p.a. USA; $50 p.a. elsewhere; student membership $20/$30 p.a. (available to anyone 25 years old or younger)

An organisation of Carroll admirers of all ages and interests. It is dedicated to furthering Carroll studies, increasing accessibility of research material, and maintaining public awareness of Carroll's contributions to society. The Society has a worldwide membership and meets twice a year. The Society maintains an active publication programme and members receive copies of the Society's magazine *Knight Letter*. An interest in Lewis Carroll, a simple love for Alice (or the Snark for that matter) qualifies for membership. Founded in 1974.

The Center for Children's Books

501 East Daniel Street, Champaign, IL 61820
tel +1 217-244-9331
email ccb@illinois.edu
website http://ccb.ischool.illinois.edu

CCB houses a non-circulating collection of more than 16,000 recent and historically significant trade books for children, plus review copies of nearly all trade books published in the USA in the current year.

There are over 1,000 professional and reference books on the history and criticism of literature for youth, literature-based library and classroom programming, and storytelling. The collection is available for examination by scholars, teachers, librarians, students and other educators.

Centre for Literacy in Primary Education

Webber Street, London SE1 8QW
tel 020-7401 3382/3
email info@clpe.org.uk
website www.clpe.org.uk

A centre for children's language, literacy, literature and educational assessment which provides in-service training for teachers, consultancy to educational establishments and publishers, and courses for parents. It contains a reference library of children's books plus teachers' resources. CLPE publishes teaching resources relating to literacy in the primary classroom. Book recommendations online at www.corebooks.org.uk.

The Children's Book Circle – see page 358

The Children's Book Council and Every Child A Reader

54 West 39th Street, 14th Floor, New York, NY 10018
tel +1 212-996-1990
email cbc.info@cbcbooks.org
website www.cbcbooks.org
website www.everychildareader.net

The CBC is the non-profit trade association of North American publishers and packagers of trade books and related materials for children and young adults. Every Child a Reader is its charitable component that sponsors Children's Book Week, which celebrated 100 years in May 2019; the Children's & Teen Choice Book Awards; Get Caught Reading; and the National Ambassador of Young People's Literature, in conjunction with the Library of Congress.

The CBC offers children's publishers the opportunity to work together on educational programming, diversity advocacy, and national literacy and public awareness campaigns. The CBC connects member publishers to librarians, teachers, booksellers, and caregivers across the country, providing reading lists, student resources, and community outreach in coordination with prominent national organisations.

The Children's Book Council of Australia

Level 2 State Library of Queensland, Stanley Place, South Brisbane 4101

email admin@cbca.org.au
website www.cbca.org.au
Facebook www.facebook.com/theCBCA
Twitter @theCBCA

Aims to foster children's enjoyment of books through managing the Children's Book of the Year Awards; providing information on and encouragement to authors and illustrators; organising exhibitions and activities during Children's Book Week; supporting children's library services; and promoting high standards in book reviewing, along with promoting greater equity of access to reading through community projects.

The Children's Book Guild of Washington DC

email childrensbookguild@yahoo.com
website www.childrensbookguild.org

A regional association of writers, artists, librarians and other specialists dedicated to the field of children's literature. Its aims are to uphold and stimulate high standards of writing and illustrating for children; to increase knowledge and use of better books for children in the community; and to cooperate with other groups having similar purposes. Founded 1945.

Children's Books Ireland

17 North Great George's Street, Dublin D01 R2F1, Republic of Ireland
tel +353 (0)1 872 7475
email info@childrensbooksireland.com
website www.childrensbooksireland.ie
Director Elaina Ryan, *Publications and Projects Manager* Jenny Murray, *Programme and Events Manager* Aoife Murray, *Administrator* Ciara Houlihan

The national children's books resource organisation of Ireland. Its mission is to make books part of every child's life. It champions and celebrates the importance of authors and illustrators and works in partnership with the people and organisations who enhance children's lives through books. Core projects include: the CBI Annual Conference; the CBI Book of the Year Awards and its shadowing scheme for school groups and book clubs; the annual nationwide reading campaign which promotes books and reading and which coincides with the publication of the *Inis Reading Guide*, a guide to the best books of the year; nationwide Book Clinics; the Robert Dunbar Memorial Libraries; and *Inis* magazine in print and online – a forum for discussion, debate and critique of Irish and international books. CBI administers the Laureate na nÓg project on behalf of the Arts Council and runs live literature events throughout the year. Founded 1996.

Children's Literature Association

3525 Piedmont Road, Building 5, Suite 300, Atlanta, GA 30305
tel +1 630-571-4520
email info@childlitassn.org
website https://chla.memberclicks.net
Membership $90 p.a. individual membership; retired $55 p.a.; student $40 p.a.; institutional $170 p.a.; joint $45 p.a.

An organisation encouraging high standards of criticism, scholarship, research and teaching in children's literature.

Contact An Author

2 Burns Close, Carshalton SM5 4PY
tel 020-8642 0884
email info@contactanauthor.co.uk
website https://contactanauthor.uk
Facebook www.facebook.com/contactanauthor
Twitter @contactanauthor
Contact Joe Ratzer

An author-booking agency that connects children with compassionate and creative people to enhance education. Helps schools, libraries, festivals and organisations all over the world to book authors for their events. Its mission is to celebrate books and help to arrange as many author visits as possible. Always happy for published authors to join. Founded 2006.

Coram Beanstalk

Coram Campus, 41 Brunswick Square, London WC1N 1AZ
tel 020-7729 4087
website www.beanstalkcharity.org.uk
Facebook www.facebook.com/Beanstalkreads
Twitter @beanstalkreads

Recruits, trains and supports volunteers to provide consistent, one-to-one reading support to children aged 3–13 who need help. Reading helpers give them the support they need to improve their reading skills, reading ability and confidence. Also provides training to people within the school community who want to help children learn to read for pleasure whilst improving their reading skills.

Creative Industries Federation

22 Endell Street, London WC2H 9AD
tel 020-3771 0350
website www.creativeindustriesfederation.com
Twitter @Creative_Fed

The national organisation for the UK's creative industries, cultural education and arts, spanning advertising and architecture to video games, performance and publishing. The Federation is entirely independent and works with members in towns, cities and the rural economy nationwide, as well as with politicians, mayors and local authorities on a wide range of policy issues. Founded 2014.

Societies, prizes and festivals

Creative Scotland

Waverley Gate, 2–4 Waterloo Place,
Edinburgh EH1 3EG
tel 0330 333 2000 (switchboard); 0345 603 6000
(enquiries line)
email enquiries@creativescotland.com
website www.creativescotland.com

The public body that supports the arts, screen and
creative industries across all parts of Scotland on
behalf of everyone who lives, works or visits there.
Through distributing funding from the Scottish
Government and the National Lottery, Creative
Scotland enables people and organisations to work in
and experience the arts, screen and creative industries
in Scotland by helping others to develop great ideas
and bring them to life.

Cwlwm Cyhoeddwyr Cymru

Elwyn Williams, Bryntirion Villa, Ffordd Penglais,
Aberystwyth SY23 2EU
tel 07866 834109
email elwyn_williams@btinternet.com
website www.bedwen.com
Facebook www.facebook.com/bedwenlyfrau

Represents and promotes Welsh-language publishers
and organises Bedwen Lyfrau, the only national
Welsh-language book festival, held annually in April.
Founded 2002.

Roald Dahl's Marvellous Children's Charity

website www.roalddahl.com/charity

Helps to make life better for seriously ill children in
the UK. The Roald Dahl Nurses provide support to
children with serious illnesses, and their families. The
Charity believes that every child should have the best
possible healthcare.

The website is illustrated with the artworks of
Quentin Blake, Roald Dahl's principal illustrator and
President of the charity, and includes full information
about the author, his life and his works. It also
provides details of the children's Dahlicious Dress Up
Day event and includes a free online club for children
and the online magazine *Dahl-y Telegraph*.

The Roald Dahl Museum and Story Centre
website www.roalddahl.com/museum
Houses Roald Dahl's unique archive and is situated
in the Buckinghamshire village where Roald Dahl
lived and worked for 36 years. The Museum features
three interactive galleries and the Story Centre
provides activities and events to inspire young
writers.

Walter de la Mare Society

3 Hazelwood Close, New River Crescent,
Palmers Green, London N13 5RE
website www.walterdelamare.co.uk
Honorary Secretary and Treasurer Frances Guthrie
Membership £15 p.a.

Established to promote the study and deepen the
appreciation of the works of Walter de la Mare
(1873–1956) through a magazine, talks, discussions
and other activities. Founded 1997.

Discover Children's Story Centre

383–387 High Street, Stratford, London E15 4QZ
tel 020-8536 5555
website www.discover.org.uk

The UK's first hands-on creative literacy centre for
children aged 0–11 years and their families, carers
and teachers. Its mission is to spark children's and
adults' imagination, curiosity and creativity in a
magical and stimulating environment through
creative play. It offers a variety of programmes
including schools workshops, family art activities, a
literature programme led by children's writers and
illustrators, community and education projects, artist
residencies in schools and training for professionals
that work with children and families. Artists are
commissioned to create multisensory installations
and exhibitions.

Editors' and Proofreaders' Alliance of Northern Ireland

email info@epani.org.uk
website www.epani.org.uk
Twitter @epa_ni
Coordinator Averill Buchanan

Aims to establish and maintain high professional
standards in editorial skills in Northern Ireland.
Membership is free, but a small fee is charged for
inclusion in EPANI's online directory. For services
for authors, see our directory of freelance
professional editors, proofreaders and indexers based
in Northern Ireland. Founded 2011.

Educational Publishers Council

The Publishers Association, First Floor,
50 Southwark Street, London SE1 1UN
tel 020-7378 0504
email mail@publishers.org.uk
website www.publishers.org.uk

Provides a forum for publishers of printed and
electronic learning resources for the school and
college markets. It runs events and meetings for its
members and provides an information service. It also
promotes the industry through the media.

English Association

University of Leicester, University Road,
Leicester LE1 7RH
tel 0116 229 7622
email engassoc@leicester.ac.uk
website www2.le.ac.uk/engassoc
Chair Rob Penman

Aims to further knowledge, understanding and
enjoyment of English literature and the English
language by working towards a fuller recognition of

English as an essential element in education and in the community at large; by encouraging the study of English literature and language by means of conferences, lectures and publications; and by fostering the discussion of methods of teaching English of all kinds.

The EA welcomes writers as members, and is pleased to represent all members' voices in national and international debates and discussions. Members are entitled to attend conferences and lectures, receive EA publications, and comment on and influence teaching and learning of all kinds.

Federation of Children's Book Groups – see page 359

Federation of European Publishers

Rue Montoyer 31 Bte 8, B–1000 Brussels, Belgium
tel +32 2-7701110
email info@fep-fee.eu
website www.fep-fee.eu

Represents the interests of European publishers on EU affairs; informs members on the development of EU policies which could affect the publishing industry. Founded 1967.

The Gaelic Books Council/Comhairle nan Leabhraichean

32 Mansfield Street, Glasgow G11 5QP
tel 0141 337 6211
email alison@gaelicbooks.org
website www.gaelicbooks.org
Director Alison Lang

Stimulates Scottish Gaelic publishing by awarding publication grants for new books, commissions new works from established and emerging authors and provides editorial advice and guidance to Gaelic writers and publishers. Has a bookshop in Glasgow that stocks all Gaelic and Gaelic-related books in print. All stock is listed on the website. Founded 1968.

The Greeting Card Association

United House, North Road, London N7 9DP
tel 020-7619 9266
email gca@max-publishing.co.uk
website www.greetingcardassociation.org.uk
Facebook www.facebook.com/
GreetingCardAssociation
Twitter @GCAUK
Chief Executive Sharon Little

The trade association for greeting card publishers. See website for information, including teachers' resources, lesson plans and card-making projects for children of all ages. Official magazine: *Progressive Greetings Worldwide*. Founded 1919.

Guernsey Arts Commission

Candie Museum, Candie Road, St Peter Port, Guernsey GY1 2UG
tel (01481) 709747
email info@arts.gg

The Commission's aim is to help promote, develop and support the arts in Guernsey through exhibitions, a community arts programme and public events.

House of Illustration

2 Granary Square, Kings Cross, London N1C 4BH
tel 020-3696 2020
email info@houseofillustration.org.uk
website http://houseofillustration.org.uk/
Twitter @illustrationHQ

House of Illustration empowers people through illustration. Founded by Sir Quentin Blake, it is the UK's first and only public gallery dedicated to illustration and graphic art. Its exhibitions celebrate contemporary and historic work across three galleries, amplified by a vibrant programme of talks, late openings and live drawing nights. It also supports emerging artists and runs a pioneering learning programme for children, young people, families and adults.

IBBY

Nonnenweg 12, Postfach CH–4009–Basel, Switzerland
tel +41 61-272 2917
email ibby@ibby.org
British Section Ms Liza Miller, 71 Addiscombe Court Road, Croydon CR0 6TT
email liza.miller@hachettechildrens.co.uk
website www.ibby.org
Secretary Liza Miller

IBBY (the International Board on Books for Young People) is a non-profit organisation which represents an international network of people from all over the world who are committed to bringing books and children together. Its aims are:

• to promote international understanding through children's books;
• to give children everywhere the opportunity to have access to books with high literary and artistic standards;
• to encourage the publication and distribution of quality children's books, especially in developing countries;
• to provide support and training for those involved with children and children's literature;
• to stimulate research and scholarly works in the field of children's literature.

IBBY is composed of more than 79 National Sections all over the world and represents countries with well-developed book publishing and literacy programmes, and other countries with only a few dedicated professionals who are doing pioneer work in children's book publishing and promotion. Founded 1953.

Imaginate
30B Grindlay Street, Edinburgh EH3 9AX
tel 0131 225 8050
email info@imaginate.org.uk
website www.imaginate.org.uk
Chief Executive Paul Fitzpatrick, *Festival Director* Noel Jordan

The national organisation in Scotland which promotes, develops and celebrates theatre and dance for children and young people. Imaginate wants more children in Scotland to experience work that is deeply engaging, innovative and inspiring, and believes that all children deserve the opportunity to develop their creativity, emotional intelligence and reach their true potential.

Imaginate wants more high-quality children's work made in Scotland, and so supports artists with a year-round programme of creative development. This includes a mix of events, training, residencies, mentoring and special projects. Imaginate celebrates the best of children's theatre and dance from around the world by producing the Edinburgh International Children's Festival which showcases performances that delight and inspire the young and young-at-heart.

Imaginative Book Illustration Society
email ibissec@martinsteenson.co.uk
website www.bookillustration.org
Membership enquiries Martin Steenson

IBIS was established to encourage research into, and to facilitate, the exchange of information on book and periodical illustrations, the artists and their publishers. The Society has a worldwide membership including artists, collectors, bibliographers, writers and general enthusiasts. Whilst IBIS embraces all aspects of illustrative art, the main emphasis is on the illustration of texts in English since the 1830s. Founded 1995.

Independent Publishers Guild
PO Box 12, Llain, Login SA34 0WU
tel (01437) 563335
email info@ipg.uk.com
website www.ipg.uk.com
Chief Executive Bridget Shine
Membership Open to new and established publishers and book packagers

The IPG provides an information and contact network for independent publishers. Also voices concerns of member companies within the book trade. Founded 1962.

Independent Theatre Council
The Albany, Douglas Way, London SE8 4AG
tel 020-7403 1727
email admin@itc-arts.org
website www.itc-arts.org/
Twitter @itc_arts

Enables the creation of high-quality professional performing arts by supporting, representing and developing the people who manage and produce it. It has around 500 members from a wide range of companies, venues and individuals in the fields of drama, dance, opera, musical theatre, puppetry, mixed media, mime, physical theatre and circus. Founded 1974.

International Authors Forum
5th Floor, Shackleton House, 4 Battle Bridge Lane, London SE1 2HX
tel 020-7264 5707
email luke.alcott@internationalauthors.org
website www.internationalauthors.org
Executive Administrator Luke Alcott

A forum for discussion, where authors' organisations can share information and take action on issues affecting them worldwide. Organises events, publications and discussions, and collaborates with other organisations representing authors to promote the importance of creative work financially, socially and culturally. Keeps members up to date with international developments in copyright law.

International Publishers Association
23 Avenue de France, 1202 Geneva, Switzerland
tel +41 22-704 1820
email info@internationalpublishers.org
website www.internationalpublishers.org
President Hugo Setzer, *Secretary-General* José Borghino

The IPA is a federation of national, regional and international publishers associations. It promotes and protects publishing worldwide, with a focus on copyright and freedom to publish. Its membership comprises 81 organisations from 69 countries worldwide. Founded 1896.

Irish Writers Centre
19 Parnell Square, Dublin D01 E102, Republic of Ireland
tel +353 (0)1 872 1302
email info@writerscentre.ie
website www.irishwriterscentre.ie
Director Valerie Bistany

The national resource centre for Irish writers, the Irish Writers Centre supports and promotes writers at all stages of their development. It runs workshops, seminars and events related to the art of writing which are run by established writers across a range of genres. It hosts professional development seminars for writers, and provides space for writers, writing groups and other literary organisations.

The Kipling Society

Bay Tree House, Doomsday Garden, Horsham, West Sussex RH13 6LB
tel (07866) 867710
email mike@kipling.me.uk
website www.kiplingsociety.co.uk
Chairman Mike Kipling
Membership £29 p.a.; £14 aged under 23; £31 Europe or rest of world

Encourages discussion and study of the work and life of Rudyard Kipling (1865–1936), to assist in the study of his writings, to hold discussion meetings, to publish a quarterly journal and website (with a Readers' Guide to Kipling's work) and to maintain a Kipling Library at Haileybury School in Hertfordshire.

The C.S. Lewis Society (New York)

84–23, 77th Avenue, Glendle, NY 11385–7706, USA
email subscribe@nycslsociety.com
email csarrocco@aol.com
website www.nycslsociety.com
Secretary Clare Sarrocco

The oldest society for the appreciation and discussion of C.S. Lewis (1898–1963). Founded 1969.

Literature Wales

Glyn Jones Centre, Wales Millennium Centre, Bute Place, Cardiff CF10 5AL
tel 029-2047 2266
email post@literaturewales.org
website www.literaturewales.org
Facebook www.facebook.com/LlenCymruLitWales/
Twitter @LitWales
Chief Executive Lleucu Siencyn

Literature Wales is the national company for the development of literature in Wales. Working to inspire communities, develop writers and celebrate Wales' literary culture, its vision is a Wales where literature empowers, improves and brightens lives. Activities include the Wales Book of the Year Award, creative writing courses at Tŷ Newydd Writing Centre, writer's bursaries and mentoring, the National Poet of Wales initiative, and more. The organisation is a member of the Arts Council of Wales' Arts Portfolio Wales.

Little Theatre Guild of Great Britain

tel (01207) 545280
email caroline.chapman1816@gmail.com
website www.littletheatreguild.org
Secretary Caroline Chapman

Promotes closer cooperation amongst the little theatres constituting its membership; acts as a coordinating and representative body on behalf of the little theatres; maintains and advances the highest standards in the art of theatre; and assists in encouraging the establishment of other little theatres.

Magazines Canada

Mailbox 201, 555 Richmond Street West, Suite 604, Toronto, Ontario M5V 3B1
tel +1 416-504-0274
email info@magazinescanada.ca
website www.magazinescanada.ca
Executive Director Melanie Rutledge

The national trade association representing Canadian consumer, cultural, speciality, professional and business media magazines.

The Mythopoeic Society

website www.mythsoc.org

A non-profit international literary and educational organisation for the study, discussion and enjoyment of fantastic and mythic literature, especially the works of Tolkien, C.S. Lewis and Charles Williams. 'Mythopoeic' (myth-oh-PAY-ik or myth-oh-PEE-ic) means 'mythmaking' or 'productive of myth' and aptly describes much of the fictional work of the three authors who were also prominent members of an informal Oxford literary circle (1930s–1950s) known as the Inklings. Membership is open to all scholars, writers and readers of these literatures. The Society sponsors three periodicals: *Mythprint* (a bulletin of book reviews, articles and events), *Mythlore* (scholarly articles on mythic and fantastic literature), and *Mythic Circle* (a literary annual of original poetry and short stories). Each summer the Society holds an annual conference, Mythcon. Founded 1967.

National Association for the Teaching of English

Aizlewood Mill, Nursery Street, Sheffield S3 8GG
tel 0114 282 3545
email info@nate.org.uk
website www.nate.org.uk

NATE works to: promote standards of excellence in the teaching of English from early years to university; promote innovative and original ideas that have practical classroom outcomes; support teachers' professional development through access to current research, publications and national and regional conferences; provide an informed national voice on matters concerning the teaching of English and its related subjects; encourage sharing and collaboration between teachers and learners of English and its related subjects.

National Association of Writers' Groups

Old Vicarage, Scammonden, Huddersfield HD3 3FT
email info@nawg.co.uk
website www.nawg.co.uk
Facebook www.facebook.com/NAWGNews/
Twitter @NAWGnews
Secretary Chris Huck
Membership £50 p.a. per group; £25 p.a. individuals

NAWG aims to advance the education of the general public throughout the UK, including the Channel Islands, by promoting the study and art of writing in all its aspects. Publishes *LNK*, a bi-monthly magazine. Festival of Writing held annually in August/September. New members always welcome. Founded 1995.

National Association of Writers in Education

Tower House, Mill Lane, off Askham Fields Lane, Askham Bryan, York, YO23 3FS
tel 0330 333 5909
email admin@nawe.co.uk
website www.nawe.co.uk

National membership organisation which aims to further knowledge, understanding and enjoyment of creative writing and to support good practice in its teaching and learning at all levels. NAWE promotes creative writing as both a distinct discipline and an essential element in education generally. Its membership includes those working in Higher Education, the many freelance writers working in schools and community contexts, and the teachers and other professionals who work with them. It runs a national database of writers, produces a weekly opportunities bulletin, publishes two journals – *Writing in Education* and *Writing in Practice* – and holds a national conference. Professional membership includes public liability insurance cover.

National Centre for Research in Children's Literature

website www.roehampton.ac.uk/research-centres/national-centre-for-research-in-childrens-literature

NCRCL promotes research excellence in the field of children's literature. News of regular conferences and events can be found at the NCRCL Blog. Founded 1995.

National Centre for Writing

Dragon Hall, 115–123 King Street, Norwich NR1 1QE
email info@nationalcentreforwriting.org.uk
website www.nationalcentreforwriting.org.uk
Facebook www.facebook.com/NationalCentreforWriting
Twitter @WritersCentre

Celebrates and explores the artistic and social power of creative writing and literary translation. An ongoing programme of innovative collaborations engages writers, literary translators and readers in projects that support new voices and new stories and respond to the rapidly changing world of writing. Based at the historic Dragon Hall in Norwich, where workshops and mentoring are regularly available for writers at all levels, both face-to-face and online. Projects range from major international partnerships to vibrant festivals such as the Noirwich Crime Writing Festival and the Norfolk & Norwich Festival. Founded 2018.

National Literacy Trust – see page 361

National Society for Education in Art and Design

3 Mason's Wharf, Potley Lane, Corsham, Wilts. SN13 9FY
tel (01225) 810134
email info@nsead.org
website www.nsead.org
Facebook www.facebook.com/groups/NSEADOnline
Twitter @NSEAD1
General Secretary Michele Gregson, *Assistant General Secretary* Sophie Leach

The leading national authority concerned with art, craft and design across all phases of education in the UK. Offers the benefits of membership of a professional association, a learned society and a trade union. Has representatives on national and regional committees concerned with art and design education. Publishes *International Journal of Art and Design Education* online (three p.a.; Wiley Blackwell) and *AD* magazine for teachers. Founded 1888.

The Edith Nesbit Society

21 Churchfields, West Malling, Kent ME19 6RJ
email edithnesbit@gmail.com
website www.edithnesbit.co.uk
Membership £10 p.a. individual; £12 p.a.; joint; £15 p.a. organisations

Promotes an interest in the life and works of Edith Nesbit (1858–1924) by means of talks, a regular newsletter and other publications, and visits to places associated with her. Founded 1996.

New Writing North

email office@newwritingnorth.com
website www.newwritingnorth.com

The literature development agency for the North of England. Specialises in developing writers and acts as a broker between writers, producers, publishers and broadcasters. Flagship projects include Northern Writers' Awards, Gordon Burn Prize and Durham Book Festival.

New Zealand Association of Literary Agents
PO Box 6292, Dunedin North 9059
email tfs@elseware.co.nz
website www.elseware.co.nz/nzala

Set up to establish standards and guidelines for literary agents operating in New Zealand. All members subscribe to a code of ethics which includes working on commission and not charging upfront fees for promotion or manuscript reading.

Newcastle University Library
Robinson Library, Newcastle University, Newcastle upon Tyne NE2 4HQ
tel 0191 208 7662
email libraryhelp@ncl.ac.uk
website www.ncl.ac.uk/library

A modern academic library with multi-disciplinary collections, including historical children's books.

The Special Collections
tel 0191 208 7712
email lib-specenq@ncl.ac.uk
website www.ncl.ac.uk/library/special-collections
The Library's Special Collections hold many unique archives and rare books. These materials provide great scope for original research for many subject areas and the potential to complement teaching and learning at the university. There are a number of collections and archives dedicated to children's literature. See website for details.

The Office for Standards in Education, Children's Services and Skills
Piccadilly Gate, Store Street, Manchester M1 2WD
tel 0300 123 1231
email enquiries@ofsted.gov.uk
website www.gov.uk/ofsted

Ofsted is a non-ministerial government department. It regulates and inspects to achieve excellence in the care of children and young people, and in education and skills for learners of all ages. It regulates and inspects childcare and children's social care, and inspects the Children and Family Court Advisory and Support Service (Cafcass), schools, colleges, initial teacher training, further education and skills, adult and community learning, and education and training in prisons and other secure establishments. It assesses council children's services, and inspects services for looked after children, safeguarding and child protection.

PICSEL (Picture Industry Collecting Society for Effective Licensing)
112 Western Road, Brighton, East Sussex BN1 2AB
tel (01273) 746564
email info@picsel.org.uk
website www.picsel.org.uk

PICSEL is a not-for-profit organisation that ensures that all visual artists, creators and representative rights holders of images receive fair payment for various secondary uses of their works. It works to ensure that all licence fees collected are distributed equitably, efficiently and in a transparent manner. Founded 2016.

The Poetry Book Society – see page 219

The Poetry Society – see page 219

Poetry Society Education – see page 223

Pop Up Projects
Chauffeurs Cottage, 1 St Peters Road, Peterborough PE1 1YX
email info@pop-up.org.uk
website www.pop-up.org.uk
Facebook www.facebook.com/popupfestival
Twitter @PopUpFestival

A not-for-profit community interest company which works with educational, literary and cultural organisations on projects and literature programmes that enable children, empower teachers and engage families from all walks of life to read more widely, write more creatively and develop visual storytelling skills. To find out more about the Pop Up Festival, bespoke projects for schools or professional development opportunities, contact education@pop-up.org.uk. Founded 2011.

The Beatrix Potter Society
email info@beatrixpottersociety.org.uk
website www.beatrixpottersociety.org.uk

Promotes the study and appreciation of the life and works of Beatrix Potter (1866–1943) as author, artist, diarist, farmer and conservationist. Regular lecture meetings, conferences and events in the UK and USA. Quarterly newsletter. Small publishing programme. Founded 1980.

The Publishers Association
First Floor, 50 Southwark Street, London SE1 1UN
tel 020-7378 0504
email mail@publishers.org.uk
website www.publishers.org.uk
Twitter @PublishersAssoc
President Peter Phillips, *Ceo* Stephen Lotinga

The leading representative voice for book, journal, audio and electronic publishers in the UK. The Association has over 100 members and its role is to support publishers in their political, media and industry stakeholder communications. Founded 1896.

Publishers Association of New Zealand

PO Box 33319, Takapuna, Auckland 0740
tel +64 (0)9 280 3212
email catriona@publishers.org.nz
website www.publishers.org.nz
Association Director Catriona Ferguson

PANZ represents book, educational and digital publishers in New Zealand. Members include both the largest international publishers and companies in the independent publishing community.

Publishing Ireland/Foilsiú Éireann

63 Patrick Street, Dun Laoghaire,
Co Dublin A96 WF25, Republic of Ireland
tel +353 (0)1 639 4868
email info@publishingireland.com
website www.publishingireland.com

Publishing Ireland enables publishers to share expertise and resources in order to benefit from opportunities and solve problems that are of common concern to all. It comprises most of the major publishing houses in Ireland with a mixture of trade, general and academic publishers as members.

Publishing Scotland

Scott House, 10 South St Andrew Street,
Edinburgh EH2 2AZ
tel 0131 228 6866
email enquiries@publishingscotland.org
website www.publishingscotland.org
Chief Executive Marion Sinclair

A network for trade, training and development in the Scottish publishing industry. Founded 1973.

The Arthur Ransome Society Ltd

Abbot Hall Art Gallery & Lakeland Museum, Kendal, Cumbria LA9 5AL
website www.arthur-ransome.org.uk

Exists to celebrate the life, promote the works and diffuse the ideas of Arthur Ransome (1884–1967), author of the world-famous *Swallows and Amazons* series of books for children. The Society seeks in particular to encourage children and others to engage, with due regard to safety, in adventurous pursuits; educate the public generally about Ransome and his work; sponsor research in relevant areas; be a communications link for those interested in any aspect of Arthur Ransome's life and works. Founded 1990.

Read for Good

26 Nailsworth Mills, Avening Road, Nailsworth, Glos. GL6 0BS
tel (01453) 839005
email reading@readforgood.org
website www.readforgood.org

Read for Good aims for all children in the UK to be given the opportunity, space and motivation to develop their own love of reading, benefiting them throughout their lives. Many studies show that reading changes lives: from educational outcomes and social mobility to emotional wellbeing. Runs a readathon programme in schools and a hospital programme, which focuses on the supply of books and storyteller visits to brighten up the days of children in the UK's main children's hospitals.

The Reading Agency

Free Word Centre, 60 Farringdon Road,
London EC1R 3GA
info@readingagency.org.uk
website www.readingagency.org.uk
Twitter @readingagency

A charity whose mission is to inspire more people to read more, encourage them to share their enjoyment of reading and celebrate the difference that reading makes to everyone's lives. It has a close partnership with public libraries in creating equal access to reading, and works closely with publishers to bring author events and reading promotions to every kind of community. Funded by the Arts Council.

Supports a wide range of reading initiatives for children, young people and adults including: the Summer Reading Challenge, run in partnership with libraries, which helps get three-quarters of a million children reading each year; Reading Ahead, designed to build people's reading confidence and motivation; and World Book Night, an annual celebration of books and reading which takes place on 23 April.

RNIB National Library Service

tel 0303 123 9999
website www.rnib.org.uk/library

The largest specialist library for readers with sight loss in the UK. It offers a comprehensive range of books and accessible information for children and adults in a range of formats including braille, large print and unabridged audio. Members have access to a free bi-annual magazine, an online library catalogue and a reader services team.

The Malcolm Saville Society

11 Minster Court, Windsor Close, Taunton TA1 4LW
email mystery@witchend.com
website www.witchend.com
Facebook www.facebook.com/MalcolmSaville
Twitter @MSavilleSociety
Membership £15 p.a. UK; £17.50 p.a. Europe; £21 p.a. elsewhere

Promotes interest in the work of Malcolm Saville (1901–82), children's author. Regular social activities, library, contact directory and magazine (four p.a.). Founded 1994.

Scattered Authors' Society

email scatteredauthorssociety@gmail.com
website www.scatteredauthors.org

Provides a forum for informal discussion, contact and support for professional writers in children's fiction. Founded 1998.

School Library Association
1 Pine Court, Kembrey Park, Swindon SN2 8AD
tel (01793) 530166
email info@sla.org.uk
website www.sla.org.uk

Promotes the development of school libraries and information literacy as central to the curriculum. SLA provides training, networking and an information service. Publishes guidelines for school library and resource centres, book lists and a quarterly journal which includes current book and digital resources reviews for all school-age children.

Scottish Book Trust
Sandeman House, Trunk's Close, 55 High Street, Edinburgh EH1 1SR
tel 0131 524 0160
email info@scottishbooktrust.com
website www.scottishbooktrust.com
Facebook www.facebook.com/scottishbktrust
Twitter @ScottishBkTrust

Scotland's national agency for the promotion of reading, writing and literature. Programmes include: Bookbug, a free universal book-gifting programme which encourages families to read with their children from birth; an ambitious schools programme including national tours, the virtual events programme Authors Live and the Bookbug Picture Book Prize; the Scottish Teenage Book Prize; the Live Literature funding programme, a national initiative enabling Scottish citizens to engage with authors, playwrights, poets, storytellers and illustrators; a writer development programme, offering mentoring and professional development for emerging and established writers; and a readership development programme featuring a national writing campaign, as well as Book Week Scotland, during the last week in November.

Scottish Storytelling Forum
Scottish Storytelling Centre, 43–45 High Street, Edinburgh EH1 1SR
tel 0131 556 9579
email reception@scottishstorytellingcentre.com
website www.scottishstorytellingcentre.co.uk
website www.storytellingforum.co.uk
Facebook www.facebook.com/ScotStoryForum
Twitter @ScotStoryCentre

Scotland's national charity for oral storytelling, established to encourage and support the telling and sharing of stories across all ages and sectors of society, in particular those who, for reasons of poverty or disability, are sometimes excluded from artistic experiences. The Scottish Storytelling Centre is the Forum's resource and training centre which presents a year-round programme of storytelling and traditional arts events, workshops and the Scottish International Storytelling Festival in the autumn. The Storytelling Network has over 150 professional storytellers across Scotland. Founded 1992.

Seven Stories – The National Centre for Children's Books – see page 356

Society for Editors and Proofreaders
Apsley House, 176 Upper Richmond Road, London SW15 2SH
tel 020-8785 6155
email administrator@sfep.org.uk
website www.sfep.org.uk
Facebook www.facebook.com/EditProof
Twitter @TheSfEP

The SfEP works to promote high editorial standards and achieve recognition of its members' professional status, through local and national meetings, an annual conference, discussion forums and a regular e-magazine. The Society publishes an online directory of experienced members. It also runs online courses and workshops and offers in-house training, which help newcomers to acquire basic editorial skills, and enable experienced editors and proofreaders to update their skills or broaden their competence. Training also covers aspects of professional practice and business for the self-employed. The Society supports moves towards recognised standards of training and accreditation for editors and proofreaders and is working towards chartership. It has close links with the Publishing Training Centre and the Society of Indexers, is represented on the BSI Technical Committee dealing with copy preparation and proof correction (BS 5261), and works to foster good relations with all relevant bodies and organisations in the UK and worldwide. Founded 1988.

Society for Storytelling (SfS)
The Glass House, Fulcher Avenue, Cromer, Norfolk NR27 7SG
tel 07775 068886
website https://sfs.org.uk
Facebook www.facebook.com/societyforstorytelling/
Twitter @sfs_uk

SfS provides information on oral storytelling, events, storytellers and traditional stories. Its volunteers have specialist knowledge of storytelling in education, health, therapy and business settings. To increase public awareness of the art of storytelling it promotes National Storytelling Week. The SfS provides a network for anyone interested in the art of oral storytelling whether they are full-time storytellers, use storytelling in their work, tell stories for the love of it or just want to listen. It holds an annual conference and produces a quarterly newsletter. Founded 1993.

Society of Artists Agents

website www.saahub.com

Formed to promote professionalism in the illustration industry and to forge closer links between clients and artists through an agreed set of guidelines. The Society believes in an ethical approach through proper terms and conditions, thereby protecting the interests of the artists and clients. Founded 1992.

The Society of Authors

– see page 349

Society of Children's Book Writers and Illustrators (SCBWI) – see page 353

Society of Editors

University Centre, Granta Place, Mill Lane, Cambridge CB2 1RU
tel (01223) 304080
email office@societyofeditors.org
website www.societyofeditors.org
Executive Director Ian Murray
Membership up to £230 p.a. depending on category

Formed from the merger of the Guild of Editors and the Association of British Editors, the Society of Editors has members in national, regional and local newspapers, magazines, broadcasting and digital media, journalism education and media law. It campaigns for media freedom, self regulation, the public's right to know and the maintenance of standards in journalism.

Society of Young Publishers

c/o The Publishers Association, First Floor, 50 Southwark Street, London SE1 1UN
email sypchair@thesyp.org.uk
website www.thesyp.org.uk
Twitter @SYP_UK
Membership Open to anyone employed in publishing or hoping to be soon, catering specifically to those in the first ten years of their career; £30 p.a. standard; £24 p.a. student/unwaged; £18 p.a. digital only

SYP organises monthly events which offer the chance to network, develop skills and hear senior figures talk on topics of key importance to the publishing industry. Organises industry mentor schemes, book clubs and two annual conferences. Publishes a quarterly print magazine *InPrint*. Provides a job database advertising the latest vacancies and internships; online forum The Network; and a blog, PressForward. Has branches in London, Oxford, Scotland, Ireland, the South West and North (Manchester/Leeds), overseen by a UK steering committee. Founded 1949.

Speaking of Books

44 Blackheath Park, London SE3 9SJ
tel 07931 929325
email jan@speakingofbooks.co.uk
website www.speakingofbooks.co.uk

Arranges school visits by writers, illustrators and storytellers. Also in-service training days relating to literacy.

Spread the Word

The Albany, Douglas Way, London SE8 4AG
tel 020-8692 0231 extension 249
email hello@spreadtheword.org.uk
website www.spreadtheword.org.uk
Facebook www.facebook.com/spreadthewordwriters
Twitter @STWevents
Instagram spreadthewordwriters

London's writer development agency, helping writers make their mark on the page, the screen and in the world. Kick-starts the careers of London's best new writers, and energetically campaigns to ensure mainstream publishing truly reflects the diversity of the city. Supports the creative and professional development of talent, by engaging those already interested in literature and those who will be, and by advocating on behalf of both.

The Robert Louis Stevenson Club

website http://robert-louis-stevenson.org/rls-club/

Aims to foster interest in Robert Louis Stevenson's life (1850–94) and works through various events and its newsletter. Founded 1920.

The Story Museum

42 Pembroke Street, Oxford OX1 1BP
tel (01865) 807600
email onceuponatime@storymuseum.org.uk
website www.storymuseum.org.uk
Facebook www.facebook.com/TheStoryMuseum
Twitter @TheStoryMuseum

The Story Museum celebrates story in all forms and explores their enduring power to teach and delight. It aims to inspire present and future generations by providing great ways of engaging with great stories. Also runs an active education and outreach programme alongside exhibition and events. The Museum is fully reopening in spring 2020 following a £6 million major redevelopment project with ten new story-themed gallery and activity spaces including a 120-seat performance space.

Story Therapy®

1 Sugworth Lane, Radley, Abingdon-on-Thames, Oxon OX14 2HZ
email admin@storytherapyresources.co.uk
website www.storytherapyresources.co.uk
Facebook www.facebook.com/storytherapy
Twitter @StoryTherapyR
Contact Hilary Hawkes

A non-profit social enterprise creating resources, especially story-themed resources, that support children's emotional health and mental wellbeing. Founded 2016.

The Swedish Institute for Children's Books
email info@barnboksinstitutet.se
website http://barnboksinstitutet.se

Svenska barnboksinstitutet is a research and information centre for children's and young adult literature with a special library open to the public. Founded 1965.

The Tolkien Society
website www.tolkiensociety.org
Membership £30 p.a.; £45 p.a. families; £10 p.a. students

An educational charity and literary society devoted to the study and promotion of the life and works of J.R.R. Tolkien.

United Kingdom Literacy Association
Room 9 c/o VAL, 9 Newarke Street,
Leicester LE1 5SN
tel 0116 254 4116
website www.ukla.org
Twitter @The_UKLA

UKLA is a registered charity, which has as its sole object the advancement of education in literacy. It is committed to promoting good practice nationally and internationally in literacy and language teaching and research. Founded in 1963, renamed in 2003.

V&A Museum of Childhood
Cambridge Heath Road, London E2 9PA
tel 020-8983 5200
email moc@vam.ac.uk
website www.vam.ac.uk/moc
Facebook www.facebook.com/museumchildhood
Twitter @MuseumChildhood

Holds one of the largest and oldest collections of toys and childhood artefacts in the world. As well as its permanent displays, the museum has temporary exhibitions, workshops and activities for all.

Voice of the Listener & Viewer
The Old Rectory Business Centre, Springhead Road, Northfleet DA11 8HN
tel (01474) 338716
email info@vlv.org.uk
website www.vlv.org.uk
Twitter @vlvuk
Administrator Sarah Stapylton-Smith
Membership £30 p.a.; £45 p.a. joint; academic, corporate and student rates available

VLV's mission is to campaign for accountability, diversity and excellence in UK broadcasting, seeking to sustain and strengthen public service broadcasting to the benefit of civil society and democracy in the UK. It holds regular conferences and seminars and publishes a bulletin and an e-newsletter. Founded 1983.

Welsh Books Council/Cyngor Llyfrau Cymru
Castell Brychan, Aberystwyth, Ceredigion SY23 2JB
tel (01970) 624151
email castellbrychan@books.wales
website www.books.wales
website www.gwales.com
Ceo Helgard Krause

A national body funded directly by the Welsh Government which provides a focus for the publishing industry in Wales. Awards grants for publishing in Welsh and English. Provides services to the trade in the fields of editing, design, marketing and distribution. The Council is a key enabling institution in the world of books and provides services and information in this field to all who are associated with it. Founded 1961.

The Henry Williamson Society
email paulmcglonegoshawk@gmail.com
email margaretmurphy567@gmail.com
website www.henrywilliamson.co.uk
General Secretary Paul McGlone, *Membership Secretary* Margaret Murphy

Encourages a wider readership and greater understanding of the literary heritage left by Henry Williamson (1895–1977). Founded 1980.

Writers Advice Centre for Children's Books
Shakespeare House, 168 Lavender Hill, London SW11 5TG
tel 020-7801 6300
email info@writersadvice.co.uk
website www.writersadvice.co.uk
Facebook www.facebook.com/writersadvice
Twitter @writersadvice
Managing Editor Louise Jordan

Dedicated to helping new and published children's writers by offering both editorial advice and tips on how to get published. The Centre also runs workshops, an online children's writing correspondence course and publishes a small list of its own under the name of Wacky Bee Books (www.wackybeebooks.com). Founded 1994.

WGGB - The Writers' Union
First Floor, 134 Tooley Street, London SE1 2TU
tel 020-7833 0777
email admin@writersguild.org.uk
website www.writersguild.org.uk
General Secretary Ellie Peers
Membership Full, Candidate and Affiliate membership available

WGGB (Writers' Guild of Great Britain) is a trade union for professional and aspiring writers in TV, radio, film, theatre, books, poetry, comedy, animation and video games with 2,200 members;

affiliated to the Trades Union Congress. WGGB negotiates collective minimum terms agreements with the main broadcasters and trade bodies for film, TV, radio and theatre – these cover fees, advances, royalties, residuals, pension contributions, rights, credits and other matters. WGGB members have access to free contract vetting, legal advice and representation in work-related disputes, and the Writers' Guild Welfare Fund gives emergency assistance to members in financial trouble. Members receive a weekly email bulletin containing news and work opportunities.

Young at Art

Cotton Court, 30–42 Waring Street, Belfast BT1 2ED
tel 028-9023 0660
email manager@youngatart.co.uk
website www.youngatart.co.uk

Coordinates the annual Belfast Children's Festival as well as a wide variety of projects that encourage children and young people under 18 to enjoy the arts, develop awareness of its impact on their lives, and have a say in what their arts provision should be. These include engagement programmes, workshop programmes, commissions, seminars, training, research and online resources. Founded 2000.

Youth Libraries Group

CILIP, 7 Ridgmount Street, London WC1E 7AE
email secretary.YLG@cilip.org.uk
website www.cilip.org.uk/ylg
Twitter @youthlibraries
Secretary Sue Polchow

YLG is open to all members of the Chartered Institute for Library and Information Professionals (CILIP) who are interested in children's work. At a national level its aims are:

• to influence the provision of library services for children and the provision of quality literature;
• to inspire and support all librarians working with children and young people;
• to liaise with other national professional organisations in pursuit of such aims.

At a local level, the YLG organises regular training courses, supports professional development and provides opportunities to meet colleagues. It holds an annual conference and judges the CILIP Carnegie and Kate Greenaway Awards (see page 382).

Children's book and illustration prizes and awards

This list provides details of prizes, competitions and awards relevant to children's writers and artists.

Academy of British Cover Design: Annual Cover Design Competition

website https://abcoverd.co.uk
Twitter @abcoverd

The Academy of British Cover Design's annual competition awards covers produced for any book published between 1 January and 31 December each year, by any designer in the UK, for a UK or overseas publisher. Ebooks are eligible. Designers may enter their own work or the work of designers. There are ten categories: children's, young adult, sci-fi/fantasy, mass market, literary fiction, crime/thriller, non-fiction, series design, classic/reissue and women's fiction. A cover can only be submitted in one category unless it is entered as an individual cover and again as part of a series design. Entry is free.

ALCS Educational Writers' Award

The Society of Authors, 24 Bedford Row,
London WC1R 4TQ
tel 020-7373 6642
email prizes@societyofauthors.org
website www.societyofauthors.org/ALCS-award

This is an annual award alternating each year between books in the 5–11 and 11–18 age groups. It is given to an outstanding example of traditionally published non-fiction (with or without illustrations) that stimulates and enhances learning. The work must have been first published in the UK, in the English language, within the previous two calendar years. Deadline 10 June.

The Hans Christian Andersen Awards

International Board on Books for Young People,
Nonnenweg 12, Postfach CH–4009 Basel, Switzerland
tel +41 61 272 2917
email ibby@ibby.org
website www.ibby.org

Given every other year by IBBY, the Hans Christian Andersen Awards recognise lifelong achievement and are presented to an author and an illustrator whose complete works have made an important, lasting contribution to children's literature. The Author's Award has been given since 1956 and the Illustrator's Award since 1966.

Arts Council England

tel 0161 934 4317
website www.artscouncil.org.uk

Arts Council England is the national development agency for the arts in England, providing funding for a range of arts and cultural activities. It supports creative writing including poetry, fiction, storytelling, spoken word, digital work, writing for children and literary translation. It funds a range of publishers and magazines as well as providing grants to individual writers. Contact the enquiries team for more information on funding support and advice.

Association for Library Service to Children Awards

American Library Association, 50 East Huron Street,
Chicago, IL 60611
tel +1 800-545-2433 ext. 2163
email alscawards@ala.org
website www.ala.org/alsc

The following awards are administered by ALSC:

• The Caldecott Medal (named in honour of the 19th-century English illustrator Randolph Caldecott) is awarded annually to the artist of the most distinguished US picture book for children.
• The Newbery Medal (named after the 18th-century British bookseller John Newbery) is awarded annually to the author of the most distinguished contribution to US literature for children.
• The Geisel Award (named after the world-renowned children's author a.k.a. Dr Seuss) is given annually to the author(s) and illustrator(s) of the most distinguished contribution to the body of children's literature known as beginning reader books published in the USA during the preceding year.
• The Robert F. Sibert Informational Book Award is given annually to the author of the most distinguished informational book published in English during the preceding year.
• The Children's Literature Legacy Award honours authors and illustrators published in the US whose books have made a substantial and lasting contribution to literature for children.
• The Excellence in Early Learning Digital Media Award will be given in 2020 to a digital media producer that has created distinguished digital media for an early learning audience.
• The Batchelder Award is awarded annually to an outstanding children's book translated from a language other than English and originally published in a country other than the United States.
• The Belpré Awards are presented annually to a Latino/Latina writer and illustrator whose work best

portrays, affirms and celebrates the Latino cultural experience.

• The Odyssey Award is given for the best audio book produced for children and/or young adults. Co-administrered with YALSH and sponsored by Book list.

• The Wilder Award is given to an author or illustrator whose books have made a substantial and lasting contribution to children's literature.

Bardd Plant Cymru (Welsh-Language Children's Poet Laureate)

Welsh Books Council, Castell Brychan, Aberystwyth, Ceredigion SY23 2JB
tel (01970) 624151
email castellbrychan@books.wales
website www.books.wales

The main aim is to raise the profile of poetry amongst children and to encourage them to compose and enjoy poetry. During his/her term of office the bard will visit schools as well as help children to create poetry through electronic workshops. The scheme's partner organisations are: S4C, the Welsh Government, the Welsh Books Council, Urdd Gobaith Cymru and Literature Wales.

J.M. Barrie Award

email admin@childrensarts.org.uk
website www.childrensarts.org.uk/what-we-do/awards/
Twitter @childrensarts

The Action for Children's Arts J.M. Barrie Award is given annually to a children's arts practitioner or organisation for a lifetime's achievement in delighting children whose work, in the view of the trustees, will stand the test of time. *2018 winners*: Stuart and Kadie Kanneh-Mason.

The Bath Children's Novel Award

PO Box 5223, Bath BA1 0UR
email info@bathnovelaward.co.uk
website www.bathnovelaward.co.uk
Twitter @bathnovelaward

This annual international prize is for unpublished or independently published writers of novels for children or young adults. Submissions: first 5,000 words plus one-page synopsis. Entries open June until November. Entry fee: £28 per novel. Children and teenagers vote for the shortlist, with the winner chosen by a literary agent. Prize: £2,500 plus introductions to literary agents.

BBC Radio 2 500 Words

email 500words@bbc.co.uk
website www.bbc.co.uk/programmes/p00rfvk1

The UK's most successful short story-writing competition for children between the ages of 5 and 13. It seeks to get children excited about reading and writing, no matter what their ability, experience or background. Entrants must write an original story, on any subject, of no more than 500 words in length and submit it online. Stories are judged anonymously, without regard to grammar, punctuation or spelling. The final is broadcast live on BBC Radio 2. A full list of FAQs regarding entries and submissions can be found on the website. Founded 2011.

BBC Young Writers' Award

email bbcywa@bbc.co.uk
website www.bbc.co.uk/ywa

The BBC Young Writers' Award seeks out writers between 14 and 18 who submit a story of no more than 1,000 words on any topic they choose. The winner receives a mentorship with an author and their story is broadcast on a BBC Radio 1 podcast and published in an anthology.

Blue Peter Book Awards

BookTrust, G8 Battersea Studios, 80 Silverthorne Road, London SW8 3HE
tel 020-7801 8843
email bluepeter@booktrust.org.uk
website www.booktrust.org.uk/books/awards-and-prizes

Awarded annually, winners are shortlisted by a panel of expert adult judges, then a group of young *Blue Peter* viewers judge the two categories, which are: the Best Story and the Best Book with Facts. Winning books are announced on *Blue Peter* in March. Founded 2000.

International Award for Illustration Bologna Children's Book Fair

email illustratori@bolognafiere.it
website www.bolognachildrensbookfair.com

The aim of the award is to support the illustration work of young artists, the special quality of whose work has yet to be acknowledged. This annual award is granted to one of the young illustrators selected each year from the Bologna Children's Book Fair Illustrators Exhibition. Founded 2009.

BolognaRagazzi Award

Piazza Costituzione 6, 40128 Bologna, Italy
tel +39 051-282111
email bookfair@bolognafiere.it
website www.bolognachildrensbookfair.com

Prizes are awarded each April to encourage excellence in children's publishing in the categories of Fiction, Non-fiction, New Horizons and Opera Prima, which is devoted to new authors and illustrators and aims to acknowledge publishers' efforts at finding new talent. The Digital Award recognises innovation and excellence in global digital children's publishing. The BOP (Best Children Publisher of the Year) prize has also been created to acknowledge publishers at the forefront of innovation in their activity for the creative nature of the editorial choices they have made during the previous year's editions of the fair.

Bookbug Picture Book Prize

Scottish Book Trust, Sandeman House,
Trunk's Close, 55 High Street, Edinburgh EH1 1SR
tel 0131 524 0160
email info@scottishbooktrust.com
website www.scottishbooktrust.com

Scotland's national picture book prize which recognises the favourite picture book of children in Scotland by writers and illustrators resident in Scotland. Visit the Scottish Book Trust website for more details.

BookTrust Storytime Prize

BookTrust, G8 Battersea Studios,
80 Silverthorne Road, London SW8 3HE
tel 020-7801 8826
email StoryTimePrize@booktrust.org.uk
website www.booktrust.org.uk/prizes

An annual prize to celebrate the best books for sharing with young children aged 0–5 with a particular focus on books that have a wide appeal to parents and carers across our diverse nation, and for stories which can be read and enjoyed over and over again. The prize is run in collaboration with Youth Library Group (YLG) and the shortlisted titles are shared with families by public librarians across the UK to find the best book. Publishers are invited to enter up to five books per imprint. See website for further details and timings.

The Branford Boase Award

8 Bolderwood Close, Bishopstoke, Eastleigh,
Hants SO50 8PG
tel 023-8060 0439
email anne.marley@tiscali.co.uk
website www.branfordboaseaward.org.uk

An annual award of £1,000 is made to a first-time writer of a full-length children's novel (age 7+) published in the preceding year; the editor is also recognised. Its aim is to encourage new writers for children and to recognise the role of perceptive editors in developing new talent. The Award was set up in memory of the outstanding children's writer Henrietta Branford and the gifted editor and publisher Wendy Boase who both died in 1999. Closing date for nominations: end of December.

The Carmelite Prize

website www.carmeliteprize.co.uk

The Carmelite Prize is an annual award run by Hachette Children's Group which recognises excellence in children's book illustration. The competition is open to all students aged 18 and over who are studying illustration and design in the UK in further or higher education. Only one entry per person. Entries will not be accepted from agents, third parties or in bulk. The winner and two runners-up will be chosen from the top five entries: first prize

£1,000, first runner-up £500, second runner-up £250. See website for full terms and conditions.

Carnegie Medal – see The CILIP Carnegie and Kate Greenaway Children's Book Awards

The Caterpillar Poetry Prize

email enquiries@thecaterpillarmagazine.com
website www.thecaterpillarmagazine.com

The Caterpillar Poetry Prize is for a single unpublished poem written by an adult for children. The writer of the winning poem receives €1,000 and has their poem published in *The Caterpillar*. The prize is open to anyone over the age of 16. The entry fee is €12 and writers can submit as many poems as they like. Closing date 31 March. For full entry details and guidelines, see the website.

The Caterpillar Story for Children Prize

email enquiries@thecaterpillarmagazine.com
website www.thecaterpillarmagazine.com

An annual prize for a single story written by an adult for children. The writer receives €1,000 and has their story published in *The Caterpillar*. The prize is open to anyone over the age of 16. The entry fee is €12 and writers can submit as many stories as they like. Closing date 30 September. For full entry details and guidelines, see the website.

The CBI Book of the Year Awards

Children's Books Ireland,
17 North Great George's Street, Dublin 1 D01 R2F1,
Republic of Ireland
tel +353 (0)1 872 7475
email info@childrensbooksireland.ie
website www.childrensbooksireland.ie

The CBI Book of the Year Awards (formerly the Bisto Awards) are the leading annual children's book awards in Ireland. The awards are: CBI Book of the Year, the Eilís Dillon Award (for a first children's book), the Honour Award for Fiction, the Honour Award for Illustration, the Judges' Special Award and the Children's Choice Award. Schools and reading groups nationwide take part in a shadowing scheme: each group reads the shortlisted books and engages with them using the suggested questions and activities in the CBI shadowing packs. Each group then votes for their favourite book, the results of which form the basis for the Children's Choice Award. Closing date: December for work published between 1 January and 31 December of an awards year. Shortlist announced in March; winners announced in May. Founded 1990.

Cheltenham Illustration Awards

email eevans@glos.ac.uk
website www.cheltenham-illustration-awards.com

Exhibition and Annual submissions are invited and can be freely interpreted in a narrative context.

Submissions of work are free and open to all students, emerging and established illustrators and graphic novelists. A selection panel will assess entries. The selected work will be showcased in an exhibition and published in the *Cheltenham Illustration Awards Annual*, which will be distributed to education institutions and publishers. Deadline for submissions: June.

The Children's Book Award
1 Oakwell Close, Bragbury End, Stevenage, Herts. SG2 8UG
email contact@childrensbookaward.org.uk
website www.fcbg.org.uk

This award, founded by Pat Thomson and run by the Federation of Children's Book Groups, is given annually to authors and illustrators of children's fiction published in the UK. Children participate in the judging of the award. Awards are made in the following categories: Books for Younger Children, Books for Young Readers and Books for Older Readers. Founded 1980.

The Children's Laureate
BookTrust, Studio G8, Battersea Studios, 80 Silverthorne Road, London SW8 3HE
tel 020-7801 8800
email childrenslaureate@booktrust.org.uk
website www.childrenslaureate.org.uk
Contact Charlotte Copping

The idea for the Children's Laureate originated from a conversation between (the then) Poet Laureate Ted Hughes and children's writer Michael Morpurgo. The post was established to celebrate exceptional children's authors and illustrators and to acknowledge their importance in creating the readers of tomorrow. Quentin Blake was the first Children's Laureate (1999–2001), followed by Anne Fine (2001–2003), Michael Morpurgo (2003–2005), Jacqueline Wilson (2005–2007), Michael Rosen (2007–2009), Anthony Browne (2009–2011), Julia Donaldson (2011–2013), Malorie Blackman (2013–2015), Chris Riddell (2015–2017) and Lauren Child (2017–2019). Founded 1999.

The CILIP Carnegie and Kate Greenaway Children's Book Awards
CILIP, 7 Ridgmount Street, London WC1E 7AE
tel 020-7255 0650
email ckg@cilip.org.uk
website www.ckg.org.uk

Nominations for the following two awards are invited from members of CILIP (the library and information association), who are asked to submit up to two titles for each award, accompanied by a 50-word appraisal justifying the recommendation of each book. The awards are selected by judges from the Youth Libraries Group of CILIP. One title from each shortlist will receive a prize awarded by children who take part in the Awards shadowing scheme who vote for their favourites.

Carnegie Medal
Awarded annually for an outstanding book for children (fiction or non-fiction) written in English and first published in the UK during the preceding year or co-published elsewhere within a three-month time lapse. The Carnegie Medal winner is awarded £5,000 prize money from the Colin Mears Award annually.

Kate Greenaway Medal
Awarded annually for an outstanding illustrated book for children first published in the UK during the preceding year or co-published elsewhere within a three-month time lapse. Books intended for older as well as younger children are included, and reproduction will be taken into account. The Colin Mears Award (£5,000) is awarded annually to the winner of the Kate Greenaway Medal.

CLiPPA (Centre for Literacy in Primary Poetry Award)
CLPE, 44 Webber Street, London SE1 8QW
tel 020-7401 3382/3
email info@clpe.org.uk
website www.clpe.org.uk
Twitter @clpe1

CLiPPA is an award that honours excellence in children's poetry. Organised by the Centre for Literacy in Primary Education (CLPE), it is presented annually in July for a book of poetry published in the preceding year. The book can be a single-poet collection or an anthology. Submissions deadline: end of January.

Costa Book Awards
The Booksellers Association, 6 Bell Yard, London WC2A 2JR
tel 020-7421 4693
email naomi.gane@booksellers.org.uk
website www.costa.co.uk/costa-book-awards
Contact Naomi Gane

The awards celebrate and promote the most enjoyable contemporary British writing. There are five categories: Novel, First Novel, Biography, Poetry and Children's, plus one overall winner. Each category is judged by a panel of judges and the winner in each category receives £5,000. Judges then choose the Costa Book of the Year from the five category winners. The overall winner receives £30,000. There is also a seventh award, the Short Story Award, given for a single short story. Total prize money for the Costa Book Awards is £60,000. Submissions must be received from publishers. Shortlist announced: November. Closing date: end of June. For full eligibility and submission guidelines, see the website. Founded 1971.

East Sussex Children's Book Award

website www.eastsussex.gov.uk/libraries/activities-and-events/book-award

Each year children in East Sussex can vote for their favourite read from five fiction paperbacks. Participating schools read and discuss shortlisted books and the winner is announced in June.

English Association English 4–11 Children's Book Awards

email engassoc@leicester.ac.uk
website www2.le.ac.uk/offices/english-association/primary/english-4-11-book-awards

The Awards recognise the best children's picture books of the year in four categories: Fiction and Non-Fiction in age ranges 4–7 years and 7–11 years. The prizes are presented at the Association's annual general meeting each May, and the winning and shortlisted books are featured in a full-colour insert in the summer issue of the *English 4–11* journal. The winning books are chosen by the editorial board of *English 4–11*, which is published in collaboration with the UK Literacy Association.

Etisalat Award for Arabic Children's Literature

email info@uaebby.org.ae
website www.etisalataward.ae

The prize of 1.2 million UAE Dirham is open only to children's literature written in the Arabic language; translated content is not eligible. The Award has widened its scope since its inception, adding new categories in order to highlight the individual achievements of writers illustrators and publishers. The value of the Award is distributed between six categories: best text, best illustration, best production, children's book of the year, young adult book of the year, and digital award of the year. The Award is organised by The UAE Board on Books for Young People and sposored by Etisalat Telecom.

FAB Prize for Undiscovered BAME Talent

email fab@faber.co.uk
website www.fabprize.org

The FAB Prize, set up by Faber Children's and Andlyn Literary Agency is an annual competition for unagented and unpublished writers and illustrators from black, Asian and/or minority ethnic backgrounds. Now with the additional backing of BookTrust, the competition winners and runners up are not only offered mentoring, but also exposure to literary agents and editors alongside access to training and shadowing schemes. The prize offers a unique opportunity to kick start a writing or illustrating career and get a foot in the door. Entries must be text or artwork for children aged 1 to 18 years. First prize of £500 for text and £500 for illustration. To follow

the results of the 2019 prize and for information about future prizes, visit the website. Founded 2017.

The Eleanor Farjeon Award

website www.childrensbookcircle.org.uk

An annual award which may be given to an individual or an organisation. Librarians, authors, publishers, teachers, reviewers and others who have given exceptional service to the children's book industry are eligible for nomination. It was instituted in 1965 by the Children's Book Circle (page 358) for distinguished services to children's books and named after the much-loved children's writer Eleanor Farjeon.

The Klaus Flugge Prize

website www.klausfluggeprize.co.uk/

This prize is awarded to the most promising and exciting newcomer to children's book illustration. It honours the work of publisher Klaus Flugge in the field of illustration and children's picture books, and the winning debut illustrator receives £5,000. For full details see the website.

Foyle Young Poets of the Year Award – see page 223

Grampian Children's Book Award

website www.gcbookaward.wixsite.com
Twitter @GrampBookAward

This award is for best fiction book, judged solely by pupils in participating secondary schools in Aberdeen City, Aberdeenshire and Moray and children in Aberdeen Central Children's Library.

Kate Greenaway Medal – see The CILIP Carnegie and Kate Greenaway Children's Book Awards

Independent Bookshop Week Book Awards

6 Bell Yard, London WC2A 2JR
tel 020-7421 4694
email emma.bradshaw@booksellers.org.uk
website www.indiebookshopweek.org.uk
Twitter @booksaremybag

Awards are given in three categories: adult, children's and picture book. For entry guidelines and shortlist details see the website.

Jhalak Prize

email jhalakprize@mediadiversified.org
website www.mediadiversified.org/about-us/jhalak-prize/

Awarded annually, this prize seeks out the best books by British/British resident BAME writers and awards one winner £1,000. Entries can be for fiction, non-fiction, short story, graphic novel, poetry, children's books, YA, teen and all genres. Started by authors Sunny Singh and Nikesh Shukla and Media Diversified, with support from The Authors' Club and a prize donated by an anonymous benefactor, the prize exists to celebrate the achievements of writers of colour. For submission guidelines and details of key dates see the website. Founded 2016.

Kelpies Prize

Floris Books, 2a Robertson Avenue,
Edinburgh EH11 1PZ
tel 0131 337 2372
email kelpiesprize@florisbooks.co.uk
website www.florisbooks.co.uk/kelpiesprize

An annual award for emerging writers who are committed to developing their writing craft, their book promotion skills and their profile as a children's author. The Kelpies Prize is open to anyone who lives or works in Scotland. The winner will receive £1,000 cash, a year of mentoring with an experienced editorial team, a publishing contract with Floris Books and a week-long writing retreat Moniack Mhor. Submit writing samples and entry form online, see website for full details. Closing date: end February. Winner announced August. 2018 winner: *The Lost Wizard of Nine-Witches Wood* by Hannah Foley.

Kindle Storyteller Prize

website www.amazon.co.uk

The Kindle Storyteller Prize is open to submissions of new English-language books in any genre. Titles must be previously unpublished and be available as an ebook and in print via Kindle Direct Publishing or CreateSpace (print edition only). The winning author will receive £20,000 and will be recognised at a central London award ceremony. Competition entry period runs from 1 May to 31 August.

Lancashire Book of the Year Award

tel 0300 123 6703
email enquiries@lancashire.gov.uk
website www.lancashire.gov.uk

This annual prize is awarded to the best work of fiction for children in the 12–14 year group, written by a UK author. It is the longest-running regional book award in the country and the award is is voted for by Year 9 students in high schools around the county of Lancashire. The winner is announced in June.

The Astrid Lindgren Memorial Award

Swedish Arts Council, PO Box 27215,
SE–102 53 Stockholm, Sweden
tel +46 8-51926400
email literatureaward@alma.se
website www.alma.se

An award to honour the memory of Astrid Lindgren, Sweden's favourite author, and to promote children's and youth literature around the world. The award is five million Swedish kronas, the world's largest for children's and youth literature, and the second-largest literature prize in the world. It is awarded annually to one or more recipients, regardless of language or nationality.

Authors, illustrators, storytellers and promoters of reading are eligible. The award is for life-long work or artistry rather than for individual pieces. The prize can only be awarded to living people. The body of work must uphold the highest artistic quality and evoke the deeply humanistic spirit of Astrid Lindgren.

The winner is selected by a jury based on nominations for outstanding achievement from selected nominating bodies around the world. The jury has the right to suggest nominees of their own. Neither individuals nor organisations may nominate themselves. The Astrid Lindgren Memorial Award is administered by the Swedish Arts Council. Founded 2002.

Little Rebels Children's Book Award

email info@letterboxlibrary.com
website https://littlerebels.org
website https://littlerebels.org/submitting-a-book/
Twitter @littlerebsprize

The Little Rebels Children's Book Award recognises children's fiction for readers aged 0 to 12 years which promotes social justice or social equality, challenges stereotypes or is informed by anti-discriminatory concerns. The award is given by the Alliance of Radical Booksellers. See website for submission guidelines. Founded 2010.

The Macmillan Prize for Children's Picture Book Illustration

Macmillan Children's Books, 20 New Wharf Road,
London N1 9RR
email macmillanprize@macmillan.co.uk
website www.panmacmillan.com/macmillanprize

Three prizes are awarded annually for unpublished children's book illustrations by art students in higher education establishments in the UK. Prizes: 1st: £1,000, 2nd: £500 and 3rd: £250.

The Mythopoeic Fantasy Award for Children's Literature

email awards@mythsoc.org
website www.mythsoc.org

This award honours books for younger readers (from young adults to picture books for beginning readers), in the tradition of *The Hobbit* or *The Chronicles of Narnia*.

The Mythopoeic Awards are chosen from books nominated by individual members of the Mythopoeic Society and selected by a committee of Society members. Authors, publishers, and their representatives may not nominate their own books for any of the awards, nor are books published by the

Mythopoeic Press eligible for the awards. The Mythopoeic Society does not accept or review unsolicited manuscripts.

New Zealand Book Awards for Children and Young Adults

c/o NZ Book Awards Trust, 72 Waripori Street, Wellington 6023
tel +64 (0)27 733 9855
email childrensawards@nzbookawards.org.nz
website www.nzbookawards.nz/new-zealand-book-awards-for-children-and-young-adults/

Annual awards to celebrate excellence in, and provide recognition for, the best children's books published annually in New Zealand. Awards are presented in six categories: Picture Book, Junior Fiction (the Wright Family Foundation Esther Glen Award), Young Adult Fiction, Non-Fiction (the Elsie Locke Award), Illustration (the Russell Clark Award) and te reo Māori (the Wright Family Foundation Te Kura Pounamu Award). Each of these awards carries prize money of $7,500. The overall prize, the Margaret Mahy Book of the Year award, carries a further prize of $7,500. A Best First Book prize of $2,000 is also awarded to a previously unpublished author or illustrator. Eligible books must have been published in New Zealand between April and March in the period preceding the awards' August ceremony date.

North East Book Award

Cramlington Learning Village, Cramlington, Northumberland NE23 6BN
tel (01670) 712311
email earmstrong@cramlingtonlv.co.uk
website http://northeastbookaward.wordpress.com
Contact Eileen Armstrong

Awarded to a book written by a UK/Ireland resident author and first published in paperback the previous year. The shortlist is selected by school librarians, teachers and the previous year's student judges. The final winner is decided entirely by the student judges (Year 7/8) and is announced in June. 2018 winner: *A Place Called Perfect* by Helena Duggan (Usborne).

North East Teen Book Award

Cramlington Learning Village, Cramlington, Northumberland NE23 6BN
tel (01670) 712311
email earmstrong@cramlingtonlv.co.uk
website http://northeastteenagebookaward.wordpress.com
Contact Eileen Armstrong

Awarded to a book written by a UK/Ireland resident author and first published in paperback during the previous year. The shortlist is selected by school librarians, teachers and the previous year's student judges. The final winner is decided entirely by the student judges (Year 9+) and is announced in March. 2018 winner: *Shell* by Paula Rawsthorne (Scholastic).

Nottingham Children's Book Awards

Nottingham Library Service, Culture and Libraries, Nottingham Central Library, Angel Row, Nottingham NG1 6HP
tel 0115 876 1941
email sandra.edis@nottinghamcity.gov.uk
website www.nottinghamcity.gov.uk/ncba
Facebook www.facebook.com/NottinghamLibraries
Twitter @readingnottm
Contact Sandra Edis

Nottingham children aged 2–4 years choose their favourite picture books from books published the previous year. The shortlist of titles is drawn up by the end of November with the help of local nurseries and children's centres. Voting takes place in under-5 settings and libraries in spring, with the winner announced on the website. The book award focuses on children's literature for different ages, this year concentrating on preschool children. Launched 1999.

Oscar's Book Prize

website www.oscarsbookprize.co.uk

This £5,000 prize supported by Amazon and The National Literacy Trust, in partnership with the *Evening Standard*, is awarded to the preschool book published in the UK the previous year that the judges consider to be the best.

Publishers may enter up to three books per imprint. Collections and anthologies are not eligible. Previously published, self-published books and ebooks are not eligible. Full terms and conditions and a downloadable entry form are available on the website. Founded 2013.

The People's Book Prize

email thepeoplesbkpr@aol.com
website www.peoplesbookprize.com
Facebook www.facebook.com/pages/The-Peoples-Book-Prize/200637717319384/
Twitter @PeoplesBkPrize
Founder and Prize Administrator Tatiana Wilson, *Patron* Frederick Forsyth CBE, *Founding Patron* Dame Beryl Bainbridge DBE

The People's Book Prize awards prizes in six categories: fiction, non-fiction, children's, first-time author (the Beryl Bainbridge First Time Author Award), TPBP Best Achievement Award and TPBP Best Publisher Award. Titles must be submitted by publishers, with a limit of three titles per category, per collection. Winners are announced at an awards ceremony in May at the Worshipful Company of Stationers and Newspaper Makers, Stationers' Hall, London.

Phoenix Award

Children's Literature Association,
3525 Piedmont Road, Building 5, Suite 300,
Atlanta GA 30305
tel +1 630-571-4520

email info@childlitassn.org
website www.childlitassn.org

This Award is presented by the Children's Literature Association (ChLA) for the most outstanding book for children originally published in the English language 20 years earlier which did not receive a major award at the time of publication. It is intended to recognise books of high literary merit. 2019 winner: *Black Cat* by Christopher Myers (Scholastic, 1999). Founded 1985.

The Royal Society Young People's Book Prize

The Royal Society, 6–9 Carlton House Terrace, London SW1Y 5AG
tel 020-7451 2500
email sciencebooks@royalsociety.org
website www.royalsociety.org/young-peoples-book-prize
Facebook www.facebook.com/theroyalsociety
Twitter @royalsociety

This prize is open to books for under-14s that have science as a substantial part of their content, narrative or theme. An expert adult panel choose the shortlist, but the winner is chosen by groups of young people in judging panels across the UK. The winning entry receives £10,000 and shortlisted entries receive £2,500. Entries open in December each year. Pure reference works including encyclopedias, educational textbooks and descriptive books are not eligible. The Prize is offered thanks to the generosity of an anonymous donor. Founded 1988.

RSPCA Young Photographer Awards

Brand Marketing and Content Department, RSPCA, Wilberforce Way, Southwater, Horsham, West Sussex RH13 9RS
email ypa@rspca.org.uk
website www.rspca.org.uk/ypa

Annual awards open to anyone aged 18 or under. The aim of the competition is to encourage young people's interest in photography and to show their appreciation and understanding of the animals around them. See website for a full list of categories and submission guidelines. Founded 1990.

Scholastic Laugh Out Loud Book Prize

email laughoutloud@scholastic.co.uk
website https://shop.scholastic.co.uk/lollies

Known as The Lollies, the Laugh Out Loud Book Prize is awarded to books in three categories: Best Picture Book, Best Book for 6–8 year olds and Best Book for 9–13 year olds. A judging panel selects four books to make up a shortlist for each category, but winners are decided entirely by children's votes, with voting taking place via the website and promoted through Scholastic Book Clubs and Book Fairs. See website for full entry and submission guidelines.

Sheffield Children's Book Award

Schools & Young People's Library Service, Stadia Technology Park, 60 Shirland Lane, Sheffield S9 3SP
tel 0114 250 6844
email jennifer.wilson@sheffield.gov.uk
website www.sheffield.gov.uk/content/sheffield/home/libraries-archives/book-awards.htm

Presented annually in November to the book chosen as the most enjoyable by the children of Sheffield. In 2018 there were seven category winners and an overall winner. Baby Book Award: *Milo's Mix & Match* by Faye Williamson; Toddler Books: *Yoga Babies* by Fearne Cotton & Sheema Dempsey; Picture Book: *Game of Stones* by Rebecca Lisle & Richard Watson; Emerging Reads: *Press Start* by Thomas Flintham; Shorter Novel: *Letters from the Lighthouse* by Emma Carroll; Longer Novel: *The Island at the End of Everything* by Kiran Milwood Hargrave; Young Adult and Overall Winner: *We Come Apart* by Sarah Crossan & Brian Conaghan.

The Times/Chicken House Children's Fiction Competition

Chicken House, 2 Palmer Street, Frome, Somerset BA11 1DS
tel (01373) 454488
email hello@chickenhousebooks.com
website www.chickenhousebooks.com
Twitter @chickenhsebooks
Contact Kesia Lupo

This annual competition is open to unpublished writers of a full-length children's novel (age 7–18). Entrants must be over 18 and novels must not exceed 80,000 words in length. The winner will be announced in *The Times* and will receive a worldwide publishing contract with Chicken House with a royalty advance of £10,000. The winner is selected by a panel of judges which includes children's authors, journalists, publishers, librarians and other key figures from the world of children's literature.

Submissions are invited between September and February, with a shortlist announced in May and the winner chosen in August.

Tir na n-Og Awards

Welsh Books Council, Castell Brychan, Aberystwyth, Ceredigion SY23 2JB
email wbc.children@books.wales
website www.wbc.org.uk
Facebook www.facebook.com/LlyfrDaFabBooks
Twitter @LlyfrDaFabBooks

The Tir na n-Og Awards were established with the intention of promoting and raising the standard of children's and young people's books in Wales. Three awards are presented annually by the Welsh Books Council and are sponsored by the Chartered Institute of Library and Information Professionals Cymru/Wales:

• The best English-language book of the year with an authentic Welsh background. Fiction and factual books originally in English are eligible; translations from Welsh or any other language are not eligible. Prize: £1,000.
• The best original Welsh-language book aimed at the primary school sector. Prize: £1,000.
• The best original Welsh-language book aimed at the secondary school sector. Prize: £1,000. Founded 1976.

Christopher Tower Poetry Prize – see page 223

UKLA Book Awards
website www.ukla.org
Twitter @The_UKLA

The UKLA Book Award is a national, annual award for children's books and is judged by teachers. There are three categories covering the age range of 3–16+. Teachers are looking for books which evocatively express ideas and offer layered meanings through the use of language, imaginative expression and rich illustration/graphics. Detailed submission criteria can be found on the website.

The V&A Illustration Awards
Victoria & Albert Museum, London SW7 2RL
email villa@vam.ac.uk
website www.vam.ac.uk/illustrationawards

These annual awards are open to illustrators living or publishing in the UK market and students who have attended a course in the UK over the last two years. Awards are made in the following categories: best illustrated book, book cover design, illustrated journalism and student illustrator.

Waterstones Children's Book Prize
Waterstones, 203–206 Piccadilly, London W1J 9HD
tel 020-7071 6300
email childrensbookprize@waterstones.com
website www.waterstones.com

The aim of the prize is to reward and champion new and emerging children's writers, voted for by booksellers. In 2019, the Children's Book Proze celebrates its 15th anniversary. For the 2020 prize, books must be new during 2019. There are three categories: Illustrated Books, Younger Fiction and Older Fiction. Submission criteria:

Illustrated Books. Illustrated books authored and illustrated by the same person: The author/illustrator may not have previously published more than two titles of any fiction genre worldwide (educational titles are exempt). Author/illustrator partnerships: Neither the author nor illustrator may have previously solely published more than two titles of any fiction genre (which includes picture books) worldwide (educational titles are exempt). Author/illustrator partnerships may not have previously published more than two titles together.

Younger Fiction and *Older Fiction*. No more than one previously published title of any fiction genre worldwide (educational titles are exempt). The title must make sense as a standalone novel. If the title is illustrated, and the illustrator matches submission criteria for Illustrated Books, then the illustrator will be considered eligible for this category.

2020 shortlist announced February 2020. Winners announced March 2020. Publishers to declare any titles written under another name including series fiction. Writing and concept must be solely the work of the author. Titles must have been published in 2019. There will be one winner in each category. There will be an overall winner from the category winners.

Wildlife Photographer of the Year
The Natural History Museum, Cromwell Road, London SW7 5BD
website www.nhm.ac.uk/visit/wpy/competition.html

This annual award is given to the photographer whose individual image is judged to be the most striking and memorable. There is an adult competition for photographers aged 18 or over and a young competition for photographers aged 17 or under. See website for submission guidelines.

Winchester Writers' Festival Competitions and Scholarships
University of Winchester, Winchester, Hants SO22 4NR
tel (01962) 826327
email sara.gangai@winchester.ac.uk
website www.writersfestival.co.uk
Festival Director Sara Gangai

The annual Winchester Writers' Festival runs a number of competitions and bursaries for writers. For full details, visit www.writersfestival.co.uk or contact the Festival Director.

World Illustration Awards
Association of Illustrators, Somerset House, Strand, London WC2R 1LA
tel 020-7759 1010
email awards@theaoi.com
website www.theaoi.com/world-illustration-awards/
Facebook www.facebook.com/theaoi
Twitter @theaoi

The World Illustration Awards, in partnership with the *Directory of Illustration*, is an awards programme that sets out to celebrate contemporary illustration across the globe. A panel of international judges create a shortlist, which is displayed at an exhibition in Somerset House and subsequently tours the UK and internationally. For submission guidelines, categories and prizes, see the website.

YouWriteOn.com Book Awards
tel 07948 392634
email edward@youwriteon.com
website www.youwriteon.com

Societies, prizes and festivals

Arts Council-funded site publishing awards for new fiction writers. Random House and Orion, the publishers of authors such as Dan Brown and Terry Pratchett, provide free professional critiques for the highest rated new writers' opening chapters and short stories on YouWriteOn.com each month. The highest rated writers of the year are then published, three in each of the adult and children's categories, through YouWriteOn's free paperback publishing service for writers. The novel publishing awards total £1,000. Writers can enter at any time throughout the year: closing date is 31 December each year. Join YouWriteOn.com to participate. Previous YouWriteOn.com winners have been published by mainstream publishers such as Random House, Orion, Penguin and Hodder including Channel 4 TV Book Club winner and bestseller *The Legacy* by Katherine Webb. Founded 2005.

PRIZE WINNERS

This is a selection of high-profile literary prize winners from the last year presented chronologically. Entries for many of these prizes are included in the *Yearbook*, starting on page 379.

May 2018
CBI Book of the Year Award
Tangleweed and Brine by Deirdre Sullivan, illustrated by Karen Vaughan
Tir na n-Og Awards
The Nearest Faraway Place by Hayley Long
The V&A Illustration Awards
Suzanne Dean for the cover of *Bluets* (Jonathan Cape 2017) (Book Cover Design Award); John Vernon Lord for *Ulysses* (The Folio Society 2017) (Book Illustration and Moira Gemmill Illustrator of the Year); Cat O'Neil for the illustration *RSA Benefits* commissioned by *Libération*, 10 Apr 2017 (Editorial Illustration Award); Joseph Namara Hollis for *The Big City* (Student Illustrator of the Year)

June
The Macmillan Prize for Children's Picture Book Illustration
Paloma Flew by María J. Guarda
The CILIP Carnegie Medal
Where the World Ends by Geraldine McCaughrean
The CILIP Kate Greenaway Medal
Town Is by the Sea illustrated by Sydney Smith
East Sussex Children's Book Awards
Evie's Ghost by Helen Peters

July
Lancashire Book of the Year Award
See How They Lie by Sue Wallman
UKLA Book Awards
Colin & Lee, Carrot and Pea by Morag Hood (3–6 years); *Welcome to Nowhere* by Elizabeth Laird and *Lesser Spotted Animals* by Martin Brown (7–11

years); *We Come Apart* by Sarah Crossan and Brian Conaghan (12–16+ years)
CLiPPA The CLPE Poetry Award
Rhythm and Poetry by Karl Nova
Branford Boase Award
Kick by Mitch Johnson (and his editors Rebecca Hill and Becky Walker)

August
Mythopoeic Fantasy Award for Children's Literature (USA)
Frogkisser! by Garth Nix
Kelpies Prize
The Lost Wizard of Nine Witches Wood by Hannah Foley

December
Eleanor Farjeon Award
Michael Morpurgo
Sheffield Children's Book Award
Game of Stones by Rebecca Lisle (Picture Book); *Press Start!* by Thomas Flintham (Emerging Read); *Letters From the Lighthouse* by Emma Carroll (Shorter novel); *The Island at the End of Everything* by Kiran Millwood Hargrave (Longer Novels); *We Come Apart* by Sarah Crossan and Brian Conaghan (Young Adult and Overall Winner)

January 2018
Costa Book of the Year
The Skylarks' War by Hilary McKay (Costa Children's Book of the Year)
BookBug Picture Book Prize (Scottish Book Trust)
One Button Benny by Alan Windram, illustrated by Chloë Howill-Hunter

February
North East Teenage Book Awards
Shell by Paula Rawsthorne
Scottish Teen Book Prize (Scottish Book Trust)
Farewell Tour of the Terminal Optimist by John Young

March
Blue Peter Book Awards
The Boy at the Back of the Class by Onjali Q. Raúf (Best Story); *The Colours of History* by Clive Gifford, illustrated by Marc-Etienne Peintre (Best Book with Facts)

April
BolognaRagazzi Award
Puppet, Plum Pit, Plum, Plank, and back to Puppet by Vojtěch Mašek, illustrated by Chrudoš Valoušek (Fiction); *Atlas das viagens e dos exploradores* by Isabel Minhós Martins, illustrated by Bernardo P. Carvalho (Non-fiction); *A History of Pictures for Children* by David Hockney and Martin Gayford, illustrated by Rose Blake (New Horizons); *Julian Is a Mermaid* by Jessica Love (Opera Prima)

International Award for Illustration Bologna Children's Book Fair
Sarah Mazzetti

Waterstones Children's Book Prize
Children of Blood and Bone by Tomi Adeyemi (Best Older Fiction); *The Girls* by Lauren Ace, illustrated by Jenny Løvlie (Best Illustrated Book); *The Boy at the Back of the Class* by Onjali Q. Raúf (Best Younger Fiction and Overall Winner)

May

British Book Awards
The Ice Monster by David Walliams, illustrated by Tony Ross (Children's fiction); *You Are Awesome* by Matthew Syed, illustrated by Toby Triumph (Illustrated & Non-Fiction); Judith Kerr (Illustrator of the Year)

Grampian Children's Book Award
The 1,000 Year-Old Boy by Ross Welford

Children's literature festivals and trade fairs

Some of the literature festivals in this section are specifically related to children's books and others are general arts festivals which include literature events for children.

Aspects Irish Literature Festival
website www.aspectsfestival.com
Facebook www.facebook.com/aspectsfestival/

An annual celebration of contemporary Irish writing with novelists, poets and playwrights. Includes writers' visits to schools and Young Aspects Showcase, where young people are given the opportunity to publicly read their own work.

Barnes Children's Literature Festival
website www.barneskidslitfest.org
Facebook www.facebook.com/BarnesKidsLitFest
Twitter @kidslitfest
Takes place May

The Barnes Children's Literature Festival is London's largest dedicated literature event. The Festivals have starred some of the best-known names in children's literature including Axel Scheffler, Piers Torday, Sally Gardner, Roger McGough, Lauren Child, Jacqueline Wilson, Philip Reeve, Cornelia Funke and Danny Wallace. Offers a full schedule of family-friendly events.

Bath Children's Literature Festival
Bath Festivals, 9/10 Bath Street, Bath BA1 1SN
tel (01225) 614180
email info@bathfestivals.co.uk
website www.bathfestivals.org.uk/childrens-literature
Takes place 27 September – 6 October 2019

Europe's largest annual dedicated children's literature festival.

Beyond the Border: The Wales International Storytelling Festival
tel (02921) 660501
website www.beyondtheborder.com

An international festival celebrating oral tradition and bringing together storytellers, poets and musicians from around the world. This is the largest event of its type in the UK and features storytelling, poetry, music, singing, theatre, circus and film.

Big Wig Children's Festival
Wigtown Festival Company, 11 North Main Street, Wigtown DG8 9HN
tel (01988) 402036
email mail@wigtownbookfestival.com
website www.wigtownbookfestival.com
Facebook www.facebook.com/WigtownBookFestival

Twitter @wigtownbookfest
Operational Director Anne Barclay
27 September–6 October 2019 (main festival)

Big Wig Children's Festival welcomes authors from across the UK to inspire the next generation of readers and writers at the annual Wigtown Book Festival each autumn. Loved by children and families, the programme of more than 30 events with children's authors, illustrators, storytellers and artists sparks the imagination.

Bologna Children's Book Fair
Piazza Costituzione 6, 40128 Bologna, Italy
tel +39 051-282111
email bookfair@bolognafiere.it
website www.bolognachildrensbookfair.com
Takes place Spring

Held annually, the Bologna Children's Book Fair is the leading children's publishing event. Publishers, authors and illustrators, literary agents, app developers, e-publishing professionals, licensors and licensees, and many other members of the children's content community meet in Bologna to buy and sell copyrights, establish new contacts and strengthen their professional relationships, discover new illustrators, develop new business opportunities, learn about the latest trends and developments and explore children's educational materials, including new media products. Entry is restricted to professionals in children's content.

Selected by a jury, the Bologna Illustrators' Exhibition showcases fiction and non-fiction children's book illustrators, both new and established, from all over the world. Many illustrators also visit the Fair to show their latest portfolios to publishers.

Borders Book Festival
Harmony House, St Mary's Road, Melrose TD6 9LJ
tel (01896) 822644
email info@bordersbookfestival.org
website www.bordersbookfestival.org
Takes place June

An annual festival with a programme of events featuring high-profile and bestselling writers. Winner of the Walter Scott Prize for Historical Fiction is announced during the festival. Founded 2004.

Cambridge Literary Festival
7 Downing Place, Cambridge CB2 3EL
email info@cambridgeliteraryfestival.com
website www.cambridgeliteraryfestival.com

Takes place April and November

The Cambridge Literary Festival welcomes writers and readers from around the world and provides a space for debate and diversity, and showcases creativity. It encourages children and young people to be enthused by reading and writing, and provides a forum for authors and readers to mingle, converse and develop their craft.

Cardiff Children's Lit Fest

County Hall, Cardiff, CF10 4UW
email events@cardiff.gov.uk
website www.cardiffkidslitfest.com
Twitter @CDFKidsLitFest
Takes place March/April

The Cardiff Children's Literature Festival is an annual event aimed at young people who appreciate the magic of books and grown-ups who want to write them. The festival includes events with local and national authors and comprises a number of educational sessions for schools.

The Times and The Sunday Times Cheltenham Literature Festival

109–111 Bath Road, Cheltenham, Glos. GL53 7LS
tel (01242) 511211
website www.cheltenhamfestivals.com/literature
Facebook www.facebook.com/cheltenhamfestivals
Twitter @cheltlitfest
Takes place 4–13 October 2019

This annual festival is one of the oldest literary events in the world. The festival features adult, family and schools programmes for everyone with around 500 events over 10 days. Events for families and schools include presentations from the very best children's authors and illustrators alongside workshops, shows, storytellers, story trails, discussions and free drop-in craft activities. Founded 1949.

Edinburgh International Book Festival

Charlotte Square, Edinburgh EH2 4DR
tel 0131 718 5666
email admin@edbookfest.co.uk
website www.edbookfest.co.uk
Twitter @edbookfest
Takes place August

The largest celebration of books and reading in the world. In addition to a unique independent bookselling operation, around 1,000 UK and international writers appear in over 900 events for adults and children. Programme details available in June.

Edinburgh International Children's Festival

30B Grindlay Street, Edinburgh, EH3 9AX
tel 0131 225 8050
email info@imaginate.org.uk
website www.imaginate.org.uk

Takes place May/June

The Edinburgh International Children's Festival presents the world's best theatre and dance for young audiences aged 0–15, with performances that are deeply engaging, innovative and inspiring.

The Festival of Writing

Prama House, 267 Banbury Road, Oxford OX2 7HT
tel 0345 459 9560
email info@jerichowriters.com
website https://jerichowriters.com/festival-of-writing
Takes place 6–8 September 2019

A festival for aspiring writers providing the opportunity to meet literary agents, publishers and professional authors. It is the country's biggest writing festival specifically for writers looking to get published.

Folkestone Book Festival

Quarterhouse, Mill Bay, Folkestone, Kent CT20 1BN
tel (01303) 760740
email info@creativefolkestone.org.uk
website www.creativefolkestone.org.uk/folkestone-book-festival/
Facebook www.facebook.com/FolkestoneBookFestival
Twitter @FstoneBookFest
Takes place 15–24 November 2019

Folkestone Book Festival holds a special place amongst the UK book festivals' scene. Taking place annually in November, the festival is an opportunity to gather, tell stories and exchange ideas.

The Hay Festival

The Drill Hall, 25 Lion Street, Hay-on-Wye HR3 5AD
tel (01497) 822620
email admin@hayfestival.org
website www.hayfestival.org
Takes place May/June

This annual festival of literature and the arts in Hay-on-Wye, Wales, brings together writers, musicians, film-makers, historians, politicians, environmentalists and scientists from around the world to communicate challenging ideas. Hundreds of events over ten days. Within the annual festival is a festival for families and children, HAYDAYS, which introduces children, from toddlers to teenagers, to their favourite authors and holds workshops to entertain and educate. Programme published April.

Ilkley Literature Festival

9 The Grove, Ilkley LS29 9LW
tel (01943) 601210
email info@ilkleyliteraturefestival.org.uk
website www.ilkleyliteraturefestival.org.uk
Facebook www.facebook.com/ilkleyliteraturefestival/
Twitter @ilkleylitfest
Assistant Festival Director Erica Morris, *Programme Coordinator* Pakeezah Zahoor

Takes place 4–20 October 2019

The North of England's oldest and largest literature festival with over 250 events, from author discussions to workshops, readings, literary walks, children's events and a festival fringe. Founded 1973.

Imagine: Writers and Writing for Children

Southbank Centre, London SE1 8XX
tel 020-7960 4200
website www.southbankcentre.co.uk/whatson/festivals-series/imagine-childrens-festival
Takes place February

An annual festival celebrating writing for children featuring a selection of poets, storytellers and illustrators.

Independent Bookshop Week

website www.indiebookshopweek.org.uk
Facebook www.facebook.com/booksaremybag/
Twitter @booksaremybag
Takes place June

An annual celebration of independent bookshops and is part of the IndieBound campaign to promote independent bookshops, strong reading communities and the idea of shopping locally and sustainably. Independent Bookshop Week brings together bookshops, publishers and consumers through events such as National Reading Group Day, author visits and storytime sessions, and offers from publishers.

Jewish Book Week

Jewish Book Week, ORT House, 126 Albert Street, London NW1 7NE
tel 020-7446 8771
email info@jewishbookweek.com
website www.jewishbookweek.com
Head of Production Sarah Fairbairn
Takes place February/March

A 10-day festival of writing, arts and culture, with contributors from around the world and sessions in London and nationwide. Includes events for children and teenagers.

Laureate na nÓg/Ireland's Children's Laureate

Children's Books Ireland,
17 North Great George's Street, Dublin 1, D01 R2F1
tel +353 (0)18 727475
email info@childrenslaureate.ie
email info@childrensbooksireland.ie
website www.childrenslaureate.ie

This is a project recognising the role and importance of literature for children in Ireland, established to engage young people with high-quality literature and to underline the importance of children's literature in Ireland's cultural and imaginative life. It was awarded for the first time in 2010. The laureate participates in selected events and activities around Ireland and internationally during their two-year term.

The laureate is chosen in recognition of their widely recognised high-quality children's writing or illustration and the positive impact they have had on readers as well as other writers and illustrators. Laureate na nÓg 2010–2012, Siobhán Parkinson; 2012–2014, Niamh Sharkey; 2014–2016, Eoin Colfer; 2016–2018, PJ Lynch; 2018–2020, Sarah Crossan.

Manchester Children's Book Festival

Manchester Metropolitan University,
Rosamond Street West, Off Oxford Road,
Manchester M15 6LL
email mcbf@mmu.ac.uk
website www.mcbf.org.uk
Twitter @MCBFestival
Instagram @mcbfestival

A festival of year-round activities celebrating the very best writing for children, inspiring young people to engage with literature and creativity across the curriculum, and offering extended projects and training to ensure the event has an impact and legacy in classrooms.

May Festival

Festivals and Events Team, University of Aberdeen, King's College, Aberdeen AB24 3FX
tel (01224) 273233
email festival@abdn.ac.uk
website www.abdn.ac.uk/mayfestival
Takes place May

The May Festival offers more than 120 events spanning popular themes including literature, music, film, science, visual arts and sport. The University of Aberdeen offers a *Discover* strand of events which gives audiences the opportunity to gain an insight into the research going on at the university. In addition, the Festival features a tours programme and historic exhibitions. Now in its 6th year, the Festival welcomes famous faces and offers a programme of events to celebrate and showcase north east Scotland's unique cultural landscape.

Off the Shelf Festival of Words Sheffield

Cathedral Court, 46 Church Street, Sheffield S1 2GN
tel 0114 222 3895
email offtheshelf@sheffield.ac.uk
website www.offtheshelf.org.uk
Takes place 5–26 October 2019

Meet great writers, historians, artists, scientists, journalists and musicians at this diverse and innovative festival. Events city-wide for all ages.

Oundle Festival of Literature

email oundlelitfestival@hotmail.co.uk
website www.oundlelitfest.org.uk
Facebook www.facebook.com/OundleFestivalOfLiterature/
Twitter @OundleLitFest
Festival Manager Helen Shair
Takes place early March

Kid Lit Week includes a writing competition and events for a variety of age groups. The Festival also runs a programme of all year talks, discussions and workshops by award-winning and local authors and poets. The Festival uses a variety of venues in the market town of Oundle.

FT Weekend Oxford Literary Festival
c/o Critchleys, Beaver House,
23–28 Hythe Bridge Street, Oxford OX1 2EP
email info@oxfordliteraryfestival.org
website www.oxfordliteraryfestival.org
Takes place March/April

An annual festival for adults and children held in venues across the city and university. Presents topical debates, fiction and non-fiction discussion panels, and adult and children's authors who have recently published books.

Richmond upon Thames Literature Festival
email artsinfo@richmondandwandsworth.gov.uk
website www.richmondlitfest.com
Twitter @richmondlitfest
Takes place November

An annual literature festival featuring a diverse programme of authors in venues across the borough. The festival includes an exciting programme of author events for children and families as well as opportunities to explore creativity in literature through workshops and interactive sessions.

Scottish International Storytelling Festival
43–45 High Street, Edinburgh EH1 1SR
tel 0131 556 9579
email reception@scottishstorytellingcentre.com
website www.scottishstorytellingcentre.co.uk
Festival Director Donald Smith
Takes place October

A celebration of Scottish storytelling set in its international context, complemented by music, ballad and song. Takes place at the Scottish Storytelling Centre and partner venues across Edinburgh and Scotland.

The Self-Publishing Conference
tel 0116 279 2299
email books@troubador.co.uk
website www.selfpublishingconference.org.uk
Twitter @Selfpubconf

The UK's only dedicated self-publishing conference. This annual event covers all aspects of self-publishing from production through to marketing and distribution. Founded 2013.

StAnza: Scotland's International Poetry Festival
tel (01334) 475000 (box office), (01334) 474610 (programmes)
email stanza@stanzapoetry.org
website www.stanzapoetry.org
Facebook www.facebook.com/stanzapoetry
Twitter @StAnzaPoetry
Instagram stanzapoetry
Festival Director Eleanor Livingstone
Takes place March

The festival engages with all forms of poetry: read and spoken verse, poetry in exhibition, performance poetry, cross-media collaboration, schools work, book launches and poetry workshops, with numerous UK and international guests and weekend children's events. Founded 1997.

Stratford-upon-Avon Poetry Festival
website www.shakespeare.org.uk/poetryfest
Takes place June

This annual festival celebrates Shakespeare's creative genius. Organised by the Shakespeare Birthplace Trust, the festival presents an exciting line-up of readings, performances and workshops showcasing the talents of inspirational and award-winning artists from all over the world. It also includes a special programme of family-friendly events.

The Winchester Writers' Festival
University of Winchester, Winchester,
Hants SO22 4NR
tel (01962) 826367
email sara.gangai@winchester.ac.uk
website www.writersfestival.co.uk
Twitter @WinWritersFest
Festival Director Sara Gangai
Takes place Third weekend in June

This major festival of writing, celebrating its 39th year in 2019, attracts new and emerging writers from the UK and around the world who come for day-long courses, talks, workshops and up to four one-to-one appointments each with literary agents, commissioning editors and established novelists, poets and screenwriters to help them harness their creativity, develop their writing and editing skills and pitch their work to industry professionals.

World Book Day
email wbd@education.co.uk
website www.worldbookday.com
Facebook www.facebook.com/worldbookdayuk
Twitter @WorldBookDayUK
Takes place First Thursday in March

An annual celebration of books and reading aimed at promoting their value and creating the readers of the future. Every schoolchild in full-time education receives a £1 (€1.50) book token and events take place all over the UK and Ireland in schools, bookshops and libraries.

YALC (Young Adult Literature Convention)
email yalc@showmastersevents.com
website www.londonfilmandcomiccon.com/index.php/zones/yalc
Facebook www.facebook.com/ukYALC
Twitter @yalc_uk
Takes place Annually in July

YALC is a celebration of the best young adult books and authors. It is an interactive event where YA fans can meet their favourite authors, listen to panel discussions and take part in workshops.

Societies, prizes and festivals

Children's writing courses and conferences

Contact your local library, college or university for further information about the courses that might be most suited to you and the stage you are at with your writing.

Blue Elephant Storyshaping

website www.blueelephantstoryshaping.com
Contact Natascha Biebow, Editor, Coach and Mentor

Offers one-to-one coaching, individual manuscript reviews and marketing advice to writers of picture books up to middle grade fiction. The Cook Up a Picture Book online course offers coaching and mentoring, and is aimed at picture book writers who wish to fine-tune their work, plus illustrators who would like to write and illustrate. The Small-Group Coaching Course is a six-week course featuring weekly, one-to-one detailed editorial feedback and top tips on key aspects of picture book craft and publishing. The aim is to create at least one marketable picture book. There is the opportunity to submit to an editor or agent at the end of this course. See website for full details of services available.

The Federation of Children's Book Groups Conference

1 Oakwell Close, Bragbury End, Stevenage, Herts. SG2 8UG
tel 0300 102 1559
email info@fcbg.org.uk
website www.fcbg.org.uk
Twitter @FCBGnews
Takes place April

Held annually, guest speakers include well-known children's authors as well as experts and publishers in the field of children's books. Publishers also exhibit their newest books and resources.

The Golden Egg Academy

email info@goldeneggacademy.co.uk
website www.goldeneggacademy.co.uk
Founder and Managing Director Imogen Cooper

The Golden Egg Academy runs writing courses for authors who want to develop their writing to publication standard. Golden Egg has helped more than 40 writers gain contracts with publishers since 2015. The fiction plan comprises a one-year 'Story Foundations' course, followed by an optional one-year 'Work on Your Novel' course. The picture book plan is a nine-month course. Both courses combine three all-day workshops in London with one-to-one editorial surgeries and regular online group seminars. Students also have the opportunity to meet industry professionals and benefit from presentations by some

of the best writers in their field. Fiction writers enjoy an exclusive non-binding 'First Look' deal with Chicken House and The Viney Shaw Agency; picture book writers enjoy an exclusive non-binding 'First Look' deal with Andersen Press and Peters, Fraser and Dunlop. All students are invited to participate in Golden Egg Academy social events during the academic year.

The Golden Egg Academy is a curated writing programme; all applicants receive a written assessment on their submissions. The picture book programme is led by Tessa Strickland, co-founder and former editor-in-chief of independent children's publisher, Barefoot Books. For more details, visit the website.

IBBY Congress

Nonnenweg 12, Postfach CH-4009-Basel, Switzerland
tel +41 61-272 2917
email ibby@ibby.org
website www.ibbycongress2020.org

IBBY's biennial international congresses bring together IBBY (the International Board on Books for Young People) members and other people involved in children's books and reading development from all over the world. The congresses are excellent occasions to make contacts, exchange ideas and open horizons. Every two years a different National Section hosts the Congress. Several hundred people attend the lectures, panel discussions, seminar sessions and workshops on current congress themes. An IBBY International Congress also serves as a framework not only for the General Assembly and other meetings, but also for the presentation of different exhibitions and celebrations such as the Hans Christian Andersen Awards and the IBBY Honour List.

The 37th IBBY International Congress will be held 5–7 September 2020 at the Trade Centre in Moscow; the theme is Great Big World Through Children's Books: National and Foreign Literature. page 369.

Jericho Writers

Prama House, 267 Banbury Road, Oxford OX2 7HT
tel 0345 459 9560
email info@jerichowriters.com
website https://jerichowriters.com
Twitter @Jerichowriters
Founder Harry Bingham *Operations* Samantha Novak

A writers' club which helps members to grow their careers through access to the best teaching materials, tools and practical advice. Membership benefits include access to video courses, masterclasses with advice from industry experts, information about UK literary agents and discounts and priority booking on editorial services, tutored courses and events.

Oxford University Day and Weekend Schools

Oxford University Department of Continuing Education, Rewley House, 1 Wellington Square, Oxford OX1 2JA
tel (01865) 270368
email ppdayweek@conted.ox.ac.uk
website www.conted.ox.ac.uk/about/day-and-weekend
Contact Day School Administrator

Effective Writing: a series of three-day accredited courses for creative writing. Topics vary from year to year. Courses always held on Fridays. See website for further courses on creative writing.

SCBWI-BI Annual Conference and Masterclass Series

email scbwi@scbwi.org
website www.britishisles.scbwi.org/events
website https://britishisles.scbwi.org/events/illustration-masterclass-writing-for-illustrators/
website https://britishisles.scbwi.org/events/author-masterclass-whole-series-booking/
Contact Natascha Biebow

The SCBWI-BI (Society of Children's Book Writers and Illustrators – British Isles) annual conference offers a mix of inspiration, networking and fun for writers and illustrators, both published and unpublished. Offers the opportunity for published authors and illustrators to meet librarians and booksellers and market their books. Features a faculty of award-winning authors, illustrators and other industry professionals.

The Masterclass Series offers sessions for authors and illustrators to develop their knowledge and skills in a variety of areas covering a range of topics including fiction, series fiction, picture books, illustration and poetry.

Swanwick, The Writers' Summer School

Hayes Conference Centre, Swanwick, Derbyshire DE55 1AU
tel 07452 283652
email secretary@swanwickwritersschool.org.uk
website www.swanwickwritersschool.org.uk
Facebook www.facebook.com/SwanwickWriters
Twitter @swanwickwriters
Takes place August

Operating for over 70 years, Swanwick offers the opportunity to learn new skills and hone existing ones. There is an extensive choice of courses, talks and workshops. Offers several highly subsidised places for writers aged between 18 and 30, and assistance for writers unable to afford the full course fee. Full details of the programme and information on how to apply for the TopWrite Programme and Assisted Places Scheme are available on the website.

Tŷ Newydd Writing Centre

Tŷ Newydd, Llanystrndwy, Cricieth, Gwynedd LL52 0LW
tel (01766) 522811
email tynewydd@leteraturewales.org
website www.tynewydd.wales
Twitter @ty_newydd

Tŷ Newydd, the former home of Prime Minister David Lloyd George, has hosted residential creative writing courses for writers of all abilities for over 25 years. Whether you are interested in a poetry masterclass, writing for the theatre, developing a novel for young adults or conquering the popular fiction market, there will be a course in the programme suitable for you. Courses are open to everyone over the age of 16 and no qualifications are necessary. Staff can advise on the suitability of courses, and further details about each individual course can be obtained by visiting the website, or contacting the team by phone or email. Tŷ Newydd also offers courses for schools, corporate courses and away days for companies. Tŷ Newydd Writing Centre is run by Literature Wales, the national company for the development of literature in Wales.

Writers & Artists

Bloomsbury Publishing plc, 50 Bedford Square, London WC1B 3DP
tel 020-7631 5985
email writersandartists@bloomsbury.com
website www.writersandartists.co.uk
Facebook www.facebook.com/WritersArtistsYearbook
Twitter @Writers_Artists
Contacts James Rennoldson, Clare Povey

Writers & Artists (W&A) runs events and courses throughout the year across the UK and at its offices in London. Collaborates with literary festivals, universities and charities such as York Literature Festival, Book Aid International, Literature Works, Arts University Bournemouth and the Open University. An annual How to Write For Children & Young adults conference is held in February and a children's fiction evening writing course, Your Children's Book, takes place twice a year. W&A also offers editing services, bespoke mentoring and literary agent events and lunches throughout the year including an agent event dedicated solely to children's fiction. See website for full details.

Societies, prizes and festivals

UNIVERSITY COURSES

Bath Spa University

Bath Spa University, Newton Park, Newton St Loe, Bath BA2 9BN
tel (01225) 876180
email admissions@bathspa.ac.uk
website www.bathspa.ac.uk

MA Writing for Young People, PhD in Creative Writing.

University of Bolton

Deane Road Campus, Bolton BL3 5AB
tel (01204) 903903
website www.bolton.ac.uk
Facebook www.facebook.com/UniversityofBolton
Twitter @BoltonUni
Contact Dr Jill Marsden and Dr Ben Wilkinson, Admission Tutors, Creative Writing

MPhil/PhD Creative Writing Specialisms.

University of Central Lancashire

School of Art, Design and Fashion,
University of Central Lancashire, Preston PR1 2HE
tel (01772) 893364
email swilkin@uclan.ac.uk
website www.uclan.ac.uk
Contact Steve Wilkin, Course Leader

The MA Children's Book Illustration is a taught master's course that was founded in 2005 and which explores the practice of illustration for children's picture and story books. The course is designed to encourage pursuit of a unique and personal line of research into an artist's chosen area of children's book illustration. Many graduates have gone on to careers as published illustrators. The course runs both full and part time.

University of London, Goldsmiths

Goldsmiths, University of London,
London SE14 6NW
tel 020-7919 7171
website www.gold.ac.uk
Facebook www.facebook.com/GoldsmithsUoL/
Twitter @GoldsmithsUoL

Postgraduate courses include Artists' Film and Moving Image, Children's Literature, Children's Illustration, Computer Games Art and Design, Creative and Life Writing, Digital Media, Film and Screen Studies, Film-making, Journalism, Performance Making, Radio, Scriptwriting, Television.

The Manchester Writing School at Manchester Metropolitan University

70 Oxford Street, Manchester M1 5NH
tel 0161 247 1787
email writingschool@mmu.ac.uk
website www.manchesterwritingschool.co.uk
Twitter @McrWritingSchl
Contact (admission and general enquiries) James Draper, Manager

Master of Fine Arts (MFA) and Master of Arts (MA) in Writing for Children & Young Adults, campus-based and international online distance learning, available to study full-time (MA: one year, MFA: two years) or part-time (MA: two years; MFA: three years). September and January enrolment. Scholarships available (including Joyce Nield Fund for non-UK Commonwealth students). Evening taught, with strong industry links. MFA students complete a full-length book. Optional unit in Teaching Creative Writing. PhD in Creative Writing – including PhD by practice and PhD by published work: Children's Writing. Tutors include Catherine Fox, Livi Michael and Alex Wheatle. Visiting Teaching Fellows: Sherry Ashworth, Mandy Coe and Paul Dowswell.

Home of the Manchester Children's Book Festival (mcbf.org.uk), anthology publishing projects, and Carol Ann Duffy's national and international Laureate Education Projects.

Nottingham Trent University

School of Arts and Humanities,
Nottingham Trent University, Clifton Lane, Nottingham NG11 8NS
tel 0115 848 4200
email rory.waterman@ntu.ac.uk
email hum.enquiries@ntu.ac.uk
website www.ntu.ac.uk/creativewriting
Facebook www.facebook.com/ntucreative/
Twitter @ntuhum
Contact Dr Rory Waterman, Programme Leader

MA Creative Writing. A practice-based course in Nottingham UNESCO City of Literature, and one of the longest-established and successful programmes of its kind in the UK (currently celebrating 25 years), with close links to the writing industry, an annual anthology, a programme of guest talks and workshops, and many highly successful graduate writers. Diverse module options include: Fiction; Poetry; Writing for Stage, Radio and Screen; Children's and Young Adult Fiction.

University of Roehampton

Grove House, Roehampton Lane, London SW15 5PJ
tel 020-8392 3000
website www.roehampton.ac.uk
Facebook www.facebook.com/roehamptonuni/
Twitter @RoehamptonUni

Postgraduate courses include Children's Literature, Journalism, Creative Writing, Publishing, Film and Screen Cultures.

University of Winchester

Sparkford Road, Winchester SO22 4NR
tel (01962) 841515
email enquiries@winchester.ac.uk
website www.winchester.ac.uk
Facebook www.facebook.com/universityofwinchester
Twitter @_UoW

MA Writing for Children and Young Adults.

Publishing practice
ISBNs: what you need to know

The Nielsen ISBN Agency for UK & Ireland receives a large number of enquiries about the ISBN system. The most frequently asked questions are answered here and for more information visit www.nielsenisbnstore.com.

What is an ISBN?
An ISBN is an International Standard Book Number and is 13 digits long.

What is the purpose of an ISBN?
An ISBN is a product number, used by publishers, booksellers and libraries for ordering, listing and stock control purposes. It enables them to identify a particular publisher and allows the publisher to identify a specific edition of a specific title in a specific format within their output.

Contact details

Nielsen ISBN Agency for UK and Ireland
3rd Floor, Midas House, 62 Goldsworth Road,
Woking GU21 6LQ
tel (01483) 712215
email isbn.agency@nielsen.com
website www.nielsenisbnstore.com

What is a publisher?
The publisher is generally the person or organisation taking the financial and other risks in making a product available. For example, if a product goes on sale and sells no copies at all, the publisher loses money. If you get paid anyway, you are likely to be a designer, printer, author or consultant of some kind.

What is the format of an ISBN?
The ISBN is 13 digits long and is divided into five parts, as shown below, separated by spaces or hyphens.
• Prefix element: for the foreseeable future this will be 978 or 979
• Registration group element: identifies a national, geographic, or national grouping. It shows where the publisher is based
• Registrant element: identifies a specific publisher or imprint
• Publication element: identifies a specific edition of a specific title in a specific format
• Check digit: the final digit which mathematically validates the rest of the number
The four parts following the prefix element can be of varying length.
Prior to 1 January 2007 ISBNs were ten-digit numbers; any existing ten-digit ISBNs must be converted by prefixing them with '978' and the check digit must be recalculated using a Modulus 10 system with alternate weights of 1 and 3. The ISBN Agency can help you with this.

Do I *have* to have an ISBN?
There is no legal requirement in the UK and Ireland for an ISBN and it conveys no form of legal or copyright protection. It is simply a product identification number.

Why should I use an ISBN?
If you wish to sell your publication through major bookselling chains, independent bookshops or internet booksellers, they will require you to have an ISBN to assist their internal processing and ordering systems.

The ISBN also provides access to bibliographic databases, such as the Nielsen Book Database, which use ISBNs as references. These databases help booksellers and libraries to provide information for customers. Nielsen Book has a range of information, electronic trading and retail sales monitoring services which use ISBNs and are vital for the dissemination, trading and monitoring of books in the supply chain. The ISBN therefore provides access to additional marketing opportunities which could help sales of your product.

Where can I get an ISBN?

ISBNs are assigned to publishers in the country where the publisher's main office is based. This is irrespective of the language of the publication or the intended market for the book.

The ISBN Agency is the national agency for the UK and Republic of Ireland and British Overseas Territories. A publisher based elsewhere will not be able to get numbers from the UK Agency (even if you are a British Citizen) but can contact the Nielsen ISBN Agency for details of the relevant national Agency.

If you are based in the UK and Ireland you can purchase ISBNs online from the Nielsen ISBN Store: www.nielsenisbnstore.com.

How long does it take to get an ISBN?

If you purchase your ISBNs online from the Nielsen ISBN Store you will receive your ISBN allocation within minutes. If you are purchasing ISBNs direct from the ISBN Agency via an off-line application, it can take up to five days. The processing period begins when a correctly completed application is received in the ISBN Agency and payment is received.

How much does it cost to get an ISBN?

Please refer to www.nielsenisbnstore.com or email the ISBN Agency: isbn.agency@nielsen.com.

What if I only want one ISBN?

ISBNs can be bought individually or in blocks of ten or more; visit the ISBN Store to find out more.

Who is eligible for ISBNs?

Any individual or organisation who is publishing a qualifying product for general sale or distribution to the market. By publishing we mean making a work available to the public.

Which products do NOT qualify for ISBNs?

Any publication that is without a defined end should not be assigned an ISBN. For example, publications that are regularly updated and intended to continue indefinitely are ineligible for ISBN.

Some examples of products that do not qualify for ISBN are:

• Journals, periodicals, serials, newspapers in their entirety (single issues or articles, where these are made available separately, may qualify for ISBN);

• Abstract entities such as textual works and other abstract creations of intellectual or artistic content;

• Ephemeral printed materials such as advertising matter and the like;

• Customised print-on-demand publications (Publications that are available only on a limited basis, such as customised print on demand publications with content specifically tailored to a user's request shall not be assigned an ISBN. If a customised publication is being made available for wider sale, e.g. as a college course pack available through a college book store, then an ISBN may be assigned);

- Printed music;
- Art prints and art folders without title page and text;
- Personal documents (such as a curriculum vitae or personal profile);
- Greetings cards;
- Music sound recordings;
- Software that is intended for any purpose other than educational or instructional;
- Electronic bulletin boards;
- Emails and other digital correspondence;
- Updating websites;
- Games;
- Non text-based publications.

Following a review of the UK market, it is now permissible for ISBNs to be assigned to calendars and diaries, provided that they are not intended for purely time-management purposes and that a substantial proportion of their content is textual or graphic.

What is an ISSN?

An International Standard Serial Number. This is the numbering system for journals, magazines, periodicals, newspapers and newsletters. It is administered by the British Library, *tel* (01937) 546959; *email* issn-uk@bl.uk; *website* www.bl.uk/bibliographic/issn.html

Public Lending Right

Under the PLR system, payment is made from public funds to authors and other contributors (writers, illustrators/photographers, translators, adapters/retellers, ghostwriters, editors/compilers/abridgers/revisers, narrators and producers) whose books (print, audiobook and ebook) are lent from public libraries. Payment is annual; the amount authors receive is proportionate to the number of times that their books were borrowed during the previous year (July to June).

How the system works

From the applications received, the PLR office compiles a database of authors and books (the PLR Register). A representative sample of book issues is recorded, consisting of all loans from selected public libraries. This is then multiplied in proportion to total library lending to produce, for each book, an estimate of its total annual loans throughout the country. The estimated loans are matched against the database of registered authors and titles to discover how many loans are credited to each registered book for the calculation of PLR payments, using the ISBN printed in the book (see below).

Parliament allocates a sum each year (£6.6 million for 2018/19) for PLR. This fund pays the administrative costs of PLR and reimburses local authorities for recording loans in the sample libraries (see below). The remaining money is divided by the total estimated national loan figure for all registered books in order to work out how much can be paid for each estimated loan of every registered ISBN.

Since July 2014 the UK PLR legislation has been extended to include public library loans of audiobooks and ebooks downloaded to library premises for taking away as loans ('on-site' ebook loans). On 27 April 2017 the Digital Economy Bill, which included provision to extend the UK PLR legislation to include remote loans of ebooks from public libraries, received Royal Assent. The new arrangements took effect officially from 1 July 2018, when remote ebook loans data began to be collected, and any payments arising from the newly eligible loans will be made in February 2020. The PLR website provides updated information on this legislation.

Limits on payments

If all the registered interests in an author's books score so few loans that they would earn less than £1 in a year, no payment is due. However, if the books of one registered author score so high that the author's PLR earnings for the year would exceed £6,600, then only £6,600 is paid. (No author can earn more than £6,600 in PLR in any one year.) Money

Further information

Public Lending Right
Public Lending Right, British Library, Boston Spa,
Wetherby, West Yorkshire LS23 7BQ
tel (01937) 546030
website www.bl.uk/pl
website www.plrinternational.com
Contact Head of PLR Operations

The UK PLR scheme is administered by the British Library from its offices in Boston Spa. The UK PLR office also provides registration for the Irish PLR scheme on behalf of the Irish Public Lending Remuneration office.
Application forms, information and publications are all obtainable from the PLR Office. See website for further information on eligibility for PLR, loans statistics and forthcoming developments.

British Library Advisory Committee for Public Lending Right
Advises the British Library Board, the PLR Head of Policy and Engagement and Head of PLR Operations on the operation and future development of the PLR scheme.

that is not paid out because of these limits belongs to the fund and increases the amounts paid that year to other authors.

The sample

Because it would be expensive and impracticable to attempt to collect loans data from every library authority in the UK, a statistical sampling method is employed instead. The sample represents only public lending libraries – academic, school, private and commercial libraries are not included. Only books which are loaned from public libraries can earn PLR; consultations of books on library premises are excluded.

The sample consists of the entire loans records for a year from libraries in more than 30 public library authorities spread through England, Scotland and Wales, and whole data is collected from Northern Ireland. Sample loans represent around 20% of the national total. All the computerised sampling points in an authority contribute loans data ('multi-site' sampling). The aim is to increase the sample without any significant increase in costs. In order to ensure representative sampling, at least seven libraries are replaced every year and a library cannot stay in the sample for more than four years. Loans are totalled every 12 months for the period 1 July–30 June.

An author's entitlement to PLR depends on the loans accrued by his or her books in the sample. This figure is averaged up to produce first regional and then finally national estimated loans.

ISBNs

The PLR system uses ISBNs (International Standard Book Numbers) to identify books lent and correlate loans with entries on the PLR Register so that payments can be made. ISBNs are required for all registrations. Different editions (e.g. 1st, 2nd, hardback, paperback, large print) of the same book have different ISBNs. See *ISBNs: what you need to know* on page 397.

Most borrowed authors and books

- The most borrowed children's author in 2016–17 was Julia Donaldson.
- The most borrowed classic author overall was children's writer Roald Dahl.
- The most borrowed children's title was *Diary of a Wimpy Kid: Old School* by Jeff Kinney.

(2017–18 data not available before going to press. The 2017-18 figures will be published on the PLR website in summer 2019)

Authorship

In the PLR system the author of a printed book or ebook is any contributor such as the writer, illustrator, translator, compiler, editor or reviser. Authors must be named on the book's title page, or be able to prove authorship by some other means (e.g. receipt of royalties). The ownership of copyright has no bearing on PLR eligibility. Narrators, producers and abridgers are also eligible to apply for PLR shares in audiobooks and e-audiobooks.

Co-authorship/illustrators. In the PLR system the authors of a book are those writers, translators, editors, compilers and illustrators as defined above. Authors must apply for registration before their books can earn PLR and this can be done via the PLR website. There is no restriction on the number of authors who can register shares in any one book as long as they satisfy the eligibility criteria.

Writers and/or illustrators. At least one contributor must be eligible and they must jointly agree what share of PLR each will take based on contribution. This agreement is necessary even if one or two are ineligible or do not wish to register for PLR. The eligible authors will receive the share(s) specified in the application.

Translators. Translators may apply for a 30% fixed share (to be shared equally between joint translators).

Editors and compilers. An editor or compiler may apply to register a 20% share if they have written at least 10% of the book's content or more than ten pages of text in addition to normal editorial work and are named on the title page. Alternatively, editors may register 20% if they have a royalty agreement with the publisher. In the case of joint editors/compilers, the total editor's share should be divided equally.

Audiobooks. PLR shares in audiobooks are fixed by the UK scheme and may not be varied. *Writers* may register a fixed 60% share in an audiobook, providing that it has not been abridged or translated. In cases where the writer has made an additional contribution (e.g. as narrator), he/she may claim both shares. *Narrators* may register a fixed 20% PLR share

---

Summary of the 36th year's results

Registration: authors. When registration closed for the 36th year (30 June 2018) there were 62,564 authors and assignees.

Eligible loans. The loans from UK libraries credited to registered books – approximately 42% of all library borrowings – qualify for payment. The remaining loans relate to books that are ineligible for various reasons, to books written by dead or foreign authors, and to books that have simply not been applied for.

Money and payments. PLR's administrative costs are deducted from the fund allocated to the British Library Board annually by Parliament. Total government funding for 2017/18 was £6.6 million. The amount distributed to authors was just over £6 million. The Rate per Loan for 2017/18 was 8.52 pence.

The numbers of authors in various payment categories are as follows:

*297	payments at	£5,000–6,600
366	payments between	£2,500–4,999.99
790	payments between	£1,000–2,499.99
843	payments between	£500–999.99
3,213	payments between	£100–499.99
16,792	payments between	£1–99.99
22,301	TOTAL	

* Includes 199 authors whose book loans reached the maximum threshold

---

Most borrowed children's authors

1	Julia Donaldson	11	Claire Freedman
2	Daisy Meadows	12	Enid Blyton
3	Roald Dahl	13	Jeff Kinney
4	Roderick Hunt	14	Jeanne Willis
5	Francesca Simon	15	Lucy Cousins
6	Adam Blade	16	Holly Webb
7	Jacqueline Wilson	17	Kes Gray
8	David Walliams	18	Liz Pichon
9	Fiona Watt	19	Mick Inkpen
10	Michael Morpurgo	20	Terry Deary

This list is of the most borrowed authors in UK public libraries. It is based on PLR sample loans in the period July 2016–June 2017 (data for 2017–18 not available before going to press; this will be published on the PLR website in summer 2019). It includes all writers, both registered and unregistered, but not illustrators where the book has a separate writer. Writing names are used; pseudonyms have not been combined.

Please note that this top 20 listing is based on the February 2018 UK PLR payment calculations.

in an audiobook. *Producers* may register a fixed 20% share in an audiobook. *Abridgers* (in cases where the writer's original text has been abridged prior to recording as an audiobook) qualify for 12% (20% of the writer's share). *Translators* (in cases where the writer's original text has been translated from another language) qualify for 18% (30% of the writer's share). If there is more than one writer, narrator, etc the appropriate shares should be divided equally. If more than one contribution has been made, e.g. writer and narrator, more than one fixed share may be applied for.

Dead or missing co-authors. Where it is impossible to agree shares with a co-author because that person is dead or untraceable, then the surviving co-author or co-authors may submit an application to register a share which reflects their individual contribution to the book.

Transferring PLR after death. First applications may not be made by the estate of a deceased author. However, if an author registers during their lifetime the PLR in their books can be transferred to a new owner and continues for up to 70 years after the date of their death. The new owner can apply to register new titles if first published one year before, or up to ten years after, the date of the author's death. New editions of existing registered titles can also be registered posthumously.

Most borrowed children's fiction titles

	Author	Title	Publisher	Year
1	Jeff Kinney	*Diary of a Wimpy Kid: Old School*	Puffin	2015
2	Jeff Kinney	*Diary of a Wimpy Kid*	Puffin	2008
3	David Walliams (illus. Tony Ross)	*Grandpa's Great Escape*	HarperCollins	2015
4	David Walliams (illus. Tony Ross)	*The World's Worst Children*	HarperCollins	2016
5	Jeff Kinney	*Diary of a Wimpy Kid: Roderick Rules*	Puffin	2009
6	Roald Dahl (illus. Quentin Blake)	*The BFG*	Puffin	2016
7	Jeff Kinney	*Diary of a Wimpy Kid: The Long Haul*	Puffin	2006
8	Jeff Kinney	*Diary of a Wimpy Kid: Cabin Fever*	Puffin	2013
9	Jeff Kinney	*Diary of a Wimpy Kid: Hard Luck*	Puffin	2015
10	Jeff Kinney	*Diary of a Wimpy Kid: Dog Days*	Puffin	2010
11	Roald Dahl (illus. Quentin Blake)	*Charlie and the Chocolate Factory*	Puffin	2016
12	Jeff Kinney	*Diary of a Wimpy Kid: The Ugly Truth*	Puffin	2012
13	David Walliams (illus. Quentin Blake)	*Mr Stink*	HarperCollins	2010
14	Liz Pichon	*The Brilliant World of Tom Gates*	Scholastic	2011
15	David Walliams (illus. Tony Ross)	*Billionaire Boy*	HarperCollins	2011
16	Jeff Kinney	*Diary of a Wimpy Kid: The Last Straw*	Puffin	2009
17	J.K. Rowling	*Harry Potter and the Philosopher's Stone*	Bloomsbury	2014
18	Jeff Kinney	*Diary of a Wimpy Kid: The Third Wheel*	Puffin	2014
19	David Walliams (illus. Quentin Blake)	*The Boy in the Dress*	HarperCollins	2009
20	Roald Dahl (illus. Quentin Blake)	*The Twits*	Puffin	2016

(Data for 2017–18 not available before going to press; this will be published on the PLR website in summer 2019)

Publishing practice

Residential qualifications. To register for the UK PLR scheme, at the time of application authors must have their only home or principal home in the UK or in any of the other countries within the European Economic Area (i.e. EC member states plus Iceland, Norway and Liechtenstein).

Eligible books

In the PLR system each edition of a book is registered and treated as a separate book. A book is eligible for PLR registration provided that:
• it has an eligible author (or co-author);
• it is printed and bound (paperbacks counting as bound);
• it has already been published;
• copies of it have been put on sale, i.e. it is not a free handout;
• the authorship is personal, i.e. not a company or association, and the book is not crown copyright;
• it has an ISBN;
• it is not wholly or mainly a musical score;
• it is not a newspaper, magazine, journal or periodical.

Audiobooks. An audiobook is defined as an 'authored text' or 'a work recorded as a sound recording and consisting mainly of spoken words'. Applications can therefore only be accepted to register audiobooks which meet these requirements and are the equivalent of a printed book. Music, dramatisations and live recordings do not qualify for registration. To qualify for UK PLR in an audiobook contributors should be named on the case in which the audiobook is held; OR be able to refer to a contract with the publisher; OR be named within the audiobook recording.

Ebooks. Previously only ebooks downloaded to fixed terminals in library premises and then taken away on loan on portable devices to be read elsewhere qualified for PLR payment. Information provided by libraries suggested that the vast majority of ebook and digital audio lending was carried out 'remotely' to home PCs and mobile devices, which meant the loan did not qualify for PLR.

On 27 April 2017 the Digital Economy Bill, which included provision to extend the UK PLR legislation to include remote loans of ebooks from public libraries, received Royal Assent. The new arrangements took effect officially from 1 July 2018, and remote ebook loans is now collected, and the first payments arising from the newly eligible loans will be made in February 2020. The PLR website provides updated information on this legislation.

Statements and payment

Authors with an online account may view their statement online. Registered authors without an online account receive a statement posted to their address if a payment is due.

Sampling arrangements

To help minimise the unfairness that arises inevitably from a sampling system, the scheme specifies the eight regions within which authorities and sampling points have to be designated and includes libraries of varying size. Part of the sample drops out by rotation each year to allow fresh libraries to be included. The following library authorities were designated for the year beginning 1 July 2017 (all are multi-site authorities). This list is based on the nine government regions for England plus Northern Ireland, Scotland and Wales.
• East – Bedfordshire/Bedford, Hertfordshire

- East Midlands – Derbyshire, Rutland
- London – Greenwich, Hounslow, Lambeth, Luton
- North East – Durham, North Tyneside, Sunderland
- North West & Merseyside – Cumbria, Lancashire, Stockport
- South East – Kent
- South West – Bournemouth, Devon, Poole
- West Midlands – Worcestershire
- Yorkshire & The Humber – Barnsley, Wakefield
- Northern Ireland – The Northern Ireland Library Authority
- Scotland – Aberdeenshire, Falkirk, Fife, South Lanarkshire
- Wales – Caerphilly, Conwy, Gwynedd.

Participating local authorities are reimbursed on an actual cost basis for additional expenditure incurred in providing loans data to the PLR Office. The extra PLR work mostly consists of modifications to computer programs to accumulate loans data in the local authority computer and to transmit the data to the PLR Office.

Most borrowed children's non-fiction titles

	Author	Title	Publisher	Year
1	Julia Donaldson (illus. Axel Scheffler)	*My First Gruffalo Spot and Say*	Macmillan	2015
2	Julia Donaldson (illus. Axel Scheffler)	*Counting*	Macmillan	2016
3	Lauren Holowaty	*Peppa's First Words*	Ladybird	2016
4	Julia Donaldson (illus. Axel Scheffler)	*Colours*	Macmillan	2016
5	Anna Milbourne (illus. Simona Dimitri)	*Peep Inside Space*	Usborne	2016
6	Sebastien Braun	*Can You Say it Too? Brr! Brr!*	Nosy Crow	2016
7	Axel Scheffler	*Pip and Posy: Look and Say*	Nosy Crow	2015
8	Fiona Watt (illus. Stella Baggot)	*Baby's Very First Play Book: Animal Words*	Usborne	2016
9	Eric Carle	*The Very Hungry Caterpillar's ABC*	Puffin	2015
10	——	*Follow the Trail: Trucks*	DK	2016
11	Mike Brownlow (illus. Simon Rickerty)	*Ten Little Dinosaurs*	Orchard Books	2015
12	Rebecca Gerlings	*Peppa Pig: Colours with Peppa*	Ladybird	2015
13	Sebastien Braun	*Can You Say it Too? Twit! Twoo!*	Nosy Crow	2015
14	Rod Campbell	*Early Starters: Who's That?*	Macmillan	2016
15	Rebecca Gerlings	*Peppa Pig: Shapes with Peppa*	Ladybird	2015
16	Kes Gray (illus. Jim Field)	*How Many Legs?*	Hodder	2016
17	——	*Follow the Trail: Wild Animals*	DK	2016
18	Dawn Sirett	*Follow the Trail: Farm*	DK	2016
19	Rod Campbell	*Early Starters: 123*	Macmillan	2015
20	Rod Campbell	*Early Starters: Let's Name*	Macmillan	2016

(Data for 2017–18 not available before going to press; this will be published on the PLR website in summer 2019.)

Publishing practice

Reciprocal arrangements

Reciprocal PLR arrangements now exist with the German, Dutch, Austrian and other European PLR schemes. Authors can apply for overseas PLR for most of these countries through the ALCS (Authors' Licensing and Collecting Society; see page 425). The exception to this rule is Ireland. Authors should now register for Irish PLR through the UK PLR Office. Further information on PLR schemes internationally and recent developments within the EC towards wider recognition of PLR is available from the PLR Office or on the international PLR website.

See also...

- *Prize winners, page 388*

Glossary of publishing terms

The selected terms in this glossary relate to the content of this *Yearbook.*

advance

Money paid by a publisher to an author before a book is published which will be covered by future royalties. A publishing contract often allows an author an advance payment against future royalties; the author will not receive any further royalties until the amount paid in advance has been earned by sales of the book.

advance information (AI) sheet

A document that is put together by a publishing company to provide sales and marketing information about a book before publication and can be sent several months before publication to sales representatives. It can incorporate details of the format and contents of the book, key selling points and information about intended readership, as well as information about promotions and reviews.

backlist

The range of books already published by a publisher that are still in print.

blad (book layout and design)

A pre-publication sales and marketing tool. It is often a printed booklet that contains sample pages, images and front and back covers which acts as a preview for promotional use or for sales teams to show to potential retailers, customers or reviewers.

blurb

A short piece of writing or a paragraph that praises and promotes a book, which usually appears on the back or inside cover of the book and may be used in sales and marketing material.

book club edition

An edition of a book specially printed and bound for a book club for sale to its members.

co-edition

The publication of a book by two publishing companies in different countries, where the first company has originated the work and then sells sheets to the second publisher (or licenses the second publisher to reprint the book locally).

commissioning editor

A person who asks authors to write books for the part of the publisher's list for which he or she is responsible or who takes on an author who approaches them direct or via an agent with a proposal. Also called acquisitions editor or acquiring editor (more commonly in the USA). A person who signs-up writers (commissions them to write) an article for a magazine or newspaper.

copy-editor

A person whose job is to check material ready for printing for accuracy, clarity of message and writing style and consistency of typeface, punctuation and layout. Sometimes called a desk editor.

copyright

The legal right, which the creator of an original work has, to only allow copying of the work with permission and sometimes on payment of royalties or a copyright fee. An amendment to the Copyright, Designs and Patents Act (1988) states that in the UK most works are protected for 70 years from the creator's death. The 'copyright page' at the start of a book asserts copyright ownership and author identification.

distributor

Acts as a link between the publisher and retailer. The distributor can receive orders from retailers, ship books, invoice, collect revenue and deal with returns. Distributors often handle books from several publishers. Digital distributors handle ebook distribution.

editor

A person in charge of publishing a newspaper or magazine who makes the final decisions about the content and format. A person in book publishing who has responsibility for the content of a book and can be variously a senior person (editor-in-chief) or day-to-day contact for authors (copy-editor, development editor, commissioning editor, etc).

endmatter

Material at the end of the main body of a book which may be useful to the reader, including references, appendices indexes and bibliography. Also called back matter.

extent

The number of pages in a book.

folio

A large sheet of paper folded twice across the middle and trimmed to make four pages of a book. Also a page number.

frontlist

New books just published (generally in their first year of publication) or about to be published by a publisher. Promotion of the frontlist is heavy, and the frontlist carries most of a publisher's investment. On the other hand, a backlist which continues to sell is usually the most profitable part of a publisher's list.

imprint

The publisher's or printer's name which appears on the title page of a book or in the bibliographical details; a brand name under which a book is published within a larger publishing company, usually representing a specialised subject area.

inspection copy

A copy of a publication sent or given with time allowed for a decision to purchase or return it. In academic publishing, lecturers can request inspection copies to decide whether to make a book/textbook recommended reading or adopt it as a core textbook for their course.

ISBN

International Standard Book Number.

ISSN

International Standard Serial Number. An international system used on periodicals, magazines, learned journals, etc. The ISSN is formed of eight digits, which refer to the country in which the magazine is published and the title of the publication.

literary agent

Somebody whose job is to negotiate publishing contracts, involving royalties, advances and rights sales on behalf of an author and who earns commission on the proceeds of the sales they negotiate.

moral right

The right of people such as editors or illustrators to have some say in the publication of a work to which they have contributed, even if they do not own the copyright.

out of print or o.p.

Relating to a book of which the publisher has no copies left and which is not going to be reprinted. Print on demand technology, however, means that a book can be kept 'in print' indefinitely.

packager

A company that creates a finished book for a publisher.

PDF

Portable Document Format. A data file generated from PostScript that is platform-independent, application-independent and font-independent. Acrobat is Adobe's suite of software used to generate, edit and view pdf files.

picture researcher

A person who looks for pictures relevant to a particular topic, so that they can be used as illustrations in, for example, a book, newspaper or TV programme.

prelims

The initial pages of a book, including the title page and table of contents, which precede the main text. Also called front matter.

pre-press

Before a book goes to press.

print on demand or POD

The facility to print and bind a small number of books at short notice, without the need for a large print run, using digital technology. When an order comes through, a digital file of the book can be printed individually and automatically.

production controller

A person in the production department of a publishing company who deals with printers and other suppliers.

proofreader

A person whose job is to proofread texts to check typeset page presentation and text for errors and to mark up corrections.

publisher

A person or company that publishes books, magazines and/or newspapers.

publisher's agreement

A contract between a publisher and the copyright holder, author, agent or another publisher, which lays down the terms under which the publisher will publish the book for the copyright holder.

publishing contract

An agreement between a publisher and an author by which the author grants the publisher the right to publish the work against payment of a fee, usually in the form of a royalty.

reading fee

Money paid to somebody for reading a manuscript and commenting on it.

recto

Relating to the right-hand page of a book, usually given an odd number.

reprint

Copies of a book made from the original, but with a note in the publication details of the date of reprinting and possibly a new title page and cover design.

rights

The legal right to publish something such as a book, picture or extract from a text.

rights manager

A person who negotiates and coordinates rights sales (e.g. for subsidiary, translation or foreign rights). Often travels to book fairs to negotiate rights sales.

royalty

Money paid to a writer for the right to use his or her property, usually a percentage of sales or an agreed amount per sale.

royalty split

The way in which a royalty is divided between several authors or between author and illustrator.

royalty statement

A printed statement from a publisher showing how much royalty is due to an author.

sans serif

A style of printing letters with all lines of equal thickness and no serifs. Sans faces are less easy to read than seriffed faces and they are rarely used for continuous text, although some magazines use them for text matter.

serialisation

Publication of a book in parts in a magazine or newspaper.

serif

A small decorative line added to letters in some fonts; a font that uses serifs, such as Times. The addition of serifs (1) keeps the letters apart while at the same time making it possible to link one letter to the next, and (2) makes the letters distinct, in particular the top parts which the reader recognises when reading.

slush pile

Unsolicited manuscripts which are sent to publishers or agents, and which may never be read.

style sheet

A guide listing all the rules of house style for a publishing company which has to be followed by authors and editors.

sub-editor

A person who corrects and checks articles in a newspaper before they are printed.

subsidiary rights

Rights other than the right to publish a book in its first form, e.g. paperback rights; rights to adapt the book; rights to serialise it in a magazine; film and TV rights; audio, ebook, foreign and translation rights.

territory

Areas of the world that the publisher has the rights to publish or can make foreign rights deals.

trade discount

A reduction in price given to a customer in the same trade, as by a publisher to another publisher or to a bookseller.

trade paperback (B format)

A paperback edition of a book that is superior in production quality to a mass-market paperback edition and is similar to a hardback in size 198 x 129mm.

trim size or trimmed size

The measurements of a page of a book after it has been cut, or of a sheet of paper after it has been cut to size.

typesetter

A person or company that 'sets' text and prepares the final layout of the page for printing. It can also now involve XML tagging for ebook creation.

typographic error or typo

A mistake made when keying text or typesetting.

verso

The left-hand page of a book, usually given an even number.

volume rights

The right to publish the work in hardback or paperback (this can now sometimes include ebook).

XML tagging

Inserting tags into the text that can allow it to be converted for ebooks or for use in electronic formats.

Editing your work

If you are publishing, via a traditional publisher or independently, editing your work is an essential part of the process. This article outlines for authors what is involved.

What is editing?

Broadly speaking, editing involves refining your writing ('copy') to make it as readable as possible and thus ready to be published. There are four main editorial stages:

• **Manuscript assessment/critique** is an initial assessment of the strengths and weaknesses of your work, with general suggestions for improvement.

• **Developmental/structural editing** gives more in-depth feedback on aspects of your work such as pace, writing style and appropriate language for your readership, and technical features such as characterisation (fiction) or reference styles (non-fiction).

• **Copy-editing** focuses on the detail, accuracy, completeness and consistency of your text, including grammar, spelling and punctuation.

• **Proofreading** is the final check of the layout and also picks up anything overlooked earlier.

Should I edit my work before submitting it to an agent or publisher?

Most fiction is not submitted direct to a publisher but will find its way to a commissioning or acquisitions editor via a literary agent (see the articles in this *Yearbook* in the *Literary agents* section, which starts on page 247). Some specialist non-fiction can be submitted directly to an appropriate publisher. The listings under *Children's book publishers*, starting on page 21, will indicate if a company accepts unsolicited scripts. In all cases it is important to follow the agent or publisher submission guidelines.

You should always check any submission for basic spelling and grammatical mistakes ('typos') and to ensure that there are no blatant inconsistencies or factual inaccuracies. It is up to you whether you pay a professional editor to do this for you, but you are unlikely to need a full copy-edit of your whole work at this stage. It may help, though, to have an outsider or beta-reader give you feedback.

What if I am self-publishing?

Independent authors do not have to obtain or pay for editorial advice, but if you want to sell a book that looks as good and reads as well as a professionally produced one, you are unlikely to achieve this on your own. There are a host of individuals and companies available to review and edit your work at all stages in the writing process, and to guide you through design and layout to publication and marketing.

When engaging a professional editor, be cautious and read the small print about what services are being offered and what qualifications the provider has to do the job. Decide what type of help you require and employ people with a track record and recommendations. Importantly, agree a fair price for the work. If you seek out the cheapest offering you are unlikely to get the best result. Writers & Artists offer editorial services for authors. Look also at the advice, rates, and directory of editorial professionals provided by the Society for Editors and Proofreaders (www.sfep.org.uk).

What happens during editing?

While processes differ from publisher to publisher, the sequence of events from draft manuscript to published copy is roughly similar. If you are self-publishing and working direct with an editor the sequence of events will be determined by which services you buy.

• If your work needs structural or developmental editing the publisher or freelance editor will make suggestions and you will need to revise your work accordingly.

• You will then submit the finished work for copy-editing. You should make sure you follow your publisher's style and formatting guidelines or ask your freelance editor to devise a style guide for you. This will save time in the detailed copy-edit, and therefore save you money.

• The editor or publisher may ask you to answer queries that arise during copy-editing.

• When the text is finalised it will be sent for typesetting or layout. If you are publishing independently, unless you are very experienced, you should find a reputable professional to do your interior page layout for print and ebook and commission a professional cover designer.

• You may be sent one or more sets of proofs of the layout, or your publisher may handle this stage. Again, if you are self-publishing then checking the proofs carefully is up to you. See the handy checklist in the 'Mistakes to look out for' box.

• Your work is now ready for publication – and the all-important marketing.

What are the differences between copy-editing and proofreading?

Copy-editing and proofreading are crucial stages in the publishing process and, while the two can often be confused or referred to interchangeably, there are important differences. The copy-editing function normally takes place when your work is complete but before typesetting or design, allowing substantial revisions to be made at minimal cost. Proof-reading, on the other hand, typically takes place after your work has been copy-edited and typeset and serves to 'fine-polish' the text to ensure that it is free from editorial and layout inaccuracies.

Copy-editing

This is the essential stage for all writers and should be done after you are happy with the general structure and content of your work. As this is the detailed, line-by-line edit, if you rewrite or add material after this stage your work will need to be edited again. The aim of copy-editing is to ensure that whatever appears in public is accurate, easy to follow, fit for purpose and free of error, omission, inconsistency and repetition. This process picks up embarrassing mistakes, ambiguities and anomalies, alerts you to possible legal problems and marks up your work for the typesetter/designer. Typically, copy-editing involves:

• checking for mistakes in spelling, grammar and punctuation;
• creating a style sheet; applying consistency in spelling, punctuation, capitalisation, etc;
• making sure the text flows well, is logically ordered and is appropriate for your target audience;
• marking up or formatting the structure for the designer – e.g. headings, tables, lists, boxed items, quotes;
• checking any illustrations and figures correspond with what's written in the text;

• checking that any bibliographical references and notes are correctly ordered and styled and that none are missing;
• making sure you have any necessary introductory pages (prelims);
• querying obvious errors of fact, misleading information or parts that are unclear.

How much editing your copy will require (and therefore how long it will take) depends on a number of factors, including:
• the complexity of the subject matter;
• how consistent you have been;
• whether you have correctly followed a publisher's house style (or your own);
• the quality of your writing.

In the past, manuscripts were copy-edited on paper, which was labour-intensive and time-consuming. These days, nearly all copy-editing is carried out electronically, usually using Microsoft Word (or sometimes a bespoke publishing system). Suggested changes are usually made using the Track Changes function; queries for the author or publisher are often inserted using Comments. Copy-editors and publishers work in different ways. You may be asked to work through the changes and comments accepting, rejecting or answering

Common mistakes to look out for when editing and proofreading

• Punctuation mistakes, especially with direct speech and quotations.
• Inadvertently repeated words, e.g. 'and and . . .'.
• Phrases used inappropriately, e.g. 'should of' instead of 'should have' or 'compare to' instead of 'compare with'.
• Apostrophe misuse, e.g. its/it's and plurals (*not* banana's).
• Words with similar spelling or pronunciation but with different meanings used incorrectly, e.g. their/they're/there and effect/affect.
• Mixed use of past and present tenses.
• Use of plural verbs with single subjects (or vice versa), e.g. 'one in five children *are*. . . ' instead of 'one in five children *is*. . .' or '[the company] *has* 100 employees and [the company] *provide* free childcare' instead of 'provides' (or 'have' and 'provide').
• Obvious factual errors, e.g. 'the Battle of Hastings in 1766'.
• Inconsistent use of abbreviations and acronyms.
• Abbreviations/acronyms that have not been defined at least once in full.
• Missing bullet points or numbers in a sequenced list.
• Typing errors, e.g. '3' instead of '£'.
• Inconsistent layout of names, addresses, telephone numbers and email/web addresses.
• Incorrect or no use of trademarks, e.g. 'blackberry' instead of 'BlackBerry™'.
• References in the text that do not correspond to footnotes.
• Inaccurate or inadequate cross-referencing.
• Index listings not found on the page given in the index.
• Text inadvertently reordered or cut during the typesetting process.
• Headings wrongly formatted as body text.
• Running heads (at the top of pages) that do not correspond to chapter headings.
• Fonts and font sizes used incorrectly.
• Formatting inconsistencies such as poorly aligned margins or uneven columns.
• Captions/headings omitted from illustrations, photographs or diagrams.
• Illustrations/photographs/diagrams without appropriate copyright references.
• Widows and orphans, i.e. text which runs over page breaks and leaves a word or a line stranded.

each one; you may be sent a 'clean' edited version to approve; or you may just be sent queries to answer.

Proofreading

As this is the final check for errors and layout problems, you should not make major changes at this stage. These days you will normally receive proofs as pdf documents, which should be marked up using in-built commenting tools or the correct proof correction marks (see below) – check with your publisher or editor which method you are expected to use. Some publishers still work with hard copy paper proofs, or you may prefer to work this way yourself, in which case you should learn to use the main proof correction marks.

What are proofreading symbols and why do I need to know them?

Proofreading symbols (proof correction marks) are the 'shorthand' that copy-editors and proofreaders use for correcting written material and they are set by the British Standards Institution (BSi). Typesetters, designers and printers also require this knowledge as part of correcting page layout, style and format.

If you are sent a set of page proofs it is important that you have at least a basic understanding of the main marks so that you can interpret corrections that have been made or add your own corrections quickly, uniformly and without any ambiguity. The main proof correction marks you need to know are shown in the tables which follow.

Using the marks

•When proofreading, make a mark in the text to show exactly where the correction needs to be made. The marginal mark is used to specify what needs to be done.
• If there is more than one mark in a line, mark from left to right and use both margins if you need to.
• Every marginal mark should be followed by an oblique stroke, unless it is already followed by the insert mark or the amendment is a delete symbol.
• Circle any comments or notes you write in the margins to distinguish them from the corrections.
• For copy-editing (on hard copy), marks are made in the text only.

Handy proofreading tips

Effective proofreading takes time and practice but by following these tips you'll be able to spot mistakes more quickly and accurately:
• Set aside adequate time for proofreading. It requires concentration and should not be rushed.
• Before starting on a proofreading task, make sure you have easy access to a dictionary and thesaurus, and ensure that you have any relevant style guides for spellings, use of capitals and format/design.
• If possible, proofread the document several times and concentrate on different aspects each time, e.g. sense/tone, format, grammar/punctuation/use of language.
• Always double-check scientific, mathematical or medical symbols as they can often be corrupted during the typesetting process. Accented characters and currency symbols can also cause problems.
• If possible, have a version of the copy-edited text to refer to while you proofread – it might help solve minor inaccuracies or inconsistencies more quickly.

Marks/symbols for general instructions

INSTRUCTIONS	MARGIN	TEXT
Leave the text in its original state and ignore any marks that have been made, commonly referred to as 'stet'	⊘	– – – – under the characters to be left as they were
Query for the author/typesetter/printer/publisher.	⟨?⟩	A circle should be placed around text to be queried
Remove non-textual marks	✕	A circle should be placed around marks to be removed
End of change	/	None

Marks/symbols for inserting, deleting and changing text

INSTRUCTIONS	MARGIN	TEXT
Text to be inserted	New text, followed by ⋀	⋀
Additional text supplied separately	⋀ followed by a letter in a diamond which identifies additional text ◇Ⓐ	⋀
Delete a character	ℐ	/ through the character
Delete text	ℐ	⊢⊣ through text
Delete character and close space	ℐ	⊥ through the character
Delete text and close space	ℐ	⊟ through text
Character to replace marked character	New character, followed by /	/ through the character
Text to replace marked text	New text, followed by /	⊢⊣ through text

Marks/symbols for grammar and punctuation

INSTRUCTIONS	MARGIN	TEXT
Full stop	⊙	⋀ at insertion point or / through character
Comma	,	As above
Semi-colon	;	As above
Colon	⊙	As above
Hyphen	⊏⊐	As above
Single quote marks	⌄ or ⌄	As above
Double quote marks	⌄⌄ or ⌄⌄	As above
Apostrophe	⌄	As above
Ellipses or leader dots	⟨· · ·⟩	As above
Insert/replace dash	⊢16M⊣ Size of dash to be stated between uprights	As above

Marks/symbols for altering the look/style/layout of text

INSTRUCTIONS	MARGIN	TEXT
Put text in italics	⌐⌐⌐	 ——— under text to be changed
Remove italics, replace with roman text	 ⌐⌐⌐	Circle text to be changed
Put text in bold	 ∿∿∿	 ∿∿∿ under text to be changed
Remove bold	 ∿∿∿	Circle text to be changed
Put text in capitals	≡	≡ under text to be changed
Put text in small capitals	⹀	⹀ under text to be changed
Put text in lower case	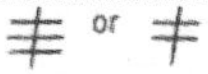 ⌿ or ⌿	Circle text to be changed
Change character to superscript	Y under character	/ through character to be changed
Insert a superscript character	Y under character	⋏ at point of insertion
Change character to subscript	⋏ above character	/ through character to be changed
Insert a subscript character	⋏ above character	⋏ at point of insertion
Remove bold and italics	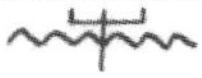 ∿�∿	Circle text to be changed
Paragraph break	 ⌐⌐	⌐⌐
Remove paragraph break, run on text	 ∼	∼
Indent text	⌐	⌐
Remove indent	⌐	⌐
Insert or replace space between characters or words	Y	⋏ at relevant point of insertion or / through character
Reduce space between characters or words	⋔	|
Insert space between lines or paragraphs	Mark extends into margin	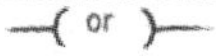 —(or)—
Reduce space between lines or paragraphs	Mark extends into margin	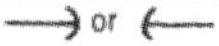 →) or (←
Transpose lines	⩵	⩵
Transpose characters or words	⌐⌐	⌐⌐
Close space between characters	⌣	character ⌣ character
Underline words	 (underline)	⬭ circle words
Take over character(s) or word(s) to next line/column/page	Mark extends into margin	⌐
Take back character(s) or word(s) to previous line/column/page	Mark extends into margin	⌐

Further resources

Butcher, Judith; Drake, Caroline and Leach, Maureen, *Butcher's Copy-editing: The Cambridge Handbook for Editors, Copy-editors and Proofreaders* (Cambridge University Press, 4th edn 2006)

Butterfield, J., *Fowler's Dictionary of Modern English Usage* (Oxford University Press, 4th edn 2015)

Ritter, R.M., *New Oxford Dictionary for Writers and Editors: The Essential A-Z Guide to the Written Word* (Oxford University Press, 2nd revised edn 2014)

The Chicago Manual of Style: The Essential Guide for Writers, Editors, and Publishers (University of Chicago Press, 17th edn 2017; www.chicagomanualofstyle.org/home.html)

Waddingham, Anne (ed.), *New Hart's Rules: The Oxford Style Guide* (Oxford University Press, 2nd edn 2014)

The Society for Editors and Proofreaders (SfEP), offers training, mentoring, support and advice for editors and proofreaders and a freely searchable directory of editorial professionals, www.sfep.org.uk (see page 375)

This article has been written by three professional editors. **Lauren Simpson** (lauren.simpson73@gmail.com) is a freelance editor, writer, publishing consultant and proofreader with over 20 years' experience. **Margaret Hunter** (daisyeditorial.co.uk) offers copy-editing, proofreading and layout services to businesses, organisations and independent authors. She joined the SfEP council in 2015. **Gerard M-F Hill** (much-better-text.com) served on the SfEP council from 2007 to 2016 and is currently its chartership adviser. He has worked as a copy-editor, indexer, proofreader, consultant and ghostwriter.

Copyright
Copyright questions

Gillian Haggart Davies answers questions to draw out some of the legal issues and explain the basics of how copyright works, or should work, for the benefit of the writer.

What is copyright?

Copyright is a negative right in the sense that it is not a right of possession but is a right of *exclusion*. However, if you know your rights it can be a strong legal tool because copyright law affords remedies in both the civil and criminal courts. Material will automatically be protected by copyright without registration (in the UK) if it is original, i.e. not copied. The onus is on you, the writer, and your publisher to do the work of protecting, policing and enforcing your valuable intellectual property. Copyright is different in every country – registration is not possible in the UK, Japan or the Netherlands; it is optional in the USA (for some works), China and India; and mandatory for some works in other jurisdictions (e.g. for some works in the Kyrgyz Republic, Mauritius and Nepal). Unfortunately, generally speaking, people do not respect copyright and there are ongoing issues to do with copyright, especially online, with large expanses of 'grey areas'.

I am a freelance writer and submitted an article to a magazine editor and heard nothing back. Six months later I read a feature in a Sunday newspaper which looks very similar. Can I sue someone?

Pitching ideas can be fraught with difficulty. In legal terms you do not have any protection under copyright law for 'ideas', but only for 'the expression of those ideas' – for the way in which the ideas have been 'clothed in words' to paraphrase a Learned Judge. It could be argued that in many ways this distinction between ideas and their expression does not work for writing and 'literary works'. But that won't help you in court or get you legal recompense if you are ripped off.

In the situation described, you would need to prove that your work came first in time; that your work was seen by the second writer or publisher; and that the second person copied unlawfully a 'substantial part' of your work (this is qualitative not quantitative), which these days involves a very woolly and subjective judicial comparison of one work weighed against the other. You would also need to be able to counter any claims that the subject matter is not capable of being monopolised by you and show that there is actual language copying. Further, you might then have to fend off counter-arguments from the other party that you did not have copyright in the first place. The other writer can rely on a 'defence' that she has 'incidentally included' the text; or that her use is 'fair dealing' (because she is using it for a permitted purpose, for example of reporting news or current affairs; or that it is for research for non-commercial purposes; is included in educational materials (Indian case); or for private use; or for 'criticism or review'; or that it is parody, pastiche or satire). These defences are actually referred to in the legislation as 'exceptions' and are very strict, i.e. they have always been difficult to make out. On parody and pastiche see a recent situation on using Enid Blyton headings in an Edinburgh Fringe performance

'Five Go Off on One!', reminding us that trade mark law also protects headings, which are generally too short to be protected by copyright law (www.thetimes.co.uk/article/five-go-to-their-solicitor-so-now-there-are-four-for-fringe-show-kwwdjwstr).

In addition, the person doing the 'copying' or publishing could say that she had an 'implied licence' from you to do so; or that she had a common law right under trusts law: this would arise, say, if she and you had been accustomed to dealing with each other in such a way that you commonly gave her original work and she used/copied it.

Avoid these difficulties by taking practical pre-emptive steps: mark your speculative pieces 'in confidence' and add '© Your Name 201X/202X'. Using the © symbol puts people on notice that you are aware of your rights. It would also have an effect later on if it came to litigation evidentially, i.e. if a person sees the copyright sign but nevertheless goes ahead and uses work without permission, the defence of 'innocent dissemination' cannot be relied upon.

You did not have copyright in the first place: if the subject matter is 'out there', i.e. common knowledge, copyright law may not protect the first work. The law is very contradictory in this area, as can be seen in these three cases which went to court: the persistent lifting of facts from another newspaper, even with rewriting, was deemed a copyright infringement; but copyright did protect a detailed sequence of ideas where precise wording was not copied; the fact that an author went to primary sources did not necessarily ensure that he was not copyright-infringing. However, copyright law does weigh heavily in favour of protecting the originator.

If a newspaper pays for an article and I then want to sell the story to a magazine, am I free under copyright law to do so?

Yes, provided that you have not assigned copyright or licensed exclusive use to the newspaper. When selling your work to newspapers or magazines, make it clear in writing that you are selling only First or Second Serial Rights, not your copyright.

Does being paid a kill fee affect my copyright in a given piece?

No, provided that you have not assigned or licensed your copyright to the magazine or newspaper. Broadly, never agree to an assignation; it is irreversible. Always license: those parts of copyright you want to license, for example print-only; UK only; not television rights, etc. Copyright rights are infinitely divisible and negotiable. If you have inadvertently or purposely granted copyright permission to the publisher and the publisher prints the piece, and you have taken a kill fee, don't forget that you can at least also claim 'secondary licence' income from the collective pool of monies collected on behalf of UK authors by both the ALCS (see page 425) and PLR (see page 400) if you are named on the piece. This may amount to only a tiny amount of money but it may take the sting out of the tail.

I am writing an (unauthorised) biography of a novelist. Can I quote her novels – since they are published and 'public domain'?

Using extracts and quotes is a very difficult area and there is no easy answer to this. If the author has definitely been deceased for 70 years or more, you may be fine; the work may have passed into the 'public domain'. However, unpublished works require caution. In general, unpublished works are protected by copyright as soon as they are 'expressed' and copyright belongs to the author until/unless published and rights are transferred to a publisher. Protection for unpublished works lasts for 50 years (usually); Crown copyright lasts for 125 years for unpublished works, etc.

Generally, copyright law requires you to ask permission and (usually) pay a fee for reuse. There is no exact recipe for the amount of money payable or the number of words you can 'take' before you need to pay. A law passed on 1 October 2014 says, somewhat vaguely, that you can take 'no more than is required for the specific purpose for which it is needed'. To quote from the legislation: 'Copyright in a work is not infringed by the use of a quotation from the work (whether for criticism or review or otherwise) provided that (a) the work has been made available to the public, (b) the use of the quotation is fair dealing with the work, (c) *the extent of the quotation is no more than is required by the specific purpose for which it is used* [emphasis added], and (d) the quotation is accompanied by a sufficient acknowledgement (*unless this would be impossible for reasons of practicality or otherwise* [emphasis added])' [Copyright and Rights in Performances (Quotation and Parody) Regulations 2014, No. 2356 (in force since 1 October 2014)]. But does this help? Is it not a bit woolly? In the biography example here, how much would 'no more than is necessary' be? A line from every work? A paragraph from every work? A page? The entirety of one work but excerpts only of others … or none at all? What if the biography is authorised, not unauthorised? These are all unanswered questions and untried by case law.

I want to use a quote from another book but don't know who owns the copyright. Can I just put it in quotes and use it?

If you cannot identify the source of the quote, we enter the murky waters of 'orphan works'. A scheme is now in place whereby you can buy a non-exclusive licence for the UK commercial or non-commercial use of an 'orphan work' from the IPO (Intellectual Property Office), for an application fee of £20 (for a single 'work', e.g. book), up to £80 for 30 'works', plus a licence fee, which will depend on the work and what you say about its use on the application form. The licence will last for seven years, which is the window of time allowed for a copyright owner to 'claim' the work (which goes on the IPO orphan works register when it becomes a licensed subject under the scheme).

The IPO will not grant an orphan-use licence if it thinks your use will be 'derogatory' of the copyright work, or if you are unable to show that you have made diligent attempts to trace the copyright owner, so the old rules about making such efforts now apply in statutory form. 'Diligent' efforts to trace the copyright owner could include contacting publishers, searching the WATCH (Writers Artists and their Copyright Holders) database (http://norman.hrc.utexas.edu/watch), and placing an advertisement in the *TLS*, the *Bookseller*, etc). Keep a record of all your efforts in case the copyright question comes back to bite you later, and use a disclaimer on your material. In an ideal world, all content would be tagged with details of what is permissible and how to contact the owner. [See IPO orphan works guidance at /www.gov.uk/government/collections/orphan-works-guidance; and the section above relating to quoting from a novel.]

The US Supreme Court ruled in 2015 that Google's use of scanned text extracts and images, used in its search engine to let users choose whether to go ahead and read/see the full work, was not in breach of copyright. The US Copyright Office said the defence is decided on a case-by-case basis. 'The distinction between what is fair use and what is infringement in a particular case will not always be clear or easily defined. There is no specific number of words, lines, or notes that may safely be taken without permission.

Acknowledging the source of the copyrighted material does not substitute for obtaining permission,' the US Copyright Office said. There are, however, at least four factors that judges must consider when deciding fair use: the purpose of use, the nature of the copyrighted work, the amount and substantiality of the portion taken, and the effect of the use upon the potential market. Google had urged the justices to side against the writers because, in the end, their works would be more readily discovered: 'Google Books gives readers a dramatically new way to find books of interest.' Google has stated that 'By formulating their own text queries and reviewing search results, users can identify, determine the relevance of, and locate books they might otherwise never have found.'

My publisher has forgotten to assert my copyright on the imprint page. What does that mean for me?

Technically, what is usually asserted on the imprint page is the moral right to be identified as author of the work. This 'paternity right' is lost if it is not 'asserted', so if it is not on the imprint page or anywhere else you lose the right. Moral rights are copyrights, separate to and additional to what we normally refer to as '('economic') copyright': they protect the personal side of creation, in that they are about the integrity of the work and the person/reputation of the creator; whereas the 'main'/economic copyright protection is there to ensure you get revenues from your work, for example licence fees and royalties. Both economic copyrights and moral rights were conferred by the 1988 UK statute and Berne Convention. They exist separately, so you can keep moral rights and 'licence away' copyright (economic copyrights). And so in reverse, even if your moral right to be identified as author is lost, your other rights – economic copyright and the moral right to not have your work subjected to 'derogatory treatment' – remain with you. Moral rights cannot be licensed or assigned because they are personal to the author, but they can be 'waived'; for example, a ghostwriter may well waive the right to be identified as author. Moral rights are very flexible and useful, but are not widely used.

I've found an illustration I want to use for the cover of a book that I'm self-publishing. I chose the picture (dated 1928) on purpose because the artist is out of copyright and the picture is in the 'public domain'. Why is the picture library, which holds the image, charging a reproduction fee?

You have to pay a reproduction fee under copyright law because of the separate copyright issue for photography. Because the original artwork was photographed, copyright vests separately in the photograph (of the artwork) as opposed to the artwork itself. It is a controversial area and one where the UK/US legal systems are split. Make sure that standing behind this is a contract with your publishing services provider identifying you as the copyright holder. Do not cede any rights. You should be granting the publisher a non-exclusive licence to publish your book only.

You should also be aware of changes which took effect in the UK in July 2016, which apply to all publishers of any illustrative or photographic pictures of 2D objects (e.g. chairs and furniture), 3D artworks, and possibly architecture (widely held by the design community as absurd). Publishers must now clear UK copyright permissions and pay any relevant fees for use of such images, unless that change to the law is undermined by judicial review, a sort of appeal procedure which could be instigated by, for example, the Publishers Association and/or the designers themselves, artists, photographers, publishers or authors.

I included someone's work on my blog, but as I blog for free and it's not a money-making thing, can I be sued for copyright infringement?

Yes you can. If the person alleging copyright infringement can show she has copyright in the work, that you had access to her work, can show you copied the whole of that work or a 'substantial part' of it, and that you did not have permission, you could well be infringing criminal and civil copyright laws. The point of copyright law – the economic as opposed to the moral rights aspect – is to protect the economic interests of the original copyright owner. If she can demonstrate that her position has been undermined by your blog in terms of her market share having diminished and/or that sales have been adversely affected, etc or if she can show that you have not paid her any reuse fee or asked permission or acknowledged her authorship, you are on very thin ice. Blogging news links, headlines, snippets of text and photos could soon be unlawful if a new EU Directive is passed, this is, however, subject to Brexit.

I retweeted, edited, two lines from Twitter. I tweet for free and it's not a money-making exercise; can I be sued for copyright infringement?

A similar answer to the above. 'Yes' or at least 'probably yes'. A ruling of the Court of Justice of the European Union (CJEU) interpreting EU copyright law strongly suggests copyright vests in anything that is the original author's creation, and in the EU case in point (*Infopaq*, 2009) that applied to an 11-word extract. This is in spite of the fact that there is a broader general principle in copyright that an 'insubstantial part' of a work does not enjoy copyright protection in the first place, and therefore there could be no breach. A good lawyer could argue either way as this is a grey area. The situation in the USA may be different but seems certainly arguable. An alternative way of viewing the situation is that this is a 'quote', and therefore 'exceptional', i.e. non-infringing under legislation introduced in 2014 (see above). But the issues have not been tested in court and, again, are wide open to argument. Keep an eye on the Great Repeal [Brexit] Bill.

In the UK, the courts have moved in a different direction on this matter. The old 'test' looked at the author's 'labour', skill and effort. In continental EU countries a literary, dramatic or artistic work must generally possess a creative element or express its author's personality. Blogging news links, headlines, snippets of text and photos could soon be unlawful if a new EU Directive is passed, subject to Brexit.

My book has been made available by a free book download site but I never agreed to this. What can I do?

Contact your publisher or ask the site direct (if it's a self-published work) to remove it from their website. If they do not act or do not respond, get legal advice: a lawyer will be able to issue a warning followed by a 'take down notice', followed if necessary by a court injunction. However, this is very difficult for cases worth under £10,000. And it is no understatement to say that the present system of access to justice and costs of lawyers and litigation will prove to be a significant hurdle for most writers. Take practical steps to protect copyright in your own works yourself by setting up a Google Alert for every title you own.

May I reproduce and share a selfie taken in an art gallery or museum?

If you take a selfie in front of a sculpture and use the photo for a T-shirt and post and share it on Facebook, that picture violates the sculptor's copyright protection against high-commercialisation. **Artists, designers, photographers and crafters are protected too**. Since 28 July 2016, those creating for sale reproduction furniture have been restricted by a tighter UK copyright law, and those designers now enjoy the same protection as is afforded to makers of 'plastic graphic works', musicians, writers, broadcasters and film-makers, i.e. 75 years (not 25) post creator's death, following the repeal of section 52 of the 1988 UK Act which applies to reproductions of e.g. anglepoise lamps, the 'Barcelona' chair, and Eames' furniture, all going up in price x12. In line with 'the rest of the EU', the loop exempting pre-1957 designs closed. The repeal of section 52 of the 1988 Act became effective on 28 July 2016 (see www.gov.uk/government/uploads/system/uploads/attach-ment_data/file/606207/160408_guidance_s52_final_web_accessible.pdf; www.klemchuk.com/ip-law-trends/selfie-legal-issues).

Gillian Haggart Davies MA (Hons), LLB is the author of *Copyright Law for Artists, Designers and Photographers* (A&C Black 2010) and *Copyright Law for Writers, Editors and Publishers* (A&C Black 2011).

See also...
- *Copyright Licensing Agency Ltd*, page 423
- *DACS (Design and Artists Copyright Society)*, page 427

Copyright Licensing Agency Ltd

Since 1983, CLA has been the recognised UK collective rights licensing body for text and images from book, journal and magazine content.

CLA provides rights, content and licensing services to customers in the academic, professional and public sectors. It performs collective licensing on behalf of its four members: ALCS (the Authors' Licensing and Collecting Society), PLS (Publishers' Licensing Services), DACS (The Design and Copyright Society) and PICSEL (Picture Industry Collecting Society for Effective Licensing). With streamlined workflow systems and over 35 years' experience, CLA is uniquely positioned to help content users access, copy and share the content they need while making sure copyright owners are paid the royalties they are due.

CLA's licences permit limited copying from print and digital publications. This copying includes photocopying, scanning and emailing of articles and extracts from books, journals and magazines, as well as digital copying from electronic publications, online titles and websites. CLA issues its licences to schools, further and higher education, businesses and government bodies. The money collected is distributed to the copyright owners to ensure that they are fairly rewarded for the use of their intellectual property.

Why was CLA established?

How CLA helps creators and users of copyright work

CLA provides content users with access to millions of titles worldwide. In return, CLA ensures that creators, artists, photographers and writers, along with publishers, are paid royalties for the copying, sharing and re-use of limited extracts of their published work.

Through this collective licensing system CLA is able to provide users with the simplest and most cost-effective means of obtaining authorisation for the use of their work.

CLA has licences which enable digitisation of existing print material, enabling users to scan and electronically send extracts from print copyright works as well as copy digital electronic and online publications, including websites.

Further information

The Copyright Licensing Agency Ltd
5th Floor, Shackleton House,
4 Battle Bridge Lane, London SE1 2HX
tel 020-7400 3100
email cla@cla.co.uk
website www.cla.co.uk

Who is licensed?

CLA offers licences to three principal sectors:
• education (schools, further and higher education);
• government (central departments, local authorities, public bodies); and
• business (businesses, industry and the professions).

The licences meet the specific needs of each sector and user groups within each sector. Depending upon the requirement, there are both blanket and transactional licences available. Every licence allows copying from most print and digital books, journals, magazines and periodicals published in the UK.

The international dimension

Many countries have established equivalents to CLA and the number of such agencies is set to grow. Nearly all these agencies, including CLA, are members of the International Federation of Reproduction Rights Organisations (IFRRO).

Through reciprocal arrangements covering 36 overseas territories, including the USA, Canada and most EU countries, CLA's licences allow copying from an expanding list of international publications. CLA receives monies from these territories for the copying of UK material abroad, passing it on to UK rights holders.

Distribution of licence fees

The fees collected from licensees are forwarded to ALCS, PLS, DACS and PISCEL for distribution to publishers, writers and visual artists. The allocation of fees is based on subscriptions, library holdings and detailed surveys of copying activity (see www.cla.co.uk/who-we-represet and read the 'Distribution Model Report'). CLA has collected and distributed over £1.4 billion as royalties to copyright owners since 1983. For the year 2016/17, £65.5 million was paid to creators and publishers in the UK and abroad.

Copyright. Made simple

The CLA exists to simplify copyright for content users and copyright owners. They help their customers to legally access, copy and share published content while making sure copyright owners are paid royalties for the use of their work.

Their rights, licences and innovative digital services (including the Digital Content Store for Higher Education; and the Education Platform for UK schools) make it easy for content users across the academic, professional and public sectors to use and manage content from books, journals, magazines and online publications, including websites. By doing so they simplify access to the work of 87,000 authors, 25,000 visual artists and 3,500 publishers and play an important part in supporting the creative industries.

See also...

- *Copyright questions,* page 417
- *Authors' Licensing and Collecting Society,* page 425
- *DACS (Design and Artists Copyright Society),* page 427

Authors' Licensing and Collecting Society

ALCS is the rights management society for UK writers.

ALCS is the largest writers' organisation in the UK with a membership of over 100,00. In the financial year of 2018/19, it paid 85,000 writers over £31.5 million (net) in royalties. Once you've paid your £36 lifetime membership fee, whatever you've earned in secondary royalties is paid into your bank account during twice yearly distributions. You can be part of this organisation which is committed to ensuring that writers' intellectual and moral rights are fully respected and fairly rewarded. ALCS represents all types of writers and includes educational, research and academic authors drawn from the professions - scriptwriters, adapters, playwrights, poets, editors and freelance journalists, across the print and broadcast media.

Established in 1977, ALCS (a non-profit company) was set up in the wake of the campaign to establish a Public Lending Right (see page 400) to help writers protect and exploit their collective rights. The organisation now represents the interests of all UK writers and aims to ensure that they are fairly compensated for any works that are copied, broadcast or recorded.

Internationally recognised as a leading authority on copyright matters and authors' interests, ALCS is committed to fostering an awareness of intellectual property issues among the writing community. It maintains a close watching brief on all matters affecting copyright, both in the UK and internationally, and makes regular representations to the UK government and the European Union.

ALCS collects fees that are difficult, time-consuming or legally impossible for writers and their representatives to claim on an individual basis, money that is nonetheless due to them. To date, it has distributed over £450 million in secondary royalties to writers. Over the years, ALCS has developed highly specialised knowledge and sophisticated systems that can track writers and their works against any secondary use for which they are due payment. A network of international contacts and reciprocal agreements with foreign collecting societies also ensures that UK writers are compensated for any similar use overseas.

The primary sources of fees due to writers are secondary royalties from the following:

Membership

Authors' Licensing and Collecting Society Ltd
5th Floor, Shackleton House,
4 Battle Bridge Lane, London SE1 2HX
tel 020-7264 5700
email alcs@alcs.co.uk
website www.alcs.co.uk
Chief Executive Owen Atkinson

Membership is open to all writers and successors to their estates at a one-off fee of £36 for Ordinary membership. Members of the Society of Authors, the Writers' Guild of Great Britain, National Union of Journalists, Chartered Institute of Journalists and British Association of Journalists have free Ordinary membership of ALCS. Operations are primarily funded through a commission levied on distributions and membership fees. The commission on funds generated for Ordinary members is currently 9.5%. Most writers will find that this, together with a number of other membership benefits, provides good value.

Photocopying and scanning

The single largest source of income, this is administered by the Copyright Licensing Agency (CLA; see page 423). Created in 1982 by ALCS and the Publishers' Licensing Services (PLS), CLA grants licences to users for copying books and serials. This includes schools, colleges, universities, central and local government departments, as well as the British Library, businesses and other institutions. Licence fees are based on the number of people who benefit and the number of copies made. The revenue from this is then split between the rights holders: authors, publishers and artists. Money due to authors is transferred to ALCS for distribution. ALCS also receives photocopying payments from foreign sources.

Foreign Public Lending Right

The Public Lending Right (PLR) system pays authors whose books are borrowed from public libraries. Through reciprocal agreements, ALCS members receive payment whenever their books are borrowed from German, Belgian, Dutch, French, Austrian, Estonian and Irish libraries. Please note that ALCS does not administer the UK Public Lending Right; this is managed directly by the UK PLR Office (see page 400).

ALCS also receives other payments from Germany. These cover the loan of academic, scientific and technical titles from academic libraries; extracts of authors' works in textbooks and the press, together with other one-off fees.

Simultaneous cable retransmission

This involves the simultaneous showing of one country's television signals in another country, via a cable network. Cable companies pay a central collecting organisation a percentage of their subscription fees, which must be collectively administered. This sum is then divided by the rights holders. ALCS receives the writers' share for British programmes containing literary and dramatic material and distributes it to them.

Educational recording

ALCS, together with the main broadcasters and rights holders, set up the Educational Recording Agency (ERA) in 1989 to offer licences to educational establishments. ERA collects fees from the licensees and pays ALCS the amount due to writers for their literary works.

Other sources of income include a blank tape levy and small, miscellaneous literary rights.

Tracing authors

ALCS is dedicated to protecting and promoting authors' rights and enabling writers to maximise their income. It is committed to ensuring that royalties due to writers are efficiently collected and speedily distributed to them. One of its greatest challenges is finding some of the writers for whom it holds funds and ensuring that they claim their money.

Any published author or broadcast writer could have some funds held by ALCS for them. It may be a nominal sum or it could run into several thousand pounds. Either call or visit the ALCS website – see **Membership** box for contact details.

DACS (Design and Artists Copyright Society)

Established by artists for artists, DACS is the UK's leading visual artists' rights management organisation.

As a not-for-profit organisation, DACS translates rights into revenues and recognition for a wide spectrum of visual artists. It collects and distributes royalties to visual artists and their estates through its different services, including Payback, Artist's Resale Right, Copyright Licensing and Artimage – in addition to lobbying, advocacy and legal advice for visual artists.

Contact details

DACS
33 Old Bethnal Green Road, London E2 6AA
tel 020-7336 8811
email info@dacs.org.uk
website www.dacs.org.uk

DACS is part of an international network of rights management organisations. Today DACS acts as a trusted broker for over 100,000 artists worldwide and in 2017 it distributed £15 million in royalties to artists and estates. See website for more information about DACS and its services.

Payback

Each year DACS pays a share of royalties to visual artists whose work has been reproduced in UK magazines and books or broadcast on UK television channels. DACS operates this service for situations where it would be impractical or near impossible for an artist to license their rights on an individual basis, for example when a university student wants to photocopy pages from a book that features their work.

Artist's Resale Right

The Artist's Resale Right entitles artists to a royalty each time their work is resold for more than €1,000 by an auction house, gallery or dealer. DACS ensures artists receive their royalties from qualifying sales not just in the UK but also from other countries in the European Economic Area (EEA). Since 1 January 2012 in the UK, artists' heirs and beneficiaries can now benefit from these royalties. (See website for details of eligibility criteria.)

Copyright Licensing

This service benefits artists and their estates when their work is reproduced for commercial purposes, for example on t-shirts or greetings cards, in a book or on a website. DACS can take care of everything on behalf of the artist, ensuring terms, fees and contractual arrangements are all in order and in their best interests. Artists who use this service are also represented globally through the DACS international network of rights management organisations.

Copyright facts

• Copyright is a right granted to visual artists under law.
• Copyright in all artistic works is established from the moment of creation – the only qualification is that the work must be original.

• There is no registration system in the UK; copyright comes into operation automatically and lasts the lifetime of the visual artist plus a period of 70 years after their death.

• After death, copyright is usually transferred to the visual artist's heirs or beneficiaries. When the 70-year period has expired, the work then enters the public domain and no longer benefits from copyright protection.

• The copyright owner has the exclusive right to authorise the reproduction (or copy) of a work in any medium by any other party.

• Any reproduction can only take place with the copyright owner's consent.

• Permission is usually granted in return for a fee, which enables the visual artist to derive some income from other people using his or her work.

• If a visual artist is commissioned to produce a work, he or she will usually retain the copyright unless an agreement is signed which specifically assigns the copyright. When visual creators are employees and create work during the course of their employment, the employer retains the copyright in those works.

See also...
• *Copyright questions,* page 417
• *Copyright Licensing Agency Ltd,* page 423

Finance
FAQs for writers

Peter Vaines, a tax barrister, addresses some frequently asked questions.

What can a working writer claim against tax?

A working writer is carrying on a business and can therefore claim all the expenses which are incurred wholly and exclusively for the purposes of that business. A list showing most of the usual expenses can be found in the article on *Income tax* (see page 431) but there will be other expenses that can be allowed in special circumstances. Strictly, only expenses which are incurred for the sole purpose of the business can be claimed; there must be no 'duality of purpose' so an item of expenditure cannot be divided into private and business parts. However, HM Revenue & Customs are now able to allow all reasonable expenses (including apportioned sums) where the amounts can be commercially justified.

Allowances can also be claimed for the cost of business assets such as a car, personal computers, printers and scanners and all other equipment (including books) which may be used by the writer. An allowance of 100% of the cost can now be claimed for most assets except cars, for which a lower allowance can be claimed. See the article on *Income tax* for further details of the deductions available in respect of capital expenditure.

Can I request interest on fees owed to me beyond 30 days of my invoice?

Yes. A writer is like any other person carrying on a business and is entitled to charge interest at a rate of 8% over bank base rate on any debt outstanding for more than 30 days – although the period of credit can be varied by agreement between the parties. It is not compulsory to claim the interest; it is your decision whether to enforce the right.

What can I do about bad debts?

A writer is in exactly the same position as anybody else carrying on a business over the payment of his or her invoices. It is generally not commercially sensible to insist on payment in advance but where the work involved is substantial (e.g. a book), it is usual to receive one third of the fee on signature, one third on delivery of the manuscript and the remaining one third on publication. On other assignments, perhaps not as substantial as a book, it could be worthwhile seeking 50% of the fee on signature and the other 50% on delivery. This would provide a degree of protection in case of cancellation of the assignment because of changes of policy or personnel at the publisher.

What financial disputes can I take to the Small Claims Court?

If somebody owes you money you can take them to the Small Claims section of your local County Court, which deals with financial disputes up to £10,000. It is much less formal than normal court proceedings and involves little expense. It is not necessary to have a solicitor. You fill in some forms, turn up and explain why you are owed the money (see www.gov.uk/make-court-claim-for-money/overview).

If I receive an advance, can I divide it between two tax years?

Yes. There is a system known as 'averaging'. This enables writers (and others engaged in the creation of literary or dramatic works or designs) to average the profits of two or more consecutive years if the profits for one year are less than 75% of the profits for the highest year. This relief can apply even if the work takes less than 12 months to create and it allows the writer to avoid the higher rates of tax which might arise if the income in respect of a number of years' work were all to be concentrated in a single year.

How do I make sure I am taxed as a self-employed person so that tax and National Insurance contributions are not deducted at source?

To be taxed as a self-employed person you have to make sure that the contract for the writing cannot be regarded as a contract of employment. This is unlikely to be the case with a professional author. The subject is highly complex but one of the most important features is that the publisher must not be in a position to direct or control the author's work. Where any doubt exists, the author might find the publisher deducting tax and National Insurance contributions as a precaution and that would clearly be highly disadvantageous. The author would be well advised to discuss the position with the publisher before the contract is signed to agree that he or she should be treated as self-employed and that no tax or National Insurance contributions will be deducted from any payments. If such agreement cannot be reached, professional advice should immediately be sought so that the detailed technical position can be explained to the publisher.

Is it a good idea to operate through a limited company?

It can be a good idea for a self-employed writer to operate through a company but generally only where the income is quite large. The costs of operating a company can outweigh any benefit if the writer is paying tax only at the basic rate. Where the writer is paying tax at the higher rate of 40% (or 45%), being able to retain some of the income in a company at a tax rate of only 19% is obviously attractive. However, this will be entirely ineffective if the writer's contract with the publisher would otherwise be an employment. The whole subject of operating through a company is complex and professional advice is essential.

When does it become necessary to register for VAT?

Where the writer's self-employed income (from all sources, not only writing) exceeds £85,000 in the previous 12 months or is expected to do so in the next 30 days, he or she must register for VAT and add VAT to all his/her fees. The publisher will pay the VAT to the writer, who must pay the VAT over to HM Revenue & Customs each quarter. Any VAT the writer has paid on business expenses and on the purchase of business assets can be deducted. It is possible for some authors to take advantage of the simplified system for VAT payments which applies to small businesses. This involves a flat rate payment of VAT without any need to keep records of VAT on expenses.

If I make a loss from my writing can I get any tax back?

Where a writer makes a loss, HM Revenue & Customs may suggest that the writing is only a hobby and not a professional activity, thereby denying any relief or tax deduction for the loss. However, providing the writing is carried out on a sensible commercial basis with an expectation of profits, any resulting loss can be offset against any other income the writer may have for the same or the previous year.

Income tax

Despite attempts by successive governments to simplify our taxation system, the subject has become increasingly complicated. Peter Vaines, a chartered accountant and barrister, gives a broad outline of taxation from the point of view of writers and other creative professionals. The proposals in the October 2018 Budget are broadly reflected in this article.

How income is taxed

Generally

Authors are usually treated for tax purposes as carrying on a profession and are taxed in a similar fashion to other self-employed professionals. This article is directed to self-employed persons only, because if a writer is employed he or she will be subject to the much less advantageous rules which apply to employment income.

Employed persons may try to shake off the status of 'employee' to attain 'freelance' status so as to qualify for the tax advantages, but such attempts meet with varying degrees of success. The problems involved in making this transition are considerable and space does not permit a detailed explanation to be made here – individual advice is necessary if difficulties are to be avoided.

Particular attention has been paid by HM Revenue & Customs (HMRC) to journalists and a number of sectors such as those engaged in the entertainment industry with a view to reclassifying them as employees so that PAYE is deducted from their earnings. This blanket treatment has been extended to other areas and, although it is obviously open to challenge by individual taxpayers, it is always difficult to persuade HMRC to change its views.

There is no reason why employed people cannot carry on a freelance business in their spare time. Indeed, aspiring authors, artists, musicians, etc often derive so little income from their craft that the financial security of an employment, perhaps in a different sphere of activity, is necessary. The existence of the employment is irrelevant to the taxation of the freelance earnings, although it is most important not to confuse the income or expenditure of the employment with that of the self-employed activity. HMRC is aware of the advantages which can be derived by an individual having 'freelance' income from an organisation of which he or she is also an employee, and where such circumstances are contrived, it can be extremely difficult to convince an Inspector of Taxes that a genuine freelance activity is being carried on. Where the individual operates through a company or partnership providing services personally to a particular client, and would be regarded as an employee if the services were supplied directly by the individual, additional problems arise from the notorious IR35 legislation and professional advice is essential.

For those starting in business or commencing work on a freelance basis there is a useful section called 'Working for yourself' on the GOV.UK website (www.gov.uk/working-for-yourself/overview).

Income

For income to be taxable it need not be substantial, nor even the author's only source of income; earnings from casual writing are also taxable but this can be an advantage because occasional writers do not often make a profit from their writing. The expenses incurred in connection with writing may well exceed any income receivable and the resultant loss may then be used to reclaim tax paid on other income. Certain allowable expenses and capital allowances may be deducted from the income, and these are set out in more detail below. The possibility of a loss being used as a basis for a tax repayment is fully appreciated by HMRC, which sometimes attempts to treat casual writing as a hobby so that any losses incurred cannot be used to reclaim tax; of course by the same token any income receivable would not be chargeable to tax. This treatment may sound attractive but it should be resisted vigorously because HMRC would not hesitate to change its mind when profits begin to arise. However, in exceptional or non-recurring writing, such as the autobiography of a sports personality or the memoirs of a politician, it could be better to be treated as pursuing a hobby and not as a professional author. Sales of copyright cannot be charged to income tax unless the recipient is a professional author – but the proceeds of sale of copyright may be charged to capital gains tax in the hands of an individual who is not a professional author.

Royalties

Where the recipient is a professional author, the proceeds of sale of copyright are taxable as income and not as capital receipts. Similarly, lump sums on account of, or in advance of royalties are also taxable as income in the year of receipt, subject to a claim for averaging relief (see below).

Copyright royalties are generally paid without deduction of income tax. However, if royalties are paid to a person who normally lives abroad, tax must be deducted by the payer or his agent at the time the payment is made unless arrangements are made with HMRC for payments to be made gross under the terms of a Double Taxation Agreement with the other country.

Grants, prizes and awards

Persons in receipt of grants from the Arts Council or similar bodies will be concerned whether or not such grants are liable to income tax. Many years ago HMRC issued a Statement of Practice after detailed discussions with the Arts Council regarding the tax treatment of the awards. Grants and other receipts of a similar nature were divided into two categories (see box) – those which were to be treated by HMRC as chargeable to tax and those which were not. Category A awards were considered to be taxable; awards made under category B were not chargeable to tax.

The Statement of Practice has not been withdrawn but it is no longer publicly available – although there is nothing to suggest that the treatment of awards in these categories will not continue to be treated in this way. In any event, the statement had no legal force and was merely an expression of the view of HMRC. It remains open to anybody in receipt of a grant or award to challenge the HMRC view on the merits of their own case.

The tax position of persons in receipt of literary prizes will generally follow a decision by the Special Commissioners in connection with the Whitbread Book Awards (now called the Costa Book Awards). In that case it was decided that the prize was not part of the author's professional income and accordingly not chargeable to tax. The precise details are not available because decisions of the Special Commissioners were not, at that time, reported unless an appeal was made to the High Court; HMRC chose not to appeal against this decision. Details of the many literary awards that are given each year start on page 379, and this decision is of considerable significance to the winners of these prizes. It would be unwise to assume that all such awards will be free of tax as the precise facts which were present in the case of the Whitbread awards may not be repeated in another case; however, it is clear that an author winning a prize has some very powerful arguments in his or her favour, should HMRC seek to charge tax on the award.

Allowable expenses

To qualify as an allowable business expense, expenditure has to be laid out wholly and exclusively for business purposes. Strictly there must be no 'duality of purpose', which means that expenditure cannot be apportioned to reflect private and business usage, for example food, clothing, telephone, travelling expenses, etc. However, HMRC will usually allow all reasonable expenses (including apportioned sums) where the amounts can be commercially justified.

It should be noted carefully that the expenditure does not have to be 'necessary', it merely has to be incurred 'wholly and exclusively' for business purposes. Naturally, however, expenditure of an outrageous and wholly unnecessary character might well give rise to a presumption that it was not really for business purposes. As with all things, some expenses are unquestionably allowable and some expenses are equally unquestionably not allowable – it is the grey area in between which gives rise to all the difficulties and the outcome invariably depends on negotiation with HMRC.

Arts Council awards

Arts Council category A awards

• Direct or indirect musical, design or choreographic commissions and direct or indirect commission of sculpture and paintings for public sites.
• The Royalty Supplement Guarantee Scheme.
• The Contract Writers' Scheme.
• Jazz bursaries.
• Translators' grants.
• Photographic awards and bursaries.
• Film and video awards and bursaries.
• Performance Art Awards.
• Art Publishing Grants.
• Grants to assist with a specific project or projects (such as the writing of a book) or to meet specific professional expenses such as a contribution towards copying expenses made to a composer or to an artist's studio expenses.

Arts Council category B awards

• Bursaries to trainee directors.
• Bursaries for associate directors.
• Bursaries to people attending full-time courses in arts administration (the practical training course).
• In-service bursaries to theatre designers and bursaries to trainees on the theatre designers' scheme.
• In-service bursaries for administrators.
• Bursaries for actors and actresses.
• Bursaries for technicians and stage managers.
• Bursaries made to students attending the City University Arts Administration courses.
• Awards, known as the Buying Time Awards, made not to assist with a specific project or professional expenses but to maintain the recipient to enable him or her to take time off to develop his or her personal talents. These include the awards and bursaries known as the Theatre Writing Bursaries, awards and bursaries to composers, awards and bursaries to painters, sculptors and print makers, literature awards and bursaries.

Finance

Great care should be taken when claiming a deduction for items where there may be a duality of purpose and negotiations should be conducted with more than usual care and courtesy – if provoked, the Inspector of Taxes may well choose to allow nothing. An appeal is always possible although unlikely to succeed as a string of cases in the Courts has clearly demonstrated. An example is the case of *Caillebotte* v. *Quinn* where the taxpayer (who normally had lunch at home) sought to claim the excess cost of meals incurred because he was working a long way from his home. The taxpayer's arguments failed because he did not eat only in order to work, one of the reasons for his eating was in order to sustain his life; a duality of purpose therefore existed and no tax relief was due.

Other cases have shown that expenditure on clothing can also be disallowed if it is the kind of clothing which is in everyday use, because clothing is worn not only to assist the pursuit of one's profession but also to accord with public decency. This duality of purpose may be sufficient to deny relief – even where the particular type of clothing is of a kind not otherwise worn by the taxpayer. In the case of *Mallalieu* v. *Drummond* a barrister failed to obtain a tax deduction for items of sombre clothing that she purchased specifically for wearing in Court. The House of Lords decided that a duality of purpose existed because clothing represented part of her needs as a human being.

Allowances

Despite the above, Inspectors of Taxes are not usually inflexible and the following list of expenses are among those generally allowed.

(a) Cost of all materials used up in the course of the work's preparation.

(b) Cost of typewriting and secretarial assistance, etc; if this or other help is obtained from one's spouse then it is entirely proper for a deduction to be claimed for the amounts paid for the work. The amounts claimed must actually be paid to the spouse and should be at the market rate, although some uplift can be made for unsocial hours, etc. Payments to a spouse are of course taxable in their hands and should therefore be most carefully considered. The spouse's earnings may also be liable for National Insurance contributions and it is important to take care because otherwise you may find that these contributions outweigh the tax savings. The impact of the National Minimum Wage should also be considered.

(c) All expenditure on normal business items such as postage, stationery, telephone, email, printers and scanners, agent's fees, accountancy charges, photography, subscriptions, periodicals, magazines, etc may be claimed. The cost of daily papers should not be overlooked if these form part of research material. Visits to theatres, cinemas, etc for research purposes may also be permissible (but not the costs relating to guests). Unfortunately, expenditure on all types of business entertaining is specifically denied tax relief.

(d) If work is conducted at home, a deduction for 'use of home' is usually allowed providing the amount claimed is reasonable. If the claim is based on an appropriate proportion of the total costs of rent, light and heat, cleaning and maintenance, insurance, etc (but not the Council Tax), care should be taken to ensure that no single room is used 'exclusively' for business purposes, because this may result in the Capital Gains Tax exemption on the house as the only or main residence being partially forfeited. However, it would be a strange household where one room was in fact used exclusively for business purposes and for no other purpose whatsoever (e.g. storing personal bank statements and other private papers); the usual practice is to claim a deduction on the basis that most or all of the rooms in the house are used at one time or another for business purposes, thereby avoiding any suggestion that any part was used exclusively for business purposes.

(e) The appropriate business proportion of motor running expenses may also be claimed although what is the appropriate proportion will naturally depend on the particular circumstances of each case. It should be appreciated that the well-known scale of benefits, whereby employees are taxed according to the size of the car's CO_2 emissions, do not apply to self-employed persons.

(f) It has been long established that the cost of travelling from home to work (whether employed or self-employed) is not an allowable expense. However, if home is one's place of work then no difficulties are likely to arise.

(g) Travelling and hotel expenses incurred for business purposes will normally be allowed but if any part could be construed as disguised holiday or pleasure expenditure, considerable thought would need to be given to the commercial reasons for the journey in order to justify the claim. The principle of 'duality of purpose' will always be a difficult hurdle in this connection – although not insurmountable.

(h) If a separate business bank account is maintained, any overdraft interest on the account will be an allowable expense. This is the only circumstance in which overdraft interest is allowed for tax purposes.

(i) Where capital allowances (see below) are claimed for a personal computer, laptop, tablet, printer, mobile phone, television, CD or DVD player, etc used for business purposes, the costs of maintenance and repair of the equipment may also be claimed.

Clearly many other allowable items may be claimed in addition to those listed. Wherever there is any reasonable business motive for some expenditure it should be claimed as a deduction although it is necessary to preserve all records relating to the expense. It is sensible to avoid an excess of imagination as this would naturally cause the Inspector of Taxes to doubt the genuineness of other expenses claimed.

The question is often raised whether the whole amount of an expense may be deducted or whether the VAT content must be excluded. Where VAT is reclaimed from HMRC by someone who is registered for VAT, the VAT element of the expense cannot be treated as an allowable deduction. Where the VAT is not reclaimed, the whole expense (inclusive of VAT) is allowable for income tax purposes.

Capital allowances

Where expenditure of a capital nature is incurred, it cannot be deducted from income as an expense – a separate and sometimes more valuable capital allowance being available instead. Capital allowances are given for many different types of expenditure, but authors and similar professional people are likely to claim only for 'plant and machinery'; this is a very wide expression which may include cars, desks, personal computers, laptops, tablets, printers, televisions, CD and DVD players used for business purposes. Plant and machinery will normally qualify for an allowance of 100%.

The reason capital allowances can be more valuable than allowable expenses is that they may be wholly or partly disclaimed in any year that full benefit cannot be obtained – ordinary business expenses cannot be similarly disclaimed. Where, for example, the income of an author is not large enough to bring him above the tax threshold, he would not be liable to tax and a claim for capital allowances would be wasted. If the capital allowances were to be disclaimed their benefit would be carried forward for use in subsequent years.

This would also be advantageous where the income is likely to be taxable at the higher rate of 40% (or the 45% rate) in a subsequent year. Careful planning with claims for capital allowances is therefore essential if maximum benefit is to be obtained.

Leasing is a popular method of acquiring fixed assets, and where cash is not available to enable an outright purchase to be made, assets may be leased over a period of time. Whilst leasing may have financial benefits in certain circumstances, in normal cases there is likely to be no tax advantage in leasing an asset where the alternative of outright purchase is available.

Books

The question of whether the cost of books is eligible for tax relief has long been a source of difficulty. The annual cost of replacing books used for the purposes of one's professional activities (e.g. the cost of a new *Children's Writers' & Artists' Yearbook* each year) has always been an allowable expense; the difficulty arose because the initial cost of reference books, etc (e.g. when commencing one's profession) was treated as capital expenditure but no allowances were due as the books were not considered to be 'plant'. However, the matter was clarified by the case of *Munby* v. *Furlong* in which the Court of Appeal decided that the initial cost of law books purchased by a barrister was expenditure on 'plant' and eligible for capital allowances. This is clearly a most important decision, particularly relevant to any person who uses expensive books in the course of exercising his or her profession.

Pension contributions

Where a self-employed person makes contributions to a pension scheme, those contributions are usually deductible.

These arrangements are generally advantageous in providing for a pension as contributions are usually paid when the income is high (and the tax relief is also high) and the pension (taxed as earned income when received) usually arises when the income is low and a lower rate of tax may be payable. There is also the opportunity to take part of the pension entitlement as a tax-free lump sum. It is necessary to take into account the possibility that the tax advantages could go into reverse. When the pension is paid it could, if rates rise again, be taxed at a higher rate than the rate of tax relief presently available for the contributions.

Each individual is allowed a lifetime pension pot (which has been gradually reduced and is now down to £1.03 million). When benefits crystallise, which will generally be when a pension begins to be paid, this is measured against the individual's lifetime pension pot with any excess being taxed on the individual at up to 55%.

Each individual also has an annual allowance for contributions to the pension fund, which is £40,000 but this is severely reduced for those paying the higher rates of tax. If the annual increase in an individual's rights under all registered schemes of which he is a member exceeds the annual allowance, the excess is chargeable to tax.

For many writers and artists this means that they can contribute a significant part of their earnings to a pension scheme (if they can afford to do so) without any of the previous complications. It is still necessary to be careful where there is other income giving rise to a pension because the whole of the pension entitlement has to be taken into account.

Flexible retirement is possible allowing members of occupational pension schemes to continue working while also drawing retirement benefits.

Class 4 National Insurance contributions

Allied to pensions is the payment of Class 4 National Insurance contributions, which are payable in addition to the normal Class 2 (self-employed) contributions. The rates are changed each year and for 2019/20 self-employed persons will be obliged to contribute 9% of their profits between the range £8,632–£50,000 per annum plus 2% on earnings above £50,000. This amount is collected in conjunction with the annual income tax liability.

Averaging relief
Relief for copyright payments

Professional authors and artists engaged in the creation of literary or dramatic works or designs may claim to average the profits of two or more consecutive years if the profits for one year are less than 75% of the profits for the highest year. This relief can apply even if the work took less than 12 months to create and is available to people who create works in partnership with others. It enables the creative artist to utilise their allowances fully and to avoid the higher rates of tax which might apply if all the income were to arise in a single year.

Collection of tax: self-assessment

Under 'self-assessment' you submit your tax return and work out your tax liability for yourself. If you get it wrong, or if you are late with your tax return or the payment of tax, interest and penalties will be charged. Completing a tax return is a daunting task but the term 'self-assessment' is not intended to imply that individuals have to do it themselves; they can (and often will) engage professional help. The term is only intended to convey that it is the taxpayer, and not HMRC, who is responsible for getting the tax liability right and for it to be paid on time.

The deadline for filing your tax return is 31 January following the end of the tax year. You must now file online; a paper tax return cannot be filed in most cases.

Income tax on self-employed earnings remains payable in two instalments on 31 January and 31 July each year. Because the accurate figures may not necessarily be known, these payments in January and July will therefore be only payments on account based on the previous year's liability. The final balancing figure will be paid the following 31 January together with the first instalment of the liability for the following year.

When HMRC receives the self-assessment tax return, it is checked to see if there is anything obviously wrong; if there is, a letter will be sent to you immediately. Otherwise, HMRC has 12 months from the filing date in which to make further enquiries; if it doesn't, it will have no further opportunity to do so and your tax liabilities are final – unless there is an error or an omission. In that event, HMRC can raise an assessment later to collect any extra tax together with appropriate penalties. It is essential that all records relevant to your tax return are retained for at least 12 months after the filing date in case they are needed by HMRC. For the self-employed, the record-keeping requirement is much more onerous because the records need to be kept for nearly six years. If you claim a tax deduction for an expense, it will be necessary to have a receipt or other document proving that the expenditure has been made. Because the existence of the underlying records is so important to the operation of self-assessment, HMRC will treat them very seriously and there are penalties for a failure to keep adequate records.

Finance

Interest

Interest is chargeable on overdue tax at a variable rate, which is presently 3.25% per annum. It does not rank for any tax relief, which can make HMRC an expensive source of credit.

However, HMRC can also be obliged to pay interest (known as repayment supplement) tax-free where repayments are delayed. The rules relating to repayment supplement are less beneficial and even more complicated than the rules for interest payable but they do exist and can be very welcome if a large repayment has been delayed for a long time. Unfortunately, the rate of repayment supplement is only 0.5% and is always less than the rate charged by HMRC on overdue tax.

Value added tax

The activities of writers, painters, composers, etc are all 'taxable supplies' within the scope of VAT and chargeable at the standard rate. (Zero rating which applies to publishers, booksellers, etc on the supply of books does not extend to the work performed by writers.) Accordingly, authors are obliged to register for VAT if their income for the past 12 months exceeds £85,000 or if their income for the coming month will exceed that figure.

Delay in registering can be a most serious matter because if registration is not effected at the proper time, HMRC can (and invariably do) claim VAT from all the income received since the date on which registration should have been made. As no VAT would have been included in the amounts received during this period the amount claimed by HMRC must inevitably come straight from the pocket of the author.

The author may be entitled to seek reimbursement of the VAT from those whom he or she ought to have charged VAT but this is obviously a matter of some difficulty and may indeed damage his or her commercial relationships. Apart from these disadvantages there is also a penalty for late registration. The rules are extremely harsh and are imposed automatically even in cases of innocent error. It is therefore extremely important to monitor the income very carefully because if in any period of 12 months the income exceeds the £85,000 limit, HMRC must be notified within 30 days of the end of the period. Failure to do so will give rise to an automatic penalty. It should be emphasised that this is a penalty for failing to submit a form and has nothing to do with any real or potential loss of tax. Furthermore, whether the failure was innocent or deliberate will not matter. Only the existence of a 'reasonable excuse' will be a defence to the penalty. However, a reasonable excuse does not include ignorance, error, a lack of funds or reliance on any third party.

However, it is possible to regard VAT registration as a privilege and not a penalty, because only VAT registered persons can reclaim VAT paid on their expenses such as stationery, telephone, professional fees, etc and even computers and other plant and machinery (excluding cars). However, many find that the administrative inconvenience – the cost of maintaining the necessary records and completing the necessary forms – more than outweighs the benefits to be gained from registration and prefer to stay outside the scope of VAT for as long as possible.

Overseas matters

The general observation may be made that self-employed persons resident and domiciled in the UK are not well treated with regard to their overseas work, being taxable on their worldwide income. It is important to emphasise that if fees are earned abroad, no tax saving can be achieved merely by keeping the money outside the country. Although exchange control regulations no longer exist to require repatriation of foreign earnings, such income remains taxable in the UK and must be disclosed to HMRC; the same applies to interest or other income arising on any investment of these earnings overseas. Accordingly, whenever foreign earnings are likely to become substantial, prompt and effective action is required to limit the impact of UK and foreign taxation. In the case of non-resident authors it is important that arrangements concerning writing for publication in the UK, for example in newspapers, are undertaken with great care. A case concerning the wife of one of the great train robbers who provided detailed information for a series of articles published in a Sunday newspaper is most instructive. Although she was acknowledged to be resident in Canada for all the relevant years, the income from the articles was treated as arising in this country and fully chargeable to UK tax.

The UK has double taxation agreements with many other countries and these agreements are designed to ensure that income arising in a foreign country is taxed either in that country or in the UK. Where a withholding tax is deducted from payments received from another country (or where tax is paid in full in the absence of a double taxation agreement), the amount of foreign tax paid can usually be set off against the related UK tax liability.

Many successful authors can be found living in Eire because of the complete exemption from tax which attaches to works of cultural or artistic merit by persons who are resident there. However, such a step should only be contemplated after giving careful regard to all the other domestic and commercial considerations, and specialist advice is essential if the exemption is to be obtained and kept; a careless breach of the conditions could cause the exemption to be withdrawn with catastrophic consequences. Consult the Revenue Commissioners in Dublin (www.revenue.ie) for further information concerning the precise conditions to be satisfied for exemption from tax in the Republic of Ireland.

Companies

When authors become successful the prospect of paying tax at high rates may drive them to take hasty action, such as the formation of a company, which may not always be to their advantage. Indeed some authors seeing the exodus into tax exile of their more successful colleagues even form companies in low tax areas in the hope of saving large amounts of tax. HMRC is fully aware of these possibilities and has extensive powers to charge tax and combat avoidance. Accordingly, such action is just as likely to increase tax liabilities and generate other costs and should never be contemplated without expert advice; some very expensive mistakes are often made in this area which are not always able to be remedied.

To conduct one's business through the medium of a company can be a very effective method of mitigating tax liabilities, and providing it is done at the right time and under the right circumstances very substantial advantages can be derived. However, if done without due care and attention the intended advantages will simply evaporate. At the very least it is essential to ensure that the company's business is genuine and conducted properly with regard to the realities of the situation. If the author continues his/her activities unchanged, simply paying all the receipts from his/her work into a company's bank account, he/she cannot expect to persuade HMRC that it is the company and not himself/herself who is entitled to, and should be assessed to tax on, that income.

It must be strongly emphasised that many pitfalls exist which can easily eliminate all the tax benefits expected to arise by the formation of the company. For example, company

Finance

directors are employees of the company and will be liable to pay much higher National Insurance contributions; the company must also pay the employer's proportion of the contribution and a total liability of nearly 26% of gross salary may arise. This compares most unfavourably with the position of a self-employed person. Moreover, on the commencement of the company's business the individual's profession will cease and the possibility of revisions being made by HMRC to earlier tax liabilities means that the timing of a change has to be considered very carefully.

The tax return

No mention has been made above of personal reliefs and allowances; this is because these allowances and the rates of tax are subject to constant change and are always set out in detail in the explanatory notes which accompany the tax return. The annual tax return is an important document and should be completed promptly with extreme care. If filling in the tax return is a source of difficulty or anxiety, *Money Which? – Tax Saving Guide* (Consumer Association, annual, March) is very helpful.

Peter Vaines is a barrister at Field Court Tax Chambers in Gray's Inn. He writes and speaks widely on tax matters.

See also...

- *FAQs for writers*, page 429
- *National Insurance contributions and social security benefits*, page 441

Finance

National Insurance contributions and social security benefits

Most people who work in Great Britain either as an employee or as a self-employed person are liable to pay Class 1 National Insurance contributions. The law governing this subject is complex and Peter Arrowsmith FCA and Sarah Bradford BA (HONS), FCA, CTA (FELLOW) summarise it here for the benefit of writers and artists. This article also contains an outline of the benefits system and should be regarded as a general guide only.

All contributions are payable in respect of years ending on 5 April. See box (below) for the classes of contributions.

Employed or self-employed?

Employed earners pay Class 1 contributions and self-employed earners pay Class 2 and Class 4 contributions. It is therefore essential to know the status of a worker to ensure that the correct class of contribution is paid. The question as to whether a person is employed under a contract *of* service and is thereby an employed earner liable to Class 1 contributions, or performs services (either solely or in partnership) under a contract *for* service and is thereby self-employed and liable to Class 2 and Class 4 contributions, often has to be decided in practice. One of the more longstanding guides can be found in the case of *Market Investigations Ltd* v. *Minister of Social Security* (1969 2 WLR 1) when Cooke J. remarked:

Classes of contributions

Class 1 Payable by employees (primary contributions) and their employers (secondary contributions), based on earnings.

Class 1A Payable only by employers in respect of all taxable benefits in kind.

Class 1B Payable only by employers in respect of PAYE Settlement Agreements entered into by them.

Class 2 Weekly flat rate contributions payable by the self-employed.

Class 3 Weekly flat rate contributions, payable on a voluntary basis in order to provide, or make up entitlement to, certain social security benefits.

Class 3A Voluntary contributions payable from 12 October 2015 until 5 April 2017 by those reaching state pension age before 6 April 2016. Amount depends on age.

Class 4 Payable by the self-employed in respect of their trading or professional income, based on earnings.

'…the fundamental test to be applied is this: "Is the person who has engaged himself to perform these services performing them as a person in business on his own account?" If the answer to that question is "yes", then the contract is a contract for services. If the answer is "no", then the contract is a contract of service. No exhaustive list has been compiled and perhaps no exhaustive list can be compiled of the considerations which are relevant in determining that question, nor can strict rules be laid down as to the relative weight which the various considerations should carry in particular cases. The most that can be said is that control will no doubt always have to be considered, although it can no longer be regarded as the sole determining factor; and that factors which may be of importance are such matters as:

• whether the man performing the services provides his own equipment,
• whether he hires his own helpers,
• what degree of financial risk he takes,
• what degree of responsibility for investment and management he has, and

• whether and how far he has an opportunity of profiting from sound management in the performance of his task.'

The above case has often been considered subsequently in Tribunal cases, but there are many factors to take into account. Increasingly, workers do not fit neatly into either category, and following the Taylor Review into Modern Working Practices, the government consulted on proposals to make the employment status rules clearer. The consultation document is available on the GOV.UK website at www.gov.uk/government/consultations/employment-status. Further guidance on employment status can be found on the GOV.UK website at www.gov.uk/government/collections/employed-or-self-employed. HMRC also produce a check employment status for tax (CEST) tool which can be used to determine if a worker is an employed or self-employed earner. This tool can be accessed at www.gov.uk/guidance/check-employment-status-for-tax.

Exceptions

There are exceptions to the above rules, those most relevant to artists and writers being:
• the employment of a spouse or civil partner is disregarded for National Insurance purposes unless it is for the purposes of a trade or profession (e.g. the employment of their spouse by an author would not be disregarded and would result in a liability for contributions if their spouse's salary reached the minimum levels);
• the employment of certain relatives in a private dwelling house in which both employee and employer reside is disregarded for social security purposes provided the employment is not for the purposes of a trade or business carried out at those premises by the employer. This would cover the employment of a relative (as defined) as a housekeeper in a private residence.

Personal service companies

Since 6 April 2000, those who have control of their own 'one-man service companies' are subject to special rules (commonly referred to as IR35). If the work carried out by the owner of the company for the company's customers would be – but for the one-man company – considered as an employment of that individual (i.e. rather than self-employment), a deemed salary may arise. If it does, then some or all of the company's income will be treated as salary liable to PAYE and National Insurance contributions (NICs). This will be the case whether or not such salary is actually paid by the company. The same situation may arise where the worker owns as little as 5% of a company's share capital.

The calculations required by HMRC are complicated and have to be done very quickly at the end of each tax year (even if the company's year-end does not coincide). It is essential that affected businesses seek detailed professional advice about these rules which may also, in certain circumstances, apply to partnerships.

The rules, as they apply where the end client is a public service body, were reformed from 6 April 2017. Under these rules, the responsibility for deciding whether IR35 applies (i.e. would the worker be an employee if employed under a direct contract) is shifted to the public sector body and responsibility for deducting PAYE and NIC due on the deemed payment (which is calculated without the 5% cost allowance) is transferred to the fee-payer, which may be an agency.

Following an announcement at the time of the 2018 Spring Statement, the government confirmed that they would be consulting on reforms where the end client is in the private sector, and looking at extending the scope of the public sector reforms where services are provided via an intermediary to a private-sector end client. An initial consultation ran from May to August 2018, a summary of responses to which was published at the time of the Autumn 2018 Budget (see www.gov.uk/government/consultations/off-payroll-working-in-the-private-sector). Also at the time of the Autumn 2018 Budget, the government announced that the private sector reforms would apply from April 2020 but would only apply to medium and large companies. A further consultation document was published in March 2019 seeking views on the scope and operation of the reforms. Comments were sought by 28 May 2019. The consultation document is available on the gov.uk website at www.gov.uk/government/consultations/off-payroll-working-rules-from-april-2020.

In order to escape the application of the IR35 rules, a number of workers arranged their engagements through 'managed service companies', etc where the promoter is heavily involved in all the company management to the exclusion of the workers themselves. Such companies are subject to similar, but different, rules, which apply from 6 April 2007 for tax and 6 August 2007 for NICs. See www.gov.uk/business-tax/ir35.

State pension age

Workers, both employed and self-employed, stop paying NICs once they reach state pension age. However, employers must continue to pay secondary Class 1 contributions in respect of earnings paid to employees who have reached state pension age.

The current state pension age for men and women was equalised at age 65 on the 6 November 2018; the state pension age for women having gradually increased from 60 to 65 during the period from 6 April 2010 to 5 November 2018. The state pension age for both men and women will gradually rise to 66, reaching this on 6 September 2020. The state pension age will be further increased from 66 to 67 between 2026 and 2028. Provisions included in the Pensions Act 2014 provide for the state pension age to be reviewed every 5 years. In July 2017, following such a review, the government announced plans to bring forward the increase in the state pension age to 65 to between 2037 and 2039, rather than between 2044 and 2046 as under existing legislation. Until November 2018, women will reach state pension age on the dates shown below, depending on their date of birth. The state pension age for women will be equalised with men from November 2018. Men will reach state pension age at age 65 until November 2018. Thereafter, the state pension age for both men and women will increase from 65 to 66.

Date of birth	Date state pension age reached	Pension age
6 Jan. 1954 to 5 Feb. 1954	6 May 2019	65 yrs 3 mths–65 yrs 4 mths
6 Feb. 1954 to 5 March 1954	6 July 2019	65 yrs 4 mths–65 yrs 5 mths
6 March 1954 to 5 April 1954	6 Sept. 2019	65 yrs 5 mths - 65 yrs 6 mths
6 April 1954 to 5 May 1954	6 Nov. 2019	65 yrs 6 mths - 65 yrs 7 mths
6 May 1954 to 5 June 1954	6 Jan. 2020	65 yrs 7 mths - 65 yrs 8 mths
6 June 1954 to 5 July 1954	6 March 2020	65 yrs 8 mths - 65 yrs 9 mths

The state pension age for **men** born before 6 December 1953 is 65.

Men and women born between 6 December 1953 and 5 January 1954 reached state pension age on 6 March 2019 (65 yrs 2 mths–65 yrs 3 mths).

Finance

Class 1 contributions

Primary Class 1 contributions are payable by employed earners and secondary Class 1 contributions are payable by self-employed workers by reference to their earnings.

Primary Class 1 National Insurance contributions are payable by employees on earnings that exceed the primary threshold (£166 per week for 2019/20) and by employers on earnings that exceed the secondary threshold (£166 per week for 2019/20). However, where the employee is under the age of 21 or an apprentice under the age of 25, employer contributions are only payable on earnings that exceed, respectively, the upper secondary threshold for under 21s or the apprentice upper secondary threshold. Both thresholds are aligned with the upper earnings limit for primary Class 1 contributions (£962 per week for 2019/20). Contributions are normally collected via the PAYE tax deduction machinery, and there are penalties for late submission of returns and for errors therein and also for PAYE and NICs paid late on more than one occasion in the tax year. Interest is charged automatically on PAYE and social security contributions paid late.

Employees' liability to pay

Contributions are payable by any employee who is aged 16 years and over (even though they may still be at school) and who is paid an amount equal to, or exceeding, the primary earnings threshold (£166 per week for 2019/20). Where the employee has earnings between the lower earnings limit and the primary threshold, contributions are payable at a notional zero rate. This preserves the employee's contributions record and entitlement to the state pension and contributory benefits. Nationality is irrelevant for contribution purposes and, subject to special rules covering employees not normally resident in Great Britain, Northern Ireland or the Isle of Man, or resident in EEA countries or those with which there are reciprocal agreements, contributions must be paid whether the employee concerned is a British subject or not provided he/she is gainfully employed in Great Britain.

Persons over state pension age are exempt from liability to pay primary contributions, even if they have not retired. However, the fact that an employee may be exempt from liability does not relieve an employer from liability to pay secondary contributions in respect of that employee.

Employees' (primary) contributions

From 6 April 2019, the rate of employees' contributions on earnings from the employee earnings threshold (£166 per week) to the upper earnings limit (£962 per week) is 12%. Contributions are payable at a rate of 2% on earnings above the upper earnings limit. Certain married women who made appropriate elections before 12 May 1977 may be entitled to pay a reduced rate of 5.85% on earnings between the primary threshold and upper earnings limit. However, they have no entitlement to benefits in respect of these contributions. Where a reduced rate election is in force, contributions are payable at the additional rate of 2% on earnings above the upper earnings limit.

Employers' (secondary) contributions

All employers are liable to pay contributions on the gross earnings of employees above the age of 16 where their earnings exceed the secondary earnings threshold (£166 per week for 2019/20). However, where the employee is under 21 or an apprentice under the age of 25, employer contributions are only payable on earnings in excess of, respectively, the upper secondary threshold for under 21s or the apprentice upper secondary threshold (AUST).

Both thresholds are set at £962 per week for 2019/20. As mentioned above, an employer's liability is not reduced as a result of employees being exempted from contributions, or being liable to pay only the reduced rate (5.85%) of contributions.

For earnings paid on or after 6 April 2019, employers are liable at a rate of 13.8% on earnings paid above the secondary earnings threshold (or, where the employee is under 21 or an apprentice under the age of 25, above, respectively, the upper secondary threshold under 21a or the AUST). Most employers are entitled to an annual employment allowance, which is set at £3,000 for 2019/20 and which is offset against their secondary Class 1 liability. However, the allowance is not available to employers where the sole employee is a director. From 6 April 2020, availability of the employment allowance will be restricted to employers with a national insurance contributions bill below £100,000 in the previous tax year. The allowance is claimed through the employer's real time information (RTI) software.

The employer is responsible for the payment of both employees' and employer's contributions, but is entitled to deduct the employees' contributions from the earnings on which they are calculated. Effectively, therefore, the employee suffers a deduction in respect of his or her social security contributions in arriving at his weekly or monthly wage or salary. Special rules apply to company directors and persons employed through agencies.

Items included in, or excluded from, earnings

Contributions are calculated on the basis of a person's gross earnings from their employment.

Earnings include salary, wages, overtime pay, commissions, bonuses, holiday pay, payments made while the employee is sick or absent from work, payments to cover travel between home and office, and payments under the statutory sick pay, statutory maternity pay, statutory paternity pay and statutory adoption pay schemes.

However, certain payments, some of which may be regarded as taxable income for income tax purposes, are ignored for Class 1 purposes. These include:
• certain gratuities paid other than by the employer;
• redundancy payments and some payments in lieu of notice;
• certain payments in kind;
• reimbursement of specific expenses incurred in the carrying out of the employment;
• benefits given on an individual basis for personal reasons (e.g. birthday presents);
• compensation for loss of office.

Rates of Class 1 contributions and earnings limits from 6 April 2019

Earnings per week	Rates payable on earnings in each band	
	Employee	Employer
£	%	%
Below 118.00	–	–
118.00–165.99	0**	–
166.00–961.99	12	13.8***
Over 962.00	2	13.8

** Contributions payable at a notional zero rate.
*** No employer contributions where employee is under 21 or an apprentice under 25.

Booklet CWG 2 (updated annually) gives a list of items to include in or exclude from earnings for Class 1 contribution purposes (available from www.gov.uk). Some such items may, however, be liable to Class 1A (employer-only) contributions.

Class 1A and Class 1B contributions

Class 1A contributions are employer-only contributions payable in respect of most taxable benefits. All taxable benefits provided to employees regardless of the employee's earnings rate are liable to Class 1A National Insurance contributions unless the benefit in question is within the charge to Class 1 or 1B or specifically exempt. Class 1A contributions are payable at a rate of 13.8%.

Class 1B contributions are payable by employers using PAYE Settlement Agreements in respect of small and/or irregular expense payments and benefits, etc. This rate is also 13.8%.

Class 2 contributions

Class 2 contributions are payable at the weekly rate of £3.00 as from 6 April 2019. They provide the mechanism by which the self-employed earn entitlement to the state pension and certain contributory benefits. They are payable annually with income tax and Class 4 contributions via the self-assessment system and are due by 3 January after the end of the tax year to which they relate. The liability is based on the number of weeks of self-employment in the tax year. Certain persons are exempt from Class 2 liability as follows:
• a person over state pension age;
• a person who has not attained the age of 16;
• a married woman or, in certain cases, a widow, either of whom elected prior to 12 May 1977 not to pay Class 2 contributions;
• persons with earnings below the small profits threshold (see below);
• persons not ordinarily self-employed (see below).
Plans to reform National Insurance contributions for the self-employed, which involved the abolition of Class 2 contributions and the reform of Class 4 contributions, which were due to take place from 6 April 2019 have been put on hold. Consequently, the self-employed will, where their profits are in excess of the relevant thresholds, continue to pay Class 2 and Class 4 contributions for 2019/20.

Small profits threshold

No liability to Class 2 contributions arises unless earnings from self-employment exceed the small profits threshold, which is set at £6,365 for 2019/20. However, those with earnings from self-employment which are below the small profits threshold have the option to pay Class 2 contributions voluntarily. This can be a cheap way of preserving their state pension record where the person is not also paying Class 1 contributions or recieiving NIC credits.

Persons not ordinarily self-employed

Part-time self-employed activities (including as a writer or artist) are disregarded for contribution purposes if the person concerned is not ordinarily employed in such activities and has a full-time job as an employee. There is no definition of 'ordinarily employed' for this purpose.

Payment of contributions

Class 2 contributions are payable via the self-assessment system with income tax and Class 4 contributions. Class 2 contributions for 2019/20 are due by 31 January 2021.

Class 3 and Class 3A contributions

Class 3 contributions are payable voluntarily. For 2019/20 they are payable at the weekly rate of £15.00 per week by persons aged 16 or over with a view to enabling them to qualify for a limited range of benefits if their contribution record is not otherwise sufficient. In general, Class 3 contributions can be paid by employees, the self-employed and the non-employed.

Broadly speaking, no more than 52 Class 3 contributions are payable for any one tax year, and contributions cannot be paid in respect of tax years after the one in which the individual concerned reaches state pension age. Class 3 contributions may be paid by monthly direct debit, quarterly bill or by annual cheque in arrears.

Class 3A contributions were introduced from October 2015, payable for a limited window, and provided those who reach state pension age before 6 April 2016 with an opportunity to top up their state pension. The Class 3A contribution 'bought' up to £25 per week of additional state pension. The amount of the Class 3A contribution depends on the contributor's age and was payable by 5 April 2017.

Class 4 contributions

In addition to Class 2 contributions, self-employed persons are liable to pay Class 4 contributions. These are calculated at the rate of 9% on the amount of profits or gains chargeable to income tax which exceed the lower profits limit (£8,632 per annum for 2019/20) but which do not exceed the upper profits limit (£50,000 per annum for 2019/2020). Profits above the upper profits limit attract a Class 4 charge at the rate of 2%. The income tax profit on which Class 4 contributions are calculated is after deducting capital allowances and losses, but before deducting personal tax allowances or retirement annuity or personal pension or stakeholder pension plan premiums.

Class 4 contributions produce no additional benefits. As part of the proposed reforms to National Insurance contributions for the self-employed, Class 2 contributions were to have been abolished from April 2019 and Class 4 contributions are to be reformed from the same time to provide benefit entitlement. However, the reforms have been put on hold and the exisiting regime for national insurance for the self-employed, under which Class 4 contributions confer no state pension or benefit entitlement, remains in place for 2019/20.

Payment of contributions

In general, Class 4 contributions are self-assessed and paid to HMRC together with the income tax as a result of the self-assessment income tax return, and accordingly the contributions are due and payable at the same time as the income tax liability on the relevant profits. Under self-assessment, payments on account of Class 4 contributions are payable at the same time as interim payments of tax.

Class 4 exemptions

The following persons are exempt from Class 4 contributions:
• persons over state pension age at the start of the tax year (i.e. on 6 April);

- an individual not resident in the UK for income tax purposes in the year of assessment;
- persons whose earnings are not 'immediately derived' from carrying on a trade, profession or vocation;
- a person under 16 years old on 6 April of the year of assessment;
- persons not ordinarily self-employed.

Married persons, civil partners and partnerships

Under independent taxation, each spouse or civil partner is responsible for his or her own Class 4 liability.

In partnerships, each partner's liability is calculated separately. If a partner also carries on another trade or profession, the profits of all such businesses are aggregated for the purposes of calculating their Class 4 liability.

When an assessment has become final and conclusive for the purposes of income tax, it is also final and conclusive for the purposes of calculating Class 4 liability.

Maximum contributions

There is a limit to the total liability for social security contributions payable by a person who is employed in more than one employment, or is also self-employed or a partner. Where a person would otherwise pay more than the permitted maximum it may be possible to defer some contributions. The calculations are complex and guidance on the permitted maximum and deferment can be found on the GOV.UK website (see www.gov.uk/defer-self-employed-national-insurance).

Social security benefits

Benefits may be contributory (i.e. dependent upon set levels of social security contributions and/or NIC-able earnings arising in all or part of one or more tax years) or means-tested (i.e. subject to a full assessment of the income and capital of the claimant and their partner). Child benefit is one of a handful falling outside either category being neither contributory nor means-tested, although the high income child benefit tax charge claws back child benefit where anyone in the household has taxable income over £50,000 per annum. The benefit is clawed back at a rate of 1% for each £100 of income over £50,000 such that the tax is equal to the child benefit received where income is £60,000 or above. However, it is important those eligible to recieve child benefit register for child benefit, even if the recipient elects not to recieve it, as NIC credits are given automatically to a parent registered for child benefit for a child under the age of 12, allowing the parent to build up qualifying years for state pension purposes.

Most benefits are administered by the Department for Work and Pensions and its agencies (such as Jobcentre Plus and The Pension Service). Some are administered wholly or partly by HMRC and the latter are marked with an asterisk in the following lists.

Universal Credit is replacing a number of benefits and is in the process of being phased in.

Universal benefits

- Child Benefit*
- Carer's Allowance (for those looking after a severely disabled person)
- Disability Living Allowance (DLA) – progressively being replaced by Personal Independence Payment (PIP)
- Personal Independence Payment (PIP) (help with some of the extra costs caused by long-term ill-health or disability for those aged 16–64)

Contributory benefits

- State Pension – basic and earnings-related
- Bereavement benefits
- Contribution-based Jobseeker's Allowance (JSA) (time limited, i.e. unemployment)
- Contribution-based Employment and Support Allowance (ESA) (time limited for some, i.e. sickness and incapacity)
- Statutory Sick Pay* (SSP) (for employees only, paid by the employer)
- Statutory Maternity Pay* (SMP) (for employees only, paid by the employer)
- Maternity Allowance (for self-employed and others meeting the conditions)
- Statutory Paternity Pay* (SPP) (for employees only, paid by the employer)
- Shared Parental Pay* (ShPP) (for employees only, paid by the employer)
- Statutory Adoption Pay* (SAP) (for employees only, paid by the employer)
- Guardian's Allowance*

Further information

GOV.UK
www.gov.uk/national-insurance
For guidance on National Insurance.

DWP benefits
www.gov.uk/browse/benefits

Tax Credits
www.gov.uk/browse/benefits/tax-credits

Child benefit
www.gov.uk/child-benefit

Statutory payments
For SSP, SMP, SPP, SAP and ShPP contact your employer in the first instance.

National Insurance Contributions & Employer Office, International Caseworker
HM Revenue and Customs BX9 1AN
tel 0300 200 3500
For enquiries for individuals resident abroad.

Means-tested benefits

- Income-based Jobseeker's Allowance (JSA) (i.e. unemployment)
- Income-based Employment and Support Allowance (ESA) (i.e. sickness and incapacity)
- Income Support (low-income top up for those of working age, not working but neither unemployed nor sick/incapacitated)
- Working Tax Credits* (WTC) (low-income top up for those of working age)
- Child Tax Credit* (low-income top up for those of working age with children, in addition to Working Tax Credit if applicable)
- Disabled Person's Tax Credits* (DPTC) (low-income top up for disabled people)
- Pension Credit (low-income top up for those of pension age)
- Social Fund grants (one-off assistance for low-income household with unexpected, emergency expenditure)

In addition, help with rent and rates is available on a means-tested basis from local authorities.

Many of the working age benefits are in the process of being replaced with 'Universal Credit', starting with new claimants. Universal Credit will eventually replace Income-based Jobseeker's Allowance, Income-related Employment and Support Allowance, Income Support, Working Tax Credit, Child Tax Credit and Housing Benefit.

Peter Arrowsmith FCA is a former sole practitioner specialising in National Insurance matters, and member and former chairman of the Employment Taxes and National Insurance Committee of the Institute of Chartered Accountants in England and Wales. **Sarah Bradford** BA (Hons), FCA CTA (Fellow) is the director of Writetax Ltd and the author of *National Insurance Contributions 2019/20* (and earlier editions) published by Bloomsbury Professional. She writes widely on tax and National Insurance contributions and provides tax consultancy services.

Finance

Index